OLOGY
IN PERSPECTIVE

PSYCHOLOGY
IN PERSPECTIVE

Third Edition

Carol Tavris

Carole Wade

Dominican University of California

Prentice
Hall

4/01

Upper Saddle River, New Jersey 07458

43787428

Library of Congress Cataloging-in-Publication Data

Tavris, Carol.
  Psychology in perspective / Carol Tavris, Carole Wade.—3rd ed.
    p. cm.
  Includes bibliographical references and index.
  ISBN 0-13-028326-6
  1. Psychology.   I. Wade, Carole.   II. Title.

  BF121.T33 2000
  150—dc21

                                         00-037310

VP/Editorial Director: *Laura Pearson*
Sr. Acquisitions Editor: *Jennifer Gilliland*
Editorial Assistant: *Nicole Girrbach*
AVP/Director of Production and Manufacturing:
  Barbara Kittle
Project Manager: *Maureen Richardson*
Managing Editor: *Mary Rottino*
Manufacturing Manager: *Nick Sklitsis*
Prepress and Manufacturing Buyer: *Tricia Kenny*
Creative Design Director: *Leslie Osher*

Interior Design: *Ximena Tamvakopoulos*
Cover Art and Design: *John Odam*
Photo Researcher: *Diana Gongora*
Interior Image Specialist: *Beth Boyd*
Manager, Rights & Permissions: *Kay Dellosa*
Director, Image Resource Center: *Melinda Reo*
Production/Formatting/Art Manager: *Guy Ruggiero*
Electronic Art Corrections: *Maria Piper*
Director of Marketing: *Beth Gillett Mejia*
Sr. Marketing Manager: *Sharon Cosgrove*

Credits appear on pp. 603–604, which constitute a continuation of the copyright page.

 This book was set in 10.5/13 Minion by TSI Graphics, Inc. and was printed
and bound by Von Hoffman Press, Inc. The cover was printed by The Lehigh Press, Inc.

Prentice Hall © 2001 by Prentice-Hall, Inc.
A Division of Pearson Education
Upper Saddle River, New Jersey 07458

Printed in the United States of America

10 9 8 7 6 5 4 3 2 1

ISBN 0-13-028326-6

Prentice-Hall International (UK) Limited, *London*
Prentice-Hall of Australia Pty. Limited, *Sydney*
Prentice-Hall Canada Inc., *Toronto*
Prentice-Hall Hispanoamericana, S.A., *Mexico*
Prentice-Hall of India Private Limited, *New Delhi*
Prentice-Hall of Japan, Inc., *Tokyo*
Pearson Education Asia Pte. Ltd., *Singapore*
Editora Prentice-Hall do Brasil, Ltda., *Rio de Janeiro*

BRIEF CONTENTS

DETAILED CONTENTS

Essay Six   The Whole Elephant   538

*P*ut any group of introductory psychology teachers together, and you are bound to hear two familiar complaints. "Introductory psychology is supposed to be a smorgasbord," one will say, "but my students are overwhelmed by the dozens of dishes; the meal has become indigestible." Another will venture, "My students complain that there's no 'big picture' in psychology; how can we bring some sort of order to our courses?"

Nearly all of the introductory books on the market—including our own text, *Psychology*—take a topical approach to psychology: a chapter on the brain, a chapter on emotions, a chapter on child development, and so forth. There is certainly a place for such encyclopedias of psychology; we're quite fond of ours! Yet, for many teachers, this conventional organization has grown increasingly problematic. As findings in psychology have burgeoned, and the number of specialty areas has grown as well, textbooks have had to become longer and longer.

And so we thought it was time for a reconceptualization of the introductory course and a true alternative to the traditional, topic-by-topic way of teaching it. Many scientists and educators agree. Several years ago, the American Association for the Advancement of Science launched Project 2061, an effort to determine the best ways of increasing scientific literacy. To this end, they commissioned the National Council on Science and Technology Education to survey hundreds of scientists, engineers, and educators and draw up a report of their recommendations. The result, *Science for All Americans,* calls on instructors to aim for *depth* rather than *breadth* in their introductory courses; to "reduce the sheer amount of material covered"; to "present the scientific endeavor as a social enterprise that strongly influences—and is influenced by—human thought and action"; and "to foster scientific ways of thinking" (AAAS Project 2061, 1990; for the report from the social and behavioral sciences panel, see Appley & Maher, 1989).

TEACHING FOR DEPTH

Psychology in Perspective represents our effort to meet this challenge. Typically, courses and textbooks are constructed around the question, "What do I want students to know about my field?" With the question phrased that way, the answer can only be "Everything!" None of us likes the idea of "leaving something out," especially if the introductory course is the only one a student might ever take. In this book, however, we accepted the premise of Project 2061 and asked a different question: "What should an educated citizen know about psychology?" With the question phrased that way,

"Everything!" is no longer such a useful answer. For one thing, students can't remember everything. For another, specific findings change yearly, and in some areas (such as genetics and memory) they change faster than that. So we asked ourselves what kind of framework we could provide students that would help them evaluate the psychological findings and claims they will encounter when they leave the classroom. What, for example, should students know about genetics in particular, and biological approaches to behavior in general, that will help them assess someone's claim to have found "the" gene for aggression or homosexuality?

To teach for depth rather than breadth, and for ideas rather than facts alone, we have organized material not by topics or psychological specialties but by what we regard as the five major perspectives in the field: biological, cognitive, learning, socio-cultural, and psychodynamic. Our aim is to provide a true introduction to how researchers in each perspective go about their business: the kinds of questions they ask, the methods they use, the assumptions they make, and their major findings. We have included many classic studies along with groundbreaking new ones, but we do not attempt to be encyclopedic. Instead, we are trying to show students the different ways of "doing" psychology. We do not wish to imply that every perspective is monolithic; we discuss many conflicting views and debates within each field. But we also show that the perspectives do differ from one another in certain key assumptions about human behavior and human nature, and in the methods they use to study them.

Writing a book for depth of concept rather than breadth of coverage means, we realize, that many instructors will find some of their favorite studies or even topics omitted entirely. Nevertheless, most of the topics of introductory psychology are in this book, although sometimes in unfamiliar places. Therefore, we encourage instructors to review the table of contents and look up topics in the index before becoming alarmed that their favorite subject is missing.

For instance, subjects that would ordinarily be in a traditional child development chapter have been broken up: Piaget and the development of reasoning abilities are in the cognitive perspective (Chapter 7); moral reasoning and the internalization of moral standards are topics we always thought appropriate for a social-cognitive learning analysis (Chapter 6); and human attachment needs, which start with the baby's innate need for contact comfort and what John Bowlby called a "secure base," are in the biological perspective (Chapter 3).

CONFRONTING THE CONTROVERSIES

Psychology in Perspective differs from traditional textbooks in yet another way. We want students to understand and appreciate the real debates and controversies within psychology—the ones psychologists talk about all the time but rarely discuss with their students. For example, the gap between research psychologists and certain psychotherapists is widening, as the split between the clinical and research constituencies of the American Psychological Association dramatically illustrates. Many researchers no longer even consider themselves "psychologists," preferring such labels as "cognitive scientist," "neuroscientist," and the like. This book candidly discusses this split—its origins, the reasons for it, and its consequences for the public (see especially Essay 5, "Evaluating the Psychodynamic Perspective," and Chapter 12, which includes a discussion of the scientist–practitioner gap).

Further, each unit concludes with an essay that critically evaluates each perspective's contributions and limitations. Each evaluation cautions against the temptation to reduce behavior to only one level of explanation. Most people are familiar with the appeal of biological reductionism, but we also examine environmental reductionism ("With the right environment, anyone can become anything"), cognitive reductionism ("The mind can control everything"), sociocultural reductionism ("My culture or The System made me do it"), and psychodynamic reductionism ("Psychic reality is all that matters").

PUTTING THE PERSPECTIVES TOGETHER

In the last unit, we offer an alternative to reductionism. In Chapter 12, we show how researchers and practitioners in each perspective study, diagnose, and treat various mental disorders. And in Essay 6, we show how research from all five perspectives might be applied to understanding two universal human pleasures: music and sex. We know that many other issues lend themselves to a multiperspective analysis and would make excellent assignments for term papers, including, just for starters, love, drug use and abuse, aggression, emotional experiences, eating habits, and achievement.

Naturally, we recognize that many psychologists travel across perspectives when they do research; for example, most psychologists who study emotion are well aware that emotion involves physiology, learning, cognition, culture, and nonconscious processes. But, in practice, most psychologists do research from the vantage point of the perspective they were trained in. Biopsychologists study the physiology of emotion, social psychologists study the social construction and display of emotion, cognitive psychologists study how attributions create emotions, and so forth.

We learned quickly enough from some of our reviewers how attached psychologists can be to their favored perspective! One reviewer thought that we weren't making it clear enough that biology is the most important one, because it underlies all the others. One thought that we should have begun with the sociocultural perspective, because it influences all the others. One thought that we should have begun with learning, because the laws of classical and operant conditioning are fundamental . . . you get the idea. And, reflecting the anomalous position of psychoanalysis in a field otherwise devoted to the scientific method, almost everyone had questions about our treatment of the psychodynamic perspective: Why did we treat it so kindly? Why did we treat it so harshly? Why did we include it at all? Of course, our goal is not to be "kind" or "harsh" but to show students how researchers within each perspective see the world. We inform readers that many empirically oriented psychologists do not consider psychodynamic approaches worth considering, but we feel that students need to understand and be able to assess critically the continuing legacy and influence of Freud and his followers.

WHAT'S NEW IN THE THIRD EDITION

In response to suggestions and reactions from reviewers and adopters of the first two editions of *Psychology in Perspective,* we have made two major changes:

✦ **WE ADDED A NEW CHAPTER** (Chapter 12) on the diagnosis and treatment of mental disorders. This material had been covered in the second edition, but it was divided up and discussed in the various perspectives (for example, cognitive therapy was discussed in evaluating the cognitive perspective; medications for mental and emotional disorders in the biological perspective). Instructors wanted all the material in one place, and we agree that this is a better idea. Also, because so many students are interested in clinical psychology or are planning to become mental-health practitioners, we felt it was important to add a unit on clinical issues in diagnosis and therapy.

✦ **WE REDUCED THE LENGTH OF THE EVALUATION ESSAYS.** Instead of being a full chapter that contained new material and applications of the perspective, each evaluation is now a much briefer assessment simply of the strengths and limitations of the perspective. Many of the specific applications of the perspective that the evaluation chapters used to contain, such as findings about children's eyewitness testimony or IQ testing, have been moved into the chapters themselves. The evaluation essays are thus briefer, punchier, and, we hope, better summaries and assessments of each perspective.

PEDAGOGICAL HELP FOR STUDENTS

As before, we include a *running glossary,* which defines bold-faced terms on the pages where they occur, for handy reference and study; chapter *summaries* and *key terms* at the end of each chapter, where students will find them easily; and self-tests called *What Do You Know?,* which encourage students to check their progress, and to go back and review if necessary. These questions do more than just test for memorization of definitions; they tell students whether they comprehend the issues. We have varied the formats and included entertaining examples to motivate students to assess their progress. Many of these self-tests also include critical-thinking items, identified by the symbol in the margin. These items invite the student to reflect on the implications of findings and consider how psychological principles might illuminate real-life issues. Although we offer some possible responses to such questions, most of them do not have a single correct answer, and students may have valid, well-reasoned answers that differ from our own.

SUPPLEMENTS

Psychology in Perspective can be used on its own, or it can serve as a core book together with additional materials. Prentice Hall has provided a comprehensive supplements package coordinated by Nicole Girrbach:

For the Instructor

✦ **INSTRUCTOR'S RESOURCE MANUAL.** Written by Carolyn Meyer of Lake-Sumter Community College, this manual addresses concerns that teachers may have when organizing their course in terms of perspectives rather than topics. For each chapter, the Instructor's Resource Manual includes a sample course syllabus, chapter summaries and outlines, teaching suggestions, classroom activities, discussion questions, suggested readings, and a listing of films and videos.

✦ **TEST ITEM FILE.** Prepared by William H. Calhoun of the University of Tennessee, Knoxville, this Test Item File contains approximately 2,500 multiple-choice, true/false, matching, short-answer, and essay questions. Each item is referenced by page, topic, and the skill it addresses—conceptual, factual, or applied.

✦ **PRENTICE HALL TEST MANAGER.** One of the best-selling test-generating software programs on the market, Test Manager is available free to adopters in Windows and Macintosh formats and contains a Gradebook, Online Network Testing, and many tools to help you edit and create tests. The program comes with full Technical Support and telephone "Request a Test" service.

✦ **PRENTICE HALL'S INTRODUCTORY PSYCHOLOGY TRANSPARENCIES, SERIES V.** Designed in large-type format for lecture settings, these full-color overhead transparencies add visual appeal to your lectures by augmenting the visuals in the text with a variety of new illustrations.

✦ **PRENTICE HALL VIDEO LIBRARIES.** Prentice Hall has assembled a superior collection of video materials that range from short lecture launchers to full-length detailed features for use in the Introductory Psychology course. The videos below are available to qualified adopters.

ABC NEWS VIDEOS FOR INTRODUCTORY PSYCHOLOGY, SERIES III consists of segments from *ABC's World News Tonight, Nightline, 20/20, Prime Time Live,* and *The Health Show.* A summary, and questions designed to stimulate critical thinking for each segment, are included in the Instructor's Resource Manual.

THE ALLIANCE SERIES: THE ANNENBERG/CPB COLLECTION is the most extensive collection of professionally produced videos available with any introductory psychology textbook. Selections include videos in the following Annenberg series: The Brain, The Brain Teaching Modules, Discovering Psychology, The Mind, and The Mind Teaching Modules.

FILMS FOR THE HUMANITIES AND SCIENCES A wealth of videos from the extensive library of Film for the Humanities and Sciences, on a variety of topics in psychology, is available to qualified adopters. Contact your local Prentice Hall representative for a list of videos.

Media Support for Instructors and Students

✦ THE PSYCHOLOGY PLACE, SPECIAL EDITION. This premier web resource for Introductory Psychology provides interactive learning activities, practice tests, "Best of the Web" site listings, current research news, an online glossary, FAQs about psychology, and other resources. Students get their subscription with the purchase of a new textbook; faculty get their subscription upon adoption of this text.

✦ WWW.PRENHALL.COM/TAVRIS COMPANION WEBSITE. This *free* online Study Guide allows students to review each chapter's material, take practice tests, research topics for course projects, and more.

For the Student

✦ STUDY GUIDE. Prepared by Christopher Kilmartin of Mary Washington College, this Study Guide is designed to reinforce the text material by providing students with a complete array of learning tools and study aids. It begins with a chapter on how to study, and it contains chapter summaries, fill-in-the-blank chapter reviews, practice tests, answer keys, learning objectives, key terms with definitions, suggested readings, and research projects.

✦ PSYCHOBABBLE AND BIOBUNK, SECOND EDITION by Carol Tavris. This expanded and updated collection of opinion essays, written for *The Los Angeles Times, The New York Times, Scientific American,* and other publications, encourages debate in the classroom by applying psychological research and the principles of scientific and critical thinking to issues in the news.

✦ PSYCHOLOGY ON THE INTERNET: EVALUATING ONLINE RESOURCES. This "hands-on" internet tutorial features Web sites related to psychology and general information about using the Internet for research and how to differentiate between good and bad sources. This supplement is available *free* when packaged with the text and helps students capitalize on all the resources that the World Wide Web has to offer.

ACKNOWLEDGMENTS

Our many reviewers, generalists and specialists alike, were invaluable to the writing of the three editions of *Psychology in Perspective.* Their advice, their attention to detail, and their approval of our departures from convention were enormously helpful both as moral support and as constructive criticism. We thank them all. (Please note that affiliations of some individuals may have changed since they reviewed our book.)

SPECIALIST REVIEWERS

Biological perspective

William Byne, The Albert Einstein College of Medicine
Ruth Hubbard, Harvard University
Linda Mealey, College of St. Benedict
Richard F. Thompson, University of Southern California

Learning perspective

Albert Bandura, Stanford University
Beverly I. Fagot, University of Oregon-Eugene [deceased]

Cognitive perspective

Karen S. Kitchener, University of Denver
Debra Ann Poole, Central Michigan University
Keith E. Stanovich, The Ontario Institute for Studies in Education

Sociocultural perspective

Patricia Devine, University of Wisconsin-Madison
Halford H. Fairchild, Pitzer College
Walter J. Lonner, Western Washington University
Steven R. López, University of California, Los Angeles

Psychodynamic perspective

Sarah Cirese, College of Marin
Gail Hornstein, Mount Holyoke College
Hans H. Strupp, Vanderbilt University

Overall manuscript

Emir Andrews, Memorial University of Newfoundland
James R. Antes, University of North Dakota
Susan L. Boatright-Horowitz, University of Rhode Island
Karen Christoff, University of Mississippi
Florence L. Denmark, Pace University
Thomas G. Fikes, University of Puget Sound
Christopher Kilmartin, Mary Washington College
Patrick Latham, Boston University
Anne L. Law, Rider University
Douglas Leber, University of Denver
Ben Lim, University of Massachusetts
Vira Lozano, College of the Sequoias
Vance Maloney, Taylor University
Roy S. Malpass, University of Texas at El Paso

Steven E. Meier, University of Idaho
Timothy E. Moore, Glendon College, York University
John B. Nezlek, College of William and Mary
Robert Patterson, Washington State University
Gordon Pitz, Southern Illinois University
Matthew J. Sharps, California State University-Fresno
Ray H. Starr, Jr., University of Maryland, Baltimore Campus
Barbara Watters, Mercyhurst College
Richard Wiebe, Northeastern University
Mark Worden, Fairfield University
Steven A. Wygant, Brigham Young University

This edition was our first outing from start to finish with our new publisher, Prentice Hall, and we are indebted to the skills and support provided by the editorial, art, and production teams. Our deepest thanks, first, to those who worked in the trenches with us daily: Senior Acquisitions Editor Jennifer Gilliland, who supervised and encouraged us so beautifully, and her capable assistant Nicole Girrbach; Production Editor Maureen Richardson and Managing Editor Mary Rottino who were so dazzlingly efficient; and our loyal and witty copy editor, Shari Dorantes Hatch, who has been minding our prose now for many years. We also know how much work went on before we ever began this edition and after we finished it. Our special thanks to Vice President and Editorial Director of Social Sciences and Psychology, Laura Pearson, and to Senior Marketing Manager Sharon Cosgrove, who have enthusiastically supported the vision of this book.

We are absolutely delighted with the book's design, inside and out. Our heartfelt thanks to Art Director Ximena Tamvakopoulos, who gave this edition a smashing new look while keeping its connection to earlier editions; Maria Piper, for executing the line art so well; and John Odam, for designing such a magnificent, witty, and provocative cover, one that conveys exactly the message we had hoped for. As they did on the sixth edition of *Psychology,* Connie Blacker and her associates at TSI Graphics did the layouts with astonishing efficiency and skill.

Finally, we thank Ronan O'Casey and Howard Williams, who uncomplainingly supported us from start to finish, and who helped us meet our deadlines by providing ample amounts of coffee, food, wine, humor, and love—the necessities of life.

This book has been a labor of love for us, and we hope that you will enjoy reading and using it. We welcome your reactions, experiences using it, and suggestions for improvements.

Carol Tavris & Carole Wade

TO THE STUDENT

*O*ur goal in writing this book is to encourage you to learn to think critically and imaginatively about a fabulous, complex subject: the human being. As you will see right away in Chapter 1, this is not going to be a book about psychobabble—all that vague psychological analysis you hear on talk shows or get from pop-psych books and self-appointed experts. We are going to give you the straight stuff about real psychology. We think it will surprise you.

This book is unconventional in another way, too. It is not only a book of answers; it is also, perhaps primarily, a book of questions. We have organized this book according to the five perspectives that psychologists use as they go about studying human beings: Some are mostly interested in biological contributions to behavior, others in environmental explanations, others in cultural influences, and so forth. In each section, we try to show you how psychologists in that perspective see the world, so that you will say, as they do, "Yes! Obviously, this approach makes the most sense!" But we do not stop there; we include a critical evaluation of the perspective's contributions, limitations, and even misuses. The point of this assessment is not to cause you to throw up your hands and say, "Nothing is true! No one has the answers!" Rather, we want you to appreciate what some psychologists themselves do not—that all perspectives together are necessary to understand and appreciate the whole human being. We want you to learn to resist single, one-note explanations of anything.

We have done everything we can think of to make this subject as absorbing for you as it has always been for us. However, what you bring to this book is as important as what we have written. We can only be the pitchers; you're the ones at bat. The more actively you are involved with your own learning, the more successful the book and your course will be, and the more enjoyable, too.

In our years of teaching (and of having been students), we have found that certain study strategies can vastly improve learning. One key strategy is to make sure you are *reading actively,* not just nodding along saying "Hmmmm" to yourself. We have tried to write this book in a lively and interesting manner, but some of our own students said that they were occasionally deceived by the style, thinking they got the major points of a discussion when they actually had not. We therefore advise you to read a chapter through to get its overall content and message, but then reread it carefully, section by section. Instead of reading silently, restate what you have read in your own words at the end of each major section. Try to describe what you have learned to an interested friend or roommate, or even a patient pet, and you will find out at once what you still don't understand. Some people find it helpful to write down the main points of each chapter, and later use them in reviewing for exams.

To aid your learning, every chapter contains several self-tests, called *What Do You Know?,* that permit you to test your understanding and retention of what you have just read and your ability to apply the material to examples. These quizzes are for your practical use and, we hope, for your enjoyment, too. When you can't answer a question, do not go on to the next section; pause right there, review what you have read, and try again. Some of these self-tests contain a *critical-thinking item,* denoted by a symbol such as the one in the margin. The answers we give for these items are only suggestions; feel free to come up with different ones. We think that if you take the time to respond thoughtfully to these special questions, you will learn more and become a more sophisticated user of psychology.

At the end of each chapter you will find two other important study aids: numbered *summaries* of the highlights of the chapter and *key terms* you need to know, with the pages on which they first appear. If you can define or identify each key term, the chances are good that you are mastering the material. The fact that we provide chapter summaries, by the way, should not stop you from making your own; some students find it very helpful to compare their own chapter summaries with ours.

There are some other features of this book you should know about. The most important new terms are printed in **boldface** and defined at the bottom of the pages on which they appear, which permits you to find these terms easily. A full *glossary* also appears at the end of the book.

You will notice that discussions of studies and theories are followed by one or more *citations* in parentheses, like this: (Smedley & Dooright, 2001). A citation tells the reader who the authors of the paper are and when their paper or book was published. The full reference can then be looked up in the *references* at the end of this book. Students often find citations useful, especially for locating material for term projects and reports.

At the back of the book you will also find a *name index* and a *subject index.* The name index lists the name of every author cited and the pages where the person's work is discussed. If you remember the name of a psychologist but you can't recall where he or she was mentioned, look up the name in the name index. The subject index provides a listing of all the major topics mentioned in the book. If you want to review material on, say, aspects of gender, which might appear in several chapters, you can look up "gender" in the subject index.

We also recommend the *Study Guide* that is available at your bookstore, and the companion website for this book **www.prenhall.com/tavris.** They will help you study and further explore the information in this book, give you practice in taking tests, and help you review material for exams.

We have done our best to make your introduction to psychology a lively and provocative one. In the end, though, it is your efforts as much as ours that will determine whether you find psychology to be exciting or boring, and whether the field will matter in your own life. We welcome your ideas and reactions so that we will learn what works for you and what doesn't. In the meantime, welcome to psychology!

Carol Tavris & Carole Wade

ABOUT THE AUTHORS

CAROL TAVRIS earned her Ph.D. in the social psychology program at the University of Michigan, and as a writer and lecturer she has sought to educate the public about the importance of critical and scientific thinking in psychology. She is author of *The Mismeasure of Woman; Anger: The Misunderstood Emotion;* and, with Carole Wade, *Psychology; Invitation to Psychology;* and *The Longest War: Sex Differences in Perspective.* She has written on psychological topics for a wide variety of magazines and professional publications; many of her opinion essays and book reviews for *The Los Angeles Times, The New York Times Book Review, Scientific American,* and other publications have recently been collected in *Psychobabble and Biobunk: Using Psychology to Think Critically About Issues in the News.* Dr. Tavris lectures widely on, among other topics, critical thinking, pseudoscience in psychology and psychiatry, anger, and the science and politics of research on gender. She has taught in the psychology department at UCLA and at the Human Relations Center of the New School for Social Research in New York. She is a Fellow of the American Psychological Association and a charter Fellow of the American Psychological Society; a member of the board of the Council for Scientific Clinical Psychology and Psychiatry; and a member of the editorial board of the APS's *Psychological Science in the Public Interest.* When she is not writing or lecturing, she can be found walking the trails of the Hollywood Hills with her border collie, Sophie.

CAROLE WADE earned her Ph.D. in cognitive psychology at Stanford University. She began her academic career at the University of New Mexico, where she taught courses in psycholinguistics and developed the first course at the university on the psychology of gender. She was professor of psychology for ten years at San Diego Mesa College, then taught at the College of Marin, and is now affiliated with Dominican University of California. She is author, with Carol Tavris, of *Psychology, Invitation to Psychology,* and *The Longest War: Sex Differences in Perspective.* Dr. Wade has a long-standing interest in making psychology accessible to students and the general public through lectures, workshops, and general interest articles. For many years she has focused her efforts on the teaching and promotion of critical-thinking skills, diversity issues, and the enhancement of undergraduate education in psychology. She chaired the APA Board of Educational Affairs Task Force on Diversity Issues at the Precollege and Undergraduate Levels of Education in Psychology, is a past chair of the APA's Public Information Committee, has been a G. Stanley Hall Lecturer, and currently serves on the steering committee for the National Institute on the Teaching of Psychology. Dr. Wade is a Fellow of the American Psychological Association and a charter member of the American Psychological Society. When she isn't busy with her professional activities, she can be found riding the trails of northern California on her Arabian horse, Condé.

PSYCHOLOGY
IN PERSPECTIVE

PART I

Invitation to Psychology

The Blind Men and the Elephant

It was six men of Indostan
To learning much inclined,
Who went to see the elephant
(Though all of them were blind),
That each by observation
Might satisfy his mind.

The First approached the elephant,
And, happening to fall
Against his broad and sturdy side,
At once began to bawl:
"God bless me! but the elephant
Is nothing but a wall!"

The Second, feeling of the tusk,
Cried, "Ho! what have we here
So very round and smooth and sharp?
To me 'tis mighty clear
This wonder of an elephant
Is very like a spear!"

The Third approached the animal,
And, happening to take
The squirming trunk within his hands,
Thus boldly up and spake:
"I see," quoth he, "the elephant
Is very like a snake!"

The Fourth reached out his eager hand,
And felt about the knee:
"What most this wondrous beast is like

Is mighty plain," quoth he;
"'Tis clear enough the elephant
Is very like a tree."

The Fifth, who chanced to touch the ear,
Said, "E'en the blindest man
Can tell what this resembles most;
Deny the fact who can,
This marvel of an elephant
Is very like a fan!"

The Sixth no sooner had begun
About the beast to grope,
Than, seizing on the swinging tail
That fell within his scope,
"I see," quoth he, "the elephant
Is very like a rope!"

And so these men of Indostan
Disputed loud and long,
Each in his own opinion
Exceeding stiff and strong,
Though each was partly in the right,
And all were in the wrong!

So, oft in theologic wars
The disputants, I ween,
Rail on in utter ignorance
Of what each other mean,
And prate about an elephant
Not one of them has seen!

—John Godfrey Saxe

CHAPTER ONE

Explaining Human Behavior

What is psychology? If you were to wander through the psychology section of your local bookstore (perhaps called "psychology and self-help" or "personal growth") you would find the following answers:

✦ Psychology is all about finding happiness. It will teach you that *You Can Be Happy No Matter What*, presumably if you also read *I Don't Have to Make Everything All Better*. And if you are feeling that nothing will ever get better, you might be cheered up by *The Joy of Stress* and *The Joy of Failure*.

✦ Psychology will make you rich and successful if you read *Baby Steps to Success* or *Giant Steps* or *How to Succeed in Life*. You can learn *How to Make the Impossible Possible* and how to *Get What You Deserve*.

✦ Psychology will help you fall in love, stay in love, or get over love. *Love Is the Answer*, but only if you are *Learning to Love Yourself* first and don't develop *Obsessive Love*. You can learn *How to Make Anyone Fall in Love with You* as long as you *Don't Say Yes When You Want to Say No*. Once you're in love, of course, you will need *The Art of Intimacy* and *The Art of Staying Together*.

✦ Psychology is full of contradictory advice. It provides *Toughness Training for Life* and will show you how to say *Good-bye to Guilt* but will also teach you *How to Turn the Other Cheek and Still Survive in Today's World*. You can develop your inner child, *The Animal in You*, or maybe even *Grow Up!*

The psychology that you are about to study, however, bears little relation to the popular psychology ("pop psych") found in many self-help books and on many TV and radio talk shows. It is more complex, more informative, and, we think, far more helpful because it is based on scientific research and **empirical** evidence, gathered by careful observation, experimentation, and measurement.

The psychology in this book also addresses a far broader range of issues than does popular psychology. When people think of psychology, they often think of mental and emotional disorders, abnormal acts, personal problems, and psychotherapy. But psychologists do not confine their attention to mental and emotional problems. They take as their subject the entire spectrum of brave and cowardly, intelligent and foolish, beautiful and brutish things that people do. Their aim is to examine and explain how human beings (and other animals, too) learn, remember, solve problems, perceive, feel, and get along (or fail to get along) with others. They are therefore as likely to study commonplace experiences as exceptional ones: rearing children, gossiping, remembering a shopping list, daydreaming, making love, and making a living.

Psychology can be defined as *the discipline concerned with behavior and mental processes and how they are affected by an organism's physical state, mental state, and external environment.* This definition, however, is a little like defining a car as a vehicle for transporting people from one place to another, without explaining how a car differs from a train or a bus, how a Ford differs from a Ferrari, or how a catalytic converter works. To get a clear picture of what psychology is, you are going to need to know more about its methods, its findings, and its ways of interpreting information. We will begin by looking more closely at what psychology is *not*.

PSEUDOSCIENCE AND PSYCHOBABBLE

In recent decades, the public's appetite for psychological information has created a huge market for what R. D. Rosen (1977) called *"psychobabble"*: pseudoscience and quackery covered by a veneer of psychological language. The examples that Rosen analyzed in the 1970s included group encounters designed to transform a person's rotten life in one weekend; "primal scream therapy," in which people are supposed to link their current unhappiness to the trauma of being born (this therapy still exists); and "Theta," a "rebirthing" therapy whose leader asserted that "no one dies if they don't want to"—certainly the ultimate belief in mind over matter!

The particular programs and groups based on psychobabble have changed their names and leaders over the years, but the common elements remain. All promise quick, simple fixes for emotional problems. All rely on vaguely psychological and scientificky-sounding language, such as "repression of feelings," "getting in touch with your real self," "reprogramming your brain," "identifying your unconscious talents," and so forth. Some forms of psychobabble take advantage of people's trust in technology. Thus, all sorts of electrical gizmos have been marketed with the promise that they will get both

---

empirical Relying on or derived from observation, experimentation, or measurement.

psychology The discipline concerned with behavior and mental processes and how they are affected by an organism's physical state, mental state, and external environment; often represented by Ψ, the Greek letter psi (usually pronounced "sy").

halves of your brain working at their peak (Chance, 1989): the Graham Potentializer, the Tranquilite, the Floatarium, the Transcutaneous Electro-Neural Stimulator, the Brain SuperCharger, and the Whole Brain Wave Form Synchro-Energizer (we're not making these up). And of course there are dozens and dozens of so-called "subliminal" tapes that promise to make you happy, thin, rich, successful, healthy, and able to speak four languages, all while you sleep. (For the record, research shows that they don't deliver on any of these promises [Moore, 1995].)

Because so many pop-psych ideas have filtered into public consciousness, the media, education, and even the law, we all need to distinguish between psychobabble and serious psychology, and between unsupported *popular opinion* and findings based on *research evidence.* Are unhappy memories "repressed" and then accurately recalled years later, as if they had been tape recorded? Do most women suffer from emotional symptoms of "PMS (premenstrual syndrome)"? Does a difficult childhood inevitably lead to an unhappy adulthood? As you will learn in this book, all of these common beliefs and many others are contradicted by the evidence.

Psychology has many nonscientific competitors: palm reading, graphology, fortune-telling, numerology, and the most popular, astrology. Like psychologists, promoters of these competing systems try to explain people's problems and predict their behavior. If you are having romantic problems, for example, an astrologer may advise you to choose an Aries instead of an Aquarius as your next love, and a "past-lives channeler" may say it's because you were jilted in a former life. But whenever the claims of psychics, astrologers, and the like are put to the test, they turn out to be so vague that they are meaningless, or they are just plain wrong (Dean, 1987; Rowe, 1993).

For example, psychics predicted that 1999 was going to be the year that Wynonna Judd quit country music to become a female wrestler, marijuana replaced petroleum as the nation's chief source of energy, O. J. Simpson confessed to Howard Stern on the air that he killed his ex-wife, and a pollution cloud forced New York City to be quarantined (*Skeptical Inquirer,* March/April 2000). Obviously, the psychics were mistaken! On the other hand, no psychic predicted the devastating earthquake that year in Turkey; the deaths of John F. Kennedy, Jr., his wife, and sister-in-law (on the contrary, one psychic predicted that the Kennedys would have twins that year); the impeachment trial of President Clinton; or the terrible shootings at Columbine High School in Colorado. Nor has any psychic ever found a missing child, identified a serial killer, or helped police solve any other crime solely by using "psychic powers," in spite of frequent reports in the mass media that this happens all the time (Rowe, 1993; Shermer, 1997).

Perhaps the ultimate difference between psychobabble and scientific psychology is that psychobabble *confirms* our existing beliefs and prejudices (which is why it is so appealing), whereas psychology often *challenges* them. You do not have to be a psychologist to know that people don't always take kindly to having their beliefs challenged. You rarely hear someone say, cheerfully, "Oh, thank you for explaining to me why my lifelong philosophy of child rearing is wrong! I'm so grateful for your facts!" The person is more likely to say, "Oh, buzz off, and take your stupid ideas with you." (In Chapter 7 you will learn why this is so.)

I see you being less gullible in the future.

However, although psychologists often challenge prevailing beliefs, they also seek to extend and deepen our understanding of generally accepted facts. After all, everyone knows that an apple will fall to the ground if it drops from a tree, but it took Isaac Newton to discover the laws of gravity and to explain why the apple falls and why it travels at a particular speed. Psychologists, like scientists in other fields, strive not only to discover new phenomena, but also to deepen or change our understanding of an already familiar world. As philosopher Paul Valéry once put it, "The purpose of psychology is to give us a completely different idea of the things we know best."

THINKING CRITICALLY AND CREATIVELY ABOUT PSYCHOLOGY

In this book, you will gain practice in distinguishing scientific psychology from pseudoscience by thinking critically. **Critical thinking** is the ability and willingness to assess claims and make objective judgments on the basis of well-supported reasons and evidence, rather than emotion and anecdote. Critical thinkers are able to look for flaws in arguments and to resist claims that have no support. Critical thinking, however, is not merely negative thinking. It includes the ability to be creative and constructive—the ability to come up with various possible explanations for events, think of implications of research findings, and apply new knowledge to social and personal problems.

Most people know that you have to exercise the body to keep it in shape, but they may not realize that clear thinking also requires effort and practice. Unlike breathing,

---

critical thinking The ability and willingness to assess claims and make judgments on the basis of well-supported reasons and evidence, rather than emotion or anecdote.

it is not automatic. All around us we can see examples of flabby thinking. Sometimes people justify their mental laziness by proudly telling you they are open-minded. "It's good to be open-minded," many philosophers reply, "but not so open that your brains fall out."

One prevalent misreading of what it means to be open-minded is the idea that all opinions are created equal and that everybody's beliefs are as good as everybody else's. On matters of personal preferences, that is true; if you prefer the look of a Ford Explorer to the look of a Honda Civic, no one can argue with you. But if you say, "The Ford is a better car than a Honda," you have uttered more than mere opinion. Now you have to support your belief with evidence of the car's reliability, track record, and safety (Ruggiero, 1997). And if you say, "Fords are the best in the world and Hondas do not exist; they are a conspiracy of the Japanese government," you forfeit the right to have your opinion taken seriously. Your opinion, if it ignores reality, is *not* equal to any other.

Unfortunately, many people forget this. Journalists and college newspaper editors sometimes feel obliged to cover "both sides of a story" even when there aren't two reasonable sides. For example, some feel they should give "equal time" to people who claim that the Holocaust never occurred, even though this is like saying that slavery in America never existed. In democratic societies, free speech is protected of course, but as one writer noted, the right to free speech "says nothing about a paper's obligation to publish every absurd claim that comes its way," nor does it require that every half-baked opinion be given a hearing (Lipstadt, 1994).

Critical thinking will help you distinguish arguments based on solidly grounded evidence from those that float along on delusion or wishful dreams. Although many of these skills depend on mental maturity and education (see Chapter 7), even young children have the basic capacity to think critically, although they may not get much credit for it. We know one fourth grader who, when told that ancient Greece was the "cradle of democracy," replied, "But what about women and slaves, who couldn't vote and had no rights? Was Greece a democracy for them?" That's certainly critical thinking. And it is also creative thinking, for once you question the assumption that Greece was a democracy for everyone, you can begin to construct a more accurate picture of Greek civilization.

Many educators, philosophers, and psychologists believe that contemporary education often shortchanges students by treating the mind as a sponge for "soaking up knowledge." The mind is not just a sponge; remembering, thinking, and understanding require judgment, choice, and the weighing of evidence. Many high school and college graduates have learned to memorize the "right" answers but cannot formulate a rational argument or see through misleading advertisements that play on their emotions. They may not know how to assess a political proposal or candidate, decide whether or when to have children, or come up with constructive solutions to their problems. Many spend huge amounts of money on medical remedies that lack any evidence of effectiveness and that can even be life-threatening (Halpern, 1998).

Critical thinking is not only indispensable in ordinary life, but also fundamental to all science. And it is particularly relevant in psychology. For one thing, the field itself includes the study of reasoning, problem solving, creativity, curiosity, and other aspects of critical thought. It also includes the study of *barriers* to clear thinking, such as the human propensity for rationalization, self-deception, and misperception. Most important, psychologists generate many competing findings on hot topics of personal and social relevance, such as addiction, memory, sexual orientation, and the role of genetics in behavior; people need to know how to think critically in order to evaluate these findings and their possible implications.

Critical thinking requires logical reasoning, but other kinds of skills are also important (Ennis, 1985; Halpern, 1995; Levy, 1997; Paul, 1984; Ruggiero, 1997). Here are eight essential guidelines to critical thinking that we will be emphasizing throughout this book.

1 **ASK QUESTIONS; BE WILLING TO WONDER.** What is the one kind of question that most exasperates parents of young children? "Why is the sky blue, Mommy?" "Why doesn't the plane fall?" "Why don't pigs have wings?" Unfortunately, as children grow up, they tend to stop asking "why" questions. (Why do you think this is?)

"The trigger mechanism for creative thinking is the disposition to be curious, to wonder, to inquire," observed Vincent Ruggiero (1988). "Asking 'What's wrong here?' and/or 'Why is this the way it is, and how did it come to be that way?' leads to the identification of problems and challenges." Psychologist Bob Perloff (1992) once reflected on a few questions he would like to have answered. "Why are moths attracted to wool but indifferent to cotton?" he wondered. "Why [is there] dust? Why is a rainbow arched? I used to feel foolish, even dumb, because I didn't know why or how the sun shines until I learned very recently that the astrophysicists themselves are in a quandary about this."

Critical thinkers frame their questions in a way that permits many answers, including unexpected ones. An advocate of hypnosis might ask, "How does hypnosis improve memory for events?"—a question that already presupposes that hypnosis reliably improves memory. But a critical thinker would ask a more neutral question, allowing for other results: "Does hypnosis affect memory, and if so, how?" (As we will see in Chapter 8, it turns out that hypnosis can increase memory *errors,* and many hypnotized people will make up details of an event that never happened.)

We hope that you will not approach psychology as "received wisdom" but will ask many questions about the theories and findings presented in this book. Be on the lookout, too, for questions about human behavior that have *not* yet been asked. If you do that, you will be not only learning psychology, but also learning to think the way psychologists do.

2 **DEFINE YOUR TERMS.** Once you have raised a general question, the next step is to frame it in clear and concrete terms. "What makes people happy?" is a fine question for midnight reveries, but it will not lead to answers until you have defined what you mean by "happy." Do you mean being in a state of euphoria most of the time? Do you mean feeling pleasantly content with life? Do you mean the absence of serious problems or pain?

Poorly defined terms can produce misleading or incomplete answers. For example, can animals use language? The answer depends on how you define "language." If you mean "a system of communication," then birds do it, bees do it, and even plants do it. If you define language as "a system of communication that combines sounds or gestures into an infinite number of structured utterances that convey meaning" (which is the way linguists define it), then as far as anyone can tell, only people do it. And if, instead of looking at language as a whole, you focus instead on specific aspects of language, asking which aspects some animals might be able to acquire in special settings, you will discover some similarities between humans and other primates, which you might never have imagined, as we will see in Chapter 7.

3 **EXAMINE THE EVIDENCE.** Have you ever heard someone in the heat of argument exclaim, "I just know it's true, no matter what you say" or "That's my opinion; nothing's going to change it"? Have you ever made such statements yourself? Accepting a conclusion without evidence, or expecting others to do so, is a sure sign of lazy thinking. A critical thinker asks, "What evidence supports or refutes this argument and its opposition? How reliable is the evidence?" If it is not possible to check the reliability of the evidence directly, the person considers whether it came from a reliable source.

Some pop-psych ideas have been widely accepted on the basis of poor evidence or even no evidence at all. For example, many people think it is healthy to ventilate their anger at the first person, pet, or piece of furniture that gets in their way. Actually, studies across many fields show that ventilation often makes the angry person angrier, makes the target of the anger become angry in return, lowers everybody's self-esteem, and fosters hostility and aggression (Bushman, Baumeister, & Stack, 1999; Tavris, 1989). Yet the belief that expressing anger is always healthy persists, despite the evidence to the contrary. Perhaps you can think of some reasons why this might be so.

4 **ANALYZE ASSUMPTIONS AND BIASES.** Critical thinkers try to identify the unspoken assumptions on which claims and arguments may rest. An assumption is any belief that is taken for granted: for example, "All Democrats (or Republicans) are idiots"; or "People have free will and are therefore entirely responsible for any crimes they commit" (or, conversely, "People's behavior is a result of their biology or upbringing, so they aren't responsible for anything they do"); or "I was brought up to believe that the best way to discipline children is to spank them." Everyone, of course, makes assumptions; we could not function otherwise. But if we do not make our own and other people's assumptions explicit, our ability to judge an argument's merits may be impaired.

When an assumption or belief keeps us from considering the evidence fairly, or causes us to ignore the evidence completely, it becomes a *bias*. Sometimes we are unaware that we have a bias until someone challenges our belief and we get defensive and angry. For example, most people believe that parents are the most important influence in shaping a child's personality and behavior. In 1998, in her book *The Nurture Assumption*, Judith Rich Harris dared to question that assumption. Genes and peers, she argued, are more important influences than how parents raise their children. This idea immediately provoked a storm of outrage and scorn. Some critics focused on Harris's lack of credentials instead of her facts or her logic (she does not have a Ph.D.), and some attacked the book without even bothering to read it. That is the nature of a bias: It causes us to put on intellectual blinders. (In later chapters we will consider the influence of genes, parents, and peers on children's development.)

5 Avoid emotional reasoning. Emotion has a place in critical thinking. Passionate commitment to a view can motivate a person to think boldly, defend an unpopular idea, and seek evidence for a creative new theory. But when gut feelings replace clear thinking, the results can be dangerous. "Persecutions and wars and lynchings," observed Edward de Bono (1985), "are all a result of gut feeling."

Because our feelings feel so *right*, so natural, we may not realize that people who hold an opposing viewpoint feel just as strongly as we do. But they usually do, which means that emotional conviction alone cannot settle arguments. You probably hold strong feelings about drugs, the causes of crime, racism, the origins of intelligence, gender differences, homosexuality, and many other issues of concern to psychologists. As you read this book, you may find yourself quarreling with findings that you dislike. Disagreement is fine; it means that you are reading actively. All we ask is that you think about why you are disagreeing: Is it because the evidence is unpersuasive or because the results make you feel anxious or annoyed?

6 Don't oversimplify. A critical thinker looks beyond the obvious, resists easy generalizations, and rejects either/or thinking. For example, is it better to feel you have control over everything that happens to you, or to accept with tranquility whatever life serves up? Either position oversimplifies. As we will see in Chapter 6, a sense of control has many important benefits, but sometimes it is wiser and healthier to "go with the flow."

One common form of oversimplification is *argument by anecdote*, generalizing from a personal experience or a few examples to everyone. One crime committed by a paroled ex-convict means that parole should be abolished; one friend who hates her school means that everybody who goes there hates it. Anecdotes are often the source of stereotyping, as well: One dishonest welfare mother means they are all dishonest; one encounter with an unconventional Californian means they are all flaky. Critical thinkers want more evidence than one or two stories before drawing such sweeping conclusions.

7 Consider other interpretations. Critical thinkers generate as many interpretations of the evidence as possible before settling on the most likely one. For example, suppose you hear a report that chronically depressed people are more likely than nondepressed people to develop cancer. Before concluding that depression causes cancer, you would need to consider some other possibilities. Perhaps depressed people are more likely to smoke and drink too much, and it is those unhealthful habits that increase their cancer risk. Perhaps, in studies of depression and cancer, early undetected cancers have been responsible for people's feelings of depression. Alternative explanations such as these must be ruled out by further investigation before we can conclude that depression is a direct cause of cancer.

Once several explanations of a phenomenon have been generated, a critical thinker chooses the one that accounts for the most evidence and makes the fewest unverified assumptions. This is the principle of *Occam's razor,* named after the fourteenth-century philosopher who proposed it, William of Occam. The "razor" pares away the unverified assumptions. For example, suppose that a fortune-teller reads your palm and predicts that soon you will fall in love on a blind date, travel to Zanzibar, and have twins. One of two things must be true (Steiner, 1989):

✦ The fortune-teller can actually sort out the infinite number of interactions among people, animals, events, objects, and circumstances that could affect your life and can know for sure the outcome. Moreover, this fortune-teller is able to alter all the known laws of physics and defy the hundreds of studies showing that no one, under proper procedures for validating psychic predictions, has been able to predict the future for any given individual.

OR

✦ The fortune-teller is faking it.

A critical thinker chooses the second alternative because it requires fewer assumptions and has the most supporting evidence.

8 TOLERATE UNCERTAINTY. Ultimately, learning to think critically teaches us one of the hardest lessons of life: how to live with uncertainty. Sometimes there is little or no evidence to examine. Sometimes the evidence permits only tentative conclusions. Sometimes the evidence seems strong enough to permit conclusions until, exasperatingly, new information throws our beliefs into disarray. Critical thinkers are willing to accept this state of uncertainty. They are not afraid to say, "I don't know" or "I'm not sure" or, the hardest, "I was wrong." This admission is not an evasion but a spur to further creative inquiry.

The desire for certainty often makes people uncomfortable when experts cannot give them "the" answer to a question. Patients may demand of their doctors, "What do you mean you don't know what's wrong with me? Find out and fix it!" Students may demand of their professors, "What do you mean it's a controversial issue? Just tell me the answer!" Critical thinkers know that the more important the question, the less likely it is to have a single simple answer.

Does this mean that there is no such thing as intellectual progress? Not at all. When a theory falls apart, a new and better theory often arises from its ashes, explaining more facts, solving more puzzles. This process of discovery and revision of ideas can be frustrating for those who want psychology and other sciences to hand them only absolute truths. But it is exciting for those who love the pursuit of understanding as much as the collection of facts.

The need to accept a certain amount of uncertainty, however, does not mean that we must live without beliefs and convictions. That would be impossible, in any case: We all need values and principles to guide our actions. As Vincent Ruggiero (1988) wrote, "It is not the embracing of an idea that causes problems—it is the refusal to relax that embrace when good sense dictates doing so. It is enough to form convictions with care and carry them lightly, being willing to reconsider them whenever new evidence calls them into question."

Of course, critical thinking cannot provide answers to all of life's quandaries. Some questions, such as whether there is a God and what the nature of God might be, are ultimately matters of faith (Shermer, 2000). Moreover, critical thinking is a process, not a once-and-for-all accomplishment. No one ever becomes a perfect critical thinker, entirely unaffected by emotional reasoning and wishful thinking. We are all less open-minded than we think; it is always easier to poke holes in another person's argument than to critically examine our own position. In the words of philosopher Richard Paul (1984), critical thinking is really "fair-mindedness brought into the heart of everyday life."

As you read this book, keep our eight guidelines in mind. In some of the "What Do You Know?" quizzes, you will find questions that ask you to use one or more of the guidelines in answering. And throughout every chapter, you will have many other opportunities to apply the guidelines to psychological theories and to the personal and social issues that affect us all.

What Do You Know?

Amelia and Harold are arguing about the death penalty. "Look, I just feel strongly that it's barbaric, ineffective, and wrong," says Harold. "You're nuts," says Amelia, "I believe in an eye for an eye, and besides, I'm absolutely sure it's a deterrent to further crime." Which lapses of critical thinking might Amelia and Harold be committing?

ANSWERS:

Here are some problems in their style of argument: feel free to think of others. (1) They are reasoning emotionally ("I feel strongly about this, so I'm right and you're wrong"). (2) They have not examined evidence that supports or contradicts their arguments. What do studies show about the link between the death penalty and crime? Is the death penalty applied fairly to rich and poor, men and women, blacks and whites? (3) They have not examined the assumptions and biases they bring to the discussion. For example, are they assuming that the main goal of the death penalty is to deter criminals, to satisfy the public desire for revenge, or to keep criminals from being paroled and returned to the streets?

PSYCHOLOGY PAST AND PRESENT

Now that you know what psychology is and what it isn't, and why studying it requires critical thinking, let us see how psychology developed into a modern discipline.

Until the nineteenth century, psychology was not a formal profession with explicit rules about how it was to be conducted. Of course, most of the great thinkers of history, from Aristotle to Zoroaster, raised questions that today would be called psychological. They wanted to know how people take in information through their senses, use information to solve problems, and become motivated to act in brave or villainous ways. They wondered about the elusive nature of emotion, and whether it controls us or is something we can control. Like today's psychologists, they wanted to *describe, predict, understand,* and *modify* behavior in order to add to human knowledge and increase human happiness. But unlike modern psychologists, scholars of the past did not rely heavily on empirical evidence. Often, their observations were based simply on anecdotes or descriptions of individual cases.

This does not mean that the forerunners of modern psychology were always wrong. On the contrary, they often had insights and made observations that were verified by later work. Hippocrates (c. 460 B.C.–c. 377 B.C.), the Greek physician known as the founder of modern medicine, observed patients with head injuries and inferred that the brain must be the ultimate source of "our pleasures, joys, laughter, and jests as well as our sorrows, pains, griefs, and tears." And so it is. In the first century A.D., the Stoic philosophers observed that people do not become angry or sad or anxious because of actual events, but because of their explanations of those events. And so they do. In the seventeenth century, the French philosopher René Descartes (1596–1650) promoted scientific thinking by searching for physical explanations of behavior. Later in the same century, the English philosopher John Locke (1643–1704) argued that the mind works by associating ideas arising from experience, a notion that continues to influence many psychologists today.

But without empirical methods, the forerunners of psychology also committed some terrible blunders. A good example comes from the early 1800s, when the theory of *phrenology* (Greek for "study of the mind") became wildly popular. Inspired by the writings and lectures of Austrian physician Joseph Gall (1758–1828), phrenologists argued that different brain areas accounted for specific character and personality traits, such as "stinginess" and "religiosity," and that such traits could be "read" from bumps on the skull. Thieves, for example, supposedly had large bumps above the ears. When phrenologists examined people with "stealing bumps" who were *not* thieves, they simply explained away this counterevidence by saying that other brain bumps represented positive traits that must be holding the person's thieving impulses in check.

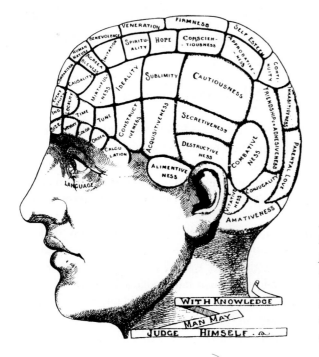

Phrenology, a nineteenth-century pseudoscientific fad, linked bumps on the skull with character traits. On this phrenological "map," notice the tiny space allocated to self-esteem and the large one devoted to cautiousness!

In the United States, all sorts of people eagerly sought the services of phrenologists. Parents used them to make decisions about whether their children could benefit from music lessons; schools used them to decide which teachers to hire; young people used them when deciding on a career or a mate; and businesses used them to find out which employees were likely to be loyal and honest (Benjamin, 1998). Some phrenologists traveled around the country giving readings, and some offered classes or self-study programs for people who wanted to overcome their deficiencies—a forerunner of today's many self-improvement programs. Enthusiasm for phrenology did not disappear until well into the twentieth century, even though it was a classic pseudoscience—utter nonsense.

The Birth of Modern Psychology

At the same time that phrenologists were at their peak of success, several pioneering researchers in Europe and America were starting to study psychological issues using scientific methods. Indeed, psychology has many forefathers—and several foremothers, too, although their accomplishments were often unacknowledged or were attributed to others (Scarborough & Furumoto, 1987). But credit for the establishment of psychology as a science usually goes to Wilhelm Wundt [VIL-helm Voont], who formally founded the first psychological laboratory in 1879, in Leipzig, Germany.

Wundt (1832–1920), who was trained in medicine and philosophy, wrote many volumes on psychology, physiology, natural history, ethics, and logic. But he is especially revered by psychologists because he was the first person to announce (in 1873) that he intended to make psychology a science and because his laboratory was the first to have its results published in a scholarly journal. Although the Leipzig laboratory started out as just a few rooms in an old building, it soon became the place to go for anyone who wanted to become a psychologist. Many of America's first psychologists got their training there.

Researchers in Wundt's laboratory did not study the wide gamut of topics that today's psychologists do. Most concentrated on sensation, perception, reaction times, imagery, and attention, and they avoided learning, personality, and abnormal behavior. Their overriding goal was to discover the building blocks of experience. One of Wundt's favorite research methods was *trained introspection,* in which specially trained people carefully observed, analyzed, and described their own sensations, mental images, and emotional reactions. This was not as easy as it sounds. Wundt's introspectors had to make 10,000 practice observations before they were allowed to participate in an actual study. Once trained, they might take as long as 20 minutes to report their inner experiences during a 1.5-second experiment.

Wundt hoped that trained introspection would produce solid, reliable results. Ironically, however, although he made his mark on history by declaring psychology to be an objective science, many other psychologists rejected introspection because it wasn't objective enough. Imagine that you round up some trained introspectors and ask them to report their mental experience of the word *triangle.* Most report a visual image of a form with three sides and three corners. But Elbert reports a flashing red triangle with equal angles, Endora reports a colorless form with one angle larger than the others, and Euphonia claims she can think about a triangle without forming any visual image at all. Introspection alone, therefore, doesn't give us the basic attributes of triangles. Many psychologists also found Wundt's approach too narrow. Wolfgang Köhler (1959) recalled how he and his colleagues had responded to it as students: "What had disturbed us was . . . the implication that human life, apparently so colorful and so intensely dynamic, is actually a frightful bore."

In America, Wundt's ideas were soon opposed by a school of scientific psychology called **functionalism,** which emphasized the function, or purpose, of behavior, as opposed to its analysis and description. One of functionalism's leaders was William James (1842–1910), an American philosopher, physician, and psychologist who argued that searching for building blocks of experience was a waste of time. The brain and the mind are constantly changing, he noted. Attempting to grasp the nature of the mind through introspection, wrote James (1890/1950), is "like seizing a spinning top to catch its motion, or trying to turn up the gas quickly enough to see how the darkness looks."

The functionalists were less interested in *what* happens when an organism does something than in *how* and *why* it's done. They were inspired in part by the evolutionary theories of British naturalist Charles Darwin (1809–1882), who had argued that a biologist's job is not merely to describe, say, the brilliant plumage of a peacock or the drab markings of a lizard, but also to figure out how these attributes enhance survival. Do they help the animal attract a mate or hide from its enemies? Similarly, the functionalists wanted to know how specific behaviors and mental processes help a person or animal adapt to the environment, so they looked for underlying causes and practical consequences of these behaviors and processes. They felt free to use many different methods, and they broadened the field of psychology to include the study of children, animals, religious experiences, and what James called the "stream of consciousness"—a term still used because it so beautifully describes the way thoughts flow like a river, tumbling over each other in waves, sometimes placid, sometimes turbulent. Although functionalism did not last long as a formal school, its emphasis on the causes and consequences of behavior was to set the course of psychological science.

Psychology also has roots in Vienna, Austria, where it first developed as a method of psychotherapy. While researchers in Europe and America were working in their laboratories, struggling to make psychology more scientific, Sigmund Freud (1856–1939), an obscure neurologist, was in his office listening to his patients' reports of depression, nervousness, and obsessive habits. Freud had originally hoped for a career as a medical researcher, but research did not pay well and family responsibilities forced him to go into private practice as a physician. As he listened to his patients, he became convinced that their symptoms were not physical at all, but a result of conflicts and emotional traumas that had occurred in early childhood and that were too threatening to be remembered consciously.

Freud argued that conscious awareness is merely the tip of a mental iceberg. Beneath the visible tip, he said, lies the unconscious part of the mind, containing unrevealed wishes, passions, guilty secrets, unspeakable yearnings, and conflicts between desire and

---

functionalism An early psychological approach that emphasized the function or purpose of behavior and consciousness.

duty. We are not aware of our unconscious urges and thoughts as we go about our daily business, yet they make themselves known—in dreams, slips of the tongue, apparent accidents, and even jokes. Freud (1905a) wrote, "No mortal can keep a secret. If the lips are silent, he chatters with his fingertips; betrayal oozes out of him at every pore."

Freud's proposals were not an overnight sensation; his first book, *The Interpretation of Dreams* (1900), managed to sell only 600 copies in the eight years following publication. Eventually, however, his ideas evolved into a broad theory of personality and a method of psychotherapy, both of which became known as **psychoanalysis.** Freudian concepts had a profound influence on the philosophy, literature, and art of the twentieth century, and his name is now as much a household word as Einstein's.

Psychology Today

From its early beginnings in philosophy, natural science, and medicine, psychology today has grown into a complex field encompassing many different specialties, perspectives, methods, and training programs. The field is now like a large, sprawling family. The members of this family share common great-grandparents, but some of the cousins have formed alliances, some are quarreling, and a few are barely speaking to one another.

The first thing the cousins are quarreling about is the very definition of a psychologist. To most laypeople, the word *psychologist* conjures up an image of a therapist listening intently while a client pours forth his or her troubles. Actually, the professional activities of psychologists fall into three general categories: (1) teaching and doing research in colleges and universities; (2) providing health or mental-health services, often referred to as *psychological practice;* and (3) conducting research or applying research findings in nonacademic settings such as business, sports, government, law, the military, and private research institutes (see Table 1.1). Some psychologists move flexibly across these areas: A researcher might also provide counseling services in a mental-health setting, such as a clinic or a hospital; a university professor might teach, do research, and consult on legal cases or with government policymakers.

Psychological Research. Most psychologists who do research have doctoral degrees (Ph.D.s or Ed.D.s, doctorates in education). Some, seeking knowledge for its own sake, work in **basic psychology,** doing "pure" research. Others, concerned with the practical uses of knowledge, work in **applied psychology.** A psychologist doing basic research might ask, "How do children, adolescents, and adults differ in their approach to moral issues such as honesty?" An applied psychologist might ask, "How can knowledge about moral development be used to prevent teenage violence?" A psychologist in basic science might ask, "Can a chimpanzee or a gorilla learn to use sign language?" An applied

---

psychoanalysis A theory of personality and a method of psychotherapy, originally formulated by Sigmund Freud, which emphasizes unconscious motives and conflicts.

basic psychology The study of psychological issues in order to seek knowledge for its own sake rather than for its practical application.

applied psychology The study of psychological issues that have direct practical significance and the application of psychological findings.

TABLE 1.1 ✦ What Is a Psychologist?

Many psychologists are psychotherapists, but others do research, teach, work in business, or consult.

ACADEMIC/RESEARCH PSYCHOLOGISTS	CLINICAL PSYCHOLOGISTS	PSYCHOLOGISTS IN INDUSTRY, LAW, OR OTHER SETTINGS
Specialize in areas of pure or applied research, such as:	*May work in any of these settings, or in some combination:*	*Do research or serve as consultants to institutions on, for example:*
Human development	Private practice	Sports
Psychometrics (testing)	Mental-health clinics or services	Consumer issues
Health	Hospitals	Advertising
Education	Research laboratories	Organizational problems
Industrial/organizational psychology	Colleges and universities	Environmental issues
Physiological psychology		Public policy
Sensation and perception		Survey research and opinion polls

---

psychologist might ask, "Can techniques used to teach language to a chimpanzee be used to help mentally impaired or disturbed children who do not speak?"

Psychologists doing basic and applied research have made important contributions in areas as diverse as health, education, marketing, management, consumer behavior, industrial design, worker productivity, and urban planning. Most of the findings you will be reading about in this book come from the efforts of research psychologists.

Psychological Practice. Psychological practitioners, whose goal is to understand and improve physical and mental health, work in mental hospitals, general hospitals, clinics, schools, counseling centers, and private practice. Since the 1970s, the proportion of psychologists who are practitioners has greatly increased; today, practitioners account for over two-thirds of new psychology doctorates and members of the American Psychological Association (APA), psychology's largest professional organization (APA Research Office, 1998; Shapiro & Wiggins, 1994).

Some practitioners are *counseling psychologists,* who generally help people deal with everyday problems such as test anxiety, family conflicts, or low job motivation. Others are *school psychologists,* who work with students (and sometimes their parents and teachers) to help students do better in school and resolve emotional difficulties. The majority, however, are *clinical psychologists,* who diagnose, treat, and study mental or emotional problems. Clinical psychologists are trained to do psychotherapy with highly disturbed people, as well as with those who are simply troubled or unhappy or who want to learn to handle their problems better.

To practice psychology, you need a license, and in almost all states a clinical psychology license requires a doctorate. Most clinical psychologists have a Ph.D., some have an Ed.D., and a smaller but growing number have a Psy.D. (doctorate in psychology, pronounced "sy-dee"). Clinical psychologists typically do four or five years of graduate work in psychology, plus at least a year's internship under the direction of a practicing psychologist. Clinical programs leading to a Ph.D. or Ed.D. are usually designed to prepare a person both as a scientist and as a clinical practitioner; they require completion of a dissertation, a major scholarly project (usually involving research) that contributes to knowledge in the field. Programs leading to a Psy.D. focus on professional practice and do not usually require a research dissertation, although they typically require the student to complete a study, literature review, or other scholarly project.

People often confuse *clinical psychologist* with three other terms: *psychotherapist, psychoanalyst,* and *psychiatrist,* but these terms mean different things:

✦ A *psychotherapist* is simply anyone who does any kind of psychotherapy. The term is not legally regulated; in fact, in most states, anyone can say that he or she is a "therapist" of one sort or another without having any training at all. And plenty do, promoting unvalidated "therapies" ranging from aromatherapy to age regression. When you hear or read about someone described as a "psychotherapist in private practice," keep in mind that the person could be anything from a clinical psychologist to an untrained, self-proclaimed "expert" who took a weekend "certification" course in some trendy but unvalidated technique.

✦ A *psychoanalyst* is a person who practices one particular form of therapy, psychoanalysis. To call yourself a psychoanalyst, you must get specialized training at a psychoanalytic institute and undergo extensive psychoanalysis yourself. Until recently, admission to a psychoanalytic institute required an M.D. or a Ph.D., but increasingly this requirement is being waived; for example, clinical social workers with master's degrees are often now admitted.

✦ A *psychiatrist* is a medical doctor (M.D.) who has done a 3-year residency in psychiatry, the medical specialty concerned with mental disorders. Like clinical psychologists, psychiatrists may either work with patients or conduct research on mental problems, such as depression or schizophrenia. But psychiatrists, because of their medical training, tend to focus on possible biological causes of mental disorders and to treat these problems with medication. They can write prescriptions, whereas clinical psychologists cannot (or at least not yet; in many states, they are pressing for prescription-writing privileges). Psychiatrists, however, are often untrained in current psychological theories and methods (Luhrmann, 2000).

As if all these credentials and labels were not confusing enough, many other people work in related mental-health fields, including licensed clinical social workers (LCSWs) and marriage, family, and child counselors (MFCCs). These professionals ordinarily treat general problems in adjustment, rather than severe mental disturbance, although their work may bring them into contact with people who have serious problems—violent delinquents, sex offenders, individuals involved in domestic and child abuse.

Licensing requirements vary from state to state but usually include a master's degree in psychology or social work and one or two years of supervised experience. (For a summary of the types of psychotherapists and the training they receive, see Table 1.2.)

Many research psychologists are worried about the recent increase in the number of psychotherapists who are unschooled in research methods, who know little about empirical findings, and who use unvalidated therapy techniques (Dawes, 1994; Poole et al., 1995). Some practitioners, too, are concerned about the lack of uniform standards in professional education (Fox, 1994). In 1987, such concerns contributed to the formation of the American Psychological Society (APS), an organization devoted to the needs and interests of psychology as a science. Many practitioners, on the other hand, argue that psychotherapy is an art, and that research findings are largely irrelevant to the work they do with clients. In Chapter 12, we will return to the important issue of the widening gap in training and attitudes between scientists and some therapists.

Psychology in the Community. Since World War II, psychology has expanded rapidly in terms of scholars, publications, and specialties. As the field has grown, psychologists have found ways to contribute to their communities in about as many areas as you can think of. They consult with companies to improve worker satisfaction and productivity. They establish programs to improve race relations and reduce ethnic tensions. They advise commissions on how pollution and noise affect mental health. They provide rehabilitation training for people who are physically or mentally disabled. They educate judges and juries about the reliability of eyewitness testimony. They assist the police in emergencies involving hostages or disturbed persons. They conduct public-opinion surveys. They run suicide-prevention hot lines. They advise zoos on the care and training of animals. They help coaches improve the athletic performance of their teams. And on and on. Is it any wonder that people are a little fuzzy about what a psychologist is?

TABLE 1.2 ✦ Types of Psychotherapists

Psychotherapist	A person who does psychotherapy: may have anything from no degree to an advanced professional degree; the term is unregulated
Clinical psychologist	Has a Ph.D., an Ed.D., or a Psy.D.
Psychoanalyst	Has specific training in psychoanalysis after an advanced degree (usually, but not always, an M.D. or a Ph.D.)
Psychiatrist	A medical doctor (M.D.) with a specialty in psychiatry
Licensed clinical social worker (LCSW); school psychologist; marriage, family, and child counselor (MFCC)	Licensing requirements vary; generally has at least a master's degree in psychology or social work

Because of the diversity in psychological occupations, and because the media and the public persist in equating "psychologist" with "psychotherapist," some psychological scientists want to use other labels to describe what they do and to yield the word *psychologist* to its popular meaning. Research psychologists, they say, should call themselves "cognitive scientists," "behavioral scientists," "neuroscientists," and so forth, depending on their area of study. This change is already underway. At present, however, the word *psychologist* still embraces all the cousins in psychology's sprawling family.

What Do You Know?

A. See whether psychology's past is still present in your memory.
   1. The forerunners of psychology depended heavily on (casual observation/empirical methods).
   2. Credit for founding modern psychology is generally given to (William James/Wilhelm Wundt).
   3. Early psychologists who emphasized how behavior helps an organism adapt to its environment were known as _____.

B. Can you match the specialties on the left with their defining credentials and approaches on the right?

   1. psychotherapist
   2. psychiatrist
   3. clinical psychologist
   4. research psychologist
   5. psychoanalyst

   a. Has an M.D. or Ph.D. and training in an approach started by Freud
   b. Has a Ph.D., Psy.D., or Ed.D. and does research on, or psychotherapy for, mental-health problems
   c. May have any credential or none
   d. Has an advanced degree (usually a Ph.D. or Ed.D) and does applied or basic research
   e. Has an M.D.; tends to take a medical approach to emotional problems

ANSWERS:

A. 1. casual observation 2. Wilhelm Wundt 3. functionalists B. 1. c 2. e 3. b 4. d 5. a

THE MAJOR PSYCHOLOGICAL PERSPECTIVES

Several people are discussing their problems with anger. A woman says, "I was *born* angry. I hissed at passersby when I was carried home from the hospital." A man attributes his bad temper to what he learned by observing his father. "My dad used to get drunk and blow up at us," he recalls, "and now I find myself doing just what he did." A teenage gang member explains why he attacked a stranger on the street: "I had no choice; the man dissed me." A woman confesses that she displaces her anger at her husband by yelling irrationally at her children, friends, and mother. Finally, an observer says, "The trouble with all of you is that you're American—always blowing up at the slightest provocation, like selfish children who don't get their way. In my country it would be a terrible loss of face to reveal anger. We are expected to remember how destructive anger can be."

The five views offered by these individuals correspond to the five approaches that predominate in psychology today: the *biological, learning, cognitive, psychodynamic,* and *sociocultural* perspectives. These approaches reflect different questions about human behavior, different assumptions about how the mind works, and, most important, different ways of explaining why people do what they do. You will be studying these five perspectives in more depth and detail as you read this book; here we will introduce you briefly to each of them. To make them more memorable to you at this early stage of your reading, we will point out more fully how each might approach the topic of anger.

The Biological Perspective

 Many people, when they first start studying psychology, are surprised to find that psychologists are interested not only in actions and thoughts, but also in genes, hormones, and nerve cells. Yet the biological approach to psychology has been an important one from the very beginning. Wilhelm Wundt's best-known work was called *Principles of Physiological Psychology,* and for good reason: He and most other early researchers expected their science to rest on a firm foundation of anatomy and physiology.

The **biological perspective** focuses on how bodily events affect behavior, feelings, and thoughts. Electrical impulses shoot along the intricate pathways of the nervous system. Hormones course through the bloodstream, telling internal organs to slow down or speed up. Chemical messengers flow across the tiny gaps that separate one microscopic brain cell from another. Biological psychologists want to know how these physical events interact with environmental ones to produce our thoughts and behavior. They study how biology affects learning and performance, memory, perceptions of reality, the experience of emotion, and vulnerability to emotional disorder. They take part in the age-old debate over the relative contributions made by "nature" (genetic dispositions) and "nurture" (upbringing and environment) in the development of abilities and personality traits. And in a popular new specialty, *evolutionary psychology,* researchers have been studying how our species' evolutionary past may help explain some of our present behaviors and psychological traits.

Technological advances have made it possible for biological researchers to explore areas of an organism's "inner space" where no one has ever ventured before. One result has been a better understanding of how mind and body interact in illness and in

---

biological perspective A psychological approach that emphasizes bodily events and changes associated with actions, feelings, and thoughts.

health. This is the research focus of an interdisciplinary specialty called (cumbersomely) *psychoneuroimmunology,* or *PNI* for short: "psycho" for psychological processes such as emotions and perceptions, "neuro" for the nervous and endocrine systems, and "immunology" for the immune system. Researchers in this specialty are learning that although bodily processes can affect one's moods and emotions, the converse is also true: Emotions, attitudes, and perceptions can influence the functioning of the immune system and thus a person's susceptibility to certain diseases (Andersen, Kiecolt-Glaser, & Glaser, 1994).

Many biological psychologists hope that their discoveries, along with those of biochemists and other scientists, will help solve some of the mysteries of mental and emotional problems. For example, researchers in the biological tradition would have a few questions about people like the woman who believes she was "born angry." Do such people have a physical condition that might be affecting their behavior, such as an injury to the brain or a neurological disorder? Do they have an inborn temperamental tendency to be easily aroused? Are drugs affecting their emotions? Is physical stress contributing to their anger?

People often think that the explanation for some puzzle of behavior must be *either* physiological *or* psychological, and they fail to appreciate how complex the interactions between body and mind really are. But the biological approach has a useful message for us all: We cannot know ourselves if we do not know our bodies.

The Learning Perspective

The **learning perspective** is concerned with the impact of the environment and experience on a person's (or an animal's) actions. The origins of this perspective go back to 1913, when a psychologist named John B. Watson (1878–1958) published a paper that rocked the still-young science of psychology. In "Psychology as the Behaviorist Views It," Watson argued that if psychology were ever to be an objective science, it would have to give up its preoccupation with the mind and consciousness. Psychologists, he said, should throw out introspection as a method of research and reject terms such as *mental state, mind,* or *emotion* in explanations of behavior. They should stick to what they can observe and measure directly: acts and events actually taking place in the environment. In short, they should give up mentalism for **behaviorism.** Instead of asking, say, what a pinprick feels like—Wundt's approach—psychologists should observe what happens if you stick someone's finger with a pin: tears, withdrawal of the hand, loud cursing, or whatever.

Watson was influenced by the Russian physiologist Ivan Pavlov (1849–1936), who had shown that many kinds of automatic or involuntary behavior, such as salivating at

---

learning perspective A psychological approach that emphasizes how the environment and experience affect a person's or animal's actions; it includes *behaviorism* and *social-cognitive learning theories.*

behaviorism An approach to psychology that emphasizes the study of objectively observable behavior and the role of the environment as a determinant of behavior.

the sight of food, were simply learned responses to specific events, or stimuli, in the environment. Later, another psychologist, B. F. Skinner (1904–1990), identified the behavioral laws governing voluntary acts, such as riding a bike, cooking an omelet, or having a temper tantrum. Skinner showed that the consequences of an act powerfully affect the probability of its recurring: Acts that are followed by pleasant consequences are more likely to be repeated, and acts that are followed by unpleasant consequences are likely to cease. If riding the bike is fun, cooking produces a delicious omelet, and having a tantrum produces attentive parents who give you an ice cream cone, you will keep doing those things. If you keep falling off the bike, if your omelet tastes like sawdust, and if your tantrum gets you grounded for a month, you will probably stop doing them.

Behaviorism soon became the predominant American school of experimental psychology and remained so until the early 1960s. Here, at last, was a way for the social sciences to be hardheaded and earn the respect of a skeptical world. And behaviorism also broadened psychology by fostering the study of groups that could not be studied at all through introspection, including animals, infants, and mentally disturbed persons.

Eventually, however, it became apparent to most psychologists that behavioral principles were not enough to explain learning. People also learn by observation, imitation, and insight; and they learn by thinking about what they see around them. One outgrowth of behaviorism, *social-learning theory* (now usually called **social-cognitive learning theory**), combines elements of classic behaviorism with research on thinking and consciousness. It emphasizes, for example, how people's plans, beliefs about other people and the world, and expectations influence their behavior. As Albert Bandura (1986), a leading proponent of this approach, observed, "If actions were determined solely by external rewards and punishments, people would behave like weathervanes, constantly shifting direction to conform to whatever momentary influence happened to impinge on them." According to Bandura, the fact that people don't (always) act like weathervanes means that much of what we do depends on what's going on in our minds—our thoughts, values, and goals ("I don't care that I keep falling off this bike, dammit, I'm determined to learn to ride it"). Today, many psychologists feel comfortable combining elements of behaviorism with approaches that incorporate the study of thinking and consciousness.

Researchers in the learning perspective would be interested in the man in our anger group who said he was imitating the explosive anger patterns of his father. They would look for the consequences of both men's outbursts. What are the rewards for such behavior? When these men express anger, do they get the attention and reactions they want from others? Learning theorists would also want to know how the man's father learned to associate drinking alcohol with behaving abusively. Alcohol doesn't "liberate buried rage," they would say. Rather, people learn that when they are drunk they can get away with certain actions—actions they would be held accountable for if they were sober.

As we will see in Chapters 5 and 6, the learning perspective has had many practical applications, from programs that help people get rid of unreasonable fears or quit

---

social-cognitive learning theory The theory that behavior is learned and maintained through observation and imitation of others, positive consequences, and cognitive processes such as plans and perceptions.

smoking to techniques that boost self-confidence. Historically, the behaviorists' insistence on precision and objectivity did much to advance psychology as a science, and learning research in general has given psychology some of its most reliable findings.

The Cognitive Perspective

 During the 1950s and 1960s, a new emphasis in psychology on the workings of the human mind gathered momentum from an unexpected source. At the same time that learning theorists were starting to recognize the importance of cognitive factors, the development of the computer was encouraging the study of problem solving, informational "feedback," and other mental processes. The result was the rise of the **cognitive perspective** in psychology. (The word *cognitive* comes from the Latin for "to know.")

Cognitive psychologists argued that in order to understand how people use language, acquire moral standards, experience emotions, or behave in groups, psychologists must know what is going on in people's heads. They must understand the origins and consequences of people's cognitions: their thoughts, memories, beliefs, perceptions, explanations, and other mental processes. However, cognitive researchers did not wish to return to the discredited method of introspection. Instead, they developed new ways to infer mental processes from observable behavior. For example, by examining the kinds of errors people make when they try to recall words from a list, cognitive psychologists could draw conclusions about whether words are stored in memory in terms of sound or meaning.

Cognitive psychologists have also made tremendous contributions to our understanding of the nature of memory. Memory does not work like a tape recorder, as many people believe, faithfully recording everything that happens to you and then storing it away somewhere in your brain. As we will see in Chapter 8, memory is constantly being reconstructed and reinvented. It can be incredibly accurate, allowing us to remember facts we learned in elementary school, song lyrics, and a favorite baseball player's batting average. But it can also be astonishingly inaccurate, "retouching" the picture of past events with details and emotional coloration after the fact, and even deluding us into "remembering" things that never happened at all.

Another of this perspective's important contributions has been to show how people's explanations and interpretations of events affect what they do and feel. All of us are constantly seeking to make sense of the world around us and of our own physical and mental states. Our ideas may not always be realistic or sensible, but they continually influence our actions, choices, and emotional reactions. Consider the teenager who attacked a stranger because he believed the stranger had insulted him. Although the teenager felt his anger was inevitable and that he had no choice about reacting as he did, in fact his anger depended on his own *perception* that the stranger's behavior was a sign

---

cognitive perspective A psychological approach that emphasizes mental processes in perception, memory, language, problem solving, and other areas of behavior.

of disrespect. Perhaps there were other ways of interpreting the situation. Perhaps the stranger had no intention of being disrespectful. Perhaps the stranger was nearsighted and didn't even see the teenager.

Hardly a topic in psychology has been unaffected by what is now often called the "cognitive revolution." Cognitive psychologists have studied how people explain their own behavior, understand a sentence, solve intellectual problems, reason, form opinions, and remember events. With new methods of investigation, they have been able to study phenomena that were once only the stuff of speculation, such as sleeping, dreaming, and hypnosis. They are designing computer programs that model how humans perform complex tasks; discovering what goes on in the mind of an infant; and identifying types of intelligence not measured by conventional IQ tests. The cognitive approach is one of the strongest forces in psychology today, and it has inspired an explosion of research on the intricate workings of the mind.

The Sociocultural Perspective

For the most part, the study of psychology has been the study of the individual. During the 1930s and 1940s, some psychologists began to question this focus. They wanted to know how dictators like Adolf Hitler could persuade people to commit the kinds of atrocities that led to the deaths of millions of people. They wondered why apparently nice people often hold hateful racial or ethnic stereotypes and whether such attitudes could be changed. They asked how cultural values and political systems affect everyday experience. The view that emerged from these questions is the **sociocultural perspective,** which emphasizes the social and cultural forces that shape behavior and attitudes.

Most of us tend to overlook how social contexts and the situations we are in shape nearly everything we do: how we perceive the world, express joy or grief, manage our households, treat our friends and enemies. We are like fish that are unaware they live in water, so obvious is water in their lives. Sociocultural psychologists study the water—the social and cultural environment that people "swim" in every day.

Within this perspective, *social psychologists* study social rules and roles, the influence of groups, why people obey authority, and how each of us is affected by others: spouses, lovers, friends, bosses, parents, and strangers. They examine how standards of masculinity and femininity influence the expression of emotion and how job opportunities affect a person's goals and ambitions. They study how we emulate our heroes, succumb to peer pressure, and blossom or wilt in close relationships. They may also study such influences as features of the physical environment (e.g., room design, noise level, and temperature) and the requirements of specific jobs (e.g., flexible or inflexible routines). They investigate how the right environments can help people cope better with disabilities, get along better with others, and become more creative.

---

sociocultural perspective A psychological approach that emphasizes social and cultural influences on behavior.

Cultural psychologists expand the definition of "environment" to include the cultural rules and values that affect human development, behavior, and feelings. Sometimes these rules and values are explicit ("Every adult woman must cover her face and hair in public"), and sometimes they are nonverbal and implicit ("The correct nose-to-nose distance for talking to a friend is about 20 inches"). (Try it, and see whether that is your culture's rule for conversational distance.)

Cultural psychologists have shown that there are many differences between cultures that emphasize individualism, as in the United States and Canada, and cultures that emphasize group loyalty and cooperation, as in Asian and Latino countries. Americans say, "The squeaky wheel gets the grease" (meaning, stand up and make noise to get what you want); the Japanese say, "The nail that stands up from the board gets pounded down" (meaning, don't be too noticeable; it's more important to fit in). As we will see in Chapter 10, these differences affect people's actions and attitudes in many ways.

Researchers in the sociocultural perspective would be interested in how the particular situation and prevailing cultural rules affect the expression of anger. They would ask, "What are the cultural messages about anger that are promoted by television, books, parents, and teachers?" And they would agree with that observer of our anger group who noted that American culture often encourages or tolerates the public and private ventilation of angry feelings. Cultural psychologists would go even further, by exploring *why* cultures differ in their attitudes toward angry outbursts. One explanation: When groups or societies value group harmony over individual expression, as in Japan, or when they need to cooperate in order to survive, as the Inuit of Canada do, they tend to fear and avoid direct expressions of anger if at all possible. In contrast, societies with economies that thrive on competition and endorse the value of personal freedom over group harmony often tolerate individual outbursts of anger along with other forms of individual expression.

The sociocultural perspective was once ignored by many psychologists, but in recent years its influence has grown, and today it is a dominant force in psychology. Because human beings are social animals who are profoundly affected by their history, the groups they belong to, and their different cultural worlds, the sociocultural perspective has made psychology a more representative and rigorous discipline.

The Psychodynamic Perspective

Our last perspective, the **psychodynamic perspective,** deals with unconscious dynamics within the individual, such as inner forces, conflicts, or instinctual energy. This perspective is the thumb on the hand of psychology—connected to the other fingers, but also set apart from them in terms of language, methods, and standards of acceptable evidence. Whereas the other perspectives originated

---

psychodynamic perspective A psychological approach that emphasizes unconscious dynamics within the individual, such as inner forces, conflicts, or the movement of instinctual energy.

in scientific research, the psychodynamic perspective originated in Freudian psycho-analysis. Many psychologists working from other perspectives believe that psychodynamic approaches belong in philosophy or literature rather than in social science. But psychodynamic assumptions are still held by many psychotherapists and have influenced many artists, novelists, and laypeople, which is why we include this perspective.

Psychodynamic theories share an *intrapsychic* view of the individual, emphasizing the hidden, unconscious mechanisms within the mind or "psyche." *Dynamics,* a term from physics, refers to the motion and balance of systems under the action of external or internal forces; for example, the science of thermodynamics studies the relationship between heat and mechanical energy. Freud borrowed from nineteenth-century physics the idea of the conservation of energy: Within any system, he thought, energy can be shifted or transformed, but the total amount of energy remains the same. Psychological energy—the energy it takes to carry out mental and emotional processes, such as thinking, dreaming, and worrying—was, to Freud, a form of physical energy.

Unconscious forces, Freud believed, have far more power over behavior than conscious ones do, so psychologists must probe beneath the surface, in effect becoming archeologists of the mind. For example, Freud viewed aggression (and sexuality as well) as a basic instinct that lodges in the unconscious. Aggressive energy that is not channeled into productive activity, he believed, will inevitably be released or *displaced* in violent actions, ranging from anger to war. Think back once again to our group of angry people: The woman who said she "displaces" anger by yelling at her children is using psychodynamic language.

Most of Freud's followers kept his fundamental belief in the importance of unconscious dynamics, but they broke away from many specific aspects of psychoanalytic theory. This is why we use the more general term *psychodynamic* to label this perspective rather than *psychoanalytic.* Although many psychodynamic assumptions are impossible to verify, others have generated empirical research. Some psychologists study defense mechanisms, which Freud saw as ways in which the mind protects itself from threatening information—for example, through denial or rationalization. Others are studying the nature of nonconscious processes—for example, how people can perceive something without being aware of it. Defenders of the psychodynamic perspective point out that it is the only one that tries to deal with the great existential human dilemmas, such as alienation in a lonely world and the universal fear of death. Later in this book, we will discuss more fully the many controversies surrounding psychodynamic ideas.

Two Influential Movements in Psychology

Throughout psychology's history, various movements and intellectual trends have emerged that do not fit neatly into any of the field's major perspectives. In the 1960s, for example, Abraham Maslow, Rollo May, and Carl Rogers rejected the psychoanalytic emphasis on unconscious conflict as too negative and pessimistic a view of human nature; psychoanalysts, they said, were ignoring human resilience and the capacity for joy. And they also rejected the behavioral approach as too mechanistic and "mindless"; behaviorists, they said, were ignoring what really matters to most people: their uniquely human hopes and aspirations. It was time, they said, for a "third force" in psychology, which they called **humanist psychology.**

In the humanist view, human behavior is not completely determined by either unconscious dynamics or the environment. People have free will and are therefore able to make more of themselves than either psychoanalysts or behaviorists would predict. Maslow (1971) wrote, "When you select out for careful study very fine and healthy people, strong people, creative people, saintly people, sagacious people . . . then you get a very different view of mankind. You are asking how tall can people grow, what can a human being become?" The goal of humanist psychology was to help people grow as tall as possible, to achieve their full potential.

Although humanism is no longer a dominant school in psychology, it has had considerable influence inside and outside the field. Many psychologists across all perspectives embrace some humanist ideas, although most regard humanism as a philosophy of life rather than a systematic approach to psychology. Further, many topics raised by the humanists—such as happiness, creativity, and courage—have been studied empirically by scientific psychologists in other perspectives. But humanism has had its greatest influence in psychotherapy and in the human potential and self-help movements. We will discuss it further in Chapter 12.

Another important movement, which emerged in the 1970s, was **feminist psychology.** Feminist psychologists threw an intellectual hand grenade into psychology: They documented evidence of a pervasive bias in the research methods of psychology and the very questions that researchers had been asking (Bem, 1993; Crawford & Marecek, 1989; Hare-Mustin & Marecek, 1990). Many studies had used only men as subjects—and usually only young, white, middle-class men, at that—and had inappropriately generalized to everyone else from such narrow data.

Today, women and men who call themselves feminist psychologists may identify with any of the five major perspectives, or they may draw on research from several approaches in analyzing gender relations and the behavior of the sexes. Feminist psychologists have spurred research on topics that were long ignored in psychology, including menstruation, motherhood, the dynamics of power and sexuality in close relationships, definitions of masculinity and femininity, gender roles, and sexist attitudes (Fischer & Good, 1998; Frieze & McHugh, 1998; Spence & Hahn, 1997). They have also critically examined the male bias in psychotherapy, starting with Freud's own case studies (Hare-Mustin, 1991). And they have analyzed the social consequences of psychological findings, showing how research has often been used to justify the lower status of women and other disadvantaged groups.

---

humanist psychology A psychological approach that emphasizes personal growth and the achievement of human potential, rather than the scientific understanding and assessment of behavior.

feminist psychology A psychological approach that analyzes the influence of social inequities on gender relations and on the behavior of the two sexes.

Critics, both outside and within this movement, worry that some feminists are replacing a male bias in research with a female bias—for example, by doing studies of women only and then drawing conclusions about gender differences, or by replacing the "women are inferior to men" stereotype with a "women are superior to men" stereotype (Yoder & Kahn, 1993). They also note that the goal of gender equality sometimes leads feminist psychologists to embrace conclusions that lack solid empirical support (Mednick, 1989; Peplau & Conrad, 1989; Stimpson, 1996).

Feminist psychologists, however, remind us that research and psychotherapy are social processes, affected by all the attitudes and values that people bring to any enterprise. To improve psychology and make it more socially useful, they say, we must become aware of our biases and attempt to correct them. This argument has inspired other efforts to eliminate bias in studies of ethnic groups, gay men and lesbians, old people, disabled people, and the poor.

What Do You Know?

A. Anxiety is a common problem. To test your understanding of the five major perspectives in psychology, match each possible explanation of anxiety on the left with a perspective on the right.

1. Anxious people often think about the future in distorted ways.
2. Anxiety is due to forbidden, unconscious desires.
3. Anxiety symptoms often bring hidden rewards, such as being excused from exams.
4. Excessive anxiety can be caused by a chemical imbalance.
5. A national emphasis on success and competition promotes anxiety about failure.

a. learning
b. psychodynamic
c. sociocultural
d. biological
e. cognitive

B. Different assumptions about human behavior can lead to different conclusions. What assumption distinguishes cognitive psychology from behaviorism? What assumption distinguishes the psychodynamic perspective from the sociocultural perspective?

ANSWERS:

A. 1. e 2. b 3. a 4. d 5. c **B.** Cognitive psychologists assume that thoughts and feelings can explain behavior; behaviorists reject this assumption. Psychodynamic psychologists assume that behavior is driven largely by internal (intrapsychic) factors, such as unconscious drives; sociocultural psychologists assume that behavior is determined largely by external social and cultural factors.

ABOUT THIS BOOK

The five perspectives that we have described represent very different approaches to the psychological study of thought and action. We have not presented them here or in the rest of the book in order of importance. We might have started with the sociocultural view, because babies are born into a cultural world that will influence their physical and mental development from the minute they emerge from the womb. But many students and instructors find it logical to start with biological influences on behavior and then move on to examine how a person thinks, what a person learns, and the environment the person lives in; so that is the order we have followed. We kept the psychodynamic perspective for last because it differs so significantly from the others.

Writing a book organized in terms of perspectives has many benefits but also a major limitation. Discussing each perspective separately allows us to show more clearly what each one contributes to our understanding of behavior. And frankly, it reflects how most psychologists do their work. Like professionals in other fields, psychologists have become highly specialized. Although some draw on findings and methods from several perspectives when studying a specific topic, such as memory or intelligence or depression, most focus on one approach. Someone who is trained to look for biological influences on, say, aggression is unlikely to study, or even to think much about, the cultural influences that make Sweden much less violent than the United States. Likewise, someone who is trained to look for cultural influences on patterns of alcohol use and abuse is unlikely to know much about possible genetic contributions to alcoholism. Like the blind men in the poem that begins this book, many psychologists tend to think that the part of the beast that they study is the whole animal, or at least the most important part of it.

Bent Offerings by Don Addis

Yet the central message of this book is that if we are to understand the fascinating complexities and puzzles of human experience, we need to look at them from different angles, not just one. The forces governing our behavior are as intertwined as strands of ivy on a wall. To emphasize this point, following the one or two chapters that comprise each perspective, we offer an essay that evaluates the perspective as a whole. There we describe the perspective's strengths and weaknesses, and explore its social and political implications. In each essay, we show the dangers of **reductionism,** the practice of reducing

---

reductionism The process of reducing a phenomenon to a single type of explanation or to a limited set of elements of a particular type (for example, biological or cognitive).

a phenomenon to a single explanation, be it biological, behavioral, or cultural. In the final chapter (Chapter 12), we show how the various perspectives contribute to the understanding and treatment of mental disorders (though not always equally). And in Essay 6, "The Whole Elephant," we discuss how findings from all perspectives interact to explain two perennially popular subjects: music and sex.

If you are ready to share the excitement of studying psychology; if you love mysteries and want to know not only who did it but also why they did it; if you are willing to reconsider what you think you think . . . then you are ready to read on. ◼

Summary

1. *Psychology* is the discipline concerned with behavior and mental processes and how they are affected by an organism's physical state, mental state, and external environment. Psychology's methods and reliance on *empirical evidence* distinguish it from "psychobabble" and pseudoscience.

2. Psychologists have many pseudoscientific competitors, such as astrologers and psychics, but when put to the test, the claims and predictions of these competitors turn out to be false. Psychobabble is appealing because it confirms our beliefs and prejudices. In contrast, psychology often challenges them, although it also seeks to extend our understanding of familiar facts.

3. One benefit of studying psychology is the development of *critical-thinking* skills and attitudes. Critical thinking can help people distinguish between beliefs based on matters of taste, preference, and wishful thinking, and beliefs based on good reasoning and solid evidence. The critical thinker is curious and asks well-framed questions, defines terms clearly, examines the evidence, analyzes assumptions and biases, avoids emotional reasoning, avoids oversimplification, considers alternative interpretations, and tolerates uncertainty.

4. Psychology's forerunners made some valid observations and had some useful insights, but without rigorous empirical methods, they also made serious errors in the description and explanation of behavior, as in the case of phrenology.

5. Psychology as a formal science was officially born in 1879, when Wilhelm Wundt established the first psychological laboratory, in Leipzig, Germany. Researchers in Wundt's laboratory hoped to discover the building blocks of experience. Their work relied heavily on *trained introspection,* which was soon abandoned by others as insufficiently objective.

6. An early school of psychology that opposed Wundt's ideas was known as *functionalism.* The functionalists were inspired in part by the evolutionary theories of Charles Darwin. They wanted to know how various actions help a person or animal adapt to the environment, and they looked for the underlying causes and purposes of specific behaviors and mental strategies. One of functionalism's leading proponents was William James. Although functionalism did not last long as a distinct school of psychology, it greatly affected the course of psychological science.

7. Psychology as a method of psychotherapy has its roots in the ideas of Sigmund Freud, who emphasized unconscious motives, conflicts, and desires. Freud's work eventually evolved into a broad theory of personality, and both his theory and his methods of treating people with emotional problems became known as *psychoanalysis.*

8. Today psychology is a complex field consisting of different schools, perspectives, methods, and approaches to training. Psychologists do research and teach in colleges and universities; provide mental-health services (*psychological practice*); and conduct research and apply findings in a wide variety of nonacademic settings. Many psychologists move flexibly across these areas. Some researchers do *applied psychology,* which is concerned with the practical uses of psychological knowledge; others do *basic psychology,* which is concerned with knowledge for its own sake.

9. *Psychotherapist* is an unregulated term for anyone who does therapy, including persons who have no credentials or training at all. Licensed therapists differ according to their training and approach. *Clinical psychologists* have a Ph.D., an Ed.D., or a Psy.D.; *psychiatrists* have an M.D.; *psychoanalysts* are trained in psychoanalytic institutes; and social workers and marriage, family, and child counselors may have a variety of postgraduate degrees. Many psychologists are concerned about an increase in poorly trained psychotherapists who lack credentials or an understanding of research methods and findings.

10. Five points of view predominate today in psychology, distinguished by the questions they raise, the assumptions they make, and the explanations they offer. The *biological perspective* emphasizes bodily events associated with actions, thoughts, and feelings, and with the relative contributions of "nature" and "nurture" in the development of abilities and personality traits. The *learning perspective* emphasizes how the environment and a person's history affect behavior; within this perspective, *behaviorists* study learned responses to events and the role of consequences in shaping behavior, and they reject mentalistic explanations; and *social-cognitive learning* theorists combine elements of behaviorism with the study of thoughts, values, and intentions. The *cognitive perspective* emphasizes mental processes in perception, problem solving, belief formation, and other human activities. The *sociocultural perspective* explores how the social context and cultural rules affect an individual's beliefs and behavior. The *psychodynamic perspective,* which originated with Freud's theory of psychoanalysis, emphasizes unconscious dynamics within the person, such as motives, conflicts, or instinctual energy; it differs greatly from the other perspectives in its language, methods, and standards of acceptable evidence.

11. Not all schools of psychology fit neatly into one of the five major perspectives. *Humanist psychology* emphasizes free will and human potential and has influenced psychotherapy and self-help movements. *Feminist psychology* draws on research from all five perspectives in analyzing gender relations and gender differences, and it has challenged gender biases in research.

12. Because the forces that govern behavior are intertwined, each perspective, by itself, is limited. The best way to formulate solutions for social and personal problems is to avoid *reductionism* by drawing on more than one approach.

Key Terms

CHAPTER TWO

Studying Human Behavior

Suppose that you are the parent of a 9-year-old boy who has been diagnosed as autistic. Your child lives in a silent world of his own, cut off from normal social interaction. He rarely looks you in the eye. He rocks back and forth for hours. Sometimes he does self-destructive things, like poking pencils in his ears. He does not speak, and he cannot function in a public-school classroom.

You are ecstatic, then, when you hear about a new technique, called "facilitated communication (FC)," which promises to release your child from his mental prison. According to this technique's proponents, when autistic or mentally impaired children are placed in front of a keyboard and an adult "facilitator" gently places a hand over the child's hand or forearm, amazing things happen. Children who have never used words are suddenly able to peck out complete sentences, answer questions, and divulge their thoughts. Some children, through their facilitators, have supposedly even mastered high-school-level subjects, or have written poetry of astonishing beauty. The fee is steep, but it certainly seems worth it.

Or is it?

The situation we have described is not hypothetical; thousands of hopeful parents have been drawn to the promise of facilitated communication. Psychological scientists, however, have been more cautious. Before accepting claims and testimonials about any program or therapy, they put those claims and testimonials to the test. In the case of facilitated communication, they have done studies involving hundreds of autistic children and their facilitators (Eberlin et al., 1993; Jacobson, Mulick, & Schwartz, 1995; Mulick, 1994). Their techniques have been simple: They show the child a picture to identify but show the facilitator a different picture, or no picture at all; or they keep the facilitator from hearing the questions being put to the child. Under these conditions, the child types out only what the facilitator sees or hears—not what the child does.

"Facilitated communication" is thought by some to be a breakthrough for autistic people, but what does controlled research show?

In one legal case, a researcher tested an autistic child, Betsy, who had been removed from her home after "typing" an account of being sexually abused by her entire family. Betsy, he found, could type only the names of objects the facilitator saw (e.g., "hat"), not what she herself saw (e.g., "cup"). Because of these results, which were shown on the TV program "Frontline," the facilitator stopped using FC and Betsy was reunited with her family.

This research shows that what happens in facilitated communication is exactly what happens when a medium guides a person's hand over a Ouija board to help the person receive "messages" from a "spirit": The person doing the "facilitating" is unconsciously nudging the other person's hand in the desired direction (Burgess et al., 1998; Spitz, 1997). Facilitated communication, on closer inspection, turns out to be *facilitator* communication. This finding is vitally important, because if parents waste their time and money on treatments that don't work, they may not get the genuine help that *is* available for autistic children (see Chapter 5), and they will suffer when their false hopes are finally shattered by reality.

You can see why research methods matter so much to psychologists. Some students would rather not study research methods; "let's just cut straight to the findings," they say. But these methods are the tools that allow psychologists to separate truth from unfounded belief, to sort out conflicting views, and to correct false ideas that may cause people harm. We hope that when you hear and read about psychological issues, you will consider not only what the findings say, but also how the information was obtained and how the results were interpreted, using information in this chapter.

WHAT MAKES PSYCHOLOGICAL RESEARCH SCIENTIFIC?

When we refer to psychologists as scientists, we do not mean that they work with complicated gadgets and machines or wear white lab coats (although some do). The scientific enterprise has more to do with attitudes and procedures than with apparatus and apparel. Here are a few key characteristics of the ideal scientist:

1 **PRECISION.** Scientists sometimes launch an investigation because they have a hunch about why some behavior or problem occurs. This hunch may be based on previous findings or casual observations. Often, however, they start out with a general **theory,** an organized system of assumptions and principles that purports to explain certain phenomena and how they are related. A scientific theory is not just someone's personal opinion, as people imply when they say "It's only a theory." Theories that come to be accepted by the scientific community are those that account for many empirical findings.

From a hunch or theory, the psychological scientist derives a **hypothesis,** a statement that attempts to describe or explain a given behavior. Initially, this statement may be quite general, as in, say, "Misery loves company." But before any research can be done, the hypothesis must be made more precise. For example, "Misery loves company" might be rephrased as "People who are anxious about an impending situation they find threatening tend to seek out others in the same boat."

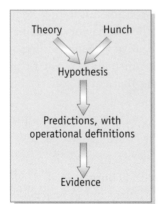

Theory   Hunch

Hypothesis

Predictions, with
operational definitions

Evidence

A hypothesis, in turn, leads to predictions about what will happen in a particular situation. In a prediction, terms such as *anxiety* or *threatening situation* are given **operational definitions,** which specify how the phenomena in question are to be observed and measured. "Anxiety" might be defined operationally as a score on an anxiety questionnaire; "threatening situation" might be defined as the threat of an electric shock. The prediction might be, "If you raise people's anxiety scores by telling them they are going to receive electric shocks and then give them the choice of waiting alone or with others in the same situation, they will be more likely to choose to wait with others than they would be if they were not anxious." The prediction can then be tested, using systematic methods.

2 **SKEPTICISM.** Scientists do not accept ideas on faith; their motto is "Show me!" Some of the greatest scientific advances have been made by those who dared to

---

theory An organized system of assumptions and principles that purports to explain a specified set of phenomena and their interrelationships.

hypothesis A statement that attempts to predict or to account for a set of phenomena; scientific hypotheses specify relationships among events or variables and are empirically tested.

operational definition A precise definition of a term in a hypothesis, which specifies the operations for observing and measuring the process or phenomenon being defined.

doubt what everyone else assumed to be true: that the sun revolves around the earth, that illness can be cured by applying leeches to the skin, or that madness is a sign of demonic possession. In the world of the researcher, skepticism means treating conclusions, both new and old, with caution. Caution, however, must be balanced by an openness to new ideas and evidence. Otherwise, the scientist may wind up as short-sighted as the famous physicist Lord Kelvin, who in 1895 reputedly declared with great confidence that radio had no future, X rays were a hoax, and "heavier-than-air flying machines" were impossible; or the head of IBM in 1958, who said, "I think there is a world market for about five computers."

3 RELIANCE ON EMPIRICAL EVIDENCE. Unlike plays and poems, scientific theories and hypotheses are not judged by how pleasing or entertaining they are. An idea may initially generate excitement because it is plausible or imaginative, but eventually it must be backed by empirical evidence if it is to be taken seriously. A collection of anecdotes or an appeal to authority will not do. Nor will the "intuitive" appeal of the idea, or its popularity. As scientist Peter Medawar (1979) wrote, "The intensity of the conviction that a hypothesis is true has no bearing on whether it is true or not."

4 WILLINGNESS TO MAKE "RISKY PREDICTIONS." A related principle is that a scientist must state an idea in such a way that it can be *refuted*, or disproved by counter-evidence. This principle, known as the **principle of falsifiability,** does not mean that the idea *will be* disproved, only that it *could be* if contrary evidence were to be discovered. Another way of saying this is that a scientist must risk disconfirmation by predicting not only what will happen, but also what will not happen. In the "misery loves company" study, the hypothesis would be refuted if most anxious people went off alone to sulk and worry, or if anxiety had no effect on their behavior. A willingness to make risky predictions forces the scientist to take negative evidence seriously. Any researcher who refuses to go out on a limb and risk disconfirmation is not a true scientist, and any theory that purports to explain everything that could conceivably happen is unscientific.

Nonscientists violate the principle of falsifiability all the time. For example, some police officers and therapists believe that murderous satanic cults are widespread, even though research psychologists, the FBI, and police investigators have been unable to substantiate this claim (Burgess et al., 1998; Spitz, 1997). Believers say they are not surprised by the lack of evidence because satanic cults cover up their activities by eating bodies or burying them. The FBI's failure to find the evidence is "proof," they say, that the FBI is part of a conspiracy to support the satanists. To believers, then, the lack of evidence of satanic cults is actually a sign of the cults' success. But if a lack of evidence can count as evidence, then what could possibly count as *counter*evidence? What could ever get believers to change their minds, to admit their hypothesis was wrong?

---

principle of falsifiability The principle that a scientific theory must make predictions that are specific enough to expose the theory to the possibility of disconfirmation; that is, the theory must predict not only what will happen, but also what will not happen.

It is not enough to say that something "could" be true. Critical thinkers decide which explanation is most likely to be true, based on the best available evidence.

5 OPENNESS. Scientists must be willing to tell others where they got their ideas, how they tested them, and what the results were. They must do this clearly and in detail so that other scientists can repeat, or *replicate,* their studies and verify—or challenge— the findings. Secrecy is a big "no-no" in science.

Sometimes replication shows that an apparently fabulous phenomenon was just a fluke. A famous example occurred many years ago, when a team of researchers trained flatworms to cringe in response to a flashing light, then killed the worms, ground them into a mash, and fed the mash to a second set of worms. This cannibalistic diet, the researchers reported, sped up acquisition of the cringe response in the second group of worms (McConnell, 1962). As you can imagine, this finding caused tremendous excitement. If worms could learn faster by ingesting the "memory molecules" of their fellow worms, what might this mean for human memory? Students joked about grinding up professors; professors joked about doing brain transplants in students. But, alas, other researchers were never able to replicate the results.

If you think about it, you will see that these principles of good science correspond to some of the critical-thinking guidelines described in Chapter 1. Formulating a prediction with operational definitions corresponds to "define your terms." Openness to new ideas encourages scientists to "consider other interpretations." The principle of falsifiability forces scientists to "analyze assumptions and biases" in a fair-minded fashion. And until their results have been replicated and verified, scientists must "tolerate uncertainty."

Do psychologists and other scientists always live up to the lofty standards expected of them? Of course not. Being human, they may put too much trust in their personal experiences. They may permit financial interests to interfere with openness, as often happens when scientists funded by private companies fail to make their negative results known (Bodenheimer, 2000). And sometimes scientists fail to put their theories fully to the test: It is always easier to be skeptical about someone else's ideas than about your own.

Commitment to one's theories is not in itself a bad thing. Passion is the fuel of progress. It motivates researchers to think boldly, defend unpopular ideas, and do the exhaustive testing that is often required to support an idea. But passion can also cloud perceptions and in some sad cases has even led to deception and fraud. That is why science is a communal activity. Scientists are expected to share their evidence and procedures with others. They are expected to submit their results to professional journals, which send the findings to experts in the field for comment before publishing them. Through this process, called *peer review,* scientists demonstrate that their position is well supported. Peer review precedes any announcements to the public through press releases or popular books. The research community—in our case, the psychological community—acts as a jury, scrutinizing and sifting the evidence, approving some viewpoints and relegating others to the scientific scrap heap.

This public process is not perfect, but it does give science a built-in system of checks and balances. Individuals are not necessarily objective, honest, or rational, but science forces them to justify their claims.

What Do You Know?

Test your understanding of science by identifying which of its rules was violated in each of the following cases.

1. For years, writer Norman Cousins told how he had cured himself of a rare, life-threatening disease through a combination of humor and vitamins. In a best-selling book, he recommended the same approach to others.

2. Benjamin Rush, an eighteenth-century physician, believed that illnesses accompanied by fever should be treated by bloodletting. Rush did not lose faith in his approach even when his patients died. He attributed each recovery to his treatment and each death to the severity of the disease (Stanovich, 1996).

3. A medical researcher first reports her results on the Internet and in a press conference, on the grounds that the findings are too important to wait for publication.

ANSWERS:

1. Cousins offered only a personal account and did not gather empirical evidence from controlled studies or consider cases of sick people who were not helped by humor and vitamins. 2. Rush violated the principle of falsifiability: He interpreted a patient's survival as support for his treatment and explained a death by saying that the person had been too ill for the treatment to work. Thus, there was no possible counterevidence that could refute the theory (which, by the way, was dead wrong—the "treatment" was actually as dangerous as the disease). 3. The researcher bypassed peer review, depriving other scientists of the opportunity to assess her methods and findings before the announcement.

DESCRIPTIVE RESEARCH

Psychologists gather evidence to support their hypotheses by using different methods, depending on the kinds of questions they want to answer. These methods are not mutually exclusive. Just as a detective may use a magnifying glass *and* a fingerprint duster *and* interviews of suspects to figure out "who done it," psychological sleuths often draw on different techniques at different stages of an ongoing investigation. As you read about these methods, we suggest that you list their advantages and disadvantages in order to remember them better. When you finish this and the next two sections, you can check your list against the one in Table 2.1, on page 59.

We will begin with **descriptive methods,** which allow psychologists to describe and predict behavior but not necessarily to choose one explanation over competing ones.

Case Studies

A **case study** (or *case history*) is a detailed description of a particular individual, based on careful observation or on formal psychological testing. It may include information about the person's childhood, dreams, fantasies, experiences, relationships, and hopes—anything that will provide insight into the person's behavior. Case studies are most commonly used by clinicians, but sometimes academic researchers use them as well, especially when they are just beginning to study a topic or when practical or ethical considerations prevent them from gathering information in other ways.

Case studies illustrate psychological principles in a way that abstract generalizations and cold statistics never can, and they produce a more detailed picture of an individual than other methods do. However, the case-study method also has many drawbacks. Vital information is often missing, so the case may be hard to interpret. Many case studies depend on people's memories of the past, and such memories may be both selective and inaccurate. Most important, this method has limited usefulness for deriving general principles of behavior, because the person who is the focus of the study may be *unrepresentative* of the group that a researcher is interested in.

When people draw conclusions solely on the basis of case studies, the results can be disastrous. To take another example involving childhood autism, physicians once believed that autism was caused by rejecting, cold, "refrigerator" mothers. Their belief was based on the writings of psychoanalyst Bruno Bettelheim (1967), who drew his conclusions from a few case histories of autistic children whose mothers had psychological problems. When proper studies were finally carried out, using objective testing procedures and a larger, representative group of autistic children and their parents, scientists learned that parents of autistic children are as psychologically healthy as any other parents. Today we know that autism stems from a neurological problem rather than from any psychological problems of the mothers. But because so many people

---

descriptive methods Methods that yield descriptions of behavior but not necessarily causal explanations.
case study A detailed description of a particular individual being studied or treated.

Case studies of people with brain damage support the idea that particular systems of brain cells are highly specialized. One man's injury left him unable to identify ordinary objects, though he had no trouble with faces. When shown this painting, he could easily see the face, but he could not see the vegetables comprising it (Moscovitch, Winocur, & Behrmann, 1997).

accepted Bettelheim's claims, thousands of women blamed themselves for their children's disorder and suffered needless guilt and remorse.

We don't want you to think that case studies are useless, however. When they are properly used, they can be enlightening. Biological psychologists, for example, study cases of patients with brain damage for clues about how the brain is organized. They have learned that brain damage can have extremely specific effects, depending on the exact location of the damage. For example, some patients can recognize manufactured items, such as photographs, tools, or books, but not natural objects, such as rocks or trees. Others can recognize most natural objects but cannot distinguish among different animals, fruits, or vegetables (Damasio, 1990). In one study (Cubelli, 1991), two patients were unable to write down correctly the vowels in words but had no trouble writing the consonants!

Ironically, then, unusual cases can sometimes increase our understanding of some general questions about human functioning. Most case studies, however, are sources, rather than tests, of hypotheses. You should be extremely cautious about pop-psych books and TV programs that present only testimonials and a few vivid case histories as evidence.

Observational Studies

In **observational studies,** the researcher observes, measures, and records behavior, taking care not to be intrusive or to interfere with the people (or animals) being observed. Unlike case studies, observational studies usually involve many participants ("subjects").

---

observational study A study in which the researcher carefully and systematically observes and records behavior without interfering with the behavior; it may involve either naturalistic or laboratory observation.

Often an observational study is the first step in a program of research; it is helpful to have a good description of behavior before you try to explain it.

The primary purpose of *naturalistic observation* is to find out how people or animals act in their normal social environments. Ethologists such as Jane Goodall have used this method to study apes and other animals in the wild. Psychologists use naturalistic observation wherever people happen to be—at home, on playgrounds or streets, in schoolrooms, or in offices. In one study, a social psychologist and his students ventured into a common human habitat: bars. They wanted to know whether people in bars drink more when they are in groups than when they are alone. They visited all 32 pubs in a midsized city, ordered beers, and recorded on napkins and pieces of newspaper how much the other patrons imbibed. They found that drinkers in groups consumed more than individuals who were alone. Those in groups did not drink any faster; they just lingered in the bar longer (Sommer, 1977).

Note that the students who did this study did not rely on their impressions or memories of how much people drank. In observational studies, you must count, rate, or measure behavior in a systematic way, in order to be sure you aren't just noticing what you expect or want to see. Careful record keeping ensures accuracy and allows different observers to cross-check their observations for consistency. You must also take pains to avoid being obvious about what you are doing and to disguise your intentions so you can see people as they really are. If the researchers who studied drinking habits had marched in with videocameras and announced that they were psychology students, the bar patrons might not have behaved naturally.

Sometimes psychologists prefer to make observations in a laboratory setting. In *laboratory observation,* psychologists have more control. They can use sophisticated equipment, determine how many people will be observed at once, maintain a clear line of vision while observing, remain hidden behind a one-way mirror, and so forth. Suppose that you wanted to know how infants of different ages respond when left with a stranger. Visiting private homes might be slow and inconvenient, and you would have to worry about interruptions. A more efficient approach might be to have parents and their infants come to your laboratory, observe them playing together for a while through a one-way window, then have a stranger enter the room and, a few minutes later, have the parent leave. You could record signs of distress, interactions with the stranger, and other behavior. If you did this, you would find that very young infants carry on cheerfully with whatever they are doing when the parent leaves. However, by the age of about 8 months, many children will burst into tears or show other signs of what child psychologists call "separation anxiety" (Ainsworth, 1979).

One shortcoming of laboratory observation is that the presence of researchers and special equipment may cause subjects to behave differently than they would in their usual surroundings. And observational studies, like other descriptive studies, are more useful for describing behavior than for explaining it. For example, the barroom results we described do not necessarily mean that being in a group makes people drink a lot. People may join a group because they are already interested in drinking and find it more comfortable to hang around the bar if they are with others. Similarly, if you observe infants protesting whenever a parent leaves the room, you cannot be sure *why* they are protesting. Is it because they have become attached to their parents and want them nearby? Is it because they learned from experience that crying brings an adult with a cookie and a cuddle? Observational studies alone cannot answer such questions.

Tests

Psychological tests, sometimes called *assessment instruments,* are procedures for measuring and evaluating personality traits, emotional states, aptitudes, interests, abilities, and values. Hundreds of psychological tests are used in industry, education, the military, and the helping professions. Typically, these tests require people to answer a series of written or oral questions. The answers may then be totaled to yield a single numerical score, or a set of scores. *Objective tests,* also called "inventories," measure beliefs, feelings, or behaviors of which an individual is aware; *projective tests* are designed to tap unconscious feelings or motives (see Essay 5).

At one time or another, most people have taken a psychological test, such as an intelligence test, an achievement test, or a vocational-aptitude test. These measures help clarify differences among people, as well as differences in the reactions of the same person on different occasions or at different stages of life. Tests may be used to promote self-understanding, to evaluate psychological treatments, or, in scientific research, to draw generalizations about human behavior. Well-constructed psychological tests are a great improvement over simple self-evaluation, because most people have a distorted view of their own abilities and traits.

One test of a good test is whether it is **standardized**—that is, whether uniform procedures exist for giving and scoring the test. It would hardly be fair to give some people detailed instructions and plenty of time and others only vague instructions and limited time. Those who administer the test must know exactly how to explain the tasks involved, how much time to allow, and what materials to use. Scoring is usually done by referring to **norms,** established standards of performance. The usual procedure for developing norms is to give the test to a large group of people who resemble those for whom the test is intended. Norms determine which scores can be considered high, low, or average.

Constructing a test is not as easy as it seems; you can't just sit around and make up some questions that interest you. For one thing, the test must be **reliable**—that is, it must produce the same results from one time and place to the next. A vocational-interest test is not reliable if it tells Tom today that he would make a wonderful engineer but a poor journalist, but then it gives different results when Tom retakes the test a week later. Psychologists can measure *test-retest reliability* by giving the test twice to the same group of people, then comparing the two sets of scores statistically. If the test is reliable,

---

psychological tests Procedures used to measure and evaluate personality traits, emotional states, aptitudes, interests, abilities, and values.

standardize In test construction, to develop uniform procedures for giving and scoring a test.

norms In test construction, established standards of performance.

reliability In test construction, the consistency of scores derived from a test, from one time and place to another.

individuals' scores will be similar from one session to another. This method has a draw-back, however: People tend to do better the second time they take a test, after they have become familiar with the strategies required and the actual test items used. A solution is to compute *alternate-forms reliability,* by giving different versions of the same test to the same group on two separate occasions. The items on the two forms are similar in format but are not identical in content. With this method, performance cannot improve because of familiarity with the items, although people may still do somewhat better the second time around because they have learned the procedures expected of them.

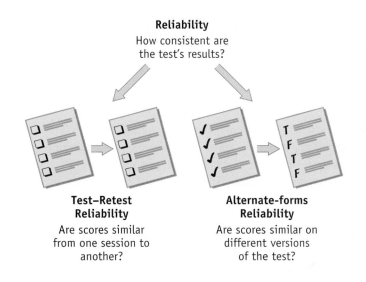

Reliability
How consistent are
the test's results?

**Test–Retest
Reliability**
Are scores similar
from one session to
another?

**Alternate-forms
Reliability**
Are scores similar on
different versions
of the test?

To be useful, a test must also be **valid;** that is, it must measure what it sets out to measure. A creativity test is not valid if what it actually measures is verbal sophistica-tion. If the items broadly represent the trait in question, the test is said to have *content validity.* If you were measuring employees' job satisfaction, and your test tapped a broad array of relevant beliefs and behaviors (e.g., "Do you feel you have reached a dead end at work?" "Are you bored with your assignments?"), it would have content validity. If the test asked only how workers felt about their salary level, it would lack content validity and would be of little use. After all, highly paid people are not always satisfied with their jobs, and people who earn low wages are not always dissatisfied.

Most tests are also judged on *criterion validity,* the ability to predict other, inde-pendent measures, or criteria, of the trait in question. The criterion for a scholastic aptitude test might be college grades; the criterion for a test of shyness might be behav-ior in social situations. To find out whether your job-satisfaction test had criterion validity, you might return a year later to see whether it correctly predicted absenteeism, resignations, or requests for job transfers.

---

validity The ability of a test to measure what it was designed to measure.

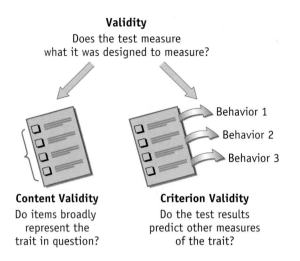

Validity
Does the test measure
what it was designed to measure?

Behavior 1
Behavior 2
Behavior 3

Content Validity
Do items broadly
represent the
trait in question?

Criterion Validity
Do the test results
predict other measures
of the trait?

Unfortunately, teachers, parents, and employers do not always stop to question a test's validity, especially when the results are summarized in a single precise-sounding number, such as an IQ score of 115 or a job applicant's ranking of 5. But among psychologists and educators, controversy exists about the validity of even some widely used tests. For example, "integrity tests," which probe for such traits as hostility to authority, conscientiousness, and "wayward impulses," are given to millions of job applicants each year, in an effort to predict dishonesty and drug use in the workplace. Such tests may be more reliable and valid than interviews, but many people who fail them are not actually dishonest, nor will they become bad employees (Camera & Schneider, 1994; Lilienfeld, 1993; Sackett, 1994).

The Scholastic Assessment Test (SAT) and the Graduate Record Exam (GRE) have also come under fire. Undergraduates can do pretty well on the SAT's reading-comprehension section even without reading the passages (although not as well as when they do read them) (Katz & Lautenschlager, 1994). This finding suggests that the items measure general knowledge and test-taking skills, not just reading comprehension. As for the GRE, it is somewhat useful for predicting first-year grades in graduate psychology programs, but it is *not* good at predicting second-year grades, professors' ratings of students, or the quality of students' dissertations (Sternberg & Williams, 1997). (See why you should know about test validity?)

Criticisms and reevaluations of psychological tests keep psychological assessment honest and scientifically rigorous. In contrast, the pop-psych tests frequently found in magazines and newspapers usually have not been evaluated for either validity or reliability. These questionnaires have inviting headlines, such as "Are You Self-destructive?" or "The Seven Types of Lover," but they are merely lists of questions that someone thought sounded good. Similarly, pseudoscientific methods of assessing personality and ability, such as handwriting analysis (graphology), lack the reliability and validity that scientists demand (Beyerstein, 1996).

Surveys

Psychological tests usually generate information about people indirectly. In contrast, **surveys** are questionnaires and interviews that gather information about people by asking them *directly* about their experiences or attitudes. Most of us are familiar with national opinion surveys, such as the Gallup and Roper polls. Surveys have been done on many topics, including consumer preferences, sexual preferences, political opinions, child-rearing practices, and use of the Internet.

Social scientists like surveys because they produce bushels of data, but they are not easy to do well. The biggest hurdle is getting a **representative sample,** a group of subjects that accurately represents the larger population that the researcher wishes to describe. Suppose you wanted to know about drug use among college sophomores. Questioning every college sophomore in the country would be impractical; instead, you would need to recruit a sample. You would use special selection procedures to ensure that this sample contained the same proportion of women, men, blacks, whites, poor people, rich people, Catholics, Jews, and so on as in the general population of college sophomores. If you questioned students only from your own school, city, or state, the results might not apply to the entire country.

Most people do not realize that a sample's size is less critical than its representativeness. A small but representative sample may yield extremely accurate results; and a survey or poll that fails to use proper sampling methods may yield questionable results, no matter how large the sample was. When MTV asks viewers to call in to vote on a controversial question or *Cosmopolitan* magazine invites its readers to tell about their sexual habits, they will not get scientifically valid results that apply to the population in general—even if thousands of people respond. Why? As a group, people who watch MTV or read *Cosmo* are likely to hold different opinions than people who watch the Discovery Channel or read *Scientific American.*

Popular polls and surveys also suffer from a **volunteer bias:** People who feel strongly enough to volunteer their opinions may differ from those who remain silent. When you read about a survey (or any other kind of study), always ask who participated. A biased, nonrepresentative sample does not necessarily mean that a survey is worthless or uninteresting, but it does mean that the results may not hold for other groups.

Another problem with surveys is that people sometimes lie, especially when the survey is about a touchy topic ("What? Me do that disgusting/dishonest/fattening thing? Never!"). The likelihood of lying is reduced when respondents are guaranteed anonymity. Also, there are ways to check for lying—for example, by asking a question

---

surveys Questionnaires and interviews that ask people directly about their experiences, attitudes, or opinions.

representative sample A group of subjects, selected from a population for study, which matches the population on important characteristics such as age and sex.

volunteer bias A shortcoming of findings derived from a sample of volunteers instead of a representative sample; the volunteers may differ from those who did not volunteer.

several times with different wording. But not all surveys use these techniques, and even when people are trying to be truthful, they may misinterpret the survey questions or misremember the past.

Every time I think I'm part of a normal relationship...

— Someone publishes a new survey.

Kohlsaat

Single Slices by Kohlsaat.

Finally, when you hear about the results of a survey or opinion poll, check to see how the questions were phrased. Political pollsters often design questions to produce the results they want. A Republican might ask people whether they support "increasing the amount spent on Medicare at a slower rate" whereas a Democrat might ask whether people favor "cuts in the projected growth of Medicare." The two phrases mean exactly the same thing, but respondents are likely to react more negatively when the word "cuts" is used (Kolbert, 1995).

As you can see, although surveys can be extremely informative, they must be conducted and interpreted carefully.

What Do You Know?

A. Which descriptive method would be most appropriate for studying each of the following topics? (All of them, by the way, have been investigated by psychologists.)

1. Ways in which the games of boys differ from those of girls
2. Changes in attitudes toward nuclear disarmament after a television movie about nuclear holocaust
3. The math skills of children in the United States versus Japan
4. Physiological changes that occur when people watch violent movies
5. The development of a male infant who was reared as a female after his penis was accidentally burned off during a routine surgery

   a. case study
   b. naturalistic observation
   c. laboratory observation
   d. survey
   e. test

B. At the start of the semester, Professor Flummox gives her new test of aptitude for studying psychology to her psychology students. At the end of the semester, she finds that those who did well on the test averaged only a C in the course. The test lacks _____.

-💡- **C.** For 55 years, a British woman sniffed large amounts of cocaine, which she obtained legally under British regulations for the treatment of addicts. Yet she appeared to show no negative effects, other than drug dependence (Brown & Middlefell, 1989). What does this case tell us about the dangers or safety of cocaine?

ANSWERS:

Critical thinking and the scientific method require that we resist generalizing from a single case.
Also, the cocaine she received may have been less potent than cocaine bought on the street.
Snorting cocaine may be relatively harmless for people like this woman, but harmful for others.
A. 1. b 2. d 3. e 4. c 5. a **B.** validity (more specifically, criterion validity) **C.** Not much.

CORRELATIONAL RESEARCH

In descriptive research, psychologists often want to know whether two or more phenomena are related and, if so, how strongly. For example, is there a relationship between the number of hours students spend watching television and students' grade-point averages? To find out, psychologists do **correlational studies.**

The word **correlation** is often used as a synonym for relationship. Technically, however, a correlation is a numerical measure of the *strength* of the relationship between two things—events, scores, or anything else that can be recorded and tallied. In psychological studies, such things are called **variables** because they can vary in quantifiable ways. Height, weight, age, income, IQ scores, number of items recalled on a memory test, number of smiles in a given time period—anything that can be measured, rated, or scored can serve as a variable.

Correlations always occur between *sets* of observations. In psychological research, these sets of observations usually come from many individuals or are used to compare groups of people. For example, in research on the origins of intelligence, psychologists look for a correlation between the IQ scores of parents and those of their children. To do this, the researchers must gather scores from a set of parents and from the children of these parents. You cannot compute a correlation if you know the IQs of only one particular parent–child pair. To say that a relationship exists, you need more than one pair of values to compare.

A **positive correlation** means that high values of one variable are associated with high values of the other, and that low values of one variable are associated with low values

---

correlational study A descriptive study that looks for a consistent relationship between two phenomena.

correlation A measure of how strongly two variables are related to one another.

variables Characteristics of behavior or experience that can be measured or described by a numeric scale; variables are manipulated and assessed in scientific studies.

positive correlation An association between increases in one variable and increases in another.

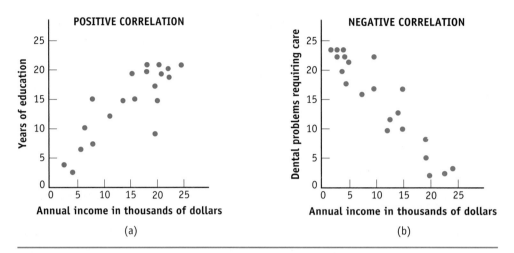

FIGURE 2.1 CORRELATIONS *Graph* a *shows a positive correlation; in general, the more education people have, the higher their income. Graph* b *shows a negative correlation; in general, the higher people's incomes, the fewer dental problems they have (from Wright, 1976).*

of the other. Height and weight are positively correlated, for example; so are IQ scores and school grades. Rarely is a correlation perfect, however, which is why correlations don't always allow us to make accurate predictions about a particular individual: Some tall people weigh less than some short ones; some people with average IQs are superstars in the classroom, and some with high IQs get poor grades. Figure 2.1a shows a positive correlation between men's educational level and their annual income. Each dot represents a man; you can find each man's educational level by drawing a horizontal line from his dot to the vertical axis. You can find his income by drawing a vertical line from his dot to the horizontal axis.

A **negative correlation** means that high values of one variable are associated with *low* values of the other. Figure 2.1b shows a negative correlation between average income and the incidence of dental disease for groups of 100 families. Each dot represents one group. In general, as you can see, the higher the income, the fewer the dental problems. In the automobile business, the older the car, the lower the price, except for antiques and models favored by collectors. As for human beings, in general, the older adults are, the fewer miles they can run, the fewer crimes they are likely to commit, and the fewer hairs they have on their heads. And remember that correlation between hours spent watching TV and grade-point averages? It's a negative one: Lots of hours in front of the television are associated with lower grades (Potter, 1987; Ridley-Johnson, Cooper, & Chance, 1983). See whether you can think of other variables that are negatively correlated. Remember, though: A negative correlation means that a relationship exists—the more of one thing, the less of another. If there is no relationship between two variables, we say that they are *uncorrelated.* Adult shoe size and IQ scores are uncorrelated.

---

negative correlation An association between increases in one variable and decreases in another.

The statistic used to express a correlation is called the **coefficient of correlation.** This number conveys both the size of the correlation and its direction. A perfect positive correlation has a coefficient of +1.00, and a perfect negative correlation has a coefficient of −1.00. Suppose you weighed ten people and listed them from lightest to heaviest, then you measured their heights and listed them from shortest to tallest. If the names on the two lists were in exactly the same order, the correlation between weight and height would be +1.00. If the correlation between two variables is +.80, it means that they are strongly (though not perfectly) related. If the correlation is −.80, the relationship is just as strong, but it is negative. When there is no association between two variables, the coefficient is zero or close to zero.

Correlational findings are common in psychology and are often reported in the news. But beware; correlations can be misleading. The important thing to remember is that *a correlation does not show causation.* It is easy to assume that if variable A predicts variable B, A must be causing B—that is, making B happen—but it's not necessarily so. The number of storks nesting in some European villages is reportedly correlated (positively) with the number of human births in those villages. Therefore, knowing when the storks nest allows you to predict when more births than usual will occur. But that doesn't mean that storks bring babies or that babies attract storks! Human births seem to be somewhat more frequent at certain times of the year (you might want to speculate on the reasons), and the peaks just happen to coincide with the storks' nesting periods.

The coincidental nature of the correlation between nesting storks and human births may seem obvious, but in other cases, unwarranted conclusions about causation are more tempting, and can even have harmful repercussions in people's lives. To continue with our autism example, many parents in the United States have become alarmed that they "caused" their children's autism by having the children vaccinated for measles, mumps, and rubella. But these parents are confusing a coincidental correlation between two events with a cause-and-effect relationship—an understandable but tragic mistake. The first signs of autism are often not apparent to adults untrained in diagnosing the disorder until a child is about 2 years old, about the same time that most children are vaccinated.

Correlations can often be interpreted in several ways. For example, television watching is positively correlated with children's aggressiveness. Therefore, many people assume that watching television (A), with its violent programs, causes aggressiveness (B):

A   B

---

coefficient of correlation A measure of correlation that ranges in value from −1.00 to +1.00.

But it is also possible that being highly aggressive (B) causes children to watch more television (A):

And there is yet another possibility: Growing up in a violent household (C) could cause children both to be aggressive *and* to watch television:

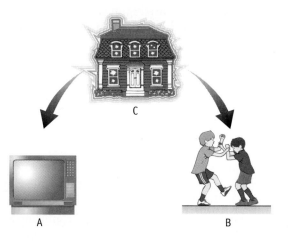

Actually, there is evidence for all three of these relationships (APA Commission on Violence and Youth, 1993; Eron, 1982, 1995).

Similarly, the negative correlation between TV watching and grades might exist because heavy TV watchers have less time to study, because they have some personality trait that attracts them to TV and makes them dislike studying, because they use TV as an escape when their grades are low, . . . you get the idea. The moral of the story: When two variables are associated, one variable may or may not be causing the other.

What Do You Know?

Are you clear about correlations?

    A. Indicate whether each of the following findings is a positive correlation or a negative one.

    1. The higher a child's score on an intelligence test, the less likely her parents are to have spanked her.

2. The higher a male monkey's level of the hormone testosterone, the more aggressive he is likely to be.

3. The older people are, the less frequently they tend to have sexual intercourse.

4. The hotter the weather, the higher the rate of muggings and assaults.

B. Now see whether you can generate two or three alternative explanations for each of the preceding findings.

ANSWERS:

A. 1. negative 2. positive 3. negative 4. positive   B. 1. Spanking may impair a child's intellectual growth; brighter children may require less physical discipline from their parents; or brighter mothers may tend to have brighter children or may be able to think of alternative methods of discipline. 2. The hormone may cause aggressiveness, or acting aggressively may stimulate hormone production. 3. Older people may have less interest in sex than younger people, have less energy or more physical ailments, or simply have more trouble finding sexual partners. 4. Hot temperatures may make people edgy and cause them to commit crimes; potential victims may be more plentiful in warm weather because more people go outside; criminals may find it more comfortable to be out committing their crimes in warm weather than in cold. (Our explanations are not the only ones possible.)

EXPERIMENTAL RESEARCH

Researchers gain plenty of illuminating information from descriptive studies, but when they want to actually track down the causes of behavior, they rely heavily on the experimental method. An **experiment** allows the researcher to *control* the situation being studied. Instead of being a passive recorder of what is going on, the researcher actively does something to affect people's behavior and then observes what happens. These procedures allow the experimenter to draw conclusions about cause and effect—about what causes what.

Experimental Variables

Suppose you are a psychologist and you come across reports suggesting that cigarette smoking improves reaction time on simple tasks. You have a hunch that nicotine has the opposite effect, however, when the task is as complex and demanding as driving a car. You know that on average, smokers have more car accidents than nonsmokers. But you realize that this relationship does not prove that smoking *causes* accidents. Smokers may simply be greater risk-takers than nonsmokers, whether the risk is lung cancer or trying to beat a red light. Or perhaps the distraction of lighting up accounts for the increased accident risk, rather than smoking itself. So you decide to do an experiment to test your hypothesis.

---

experiment A controlled test of a hypothesis in which the researcher manipulates one variable to discover its effect on another.

In a laboratory, you ask smokers to "drive" using a computerized driving simulator equipped with a stick shift and a gas pedal. The object, you tell them, is to maximize the distance by driving as fast as possible on a winding road while avoiding rear-end collisions. At your request, some of the subjects smoke a cigarette immediately before climbing into the driver's seat. Others do not. You are interested in comparing how many collisions the two groups have. The basic design of this experiment is illustrated in Figure 2.2, which you may want to refer to as you read the next few pages.

The aspect of an experimental situation manipulated or varied by the researcher is known as the **independent variable.** The reaction of the subjects—the behavior that the researcher tries to predict—is the **dependent variable.** Every experiment has at least one independent and one dependent variable. In our example, the independent variable is nicotine use: one cigarette versus none. The dependent variable is the number of collisions.

Understandably, students often have trouble keeping independent and dependent variables straight. You might think of it this way: The dependent variable—the outcome of the study—*depends* on the independent variable. When psychologists set up an experiment, they think, "If I do X, the subjects in my study will do Y." The "X" represents manipulation of the independent variable; the "Y" represents the dependent variable:

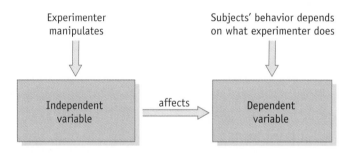

Ideally, everything in the experimental situation *except* the independent variable is held constant—that is, kept the same for all participants. You would not have some people use a stick shift and others an automatic, unless shift type were an independent variable. Similarly, you would not have some people go through the experiment alone and others perform in front of an audience. Holding everything but the independent variable constant ensures that whatever happens is due to the researcher's manipulation and nothing else. It allows you to rule out other interpretations.

Most variables may be either independent or dependent, depending on what the experimenter wishes to find out. If you want to know whether eating chocolate makes people nervous, then the amount of chocolate eaten is the independent variable. If you want to know whether feeling nervous makes people eat chocolate, then the amount of chocolate eaten is the dependent variable.

---

independent variable A variable that an experimenter manipulates.

dependent variable A variable that an experimenter predicts will be affected by manipulations of the independent variable.

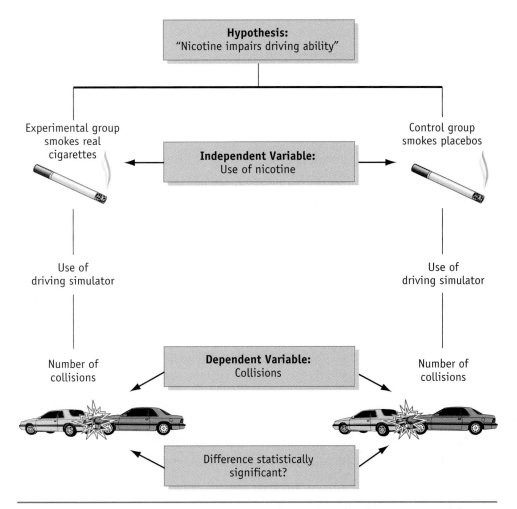

FIGURE 2.2 DO SMOKING AND DRIVING MIX? *The text describes this experimental design to test the hypothesis that nicotine in cigarettes impairs driving skills.*

Experimental and Control Conditions

Experiments usually require both an *experimental condition* and a comparison, or **control condition.** In the control condition, subjects are treated exactly as they are in the experimental condition, except that they are not exposed to the same treatment, or manipulation of the independent variable. Without a control condition, you cannot be sure that the behavior you are interested in would not have occurred anyway, even without your manipulation.

In our nicotine experiment, the people who smoke before driving make up the *experimental group,* and those who refrain from smoking make up the *control group.* We want

---

control condition In an experiment, a comparison condition in which subjects are not exposed to the same treatment as in the experimental condition.

these two groups to be roughly the same in terms of average driving skill. It would not do to start out with a bunch of reckless roadrunners in the experimental group and a bunch of tired tortoises in the control group. We probably also want the two groups to be similar in age, education, smoking history, and other characteristics so that none of these variables will affect our results. One way to accomplish this is to use **random assignment** of people to one group or another—for example, by randomly assigning them numbers and putting those with even numbers in one group and those with odd numbers in another. If we have enough participants, individual characteristics that could possibly affect the results are likely to be roughly balanced in the two groups, so we can forget about them.

Sometimes, researchers use several experimental or control groups. For example, in our nicotine study, we might want to examine the effects of different levels of nicotine by having people smoke one, two, or three cigarettes before "driving," and then comparing each of these experimental groups to each other and to a control group of nonsmokers as well. For now, however, let's focus just on experimental subjects who smoked one cigarette.

We now have two groups. We also have a problem. In order to smoke, the experimental subjects must light up and inhale. These acts might set off certain expectations—of feeling relaxed, nervous, confident, or whatever. These expectations, in turn, might affect driving performance. It would be better to have the control group do everything the experimental group does except use nicotine.

Therefore, we will change the experimental design a bit. Instead of having the control subjects refrain from smoking, we will give them a **placebo,** a fake treatment. Placebos, which are critical when testing new drugs, often take the form of pills or injections containing no active ingredients. In our study, we will use phony cigarettes that taste and smell like the real thing but contain no nicotine. Our control subjects will not know their cigarettes are fake and will have no way of distinguishing them from real ones. Now if they have substantially fewer collisions than the experimental group, we will feel safe in concluding that nicotine increases the probability of an auto accident.

Experimenter Effects

Because expectations can influence the results of a study, subjects should not know whether they are in an experimental or a control group. When this is so (as it usually is), the experiment is said to be a **single-blind study.** But subjects are not the only ones who bring expectations to the laboratory; so do researchers. And researchers' expectations and hopes for a particular result may cause them to inadvertently influence the participants' responses through facial expressions, posture, tone of voice, or some other cue.

---

random assignment A procedure for assigning people to experimental and control groups in which each individual has the same probability as any other of being assigned to a given group.

placebo An inactive substance or fake treatment used as a control in an experiment or given by a medical practitioner to a patient.

single-blind study An experiment in which subjects do not know whether they are in an experimental or a control group.

Many years ago, Robert Rosenthal (1966) demonstrated how powerful such **experimenter effects** can be. He had students teach rats to run a maze. Half the students were told that their rats had been bred to be "maze bright," and half were told that their rats had been bred to be "maze dull." In reality, there were no genetic differences between the two groups of rats, yet the supposedly brainy rats actually did learn the maze more quickly, apparently because of the way the students treated them. If an experimenter's expectations can affect a rodent's behavior, reasoned Rosenthal, surely they can affect a human being's. He went on to demonstrate this point in many other studies (Rosenthal, 1994). Even the most subtle cue from an experimenter, like a friendly smile, can affect people's responses in a study.

One solution to the problem of experimenter effects is to do a **double-blind study.** In such a study, the person running the experiment does not know which subjects are in which groups until the data have been gathered. Double-blind procedures are standard in drug research. Different doses of a drug are coded in some way, and the person administering the drug is kept in the dark about the code's meaning until after the experiment is completed. To run our nicotine study in a double-blind fashion, we would keep the person dispensing the cigarettes from knowing which ones were real and which were placebos.

Advantages and Limitations of Experiments

As we saw at the start of this chapter, a carefully conducted experiment can often keep people from leaping to unwarranted conclusions based on hearsay, "buzz," and anecdotes or case studies. A recent example, again having to do with autism, occurred when stories appeared in the news and on the Internet that a hormone called secretin could cure this disorder. One mother of an autistic child wrote an enthusiastic book about her child's experience with the drug, and its use quickly spread. But secretin failed its first controlled experimental test: Researchers could find no differences whatsoever between children taking secretin and those in a control group who were treated with plain salt water (Sandler et al., 1999).

Because experiments allow conclusions about cause and effect, and because they permit researchers to distinguish real effects from placebo effects, they have long been the method of choice in psychology. Throughout this book, you will learn many things that only experiments using control groups could have told us: why antidepressants are not always "miracle drugs," which therapy is best for which psychological problem, why people in groups are less likely to help a stranger in trouble than a single bystander is, and why children's doll play is not a reliable indicator of whether they have been sexually abused.

Like all methods, however, the experiment has its limitations. Just as in other kinds of studies, the participants are not always representative of the larger population. Most

---

experimenter effects   Unintended changes in subjects' behavior due to cues inadvertently given by the experimenter.

double-blind study   An experiment in which neither the subjects nor the individuals running the study know which subjects are in the control group and which are in the experimental group until after the results are tallied.

volunteers in psychological experiments are college students, who differ in many ways from people who are not in school. Moreover, in an experiment, the researcher determines what questions are asked and what behaviors are recorded, and the participants try to do as they are told. In their desire to cooperate with the experimenter or present themselves in a positive light, participants may act in ways that they ordinarily would not (Kihlstrom, 1995). Thus, research psychologists confront a dilemma: The more control they exercise over the situation, the more unlike real life it may be. For this reason, many psychologists are calling for more **field research,** the careful study of behavior in natural contexts such as schools and the workplace, using both descriptive and experimental methods.

As we have seen, every research method has its strengths and weaknesses. Now that we have come to the end of our discussion of these methods, how did you do on your list of their advantages and disadvantages? You can find out by comparing your list with the one in Table 2.1.

What Do You Know?

A. Name the independent and dependent variables in studies designed to answer the following questions:

1. Whether sleeping after learning a poem improves memory for the poem

2. Whether the presence of other people affects a person's willingness to help someone in distress

3. Whether people get agitated from listening to heavy-metal music

B. On a talk show, Dr. Blitznik announces a fabulous new program: Chocolate Immersion Therapy. "People who spend one day a week doing nothing but eating chocolate are soon cured of eating disorders, depression, and poor study habits," claims Dr. Blitznik. What should you find out about CIT before signing up?

ANSWERS:

A. 1. Opportunity to sleep after learning is the independent variable; memory for the poem is the dependent variable. 2. The presence of other people is the independent variable; willingness to help others is the dependent variable. 3. Exposure to heavy-metal music is the independent variable; agitation is the dependent variable. **B.** Some questions to ask: Does research show that people who go through CIT improve more than those in a control group who did not have the therapy, or who had a different therapy—say, Broccoli Immersion Therapy? If so, how many people were studied? How were they selected, and how were they assigned to the therapy and no-therapy groups? Did the people running the experiments know who was getting CIT and who was not? How long did the "cures" last? Has the research been peer reviewed? Has it been replicated?

---

field research Descriptive or experimental research conducted in a natural setting outside the laboratory.

TABLE 2.1 ✦ Research Methods in Psychology: Advantages and Disadvantages

METHOD	ADVANTAGES	DISADVANTAGES
Case study	Good source of hypotheses. Provides in-depth information on individuals. Unusual cases can shed light on situations or problems that are unethical or impractical to study in other ways.	Vital information may be missing, making the case hard to interpret. The person's memories may be selective or inaccurate. The individual may not be representative or typical.
Naturalistic observation	Allows description of behavior as it occurs in the natural environment. Often useful in first stages of a research program.	Allows researcher little or no control of the situation. Observations may be biased. Does not allow firm conclusions about cause and effect.
Laboratory observation	Allows more control than naturalistic observation. Allows use of sophisticated equipment.	Allows researcher only limited control of the situation. Observations may be biased. Does not allow firm conclusions about cause and effect. Behavior may differ from behavior in the natural environment.
Test	Yields information on personality traits, emotional states, aptitudes, abilities.	Difficult to construct tests that are valid and reliable.
Survey	Provides a large amount of information on large numbers of people.	If sample is nonrepresentative or biased, it may be impossible to generalize from the results. Responses may be inaccurate or untrue.
Correlational study	Shows whether two or more variables are related. Allows general predictions.	Does not permit identification of cause and effect.
Experiment	Allows researcher to control the situation. Permits researcher to identify cause and effect and to distinguish placebo effects from treatment effects.	Situation is artificial, and results may not generalize well to the real world. Sometimes difficult to avoid experimenter effects.

EVALUATING THE RESULTS

If you are a psychologist who has just done an observational study, a survey, or an experiment, your work has only just begun. Once you have some results in hand, you must do three things: (1) Describe them, (2) assess how reliable and meaningful they are, and (3) figure out how to explain them.

Descriptive Statistics: What's So?

Let's say that 30 people in the nicotine experiment smoked real cigarettes, and 30 smoked placebos. We have recorded the number of collisions for each person on the driving simulator. Now we have 60 numbers. What can we do with them?

The first step is to summarize the data. The world does not want to hear how many collisions each person had. It wants to know what happened in the nicotine group as a whole, compared to what happened in the control group. To provide this information, we need numbers that sum up our data. Such numbers, known as **descriptive statistics,** are often depicted in graphs and charts.

A good way to summarize the data is to compute group averages. The most commonly used type of average is the **arithmetic mean.** The mean is calculated by adding up all the individual scores and dividing the result by the number of scores. We can compute a mean for the nicotine group by adding up the 30 collision scores and dividing the sum by 30. Then we can do the same for the control group. Now our 60 numbers have been boiled down to 2. Let's assume that the nicotine group had an average of 10 collisions, whereas the control group's average was only 7.

We must be careful, however, about how we interpret these averages. It is possible that no one in our nicotine group actually had 10 collisions. Perhaps half the people in the group were motoring maniacs and had 15 collisions, whereas the others were more cautious and had only 5. Perhaps almost all the subjects had 9, 10, or 11 collisions. Perhaps the number of accidents ranged from 0 to 15. The mean does not tell us about such variability in the subjects' responses. For that, we need other descriptive statistics. These statistics—the most common one is called a **standard deviation**—tell us how clustered or spread out the individual scores are around the mean. The larger the standard deviation, the more spread out the scores are and the less "typical" the mean is. Unfortunately, when research is reported in the media, you usually hear only about the mean.

---

descriptive statistics Statistical procedures that organize and summarize a body of data.

arithmetic mean An average that is calculated by adding up a set of quantities and dividing the sum by the total number of quantities in the set.

standard deviation A commonly used measure of variability that indicates the average difference between scores in a distribution and their mean.

Inferential Statistics: So What?

At this point in our nicotine study, we have one group with an average of 10 collisions and another with an average of 7. Should we break out the champagne? Try to get on TV? Call our mothers?

Better hold off. Perhaps if one group had an average of 15 collisions and the other an average of 1, we could get excited. But rarely does a psychological study hit you between the eyes with a sensationally clear result. In most cases, it is possible that the difference between the two groups was due simply to chance. Despite all our precautions, perhaps the people in the nicotine group just happened to be a little more accident-prone, and their behavior had nothing to do with the nicotine.

To find out how impressive the data are, psychologists use **inferential statistics.** These statistics do not merely describe or summarize the data. They permit a researcher to draw *inferences* (conclusions based on evidence) about how meaningful the findings are. Like descriptive statistics, inferential statistics involve the application of mathematical formulas to the data.

The most commonly used inferential statistics are **significance tests,** which tell researchers how likely a result was to have occurred by chance. In our nicotine study, a significance test will tell us how likely it is that the difference between the nicotine group and the placebo group occurred by chance. It is impossible to rule out chance entirely, but if the likelihood that a result occurred by chance is extremely low, we can say that the result is *statistically significant.* This means that the probability is overwhelming that the difference is real—not certain, mind you, but overwhelming.

By convention, psychologists consider a result to be significant if it would be expected to occur by chance 5 or fewer times in 100 repetitions of the study. Another way of saying this is that the result is significant at the .05—"point oh five"—level. If the difference could be expected to occur by chance in 6 out of 100 studies, we would have to say that the results failed to support the hypothesis; the difference we obtained might well have occurred merely by chance. You can see that psychologists refuse to be impressed by just any old result.

Inferential statistics are necessary because a result that seems unlikely may not really be so unlikely after all. For example, how probable do you think it is that in a room of 25 people, at least two will have the same birthday? Most people think it's very unlikely, but in fact the odds are better than even. Even if there are only 10 people in the room, the chances are still 1 in 9. Or consider this: Among U.S. Presidents, two had the same birthday (Warren Harding and James Polk) and three died on the fourth of July (Johns Adams, the second president; Thomas Jefferson, the third; and James Monroe, the fifth). Surprising? No. Such "coincidences" are not statistically striking at all.

---

inferential statistics Statistical procedures that allow researchers to draw inferences about how statistically meaningful a study's results are.

significance tests Statistical tests that show how likely it is that a study's results occurred merely by chance.

Statistically significant results allow psychologists to make general predictions about human behavior. These predictions are usually stated as probabilities: "On average, we can expect 60 percent of all students to do X, Y, or Z." However, they usually do not tell us with any certainty what a particular individual will do in a particular situation. One reason is that even small, barely noticeable events can have profound but unpredictable effects on a person's behavior—as when you take a class in introductory astronomy merely because it's at the right hour, and wind up eventually working for NASA. Probabilistic results are typical not only in psychology but in all of the sciences. Medical research, for example, can tell us that the odds are high that someone who smokes will get lung cancer, but because many variables interact to produce any particular case of cancer, research cannot tell us for sure whether Aunt Bessie, a two-pack-a-day smoker, will come down with the disease.

By the way, a nicotine study similar to our hypothetical example has actually been done, using somewhat more complicated procedures (Spilich, June, & Renner, 1992). Participants who lit up before driving got a little farther on the simulated road, but they also had significantly more collisions on average (10.7) than did temporarily abstaining smokers (5.2) or nonsmokers (3.1). After hearing about this research, the head of Federal Express banned smoking on the job among all of the company's 12,000 drivers (George Spilich, personal communication).

Interpreting the Results

The last step in any study is to figure out what the findings mean. Trying to understand behavior from uninterpreted findings is like trying to become fluent in Swedish by reading a Swedish-English dictionary. Just as you need the grammar of Swedish to tell you how the words fit together, the psychologist needs hypotheses and theories to explain how the facts that emerge from research fit together.

Choosing the Best Explanation. Sometimes it is hard to choose between competing explanations. Does nicotine disrupt driving by impairing coordination, by increasing a driver's vulnerability to distraction, by interfering with the processing of information, by distorting the perception of danger, or by some combination of these factors? In interpreting any study, we must not go too far beyond the facts; several explanations may fit those facts equally well, which means that more research will be needed to determine the best one. Rarely does one study prove anything, in psychology or any other field.

Sometimes the best interpretation of a finding does not emerge until a hypothesis has been tested in different ways. Although the methods we have described tend to be appropriate for different questions (see Table 2.2), sometimes one method can be used to confirm, disconfirm, or extend the results obtained with another. If the findings of studies using various methods converge, there is greater reason to be confident about the findings. If they conflict, researchers must modify their hypotheses or do more research.

Here is an example. When psychologists compare the mental-test scores of young people and old people, they usually find that younger people outscore older ones.

TABLE 2.2 ✦ Psychological Research Methods Contrasted		
METHOD	**PURPOSE**	**EXAMPLE**
Case study	To understand the development of aggressive behavior in a particular individual; to formulate research hypotheses about the origins of aggressiveness.	Developmental history of a serial killer.
Naturalistic observation	To describe the nature of aggressive acts in early childhood.	Observation, tallying, and description of hitting, kicking, etc. during free-play periods in a preschool.
Laboratory observation	To find out whether aggressiveness in pairs of same-sex and different-sex children differs in frequency or intensity.	Observation through a one-way window of same-sex and different-sex pairs of preschoolers; pairs must negotiate who gets to play with an attractive toy that has been promised to each child.
Test	To compare the personality traits of aggressive and nonaggressive persons.	Administration of personality tests to violent and nonviolent prisoners.
Survey	To find out how common domestic violence is in the general population.	Questionnaire asking anonymous respondents (in a sample representative of the population) about the occurrence of slapping, hitting, etc. in their homes.
Correlational study	To examine the relationship between aggressiveness and television viewing.	Administration to college students of a paper-and-pencil test of aggressiveness and a questionnaire on number of hours spent watching TV weekly; computation of correlation coefficient.
Experiment	To find out whether high air temperatures elicit aggresive behavior.	Arrangement for individuals to "shock" a "learner" (actually a confederate of the experimenter) while seated in a room heated to either 72°F or 85°F.

This type of research, in which groups are compared at a given time, is called **cross-sectional.** But **longitudinal studies** can also be used to investigate mental abilities across the life span. In a longitudinal study, the same people are followed over a period of time and are reassessed at regular intervals. In contrast to cross-sectional studies, longitudinal studies find that as people age, they often perform as well as

---

cross-sectional study A study in which subjects of different ages are compared at a given time.
longitudinal study A study in which subjects are followed and periodically reassessed over time.

they ever did on many mental tests. A serious general decline in ability does not usually occur until extreme old age (Bosworth & Schaie, 1999; Salthouse, 1998). Why do results from the two types of studies conflict? Apparently, cross-sectional studies measure generational differences; younger generations may outperform older ones because they are better educated, had better nutrition as children, or are more familiar with the tests used. Without longitudinal studies, we might falsely conclude that all mental abilities inevitably decline across the adult years.

Judging the Result's Importance.   Sometimes psychologists agree on the reliability and meaning of a finding, but not on its ultimate relevance for theory or practice. Statistical significance alone does not provide the answer. A result may be statistically significant at the "point oh-five level," yet be small and of little consequence in everyday life, because the independent variable did not explain most of the variation in the subjects' behavior. On the other hand, a result may not quite reach statistical significance yet be worth following up (Falk & Greenbaum, 1995; Hunter, 1997). Because of these problems, many psychologists now prefer other statistical procedures that reveal the **effect size:** how much of the variation in the data the independent variable actually accounts for.

One popular statistical technique, called **meta-analysis,** combines and analyzes data from many studies, instead of assessing each study's results separately. Meta-analysis tells the researcher how much of the variation in scores across *all* the studies examined can be explained by a particular variable. For example, a meta-analysis of nearly 50 years of research found that gender accounts for a great deal of the variance in performance on certain spatial-visual tasks, with males doing better on the average (Voyer, Voyer, & Bryden, 1995). But other meta-analyses have shown that gender accounts for only 1 to 5 percent of the variance on tests of verbal and math ability (Feingold, 1988; Hyde, Fennema, & Lamon, 1990; Hyde & Linn, 1988). Although gender differences on these tests are reliable, they are small, and scores for males and females greatly overlap.

Meta-analysis is not a perfect technique: If you throw flawed studies into the pot along with the good ones, you might get a tasteless stew. However, it has been a useful way to find overall patterns in topics that have generated dozens and even hundreds of studies.

What Do You Know?

A. Check your understanding of the descriptive-inferential distinction by placing a check in the appropriate column for each phrase:

	DESCRIPTIVE STATISTICS	INFERENTIAL STATISTICS
1. Summarize the data	_____	_____
2. Give likelihood of data occurring by chance	_____	_____

---

effect size In an experiment, the amount of variance in the data accounted for by the independent variable.

meta-analysis A procedure for combining and analyzing data from many studies; it determines how much of the variance in scores across all studies can be explained by a particular variable.

	DESCRIPTIVE STATISTICS	INFERENTIAL STATISTICS
3. Include the mean	_____	_____
4. Give measure of statistical significance	_____	_____
5. Tell you whether to call your mother about your results	_____	_____

   B. If a researcher studies the same group over many years, the study is said to be _____.

   C. On the Internet, you read a posting about a "Fantastic Breakthrough: Five-minute Cure for Shyness!!!" Why should you be cautious about this announcement?

ANSWERS:

A. 1. descriptive 2. inferential 3. descriptive 4. inferential 5. inferential **B.** longitudinal **C.** Scientific progress, in psychology or any field, usually proceeds gradually, not all at once. (And besides, anyone can post anything on the Internet, so you will want to ask, "What's the source of this information?")

KEEPING THE ENTERPRISE ETHICAL

Rigorous research methods are the very heart of science, so it is not surprising that psychologists spend considerable time discussing and debating their procedures for collecting and evaluating data. They are also concerned about the ethics of their activities. In most colleges and universities, an ethics committee must approve all studies and be sure they conform to federal regulations. In addition, the American Psychological Association (APA) has a code of ethics that all members must follow.

The Ethics of Studying Human Beings

The APA code calls on psychological scientists to respect the dignity and welfare of human subjects. People must participate voluntarily and must know enough about the study to make an intelligent decision about participating, a doctrine known as *informed consent*. Researchers must also protect participants from physical and mental harm, and if any risk exists, they must warn the subjects in advance and give them an opportunity to withdraw at any time. (In the case of the nicotine study used as an example in this chapter, we would have to use only people who were already smokers. Exposing nonsmokers to the risks associated with smoking, a risk they would ordinarily not choose to run, would be unethical.)

However, the policy of informed consent sometimes clashes with an experimenter's need to deceive subjects about the true purpose of the study. In such cases, if the purpose were revealed in advance, the results would be ruined because the participants would not behave naturally. In social psychology, especially, a study's design sometimes calls for an elaborate deception. For example, a confederate (a research assistant masquerading as a subject) might pretend to have a seizure. The researcher can then find out whether the uninformed subjects will come to the apparent victim's aid. If they knew that the confederate was only acting, obviously they would not bother to intervene or call for assistance.

Sometimes people have been misled about procedures intentionally designed to make them uncomfortable, angry, guilty, ashamed, or anxious so that researchers can learn what people do when they feel this way. In anxiety studies, for instance, participants have been led to believe, falsely, that they failed a test or were going to get a painful shock. In studies of embarrassment and anger, people have been made to look clumsy in front of others, or have been called names, or been told they were incompetent. In studies of dishonesty, participants have been entrapped into cheating, and then confronted with evidence of their guilt.

Debate about the morality of deception escalated during the 1970s (Korn, 1998). Today, the APA's ethical guidelines require researchers to show that any deceptive procedures are justified by a study's potential value, to consider alternative procedures, and to thoroughly debrief participants about the true purpose and methods of the study afterward. But the issues raised by deception are still with us, and the APA is constantly revising its ethical code to deal with them.

The Ethics of Studying Nonhuman Animals

Another ethical issue concerns the use and treatment of nonhuman animals in research. Animals have always been used in only a small percentage of psychological studies, and in recent years, the number has declined even further (Dewsbury, 1996; Plous, 1996). Nonetheless, in certain areas of psychological research, animals still play a crucial role. Usually they are not harmed (as in research on mating in hamsters, which is fun for the hamsters), but sometimes they are (as in research on vision in kittens, when part of the animals' visual systems must be surgically removed). Some studies require the animal's death, as when rats brought up in deprived or enriched environments are sacrificed so that their brains can be examined for any effects.

Psychologists study animals for many reasons:

✦ To conduct basic research on a particular species—for example, to learn about the unusually lusty and cooperative lives of bonobo chimps.

✦ To discover practical applications—for example, to help farmers use behavioral principles to reduce crop destruction by birds and deer without resorting to their traditional method, shooting the animals.

✦ To study issues that cannot be studied experimentally with human beings because of practical or ethical considerations—for example, to discover the effects of maternal deprivation on emotional development.

◆ **To clarify theoretical questions**—for example, to determine whether life style factors or physiological factors common to all mammals are responsible for the longer life spans of women.

◆ **To improve human welfare**—for example, to help researchers develop ways to reduce chronic pain, rehabilitate patients with neurological disorders, teach people to control high blood pressure, and understand the mechanisms underlying memory loss and senility—to name only a few benefits (Feeney, 1987; Greenough, 1991; N. Miller, 1985).

Animal research, however, has provoked angry disputes. Many animal-rights activists want to eliminate all research using animals (Plous, 1991). Some extremists have vandalized laboratories or threatened and harassed researchers and their families. On the other side, some defenders of animal research have refused to acknowledge that confinement in laboratories can be psychologically and physically harmful for some species, or have branded all animal-welfare activists as terrorists. This conflict has motivated psychologists to find ways to improve the treatment of animals needed in research. The APA's ethical code covering the humane treatment of animals has been made more comprehensive, and federal laws governing the housing and care of research animals have been strengthened. The difficult task is to balance the many benefits of animal research with an acknowledgment of past abuses and a compassionate attitude toward species other than our own.

The Meaning of Knowledge

The continuing arguments over the use of deception and of animals in research show that psychology's methods can arouse as much disagreement as its findings do. Conflict exists not only about how to do studies, but even about what research can and cannot reveal. In psychology, as in many other fields, heated exchanges are taking place about the very meaning of knowledge itself.

To most psychological scientists, the purpose of their work is to map reality in as objective, value-free, and detached a manner as possible. A clear line is assumed to exist between the scientist, on one hand, and the phenomenon under study, on the other. In recent years, however, many scholars have questioned this concept of science. They have been influenced by a school of thought called **postmodernism,** which holds that detached objectivity, in any field of study, is impossible. In the postmodern view, the observer's values, judgments, and status in society inevitably affect how events are studied and how they are explained. Because scholars and researchers do their work at a particular time and in a particular culture, they bring with them shared assumptions and worldviews that influence what they count as an important fact, what parts

---

postmodernism A school of thought holding that an observer's values, culture, worldview, and status in society inevitably affect the person's observations and explanations.

of reality they notice, and how they determine standards of excellence. In the social sciences, this position has led to the view that human beings' ideas of reality are *socially constructed*—that is, based on a consensus influenced by human needs and desires. To social constructionists, knowledge is not so much discovered as it is created or invented (Gergen, 1994; Hare-Mustin & Marecek, 1990).

In psychology, postmodern debates about science are especially challenging. Psychologists have always had the goal of understanding the behavior and mental processes of human beings. Now they are being asked to analyze their own behavior as psychologists and to examine how their own values, gender, place in society, and cultural experiences affect their conclusions. Many welcome this challenge, drawing on a rich assortment of research methods to aid them. Others react to postmodern views with alarm; they acknowledge the limitations of research but worry about the tendency of some postmodernists to throw out the baby (rigorous standards of empirical research) with the bathwater (cultural bias and narrow-mindedness) (Gross & Levitt, 1994; Peplau & Conrad, 1989; Smith, 1994).

Our own position, which guides our approach in this book, falls somewhere between traditionalism and postmodernism. We think that understanding how knowledge is constructed by scholars and researchers is essential to the study of psychology, as we will try to show in the evaluation of each perspective. New ways of looking at knowledge and of doing research have the potential to expand and enrich our understanding of behavior. But for us, as for all scientific psychologists, some things must remain the same: an insistence on standards of evidence, a reliance on verifiable results, and an emphasis on critical thinking. That is why we hope that as you read the following chapters, you will resist the temptation to skip descriptions of how studies were done. If the assumptions and methods of a study are faulty, so are the results and the conclusions based on them.

Some of what you will learn in this book will confirm what you already believe; some findings will surprise you. The methods of science can help to illuminate our errors and biases and help us seek knowledge with an open mind. Biologist Thomas Huxley put it well: The essence of science, he said, is "to sit down before the fact as a little child, be prepared to give up every preconceived notion, follow humbly wherever and to whatever abyss nature leads, or you shall learn nothing." ■

Summary

1. Research methods provide a way for psychologists to separate well-supported conclusions from unfounded belief. An understanding of these methods can also help people think critically about psychological issues and become astute consumers of psychological findings and programs.

2. Scientists derive *hypotheses* from casual observations or a general *theory* of behavior, then formulate predictions using *operational definitions* of the phenomena being studied. The ideal scientist is skeptical of claims that rest solely on faith or authority, relies on empirical evidence, complies with the *principle of falsifiability*, and is open about methods and results so that findings can be replicated. In contrast,

pseudoscientists ignore these requirements. The public nature of science gives it a built-in system of checks and balances.

3. *Descriptive methods* allow psychologists to describe and predict behavior but not necessarily to choose one explanation over others. Such methods include case studies, observational studies, psychological tests, and surveys, as well as correlational methods.

4. *Case studies* are detailed descriptions of individuals. They are often used by clinicians, and they can be valuable in exploring new research topics and addressing questions that would otherwise be difficult to study. But because the person under study may not be representative of people in general, case studies are typically sources rather than tests of hypotheses.

5. In *observational studies,* the researcher systematically observes and records behavior without interfering in any way with the behavior. *Naturalistic observation* is used to find out how subjects behave in their natural settings. *Laboratory observation* allows more control and the use of special equipment; behavior in the laboratory, however, may differ in certain ways from behavior in natural contexts.

6. *Psychological tests* are used to measure and evaluate personality traits, emotional states, aptitudes, interests, abilities, and values. A good test is one that has been *standardized,* is scored using established *norms,* and is both *valid* and *reliable.* Critics have questioned the reliability and validity of even some widely used tests.

7. *Surveys* are questionnaires or interviews that ask people directly about their experiences, attitudes, and opinions. Researchers must take precautions to obtain a *sample* that is *representative* of the larger population that the researcher wishes to describe and that yields results that are not influenced by a *volunteer bias.* Findings can also be affected by the fact that respondents sometimes lie, misremember, or misinterpret the questions.

8. In descriptive research, studies that look for relationships between phenomena are known as *correlational.* A *correlation* is a measure of the strength of a positive or negative relationship between two variables, and is expressed by the *coefficient of correlation.* A correlation does *not* show a causal relationship between the variables.

9. *Experiments* allow researchers to control the situation being studied, manipulate an *independent variable,* and assess the effects of the manipulation on a *dependent variable.* Experimental studies usually require a comparison or *control condition.* *Random assignment* can be used to place people in the experimental and control groups. In some studies, control subjects receive a *placebo.* *Single-blind* and *double-blind* procedures can be used to prevent the expectations of the subjects or the experimenter from affecting the results. Because experiments allow conclusions about cause and effect, they have long been the method of choice in psychology. However, like laboratory observations, laboratory experiments create a special situation that may call forth behavior not typical in other environments. Many psychologists, therefore, have called for more *field research.*

10. Psychologists use *descriptive statistics,* such as the *arithmetic mean* and the *standard deviation,* to summarize and describe the data. They use *inferential statistics* to find out how impressive the data are. *Significance tests* tell the researchers how likely it

is that the results of a study occurred merely by chance. The results are said to be *statistically significant* if this likelihood is very low. Statistically significant results allow psychologists to make predictions about human behavior, but, as in all sciences, probabilistic results do not tell us with any certainty what a particular individual will do in a situation.

11. Choosing among competing interpretations of a finding can be difficult, and care must be taken to avoid going beyond the facts. Sometimes the best interpretation does not emerge until a hypothesis has been tested in more than one way—for example, by using both *cross-sectional* and *longitudinal* methods.

12. Statistical significance does not always imply real-world importance because the amount of variation in the data accounted for by the independent variable (the *effect size*) may be small. Conversely, a result that does not quite reach significance may be potentially useful. Therefore, many psychologists are now turning to other inferential measures. The technique of *meta-analysis,* for example, reveals how much of the variation in scores across many different studies can be explained by a particular variable.

13. The APA's ethical code requires researchers to obtain the *informed consent* of human subjects, protect them from harm, and warn them in advance of any risks. Many studies require deceptive procedures. Concern about the morality of such procedures has led to guidelines to protect participants.

14. Psychologists study animals in order to gain knowledge about particular species, discover practical applications of psychological principles, investigate issues that cannot be studied with human beings for practical or ethical reasons, clarify theoretical questions, and improve human welfare. Debate over the use of animals in research has led to more comprehensive regulations governing their treatment and care.

15. Debates are occurring in psychology, as in other fields, about the limits of research methods. Adherents of *postmodernism* argue that an observer's values, judgments, and status in society inevitably affect which events are studied, how they are studied, and how they are explained. This position has led to the view that human beings' ideas of reality are *socially constructed.* Postmodern ideas have expanded our awareness of the inherent subjectivity in studying human behavior. But scientific psychologists continue to insist on the importance of critical thinking and empirical methods.

Key Terms

theory   37

hypothesis   37

operational definition   37

principle of falsifiability   38

replicate   39

peer review   40

descriptive methods   41

case study   41

observational studies   42

naturalistic observation   43

PART II

The Biological Perspective

One rainy afternoon a young woman named Sheila Allen went to a community hospital asking for psychiatric help. Sheila Allen had virtually no strength left. She couldn't walk; she could barely sit up. For years, she had been going to doctors, getting sicker and sicker. The doctors thought her physical complaints were imaginary, and finally she agreed to enter the "kook hospital." Her diagnosis upon admission was "bizarre behavior, with looseness of thought associations and severe depression associated with suicidal thoughts."

Sheila Allen was lucky. At the hospital, she met a neurologist who suspected, correctly, that she had an uncommon disease called myasthenia gravis, which weakens the muscles. Fortunately, there is a treatment for this illness, and Sheila Allen recovered (Roueché, 1984). But others whose physical conditions have been mistaken for psychological ones have not been so lucky. The great composer George Gershwin spent years in psychoanalysis, complaining of headaches and depression. His analysts thought his problem was repressed hatred for his mother, when the real problem was a brain tumor that ultimately killed him. Similarly, songwriter Woody Guthrie ("This Land Is Your Land") was, for many years, mislabeled as an alcoholic. His real affliction was Huntington's disease, a fatal genetic condition that usually strikes people in middle age, causing involuntary spasms and twisting movements of the body, facial grimacing, memory lapses, impulsive behavior, and sometimes paranoia, depression, and other psychological symptoms.

In this psychological age, it is not uncommon for people to *over*psychologize. For example, until recently, it was generally believed that ulcers were caused by repressed anger—until the bacterium that causes most cases of ulcers was identified. Other diseases or disorders, from autism to cancer, have been blamed on psychological factors ranging from bad mothering to bad attitudes, until biological research has shown otherwise.

For psychologists who take a biological perspective on human behavior, such cases contain an important lesson: As physical creatures, we are all influenced by the workings of our bodies, and especially our brains. Therefore, in this view, to understand human beings—their temperaments, emotions, memories, perceptions, and mental disorders—we must understand the actions of genes, hormones, neurotransmitters, sensory organs, and neurons. This section explores behavior from the biological psychologist's perspective. In Chapter 3 we will consider how knowledge about genes can help account for the commonalities and differences in our personalities and abilities. In Chapter 4, we will look at how behavior is affected by the structure and biochemistry of the human nervous system.

CHAPTER THREE

The Evolution and Genetics of Behavior

*T*hink of all the ways that human beings are alike. Everywhere, no matter what their backgrounds or where they live, people love, work, argue, dance, sing, complain, and gossip. They rear families, celebrate marriages, and mourn losses. They reminisce about the past and plan for the future. They help their friends and fight with their enemies. They smile with amusement, frown with displeasure, and glare in anger. *Where do all these commonalities come from?*

Think of all the ways that human beings differ. Some are extroverts, always ready to throw a party, make a new friend, or speak up in a crowd; others are shy and introverted, preferring the safe and familiar. Some are trailblazers, ambitious and enterprising; others are placid, content with the way things are. Some take to book learning like a cat to catnip; others struggle in school but have lots of street smarts and practical know-how. Some are overwhelmed by even the most petty of problems; others, faced with severe difficulties, remain calm and resilient. *Where do all these differences come from?*

For many years, psychologists addressing these questions tended to fall into two camps. On one side were the *nativists*, who emphasized genes and inborn characteristics, or nature; on the other side were the *empiricists*, who focused on learning and experience, or nurture. Edward L. Thorndike (1903), one of the leading psychologists of the early 1900s, staked out the nativist position when he claimed that "in the actual race of life . . . the chief determining factor is heredity." But in words that became famous, his contemporary, behaviorist John B. Watson (1925), insisted that experience could write virtually any message on the blank slate of human nature: "Give me a dozen healthy infants, well-formed, and my own specified world to bring them up in and I'll guarantee to take any one at random and train him to become any type of specialist I might select—doctor, lawyer, artist, merchant-chief and yes, even beggar-man and thief, regardless of his talents, penchants, tendencies, abilities, vocations, and race of his ancestors."

In this chapter, we focus on the nature side of the debate and the findings of two related fields within the biological perspective. Researchers in **evolutionary psychology** emphasize the evolutionary mechanisms that might help explain commonalities in language learning, attention, perception, memory, sexual behavior, reasoning, and many other aspects of human psychology. Researchers in **behavioral genetics** study the contribution of heredity to individual differences in personality, mental ability, and other human characteristics. You should keep in mind, however, that today no one argues in terms of nature *or* nurture; scientists understand that heredity and environment interact to produce not only our psychological traits but even most of our physical ones.

Body weight is a good example of this interaction. At one time, most psychologists thought that being overweight was a sign of emotional disturbance. If you were fat, it was because you hated your mother, feared intimacy, or were trying to fill an emotional hole in your psyche by loading up on rich desserts. But the evidence for these notions came from flawed studies and unreliable self-reports. When researchers put this idea to the test using rigorous methods, they found that on average, fat people are no more and no less emotionally disturbed than average-weight people (Stunkard, 1980). Even more surprising, the evidence showed that *heaviness is not always caused by overeating* (C. Bouchard et al., 1990). Some heavy people eat enormous quantities of food, but so do some very thin people. Some thin people eat very little, but so do some obese people. In one study that carefully monitored everything that subjects were eating, two 260-pound women maintained their weights while consuming only 1,000 calories a day (Wooley, Wooley, & Dyrenforth, 1979). A new explanation was clearly needed.

Today, a widely accepted theory holds that a biological mechanism keeps a person's body weight at a genetically influenced **set point**—the weight you stay at when you are not consciously trying to gain or lose (Lissner et al., 1991). This biological mechanism, which involves a complex interaction of several bodily chemicals that regulate appetite and metabolism (the rate at which the body burns calories for energy), keeps people within a certain weight range, just as a thermostat keeps a house within a preset temperature range. When a heavy person diets, metabolism slows down to conserve energy (and fat reserves). When a thin person overeats, metabolism speeds up, burning energy. Set-point theory, which has been supported by dozens of studies of animals and human beings, explains why most people who go on restricted diets eventually gain their weight back; they are returning to their set point (Leibel, Rosenbaum, & Hirsch, 1995; Levitan & Ronan, 1988).

In recent years, dramatic progress has been made in identifying the specific genes and body chemicals involved in appetite, metabolic rates, weight regulation, and some

---

evolutionary psychology A field of psychology emphasizing evolutionary mechanisms that may help explain human commonalities in cognition, development, emotion, social practices, and other areas of behavior.

behavioral genetics An interdisciplinary field of study concerned with the genetic bases of behavior and personality.

set point The genetically influenced weight range for an individual, thought to be maintained by a biological mechanism that regulates food intake, fat reserves, and metabolism.

types of obesity (Chua et al., 1996; Zhang et al., 1994). But genes tell only part of the story. Despite steady increases in the number of Americans trying to lose weight, the prevalence of obesity has jumped dramatically in the past few decades, and by government standards, half the adult population is now overweight (Taubes, 1998). Obesity genes can't have changed in such a short period of time! You can probably guess the likely culprits: an increased abundance of low-cost, high-fat foods, the habit of eating high-calorie food on the run rather than eating healthy, leisurely meals, the ease of driving a car instead of walking or biking places, the popularity of television over active hobbies, and "couch potato" lifestyles (Brownell & Rodin, 1994; Hill & Peters, 1998).

It's not genes *or* the environment that determine weight, then; it's genes *and* the environment, and the same is true for most other human attributes. Throughout life, genetic factors interact with environmental ones to shape—sometimes quite literally—who we are.

Unlocking the Secrets of Genes

Let's look more closely at what genes are and how they operate. **Genes,** the basic units of heredity, are located on **chromosomes,** rod-shaped structures found in every cell of the body. Each sperm cell and each egg cell (ovum) contains 23 chromosomes, so when a sperm and an egg unite at conception, the fertilized egg and all the body cells that eventually develop from it (except for sperm cells and ova) contain 46 chromosomes, arranged in 23 pairs.

Chromosomes consist of threadlike strands of **DNA (deoxyribonucleic acid)** molecules, and genes consist of small segments of this DNA (see Figure 3.1). Each human chromosome contains thousands of genes, each with a fixed location. Estimates of the total number of human genes range from fewer than 30,000 to more than 150,000; collectively they are referred to as the human **genome.** Many of these genes are found in other animals as well; others are uniquely human, setting us apart from chimpanzees, wasps, and plants. Some genes are inherited in the same form by everyone; others vary, contributing to our individuality.

Within each gene, four basic chemical elements of DNA—identified by the letters A, T, C, and G, and numbering in the thousands or even tens of thousands—are arranged in a particular order: for example, ACGTCTCTATA. . . . This sequence forms a code that helps determine the synthesis of one of the many proteins that affect virtually every aspect of the body, from its structure to the chemicals that keep it running.

---

genes   The functional units of heredity; they are composed of DNA and specify the structure of proteins.

chromosomes   Within every body cell, rod-shaped structures that carry the genes.

DNA (deoxyribonucleic acid)   The chromosomal molecule that transfers genetic characteristics by way of coded instructions for the structure of proteins.

genome   The full set of genes in each cell of an organism (with the exception of sperm and egg cells).

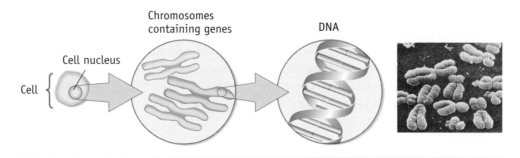

FIGURE 3.1 CHROMOSOMES, GENES, AND DNA *Chromosomes contain genes, which are the basic units of heredity, and genes are made up of DNA. The photo on the right shows human chromosomes magnified almost 55,000 times.*

Identifying even a single gene is a daunting task; biologist Joseph Levine and geneticist David Suzuki (1993) compared it to searching for someone when all you know is that the person lives somewhere on Earth. And because most human traits, even such seemingly straightforward ones as height and eye color, depend on more than one gene pair, tracking down the genetic contribution to a trait is even more difficult. Researchers must usually *clone* (produce copies of) several stretches of DNA on a chromosome, then use indirect methods to locate a given gene.

One method, which has been used to search for the genes associated with many physical and mental conditions, involves doing **linkage studies.** These studies take advantage of the tendency of genes lying close together on a chromosome to be inherited together across generations. The researchers start out by looking for **genetic markers,** DNA segments that vary considerably among individuals and whose locations on the chromosomes are already known. They then look for patterns of inheritance of these markers in large families in which a condition—say, depression or impulsive violence—is common. If a marker tends to exist only in family members who have the condition, then it can be used as a genetic landmark: The gene involved in the condition is apt to be located nearby on the chromosome, so the researchers have some idea where to search for it. The linkage method was used, for example, to locate the gene that causes Huntington's disease, the neurological disorder that killed Woody Guthrie (Huntington's Disease Collaborative Research Group, 1993). Although only one gene was involved, the search took a decade of painstaking work.

In the spring of 2000, after years of furious competition, an international collaboration of researchers called the Human Genome Project, and a private company, Celera Genomics, both announced they had completed a rough draft of a map of the entire human genome. Using high-tech methods, the researchers were able to identify

---

linkage studies Studies that look for patterns of inheritance of genetic markers in large families in which a particular condition is common.

genetic marker A segment of DNA that varies among individuals, has a known location on a chromosome, and can function as a genetic landmark for a gene involved in a physical or mental condition.

the sequence of almost all 3 billion units of DNA (those As, Cs, Ts, and Gs), and to determine the boundaries between genes and how they are arranged on the chromosomes. However, many gaps remain in the "map," and it will not be truly complete for a few more years. Moreover, even when we know where a gene is located on a chromosome, we do not automatically know its role in physical or psychological functioning. Usually, locating a gene is just the first step in understanding it.

The Genetics of Similarity

One of the questions that opened this chapter was, How can we explain our human similarities—the experiences and behaviors that seem to be universal? Evolutionary psychologists believe the answer lies in genetic dispositions that developed during the evolutionary history of our species. As British geneticist Steve Jones (1994) wrote, "Genetics is the key to the past. Every human gene must have an ancestor. . . . Each gene is a message from our forebears and together they contain the whole story of human evolution."

Evolution and Natural Selection

To read the messages from the past that are locked in our genes, we must first understand the nature of evolution itself. **Evolution** is basically a change in gene frequencies within a population over many generations. As particular genes become more common in the population or less common, so do the characteristics they influence.

Why do gene frequencies in a population change? Why don't they stay the same from one generation to another? Part of the reason is that during the division of the cells that produce sperm and eggs, if an error occurs in the copying of the original DNA sequence, genes can spontaneously change, or *mutate.* In addition, during the formation of a sperm or egg, small segments of genetic material are apt to cross over (exchange places) from one member of a chromosome pair to another, prior to the final division. As genes spontaneously mutate and recombine during the production of sperm and eggs, new genetic variations—and therefore, potential new traits—keep arising.

According to the principle of **natural selection,** first formulated in general terms by British naturalist Charles Darwin in *On the Origin of Species* (1859/1964), the fate of these genetic variations depends on the environment.[1] If, in a particular environment,

[1] Darwin did not know about genes; their discovery had not yet been widely publicized. But he realized that a species' characteristics must be transmitted from one generation to the next.

evolution A change in gene frequencies within a population over many generations; a mechanism by which genetically influenced characteristics of a population may change.

natural selection The evolutionary process in which individuals with genetically influenced traits that are adaptive in a particular environment tend to survive and to reproduce in greater numbers than other individuals; as a result, their traits become more common in the population.

individuals with a genetically influenced trait tend to be more successful than other individuals in finding food, surviving the elements, and fending off enemies—and therefore better at staying alive long enough to produce offspring—their genes will become more and more common in the population. Over many generations, their genes may even spread throughout the species. In contrast, individuals whose traits are not as adaptive in the struggle for survival will not be as "reproductively fit": They will tend to die before reproducing, and therefore their genes, and the traits influenced by those genes, will become less and less common and may eventually become extinct. Scientists debate how gradually or abruptly such changes occur and whether competition for survival is always the primary mechanism of change. But they agree on the basic processes of evolution. Over the past century and a half, Darwin's ideas have been resoundingly supported by findings in anthropology, botany, and molecular genetics (Jones, 2000). Scientists have watched evolutionary developments occurring before their very eyes in organisms that change rapidly, such as microbes, insects, and various plants. Evolutionary principles such as natural selection now guide all of the biological sciences.

Evolutionary biologists often start with an observation about some characteristic and then try to account for it in evolutionary terms. For example, why do male peacocks have such fabulous feathers, whereas females look so drab? Because during the evolution of peacocks, males who could put on the flashiest display got the attention of females, and these males therefore had a better chance of reproducing. In contrast, all females had to do was hang around and pick the guy with the fanciest feathers; they didn't even have to dress up.

Evolutionary psychologists work in the same way, but some take a slightly different tack: They start by asking what sorts of challenges human beings might have faced in their prehistoric past—having to decide which foods were safe to eat, for example, or needing to size up a stranger's intentions quickly. They then draw inferences about the behavioral tendencies that might have been selected because they helped our forebears solve these survival problems and enhanced reproductive fitness. (No assumption is made about whether the behavior is adaptive or intelligent in the *present* environment.) If such tendencies do in fact exist, that is support for an evolutionary explanation.

For example, our ancestors' need to avoid eating poisonous or rancid food might have led eventually to an innate dislike for bitter tastes and rotten smells, because those individuals who happened to be born with such dislikes would have had a better chance of surviving long enough to reproduce. Similarly, as we will see, it made good survival sense for our ancestors to develop an innate capacity for language and an ability to recognize faces and emotional expressions. But they would not have had much need for an innate ability to read or drive, inasmuch as books and cars had not yet been invented (Pinker, 1994).

The guiding assumption in evolutionary psychology is that the human mind evolved as a collection of specialized and independent "modules" to handle specific survival problems (Buss, 1995; Cosmides, Tooby, & Barkow, 1992; Mealey, 1996). Critics worry that the idea of mental modules is no improvement over instinct theory, the once-popular notion in psychology that virtually every human activity and capacity, from cleanliness to cruelty, is innate. Evolutionary psychologists, however, contend that by drawing on evidence from psychology and other disciplines, they can distinguish behavior that has a biological origin from behavior that does not. For example, as Steven Pinker (1994) explains, if a "mental module" for some behavior exists, then neuroscientists should eventually discover the brain circuits or subsystems associated with it. Further, he adds, "When children solve problems for which they have mental modules, they should look like geniuses, knowing things they have not been taught; when they solve problems that their minds are not equipped for, it should be a long hard slog." And indeed, as we will see, children acquire language without thinking twice about it, but acquiring geometry is generally a long hard slog.

Innate Human Characteristics

Because of the way our species evolved, many abilities, tendencies, and characteristics are either present at birth in all human beings or develop rapidly as a child matures, and therefore qualify as potential mental modules. These traits include not just the obvious ones, such as the ability to stand on two legs or to grasp objects with the forefinger and thumb, but also less obvious ones. Here are just a few examples:

1 INFANT REFLEXES. Babies are born with a number of *reflexes*—simple, automatic responses to specific stimuli. They will turn their heads toward a touch on the cheek or corner of the mouth and search for something to suck on, a handy "rooting" reflex that allows them to find the breast or bottle. They suck vigorously on a nipple, finger, or pacifier placed in their mouths, a response that helps them nurse. They grasp tightly a finger pressed on their palms. They follow a moving light with their eyes and turn toward a familiar sound, such as the mother's voice or the thump-thump of a heartbeat (both of which they heard in the womb). Many of these reflexes eventually disappear, but others, such as the knee-jerk, eye-blink, and sneeze reflexes, remain.

2 AN ATTRACTION TO NOVELTY. Novelty is appealing to human beings and many other species. If a rat has had its dinner, it will prefer to explore an unfamiliar wing of a maze rather than the familiar wing where food is. Human babies reveal a surprising interest in looking at and listening to unfamiliar things—which, of course, includes most of the world. A baby will even stop nursing if someone new enters his or her range of vision.

3 A DESIRE TO EXPLORE AND MANIPULATE OBJECTS. All birds, mammals, and primates have this innate inclination. Primates, especially, like to "monkey" with things, taking them apart and scrutinizing the pieces, apparently for the sheer pleasure of it (Harlow, Harlow, & Meyer, 1950). Human babies shake rattles, bang pots, and grasp whatever is put into their tiny hands. For human beings, the natural impulse to handle interesting objects can be overwhelming, which may be one reason why the command "don't touch" is so often ignored by children, museum-goers, and shoppers.

4 AN IMPULSE TO PLAY AND FOOL AROUND. Think of kittens and lion cubs, puppies and pandas, and all young primates, who will play with and pounce on one another all day until hunger or naptime calls. Play and exploration may be biologically adaptive because they help members of a species find food and other necessities of life and learn to cope with their environments. Indeed, the young of many species enjoy *practice play,* behavior that will later be used for serious purposes when they are adults (Vandenberg, 1985). A kitten, for example, will stalk and attack a ball of yarn. In human beings, play teaches children how to get along with others and gives them a chance to practice their motor and linguistic skills (Pellegrini & Galda, 1993).

5 BASIC MENTAL SKILLS. Taking advantage of the fact that infants look longer at novel or surprising stimuli than at familiar ones, psychologists have designed delightfully imaginative methods to test what tiny babies know. They find that at only 4 months of age, babies actually seem to understand some basic principles of physics! Babies will look longer at a ball if it seems to roll through a solid barrier, leap between two platforms, or hang in midair than they do when an action obeys the laws of physics, suggesting that the unusual event is surprising to them (Spelke et al., 1992). Infants as young as 2½ to 3½ months also seem to understand some of the physical properties of objects. The babies are shown a gloved hand pushing a colorful box from left to right along a striped platform. The box is pushed either until its edge reaches the end of the platform (a possible event) or until only a bit of its bottom surface rests on the platform, with the rest extending beyond the platform (an impossible event). The babies will look longer at the impossible event. Researcher Renée Baillargeon (1994) interprets this to mean that very young infants "are aware that objects continue to exist when masked by other objects, that objects cannot remain stable without support, that objects move along spatially continuous paths, and that objects cannot move through the space occupied by other objects." Pretty good for an infant, no?

Possible event

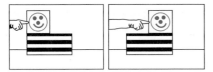

Impossible event

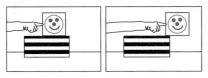

Babies also seem to have a rudimentary understanding of number. Incredibly, by the age of only 1 week, they show an understanding that a set of three items differs from a set of two items. Of course, 1-week-old babies cannot count. However, they will spend more time looking at a novel set of three items after getting used to a set of two items, or vice versa, which means that they can recognize the difference. By 18 months, infants know that four is more than three, which is more than two, which is more than one—suggesting that the brain is designed to understand "more than" and "less than" relationships for small numbers. Evolutionary psychologists believe that these fundamental arithmetic skills evolved because they were useful to our ancestors (Geary, 1995).

What Do You Know?

How evolved is your understanding of genetics and evolution?

1. What two processes during the formation of sperm and eggs help explain gene changes within a population?

2. Which is the best statement of the principle of natural selection? (a) Over time, the environment naturally selects some traits over others. (b) Genetic variations become more common over time if they are adaptive in a particular environment. (c) A species constantly improves as parents pass along their best traits to their offspring.

3. Evolutionary psychologists argue that the human mind evolved as (a) a collection of specialized modules to handle specific survival problems, (b) a general-purpose computer that adapts to any situation, (c) a collection of specific instincts for every human activity or capacity.

4. Which of the following is *not* part of our biological heritage? (a) a sucking reflex at birth, (b) a motive to explore and manipulate objects, (c) an avoidance of novel, unfamiliar objects, (d) a love of play

Answers:

1. spontaneous genetic mutations and crossover of genetic material between members of a chromosome pair, which occur before the final division 2. b 3. a 4. c

Our Human Heritage

Let's look more closely now at some human characteristics that are of special interest to evolutionary psychologists: perceptual abilities, emotional expressions, a need for sociability and attachment, a capacity for language, and (by far the most controversial) gender differences in sexual behavior.

The Origins of Perception

Shirl Jennings had been almost totally blind since early childhood, but he had adjusted well to his disability. He read Braille, enjoyed listening to sports events on the radio, and supported himself as a massage therapist. Then something happened that changed his life: At the urging of his fiancée, he agreed to undergo cataract surgery on the chance that it might restore his sight. In 1991, at the age of 51, Shirl had the operation, and it was a success.

Or was it? Oddly, although Shirl's eyes now functioned well, he seemed to have no clue about what he was seeing. To identify objects, he had to first touch or smell them.

He might see an animal's paw, nose, tail, and ears yet fail to recognize that he was looking at a cat. His own shadow confused him. His depth perception was poor, so he kept tripping. If he departed from his usual route through his own house, he became disoriented. He misread facial expressions. And when he returned to work, his clients' bodies began to disgust him! Instead of a happier, brighter world, Shirl found himself living in one that was strange and frightening. Like other people who have had their vision restored late in life, he was never able to adjust completely to this new world. In the years that followed, his eyesight deteriorated once again, and today he can make out only vague shapes. Yet he is untroubled; in fact, he is rather relieved at being released from the baffling world of sight.

Shirl's story (which inspired the 1999 movie *At First Sight*) illustrates an important distinction: It is one thing for the visual receptors in the eyes to detect and respond to changes in physical energy emitted or reflected by objects in the environment, a process called **sensation,** and quite another for the brain to interpret and organize this information, a process called **perception.** Sensation produces an immediate awareness of sound, color, form, and other building blocks of consciousness, but it takes perceptual processes to assemble those building blocks into meaningful patterns. Our sense of vision produces a two-dimensional image on the back of the eye, but we *perceive* the world in three dimensions and *perceive* where one object begins and another ends. Shirl's problems were with perception.

Psychologists are interested in cases like Shirl's for the clues they might offer in solving an old problem: Which aspects of sensation and perception have our evolutionary past prepared us for? When babies first open their eyes, do they see the same sights, hear the same sounds, smell the same odors, taste the same flavors as an adult does? Are their strategies for organizing the world wired into their brains from the beginning? Or is an infant's world, as William James once suggested, only a "blooming, buzzing confusion," waiting to be organized by experience and learning?

Unfortunately, fascinating though cases like Shirl's may be, they have some drawbacks from a scientific standpoint. Blind people who regain their sight have relied all their lives on their sense of touch, and this reliance could interfere with their ability to make sense of the visual world after their sight is restored. Also, some patients, including Shirl, have had physical damage to the eye, which could explain some of their postoperative visual problems. So to find out what happens when the usual perceptual experiences of early life fail to occur, researchers study animals whose sensory and perceptual systems are similar to our own, such as cats.

Perception, it turns out, develops abnormally in the absence of certain experiences during critical periods of development. For example, when newborn animals are reared in total darkness for a period of weeks or months, or are fitted with translucent goggles that permit only diffuse light to get through, or are allowed to see only one

---

sensation The detection of physical energy emitted or reflected by physical objects; it occurs when energy in the external environment or the body stimulates receptors in the sense organs.

perception The process by which the brain organizes and interprets sensory information.

visual pattern and no others, visual development is impaired. In one famous study, kittens were exposed to either vertical or horizontal black and white stripes. Special collars kept them from seeing anything else, even their own bodies (see Figure 3.2). After several months, the kittens exposed only to vertical stripes seemed blind to all horizontal contours; they bumped into horizontal obstacles and ran to play with a bar that an experimenter held vertically but not to a bar held horizontally. In contrast, those exposed only to horizontal stripes bumped into vertical obstacles and ran to play with horizontal bars but not vertical ones (Blakemore & Cooper, 1970).

These findings do not necessarily mean that cats are blind to horizontal and vertical lines *at birth,* however. Normal experience may merely ensure the survival of skills already present from the beginning in rudimentary form. Physiological studies suggest that this second interpretation is the correct one, at least in the case of line perception. In all mammals, complex features of the visual world, such as moving or stationary lines oriented in a particular direction, are processed by special *feature-detector cells* in the brain's visual areas (Hubel & Wiesel, 1962, 1968). The brains of newborn kittens are equipped with exactly the same kinds of feature-detector cells that adult cats have. But when kittens are kept from seeing horizontal or vertical lines during a critical period in their development, as in the study we described, the cells sensitive to those orientations deteriorate or change, and perception suffers (Hirsch & Spinelli, 1970; Mitchell, 1980). Similar critical periods probably exist in human beings as well.

Because of their ability to detect lines of different orientations, human infants are able to discriminate the edges and angles of objects. And many other visual skills are also present at birth or develop quite early, given normal experiences. For example, babies can discriminate different sizes and colors very early, possibly at birth. They can distinguish contrasts, shadows, and complex patterns after only a few weeks. Even some depth perception may be present from the beginning.

FIGURE 3.2 VISION AND EARLY EXPERIENCE *Cats are born with the ability to see horizontal and vertical lines, but without certain experiences, this ability deteriorates. Kittens were reared in darkness for five months after birth, but for several hours each day were put in a cylinder that permitted them to see only vertical lines or horizontal ones. Later on, the kittens had trouble perceiving whichever type of line they had missed out on being exposed to (Blakemore & Cooper, 1970).*

Testing an infant's perception of depth requires considerable ingenuity. One clever procedure that was used for decades was to place infants on a device called a *visual cliff* (Gibson & Walk, 1960). The "cliff" is a pane of glass covering a shallow surface and a deep one (see Figure 3.3). Both surfaces are covered by a checkerboard pattern. The infant is placed on a board in the middle, and the child's mother tries to coax the baby across either the shallow or the deep side. Babies as young as 6 months of age will crawl to their

FIGURE 3.3 THE VISUAL CLIFF *Young infants usually hesitate to crawl past the apparent edge of the visual cliff, which suggests that they are able to perceive depth.*

mothers across the shallow side but will refuse to crawl out over the "cliff." Their hesitation shows that they have depth perception.

Of course, by 6 months of age, a baby has had quite a bit of experience with the world. But infants younger than 6 months, even though they are unable to crawl, can also be tested on the visual cliff. At only 2 months of age, babies show a drop in heart rate when placed on the deep side of the cliff, but no change when they are placed on the shallow side. A slowed heart rate is usually a sign of increased attention. Thus, although these infants may not be frightened the way an older infant would be, it seems that they can perceive the difference between the "shallow" and the "deep" sides of the cliff (Banks, 1984).

Infants bring into the world other kinds of sensory and perceptual abilities as well. They will startle to a loud noise and turn their heads toward its source, showing that they perceive sound as being localized in space. They can distinguish a person's voice from other kinds of sounds. They react strongly to certain smells, such as those of garlic and vinegar, but less strongly to others, such as those of licorice and alcohol, showing that they can discriminate among odors. They can distinguish salty from sweet. They show a distinct preference for sweet tastes and, as we saw earlier, they have an innate dislike for bitter ones. Because neurological connections in infants' brains and sensory systems are not completely formed, their senses are less acute than those of an adult. However, an infant's world is clearly far from the blooming, buzzing confusion that William James took it to be.

The inborn sensory and perceptual abilities we have described all evolved to help us survive. It is enormously useful to be able to notice the edge of a cliff—or a crib, or a staircase. Our sense of smell allows us to sniff out danger by smelling smoke, spoiled food, and poison gases, and our sense of hearing helps us detect the rustle of a snake in the grass and the voice of a friend in a crowd. A sweet tooth may have evolved because sweet tastes generally belong to substances such as fruits, which are healthful and thus enhance survival. Even pain, which causes so much misery, is an indispensable part of our evolutionary heritage, for it alerts us to illness and injury. The few rare individuals who are born without a sense of pain are free of the hurts and aches that plague the rest of us, but they burn, bruise, and cut themselves more than other people do. Because they cannot feel pain's warnings, they often die young.

The Face of Emotion

In his classic book *The Expression of Emotions in Man and Animals* (1872/1965), Charles Darwin argued that certain human facial expressions of emotion—the smile, the frown, the grimace, the glare—are as biologically ordained as the wing flutter of a frightened bird, the purr of a contented cat, or the snarl of a threatened wolf. Such expressions evolved, he said, because they allowed our forebears to tell at a glance the difference between a friendly stranger and a hostile one.

Modern psychologists have supported Darwin's evolutionary explanation by confirming that certain emotional expressions are recognized the world over. For example, Paul Ekman and his colleagues have gathered abundant evidence for the universality of seven basic facial expressions of emotion: anger, happiness, fear, surprise, disgust, sadness, and contempt (Ekman, 1994; Ekman et al., 1987; Ekman & Heider, 1988). In every culture they have studied—in Brazil, Chile, Estonia, Germany, Greece, Hong Kong, Italy, Japan, New Guinea, Scotland, Sumatra, Turkey, and the United States—a large majority of people recognize the emotional expressions portrayed by those in other cultures. Even most members of isolated tribes that have never watched a movie or read *People* magazine, such as the Foré of New Guinea or the Minangkabau of West Sumatra, can recognize the emotions expressed in pictures of people who are entirely foreign to them, and we can recognize theirs.

Universal emotional expressions allow us to communicate our intentions to others and evoke a response from them, and to "read" the intentions of others. These findings do not mean, however, that everybody in a society can recognize the same expressions in all situations. Ekman (1994) called his theory of emotional expression *neurocultural,* to emphasize that two factors are involved: a universal neurophysiology in the facial muscles associated with certain emotions, and culture-specific variations in the expression of emotion. Thus, while most people in most cultures do recognize basic emotions as portrayed in photographs, sometimes a large minority does not. Across 20 studies of Western cultures, for example, fully 95 percent of the participants agreed in their judgments of happy faces, but only 78 percent agreed on expressions of sadness and anger. And across 11 non-Western societies, 88 percent recognized happiness, but only 74 percent agreed on sadness and 59 percent on anger (Ekman, 1994).

Psychologists have also found that some emotional expressions resembling those of adults are present from birth, most notably those for pleasure, anger, surprise, disgust, and possibly fear and sadness—pretty much the same ones that are universal across cultures (Campos et al., 1984). A baby's expressions of misery, angry frustration, happiness, or disgust are apparent to most parents (Izard, 1994; Stenberg & Campos, 1990). Babies, in turn, react to the facial expressions of their parents, especially when their parents are happy. American, German, Greek, Japanese, Trobriand Island, and Yanomamo mothers all "infect" their babies with happy moods by displaying happy expressions (Keating, 1994). Babies also seem primed to respond in other ways to happy facial expressions. Tiny newborns will suck longer on a pacifier if it produces a happy face than if it produces a face with a neutral or negative expression (Walker-Andrews, 1997). (If you become a parent, remember this!)

Starting at the end of their first year, babies begin to intentionally alter their own behavior in reaction to their parents' facial expressions of emotions, and this ability has obvious survival value. Recall the visual cliff that we described in the previous section. If babies are placed on a more ambiguous cliff that does not drop off sharply and does not automatically evoke fear, their behavior will depend on the mother's expression. If she assumes an expression of fear or anger, the baby will not cross. If, however, the mother smiles reassuringly, the baby is likely to cross over to her (Sorce et al., 1985). The infant's ability to recognize a parent's facial signals of alarm or safety is certainly beneficial in real situations because babies do not have the experience necessary for judging danger.

Sociability and Attachment

Unlike a tadpole or a tarantula, a human infant cannot live without care and attention from its own kind. Without other people, we languish physically and emotionally; without the universal need for affiliation and cooperation, human societies could never have survived. Human beings, therefore, are predisposed to form attachments and learn from others.

Synchrony and Sociability. Newborn babies are sociable from the moment they hatch. For one thing, they are primed to pay attention to human faces. Babies who are only 9 *minutes* old will turn their heads to watch a drawing of a face if it moves in front of them, but they will not turn if the "face" consists of scrambled features or is just the outline of a face (Goren, Sarty, & Wu, 1975; Johnson et al., 1991). This preference has a biological basis: Specific visual cells in the brain actually respond maximally to faces (Ó Scalaidhe, Wilson, & Goldman-Rakic, 1997; Young & Yamane, 1992). A preference for faces over other stimuli in the environment no doubt has survival value because it helps babies recognize where their next meal is likely to come from.

By the age of 4 to 6 weeks, babies are smiling regularly, especially in response to faces, even when they haven't yet the foggiest notion of whom they are smiling at. Babies also have rudimentary "conversations" with the people who tend them. Like many social exchanges, a baby's first "conversation" with its mother or other primary caregiver often takes place over a good meal. During nursing, babies and their mothers (or dads, or grandparents, or nannies) often play little games with each other, exchanging signals in a rhythmic pattern of sucks and pauses. During the pauses, the adult often jiggles the baby, who then starts to suck again. Like a spoken conversation, their exchange involves taking turns and waiting for a response: suck, pause, jiggle, pause, suck, pause, jiggle, pause (Kaye, 1977).

This early rhythmic dialogue illustrates a crucial aspect of all human exchanges: *synchrony,* the adjustment of one person's nonverbal behavior to coordinate with another's (Bernieri et al., 1996; Condon, 1982). People unconsciously adjust their rhythms of speech, their gestures, and their expressions to be "in sync" with each other, and these adjustments, which seem to be essential in establishing rapport between people, begin at birth. Newborn infants will synchronize their behavior and attention to adult speech but not to other sounds, such as street noise or tapping (Beebe et al., 1982). A mother and child tend to move in concert, move at the same pace and rhythm, and coordinate their movements like well-matched dance partners. Their little dance will soon develop into a full-blown dialogue.

Contact Comfort. In all primate infants, *attachment,* a deep emotional tie to caregivers, grows out of **contact comfort,** the pleasure of being touched and held. Margaret and Harry Harlow first demonstrated the importance of contact comfort by raising infant rhesus monkeys with two kinds of artificial mothers (Harlow, 1958; Harlow & Harlow, 1966). The first was a forbidding construction of wires and warming lights, with a milk bottle connected to it. The second was constructed of wire and covered in foam rubber and cuddly terry cloth. At the time, psychologists thought that babies become attached to their parents because a parent provides food and warmth. But the Harlows' baby monkeys ran to the terry-cloth "mother" when they were frightened or startled, and cuddling up to it calmed them down (see Figure 3.4).

Human infants, too, initially become attached to their mothers or other caregivers because of the contact comfort the adults provide. Indeed, for infants, cuddling is nearly as important as food. British psychiatrist John Bowlby (1969, 1973) discovered this fact years ago when he observed infants being reared in orphanages. Babies who were given adequate food, water, and warmth but who were deprived of being touched and held showed abnormal emotional and physical development. (Emotional and physical symptoms also occur in adults in our society who are "undertouched," such as the sick and the aged.) Bowlby argued that infant attachment has an adaptive purpose: It provides a *secure base* from which the child can explore the environment, a haven of safety to which the child can return when he or she is afraid. A sense of security, said Bowlby, allows children to develop cognitive skills. A sense of safety allows them to develop trust.

Many psychologists are concerned about infants who do not have secure attachments to loving adults, because these babies can develop emotional and behavioral problems that persist throughout life (Mickelson, Kessler, & Shaver, 1997; Speltz, Greenberg, & Deklyen, 1990). Some think that a baby's attachment depends entirely on how the mother treats her baby during the first year. This popularized notion is incorrect. Today we know that differences in *normal* parental child-rearing practices do not affect a child's degree of attachment. About two-thirds of all children become securely attached under a wide range of conditions: being held and cuddled constantly, being held at some times and left alone to amuse themselves at others, being cared for by many adults or by one, being cared for exclusively at home or spending hours in

---

contact comfort The innate pleasure derived from close physical contact; it is the basis of an infant's first attachment.

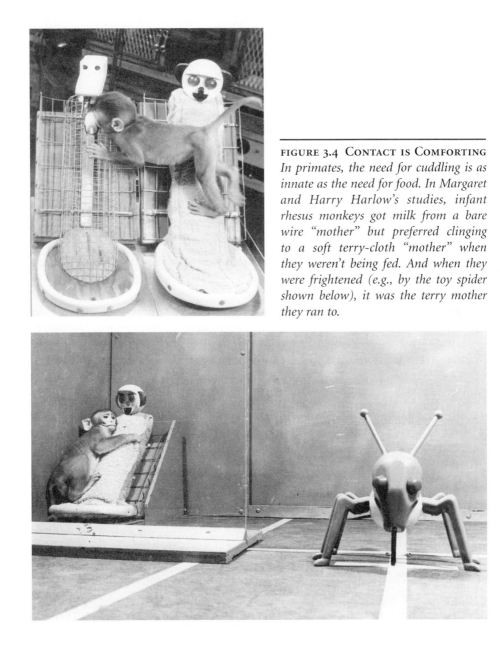

FIGURE 3.4 CONTACT IS COMFORTING
In primates, the need for cuddling is as innate as the need for food. In Margaret and Harry Harlow's studies, infant rhesus monkeys got milk from a bare wire "mother" but preferred clinging to a soft terry-cloth "mother" when they weren't being fed. And when they were frightened (e.g., by the toy spider shown below), it was the terry mother they ran to.

daycare centers (De Wolff & van Ijzendoorn, 1997; McKim et al., 1999; NICHD Early Child Care Research Network, 1997).

What, then, does cause insecure attachment? One answer is the kind of extreme neglect, abuse, and deprivation that Bowlby observed in orphanages. A child's own temperament is also a factor; some children are genetically disposed to be nervous, fearful, and difficult to comfort (Seifer et al., 1996). Finally, some children may go through phases of insecure attachment as a result of disruptive or stressful family experiences, such as the chronic illness of a parent or parental divorce (Belsky et al., 1996; Lewis, 1997).

What Do You Know?

Are you attached to quizzes yet?

1. Research with animals and human infants suggests that the ability to discriminate edges and angles of objects is (a) innate, and develops regardless of experience; (b) innate, but depends on experience for survival and development; (c) learned only after maturation of the nervous system, many months after birth.

2. What two kinds of research support Darwin's notion that certain facial expressions of emotion are part of our biological heritage?

3. A mother coos and rocks her baby, who smiles and giggles back at her. Their "conversation" shows the inherent tendency of humans to _____ their behavior.

4. Melanie is playing happily on a jungle gym when she falls off and badly scrapes her knee. She runs to her father for a consoling cuddle. Melanie seeks _____.

ANSWERS:

1. b 2. cross-cultural research on facial expressions of emotion and research on the facial expressions of newborns 3. synchronize 4. contact comfort

---

The Capacity for Language

Try to read this sentence aloud:

Kamaunawezakusomamanenohayawewenimtuwamaanasana.

Can you tell where one word begins and another ends? Unless you know Swahili, the syllables of this sentence will probably sound like gibberish.[2]

Well, to a baby learning its native tongue, *every* sentence must, at first, be gibberish. How, then, does an infant pick out discrete syllables and words from the jumble of sounds in the environment, much less figure out what the words mean and how to combine them? Is there something special about the human brain that allows a baby to discover how language works? Darwin thought so. Language, wrote Darwin (1874), is an instinctive ability unique to human beings, and many modern researchers think he was right.

To evaluate this claim, we must first appreciate that a **language** is not just any old communication system; it is a set of rules for combining elements that are in themselves meaningless into utterances that convey meaning. The elements are usually sounds, but

---

[2]*Kama unaweza kusoma maneno haya, wewe ni mtu wa maana sana,* in Swahili, means, "If you can read these words, you are a remarkable person."

---

language A system that combines meaningless elements such as sounds or gestures to form structured utterances that convey meaning.

they can also be the gestures of American Sign Language (ASL) and other manual languages used by deaf and hearing-impaired people.

Some nonhuman animals are able to acquire aspects of language if they get some help from their human friends (see Chapter 7). However, we seem to be the only species that acquires language naturally. Other primates use grunts, screeches, and gestures to warn each other of danger, attract attention, and express emotions, but the sounds are not combined to produce original sentences (at least, as far as anyone can tell). Bongo may make a sound of delight when he encounters food, but he cannot say, "The bananas in the next grove are a lot riper than the ones we ate last week and sure beat our usual diet of termites."

In contrast, language, whether spoken or signed, allows human beings to express and comprehend an infinite number of novel utterances, created on the spot. This ability is critical; except for a few fixed phrases ("How are you?" "Get a life!"), most of the utterances we produce or hear over a lifetime are new. For example, in this book you will find few, if any, sentences that you have read, heard, or spoken before in exactly the same form. Yet you can understand what you are reading, and you can produce new sentences of your own about the material.

For adults, mastering the rules of a new language can be an intimidating task. But children acquire new words at an amazingly rapid rate—about 9 a day, for a total of more than 14,000 new words during the preschool years. They absorb these words as they encounter them in conversation, typically after hearing only one or two uses of a word in context (Rice, 1989). In only a few years, a child can string all those new words together into sentences that make sense and, most impressive of all, can produce and understand an infinite number of new word combinations.

Deaf children learn sign language as easily as hearing children learn to speak. In North America, deaf children use American Sign Language (ASL) to express not only everyday meanings but also poetic and musical ones.

At one time, most psychologists assumed that children acquired their dazzling linguistic abilities by imitating adults and paying attention when adults corrected their mistakes. Then along came linguist Noam Chomsky (1957, 1980), who argued that language was far too complex to be learned bit by bit, as one might learn the world capitals. Children, said Chomsky, must not only figure out which sounds or gestures form words; they must also take the *surface structure* of a sentence—the form in which the sentence is spoken or signed—and infer an underlying *deep structure* that contains meaning. For example, although "Mary kissed John" and "John was kissed by Mary" have different surface structures, any 5-year-old knows that the two sentences have essentially the same deep structure, in which Mary is the actor and John gets the kiss. Conversely, "Bill heard the trampling of the hikers," a single-surface structure, can have two different deep structures: one in which the hikers are actors doing the trampling, and one in which they are the unfortunate objects getting trampled.

To transform surface structures into deep structures, said Chomsky, children must apply rules of grammar (*syntax*). These rules govern word order and other linguistic features that determine the role a word plays in a sentence (such as, say, kisser or kissee). Most people, even adults, cannot actually state the grammatical rules of their language ("Adjectives usually precede the noun they describe"), yet they are able to apply thousands of such rules, without even thinking about it. (No native speaker of English would say, "He threw the ball big"). Because no one explicitly teaches us these rules when we are toddlers, the human brain, Chomsky argued, must contain a **language acquisition device,** an innate mental module that allows young children to develop language if they are exposed to an adequate sampling of conversation. Just as a bird is designed to fly, human beings are designed to use language.

Over the years, linguists and *psycholinguists* (researchers who study the psychology of language) have gathered many types of evidence in support of this position (Crain, 1991; Pinker, 1994):

1 **CHILDREN IN DIFFERENT CULTURES GO THROUGH SIMILAR STAGES OF LINGUISTIC DEVELOPMENT.** For example, they will often form their first negatives by simply adding *no* or *not* at the beginning or end of a sentence ("No get dirty"); and at a later stage, they will use double negatives ("He don't want no milk") even when their language does not allow such constructions (Klima & Bellugi, 1966; McNeill, 1966). Cross-cultural similarities in sentence structure have even been reported for deaf children who have never learned a standard language, either signed or spoken, and have made up their *own* sign languages (Goldin-Meadow & Mylander, 1998). Such commonalities suggest that children are born with a *universal grammar,* which is another way of saying that the brain is disposed to notice the core features (nouns and verbs, subjects and objects, and so forth) common to all languages, even those as seemingly different as Mohawk and English, or Okinawan and Bulgarian (Baker, 1999; Cinque, 1999; Pesetsky, 1999).

---

language acquisition device According to many psycholinguists, an innate mental module that facilitates the young child's development of language.

2 CHILDREN COMBINE WORDS IN WAYS THAT ADULTS NEVER WOULD. They reduce a parent's sentences ("Let's go to the store") to their own two-word versions ("Go store") and make many charming errors that an adult would not ("The alligator goed kerplunk," "Daddy taked me," "Hey, Horton heared a Who") (Ervin-Tripp, 1964; Marcus et al., 1992). Such errors, which linguists call *overregularizations,* are not random; they show that the child has grasped a grammatical rule (e.g., add the *t* or *d* sound to make a verb past tense, as in *walked* and *hugged*) and is merely overgeneralizing it (*taked, goed*).

3 ADULTS DO NOT CONSISTENTLY CORRECT THEIR CHILDREN'S SYNTAX, YET CHILDREN LEARN TO SPEAK OR SIGN CORRECTLY ANYWAY. Learning theorists' explanations of language acquisition assume that children are rewarded for saying the right words and punished for making errors. But parents do not stop to correct every error in their children's speech, so long as they can understand what the children are trying to say (Brown, Cazden, & Bellugi, 1969). Indeed, parents often *reward* children for incorrect statements! The 2-year-old who says "Want milk" is likely to get it; most parents would not wait for a more grammatical (or polite) request.

4 EVEN CHILDREN WHO ARE PROFOUNDLY RETARDED ACQUIRE LANGUAGE. Indeed, they typically have a facility for language that exceeds by far their abilities in other areas (Bellugi et al., 1992; Smith, Tsimpli, & Ouhalla, 1993). This gap between general mental abilities and language abilities is especially striking in some children with a rare genetic disorder called Williams syndrome (Harris et al., 1997). These children, who are sometimes unable to tie their shoes or do a simple puzzle, may have extraordinary vocabularies; they may be able to talk about newts and ibexes, not just dogs and cats, and tell elaborate stories.

5 INFANTS AS YOUNG AS 7 MONTHS CAN DERIVE SIMPLE LINGUISTIC RULES FROM A STRING OF SOUNDS. If babies are repeatedly exposed to artificial "sentences" with an ABA pattern, such as *ga ti ga* or *li na li,* until they get bored, they will then prefer new sentences with an ABB pattern (such as *wo fe fe*) over new sentences with an ABA pattern (such as *wo fe wo*). (They indicate this preference by looking longer at a flashing light associated with the novel pattern than one associated with the familiar pattern.) Conversely, when the original sentences have an ABB structure, babies will prefer novel ones with an ABA structure. These responses suggest to many researchers that babies can discriminate the different types of structures (Marcus et al., 1999). Astonishingly, this ability emerges even before they can understand or produce any words.

Chomsky's ideas so revolutionized thinking about language and human nature that some linguists now refer to the initial publication of his ideas as The Event (Rymer, 1993). Chomsky completely changed the questions researchers asked about language development, and even the terms they used (language "acquisition" replaced language "learning"). Although Chomsky himself avoided the evolutionary implications, others maintain that an innate facility for language evolved in human beings because it permitted our ancestors to convey precise information about time, space, objects, and events, and to negotiate alliances that were necessary for survival (Pinker, 1994). Linkage studies of large families with inherited language disorders are now being done to try to pin down the specific genes involved in our human capacity for language (e.g., Fisher et al., 1998).

The evolutionary approach is not accepted by everyone, however. Some theorists, using computers, have been able to design models of the brain that can "learn" certain aspects of language without the help of a language acquisition device. The success of these models, say their designers, suggests that children, too, are able to acquire linguistic features without getting a head start from preprogrammed brain circuits (Rumelhart & McClelland, 1987). Other researchers argue that instead of inferring grammatical rules, children simply learn the probability that any given word or syllable will follow another (Saffran, Aslin, & Newport, 1996; Seidenberg, 1997). In this view, infants are more like statisticians than grammarians.

Even theorists who argue for an inborn grammatical capacity acknowledge that in any behavior as complex as language, both nature and nurture must play a role. Although parents may not go around correcting their children's speech all day, neither do they ignore their children's errors. For example, when a child makes a mistake or produces a clumsy sentence, parents almost invariably respond by recasting it or expanding its elements ("Monkey climbing!" "Yes, the monkey is climbing the tree") (Bohannon & Stanowicz, 1988). In turn, children are more likely to imitate adult recasts and expansions, suggesting that they are learning from them (Bohannon & Symons, 1988).

The importance of both heredity and the environment is apparent in the tragic cases of abandoned and abused children who have been isolated from normal conversation until late childhood. After they are rescued, these children may learn to use short sentences to convey their basic needs, but they rarely "catch up" grammatically. They lack the ability to use pronouns correctly, ask questions, produce proper negatives, and use all the little word endings that communicate tense, conjunction, number, and possession (Curtiss, 1977, 1982; Rymer, 1993). It's likely that these grammatical abilities must be acquired during a biologically determined *critical period* in childhood, a "make or break" period in which children must be exposed to language and must have opportunities to practice their emerging linguistic skills.

What Do You Know?

Use your human capacity for language to answer these questions.

1. The most important distinction between human language and other communication systems is that language (a) allows for the generation of an infinite number of new utterances; (b) is spoken; (c) is learned only after explicit training; (d) directly expresses a linguistic deep structure.

2. What did Chomsky mean by a "language acquisition device"?

3. What five findings support the existence of an innate "universal grammar"?

ANSWERS:

1. a 2. An innate mental module that permits young children to develop language if they are exposed to an adequate sampling of conversation. 3. Children everywhere go through similar stages of linguistic development; children combine words in ways that adults would not; adults do not consistently correct their children's syntax; even profoundly retarded children usually acquire language; and even infants only a few months old appear to distinguish different sentence structures.

Evolution, Courtship, and Mating

Genes, we have seen, contribute to many of the qualities that make us human: our pleasure in exploring and examining our environment; specific ways of seeing, tasting, smelling, and hearing the world; a need to touch and be with others; a capacity for language. When the seventeenth-century English philosopher John Locke wrote that the human mind at birth is a *tabula rasa,* a blank slate, he was mistaken; the tabula isn't rasa at all.

But what about human social customs, such as warfare, cooperation, or politics? Social scientists disagree heartily about the role biology and evolution play in such complex social behaviors. Nowhere is this disagreement more heated than in debates over the origins of male–female differences in sexual behavior, so we are going to focus on that endlessly fascinating topic.

The evolutionary viewpoint on mating practices has been strongly influenced by work in **sociobiology,** an interdisciplinary field that emphasizes evolutionary explanations of social behavior in animals, including human beings. Sociobiologists contend that evolution has bred into each of us a tendency to act in ways that maximize our chances of passing on our genes, and to help our close biological relatives, with whom we share many genes, do the same. This impulse to act in ways that ensure the survival of our personal genetic code, sociobiologists argue, is the primary motivation behind much of our social behavior, from altruism (helping others) to xenophobia (fearing strangers) (Wilson, 1975, 1978). In the sociobiological view, just as nature has selected physical characteristics that have proved adaptive, so it has selected psychological traits and social customs that aid individuals in propagating their genes. Customs that enhance the odds of such transmission survive in the form of kinship bonds, courtship rituals, dominance arrangements, taboos against female adultery, and many other aspects of social life.

Sociobiologists believe that because the males and females of most species have faced different kinds of survival and mating problems, the sexes have evolved to differ profoundly in aggressiveness, dominance, and sexual strategies (Symons, 1979; Trivers, 1972). In this view, it pays for males to compete with other males for access to young and fertile females, and to try to win and then inseminate as many females as possible. The more females a male mates with, the more genes he can pass along. (The human record in this regard was achieved by a man who fathered 899 children [Daly & Wilson,

---

sociobiology An interdisciplinary field that emphasizes evolutionary explanations of social behavior in animals, including human beings.

1983].) But according to sociobiologists, females need to shop for the best genetic deal, as it were, because they can conceive and bear only a limited number of offspring. Having such a large investment in each pregnancy, they cannot afford to make mistakes. Besides, mating with a lot of different males would produce no more offspring than staying with just one. So females try to attach themselves to dominant males, who have resources and status and are likely to have "superior" genes.

The result of these two opposite sexual strategies, in this view, is that males tend to want sex more than females do; males are often fickle and promiscuous, whereas females are usually devoted and faithful; males are drawn to sexual novelty and even rape, whereas females want stability and security; males are relatively undiscriminating in their choice of partners, whereas females are cautious and choosy; and males are competitive and concerned about dominance, whereas females are less so.

Evolutionary psychologists generally agree with these conclusions, but they differ from sociobiologists in some respects. For example, most evolutionary psychologists do not consider human beings to be "reproductive-fitness maximizers" whose main motive is to perpetuate their genes. As evolutionary psychologist David Buss (1995) pointed out, if men had a conscious or unconscious motive to maximize their reproductive fitness, they would be lining up to make donations to sperm banks! Instead, say evolutionary psychologists, the evolved behavioral tendencies described by sociobiologists are simply the consequences of evolutionary processes such as natural selection.

Evolutionary psychologists also rely less on data from nonhuman animals than sociobiologists do. Sociobiologists tend to argue by analogy. If a male scorpion fly forces himself on a female, this behavior is taken as analogous to human rape and so human rape must have the same evolutionary origins; it's basically just another mating strategy (Thornhill & Palmer, 2000). But most evolutionary psychologists recognize that such analogies are simplistic and misleading. Human rape, for example, has many motives, from revenge to sadism to selfishness, and is often committed by high-status men who could easily find consenting sexual partners.

Evolutionary psychologists tend to focus on human mating and dating practices in different cultures. For example, in one massive project, 50 scientists studied 10,000 people in 37 cultures located on six continents and five islands (Buss, 1994). Around the world, they found, men are more violent than women and more socially dominant. They are more interested in the youth and beauty of their sexual partners than women are, presumably because youth is associated with fertility. They are more sexually jealous and possessive of their partners, presumably because males can never be 100 percent sure that their children are really theirs genetically. They are quicker to have sex with partners they don't know well, and more inclined toward polygamy and promiscuity, presumably so that their sperm will be distributed as widely as possible. Women, in contrast, tend to emphasize the financial resources or prospects of a potential mate, his status, and his willingness to commit to a relationship (Bailey et al., 1994; Buss, 1994, 1996; Buunk et al., 1996; Daly & Wilson, 1983; Kenrick & Trost, 1993).

Evolutionary views of sex differences have become enormously popular (especially, for some strange reason, with men!). On a TV talk show, novelist Tom Wolfe explained that men are "genetically" wired to be promiscuous and women to be monogamous. News magazines regularly run cover stories about the supposed evolutionary advantages for males of sowing their seeds far and wide and the supposed evolutionary advantages for females of finding a man with a good paycheck.

But critics argue that evolutionary explanations are based on *stereotypes* of gender differences. The actual behavior of humans and other animals often fails to conform to the stereotypes (Hrdy, 1994; Hubbard, 1990). In many species—birds, fish, mammals, and primates, including human beings—females are sexually ardent and often have many male partners. The female's sexual behavior does not seem to depend simply on the goal of being fertilized by the male: Females have sex when they are not ovulating and even when they are already pregnant. And in many primate species, males do not just mate and run; they stick around, feeding the infants, carrying them on their backs, and protecting them against predators (Hrdy, 1988; Snowdon, 1997). These findings have sent evolutionary theorists scurrying to figure out the evolutionary benefits of male nurturance and female promiscuity. For example, they say, by having many partners, perhaps a female increases the number of males who will care for her offspring.

Critics of evolutionary theories, however, take exception to this entire line of reasoning. They point out that evolutionary explanations of complex human social customs are nonfalsifiable because they explain everything, after the fact: why females are monogamous and why they are promiscuous; why males pursue many females and why they pair up with just one.

Moreover, note the critics, human sexual behavior is amazingly varied and changeable. Cultures range from those in which women have many children to those in which they have very few; from those in which men are intimately involved in child rearing to those in which they do nothing at all; from those in which women may have many lovers to those in which women may be killed if they have sex outside of marriage (Hatfield & Rapson, 1996). In some places, the chastity of a potential mate is much more important to men than to women; but in other places, it is important to both sexes, or to neither one (see Figure 3.5). Even within a culture, sexual attitudes and practices vary

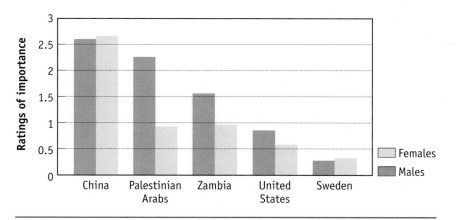

FIGURE 3.5 ATTITUDES TOWARD CHASTITY *In many places, men care more about a partner's chastity than women do, as evolutionary psychologists would predict. But culture has a powerful impact on these attitudes, as this graph shows (from Buss, 1995). Notice that in China, both sexes prefer a partner who has not yet had intercourse, whereas in Sweden, chastity is a nonissue.*

tremendously and change rapidly over time in response to changing gender roles and the economic status of women (Laumann et al., 1994). These variations, say the critics, point to the importance of economic and social factors rather than genes.

Debate over these matters can get quite intense because of worries that evolutionary arguments will be used to justify existing social and political inequalities and violent behavior. For example, such arguments have been used to argue that men, with less investment in child rearing and more interest in status and dominance, are destined to control business and politics (Wilson, 1975). (Essay 1 explores further the political implications of evolutionary arguments.)

Ultimately, what evolutionary scientists and their critics are quarreling about is the relative power of biology and culture. In *On Human Nature* (1978), Edward Wilson argued that genes hold culture on a leash. The big question, replied evolutionary theorist and social critic Stephen Jay Gould (1987), is, how long and tight is that leash? Is it too tight to allow much change, or is it long enough to permit many possible customs? To many sociobiologists, the leash is short and tight. To evolutionary psychologists, it is elastic enough to permit culture to modify evolved biological tendencies, although those tendencies can be pretty powerful (Kenrick & Trost, 1993). To critics of sociobiology and evolutionary psychology, cultural variations mean that no single, genetically determined sexual strategy exists for human beings—the leash is long and flexible.

What Do You Know?

Both sexes have evolved to be able to answer these questions.

1. Which of the following would an evolutionary psychologist expect to be more typical of males than of females? (a) promiscuity, (b) choosiness about sexual partners, (c) concern with dominance, (d) interest in young partners, (e) emphasis on physical attractiveness of partners

2. What major issue divides evolutionary theorists and their critics in debates over courtship and mating?

3. A friend of yours, who has read some sociobiology, tells you that men will always be more promiscuous than women because during evolution, the best reproductive strategy for male primates has been to try to impregnate lots of females. What kind of evidence would you need to evaluate this claim?

ANSWERS:

1. all but b 2. The relative influence of biology and culture 3. You would not want to look just for confirming evidence (recall the principle of falsifiability from Chapter 2). You would want to look also for evidence of female promiscuity and male monogamy among humans and other primates, and changes in sexual customs in response to changing social conditions. You would also want to consider non–evolutionary explanations of male promiscuity. For example, how might differences in the social, physiological, and economic consequences of male and female promiscuity help account for why men tend to be more promiscuous than women?

THE GENETICS OF DIFFERENCE

We have been focusing on the origins of human similarities. Now let's turn to the second great issue in the nature–nurture debate: the origins of the differences among us. We begin with a critical discussion of what it means to say that a trait is "heritable." Then, to illustrate how behavioral geneticists study differences that might be influenced by genes, we will examine genetic contributions to intelligence and personality.

The Meaning of Heritability

Suppose you want to measure flute-playing ability in a large group of music students, so you have some independent raters assign each student a score, from 1 to 20. When you plot the scores, you find that some people are what you might call melodically disadvantaged and should forget about a musical career; others are flute geniuses; and the rest fall somewhere in between. What causes the variation in this group of students? Why are some so musically talented and others so inept? Are these differences primarily genetic, or are they the result of experience and motivation?

To answer these questions, behavioral geneticists compute a statistic called **heritability,** which gives an estimate of the *proportion of the total variance in a trait that is attributable to genetic variation within a group.* Because the heritability of a trait is expressed as a proportion, the maximum value it can have is 1.0. Height is highly heritable; that is, within a group of equally well-nourished individuals, most of the variation among them will be accounted for by their genetic differences. In contrast, table manners have low heritability because most variation among individuals is accounted for by differences in upbringing. Our guess is that flute-playing ability falls somewhere in the middle.

Many people hold completely mistaken ideas about heritability. But as genetic findings pour in, the public will need to understand this concept more than ever. You cannot understand the nature–nurture issue without understanding the following important facts about heritability:

1 AN ESTIMATE OF HERITABILITY APPLIES ONLY TO A PARTICULAR GROUP LIVING IN A PARTICULAR ENVIRONMENT. Estimates may differ for different groups. Suppose that all the children in Community A are affluent, eat plenty of high-quality food, have kind and attentive parents, and go to the same top-notch schools. Because their environments are similar, any intellectual differences among them will have to be due largely to their genetic differences. In other words, mental ability in this group will be highly heritable. In contrast, the children in Community B are rich, poor, and in between. Some of them have healthy diets; others live on fatty foods and cupcakes. Some attend good schools; others go to inadequate ones. Some have doting parents, and some have

---

heritability A statistical estimate of the proportion of the total variance in some trait that is attributable to genetic differences among individuals within a group.

unloving and neglectful ones. These children's intellectual differences could be due largely to their environmental differences, in which case the heritability of intelligence for this group will be low.

2 HERITABILITY ESTIMATES DO NOT APPLY TO INDIVIDUALS, ONLY TO VARIATIONS WITHIN A GROUP. You inherited half your genes from your mother and half from your father, but your particular *combination* of genes is a unique genetic mosaic that has never occurred before and will never occur again (unless you have an identical twin). You also have a unique history of family relationships, intellectual training, and life experiences. It is impossible to know just how your genes and your environment have interacted to produce the person you are today. For example, if you are a great flute player, no one can say whether your ability is mainly a result of inherited musical talent, living all your life in a family of devoted flute players, a private obsession that you acquired at age 6 when you saw the opera *The Magic Flute,* or a combination of all three. For one person, genes may make a tremendous difference in some aptitude or disposition; for another, the environment may be far more important. Scientists can only try to explain the extent to which differences among people *in general* are explainable by their genetic differences.

3 EVEN HIGHLY HERITABLE TRAITS CAN BE MODIFIED BY THE ENVIRONMENT. Although height is highly heritable, malnourished children may not grow to be as tall as they would have with sufficient food. Conversely, if children eat an extremely nutritious diet, they may grow to be taller than anyone thought they could. The same principle applies to psychological traits, although biological determinists sometimes fail to realize this. They argue, for example, that because IQ is highly heritable, IQ and school achievement cannot be boosted much (Herrnstein & Murray, 1994). But even if the first part of the statement is true, the second part does not necessarily follow.

Computing Heritability

Scientists have no way to estimate the heritability of a trait or behavior directly, so they must *infer* it by studying people whose degree of genetic similarity is known. You might think that the simplest approach would be to compare blood relatives within families; after all, everyone knows of families that are famous for some talent or trait. But family traits do not tell us much, because close relatives usually share environments, not just genes. If Carlo's parents and siblings all love lasagna, that does not mean that a taste for lasagna is heritable! The same applies if everyone in Carlo's family has a high IQ, is mentally ill, or is moody.

A better approach is to study adopted children (e.g., Loehlin, Horn, & Willerman, 1996; Plomin & DeFries, 1985). Such children share half their genes with each birth parent, but they grow up in a different environment, apart from their birth parents. On the other hand, they share an environment with their adoptive parents and adoptive siblings, but not their genes. Researchers can compare correlations between the traits of adopted children and those of their biological and adoptive relatives and can use the results to estimate heritability.

Separated at birth, the Mallifert twins meet accidentally.

Another approach is to compare identical twins with fraternal twins. **Identical (monozygotic) twins** develop when a fertilized egg (zygote) divides into two parts that then develop into two separate embryos. Because the twins come from the same fertilized egg, they share all their genes. (They may differ slightly at birth, however, because of differences in the blood supply to the two fetuses or other chance factors.) In contrast, **fraternal (dizygotic) twins** develop when a woman's ovaries release two eggs instead of one, and each egg is fertilized by a different sperm. Fraternal twins are wombmates, but they are no more alike genetically than any other two siblings (they share, on average, only half their genes), and they may be of different sexes. Behavioral geneticists can estimate the heritability of a trait by comparing groups of same-sex fraternal twins with groups of identical twins. The assumption is that if identical twins are more alike than fraternal twins, the increased similarity must be genetic.

Perhaps, however, identical twins are treated differently than fraternal twins. People may treat identical twins, well, identically—or they may go to the other extreme, emphasizing the twins' differences. To avoid these problems, investigators have studied identical twins who were separated early in life and reared apart. (Until recently, adoption policies and attitudes toward illegitimacy permitted such separations to occur.)

---

identical (monozygotic) twins Twins that develop when a fertilized egg divides into two parts that develop into separate embryos.

fraternal (dizygotic) twins Twins that develop from two separate eggs fertilized by different sperm; they are no more alike genetically than are any other pair of siblings.

In theory, separated identical twins share all their genes but not their environments. Any similarities between them should be primarily genetic and should thus permit a direct estimate of heritability.

What Do You Know?

Is test-taking ability a heritable trait or a matter of motivation? Either way, be sure to take this quiz.

1. Diane hears that basket-weaving ability is highly heritable. She assumes that her own poor performance must therefore be due mostly to genes. What is wrong with her reasoning?
2. Bertram hears that basket-weaving ability is highly heritable. He concludes that schools should not bother trying to improve the skills of children who lack this talent. What is wrong with his reasoning?
3. Basket-weaving skills seem to run in Andy's family. Why shouldn't Andy conclude that his talent is genetic?
4. Why do behavioral geneticists find it useful to study twins?

ANSWERS:

1. Heritability applies only to differences among individuals within a group, not to particular individuals. 2. A trait may be highly heritable *and* still be susceptible to modification. 3. Family members share environments, as well as genes. 4. Identical twins are more alike than fraternal twins, and so do fraternal twins growing up together share an environment, and so if identical twins reared apart share only then the increased similarity is assumed to be genetic. Identical twins reared apart share only their genes, not their environment, so similarities between them should also be primarily genetic.

OUR HUMAN DIVERSITY

Behavioral-genetic research is transforming our understanding of behavior that was once explained solely in psychological terms. Let's see what this research can tell us about the origins of intelligence and personality.

Heritability and Intelligence

In heritability studies, the usual measure of intellectual functioning is an **intelligence quotient,** or **IQ** score. The term "IQ" is a holdover from the early days of psychological testing, when intelligence tests were given only to children. A child's *mental age* (MA)—

---

intelligence quotient (IQ) A measure of intelligence originally computed by dividing a person's mental age by his or her chronological age and multiplying the result by 100; it is now derived from norms provided for standardized intelligence tests.

the child's level of intellectual development relative to other children's—was divided by the child's chronological age (CA) and multiplied by 100 to yield a quotient. Thus, a child of 8 who performed like the average 6-year-old would have a mental age of 6 and an IQ of 75 ($\frac{6}{8}$ times 100); and a child of 8 who scored like an average 10-year-old would have a mental age of 10 and an IQ of 125 ($\frac{10}{8}$ times 100). All average children, regardless of age, would have an IQ of 100 because MA and CA would be the same. (In actual calculations, months were used, not years, to yield a more precise figure.)

This scoring method had a serious flaw. At one age, scores might cluster tightly around the average, whereas at another age, they might be somewhat more dispersed. As a result, the IQ score necessary to be in the top 10 or 20 or 30 percent of one's age group varied, depending on one's age. Because of this problem, and because the IQ formula did not make much sense for adults, today's intelligence tests are scored differently. Usually the average for each age group is arbitrarily set at 100, and test scores—still informally referred to as "IQs"—are computed from tables. A score still reflects how a person compares with others, either children of a particular age or adults in general. At all ages, the distribution of scores in a large population approximates a normal (bell-shaped) curve, with scores near the average (mean) most common and very high or very low scores rare (see Figure 3.6).

Most psychologists believe that IQ tests measure a general quality that affects all aspects of mental ability, but the tests have many critics. Some argue that intelligence comes in many varieties, more than can possibly be captured by a single score: musical aptitude, the ability to empathize with others, insight into oneself, and so on (Gardner, 1995). Certainly, many people are intelligent in ways not captured by standard IQ tests. They cope well with novelty, can see the larger context of a problem, and are able to pick

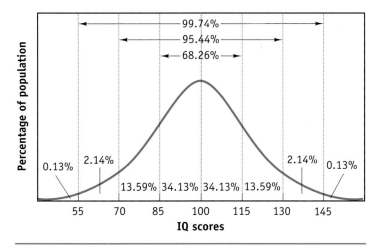

FIGURE 3.6 EXPECTED DISTRIBUTION OF IQ SCORES *In a large population, IQ scores tend to be distributed on a normal (bell-shaped) curve. On most tests, about 68 percent of all people will score between 85 and 115; about 95 percent will score between 70 and 130; and about 99.7 percent will score between 55 and 145.*

up practical strategies for achieving goals, even when those strategies are not explicitly taught (Sternberg, 1988; Sternberg et al., 1995). Other critics argue that IQ tests are biased because they tap mostly those abilities that depend on experiences in a middle-class environment and favor whites over people of other ethnicities. (In Chapter 10 we will discuss how cultures foster or ignore different kinds of "intelligences.")

Keep in mind, then, that heritability studies are estimating only the heritability of those mental skills that contribute to IQ test scores, not necessarily all aspects of mental performance, and that the tests are likely to be more valid for some groups than for others.

Genes and Individual Differences. Despite these important qualifications, it is clear that the kind of intelligence that produces high IQ scores is highly heritable. For children and adolescents, heritability estimates average around .50; that is, about half of the variance in IQ scores is explainable by genetic differences (Chipuer, Rovine, & Plomin, 1990; Devlin, Daniels, & Roeder, 1997; Plomin, 1989). For adults, the estimates are even higher—in the .60 to .80 range (Bouchard, 1995; McClearn et al., 1997; McGue et al., 1993).

In studies of twins, the scores of identical twins are always much more highly correlated than those of fraternal twins, a difference that reflects the influence of genes. In fact, the scores of identical twins reared *apart* are more highly correlated than those of fraternal twins reared *together* (see Figure 3.7). In adoption studies, the scores of adopted children are more highly correlated with those of their birth parents than with those of their biologically unrelated adoptive parents; the higher the birth parents' scores, the higher the child's score is likely to be. As adopted children grow into adolescence, the correlation between their IQ scores and those of their biologically unrelated family

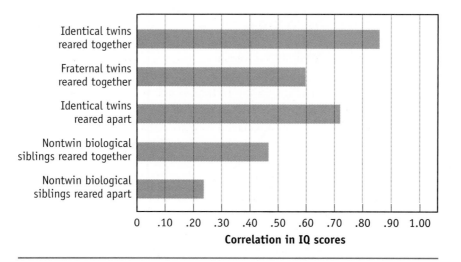

FIGURE 3.7 CORRELATIONS IN SIBLINGS' IQ SCORES *The IQ scores of identical twins are highly correlated, even when the twins are reared apart. The figures represented in this graph are based on average correlations across many studies (Bouchard & McGue, 1981).*

members diminishes. In adulthood, the correlation falls to *zero* (Bouchard, 1997b; Scarr, 1993; Scarr & Weinberg, 1994).

Recently, a research team led by psychologist Robert Plomin identified the first marker for a gene that might influence performance on IQ tests (Chorney et al., 1998). DNA analysis revealed that one form of the gene occurred twice as often in a group of children with very high IQ scores as in children with average scores. But the gene accounted for less than 2 percent of the variance among individuals, which translates to about 4 IQ points. No one knows yet how the gene might exert this small influence, or what other genes might be involved in IQ performance, and at this writing the basic finding still has to be replicated.

The Question of Group Differences. If genes influence individual differences in intelligence, do they also help account for differences between groups, as so many people assume? Unfortunately, the history of this issue has been marred by ethnic, class, and gender prejudice. As Stephen Jay Gould (1996) noted, genetic research has often been bent to support the belief that some groups are destined by "the harsh dictates of nature" to be subordinate to others.

Early in the twentieth century, for example, H. H. Goddard (1917), a leading educator, gave IQ tests to a group of immigrants at Ellis Island. Many of these immigrants knew little or no English and could neither read nor write their own language. Yet no sooner did they get off the boat after a long and tiring journey than they found themselves taking an IQ test. The results: 83 percent of the Jews, 80 percent of the Hungarians, 79 percent of the Italians, and 87 percent of the Russians scored as "feeble-minded," with a mental age lower than 12. (Note that Goddard singled out the Jews regardless of their nationality.) Goddard concluded that low intelligence and poor character were inherited and that "undesirables" should be prevented from having children.

The idea of innate group differences has continually resurfaced ever since. Most of the focus has been on black–white differences in IQ, because African-American children score, on average, some 10 to 15 points lower than do white children. (We are talking about *averages;* the distributions of scores for black children and white children overlap considerably.) A few psychologists have proposed a genetic explanation of this difference (Jensen, 1969, 1981; Rushton, 1988). In their much-discussed book *The Bell Curve: Intelligence and Class Structure in American Life* (1994), the late psychologist Richard Herrnstein and political scientist Charles Murray cited heritability studies to imply that the gap in IQ scores between the average white child and the average black child can never be closed.

You can see why heritability research provokes much more controversy than does research on, say, the sex lives of sea lions. Racists have used theories of genetic differences between groups to justify their own hatreds, and politicians have used them to argue for cuts in programs that would benefit blacks and other minorities. Herrnstein and Murray themselves concluded that there was little point in spending money on programs that were trying to raise the IQs of low-scoring children. In the 1970s, Patrick Buchanan, then an aide to President Richard Nixon, wrote a memo in which he cited an *Atlantic Monthly* article by Herrnstein to criticize compensatory education programs for blacks and poor people (reported in Levine & Suzuki, 1993).

(a) Rich soil   (b) Poor soil

FIGURE 3.8 THE TOMATO PLANT EXPERIMENT *In the hypothetical experiment described in the text, even if the differences among plants within each pot were due entirely to genetic differences, the average differences between pots could be environmental. The same general principle applies to individual and group differences among human beings.*

Genetic explanations however, have a fatal flaw: They use heritability estimates based mainly on white samples to estimate the role heredity plays in *group* differences, a procedure that is not valid. This problem sounds pretty technical, but it is not really too difficult to understand, so stay with us.

Consider, first, not people but tomatoes. (Figure 3.8 will help you visualize the following "thought experiment.") Suppose you have a bag of tomato seeds that vary genetically; all things being equal, some will produce tomatoes that are puny and tasteless, and some will produce tomatoes that are plump and delicious. Now you take a bunch of seeds in your left hand and a bunch from the same bag in your right hand. Although one seed differs genetically from another, there is no *average* difference between the seeds in your left hand and those in your right. You plant the left hand's seeds in pot A, with some soil that you have doctored with nitrogen and other nutrients, and you plant the right hand's seeds in pot B, with soil from which you have extracted nutrients. You sing to pot A and put it in the sun; you ignore pot B and leave it in a dark corner.

When the tomatoes grow, they will vary *within* each pot in terms of height, the number of tomatoes produced, and the size of the tomatoes, purely because of genetic differences. But there will also be an average difference between the plants in pot A and those in pot B. This difference *between* pots is due entirely to the different soils and the care that has been given to them—even though the heritability of the *within*-pot differences is 100 percent (Lewontin, 1970).

The principle is the same for people as it is for tomatoes. Although intellectual differences *within* groups are at least partly genetic in origin, this does not mean that differences *between* groups are genetic. Blacks and whites do not grow up, on the average, in the same "pots" (environments). Because of a long legacy of racial discrimination and de facto segregation, black children (as well as Latino and other minority children) often receive far fewer nutrients—literally, in terms of food, and figuratively, in terms of education, encouragement by society, and intellectual opportunities. Ethnic and cultural groups also differ in countless cultural ways that can affect their performance on IQ tests. And negative stereotypes about ethnic groups may cause members of these groups to doubt their own abilities, become anxious and self-conscious, and perform more poorly than they otherwise would on tests (see Chapter 10).

Doing good research on the origins of group differences in IQ is extremely difficult in the United States, where racism affects the lives of even affluent, successful African-Americans (Cose, 1994; Parker, 1997; Staples, 1994). However, the handful of studies that have overcome past methodological problems fail to reveal any genetic differences between blacks and whites in whatever it is that IQ tests measure. For example:

✦ Children who were fathered by black American soldiers and by white ones in Germany after World War II and who were reared in similar German communities by similar families did not differ significantly in IQ (Eyferth, 1961).

✦ Degree of African ancestry (which can be roughly estimated from skin color, blood analysis, and genealogy) is not related to measured intelligence, as a genetic theory of black–white differences would predict (Scarr et al., 1977).

✦ White and black infants do equally well on a test that measures their preference for novel stimuli, a predictor of later IQ scores (Fagan, 1992).

An intelligent reading of the research on intelligence, therefore, does not direct us to conclude that differences among cultural, ethnic, or national groups are permanent, genetically determined, or indicative of any group's innate superiority. On the contrary, the research suggests that we should make sure that all children grow up in the best possible soil, with room for the smartest and the slowest to find a place in the sun.

Genes and Personality

A mother we know was describing her two children: "My daughter has always been emotionally intense and a little testy," she said, "but my son is the opposite, placid and good-natured. They came out of the womb that way." Was this mother right? Is it possible to be born touchy or easygoing? What aspects of personality might have an inherited component?

Psychologists who take a biological perspective try to answer these questions in two ways: by studying temperaments in children and by doing heritability studies of twins. They hope that genes underlying temperaments and traits will one day be identified (Plomin et al., 1998).

Heredity and Temperament. Even in the first weeks after birth, infants differ in activity level, mood, responsiveness, soothability, and attention span (Belsky, Hsieh, & Crnic, 1996; Kagan, 1994). Some are irritable and cranky; others are calm and sweet-natured. Some will cuddle up in an adult's arms and snuggle; others squirm and fidget, as if they dislike being held. Some smile easily; others fuss and cry. These early differences appear even when you control for possible prenatal influences such as the mother's nutrition, drug use, or problems with the pregnancy. Most psychologists, therefore, believe that babies are born with genetically determined **temperaments,** physiological dispositions to respond to the environment in relatively stable, typical ways. Such temperaments may later form the basis of specific personality traits.

Jerome Kagan (1994, 1998a, 1998b) has been studying two temperamental styles, which he calls "reactive" and "nonreactive." About 20 percent of all children are at one extreme or the other; the rest fall somewhere in between. Highly reactive infants, even at 4 months of age, are excitable and nervous; they overreact to any little thing. If you put a colorful picture in front of them, they get aroused and upset. At 14 and 21 months, they tend to be wary and fearful of new things—toys that make a noise, odd-looking robots—even when their moms are right there with them. At 5 years, many of these children are still timid and uncomfortable in new situations. And at 7 years, many still have symptoms of anxiety. They are afraid of being kidnapped, they need to sleep with the light on, they are afraid of sleeping in an unfamiliar house—even if they have never been traumatized. In contrast, nonreactive infants, Kagan (1998a) says, are "California, laid-back babies." They lie there quietly; they never cry; they babble happily. A year later, they are outgoing and curious about new toys and events. They continue to be easygoing and extroverted throughout childhood.

Children with reactive and nonreactive temperaments have distinctive physiological patterns. During mildly stressful mental tasks, reactive children are more likely to show signs of activity in the sympathetic nervous system, the part of the nervous system that is generally responsible for physiological arousal (see Chapter 4). Their heart rate increases, the pupils of their eyes dilate, they show heightened brain activity, and they produce high levels of two stress hormones—norepinephrine and cortisol. Stephen Suomi (1987, 1991) has found exactly the same physiological symptoms in shy, anxious infant rhesus monkeys. Starting early in life, these "uptight" monkeys respond with anxiety to novelty and challenge, just as Kagan's overreactive children do. They, too, have high heart rates and elevated levels of stress hormones. When uptight rhesus monkeys grow up, they

---

temperaments Physiological dispositions to respond to the environment in certain ways; they are present in infancy and are assumed to be innate.

usually continue to be anxious when challenged, and, like Kagan's children, they act traumatized even though nothing bad has ever happened to them (Higley et al., 1991).

Heredity and Traits. Another way to study genetic influences on personality is to estimate the heritability of specific traits within groups of people. A **trait** is a habitual way of behaving, thinking, and feeling: shy, brave, reliable, friendly, hostile, confident, and so on. Each of us is a constantly shifting kaleidoscope of qualities, moods, tendencies, and preferences, and no one psychological test can possibly summarize a person's entire personality. But a variety of tests and assessment methods do provide information about such aspects of personality as needs, values, interests, and typical ways of responding to situations.

Several decades ago, Raymond B. Cattell greatly advanced the study of personality traits by applying a statistical method called **factor analysis.** Performing a factor analysis on traits is like adding water to flour: It causes the material to clump up into little balls. When applied to personality traits, this procedure identifies clusters of correlated test items that seem to be measuring some common, underlying quality. For example, the traits of assertiveness, willingness to tell jokes in large groups, and pleasure in meeting new people might share the common factor of extroversion. Using questionnaires, life descriptions, and observations, Cattell (1965, 1973) measured dozens of traits in thousands of people, including humor, intelligence, creativity, dominance, and emotional disorders. He concluded that 16 factors are necessary to describe the complexities of personality, although later in his career, he noted that only a few of them had been repeatedly confirmed.

Today, the evidence for a small cluster of fundamental personality traits is overwhelming, and most psychologists agree on the centrality of five "robust factors," known informally as the *Big Five* (Digman, 1996; Jang et al., 1998; McCrae & Costa, 1996; Wiggins, 1996). These factors are remarkably stable over a person's lifetime and have been identified all over the world, in places as diverse as China, the Netherlands, Japan, Spain, the Philippines, Hawaii, Germany, Portugal, Israel, Korea, Russia, and Australia (Benet-Martínez & John, 1998; Digman & Shmelyov, 1996; Katigbak, Church, & Akamine, 1996; McCrae & Costa, 1997; Yang & Bond, 1990):

1. *Introversion versus extroversion* describes the extent to which people are outgoing or shy. It includes such traits as being talkative or silent, sociable or reclusive, adventurous or cautious, eager to be in the limelight or inclined to stay in the shadows.

2. *Neuroticism,* or *negative emotionality,* includes such traits as anxiety, an inability to control impulses, and a tendency to feel negative emotions such as anger, guilt, scorn, and resentment. Neurotic individuals are worriers, complainers, and defeatists, even when they have no major problems. They are always ready to see the sour side of life and none of its sweetness.

---

trait A characteristic of an individual, describing a habitual way of behaving, thinking, and feeling.

factor analysis A statistical method for analyzing the intercorrelations among different measures or test scores; clusters of measures or scores that are highly correlated are assumed to measure the same underlying trait or ability (factor).

3. *Agreeableness* describes the extent to which people are good-natured or irritable, gentle or headstrong, cooperative or abrasive, secure or suspicious and jealous.

4. *Conscientiousness* describes the degree to which people are responsible or undependable, persevering or quick to give up, steadfast or fickle, tidy or careless.

5. *Openness to experience* describes the extent to which people are original, imaginative, questioning, artistic, and capable of creative thinking, or are conforming, unimaginative, and predictable.

Not everyone subscribes to the Big Five model; some researchers argue for as few as three central factors, others for as many as nine. But however they divide up the pie of personality, behavioral geneticists are finding that many traits are highly heritable. In adoption and twin studies, whether the trait in question is one of the Big Five, selflessness, aggression, or overall happiness and well-being, heritability is typically between .40 and .60 (Bouchard, 1997a; Loehlin, 1992; Lykken & Tellegen, 1996; Waller et al., 1990). This means that within a group of people, 40 to 60 percent of the variance in such traits is attributable to genetic differences. These findings have been replicated in many countries; for example, a study of Canadian and German twin samples found the same high heritability of the Big Five traits (Jang et al., 1998).

Some researchers have even reported high heritability for such specific behaviors as getting divorced (McGue & Lykken, 1992) and watching a lot of television in childhood (Plomin et al., 1990)! These findings are puzzling; how can divorce and TV watching be heritable? Our prehistoric ancestors didn't get married, let alone divorced, and they certainly didn't watch TV. What could be the personality traits or temperaments underlying these behaviors?

"THERE'S ANOTHER HEREDITARY DISEASE THAT RUNS IN THE ROYAL FAMILY. YOUR GRANDFATHER WAS A STUBBORN FOOL, YOUR FATHER WAS A STUBBORN FOOL, AND *YOU* ARE A STUBBORN FOOL."

Here is an even more startling finding: In numerous behavioral-genetic studies, the only environmental contribution to personality differences comes from having unique experiences *not shared* with other family members, such as being in Mrs. Miller's class in the fourth grade or winning the lead in the school play (Bouchard, 1997a; Hur, McGue, & Iacono, 1998; Loehlin, 1992). Shared environment—the family you grew up with and the experiences you shared with your siblings and parents—seems to have no significant effect on your personality. (We are speaking only of personality traits, though; of course, your family experiences affect your feelings toward your parents and siblings.)

Understandably, behavioral geneticists are excited about these findings, which have huge implications for the nature–nurture debate. "It will doubtless seem incredible to many readers that variables such as social class, educational opportunities, religious training, and parental love and discipline have no substantial influence on adult personality," wrote Robert McCrae and Paula Costa (1988), "but imagine for a moment that it is correct. What will it mean for research in developmental psychology? How will clinical psychology and theories of therapy be changed?" Good questions! What *do* these findings mean for education, for raising children, for psychotherapy and the treatment of personality problems? Does the environment count for nothing?

Behavioral-Genetic Research in Perspective

Findings on the heritability of intelligence and personality are impressive—so impressive that many people forget that if heredity accounts for about half of the reason people differ in their traits, then the environment (and errors in measurement) must account for the other half. As Robert Plomin (1989) observed, "The wave of acceptance of genetic influence on behavior is growing into a tidal wave that threatens to engulf the second message of this research: These same data provide the best available evidence for the importance of environmental influences."

Let's consider some other reasons not to jump to the conclusion that "genes are everything":

1 NOT ALL TRAITS ARE EQUALLY HERITABLE OR UNAFFECTED BY SHARED ENVIRONMENT. Religious orthodoxy, intellectual interests, feelings of inadequacy, adherence to traditional notions of masculinity and femininity, and many other traits are strongly affected by the environment a child shares with his or her family and larger culture (Beer, Arnold, & Loehlin, 1998).

2 SOME STUDIES MAY UNDERESTIMATE THE IMPACT OF THE ENVIRONMENT. Heritability gives us the *relative* impact of genetics and the environment on behavior. To estimate heritability, you need sensitive measures for gauging both the genetic similarity or dissimilarity of individuals *and* the similarities or differences in their environments. Measures of environmental influences on behavior are still fairly crude, often relying on vague, grab-bag categories such as "social class" or "religious training," and possibly failing to detect some important environmental influences. If the influence of the environment is underestimated, the influence of heredity will necessarily be overestimated.

3 EVEN TRAITS THAT ARE HIGHLY HERITABLE ARE NOT RIGIDLY FIXED AND CAN BE MODIFIED BY EXPERIENCE. For some traits, experiences at certain periods in life become particularly influential, and therefore heritability decreases. For example, studies of thousands of people in 10 countries find that young people, ages 16 to 21, are the most neurotic (emotionally negative) and the least agreeable and conscientious. By age 30, however, perhaps as a result of the new responsibilities of adulthood, they become more agreeable and conscientious and less negative and bitter (Costa et al., 1999).

Even individuals at the extremes of a particular temperament often change as they grow older, depending on their experiences. Kagan, who has been following reactive and nonreactive children for many years, puts it this way: What proportion of extremely reactive babies become vivacious, fearless, and extroverted? Zero. But what proportion remain extremely shy, subdued, and fearful as older children? Only about 15 percent. And what proportion become average, neither extremely shy nor extremely outgoing? All the rest. "The environment acts on fearful children to move them toward health, toward the center," Kagan (1998a) explains.

Intellectual performance, too, is modifiable by the environment (Gould, 1994; Lane, 1994; Steele, 1997). In the case of intelligence, remedial efforts have often been a matter of too little, too late; but early, intensive intervention that provides mental stimulation for children can raise mental performance (Guralnick, 1997; Ramey & Ramey, 1998). In one longitudinal study called the Abecedarian Project, inner-city children who got lots of mental enrichment at home and in child care or school, starting in infancy, had much better school performance throughout childhood than did children in a control group (Campbell & Ramey, 1995).

In developed countries, IQ scores have been climbing steadily for at least three generations (Flynn, 1987, 1999). Just as "obesity genes" cannot have changed enough to account for increases in obesity, "intelligence genes" cannot have changed enough to account for this rise in IQ scores. What might? Some of the answers that have been suggested include improvements in education, urbanization, an increasing emphasis on skills required by technology, and better nutrition (Neisser, 1998).

So . . . how confining is our biology? According to the biological perspective, the answer depends on which qualities we're talking about and how we define "confining." Many qualities are flexible and can change significantly. Others can change over time, but only within limits. And despite the claims of pop-psych books that promise you a total personality transformation in a month, some things about you probably can't be changed in 30 years, let alone 30 days.

What Do You Know?

We hope the trait of conscientiousness will motivate you to take this quiz.

1. On average, behavioral-genetic studies estimate the heritability of intelligence to be (a) about .90, (b) low at all ages, (c) about .50 for children and adolescents.

2. *True or false:* If a trait such as intelligence is highly heritable within a group, then average differences between groups must also be due mainly to heredity.

3. What two broad lines of research support the hypothesis that personality differences are due in part to genetic differences?

4. Which of the following traits are *not* among the five "robust factors" in personality? (a) introversion, (b) agreeableness, (c) psychoticism, (d) openness to experience, (e) intelligence, (f) neuroticism, (g) conscientiousness

5. A newspaper headline announces, "Couch Potatoes Born, Not Made: Kids' TV habits may be hereditary." Why is this headline misleading? What other explanations of the finding are possible? What aspects of TV watching *could* have a hereditary component?

Answers:

1. c 2. false (Can you explain why?) 3. the study of temperaments and behavioral-genetic studies of personality traits 4. c, e 5. The headline implies that there is a "TV-watching gene," but the writer is failing to consider other explanations. Perhaps some temperaments dispose people to be sedentary or passive, and this disposition can lead to a tendency to watch a lot of TV.

In Praise of Human Variation

This chapter opened with two questions: What makes us alike as human beings, and why do we differ? Today, a prevalent, but greatly oversimplified answer is that it's all in our genes. You either "have" a gene for smartness, musical ability, math genius, friendliness, or any other trait, or you don't. When researchers announced that they might have found a gene involved in mouse intelligence, *Time* magazine lost no time in putting the news on its cover, with the headline "The IQ Gene?" (September 13, 1999). In this climate, many people who believe in the importance of learning, opportunities, and experience feel that they must take an equally oversimplified position: Genes don't matter much at all.

As we have seen, however, heredity and environment always interact to produce the unique mixture of qualities that make up a human being. And once genetic and environmental influences become a part of us, they blend and become indistinguishable. We can no more speak of genes, or of the environment, "causing" personality or intelligence than we can speak of butter, sugar, or flour individually causing the taste of a cake (Lewontin, Rose, & Kamin, 1984). Many people do speak that way, however, out of a desire to make things clearer than they actually are, and sometimes to justify prejudices about culture, ethnicity, gender, or class.

An unstated assumption in many debates about nature and nurture is that the world would be a better place if certain kinds of genes prevailed. This assumption overlooks the fact that nature loves genetic diversity, not similarity. The ability of any species to survive depends on such diversity. If every penguin, porpoise, or person had exactly the same genetic strengths and weaknesses, the species could not survive changes in the environment—a new virus, or a change in weather, would wipe out the entire group. With diversity, at least some penguins, porpoises, or people have a good chance of making it.

When we view the world through an evolutionary lens, we realize that psychological diversity is adaptive, too. Each of us has something valuable to contribute, whether it is artistic talent, academic ability, creativity, social skill, athletic prowess, a sense of humor, mechanical aptitude, practical wisdom, a social conscience, or the energy to get things done. In our complicated, fast-moving world, all of these qualities are needed. The challenge, for any society, is to promote the potential of each of its members. ◪

Summary

1. From the perspective of *evolutionary psychologists* and *behavioral geneticists,* a key to understanding the qualities that unite human beings as a species and the qualities that differentiate us as individuals can be found in our genes. However, scientists understand that heredity and environment interact to produce our psychological and physical traits, as the set-point theory of body weight illustrates.

2. *Genes,* the basic units of heredity, are located on *chromosomes,* which consist of strands of *DNA.* Collectively, the thousands of human genes make up the human *genome.* Within each gene, a sequence of four basic elements of DNA constitutes a chemical code that helps determine the synthesis of a particular protein. In turn, proteins affect virtually all the structural and biochemical characteristics of the organism.

3. Most human traits depend on more than one gene pair, which makes tracking down the genetic contributions to a trait extremely difficult. One method for doing so involves the use of *linkage studies,* in which *genetic markers* are used as landmarks to locate genes that might be responsible for some trait or behavior.

4. *Evolution* depends in part on genetic *mutations* and the cross-over of genetic material from one member of a chromosome pair to the other—processes that introduce new genetic variations into a population. Evolutionary psychologists believe that the mind evolved as a collection of specialized mental modules to handle specific survival problems. They argue that many fundamental human commonalities can be explained by the evolutionary principle of *natural selection,* first formulated by Charles Darwin. These commonalities include, for example, inborn *reflexes,* an attraction to novelty, a motive to explore and manipulate objects, an impulse to play (as in *practice play*), and certain basic mental abilities, such as a rudimentary understanding of number and of the physical properties of objects.

5. Studies of animals and human infants indicate that many perceptual skills are inborn or acquired shortly after birth. By using the *visual cliff,* for example, psychologists have learned that babies have depth perception by the age of 6 months, and probably even earlier. However, in the absence of certain experiences early in life, *feature-detector cells* in the nervous system deteriorate or change, and perception is impaired.

6. The facial expressions for anger, happiness, fear, surprise, disgust, sadness, and contempt are widely found across cultures, are apparent in infancy, and are probably part of our evolutionary heritage. From birth onward, such expressions help people communicate with one another and "read" the intentions of others. However, according to the *neurocultural theory of emotion,* culture interacts with physiology to influence our emotional expressions.

7. Sociability and attachment are also necessary for human survival. Infants are naturally attracted to human faces, and soon after birth they develop *synchrony* of rhythm and pace with their caregivers. Attachment probably begins with the innate need for *contact comfort.* Infant attachment provides a *secure base* from which the child can explore the environment. The development of secure attachment is relatively unaffected by the normal range of child-rearing practices, including how much time babies spend in daycare. Factors contributing to insecure attachment include extreme

neglectfulness or rejection by parents, the child's own temperament, and stressful experiences in the family.

8. Only human beings use *language* naturally, to express and comprehend an infinite number of novel utterances. Noam Chomsky argued that the ability to take the *surface structure* of an utterance and apply rules of *syntax* to infer its underlying *deep structure* must depend on an innate faculty for language, a *language acquisition device.* Linguists and *psycholinguists* have gathered many findings in support of this view: Children from different cultures go through many similar stages of language acquisition, suggesting that they are born with a *universal grammar;* children's language is full of *overregularizations;* adults do not consistently correct children's syntax; even profoundly retarded children usually acquire language; and young infants can derive linguistic rules from strings of sounds.

9. Evolutionary psychologists believe that the human capacity for language evolved because it enhanced survival. However, some scientists have devised models of language acquisition that do not assume an innate capacity. Moreover, it seems clear that parental practices, such as repeating correct sentences verbatim, aid in language acquisition. Case studies of children deprived of exposure to language illustrate the role of both biological readiness for language and critical experiences in early childhood.

10. *Sociobiologists* and evolutionary psychologists argue that males and females have evolved different sexual and courtship strategies. In this view, it has been adaptive for males to be promiscuous, to be attracted to young partners, and to want sexual novelty, and for females to be monogamous, to be choosy about partners, and to prefer security to novelty. Cross-cultural studies support some evolutionary predictions, but critics argue that evolutionary theories are often nonfalsifiable, and that human sexual behavior is far too varied and changeable to be explained in evolutionary terms.

11. Behavioral geneticists study differences among individuals, often by using studies of *identical (monozygotic)* and *fraternal (dizygotic) twins* and adopted children to estimate the *heritability* of traits and abilities—the extent to which differences in a trait or ability within a group of individuals are accounted for by genetic differences. Heritability estimates apply only to differences within a particular group living in a particular environment, and even highly heritable traits can often be modified by the environment.

12. Heritability estimates for intelligence (as measured by *IQ* tests, which have come under fire by critics) average about .50 for children and adolescents and .60 to .80 for adults. Identical twins are more similar in IQ-test performance than are fraternal twins, and adopted children's scores correlate more highly with those of their biological parents than with those of their nonbiological relatives.

13. It is not valid to draw conclusions about between-group differences in IQ from heritability estimates based on differences *within* a group. The available evidence fails to support genetic explanations of ethnic differences in IQ-test performance.

14. Individual differences in *temperaments,* or ways of reacting to the environment, emerge early in life and can influence subsequent personality development. Temperamental differences in extremely reactive and nonreactive children (and

monkeys) are associated with variations in the responsiveness of the sympathetic nervous system to change and novelty.

15. *Factor analysis* has established strong evidence for the *Big Five* dimensions (*traits*) of personality: extroversion/introversion, neuroticism, agreeableness, conscientiousness, and openness to experience. For these and many other traits, heritability is typically around .50. In many studies, the only environmental contribution to personality differences comes from nonshared experiences.

16. Genes are not everything. If heredity accounts for only part of the variation among people in their traits, then the environment (and errors of measurement) must account for the rest. Further, not all traits are equally heritable or unaffected by shared environment; some studies may underestimate the effects of the environment because of methodological problems; and even some highly heritable traits can be modified by experience. Neither nature alone nor nurture alone can explain people's similarities or differences. Genetic and environmental influences blend and become indistinguishable in the development of any individual.

Key Terms

CHAPTER FOUR

Neurons, Hormones, and the Brain

*E*mily D., a former English teacher and poet, had a tumor in a part of the brain that processes the expressive qualities of speech, such as rhythm and intonation. Although she could understand words and sentences perfectly well, she could not tell whether a speaker was indignant, cheerful, or dejected unless she carefully analyzed the person's facial expressions and gestures. Emily D.'s brain damage had left her entirely deaf to the emotional nuances of speech, the variations of tone and cadence that can move a listener to laughter, tears, or outrage. But she had one skill that many people lack. Because she could not be swayed by verbal theatrics or tone of voice, she could easily spot a liar.

Dr. P., a cultured and charming musician of great repute, suffered damage in a part of the brain that handles visualization. Although his vision remained sharp and his reasoning abilities keen, he could no longer recognize people or objects, or even dream in visual images. He would pat the heads of water hydrants and parking meters, thinking they were children, or chat with pieces of furniture, wondering why they did not reply. He could spot a pin on the floor but did not know his own face in the mirror. Once, when looking around for his hat, he thought his wife's head was the hat and tried to lift it off. Neurologist Oliver Sacks (1985), who studied Dr. P., came to call him "the man who mistook his wife for a hat."

These two fascinating cases, reported by Sacks, show us that the brain is the bedrock of behavior. Neuropsychologists, along with neuroscientists from other disciplines, excavate the bedrock by analyzing the brain and the rest of the nervous system. Their goal is to discover the biological events underlying consciousness, perception, memory, emotion, reasoning, stress, and cognitive clarity or confusion.

At this very moment, your own brain, assisted by other parts of your nervous system, is busily taking in these words. Whether you are excited, curious, or bored, your brain is registering some sort of emotional reaction. As you continue reading, your brain will (we hope) store away much of the information in this chapter. Later your brain may enable you to smell a flower, climb the stairs, greet a friend, solve a personal problem, or chuckle at a joke. But the brain's most startling accomplishment is its knowledge that it is doing all these things. This self-awareness makes brain research different from the study of anything else in the universe. Scientists must use the cells, biochemistry, and circuitry of their own brains to understand the cells, biochemistry, and circuitry of brains in general.

Because the brain is the site of consciousness, people disagree about what language to use in describing it. If we say that "your brain" stores events or registers emotions, we imply a separate "you" that is "using" that brain. But if we leave "you" out of the picture and just say that the brain does these things, we risk implying that brain mechanisms alone explain behavior (which is untrue), and we lose sight of the person. No one has ever resolved this dilemma to everyone's satisfaction.

William Shakespeare called the brain "the soul's frail dwelling house." Actually, this miraculous organ is more like the main room in a house filled with many alcoves and passageways—the "house" being the nervous system as a whole. Before we can understand the windows, walls, and furniture of this house, we need to become acquainted with the overall floor plan. It's a pretty technical plan, which means that you will be learning many new terms, but you will need to know these terms in order to understand how biological psychologists go about explaining psychological topics. Later, we will illustrate their approach by showing how biological research in psychology is illuminating the enigma of memory and the mysteries of sleep.

THE NERVOUS SYSTEM: A BASIC BLUEPRINT

The function of a nervous system is to gather and process information, produce responses to stimuli, and coordinate the workings of different cells. Even the lowly jellyfish and the humble worm have the beginnings of such a system. In very simple organisms that do little more than move, eat, and eliminate wastes, the "system" may be no more than one or two nerve cells. In human beings, who do such complex things as dance, cook, and take psychology courses, the nervous system contains billions of cells. Scientists divide this intricate network into two main parts; the central nervous system and the peripheral (outlying) nervous system (see Figure 4.1).

The **central nervous system (CNS)** receives, processes, interprets, and stores incoming sensory information about tastes, sounds, smells, color, pressure on the skin, the state of internal organs, and so forth. It also sends out messages destined for muscles, glands, and internal organs. The CNS is usually conceptualized as having two components: the brain, which we will consider in detail later, and the **spinal cord.** The spinal cord is actually an extension of the brain. It runs from the base of

---

central nervous system (CNS) The portion of the nervous system consisting of the brain and spinal cord.

spinal cord A collection of neurons and supportive tissue running from the base of the brain down the center of the back, protected by a column of bones (the spinal column).

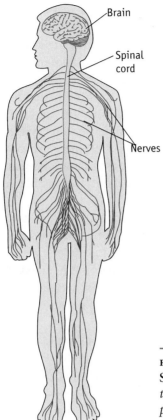

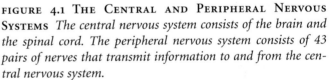

FIGURE 4.1 THE CENTRAL AND PERIPHERAL NERVOUS SYSTEMS *The central nervous system consists of the brain and the spinal cord. The peripheral nervous system consists of 43 pairs of nerves that transmit information to and from the central nervous system.*

the brain down the center of the back, protected by a column of bones (the spinal column), and it acts as a bridge between the brain and the parts of the body below the neck. It also handles some reflexes, such as the one that causes you automatically to pull your hand away from a hot iron.

The **peripheral nervous system (PNS)** handles the central nervous system's input and output. It contains all portions of the nervous system outside the brain and spinal cord, right down to nerves in the tips of the fingers and toes. A brain that could not collect information about the world by means of a peripheral nervous system would be like a radio without a receiver. In the peripheral nervous system, *sensory nerves* carry messages from special receptors in the skin, muscles, and other internal and external sense organs to the spinal cord, which sends them along to the brain. These nerves put us in touch with both the outside world and the activities of our own bodies. *Motor nerves* carry orders from the central nervous system to muscles, glands, and internal organs. They enable us

---

peripheral nervous system (PNS) All portions of the nervous system outside the brain and spinal cord; it includes sensory and motor nerves.

to move our bodies, and they cause glands to contract and to secrete substances, including chemical messengers called *hormones.*

Scientists further divide the peripheral nervous system into two parts: the somatic (bodily) nervous system and the autonomic (self-governing) nervous system. The **somatic nervous system,** sometimes called the *skeletal nervous system,* consists of nerves that are connected to sensory receptors and to the skeletal muscles that permit voluntary action. When you sense the world around you, or when you turn off a light or write your name, your somatic system is active. The **autonomic nervous system** regulates the functioning of blood vessels, glands, and internal (visceral) organs such as the bladder, stomach, and heart. When you see someone you have a crush on, and your heart starts to pound, your hands get sweaty, and your cheeks feel hot, you can blame your autonomic nervous system.

The autonomic nervous system works more or less automatically, without a person's conscious control. However, some people can learn to heighten or suppress their autonomic responses intentionally. In India, some yogis can slow their heartbeats and metabolisms so dramatically that they can survive in a sealed booth long after most of us would have died of suffocation. During the 1960s and 1970s, Neal Miller and his colleagues showed that many other people can also learn to control their visceral responses, by taking advantage of a technique called **biofeedback** (Miller, 1978).

In biofeedback, monitoring devices track the bodily process in question and produce a signal, such as a light or a tone, whenever a person makes the desired response. The person may either use a prearranged method to produce the desired response or simply try to increase the signal's frequency in any way that he or she chooses. Using biofeedback, some people have learned to control such autonomic responses as blood pressure, blood flow, heart rate, and skin temperature. Some clinicians are therefore using biofeedback training to treat high blood pressure, asthma, and migraine headaches, although there is controversy about success rates and about what, exactly, is being controlled—the actual autonomic responses, or responses that can be voluntarily produced, such as breathing, which then in turn affect the autonomic system.

The autonomic nervous system is itself divided into two parts: the **sympathetic nervous system** and the **parasympathetic nervous system.** These two parts work together, but in opposing ways, to adjust the body to changing circumstances. The sympathetic system acts like the accelerator of a car, mobilizing the body for action

---

somatic nervous system The subdivision of the peripheral nervous system that connects to sensory receptors and to skeletal muscles; sometimes called the *skeletal nervous system.*

autonomic nervous system The subdivision of the peripheral nervous system that regulates the internal organs and glands.

biofeedback A method for learning to control bodily functions, including ones usually thought to be involuntary, by attending to feedback from an instrument that monitors the function and that signals changes in it.

sympathetic nervous system The subdivision of the autonomic nervous system that mobilizes bodily resources and increases the output of energy during emotion and stress.

parasympathetic nervous system The subdivision of the autonomic nervous system that operates during relaxed states and that conserves energy.

and an output of energy. It makes you blush, sweat, and breathe more deeply, and it pushes up your heart rate and blood pressure. When you are in a situation that requires you to fight, flee, or cope with stress, the sympathetic nervous system whirls into action. The parasympathetic system is more like a brake: It does not stop the body, but it does tend to slow things down or keep them running smoothly. It enables the body to conserve and store energy. If you have to jump out of the way of a speeding motorcyclist, sympathetic nerves increase your heart rate. Afterward, parasympathetic nerves slow it down again and keep its rhythm regular.

What Do You Know?

Pause now to test your memory by mentally filling in the missing parts of the nervous system "house." Then see whether you can briefly describe what each part of the system does.

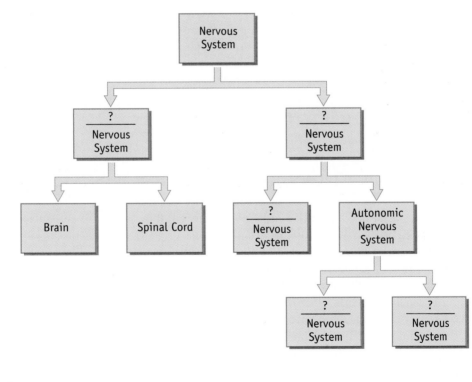

ANSWERS:

Check your answers against Figure 4.2 on the next page. If you had difficulty, or if you could label the parts but forgot what they do, review the preceding section and try again.

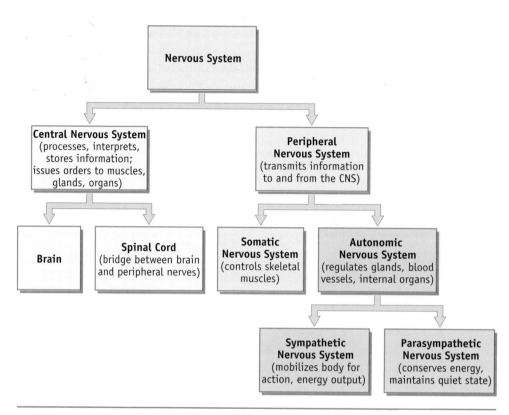

FIGURE 4.2 How the Nervous System Is Organized *Use this diagram to check your answers to the "What Do You Know?" quiz on page 121.*

COMMUNICATION IN THE NERVOUS SYSTEM

The blueprint we have just described provides only a general idea of the nervous system's structure. Now we turn to the details.

The nervous system is made up in part of **neurons,** or *nerve cells.* These neurons are held in place by **glial cells** (from the Greek for "glue"). Glial cells, which greatly outnumber neurons, also provide the neurons with nutrients, insulate the neurons, and remove cellular debris when the neurons die. Many neuroscientists suspect that glial cells carry electrical or chemical signals between parts of the nervous system, and that these signals somehow influence the activity of neighboring neurons. It is the neurons, however, that are the communication specialists, transmitting signals to, from, or within the central nervous system.

---

neuron A cell that conducts electrochemical signals; the basic unit of the nervous system; also called a *nerve cell.*

glial cells Nervous system cells that aid the neurons by providing them with nutrients, insulating them, and removing cellular debris when they die.

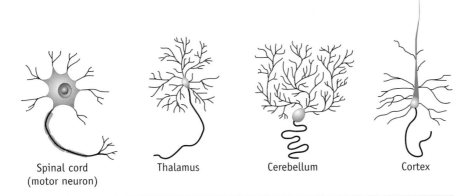

Spinal cord
(motor neuron)   Thalamus   Cerebellum   Cortex

FIGURE 4.3 DIFFERENT KINDS OF NEURONS *Neurons vary in size and shape, depending on their location and function. More than 200 types of neurons have been identified in mammals.*

Although neurons are often called the building blocks of the nervous system, in structure they are more like snowflakes than blocks, exquisitely delicate and differing from one another greatly in size and shape (see Figure 4.3). In the giraffe, a neuron that runs from the spinal cord down the animal's hind leg may be 9 feet long! In the human brain, neurons are microscopic. No one is sure how many neurons the human brain contains, but a typical estimate is 100 billion, about the same number as there are stars in our galaxy—and some estimates go much higher.

The Structure of the Neuron

As you can see in Figure 4.4 on the next page, a neuron has three main parts: *dendrites,* a *cell body,* and an *axon.* The **dendrites** look like the branches of a tree; indeed, the word *dendrite* means "little tree" in Greek. Dendrites act like antennas, receiving messages from as many as 10,000 other nerve cells and transmitting these messages toward the cell body. The **cell body,** which is shaped roughly like a sphere or a pyramid, contains the biochemical machinery for keeping the neuron alive. It also determines whether the neuron should "fire"—that is, transmit a message to other neurons—based on the number of inputs it has received. The **axon** (from the Greek for "axle") transmits messages away from the cell body to other neurons or to muscle or gland cells. Axon ends commonly divide into branches, called *axon terminals.* In adult human beings, axons vary from only 4 thousandths of an inch to a few feet in length. Dendrites and axons give each neuron a double role: As one researcher put it, a neuron is first a catcher, then a batter (Gazzaniga, 1988).

---

dendrites A neuron's branches that receive information from other neurons and transmit it toward the cell body.
cell body The part of the neuron that keeps it alive and determines whether it will fire.
axon A neuron's extending fiber that conducts impulses away from the cell body and transmits them to other neurons.

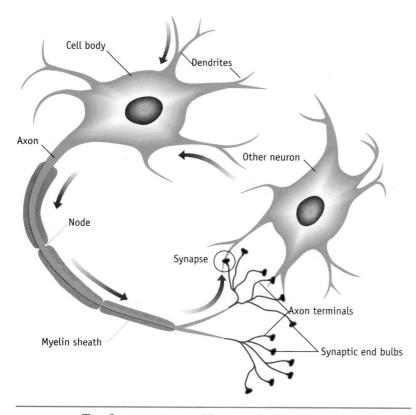

FIGURE 4.4 THE STRUCTURE OF A NEURON *Incoming neural impulses are received by the dendrites of a neuron and are transmitted to the cell body. Outgoing signals pass along the axon to the terminal branches.*

Many axons, especially the larger ones, are insulated by a surrounding layer of fatty material called the **myelin sheath,** which is derived from glial cells. This covering is divided into segments that make it look a little like a string of link sausages (see Figure 4.4 again). One purpose of the myelin sheath is to prevent signals in adjacent cells from interfering with each other. Another, as we will see, is to speed up the conduction of neural impulses. In individuals with multiple sclerosis, loss of myelin causes erratic nerve signals, leading to loss of sensation, weakness or paralysis, lack of coordination, or vision problems.

In the peripheral nervous system, the fibers of individual neurons (axons and sometimes dendrites) are collected together in bundles called **nerves,** rather like the lines in a telephone cable. The human body has 43 pairs of peripheral nerves; one nerve from each pair is on the left side of the body, and the other is on the right. Most of these nerves enter or leave the spinal cord, but the 12 pairs that are in the head—the *cranial nerves*—connect directly to the brain.

---

myelin sheath A fatty insulation that may surround the axon of a neuron.

nerve A bundle of nerve fibers (axons and sometimes dendrites) in the peripheral nervous system.

Until recently, neuroscientists thought that neurons in the central nervous system could not reproduce (multiply) or regenerate (grow back) after being injured. The assumption was that no new CNS neurons arose after infancy, and that if cells in the brain or spinal cord were damaged, nothing could be done. But then the conventional wisdom got thrown out the window. Animal studies showed that severed axons in the spinal cord *can* regrow if you treat them with certain nervous system chemicals (Schnell & Schwab, 1990). And Canadian neuroscientists working with mice discovered that immature cells, called *precursor cells,* will give birth to new neurons (a process called *neurogenesis*) when immersed in a growth-promoting protein in the laboratory. The new neurons will then continue to divide and multiply (Reynolds & Weiss, 1992). One of the researchers, Samuel Weiss, said that this result was hard to believe at first: "It challenged everything I had read; everything I had learned when I was a student" (quoted in Barinaga, 1992).

Since then, scientists have learned that the human brain also contains precursor cells (sometimes called *progenitor* or *stem cells*), and that these cells, too, give rise to new neurons when treated in the laboratory (Kirschenbaum et al., 1994). Even more astonishing, in rodents and monkeys, precursor cells in an area associated with learning and memory continue to divide and mature throughout adulthood (Gage et al., 1998; Gould et al., 1998). Researchers who studied the brains of five elderly people who had died of cancer found evidence of the very same process in human beings (Eriksson et al., 1998). Animal studies indicate that we have some control over that process, because physical and mental exercise promote the production and survival of these new cells (Gould et al., 1999; Kempermann, Brandon, & Gage, 1998; van Praag, Kempermann, & Gage, 1999). One of the researchers, psychologist Elizabeth Gould, commented, "It is a classic case of 'use it or lose it'" (quoted in *The Los Angeles Times,* February 23, 1999). Misusing it can also lose it: Stress can inhibit the production of new cells (Gould et al., 1998), and nicotine can kill precursor cells (Berger, Gage, & Vijayaraghavan, 1998).

Each year brings ever more findings that only a short time ago would have seemed like science fiction. Animal research is raising hopes that regenerated axons will someday enable people with spinal cord injuries to use their limbs again. Researchers also hope that transplanted precursor cells from embryos or adults will someday help people recover from brain damage. In 1998, the first attempt to use such cells in a human being took place: Specially prepared precursor cells extracted from a young man's tumor were implanted into the brain of a woman whose right side had been paralyzed by a stroke (Fackelmann, 1998). Since then, several similar surgeries have been performed. The results are still uncertain, but daring experiments like this one will continue. Eventually, treatments inspired by basic research on neurons may be among the most stunning contributions of biological research.

How Neurons Communicate

Neurons do not directly touch each other, end to end. Instead, they are separated by a minuscule space called the *synaptic cleft,* where the axon terminal of one neuron nearly touches a dendrite or the cell body of another. The entire site—the axon terminal, the cleft, and the covering membrane of the receiving dendrite or cell body—is called a

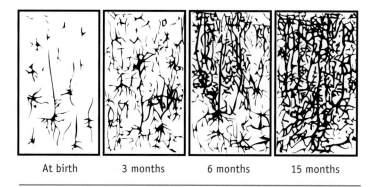

| At birth | 3 months | 6 months | 15 months |

FIGURE 4.5 GETTING CONNECTED *Neurons in a newborn's brain are widely spaced but immediately begin to form connections. These drawings show the marked increase in the number of connections from birth to age 15 months.*

synapse. Because a neuron's axon may have hundreds or even thousands of terminals, a single neuron may have synaptic connections with a great many others. As a result, the number of communication links in the nervous system runs into the trillions or perhaps even the quadrillions.

When we are born, most of these synapses have not yet formed, but during the first 15 months after birth, there is an explosion of new connections (see Figure 4.5). Throughout life, axons and dendrites continue to grow, and tiny bumplike projections on dendrites (called *spines*) increase in both size and number, resulting in new, more complex synaptic connections in the brain. Just as new learning and stimulating environments promote the production of new neurons, they also produce the greatest increases in synaptic complexity (Diamond, 1993; Greenough & Anderson, 1991; Greenough & Black, 1992; Rosenzweig, 1984). Throughout life, too, some unused synaptic connections are lost as cells or their branches die and are not replaced. Thus, the brain's circuits are continually changing in response to information, challenges, and changes in the environment.

Scientists refer to the brain's remarkable flexibility as *plasticity*. Plasticity may help explain why people with brain damage sometimes experience amazing recoveries—why individuals who cannot recall simple words after a stroke may be speaking normally within a matter of months, and why patients who cannot move an arm after a head injury may regain full use of it after physical therapy. Their brains have rewired themselves to adapt to the damage! Recent research, with 13 stroke patients who each had a paralyzed arm, suggests that the brain can actually be coaxed to perform such rewiring (Liepert et al., 2000). Scientists immobilized the patients' good arms so that the patients were forced to try to use their paralyzed limbs during intensive therapy sessions. After only a few weeks, the patients regained nearly full use of their limbs—despite the fact that some had had their strokes many years before. What's more, an

---

synapse The site where a nerve impulse is transmitted from one nerve cell to another; it includes the axon terminal, the synaptic cleft, and receptor sites in the membrane of the receiving cell.

area responsible for arm movements on the injured side of the brain had nearly doubled! Further studies of this promising therapy are currently under way.

Neurons speak to one another, or in some cases to muscles or glands, in an electrical and chemical language. When a nerve cell is stimulated, a change in electrical potential occurs between the inside and the outside of the cell. The physics of this process involves the sudden, momentary inflow of positively charged sodium ions across the cell's membrane, followed by the outflow of positively charged potassium ions. The result is a brief change in electrical voltage—an *action potential*—which produces an electric current or impulse.

If an axon is unmyelinated, the action potential at each point in the axon gives rise to a new action potential at the next point; thus, the action potential travels down the axon, somewhat as fire travels along the fuse of a firecracker. But in myelinated axons, the process is a little different. Conduction of a neural impulse beneath the sheath is impossible, in part because sodium and potassium ions cannot cross the cell's membrane except at the breaks (nodes) between the myelin's "sausages." Instead, the action potential "hops" from one node to the next. (More specifically, positively charged ions flow down the axon at a very fast rate, causing regeneration of the action potential at each node.) This arrangement allows the impulse to travel faster than it could if the action potential had to be regenerated at every point along the axon. Nerve impulses travel more slowly in babies than in older children and adults because when babies are born, the myelin sheaths on their axons are not yet fully developed.

When a neural impulse reaches the axon terminal's buttonlike tip, it must get its message across the synaptic cleft to another cell. At this point, *synaptic vesicles,* tiny sacs in the tip of the axon terminal, open and release a few thousand molecules of a chemical substance called a **neurotransmitter.** Like sailors carrying a message from one island to another, these molecules then diffuse across the synaptic cleft (see Figure 4.6).

When they reach the other side, the neurotransmitter molecules bind briefly with *receptor sites,* special molecules in the membrane of the receiving neuron, fitting these sites much as a key fits a lock. Changes occur in the receiving neuron's membrane, and the ultimate effect is either *excitatory* (a voltage shift in a positive direction) or *inhibitory* (a voltage shift in a negative direction), depending on which receptor sites have been activated. If the effect is excitatory, the probability that the receiving neuron will fire increases; if it is inhibitory, the probability decreases. Inhibition in the nervous system is extremely important. Without it, we could not sleep or coordinate our movements, and excitation of the nervous system would be overwhelming, producing convulsions.

What any given neuron does at any given moment depends on the net effect of all the messages being received from other neurons. Only when the cell's voltage reaches a certain threshold will it fire. Thousands of messages, both excitatory and inhibitory, may be coming into the cell. Essentially, the neuron must average them. But how it does this, and how it "decides" whether to fire, is still not well understand. The message that reaches a final destination depends on the rate at which individual neurons are firing,

---

neurotransmitter A chemical substance that is released by a transmitting neuron at the synapse and that alters the activity of a receiving neuron.

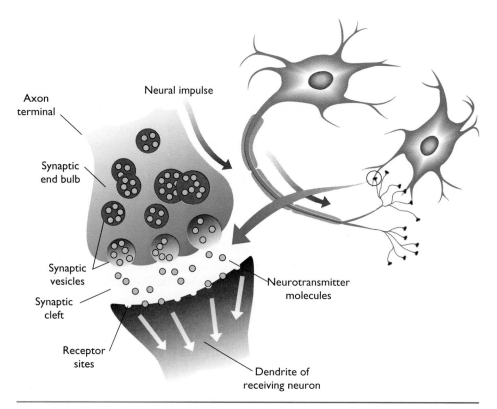

FIGURE 4.6 NEUROTRANSMITTER CROSSING A SYNAPSE *Neurotransmitter molecules are released into the synaptic cleft between two neurons from vesicles (chambers) in the transmitting neuron's axon terminal. The molecules then bind to receptor sites on the receiving neurons. As a result, the electrical state of the receiving neuron changes, and the neuron becomes either more likely to fire an impulse or less so, depending on the type of neurotransmitter.*

how many are firing, what types of neurons are firing, and where the neurons are located. It does *not* depend on how strongly the neurons are firing, however, because a neuron always either fires or it doesn't. Like the turning on of a light switch, the firing of a neuron is an *all-or-none* event.

Chemical Messengers in the Nervous System

The nervous system "house" would remain forever dark and lifeless without chemical couriers such as the neurotransmitters. Let's look more closely now at these substances and at two other types of chemical messengers: endorphins and hormones.

Neurotransmitters: Versatile Couriers. As we have seen, neurotransmitters make it possible for one neuron to excite or inhibit another. Neurotransmitters exist not only in the brain, but also in the spinal cord, the peripheral nerves, and certain glands. Through their effects on specific nerve circuits, these substances can affect mood, memory, and well-being in different ways, with the nature of the effect depending on the level of the neurotransmitter and its location. Hundreds of substances are known or suspected to be neurotransmitters, and the number keeps growing. Here are a few of the better-understood ones and some of their known or suspected effects:

✦ *Serotonin* affects neurons involved in sleep, appetite, sensory perception, temperature regulation, pain suppression, and mood.

✦ *Dopamine* affects neurons involved in voluntary movement, learning, memory, and emotion.

✦ *Acetylcholine* affects neurons involved in muscle action, cognitive functioning, memory, and emotion.

✦ *Norepinephrine* affects neurons involved in increased heart rate and the slowing of intestinal activity during stress, and neurons involved in learning, memory, dreaming, waking from sleep, and emotion.

✦ *GABA* (gamma-aminobutyric acid) functions as the major inhibitory neurotransmitter in the brain.

✦ *Glutamate* functions as an important excitatory neurotransmitter in the brain and plays a critical role in long-term memory.

Harmful effects can occur when neurotransmitter levels are too high or too low. Low levels of serotonin and norepinephrine have been associated with severe depression. Abnormal GABA levels have been implicated in sleep and eating disorders and in convulsive disorders, including epilepsy (Bekenstein & Lothman, 1993). People with *Alzheimer's disease*—a devastating condition that leads to memory loss, personality changes, and eventual disintegration of all physical and mental abilities—lose brain cells responsible for producing acetylcholine, and this deficit may help account for their memory problems.

The degeneration of brain cells that produce and use another neurotransmitter, dopamine, appears to cause the symptoms of *Parkinson's disease,* a condition characterized by tremors, muscular spasms, and increasing muscular rigidity. Patients with advanced Parkinson's may "freeze" for minutes or even hours. Injections of dopamine do not help, because dopamine molecules cannot cross the *blood–brain barrier,* a system of densely packed capillary and glial cells whose function is to prevent potentially harmful substances from entering the brain. Symptoms can be lessened by the administration of levodopa (L-dopa), which is a building block of dopamine, but patients must take larger and larger doses to achieve the desired result. After a while, adverse effects from the medication—including depression, confusion, and even episodes of psychosis—may be worse than the disease itself.

During the 1990s, surgeons pioneered a dramatic new approach to treating Parkinson's disease and potentially other diseases. They grafted dopamine-producing brain tissue from aborted fetuses into the brains of Parkinson's patients and patients who developed Parkinson's-like symptoms after using a botched synthetic mood-altering drug that killed their dopamine-producing cells (Freed et al., 1993; Lindvall et al., 1994; Uchida & Toya, 1996; Widner et al., 1993). Not all patients improved, but some who were virtually helpless before the operation can now move freely and even dress and feed themselves. Although the long-term risks and benefits of brain-tissue transplants are not yet certain, and although the technique is not currently feasible on a large scale, this work has generated a lot of excitement.

We want to warn you, however, that pinning down the relationship between neurotransmitter abnormalities and behavioral abnormalities is extremely difficult. Each neurotransmitter plays multiple roles, and the functions of different substances often overlap. Further, it is always possible that something about a disorder leads to abnormal neurotransmitter levels, instead of the other way around. Although drugs that boost or decrease levels of particular neurotransmitters are sometimes effective in treating disorders, that does not necessarily mean that abnormal neurotransmitter levels are *causing* the disorders. After all, aspirin can relieve a headache, but headaches are not caused by a lack of aspirin!

Many of us regularly do things that affect our own neurotransmitters, usually without knowing it. For example, most recreational drugs produce their effects by blocking or enhancing the actions of neurotransmitters. So do some herbal remedies. For example, St. John's wort, which many people take for depression, prevents the cells that release serotonin from reabsorbing excess molecules that have remained in the synaptic gap. As a result, serotonin levels rise. Many people do not realize that such remedies, because they affect the nervous system's biochemistry, can interact with other medications and can be harmful in high doses. Even ordinary foods can influence the availability of neurotransmitters in the brain, as we discuss in Essay 1, following this chapter.

Endorphins: The Brain's Natural Opiates. Another intriguing group of chemical messengers is known collectively as *endogenous opioid peptides,* or more popularly as **endorphins.** Endorphins have effects similar to those of natural opiates; that is, they reduce pain and promote pleasure. They are also thought to play a role in appetite, sexual activity, blood pressure, mood, learning, and memory. Some endorphins function as neurotransmitters, but most act primarily as *neuromodulators,* which alter the effects of neurotransmitters—for example, by limiting or prolonging those effects.

Endorphins were first identified in the early 1970s. Candace Pert and Solomon Snyder (1973) were doing research on morphine, a pain-relieving and mood-elevating opiate derived from heroin, which is made from poppies. They found that morphine works by binding to receptor sites in the brain. This seemed odd. As Snyder later recalled, "We doubted that animals had evolved opiate receptors just to deal with certain properties of the poppy plant" (quoted in Radetsky, 1991). Pert and Snyder reasoned that if opiate receptors exist, then the body must produce its own internally generated, or *endogenous,* morphinelike substances, which they named "endorphins." Soon they and other researchers confirmed this hypothesis.

Endorphin levels seem to shoot up when an animal or a person is afraid or under stress. This is no accident; by making pain bearable in such situations, endorphins give

---

endorphins [en-DOR-fins] Chemical substances in the nervous system that are similar in structure and action to opiates; they are involved in pain reduction, pleasure, and memory, and are known technically as *endogenous opioid peptides.*

a species an evolutionary advantage. When an organism is threatened, it needs to do something fast. Pain, however, can interfere with action: A mouse that pauses to lick a wounded paw may become a cat's dinner; a soldier who is overcome by an injury may never get off the battlefield alive. But, of course, the body's built-in system of counter-acting pain is only partly successful, especially when painful stimulation is prolonged.

A link may also exist between endorphins and the pleasures of social contact. When young puppies, guinea pigs, and chicks are injected with low doses of morphine or endorphins, the animals show much less distress than usual after separation from their mothers. (In all other respects, they behave normally.) The morphine seems to provide a biochemical replacement for the mother, or, more precisely, for the endorphin surge presumed to occur during contact with her. Conversely, when young guinea pigs and chicks receive a chemical that *blocks* the effects of opiates, their crying increases (Panksepp et al., 1980). These findings suggest that endorphin-stimulated euphoria may be a child's initial motive for seeking affection and cuddling—that, in effect, a child attached to a parent is a child addicted to love.

Hormones: Long-Distance Messengers. **Hormones,** which make up the third class of chemical messengers, are produced primarily in **endocrine glands** and are released directly into the bloodstream, which carries them to organs and cells that may be far from their point of origin. Hormones have dozens of jobs, from promoting bodily growth to aiding digestion to regulating metabolism.

Neurotransmitters and hormones are not always chemically distinct; the two classi-fications are like clubs that admit some of the same members. A particular chemical, such as norepinephrine, may belong to more than one classification, depending on where it is located and what function it is performing. Nature has been efficient, giving some sub-stances more than one task to perform.

The following hormones, among others, are of particular interest to psychologists:

1 **Adrenal hormones,** which are produced by the *adrenal glands* (organs that are perched above the kidneys), are involved in emotion and stress. These hormones will surge if you are laughing at a funny movie or playing a video game, if you are worried about an exam, if you are cheering at a rock concert, or if you are responding to an insult. They will also rise in response to nonemotional conditions, such as heat, cold, pain, injury, burns, and physical exercise, and in response to some drugs, such as caffeine and nicotine. Later, we will see that increased output of adrenal hormones can affect your memory for events taking place at the time.

The outer part of each adrenal gland produces *cortisol*, which increases blood-sugar levels and boosts energy. The inner part produces *epinephrine* (popularly known as adrenaline) and *norepinephrine.* When adrenal hormones are released in your body, they

---

hormones Chemical substances, secreted by organs called *glands*, that affect the functioning of other organs.

endocrine glands Internal organs that produce hormones and release them into the bloodstream.

adrenal hormones Hormones that are produced by the adrenal glands and that are involved in emotion and stress; they include cortisol, epinephrine, and norepinephrine.

activate the sympathetic nervous system, which in turn increases your arousal level and prepares you for action. Your pupils dilate, widening to allow in more light; your heart beats faster; your breathing speeds up; your blood-sugar level rises, providing your body with more energy. And your digestion slows down, so that blood flow can be diverted from your stomach and intestines to your muscles and the surface of your skin. This is why, when you are excited, scared, furious, or wildly in love, you may not want to eat.

2 **Melatonin,** which is secreted by the *pineal gland,* deep within the brain, promotes sleep and helps to regulate daily biological rhythms. A **biological rhythm** is a periodic fluctuation in a biological system. We've got dozens of such rhythms; a biological clock in our brains governs the waxing and waning of hormone levels, urine volume, blood pressure, and even the responsiveness of brain cells to stimulation. Biological rhythms are typically synchronized with external events, such as changes in clock time and daylight. But many rhythms continue to occur even in the absence of all external time cues; that is, they are endogenous.

Some biological rhythms occur less often than once a day, cycling, say, on a seasonal or monthly basis. (The female menstrual cycle is an example.) Other rhythms—dozens of them, including stomach contractions, alertness, verbal and spatial performance, and daydreaming, to name just a few—occur more frequently than once a day, often following roughly a 90-minute schedule, as long as social customs do not intervene. And still others, called **circadian rhythms,** occur approximately every 24 hours. Circadian rhythms, which are also found in plants, animals, and insects, reflect the adaptation of organisms to the many changes associated with the rotation of the Earth on its axis, such as changes in light, air pressure, temperature, and wind. The best-known circadian rhythm is the sleep–wake cycle, but there are hundreds of others. For example, body temperature fluctuates about 1 degree centigrade each day, peaking, on average, in the late afternoon and hitting a low point, or trough, in the wee hours of the morning.

Circadian rhythms are controlled by a biological clock, or overall coordinator, located in a tiny, teardrop-shaped cluster of cells called the **suprachiasmatic nucleus (SCN).** (The SCN is part of the *hypothalamus,* which we will be describing shortly.) Other clocks have also been identified, scattered around the body, but the SCN is the master pacemaker. Melatonin appears to help keep this clock in phase with the light–dark cycle, and in turn is regulated by the SCN (Haimov & Lavie, 1996; Lewy et al., 1992). When you go to sleep in a darkened room, your melatonin level falls; when you wake up in the morning to a lightened room, it rises. Animal studies suggest that

---

melatonin A hormone, secreted by the pineal gland, that is involved in the regulation of daily biological rhythms.

biological rhythm A periodic, more or less regular fluctuation in a biological system; it may or may not have psychological implications.

circadian [sur-CAY-dee-un] rhythm A biological rhythm with a period (from peak to peak or trough to trough) of about 24 hours; from the Latin *circa,* "about," and *dies,* "a day."

suprachiasmatic [soo-pruh-KIE-az-MAT-ick] nucleus (SCN) An area of the brain containing a biological clock that governs circadian rhythms.

"You've been charged with driving under the influence of testosterone."

In the popular view, hormones "drive" our behavior—but in reality it's not that simple.

information about light and dark reaches the pineal gland via a neural pathway that leads from the back of the eyes through the SCN and on to the pineal gland.

Melatonin also seems to directly promote sleep. Interestingly, in some blind people who lack light perception, the normal melatonin cycle is absent. As a result, their circadian rhythms are disrupted, and they suffer from insomnia and other sleep problems (Czeisler et al., 1995; Tabandeh et al., 1998). Melatonin treatments have been used to synchronize the disturbed sleep–wake cycles of such people (Sack & Lewy, 1997). However, efforts to treat the insomnia of sighted people by giving them melatonin have been sparse and the results have been mixed (UC Berkeley Wellness Letter, May 2000). Melatonin supplements sold over the counter should be used with caution, if at all, because there are no federal standards for quality, dosage, and when to take them, and the long-term safety of such treatments is not yet known.

3 **Sex hormones,** which are secreted by tissue in the gonads (testes in men, ovaries in women), and also by the adrenal glands, actually occur in both sexes, but in differing amounts and proportions in males and females after puberty. *Androgens* (the most important of which is *testosterone*) are masculinizing hormones produced mainly in the testes but also in the ovaries and the adrenal glands. Androgens set in motion the physical changes males experience at puberty—for example, a deepened

---

sex hormones Hormones that regulate the development and functioning of reproductive organs and that stimulate the development of male and female sexual characteristics; they include androgens, estrogens, and progesterone.

voice and facial and chest hair—and cause pubic and underarm hair to develop in both sexes. Testosterone also influences sexual arousal in both sexes. *Estrogens* are feminizing hormones that bring on the physical changes females experience at puberty, such as breast development and the onset of menstruation, and that influence the course of the menstrual cycle. *Progesterone* contributes to the growth and maintenance of the uterine lining in preparation for a fertilized egg, among other functions. Estrogens and progesterone are produced mainly in the ovaries but also in the testes and the adrenal glands.

Researchers are now studying the involvement of sex hormones in behavior not directly related to sex and reproduction, such as memory and mental functioning. For example, estrogens appear to promote the growth of spines on dendrites, and thus the formation of synapses, in certain brain areas, and many researchers believe they contribute to improved learning and memory (Sherwin, 1998a; Wickelgren, 1997). However, the most common beliefs about the nonsexual effects of sex hormones—that fluctuating levels of estrogen and progesterone make many women "emotional" before menstruation and that testosterone makes men irrationally angry and violent—have not been borne out by research, as we will see in Essay 1.

What Do You Know?

You can activate your neurotransmitters by taking this quiz.

A. Which word in parentheses best fits each of the following definitions?

1. Basic building blocks of the nervous system (*nerves/neurons*)

2. Cell parts that receive nerve impulses (*axons/dendrites*)

3. Site of communication between neurons (*synapse/myelin sheath*)

4. Opiate-like substance in the brain (*dopamine/endorphin*)

5. Chemicals that make communication among neurons possible (*neurotransmitters/hormones*)

6. Hormone closely associated with emotional excitement (*epinephrine/estrogen*)

B. Imagine that you are depressed, and you hear about a treatment for depression that affects the levels of several neurotransmitters thought to be involved in the disorder. Based on what you have learned, what questions would you want to ask before deciding whether to try the treatment?

ANSWERS:

A. 1. neurons 2. dendrites 3. synapse 4. endorphin 5. neurotransmitters 6. epinephrine **B.** You might want to ask, among other things, about side effects (each neurotransmitter has several functions, all of which might be affected by the treatment); about evidence that the treatment works; and about whether there is any reason to believe that your own neurotransmitter levels are abnormal or whether there might be other reasons for your depression.

THE BRAIN

We come now to the main room of the nervous system "house": the brain. "It's amazing," neurologist Robert Collins once wrote, "to think that the body feeds the brain sugar and amino acids, and what comes out is poetry and pirouettes." Amazing, indeed. A disembodied brain stored in a formaldehyde-filled container is a putty-colored, wrinkled glob of tissue that looks a little like a walnut whose growth has gotten out of hand. It takes an act of imagination to envision this modest-looking organ writing *Hamlet,* discovering radium, or inventing the paper clip.

Mapping the Brain

In a living person, of course, the brain is encased in a thick protective vault of bone. How, then, can scientists study it? One approach is to study patients who have had a part of the brain damaged or removed because of disease or injury. Another, called the *lesion method,* involves damaging or removing sections of brain in animals, then observing the effects.

The brain can also be probed with devices called *electrodes.* Some electrodes are coin-shaped and are simply pasted or taped onto the scalp. They detect the electrical activity of millions of neurons in particular regions of the brain and are widely used in research and medical diagnosis. The electrodes are connected by wires to a machine that translates the electrical energy from the brain into wavy lines on a moving piece of paper or visual patterns on a screen. That is why electrical patterns in the brain are known as "brain waves." Different wave patterns are associated with sleep, relaxation, and mental concentration.

A brain-wave recording is called an **electroencephalogram (EEG).** A standard EEG is useful but not very precise, because it reflects the activities of many cells at once. "Listening" to the brain with an EEG machine is like standing outside a sports stadium: You know when something is happening, but you cannot be sure what it is or who is doing it. Fortunately, computer technology can be combined with EEG technology to get a clearer picture of brain activity patterns associated with specific events and mental processes; the computer suppresses all the background noise, leaving only the pattern of electrical response to the event being studied.

For even more precise information, researchers use *needle electrodes,* very thin wires or hollow glass tubes that can be inserted into the brain, either directly in an exposed brain or through tiny holes in the skull. Only the skull and the membranes covering the brain need to be anesthetized; paradoxically, the brain itself, which processes all sensation and feeling, feels nothing when it is touched. Therefore, a human patient or an animal can be awake and not feel pain during the procedure. Needle electrodes can be used both to record electrical activity from the brain and to stimulate the brain with weak electrical currents. Stimulating a given area often

---

electroencephalogram (EEG) A recording of neural activity detected by electrodes.

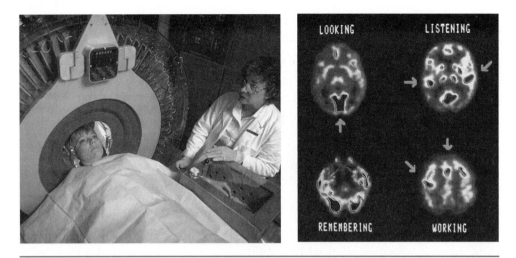

FIGURE 4.7　METABOLIC ACTIVITY IN THE BRAIN　*On the left, a woman lies with her head in a PET scanner, which will detect biochemical activity in specific brain areas. In the scan on the right, the colored areas and the arrows indicate regions that are most active when the person looks at a complicated visual scene, listens to a sound, moves the right hand, or recalls stories heard earlier.*

results in a specific sensation or movement. *Microelectrodes* are so fine that they can be inserted into single cells.

Since the mid-1970s, even more amazing doors to the brain have opened. The **PET scan (positron-emission tomography)** goes beyond anatomy to record biochemical changes in the brain as they are happening. One type of PET scan takes advantage of the fact that nerve cells convert glucose, the body's main fuel, into energy. A researcher can inject a patient with a substance that mimics glucose and contains a harmless radioactive element. This substance accumulates in brain areas that are particularly active and are therefore consuming glucose rapidly. The substance emits radiation, a telltale sign of activity, like cookie crumbs on a child's face. The radiation is detected by a scanning device, and the result is a computer-processed picture of biochemical activity on a display screen, with different colors indicating different activity levels. Other kinds of PET scans measure blood flow or oxygen consumption, which also reflect brain activity.

PET scans, which were originally designed to diagnose abnormalities, have produced evidence that certain brain areas in people with emotional disorders are either unusually quiet or unusually active. But PET technology can also show which parts of the brain are active during ordinary activities and emotions. It lets researchers see which areas are busiest when a person hears a song, recalls a sad memory, works on a math problem, or shifts attention from one task to another. The PET scans in Figure 4.7 show what an average healthy brain looks like when a person is doing different tasks.

PET scan (positron-emission tomography) A method for analyzing biochemical activity in the brain, using injections of a glucoselike substance containing a radioactive element.

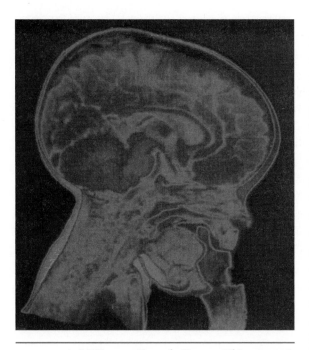

FIGURE 4.8 MRI OF A CHILD'S BRAIN   *This magnetic resonance image shows a child's brain—and the bottle he was drinking from while the image was obtained.*

Another technique used in both medical diagnosis and brain research, **MRI (magnetic resonance imaging),** allows the exploration of "inner space" without injecting chemicals. Powerful magnetic fields and radio frequencies are used to produce vibrations in the nuclei of atoms making up body organs, and the vibrations are then picked up as signals by special receivers. A computer analyzes the signals and converts them into a high-contrast picture of the organ (see Figure 4.8). A new, ultrafast version of MRI, called *functional MRI,* detects blood flow by picking up magnetic signals from blood that has given up its oxygen to active brain cells. It can capture brain changes many times a second as a person performs a task, such as reading a sentence or solving a puzzle. Other scanning techniques are becoming available with each passing year. Some of them convert still pictures into a moving picture that shows ongoing changes in the brain, on a three-dimensional image.

Brain-scanning techniques are certainly remarkable. However, after researchers find out which brain areas are active during a task, they must still figure out precisely what is happening inside the person's head, both mentally and physiologically. Enthusiasm for new technology has produced a mountain of findings, but uncritical interpretation of these findings has often led to unwarranted conclusions. One scientist (cited in Wheeler, 1998) drew this analogy: A researcher scans the brains of gum-chewing volunteers, finds out which parts of their brains are active, and concludes that he or she has found the brain's "gum-chewing center!"

Descriptive studies using brain scans, then, are just a first step in understanding brain processes. Nonetheless, they are an important and exciting first step. The brain can no longer hide from researchers behind the fortress of the skull. It is now possible to get a clear visual image of our most enigmatic organ without so much as lifting a scalpel.

MRI (magnetic resonance imaging)   A method for studying body and brain tissue, using magnetic fields and special radio receivers.

A Tour Through the Brain

All modern brain theories assume that the major brain parts perform different (though overlapping) tasks. This concept, which is known as **localization of function,** goes back at least to Joseph Gall (1758–1828). Gall was the Austrian anatomist who thought that personality traits were reflected in the development of specific areas of the brain (see Chapter 2). Gall's theory of *phrenology* was completely wrongheaded (so to speak), but his general notion of specialization in the brain had merit.

To learn about what the various brain structures do, we are going to take an imaginary stroll through the brain. Pretend, now, that you have shrunk to a microscopic size and that you are wending your way through the "soul's frail dwelling house," starting at the lower part, just above the spine. Figure 4.9, a cross-section, shows the major structures we will encounter along our tour; you may want to refer to it as we proceed.

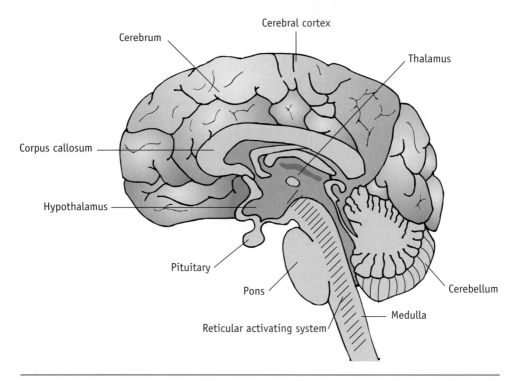

FIGURE 4.9 THE HUMAN BRAIN *This cross-section depicts the brain as if it were split in half. The view is of the inside surface of the right half and shows the structures described in the text.*

---

localization of function Specialization of particular brain areas for particular functions.

The Brain Stem.   We begin at the base of the skull with the **brain stem,** which began to evolve some 500 million years ago in segmented worms. The brain stem looks like a stalk rising out of the spinal cord. Pathways to and from upper areas of the brain pass through its two main structures, the **medulla** and the **pons.** The pons is involved in (among other things) sleeping, waking, and dreaming. The medulla is responsible for bodily functions that do not have to be consciously willed, such as breathing and heart rate. Hanging has long been used as a method of execution because when it breaks the neck, nervous pathways from the medulla are severed, stopping respiration.

Extending upward from the core of the brain stem is the **reticular activating system (RAS).** This dense network of neurons, which extends above the brain stem into the center of the brain and has connections with higher areas, screens incoming information and arouses the higher centers when something happens that demands their attention. Without the reticular activating system, we could not be alert or perhaps even conscious.

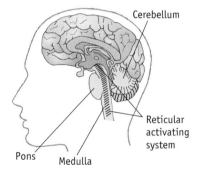

Cerebellum

Reticular activating system

Pons   Medulla

The Cerebellum.   Standing atop the brain stem and looking toward the back part of the brain, we see a two-lobed structure about the size of a small fist. It is the **cerebellum,** or "lesser brain," which contributes to a sense of balance and coordinates the muscles so that movement is smooth and precise. If your cerebellum were damaged, you would probably become exceedingly clumsy and uncoordinated. You might have trouble using a pencil, threading a needle, riding a bike, or even walking. In addition, this structure is involved in remembering certain simple skills and acquired reflexes. (Researchers have learned this in studies of rabbits and other animals, as we will see when we discuss the biology of memory.)

Some researchers think that the cerebellum is a lot less "lesser" than previously thought—that it also plays a role in such higher-order processes as analyzing sensory information, solving problems, and understanding words (Fiez, 1996; Gao et al., 1996; Müller, Courchesne, & Allen, 1998).

---

brain stem   The part of the brain at the top of the spinal cord, consisting of the medulla and the pons.

medulla [muh-DUL-uh]   A structure in the brain stem responsible for certain automatic functions, such as breathing and heart rate.

pons   A structure in the brain stem involved in, among other things, sleeping, waking, and dreaming.

reticular activating system (RAS)   A dense network of neurons found in the core of the brain stem; it arouses the cortex and screens incoming information.

cerebellum   A brain structure that regulates movement and balance, and that is involved in the learning of certain kinds of simple responses.

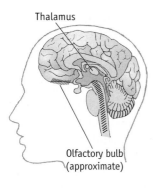

Thalamus

Olfactory bulb
(approximate)

The Thalamus. Deep in the brain's interior, we can see the **thalamus,** the busy traffic officer of the brain. The thalamus relays motor impulses from higher centers to the spinal cord. And conversely, as sensory messages come into the brain, the thalamus directs them to higher centers. For example, the sight of a sunset sends signals that the thalamus directs to a visual area, and the sound of an oboe sends signals that the thalamus sends on to an auditory area. The only sense that completely bypasses the thalamus is the sense of smell, which has its own private switching station, the *olfactory bulb.* The olfactory bulb lies near areas involved in emotion. Perhaps that is why particular odors—the smell of fresh laundry, gardenias, a steak sizzling on the grill—often rekindle memories of important personal experiences.

The Hypothalamus and the Pituitary Gland. Beneath the thalamus sits a structure called the **hypothalamus** (*hypo* means "under"). It is involved in drives associated with the survival of both the individual and the species—hunger, thirst, emotion, sex, and reproduction. It regulates body temperature by triggering sweating or shivering, and it controls the complex operations of the autonomic nervous system. As we have seen, it also contains the SCN, the neurological superclock that regulates the body's circadian rhythms.

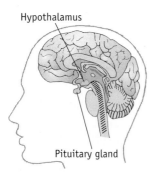

Hypothalamus

Pituitary gland

Hanging down from the hypothalamus, connected to it by a short stalk, is a cherry-sized endocrine gland called the **pituitary gland.** The pituitary is often called the body's "master gland" because the hormones it secretes affect many other endocrine glands. The master, however, is really only a supervisor. The true boss is the hypothalamus, which sends chemicals to the pituitary, telling it when to "talk" to the other endocrine glands. The pituitary, in turn, sends hormonal messages out to these glands.

The Limbic System. The hypothalamus has many connections to a set of loosely interconnected structures called the **limbic system,** shown in Figure 4.10. (*Limbic* comes from the Latin for "border"; these structures form a sort of border between the higher and the lower parts of the brain.) Some anatomists include the hypothalamus and parts of the thalamus in the limbic system. Although the usefulness of speaking of the limbic system as an integrated set of structures is now in dispute (LeDoux, 1996), it is

---

thalamus A brain structure that relays motor impulses to the spinal cord and sensory messages to the cerebral cortex.

hypothalamus A brain structure involved in emotions and drives vital to survival, such as fear, hunger, thirst, and reproduction; it regulates the autonomic nervous system.

pituitary gland A small endocrine gland at the base of the brain, which releases many hormones and regulates other endocrine glands.

limbic system A group of brain areas involved in emotional reactions and motivated behavior.

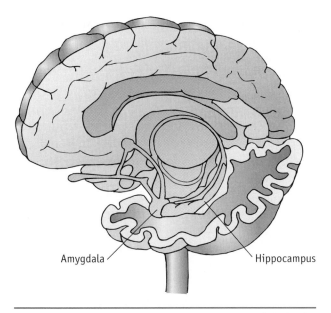

Amygdala   Hippocampus

FIGURE 4.10 THE LIMBIC SYSTEM *Structures of the limbic system play an important role in memory and emotion. The text describes two of these structures, the amygdala and the hippocampus.*

clear that structures in this region are heavily involved in emotions, such as rage and fear, that we share with other animals (MacLean, 1993).

Many years ago, James Olds and Peter Milner reported finding "pleasure centers" in the limbic system (Olds, 1975; Olds & Milner, 1954). Olds and Milner trained rats to press a lever in order to get a buzz of electricity delivered through tiny electrodes to the limbic system. Some rats would press the bar thousands of times an hour, for 15 or 20 hours at a time, until they collapsed from exhaustion. When they revived, they went right back to the bar. When forced to make a choice, the hedonistic rodents opted for electrical stimulation over such temptations as water, food, and even an attractive rat of the other sex that was making provocative gestures. Today, however, researchers believe that brain stimulation activates neural pathways rather than discrete "centers," and that changes in neurotransmitter or neuromodulator levels are involved.

One limbic structure that has important psychological functions is the **amygdala,** which is responsible for evaluating sensory information, instantly determining its emotional importance, and contributing to the initial decision to approach or withdraw from a person or situation (LeDoux, 1994, 1996). For example, the amygdala quickly assesses danger or threat, which is a good thing, because otherwise you could be standing in the street asking, "Is it wise to cross now, while that very large truck is hurtling toward me?" The amygdala's initial response may then be overridden by a more accurate appraisal from the cerebral cortex (a structure to be described shortly). That is why, after you jump with fear when you feel a hand on your back in a dark alley, your fear evaporates when the cortex registers that the hand belongs to a friend with a lousy sense of humor.

If either the amygdala or critical areas of the cortex are damaged, emotional abnormalities result. A rat with a damaged amygdala "forgets" to be afraid when it

---

amygdala [**uh-MIG-dul-uh**] A brain structure involved in the arousal and regulation of emotion, particularly fear, and the initial emotional response to sensory information.

should be. Likewise, people with damage to the amygdala often cannot experience fear or recognize fear in others. Antonio Damasio (1999) described a case of a woman with a severely damaged amygdala who "knows what fear is supposed to be, what should cause it, and even what one may do in situations of fear"—but she herself is fearless, unable to learn the "telltale signs" of danger or trouble that show up in the face of a threatening person or situation. Just the opposite problem can occur in rats or people with damage to critical areas of the cortex; they often lose the capacity to put aside their initial fear when the emotion is no longer necessary or appropriate. In people, the result can be constant, irrational feelings of impending doom or anxiety or obsessive thoughts of danger (Schulkin, 1994; Schwartz et al., 1996).

Another important limbic area is the **hippocampus,** which has a shape that must have reminded someone of a sea horse, for that is what its name means. One of its primary tasks seems to be to compare sensory messages with what the brain has learned to expect about the world. When expectations are met, the hippocampus tells the reticular activating system, the brain's arousal center, to "cool it." It wouldn't do to be highly aroused in response to *everything*. What if neural alarm bells went off every time a car went by, a bird chirped, or you felt your saliva trickling down the back of your throat? The hippocampus is also called the "gateway to memory" because it plays a major role in the formation of some kinds of memories. For example, it enables humans (and other species) to form a "spatial memory" that allows them to navigate through their environments (Maguire et al., 2000). The hippocampus is also involved in the formation of memories of facts and events, as we will see later.

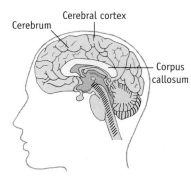

Cerebrum
Cerebral cortex
Cerebral cortex
Corpus callosum

The Cerebrum and Cerebral Cortex. At this point in our tour, the largest part of the brain still looms above us. It is the cauliflower-like **cerebrum,** where the higher forms of thinking take place. The complexity of the human brain's circuitry far exceeds that of any computer in existence, and much of its most complicated wiring is packed into this structure. Compared with many other creatures, we humans may be ungainly, feeble, and thin-skinned, but our well-developed cerebrum enables us to overcome these limitations and creatively control our environment (and, some would say, to mess it up).

The cerebrum is divided into two separate halves, or **cerebral hemispheres,** connected by a large band of fibers called the **corpus callosum.** In general, the right hemi-

---

hippocampus A brain structure involved in the storage of new information in memory.

cerebrum [suh-REE-brum] The largest brain structure, consisting of the upper part of the brain; it is in charge of most sensory, motor, and cognitive processes. (From the Latin for "brain.")

cerebral hemispheres The two halves of the cerebrum.

corpus callosum [CORE-puhss cah-LOW-suhm] The bundle of nerve fibers connecting the two cerebral hemispheres.

sphere is in charge of the left side of the body and the left hemisphere is in charge of the right side of the body. The two hemispheres also have somewhat different tasks and talents, a phenomenon known as **lateralization.**

Working our way right up through the top of the brain, we find that the cerebrum is covered by several thin layers of densely packed cells known collectively as the **cerebral cortex.** Cell bodies in the cortex, as in many other parts of the brain, produce a grayish tissue; hence the term *gray matter.* In other parts of the brain (and in the rest of the nervous system), long, myelin-covered axons prevail, providing the brain's *white matter.* Although the cortex is only about 3 millimeters thick, it contains almost three-fourths of all the cells in the human brain. The cortex has many deep crevasses and wrinkles, which enable it to contain its billions of neurons without requiring us to have the heads of giants—heads that would be too big to permit us to be born. In other mammals, which have fewer neurons, the cortex is less crumpled; in rats, it is quite smooth.

On each cerebral hemisphere, deep fissures divide the cortex into four distinct regions, or lobes (see Figure 4.11 on the next page). These lobes are:

+ The **occipital lobes** (from the Latin for "in back of the head") are at the lower back part of the brain. Among other things, they contain the *visual cortex,* where visual signals are processed. Damage to the visual cortex can cause impaired visual recognition or blindness.

+ The **parietal lobes** (from the Latin for "pertaining to walls") are at the top of the brain. They contain the *somatosensory cortex,* which receives information about pressure, pain, touch, and temperature from all over the body. The areas of the somatosensory cortex that receive signals from the hands and the face are disproportionately large because these body parts are particularly sensitive.

+ The **temporal lobes** (from the Latin for "pertaining to the temples") are at the sides of the brain, just above the ears and behind the temples. They are involved in memory, perception, and emotion, and they contain the *auditory cortex,* which processes sounds. An area of the left temporal lobe, known as *Wernicke's area,* is involved in language comprehension.

+ The **frontal lobes,** as their name indicates, are located toward the front of the brain, just under the skull, in the area of the forehead. They contain the *motor cortex,* which issues orders to the 600 muscles of the body that produce voluntary movement. In the left frontal lobe, a region known as *Broca's area* is involved in speech

---

lateralization Specialization of the two cerebral hemispheres for particular operations.

cerebral cortex A collection of several thin layers of cells covering the cerebrum; it is largely responsible for higher mental functions. (*Cortex* is Latin for "bark" or "rind.")

occipital [ahk-SIP-uh-tuhl] lobes Lobes at the lower back part of the brain's cerebral cortex; they contain areas that receive visual information.

parietal [puh-RYE-uh-tuhl] lobes Lobes at the top of the brain's cerebral cortex; they contain areas that receive information on pressure, pain, touch, and temperature.

temporal lobes Lobes at the sides of the brain's cerebral cortex, just above the ears; they contain areas involved in hearing, memory, perception, emotion, and (in the left lobe, typically) language comprehension.

frontal lobes Lobes at the front of the brain's cerebral cortex; they contain areas involved in short-term memory, higher-order thinking, initiative, social judgment, and (in the left lobe, typically) speech production.

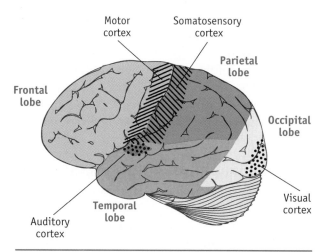

Motor cortex

Somatosensory cortex

Parietal lobe

Frontal lobe

Occipital lobe

Visual cortex

Temporal lobe

Auditory cortex

FIGURE 4.11 LOBES OF THE CEREBRUM *Deep fissures divide the cortex of each cerebral hemisphere into four regions. Within these lobes, areas are specialized for vision, hearing, and other functions.*

production. The frontal lobes are also involved in the ability to make plans, think creatively, and take initiative.

Although variations in the organization of the cerebral cortex exist, depending on people's experiences, the lobes of the cerebral cortex will respond in characteristic ways when stimulated. If a surgeon applied electrical current to the somatosensory cortex in your parietal lobes, for example, you would probably feel a tingling in the skin or a sense of being gently touched. If your visual cortex in the occipital lobes were electrically stimulated, you might report a flash of light or swirls of color. And, eerily, there are many areas of your cortex which, if stimulated, would do nothing at all; the areas are "silent."

The "silent" areas are sometimes called the *association cortex* because they are involved in higher mental processes. Psychologists are especially interested in the forwardmost part of the frontal lobes, the *prefrontal cortex*. This area barely exists in mice and rats and takes up only 3.5 percent of the cerebral cortex in cats, about 7 percent in dogs, and 17 percent in chimpanzees. In human beings, it accounts for fully 29 percent of the cortex.

Scientists have long known that the frontal lobes, and the prefrontal cortex in particular, must have something to do with personality. The first clue appeared in 1848, when a bizarre accident drove an inch-thick, 3½-foot-long iron rod clear through the head of a young railroad worker named Phineas Gage. The rod (which is still on display at Harvard University, along with Gage's skull) entered beneath the left eye and exited through the top of the head, destroying much of the prefrontal cortex (H. Damasio et al., 1994). Miraculously, Gage survived this trauma and retained the ability to speak, think, and remember. But his friends complained that he was "no longer Gage." In a sort of Jekyll-and-Hyde transformation, he had changed from a mild-mannered, friendly, energetic, and efficient worker into a foul-mouthed, ill-tempered, undependable lout who could not hold a steady job or stick to a plan. His employers had to let him go, and he was reduced to exhibiting himself as a circus attraction.

This sad case and others suggest that parts of the frontal lobes are involved in social judgment, rational decision making, and the ability to set goals and to make and carry through plans (Klein & Kihlstrom, 1998). As neurologist Antonio Damasio (1994) wrote, "Gage's unintentional message was that observing social convention, behaving ethically, and, in general, making decisions advantageous to one's survival and progress, require both knowledge of rules and strategies *and* the integrity of specific brain systems." Interestingly, the mental deficits that characterize damage to these areas are accompanied by a flattening out of emotion and feeling, which suggests that normal emotions are necessary for everyday reasoning and the ability to learn from mistakes.

The frontal lobes also govern the ability to do a series of tasks in the proper sequence and to stop doing them at the proper time. The pioneering Soviet psychologist Alexander Luria (1980) studied many cases in which damage to the frontal lobes disrupted these abilities. One man observed by Luria kept trying to light a match after it was already lit. Another planed a piece of wood in the hospital carpentry shop until it was gone . . . and then went on to plane the workbench!

Some researchers believe that damage to the prefrontal cortex caused by birth complications or physical abuse, when combined with a lack of love or other environmental stresses, might help account for some cases of criminally violent behavior (Raine et al., 1998). A study of more than 4,000 boys, followed from birth to age 18, found that many of those who became violent offenders had experienced two risk factors: birth complications that caused damage to the prefrontal cortex, and early maternal rejection. Although only 4.4 percent of the boys had both risk factors, these boys accounted for 18 percent of all violent crimes committed by the sample as a whole (Raine, Brennan, & Mednick, 1994). Such findings raise troubling legal questions: Should violent individuals who have damage in the prefrontal cortex be held responsible for their acts? And what treatment or punishment should they receive?

We have come to the end of our tour. When you think that your hardworking brain has mastered this material, pause to see how it's doing by taking the following quiz. (Table 4.1 on the next page summarizes the parts of the brain and their primary functions.)

What Do You Know?

Match each description on the left with a term on the right.

1. Filters out irrelevant information
2. Known as the "gateway to memory"
3. Controls the autonomic nervous system; involved in drives associated with survival
4. Consists of two hemispheres
5. Wrinkled outer covering of the brain
6. Site of the motor cortex; associated with planning and taking initiative

a. reticular activating system
b. cerebrum
c. hippocampus
d. cerebral cortex
e. frontal lobes
f. hypothalamus

ANSWERS:

1. a 2. c 3. f 4. b 5. d 6. e

TABLE 4.1 ✦ Functions Associated with the Major Brain Structures

The functions listed here are just some of those that have been linked with these structures.

STRUCTURE	FUNCTION(S)
Brain stem	
Pons	Sleeping, waking, dreaming
Medulla	Automatic functions such as breathing, heart rate
Reticular activating system (RAS) (extends into the center of the brain)	Screening of incoming information, arousal of higher centers, consciousness
Cerebellum	Balance, coordination, memory for simple skills and learned reflexes, possible involvement in more complex mental tasks
Thalamus	Relay of motor impulses to the spinal cord, and of incoming sensory information (except for olfactory sensations) to other brain centers
Hypothalamus	Behaviors necessary for survival, such as hunger, thirst, emotion, reproduction; regulation of body temperature and circadian rhythms; control of autonomic nervous system
Pituitary gland	Under direction of the hypothalamus, secretion of hormones that affect other endocrine glands
Limbic system	Emotions related to survival
Amygdala	Initial evaluation of sensory information to determine its importance; mediation of anxiety and depression
Hippocampus	Comparison of sensory information with expectations, modulation of the RAS; formation of new spatial memories and memories about facts and events
Cerebrum (including cerebral cortex)	Higher forms of thinking
Occipital lobes	Visual processing
Parietal lobes	Processing of pressure, pain, touch, temperature
Temporal lobes	Memory, perception, emotion, hearing, language comprehension
Frontal lobes	Movement, short-term memory, planning, setting goals, creative thinking, initiative, social judgment, rational decision making, speech production

The Brain's Two Hemispheres

We have seen that the cerebrum is divided into two hemispheres that control opposite sides of the body. As we mentioned earlier, although similar in structure, these hemispheres have some separate talents, or areas of specialization.

Split Brains: A House Divided

In a normal brain, the two hemispheres communicate with one another across the corpus callosum, the bundle of fibers that connects them. Whatever happens in one side of the brain is instantly flashed to the other side. What would happen, though, if the two sides were cut off from one another?

In 1953, Ronald E. Myers and Roger W. Sperry took the first step toward answering this question by severing the corpus callosum in cats. They also cut parts of the nerves leading from the eyes to the brain. Normally, each eye transmits messages to both sides of the brain. After this procedure, a cat's left eye sent information only to the left hemisphere and its right eye sent information only to the right hemisphere.

At first, the cats did not seem to be affected much by this drastic operation. But Myers and Sperry showed that something profound had indeed happened. They trained the cats to perform tasks with one eye blindfolded. For example, a cat might have to push a panel with a square on it to get food but ignore a panel with a circle. Then the researchers switched the blindfold to the cat's other eye and tested the animal again. Now the cats behaved as if they had never learned the trick. Apparently, one side of the brain did not know what the other side was doing; it was as if the animals had two minds in one body. Later studies confirmed this result with other species, including monkeys (Sperry, 1964).

In all the animal studies, ordinary behavior, such as eating and walking, remained normal. Encouraged by this finding, a team of surgeons decided in the early 1960s to try cutting the corpus callosum in patients with debilitating, uncontrollable epilepsy. In severe forms of this disease, disorganized electrical activity spreads from an injured area to other parts of the brain. The surgeons reasoned that cutting the connection between the two halves of the cerebrum might stop the spread of electrical activity from one side to the other.

The results of this *split-brain surgery* generally proved successful. Seizures were reduced and sometimes disappeared completely. As an added bonus, these patients gave scientists a chance to find out what each half of the brain can do when it is quite literally cut off from the other. It was already known that the two hemispheres are not mirror images of each other. In most people, language is largely handled by the left hemisphere. Thus, a person who suffers brain damage because of a stroke (a blockage in or rupture of a blood vessel in the brain) is much more likely to have language problems if the damage is in the left side than if it is in the right. How would splitting the brain affect language and other abilities?

In their daily lives, split-brain patients did not seem much affected by the fact that the two sides of their brains were incommunicado. Their personalities and intelligence remained intact; they could walk, talk, and in general lead normal lives. Apparently, connections in the undivided lower parts of the brain kept body movements normal. But in a series of ingenious studies, Sperry and his colleagues (and later other researchers) showed that perception and memory had been affected, just as they had been in earlier animal research. In 1981, Sperry won a Nobel Prize for his work.

To understand this research, you must know how nerves connect the eyes to the brain. (The human patients, unlike Myers and Sperry's cats, did not have these nerves cut.) If you look straight ahead, everything in the left side of the scene before you—the left visual field—goes to the right half of your brain, and everything in the right side of the scene goes to the left half of your brain. This is true for *both* eyes (see Figure 4.12).

The procedure was to present information to only one or the other side of the subjects' brains. In one early study the researchers took photographs of different faces, cut

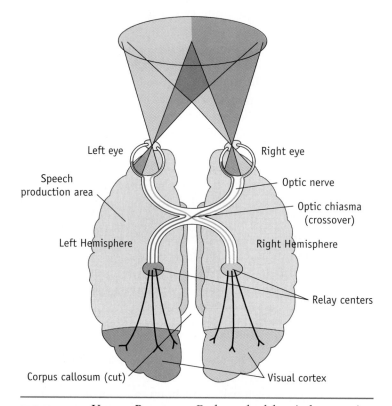

FIGURE 4.12 VISUAL PATHWAYS *Each cerebral hemisphere receives information from the eyes, by way of the optic nerves, about the opposite side of the visual field. Thus, if you stare directly at the corner of a room, everything to the left of the juncture is represented in your right hemisphere and vice versa. This is so because half the axons in each optic nerve cross over to the opposite side of the brain. Normally, each hemisphere immediately shares its information with the other one, but in split-brain patients, severing the corpus callosum prevents such communication.*

them in two, and pasted different halves together (Levy, Trevarthen, & Sperry, 1972). The reconstructed photographs were then presented on slides. The person was told to stare at a dot on the middle of the screen, so that half the image fell to the left of this point and half to the right. Each image was flashed so quickly that the person had no time to move his or her eyes. When the subjects were asked to say what they had seen, they named the person in the right part of the image (which would be the little boy in Figure 4.13). But when they were asked to *point* with their left hands to the face they had seen, they chose the person in the left side of the image (the mustached man in the figure). Further, they claimed they had noticed nothing unusual about the original photographs! Each side of the brain saw a different half-image and automatically filled in the missing part. Neither side knew what the other side had seen.

Why did the patients name one side of the picture but point to the other? Speech centers are in the left hemisphere. When the person responded with speech, it was the left side of the brain doing the talking. When the person pointed with the left hand, which is controlled by the right side of the brain, the right hemisphere was giving *its* version of what the person had seen.

In another study, the researchers presented slides of ordinary objects and then suddenly flashed a slide of a nude woman. Both sides of the brain were amused, but because only the left side has speech, the two sides responded differently. When the

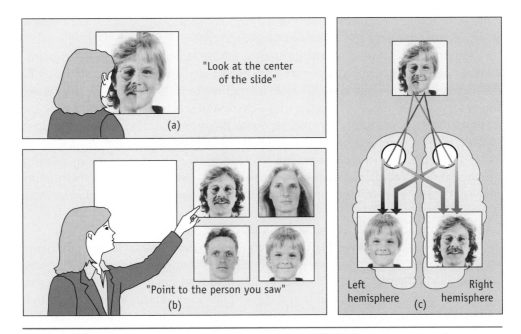

FIGURE 4.13 DIVIDED BRAIN, DIVIDED VIEW *When split-brain patients were shown composite photographs (a) and were then asked to pick out the face they had seen from a series of intact photographs (b), they said they had seen the face on the right side of the composite—yet they pointed with their left hands to the face that had been on the left. Because the two cerebral hemispheres could not communicate, the verbal left hemisphere was aware of only the right half of the picture, and the relatively mute right hemisphere was aware of only the left half (c).*

picture was flashed to her left hemisphere, one woman laughed and identified it as a nude. When it was flashed to her right hemisphere, she said nothing but began to chuckle. Asked what she was laughing at, she said, "I don't know . . . nothing . . . oh—that funny machine." The right hemisphere could not describe what it had seen, but it reacted emotionally just the same (Gazzaniga, 1967).

A Question of Dominance

Dozens of people have undergone the split-brain operation since the mid-1960s, and research on left–right differences has also been done with people whose brains are intact (Springer & Deutch, 1998). Electrodes and brain scans have been used to gauge activity in the left and right hemispheres while people perform different tasks. The results confirm that nearly all right-handed people and a majority of left-handers process language mainly in the left hemisphere. The left side is also more active during some logical, symbolic, and sequential tasks, such as solving math problems and understanding technical material. Because of its cognitive talents, many researchers refer to the left hemisphere as *dominant*. They believe that the left hemisphere usually exerts control over the right hemisphere. One well-known split-brain researcher, Michael Gazzaniga (1983), has argued that without help from the left side, the right side's mental skills would probably be "vastly inferior to the cognitive skills of a chimpanzee." He and others also believe that a mental "module" in the left hemisphere is constantly trying to explain actions and emotions generated by brain parts whose workings are nonverbal and outside of awareness.

You can see in split-brain patients how the left hemisphere concocts such explanations. In one classic example, a picture of a chicken claw was flashed to a patient's left hemisphere, a picture of a snow scene to his right. The task was to point to a related image for each picture from an array, with a chicken the correct choice for the claw and a shovel for the snow scene. The patient chose the shovel with his left hand and the chicken with his right. When asked to explain why, he responded (with his left hemisphere) that the chicken claw went with the chicken, and the shovel was for cleaning out the chicken shed. The left hemisphere had seen the left hand's response but did not know about the snow scene, so it interpreted the response by using the information it did have (Gazzaniga, 1988). In people with intact brains, says Gazzaniga, the left side's interpretations account for the sense of a unified, coherent identity.

Other researchers, including Roger Sperry (1982), have rushed to the right hemisphere's defense. The right side, they point out, is no dummy. It is superior in problems requiring spatial-visual ability, the ability you use to read a map or follow a dress pattern, and it excels in facial recognition and the ability to read facial expressions. (Dr. P. and Emily D., described at the beginning of this chapter, both had damage in the right hemisphere.) It is active during the creation and appreciation of art and music. It recognizes nonverbal sounds, such as a dog's barking. The right hemisphere also has some language ability. Typically, it can read a word briefly flashed to it and can understand an experimenter's instructions. In a few split-brain patients, the right hemisphere's language ability has been quite well developed.

Some researchers have credited the right hemisphere with having a cognitive style that is intuitive and holistic (in which things are seen as wholes), in contrast to the left hemisphere's more rational and analytic mode. However, many researchers are concerned about popular misinterpretations of this conclusion. Books and programs that promise to make you more "right-brained" tend to oversimplify and exaggerate hemispheric differences. Individuals differ in the degree of lateralization for different tasks. Moreover, the "intuitive, holistic" right hemisphere, which is often praised in popular writings, is not always a hero. For example, regions of the right hemisphere seem to be specialized for the processing of negative emotions like fear and sadness, whereas regions of the left hemisphere are specialized for positive emotions like happiness (Davidson, 1995). And left-hemisphere activation is associated with tendencies to approach other people, whereas right-hemisphere activation is associated with tendencies to withdraw (Harmon-Jones & Allen, 1998). Most important, the differences between the two sides are relative, not absolute—a matter of degree. In most real-life activities, the two hemispheres cooperate naturally, with each making a valuable contribution (Kinsbourne, 1982; J. Levy, 1985). "The left-right dichotomy," Sperry (1982) himself once noted, "is an idea with which it is very easy to run wild."

If you have mastered the information we have discussed so far, you are prepared to read popular accounts of advances in neuropsychology. We will see next how biological psychologists draw on findings about the brain and nervous system to investigate two topics that have always fascinating human beings: memory and sleep.

What Do You Know?

Use as many parts of your brain as necessary to answer these questions.

1. Keeping in mind that both sides of the brain are involved in most activities, see whether you can identify which of the following is (are) most closely associated with the left hemisphere: (a) enjoying a musical recording; (b) wiggling the left big toe; (c) giving a speech in class; (d) balancing a checkbook; (e) recognizing a long-lost friend

2. Over the past decades, thousands of people have taken courses and bought tapes that promise to develop the "creativity" and "intuition" of their right hemispheres. What characteristics of human thought might explain the eagerness of some people to glorify "right-brainedness" and disparage "left-brainedness" (or vice versa)?

ANSWERS:

1. c, d 2. One possible answer: Human beings like to make sense of the world, and one easy way to do that is to divide humanity into opposing categories. This kind of either-or thinking can lead to the conclusion that fixing up one of the categories (e.g., making "left-brained" types more "right-brained") will make individuals happier and the world a better place. If only it were that simple!

THE BIOLOGY OF MEMORY

One of the most amazing things the brain does is remember that it can do things. In Chapter 8 we will examine the psychology of memory—how it works, why it lets us down, and why we forget. But here we want to consider the biology of memory. What happens in the brain when you remember your first kiss, how to knit a sweater, or the anatomy of the brain itself?

Changes in Neurons and Synapses

Forming a memory involves chemical and structural changes at the level of neurons, and these changes differ, depending on whether the memory is retained for just a few seconds or minutes, or for longer. Studies of sea snails and other organisms that have small numbers of easily identifiable neurons show that in short-term retention, changes within neurons temporarily alter the neurons' ability to release neurotransmitters, the chemicals that carry messages from one cell to another (Alkon, 1989; Kandel & Schwartz, 1982). When these primitive animals are taught to withdraw or not withdraw parts of their bodies in response to a light touch, and the animal retains the skill for only the short term, the neurons involved temporarily show an increase or decrease in readiness to release neurotransmitter molecules, depending on the kind of response being learned.

In contrast, long-term memory involves lasting structural changes in the brain. To mimic what they think may happen during the formation of a long-term memory, researchers apply brief, high-frequency electrical stimulation to groups of neurons in the brains of animals. In various areas, especially the hippocampus, this stimulation increases the strength of synaptic responsiveness, a phenomenon known as **long-term potentiation** (McNaughton & Morris, 1987). In other words, some synaptic pathways become more excitable. Long-term potentiation seems to involve (1) an increase in the release of the neurotransmitter glutamate from transmitting neurons, and (2) chemical reactions in the glutamate receptors of receiving neurons, which make these neurons more receptive to the next signal that comes along (Bliss & Collingridge, 1993). It is a little like increasing the diameter of a funnel's neck to permit more flow through the funnel.

Other changes also occur in long-term potentiation. For example, dendrites grow and branch out, and certain types of synapses increase in number (Greenough, 1984). And in a complementary process, some neurons become *less* responsive than they were previously (Bolshakov & Siegelbaum, 1994). The neural and synaptic changes in the brain that underlie long-term memory all take time to develop, which may explain why memories remain vulnerable to disruption for a while after they are stored— why, for example, a blow to the head may disrupt new memories even though old ones are unaffected.

---

long-term potentiation A long-lasting increase in the strength of synaptic responsiveness, thought to be a biological mechanism of long-term memory.

Locating Memories

In 1996 a little study made big headlines: Researchers had their first clue that true memories might actually be located in a different part of the brain from false (mistaken) memories. PET scans showed that false and true memories for words in a list triggered different patterns of brain activity. Only true memories produced activity in left-hemisphere areas involved in processing sounds and speech; only false memories activated frontal-lobe areas thought to be involved in conscious attempts to remember information (Schacter et al., 1996). Some writers wondered whether these results would lead to a "litmus test" for distinguishing real memories from phony ones.

Such a test may never be possible. Nevertheless, this research illustrates one of the most important developments in the study of memory: the ability to use microelectrodes, brain-scan technology, and other techniques to identify the brain structures responsible for the formation and location of specific types of memories. For example, research using these techniques shows that during short-term memory tasks, areas in the frontal lobes are especially active (Goldman-Rakic, 1996).

One of the most important areas involved in memory is the hippocampus. Along with adjacent brain areas, it enables us to form long-term *declarative memories,* memories of facts and events—the kind you draw on when identifying a flower or telling someone about a vacation trip or what you had for lunch (see Chapter 8). The ultimate destinations of declarative memories seem to lie in parts of the cerebral cortex, possibly in the same cortical areas that were involved in the original perception of the information (Mishkin & Appenzeller, 1987). But the hippocampus has been called the "gateway to memory" because without it the information would never get to the cortical storage areas (Mishkin et al., 1997; Squire & Zola-Morgan, 1991).

We know about this function of the hippocampus in part from research on brain-damaged patients with severe memory problems. The case of one man, known to researchers as H. M., is probably the most intensely studied in the annals of medicine (Corkin, 1984; Corkin et al., 1997; Milner, 1970; Ogden & Corkin, 1991). In 1953, when H. M. was 27 years old, surgeons removed most of his hippocampus, along with part of the amygdala. The operation was a last-ditch effort to relieve H. M.'s severe and life-threatening epilepsy. People who have epilepsy, a neurological disorder that has many causes and takes many forms, often have seizures. Usually, the seizures are brief, mild, and controllable by drugs, but in H. M.'s case, they were unrelenting and uncontrollable.

The operation did achieve its goal: Afterward, the young man's seizures were milder and could be managed with medication. His memory, however, had been affected profoundly. Although H. M. continued to recall most events that had occurred before the operation, he could no longer remember new experiences for much longer than 15 minutes; these declarative memories vanished like water down the drain. Nor could he learn new words, songs, stories, or faces. He would read the same magazine over and over without realizing it. He could not recognize his doctors, and he could not recall the day of the week, the year, or even his last meal. Most scientists attribute these deficits to an inability to form new memories for long-term storage.

Today, many years later, H. M. will occasionally recall an unusually emotional event, such as the assassination of someone named Kennedy. He sometimes remembers that both his parents are dead, and he knows he has memory problems (which he describes as "like waking from a dream"). But, according to Suzanne Corkin, who has studied H. M. extensively, these "islands of remembering" are the exceptions in a vast sea of forgetfulness. This good-natured man still does not know the scientists who have studied him for decades. He thinks he is much younger than he is, and he can no longer recognize a photograph of his own face; he is stuck in a time warp from the past.

In contrast, the formation of *procedural memories*—memories for skills and habits—seems to involve other brain structures and pathways. For example, when rabbits are taught to blink their eyes in response to a tone, changes in electrical activity occur in parts of the cerebellum. If the affected brain tissue is removed or destroyed, the animals immediately forget the response and cannot relearn it. Moreover, if you deaden a part of the cerebellum during the initial learning, the rabbits will not learn the response in the first place (Krupa, Thompson, & Thompson, 1993; Thompson, 1986). Human patients with damage in the cerebellum are also incapable of this type of simple learning (Daum & Schugens, 1996).

Interestingly, patients like H. M., despite their inability to form new memories for facts and events, can, with sufficient practice, acquire new procedural memories; they can learn, for example, to solve puzzles or play tennis, even though they cannot remember the training sessions in which they learned these skills. Apparently, the parts of the brain involved in forming procedural memories have remained intact.

One complication in "locating" memories is that the typical declarative memory is a complex cluster of information. When you recall meeting a man yesterday, you remember his greeting, his tone of voice, how he looked, and where he was. Even a single concept, such as "shovel," includes a lot of information (about length, material, uses, etc.). These different pieces of information are probably processed separately and stored at different locations distributed across wide areas of the brain, with all the sites participating in the representation of the event or concept as a whole (H. Damasio et al., 1996; Squire, 1987). The role of the hippocampus may be to somehow bind together the diverse aspects of a memory at the time it is formed, so that even though these aspects are stored in different cortical sites, the memory can be retrieved as one coherent entity (Squire & Zola-Morgan, 1991).

Researchers are learning more and more about where memories are located; they have even been able to relate the encoding of different types of material, such as words and scenes, to specific areas in the frontal and temporal lobes (Schacter, 1999). As we noted in Chapter 2, case studies show that brain damage can have extremely specific effects on memory, depending on where the damage is. In one study of two stroke victims, one woman could read or speak verbs but had trouble writing them, whereas another could do only the reverse (Caramazza & Hillis, 1991)! Someday, neuroscientists may be able to describe the entire stream of events in the brain that occur from the moment you say to yourself "I must remember this" to the moment you actually do remember . . . or find that you can't.

Hormones and Memory

Have you ever smelled fresh cookies and recalled a tender scene from your childhood? Do you have a vivid memory of the first time you fell in love? Emotional memories such as these are often especially intense, and the explanation resides partly in our hormones.

Hormones released by the adrenal glands during stress and emotional arousal, including epinephrine (adrenaline) and certain steroids, enhance memory. If you give people a drug that prevents their adrenal glands from producing these hormones, they will remember less about emotional stories they heard than control subjects will (Cahill et al., 1994). Conversely, if you give epinephrine to animals right after learning, their memories will improve (McGaugh, 1990). The link between emotional arousal and memory makes evolutionary sense: Arousal tells the brain that an event or piece of information is important enough to encode and store for future use.

In real life, the hormones that flood our bodies during an upsetting experience may actually make the event *too* memorable. For example, high levels of epinephrine and other hormones during a traumatic experience may help explain the persistent flashbacks often suffered by people who have survived such an experience. Work is now under way to find out whether administering drugs that block these hormones immediately after a traumatic event will help prevent the later development of these troubling symptoms (McGaugh, 1999).

Hormones have a different effect on ordinary learning, however, than they do on memory for a single, striking experience. When animals are given very high dosages of adrenal hormones, their memories suffer instead of improving; a moderate dose is optimal. Similarly, if you are trying to encode, integrate, and remember information for a psychology exam, very high hormone levels could actually interfere with memory. If you want to remember such information well, you should probably aim for an arousal level somewhere between "hyper" and "laid back."

You might be wondering how hormones produced in the adrenal glands can affect the storage of information in the brain. One possibility is that epinephrine causes the level of glucose (a sugar) to rise in the bloodstream. Although epinephrine does not readily enter the brain from the bloodstream, glucose does. Once in the brain, glucose may enhance memory either directly or by altering the effects of neurotransmitters (Gold, 1987). This "sweet memories" effect occurs both in aged rats and mice and in elderly human beings. In one fascinating study, healthy older people fasted overnight, drank a glass of lemonade sweetened with either glucose or saccharin, and then took two memory tests. The saccharine-laced drink had no effect on their performance, but lemonade with glucose greatly boosted their ability to recall a taped passage 5 or 40 minutes after hearing it (Manning, Hall, & Gold, 1990).

However, the exact mechanisms involved in the hormone–memory link remain unclear and controversial. In this area, as in others in the biology of memory, many findings are still provisional, and we have much to learn. No one knows yet exactly how the brain actually stores information, how different memory circuits link up with one another, or how a student is able to locate and retrieve information at the drop of a multiple-choice item.

What Do You Know?

Find out whether your brain has recorded what you just read.

1. Is long-term potentiation associated with (a) increased responsiveness of a receiving neuron to a transmitting neuron, (b) a decrease in receptors on a receiving neuron, or (c) reaching your true potential?

2. The cerebellum has been associated with _____ memories; the hippocampus has been associated with _____ memories.

3. *True or false:* Hormone research suggests that if you want to remember well, you should be as relaxed as possible while learning.

4. After reading about glucose and memory, should you immediately start gulping down lemonade? Why or why not?

ANSWERS:

1. a 2. procedural, declarative 3. false 4. You probably should not pig out on sugar yet. Results from elderly people, using measures of memory on which older people show deficits, may not generalize to younger people with normal memories. Even if the results do generalize, you would need to know how much glucose is effective; in the elderly, there is an optimal dose (Parsons & Gold, 1992). Also, in some people, frequent glucose consumption may have adverse health consequences that would outweigh the benefits.

THE BIOLOGY OF SLEEP AND DREAMS

Earlier we saw that many bodily processes go through cycles, waxing and waning in predictable ways. Perhaps the most perplexing of these biological rhythms is the one governing sleeping and wakefulness. Sleep, after all, puts us at risk: Muscles that are usually ready to respond to danger relax, and senses grow dull. As the late British psychologist Christopher Evans (1984) noted, "The behavior patterns involved in sleep are glaringly, almost insanely, at odds with common sense." Then why is sleep such a profound necessity?

Why We Sleep

One obvious function of sleep is to provide a time-out period, so that the body can eliminate waste products from muscles, repair cells, strengthen the immune system, or recover physical abilities lost during the day. When we do not get enough sleep, our bodies operate abnormally; for example, levels of hormones that are necessary for normal muscle development and proper immune–system functioning decline (Leproult, Copinschi, et al., 1997).

Sleep deprivation that lasts for four days or longer is quite uncomfortable. In animals, forced sleeplessness leads to infections and eventually death (Rechtschaffen et al., 1983), and the same may be true for people. There is a case on record of a man who, at the age of 52, abruptly began to lose sleep. After sinking deeper and deeper into an exhausted stupor, he developed a lung infection and died. An autopsy showed he had lost almost all of the large neurons in two areas of the thalamus that have been linked to sleep and hormonal circadian rhythms (Lugaresi et al., 1986).

Sleep is also necessary for normal mental functioning. After the loss of even a single night's sleep, mental flexibility, attention, and creativity all suffer. In chronic sleep deprivation, high levels of the stress hormone cortisol may damage or impair the brain cells that are necessary for learning and memory (Leproult, Van Reeth, et al., 1997). After several days of staying awake, people may even begin to have hallucinations and delusions (Dement, 1978).

The Realms of Sleep

Until the early 1950s, little was known about the physiology of sleep. Then a breakthrough occurred in the laboratory of physiologist Nathaniel Kleitman, who at the time was the only person in the world who had spent an entire career studying sleep. Kleitman had given one of his graduate students, Eugene Aserinsky, the tedious task of finding out whether the slow, rolling eye movements that characterize the onset of sleep continue throughout the night. To both men's surprise, eye movements did indeed occur, but they were rapid, not slow (Aserinsky & Kleitman, 1955). Using the electroencephalograph to measure the brain's electrical activity, these researchers, along with another of Kleitman's students, William Dement, were able to correlate the rapid eye movements of sleepers with changes in the sleepers' brain-wave patterns. Adult volunteers were soon spending their nights sleeping in laboratories while scientists observed them and measured changes in their brain activity, muscle tension, breathing, and other physiological responses.

As a result of this research, today we know that during sleep, periods of **rapid eye movement (REM)** alternate with periods of fewer eye movements, or *non-REM (NREM)*, in a cycle that occurs about every 90 minutes or so. The REM periods last from a few minutes to as long as an hour, averaging about 20 minutes in length. Whenever they begin, the pattern of electrical activity from the sleeper's brain changes to resemble that of alert wakefulness. Non-REM periods are themselves divided into shorter, distinct stages, each one associated with a particular brain-wave pattern (see Figure 4.14).

When you first climb into bed, close your eyes, and relax, your brain emits bursts of *alpha waves*. On an EEG recording, alpha waves have a regular, slow rhythm and a high amplitude (height). Gradually, these waves slow down even further, and you drift into the Land of Nod, passing through four stages, each one deeper than the previous one.

---

rapid eye movement (REM) sleep Sleep periods characterized by quick eye movements, loss of muscle tone, and dreaming.

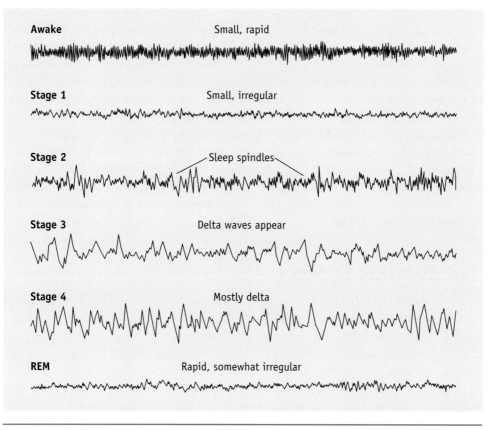

FIGURE 4.14 BRAIN-WAVE PATTERNS DURING WAKEFULNESS AND SLEEP *Most types of brain waves are present throughout sleep, but different ones predominate at different stages.*

◆ *Stage 1.* Your brain waves become small and irregular, and you feel yourself drifting on the edge of consciousness, in a state of light sleep. If awakened, you may recall fantasies or a few visual images.

◆ *Stage 2.* Your brain emits occasional short bursts of rapid, high-peaking waves called *sleep spindles.* Minor noises probably won't disturb you.

◆ *Stage 3.* In addition to the waves characteristic of Stage 2, your brain occasionally emits *delta waves,* very slow waves with very high peaks. Your breathing and pulse have slowed down, your muscles are relaxed, and you are hard to arouse.

◆ *Stage 4.* Delta waves have now largely taken over, and you are in deep sleep. It will probably take vigorous shaking or a loud noise to awaken you. Oddly, though, if you talk or walk in your sleep, this is when you are likely to do so. (The causes of sleepwalking, which occurs more often in children than adults, are still unknown.)

This sequence of stages takes about 30 to 45 minutes. Then you move back up the ladder from Stage 4 to 3 to 2 to 1. At that point, about 70 to 90 minutes after the onset of sleep, something peculiar happens. Stage 1 does not turn into drowsy wakefulness, as one might expect. Instead, your brain begins to emit long bursts of very rapid, somewhat irregular waves. Your heart rate increases, your blood pressure rises, and your breathing becomes faster and more irregular. Small, convulsive twitches in your face and fingers may occur. In men, the penis becomes somewhat erect as vascular tissue relaxes and blood fills the genital area faster than it exits. In women, the clitoris enlarges and vaginal lubrication increases. At the same time, most of your skeletal muscles go limp, preventing your aroused brain from producing physical movement. You have entered the realm of REM.

Because the brain is extremely active while the body is entirely inactive, REM sleep has also been called "paradoxical sleep." It is during these periods that you are most likely to dream. Even people who claim they never dream at all will report dreams if awakened in a sleep laboratory during REM sleep. But dreaming is also often reported during non-REM sleep, though the dreams tend to be shorter and less vivid and fantasy-like.

REM and non-REM sleep continue to alternate throughout the night, with Stages 3 and 4 tending to become shorter or even to disappear, and REM periods tending to get longer and closer together as the hours pass. This pattern explains why you are likely to be dreaming when the alarm goes off in the morning. But the cycles are far from regular. An individual may bounce directly from Stage 4 back to Stage 2, or go from REM to Stage 2 and then back to REM. Also, the time between REM and non-REM is highly variable, differing from person to person and also within any given individual.

The purpose of REM sleep is still a matter of debate, but clearly it does have a purpose. If you wake people every time they lapse into REM sleep, nothing dramatic will happen. When finally allowed to sleep normally, however, they will spend a much longer time than usual in the REM phase. Electrical brain activity associated with REM may burst through into quiet sleep and even into wakefulness. The subjects seem to be making up for something they were deprived of. Many people think that in adults, at least, this "something" has to do with dreaming.

The Dreaming Brain

Why do the images of dreams arise? Why doesn't the brain just rest, switching off all thoughts and images and launching us into a coma? Why, instead, do we spend our nights flying through the air, battling monsters, falling through elevator shafts, or having weird conversations in the fantasy world of our dreams?

Most theories of dreaming have been psychological. Freud (1900/1953) proposed that we dream to gratify unconscious wishes and longings, often sexual or aggressive. Others argue that dreams help us deal with the ongoing emotional preoccupations of waking life, such as anxieties about relationships, work, sex, health, or (in students) exams (Domhoff, 1996; Punamaeki & Joustie, 1998; Webb & Cartwright, 1978). The Student's Nightmare—the kind of dream in which you can't find your classroom or you study hard for a psychology midterm and it turns out to be on Hindu art—is a good example.

But biological theories put the emphasis instead on brain physiology. For example, Francis Crick and Graeme Mitchison (1995) believe that during REM sleep a sort of "reverse learning" occurs; unused synaptic connections in the brain, they say, become weaker, making memory more efficient and accurate and protecting us from becoming obsessed by unwanted thoughts and images. In this view, dreams are merely mental garbage. Other researchers emphasize the strengthening of synaptic connections associated with recently stored memories; they find that disruptions of REM sleep impair memory for a task and normal REM sleep enhances it (Karni et al., 1994). But this approach doesn't really explain dreaming, which is often storylike.

One leading biological theory, the **activation-synthesis theory,** proposed by Allan Hobson (1988, 1990), holds that dreams are not "children of an idle brain," as Shakespeare called them. Rather, they are the result of neurons firing spontaneously in the pons during REM sleep. These neurons control eye movement, gaze, balance, and posture, and they send messages to areas of the cerebral cortex responsible during wakefulness for visual processing and voluntary action.

According to the activation-synthesis theory, the signals originating in the pons have no psychological meaning in themselves. But the cortex tries to make sense of them by *synthesizing,* or integrating, them with existing knowledge and memories to produce some sort of coherent interpretation—just as it would if the signals had come from sense organs during wakefulness. When neurons fire in the part of the brain that handles balance, for instance, the cortex may generate a dream about falling. When signals occur that would ordinarily produce running, the cortex may manufacture a dream about being chased. Because the signals from the pons occur randomly, the cortex's interpretation—the dream—is likely to be incoherent and confusing. And because cortical neurons that control storage of new memories are turned off during sleep, we typically forget our dreams upon waking unless we write them down or immediately recount them to someone else.

Wishes, in this view, do not cause dreams; brain-stem mechanisms do. But that does not mean that dreams are meaningless. Hobson (1988) has argued that the brain "is so inexorably bent upon the quest for meaning that it attributes and even creates meaning when there is little or none to be found in the data it is asked to process." By studying these attributed meanings, you can learn about your unique perceptions, conflicts, and concerns—not by trying to dig below the surface of the dream, as a Freudian would, but by examining the surface itself. Or you can relax and just enjoy the nightly entertainment that dreams provide.

This theory, like all other theories of dreaming, has come in for criticism (Squier & Domhoff, 1998). Not all dreams are as disjointed or as bizarre as the theory predicts. And what about dreams that occur outside of REM sleep? Perhaps it will turn out that different kinds of dreams have different purposes and origins. We all know from experience that some dreams seem related to daily problems, some are vague and incoherent, and some are anxiety dreams that occur when we are tense and worried. Much remains to be learned about the functions of dreaming and even of sleep itself.

---

activation-synthesis theory The theory that dreaming results from the cortical synthesis and interpretation of neural signals triggered by activity in the lower part of the brain.

What Do You Know?

Wake up and answer these questions!

A. Match each term with the appropriate phrase:

1.	REM periods	a.	delta waves and talking in one's sleep
2.	alpha	b.	irregular brain waves and light sleep
3.	Stage 4 sleep	c.	relaxed but awake
4.	Stage 1 sleep	d.	active brain but inactive muscles

B. According to the activation-synthesis theory, dreams arise because of signals initiated in the _____ of the brain, and these signals are then synthesized with existing knowledge by the _____, to produce an interpretation.

ANSWERS:

A. 1. d 2. c 3. a 4. b **B.** pons, cerebral cortex

THE OLDEST QUESTION

When we think about the remarkable blob of tissue in our heads that allows us to remember, to dream, and to think—and to think about our memories, dreams, and thoughts—we are led, inevitably, to a question that people have pondered for thousands of years: Where, exactly, is the self?

When you say, "I am feeling unhappy," your amygdala, your serotonin receptors, your endorphins, and all sorts of other brain parts and processes are active, but who, exactly, is the "I" doing the feeling? When you say, "I've decided to have a hot dog instead of a hamburger," who is the "I" doing the choosing? When you say, "My mind is playing tricks on me," who is the "me" watching your mind play those tricks, and who is it that's being tricked? Isn't the self observing itself a little like a finger pointing at its own tip?

Most religions resolve the problem by teaching that an immortal self or soul exists, entirely apart from the mortal brain. But modern brain scientists usually consider mind to be a matter of matter. They may have personal religious convictions about a soul, but most assume that what we call "mind," "consciousness," or "self-awareness" can be explained in physical terms as a product of the activities of the cerebral cortex. They regard the brain as a fabulous, exceedingly complex machine that will one day be understood in terms of its parts, without reference to some invisible manager pulling the levers; in the words of the British philosopher Gilbert Ryle (1949), there is no "ghost in the machine."

According to some scientists, our conscious sense of a unified self may even be an illusion. Neurologist Richard Restak (1983, 1994) has noted that many of our actions

the MIND-BRAIN Question

"THEN IT'S AGREED—YOU CAN'T HAVE A MIND WITHOUT A BRAIN, BUT YOU CAN HAVE A BRAIN WITHOUT A MIND."

and choices seem to occur without direction by a conscious self. He concludes that "the brains of all creatures are probably organized along the lines of multiple centers and various levels." Cognitive scientist Daniel Dennett (1991) suggests that the brain or mind consists of independent parts that deal with different aspects of thought and perception, constantly conferring with each other and revising their "drafts" of reality. Likewise, Michael Gazzaniga (1985, 1998) proposes that the brain is organized as a loose confederation of independent modules, or mental systems, all working in parallel and most working without our conscious awareness. The sense of a unified self, he says, occurs because one verbal module, an "interpreter" (usually in the left hemisphere), is constantly coming up with theories to explain the actions, moods, and thoughts of the others.

The idea that the brain consists of modules and that the self is an illusion is consistent with the teachings of many Eastern spiritual traditions. Buddhism, for example, teaches that the self is not a unified "thing" but rather a collection of thoughts, perceptions, concepts, and feelings that shift and change from moment to moment. To Buddhists, the unity and the permanence of the self are a mirage. Such notions are contrary, of course, to what most people in the West, including psychologists, have always assumed about their "selves."

Even in these days of modern technology, details about what neural system or systems could be responsible for our sense of self remain hazy. No one yet understands how the inner life of the mind, our subjective sense of experience, is linked to the physical processes of the brain. Some brain-injured patients, like H. M., are unable to store new memories, but they can nonetheless describe what kind of person they have been since the brain damage occurred (Klein & Kihlstrom, 1998). Where in the brain does this capacity to reflect on one's own personality reside?

We are not about to settle here a question that has plagued philosophers for thousands of years. Inevitably, though, as we think about the brain, we must think about how the brain can think about itself. What do you think about the existence and location of your "self" . . . and who, by the way, is doing the thinking? Think about it! ◼

Summary

1. The brain is the bedrock of consciousness, perception, memory, emotion, and reasoning. People debate how to speak about this organ: For example, where is the "you" that is using "your brain"?

2. The function of the nervous system is to gather and process information, produce responses to stimuli, and coordinate the workings of different cells. Scientists divide it into the *central nervous system (CNS)* and the *peripheral nervous system (PNS)*. The CNS, which includes the brain and *spinal cord*, receives, processes, interprets, and stores information and sends messages destined for muscles, glands, and organs. The PNS transmits information to and from the CNS by way of *sensory* and *motor nerves*.

3. The peripheral nervous system consists of the *somatic nervous system*, which permits sensation and voluntary actions, and the *autonomic nervous system*, which regulates blood vessels, glands, and internal (visceral) organs. The autonomic system usually functions without conscious control, although some people can learn to heighten or suppress autonomic responses, using *biofeedback* techniques.

4. The autonomic nervous system is divided into the *sympathetic nervous system*, which mobilizes the body for action, and the *parasympathetic nervous system*, which conserves energy.

5. *Neurons* are the basic units of the nervous system; they are held in place, nourished, and insulated by *glial cells*. Each neuron consists of *dendrites*, a *cell body*, and an *axon* (with its *axon terminals*). In the peripheral nervous system, axons (and sometimes dendrites) are collected together in bundles called *nerves*. Many axons are insulated by a *myelin sheath* that speeds up the conduction of neural impulses and prevents signals in adjacent cells from interfering with one another. Recent research has challenged the old assumption that neurons in the human central nervous system cannot be induced to regenerate or multiply. Scientists have also learned that *precursor cells* in brain areas associated with learning and memory continue to divide and mature throughout adulthood. A stimulating environment seems to enhance this process of *neurogenesis*.

6. Communication between two neurons occurs at the *synapse*. Many synapses have not yet formed at birth. During development, axons and dendrites continue to grow as a result of both physical maturation and experience with the world, and throughout life, new learning results in new synaptic connections in the brain. Thus, the brain's circuits show *plasticity*; they are not fixed and immutable but are continually changing in response to information, challenges, and changes in the environment.

7. When a wave of electrical voltage (*action potential*) reaches the end of a transmitting axon, *neurotransmitter* molecules are released by *synaptic vesicles* into the *synaptic cleft*. When these molecules bind to *receptor sites* on the receiving neuron, that neuron becomes either more or less likely to fire. The message that reaches a final destination depends on how frequently particular neurons are firing, how many are firing, what types are firing, and where they are located.

8. Through their effects on neural circuits, neurotransmitters play a critical role in mood, memory, and psychological well-being. Abnormal levels of neurotransmitters have been implicated in several disorders, including depression, Alzheimer's disease, and Parkinson's disease.

9. *Endorphins,* which act primarily as *neuromodulators* that affect the action of neurotransmitters, reduce pain and promote pleasure. Endorphin levels seem to shoot up when an animal or person is afraid or is under stress. Endorphins may also be linked to the pleasures of social contact.

10. *Hormones,* produced mainly by the *endocrine glands,* affect and are affected by the nervous system. Psychologists are especially interested in *adrenal hormones* such as *cortisol, epinephrine,* and *norepinephrine,* which are involved in arousal, emotions, and stress; *melatonin,* which affects and is affected by the *suprachiasmatic nucleus (SCN)* and thus plays a role in the regulation of *circadian rhythms,* such as the sleep–wake cycle; and the *sex hormones,* which are involved in the physical changes of puberty, the menstrual cycle (*estrogens* and *progesterone*), sexual arousal (*testosterone,* an *androgen*), and some nonreproductive functions—including, many researchers believe, mental functioning.

11. Researchers study the brain by observing patients with brain damage; by using the *lesion method* with animals; and by using such techniques as *electroencephalograms (EEGs), positron-emission tomography (PET scans),* and *magnetic resonance imaging (MRI).*

12. All modern brain theories assume *localization of function.* In the lower part of the brain, in the *brain stem,* the *medulla* controls automatic functions such as heartbeat and breathing, the *pons* is involved in sleeping, waking, and dreaming, and the *reticular activating system (RAS)* screens incoming information and is responsible for alertness. The *cerebellum* contributes to balance and muscle coordination and may also play a role in some higher mental operations.

13. The *thalamus* relays motor impulses to the spinal cord and directs sensory messages to appropriate higher cortical centers. The *hypothalamus* is involved in emotion and in drives associated with survival. It also controls the operations of the autonomic nervous system and sends out chemicals that tell the *pituitary gland* when to "talk" to other endocrine glands.

14. The *limbic system* is involved in emotions that we share with other animals, and it contains pathways involved in pleasure. Within this system, the *amygdala* is responsible for evaluating sensory information and quickly determining its emotional importance (for example, by assessing danger or threat); it is involved in the experience and recognition of fear, and in the initial decision to approach or withdraw from a person or situation. The *hippocampus* plays a critical role in spatial memory and in the formation of long-term memories for facts and events.

15. Much of the brain's circuitry is packed into the *cerebrum,* which is divided into two hemispheres and is covered by thin layers of cells known collectively as the *cerebral cortex.* The *occipital lobes* (containing the *visual cortex*), *parietal lobes* (containing the *somatosensory cortex*), *temporal lobes* (containing the *auditory cortex* and *Wernicke's*

area), and *frontal lobes* (containing the *motor cortex* and *Broca's area*) have specialized functions. The *association cortex* appears to be responsible for higher mental processes. The frontal lobes, particularly areas in the *prefrontal cortex,* are involved in social judgment, the making and carrying out of plans, and decision making.

16. Studies of *split-brain* patients, who have had the *corpus callosum* cut, show that the two *cerebral hemispheres* have somewhat different talents, a phenomenon known as *lateralization.* In most people, language is processed mainly in the left hemisphere, which generally is specialized for logical, symbolic, and sequential tasks. The right hemisphere is associated with spatial-visual tasks, facial recognition, and the creation and appreciation of art and music. Regions of the left hemisphere seem to be specialized for the processing of positive emotions and approaching others, regions of the right hemisphere for negative emotions and withdrawing from others. However, in most mental activities, the two hemispheres cooperate as partners, with each making a valuable contribution.

17. The biological perspective offers insights into the mysteries of memory. Short-term memory appears to involve temporary changes in the ability of neurons to release neurotransmitters; long-term memory involves *long-term potentiation,* a lasting increase in the strength of synaptic responsiveness. Areas of the prefrontal cortex are especially active during short-term memory tasks. The hippocampus (the "gateway to memory") and adjacent areas play a critical role in the formation of long-term *declarative memories* (in contrast to *procedural memories,* which involve other structures), but the various components of a memory are probably stored at different sites in the cortex. Hormones released by the adrenal glands during stress or emotional arousal enhance memory, possibly by increasing glucose levels in the bloodstream, which in turn alter the effects of neurotransmitters. But very high levels of these hormones can interfere with the retention of complex information or tasks; a moderate level is optimal.

18. Biological research is also increasing our understanding of sleep and dreams. Sleep is necessary for normal mental and physical functioning. During sleep, periods of *rapid eye movement (REM)* alternate with *non-REM sleep.* During REM sleep, the brain is active and aroused, yet most of the skeletal muscles are limp; dreams are reported most often in REM sleep. Some researchers emphasize the weakening of unnecessary synaptic connections during REM sleep; others emphasize the strengthening of synaptic changes associated with memory for what has recently been learned. The *activation-synthesis theory* holds that dreams occur when the cortex tries to make sense of spontaneous neural firing initiated in the pons; the resulting interpretation, or synthesis of the signals with existing knowledge and memories, is the dream.

19. One of the oldest questions of all is where the "self" resides. Many brain researchers and cognitive scientists believe that a unified self may be something of an illusion. The brain, they argue, operates as a collection of independent modules or mental systems, perhaps with one of them functioning as an "interpreter." But much remains to be learned about the relationship between the brain and the mind.

Key Terms

Evaluating the Biological Perspective

A few decades ago, biological psychology was still in its infancy. Neurotransmitters were just being discovered, and endorphins were unknown. There were no PET scans or MRIs to help scientists peer into the brain. People suffering from brain disorders were often misdiagnosed as having psychological problems. Behavioral genetics had not yet produced its astonishing findings on the heritability of many human personality traits. The idea of identifying every single human gene would have been ridiculed as science fiction.

No longer. Since the 1970s, our understanding of the nervous system and brain chemistry has expanded astronomically; more has been learned about the brain in the past 25 years than in the previous 250. The biological perspective has given psychologists a new appreciation for the impact of physiology on temperaments, abilities, mental disorders, emotions, and many other aspects of human psychology. Sometimes, as in the study of body weight or autism, biological theories are making purely psychological theories passé. And every month sees new discoveries in genetic research.

CONTRIBUTIONS OF THIS PERSPECTIVE

As biological findings have accumulated, psychology has been moving closer to the life sciences in general, and to biology and neuroscience in particular. Here are a few of the biological perspective's major contributions to psychological science:

1 REJECTION OF EXTREME ENVIRONMENTALISM. For many years following World War II, the prevailing doctrine in psychology was that culture and environment are the primary if not the sole determinants of personality, intelligence, and behavior. This extreme environmentalism was influenced by three interlocking factors: the popularity of behaviorism (see Chapter 5), the optimistic Western belief in equality and the

perfectibility of human nature, and the historical association between biological explanations and racism.

Early in the twentieth century, eugenicists in Europe and North America had argued that government should help improve humanity by discouraging births among the lower classes and others presumed to have genetically inferior traits. Some within the eugenics movement called for the forced sterilization of people with low IQs and for strict limits on immigration. They were inspired by *Social Darwinism,* the theory that the prevailing social order reflects the "survival of the fittest." (The phrase was coined not by Darwin, but by the English political philosopher Herbert Spencer in the 1840s.) These ideas were taken to their extreme during the 1930s and 1940s by the Nazis, who used them as a rationale for exterminating 12 million people they deemed "biologically unfit" and "inferior," including Jews, Gypsies, homosexuals, the mentally ill, and the physically disabled. Nazi doctors also performed horrific "experiments" on their captives, claiming they were doing empirical biological research (Lifton, 1986). When the extent of the Nazi atrocities became known, most scholars turned away in disgust from all biological explanations of human abilities and behavior.

But now the pendulum is swinging back, as people realize that biological research should not be considered "guilty by association"—that it, like any other kind of research, can be used for good or evil. Biological researchers argue that knowledge is worth having for its own sake and that the potential for misusing knowledge is no justification for ignorance or censorship. In their view, a society bent on eliminating its enemies or suppressing a minority group will use any information it can to justify its ends, biological or otherwise. It is true that Hitler chose "the ugly language of eugenics" to rationalize the Holocaust, notes Michael Bailey (1993), but Joseph Stalin did not choose "biological inferiority" as his excuse for massacring millions; instead, he summoned the virtuous language of class revolution and the communist vision of a new egalitarian world. The Bosnian Serbs sought to exterminate their enemies in the name of "ethnic cleansing" on the grounds that their enemies were culturally, not biologically, inferior. In short, a society bent on genocide will use any rationale at hand; the claim that the enemy is biologically inferior is only one of many that tyrants have relied on to justify their actions.

Today, the biological perspective, having rejected extreme environmentalism as an explanation of behavior, reminds us that in spite of our intricate neural wiring and our spectacular mental achievements, human beings have much in common with other species. Like other animals, we are constrained by our evolutionary past: For example, as we will see in Chapter 5, it is easier for us to acquire a fear of spiders than a fear of butterflies, no doubt because during human evolution, spiders were more hazardous to human survival than butterflies were. And the findings of behavioral geneticists and neuroscientists are showing that we cannot hope to understand human personality and performance without taking the brain, the body, and genes into account.

2 **AN APPRECIATION FOR THE ROLE OF PHYSICAL HEALTH IN PSYCHOLOGICAL FUNCTIONING.** The biological perspective teaches us that our bodies and brains need proper care and maintenance to work properly; we interfere with the fine calibration of our biological systems at our peril. Lack of exercise, irregular sleep habits, or work shifts

that interfere with normal biological rhythms can all affect how we function mentally and emotionally. Conversely, good health habits tone the mind as well as the body. Aerobic exercise, for example, tends to decrease a person's physiological arousal to stress and also to reduce anxiety, depression, and irritability (Brown, 1991; McDonald, 1998). In a study of preschoolers, children who did aerobic exercises daily for eight weeks not only had better cardiovascular fitness and agility than children who spent the same time in free play, but they also had higher self-esteem (Alpert et al., 1990).

Biological findings on sleep have also raised public consciousness of the serious sleep deficit that many people suffer. In Chapter 4 we saw that sleep is necessary for normal physical and mental functioning. Not surprisingly, when people are sleepy, traffic and work accidents increase (Coren, 1996; Dement & Vaughan, 1999; Maas, 1998). In 1995, the National Transportation Safety Board reported that tired truck drivers who fall asleep at the wheel are responsible for up to 1,500 road deaths a year in the United States; driver fatigue is a greater safety problem than the use of alcohol or other drugs. Many researchers are also worried about American students, who get only about six hours of sleep a night on average, even though most people need at least eight for optimal performance and adolescents typically need ten. According to sleep researcher James Maas (1998), many students "drag themselves through high school and college like walking zombies . . . moody, lethargic, and unprepared or unable to learn."

Ordinary foods can also affect mood, alertness, and mental performance, because certain nutrients are the precursors of neurotransmitters that are essential to psychological functioning (Wurtman, 1982). For example, tyrosine, an amino acid found in protein-rich foods such as dairy products and meat, is a precursor of norepinephrine, epinephrine, and dopamine; and choline, a component of the lecithin found in egg yolks, soy products, and liver, is a precursor of acetylcholine. Because mental functioning and mood involve many different neurotransmitters, restrictive fad diets—the ones that eliminate all protein, or all carbohydrates, or all whatever—are probably a bad idea in both physiological and psychological terms. So is reliance on whatever health food or nutritional supplement is being promoted at the moment. The best "brain food," and probably the best "mood food," too, is a well-balanced diet—the sort of diet that many children do not get because of poor eating habits or poverty and neglect.

Finally, environmental toxins can affect mental abilities. Exposure to high levels of lead in early childhood is associated with many subsequent, long-lasting problems— low vocabulary and grammatical reasoning scores, slow reaction times, poor hand–eye coordination, low reading scores, attention problems, and aggressiveness—even after other possible factors are taken into account (Needleman et al., 1990, 1996; Stokes et al., 1998). (Although house paint no longer contains lead, poor children often live in rundown buildings with peeling, lead-based paint.)

In sum, then, biological findings have tremendous implications not only for our health, as in the case of sleep deprivation, but also for major social issues, such as the effects of poverty, toxins, and malnutrition on a nation's level of intelligence and its incidence of behavior problems.

3 **A MORE ACCURATE UNDERSTANDING OF SOME MENTAL AND EMOTIONAL DISORDERS.** Because of advances in biology and biological psychology, we now know that many disorders once considered to be purely psychological or the normal result of aging in fact involve genetic, neurological, or biochemical abnormalities.

For example, senility used to be regarded as an inevitable part of aging. But scientists have shown that many cases of apparent senility in the elderly are caused by prescription medications, harmful combinations of medications, and even over-the-counter drugs such as sleeping pills and antihistamines.

Other cases of senility are a result of diseases such as Alzheimer's. The brains of Alzheimer's patients contain abnormal deposits of beta-amyloid, a protein that in certain forms appears to be toxic to nerve cells or to activate other toxic compounds. Several genes have also been implicated in Alzheimer's. Genes on three different chromosomes, when mutated, may cause most cases of early-onset familial (inherited) Alzheimer's, a form of the disease that can strike as early as age 30 (Levy-Lahad et al., 1995; Sherrington et al., 1995). Another gene, on chromosome 19, seems to increase the risk of late-onset Alzheimer's (Corder et al., 1993). Research on the functions of these and several other genes associated with Alzheimer's is helping researchers in their efforts to understand and cure this terrible illness.

The Human Genome Project is also expected to reveal new details about the genetic contributions to mental and emotional disorders. Indeed, in May, 2000, members of the project reported that they had decoded chromosome 21, which is responsible for Down's syndrome, the most common genetic cause of mental retardation (Hattori et al., 2000). Most people with Down's syndrome have an extra copy of chromosome 21 in every cell of their body. In Chapter 12, we will be discussing biological contributions to other mental disorders, including depression, antisocial personality disorder, and schizophrenia. Biological researchers hope that one day, genetic therapies will offer ways of preventing or treating these debilitating conditions.

MISUSES AND LIMITATIONS OF THIS PERSPECTIVE

Advances in biological psychology have been so dazzling that it is easy to get carried away by them. Soon, we think, we'll know the genes for everything from TV watching to math genius! Soon we'll have a drug to fix any part of our personalities we want to change! Soon we'll know just which part of the brain makes some people violent! But hold on; before we go galloping off on the biological highway, we need to consider some potholes that people often stumble into when interpreting and applying the message of this perspective.

1 **BIOLOGICAL REDUCTIONISM.** When considering the accomplishments of this perspective, many people fall victim to *biological reductionism,* the tendency to explain complex personal and social problems solely in terms of a few physiological mechanisms—as

when people speak of the gene "for" this or that condition or the brain structure that "controls" some behavior. Reductionism of any kind distorts and limits our understanding of human behavior, and we will be discussing other forms of reductionism when we evaluate other perspectives. But in today's world, biological reductionism has a special appeal because it promises quick fixes—a pill, a hormone injection, a brain-tissue transplant—for what have seemed to be intractable problems. (In Chapter 12, we will critically evaluate the widespread use of medications for psychological problems.)

You can see biological reductionism at work in the way many people explain women's complaints in contrast to men's. Since the 1970s, a vague cluster of symptoms associated with the days preceding menstruation—including fatigue, headaches, irritability, and depression—has come to be thought of as an illness and has been given a label, *"premenstrual syndrome (PMS)."* Some popular books have asserted, without any evidence whatsoever, that most women suffer from "PMS." But discussions of "PMS" often fail to distinguish between physical and emotional symptoms, and this distinction is crucial. No one disputes that physical symptoms are associated with menstruation, including cramps, breast tenderness, and water retention, although women vary tremendously in this regard. And of course these physical symptoms can make some women feel grumpy or unhappy, just as back pain can make men feel grumpy or unhappy. But the evidence shows that emotional symptoms associated with menstruation are rare, which is why we put "PMS" in quotes. In fact, less than 5 percent of all women have such symptoms predictably over several cycles (Brooks-Gunn, 1986; Reid, 1991).

If true "PMS" is so uncommon, then why do so many women think they have it? For one thing, a woman may tend to notice feelings of depression or irritability when these moods happen to occur premenstrually but overlook times when such moods are *absent* premenstrually. She may label symptoms that occur before a period as "PMS," but attribute the same symptoms at other times of the month to a stressful day or a low grade on an English paper. To overcome these problems, psychologists have polled women about their emotional and physical well-being or have had them keep daily diaries without revealing the true purpose of the study (e.g., Chrisler, 2000; Hardie, 1997; McFarlane, Martin, & Williams, 1988; McFarlane & Williams, 1994; Walker, 1994). They have found that most women do not have the typical "PMS" symptoms or show a consistent "PMS" pattern across menstrual cycles, even when they firmly believe they do. And when researchers have included *men* in their studies of moods over the monthly span, guess what? They find no gender differences in mood swings (see Figure E1.1).

These results are unknown to most people and are usually ignored by doctors, therapists, and the media—so entrenched is the belief that "most women suffer from PMS." An equally popular misconception is that men suffer from "testosterone poisoning"—that testosterone is the most important cause of male anger and aggression. (It's not, as we will see in Chapter 10.) In reality, for most people of both sexes, hormones are only a small part of the story. The promise of a simple biological explanation for people's feelings of anger or frustration holds great appeal for many men and women, but it is a classic instance of biological reductionism.

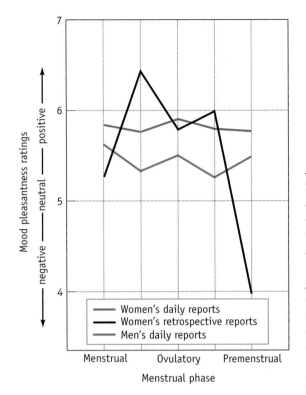

FIGURE E1.1 MOOD CHANGES IN MEN AND WOMEN *Women and men recorded their moods daily for 70 days without knowing the purpose of the study. Later, many women said they had been grumpier and more depressed premenstrually, but their own diaries did not bear them out. Both sexes experienced only moderate mood changes, and there were no significant differences between women and men at any time of the month (McFarlane, Martin, & Williams, 1988).*

2 PREMATURE CONCLUSIONS. Science is a slow, painstaking process, but sudden dramatic breakthroughs make better headlines. As a result, the media often overstate biological findings or leap to conclusions on the basis of only one or two studies. And the public, eager for quick answers, follows suit.

Thus, each time researchers think they have located a possible genetic marker or gene associated with some trait or disorder, the media announce that "the" gene for such-and-such has been found. But in many cases, further research has failed to replicate the initial finding. Everyone got excited when a gene was reported for bipolar disorder (manic depression); the finding was not replicated. A gene was reported for a kind of alcoholism—but the finding was not replicated. A gene was reported for sensation-seeking—not replicated. A marker was reported for sexual orientation in gay men with gay relatives—not replicated. A gene was reported for chronic worrying; don't worry about it. Biological findings, like psychological ones, require replication.

People are especially likely to rush to conclusions about biology and behavior when findings seem to support common assumptions about hot topics like gender differences. In 1982, two anthropologists autopsied 14 human brains and reported an average sex difference in the size and shape of the splenium, a small section at the end of the corpus callosum (the bundle of fibers dividing the two hemispheres) (de Lacoste-Utamsing & Holloway, 1982). The researchers concluded that women's brains are less lateralized for certain tasks than men's are—that men rely more heavily on one or the other side of the brain, whereas women tend to use both sides. This news was received with as much excitement as if a cure for the common cold had just been discovered. The study quickly made its way into newspapers, magazines, and even textbooks as a verified sex difference.

Today, however, we know more. In a review of the available studies, neuroscientist William Byne (1993) found that only the 1982 study reported the splenium to be larger in women. Two very early studies (in 1906 and 1909) found that it was larger in men, and 21 later studies found no sex difference at all. Findings on the shape of the splenium were also mixed: Four studies found the splenium to be more bulb-shaped in women; 1 found it to be more bulbous in men; and 6 studies found no sex difference. Likewise, a Canadian meta-analysis of 49 studies found only trivial differences between the two sexes, differences that paled in comparison with the huge individual variations within each sex (Bishop & Wahlsten, 1997). These findings did *not* make their way into most newspapers, magazines, and textbooks.

Reports of other male–female brain differences have also generated premature conclusions. In one study, 19 men and 19 women were asked to say whether pairs of nonsense words rhymed; MRI scans showed that in both sexes, an area at the front of the left hemisphere was activated. However, in 11 of the women and none of the men, the corresponding area in the right hemisphere was also active (Shaywitz et al., 1995). This finding appears to be further evidence for a sex difference in lateralization, at least for this type of task, but many questions remain unanswered. For example, why were some women, but not all, using both hemispheres? Lots of people have joked about these results ("No wonder men won't ask for directions—they can't even find their way across their own brains!" or "No wonder women's thinking is so fuzzy, unfocused, and intuitive!"). But few have paused to ask whether the findings have any implications for anyone's behavior *in real life.* In fact, in this study the men and women performed equally well on the rhyming task despite the differences in their MRIs. So what do those brain differences actually mean for anyone's behavior? No one knows. Speculations are as plentiful as ants at a picnic, but at present they remain just that—speculations (Blum, 1997; Hoptman & Davidson, 1994).

While it is important, therefore, to keep an open mind about new biological findings, it is also important to be aware of how the implications of such findings might be exaggerated.

3 UNWARRANTED INFERENCES ABOUT CAUSE AND EFFECT. Whenever people evaluate findings from biological psychology, especially correlational findings, they need to ask, in this case, is biology influencing behavior, or is it the other way around? Or both? Although the brain affects how we experience the world, we must never forget that experience also shapes and alters the brain. Consider a few examples:

✦ Bilingual people who learned both of their languages in childhood use a single uniform Broca's area when generating complex sentences in both languages; but in people who learned a second language during adolescence, Broca's area is divided into two distinct regions, one for each language (Kim et al., 1997).

◆ Years of musical training in childhood literally change the parts of the brain associated with music production (Jancke, Schlaug, & Steinmetz, 1997), as we will discuss further in Essay 6.

◆ A study of London cabdrivers found a direct relation between the size of the cabbies' posterior hippocampus, thought to store visual representations of the environment, and number of years spent driving in London (Maguire et al., 2000).

◆ Rats that learn complicated tasks or grow up playing with lots of challenging rat toys develop thicker and heavier cortexes and richer networks of synaptic connections in certain brain areas than do rats that grow up in unchallenging environments (Diamond, 1993; Greenough & Anderson, 1991; Greenough & Black, 1992; Rosenzweig, 1984). As we saw in Chapter 4, physical and mental exercise also enhance the production and survival of precursor cells in the central nervous system. These changes continue throughout life as long as the animal is in a stimulating environment.

There is also some evidence that practice on specific tasks can make the brain more efficient. PET-scan studies show that during certain intellectual tasks the brains of high performers are less active, metabolizing glucose at a lower rate than those of low performers (Haier et al., 1988; Parks et al., 1988). But is such a neurologically efficient brain the cause or the result of superior performance? The second interpretation is supported by a study in which people played a computer game over a period of several weeks. As the study progressed, their glucose metabolism rates during the sessions gradually fell (Haier et al., 1992).

These results point to an exciting—and to most people surprising—contribution of the biological perspective. Whereas many people assume that our brains determine our abilities, this work suggests that the kinds of experiences and environments we have affect our brains, to our detriment or our advantage.

4 BIOLOGICAL POLITICS. Biological findings are often cited for political purposes, as if there were a direct link between the findings and the implications for social or public policy. Of course, no research is conducted in a social and moral vacuum, nor could it be. But biological findings, which hold so much promise, also have great potential for being misinterpreted and misused for political purposes (Fausto-Sterling, 1985, 2000; Gould, 1996; Hubbard & Wald, 1993). That is why they often generate such controversy.

In general, people who are politically or socially conservative are drawn to genetic and evolutionary theories of behavior because such findings seem to support their view that male dominance, group differences in some skill or ability, and social hierarchies separating rich and poor are ordained "by nature." For example, as we saw in Chapter 3, some conservatives have misinterpreted heritability studies to argue against the use of public funds for remedial education. And Edward Wilson (1975), one of the leading proponents of sociobiology, once wrote that because of genetics, "even with identical education and equal access to all professions [for both sexes], men are likely to continue to play a disproportionate role in political life, business, and science." This is not a message that people who hope for gender equality welcome!

Liberals and egalitarians, believing in the possibility of social and economic equality between ethnic groups and the sexes, thus often feel constrained to fight vigorously against biological explanations. For example, they fear that research on a possible link between genes and criminal violence will be used to foster racism, stigmatize poor people, and draw attention and resources away from the economic and environmental causes of aggression and crime. In 1995, when the University of Maryland hosted an interdisciplinary conference on "The Meaning and Significance of Research on Genetics and Criminal Behavior," protesters disrupted the proceedings, even though the conference participants included critics as well as supporters of such research.

As long as people have passionate political commitments, they will tend to interpret research—any research—in light of what they believe. Indeed, biological findings themselves can often be used for conservative *or* liberal purposes, depending on the point of view of the people interpreting them.

For instance, consider the emotionally sensitive question of the origins of homosexuality. Exclusively *psychological* theories of sexual orientation have never been supported; homosexuality is not a result of having a "smothering mother," an absent father, homosexual role models, or emotional problems, as was once thought. Homosexuality has occurred in cultures throughout history and around the world, regardless of whether it has been barely tolerated, actively encouraged, or violently suppressed. Many gay men recall that they rejected boys' toys, games, and activities from an early age, in spite of enormous pressures from their parents and peers to conform to the traditional male role (Bailey & Zucker, 1995). Many researchers, therefore, have been turning to biological explanations of sexual orientation. Some studies have found evidence of moderate heritability in homosexuals, particularly men (Bailey & Pillard, 1995; Gladue, 1994). A few studies have reported differences in specific brain structures in gay and straight men (e.g., Allen & Gorski, 1992); and others have suggested that girls who were accidentally exposed to masculinizing hormones in the womb have an increased likelihood of becoming bisexual or lesbian (e.g., Meyer-Bahlburg et al., 1995).

However, the evidence for biological origins of homosexuality is still inconclusive and has been extremely difficult to replicate (Rice et al., 1999). The vast majority of gay men and lesbians do not have a close gay relative, and their siblings are overwhelmingly likely to be heterosexual. The large majority of "androgenized" women do not become lesbians, and most lesbians were not exposed to atypical prenatal hormones (Peplau et al., 1999; Peplau & Spalding, 2000). Further, many people (especially women) cannot be classified as exclusively homosexual or heterosexual because they have intimate experiences with partners of the same or the other sex at different times in their lives (Baumeister, 2000; Byne, 1995; Herdt, 1984). And so the origins of sexual orientation remain uncertain.

Many gay men and lesbians have welcomed biological theories on the grounds that these theories support what they have been saying all along: that sexual orientation is a fact of nature, not a matter of choice. Others, however, reject biological theories because they fear that religious fundamentalists will argue that gay people have a biological "defect" that should be "corrected." (Indeed, that is the view held by the popular talk-show host Laura Schlessinger.)

In this debate, you can see that it is *people's own attitudes toward homosexuality,* not research findings themselves, that determine whether they interpret biological findings on sexual orientation in "liberal" or "conservative" ways. Evidence that sexual orientation is a "fact of nature" can be used to help people understand that homosexuality is a universal human variation, like being left-handed; or it can be used to try to eradicate the "problem," as teachers and parents once tried to do by forcing left-handed children to use their right hands only. (It didn't work.)

Similarly, evidence that some extremely violent delinquents are brain damaged (perhaps as a result of drug use, parental blows to the head, or a genetic mutation) can be used to support programs designed to prevent or treat this problem, or it can be used to screen and stigmatize children who are merely "potentially" aggressive and to shut off funding for the study of other causes of violence. Genetic engineering, which is revolutionizing the biomedical world, can be used to eradicate horrendous diseases; gene therapy has recently been used, apparently successfully, to treat three infants who would otherwise have died within a year of immune disorders. But genetic engineering can also be used to eradicate perfectly normal human variations that some people regard as a social disadvantage, such as being shorter than average.

In sum, it is important to distinguish *scientific* questions about the biology of behavior from their *political or moral* implications (Strickland, 1995). Biological findings do not absolve either individuals or society of the responsibility for making wise political, social, and moral decisions.

What Do You Know?

1. Name three major contributions of the biological perspective.

2. Almost overnight, your 80-year-old grandmother has become confused and delusional. Before concluding that old age has made her senile or that she has Alzheimer's, what other explanation(s) should you rule out?

3. Name four common misuses of biological findings on behavior.

4. Biological reductionism is (a) the tendency to minimize the importance of biology in human functioning, (b) the reduction of complicated biological findings to a few psychological principles, (c) the reduction of complex social and personal issues to a few biological mechanisms, (d) the successful explanation of psychological findings in terms of biological processes.

ANSWERS:

1. rejection of extreme environmentalism; evidence for the role of health in physical and mental functioning; better understanding of the biological contributions to mental and emotional disorders. 2. Of course, there are many possible causes, including stroke. But you should rule out the possibility that she is taking too many medications or nonprescription drugs. 3. biological reductionism; premature conclusions; unwarranted inferences about cause and effect; and "biological politics." 4. c

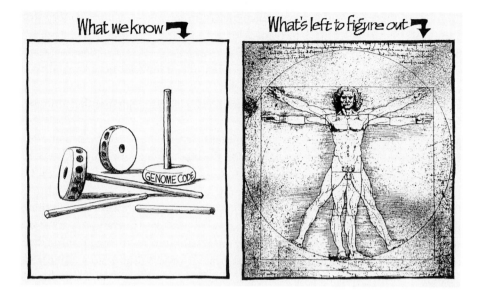

The biological perspective has vastly broadened our understanding of mental disorders and normal functioning. There is no disputing that the more we know about our physical selves—our genes, our hormones, our neurotransmitters, our neurons—the better we will understand our psychological selves. The challenge is to learn from biology without oversimplifying it. In evaluating the biological perspective, therefore, we must draw on principles of critical thinking. In particular, we must be wary of media hype, avoid premature conclusions, examine unwarranted political uses of findings, resist the temptation to "overbiologize," and, as in the case of homosexuality, live with uncertainty when we do not have "the" answers.

Analyzing a human being in terms of physiology alone is like analyzing the Taj Mahal solely in terms of the materials that were used to build it. Physiological findings are always most illuminating when they are integrated with what we know about personal development and cultural context. Even if we could monitor every cell and circuit of the brain, we would not know how we came to be who we are. We would still need to understand the circumstances, thoughts, and cultural rules that affect whether we are gripped by hatred, consumed by grief, lifted by love, or transported by joy. ■

Summary

1. Biological findings have multiplied astronomically in the past few decades, and the biological perspective is giving people a new appreciation for the role of physiology in temperaments, abilities, mental disorders, emotions, and many other aspects of psychology. This perspective shows that human beings, like other animals, are constrained by their evolutionary past and are a product, in part, of their genes, neurons, and biochemistry.

2. Among this perspective's major contributions to psychology are rejection of the extreme environmentalism that prevailed for many years (in part as a reaction to *Social Darwinism*); an appreciation for the role of physical health in psychological functioning; and new insights into biochemical and genetic factors in mental and emotional disorders.

3. This perspective and its findings can also be misused. Many people fall into the trap of *biological reductionism,* the tendency to explain complex personal and social problems solely in terms of a few physiological mechanisms, as in the acceptance of *"PMS"* as a widespread condition that explains women's feelings of anger or frustration and "testosterone poisoning" as an explanation of men's anger and aggressiveness.

4. In interpreting biological findings, people often jump to premature conclusions (for example, about the implications of reported sex differences in the brain); draw unwarranted inferences about cause and effect (for example, by assuming that the brain affects performance on mental tasks without also considering that experience and training affect brain functioning); and use findings for political purposes (as in the example of research on sexual orientation).

Key Terms

Social Darwinism   169

biological reductionism   171

"premenstrual syndrome (PMS)"   172

PART III

The Learning
Perspective

On a hot summer day, James Peters shot and killed his next-door neighbor, Ralph Galluccio. Peters had reached the end of his patience in an acrimonious 10-year dispute with Galluccio over their common property line. Shocked friends insisted that this feud was not predictable from the men's personalities. Galluccio, his employer reported, was "a likable person with a good, even disposition." Peters, said his employer, was a "very mild-mannered, cooperative" man, an "all-around good guy."

How on earth could two "nice" men like James Peters and Ralph Galluccio get into such an irrational and ultimately tragic argument? Whereas a psychologist in the biological perspective might look for clues in the men's testosterone levels or inherited temperaments, a psychologist in the learning perspective would emphasize each man's past learning and present environment. In the learning view, past learning explains why each of us winds up with the thousands of qualities and talents that commonly go by the name "personality"—why we become liberals or conservatives, rock fans or Bach buffs, gourmet cooks or fast-food fanatics, optimists or pessimists. A learning theorist, therefore, would want to know about the particular circumstances of the Peters–Galluccio feud, as well as each man's past to explain why, when hurled insults and then hurled eggs failed to bring about a resolution, all they knew how to do was to behave more violently.

Research in the learning perspective has been heavily influenced by *behaviorism,* the school of psychology that accounts for behavior in terms of observable acts and events without reference to mental entities such as "mind" or "will." Behaviorists regard such hypothetical entities as fictions; as William Baum (1994) explained, "I no more have a mind than I have a fairy godmother. I can talk to you about my mind or about my fairy godmother; that cannot make either of them less fictional. No one has ever seen either one . . . such talk is no help in a science."

For almost half a century, until the 1960s, behaviorism was *the* approach to learning. (Detractors of behaviorism like to say that during this period, psychology "lost its mind.") Today, however, other approaches, known as *social-cognitive learning theories,* continue to recognize the importance of the environment but hold that omitting mental processes from explanations of human learning is like omitting passion from descriptions of sex: You may explain the form, but you miss the substance.

In Chapter 5 we are going to take a look at some of the many principles of learning uncovered by behavioral studies, including the work of two remarkable scientists, Ivan Pavlov and B. F. Skinner. Then, in Chapter 6, we will see how social-cognitive learning theorists and other researchers have expanded on behavioral principles and added social and cognitive variables to the learning equation.

CHAPTER FIVE

Behavioral Learning

*H*ow would you explain the following incidents?

✦ A dentist decides to soothe the fears of his youngest patients by showing them animated cartoons while he drills their teeth. He thinks that if the children are distracted, they will relax and lose their fear. But decades later, a former patient, now an adult, describes an unforeseen result: "After all these years," he says, "I still can't stand watching cartoons."

✦ It's January 1, and a struggling student decides to reform his study habits. "This semester I *am* going to get all A's," he vows. "I'm going to work harder and longer every day." But within a few weeks he is back to his regular pattern, which he can't seem to change. "I just don't have the willpower to make it," he decides.

✦ A young mother's two little girls are constantly whining and quarreling, and mornings have become intolerable. When the mother wakens them, the older girl complains angrily, demands to know what's for breakfast, and orders her younger sister out of the room. This makes the younger child burst into tears. Sometimes the mother responds to her daughters' fighting by shouting at them herself; at other times she tries to smother her anger and help them resolve their conflicts. Their misbehavior only increases.

In each of these cases, an intention has missed its mark. The reason, a **behaviorist** would say, is that the dentist, the student, and the mother have all misapplied or ignored certain basic laws of learning—laws that you are going to read about in this chapter.

In ordinary speech, "learning" usually refers to classroom activities, such as memorizing the facts of geography, or to the acquisition of practical skills, such as carpentry or sewing. But to psychologists, learning is *any* relatively permanent change in behavior that occurs because of experience (except for changes due to fatigue, injury, or disease). Experience is the great teacher, providing the essential link between the past and the future, enabling an organism to adapt to changing circumstances in order to survive and thrive. Our species is more dependent on learning than is any other, but learning is a fundamental process in all animals, from the lowliest backyard bug to the most eminent human scholar.

In this chapter, we are going to explore a basic kind of learning called **conditioning,** which involves associations between environmental stimuli (Ss) and responses (Rs). Behaviorists have shown that two types of conditioning, *classical conditioning* and *operant conditioning,* can explain much of human behavior.

CLASSICAL CONDITIONING

At the turn of the century, the great Russian physiologist Ivan Pavlov (1849–1936) was studying salivation in dogs as part of a research program on digestion. His work would shortly win him the Nobel Prize in physiology and medicine. One of Pavlov's procedures was to make a surgical opening in a dog's cheek and insert a tube that conducted saliva away from the animal's salivary gland so that the saliva could be measured. To stimulate the reflexive flow of saliva, Pavlov placed meat powder or other food in the dog's mouth. This procedure was later refined by others, who used an apparatus in which salivation was measured by the movement of a needle on a revolving drum.

Pavlov was a truly dedicated scientific observer; many years later, as he lay dying, he even dictated his sensations for posterity! And he imbued his students with the same kind of attention to detail. During the salivation studies, one of these students noticed something that most people would have overlooked or dismissed as trivial. After a dog had been brought to the laboratory a number of times, it would start to salivate *before* the food was placed in its mouth. The sight or smell of the food, the dish in which the food was kept, even the sight of the person who delivered the food each day or the sound of the person's footsteps were enough to start the dog's mouth watering. This new salivary response clearly was not inborn, so it had to have been acquired through experience.

At first, Pavlov treated the dog's drooling as just an annoying secretion. But he quickly realized that his student had stumbled onto an important phenomenon, one that Pavlov came to believe was the basis of a great deal of learning in human beings and other animals. He called that phenomenon a "conditional" reflex—conditional because it depended on environmental conditions. Later, an error in the translation of his writings transformed "conditional" into "conditioned," the word most commonly used today.

---

behaviorism An approach to psychology that emphasizes the study of observable behavior and the role of the environment as a determinant of behavior.

conditioning A basic kind of learning that involves associations between environmental stimuli and the organism's responses.

Pavlov soon dropped what he had been doing and turned to the study of conditioned reflexes, to which he devoted the last three decades of his life. Why were his dogs salivating to aspects of the environment other than food?

New Reflexes from Old

Pavlov initially speculated about what his dogs might be thinking and feeling to make them drool before getting their food. Was the doggy equivalent of "Oh boy, this means chow time" going through their minds? Eventually, however, he decided that such speculation was pointless (Todes, 1997). Instead, he focused on analyzing the environment in which the conditioned reflex arose. The original salivary reflex, according to Pavlov, consisted of an **unconditioned stimulus (US),** food, and an **unconditioned response (UR),** salivation. By an *unconditioned stimulus,* Pavlov meant an event or thing that elicits a response automatically or reflexively. By an *unconditioned response,* he meant the response that is automatically produced:

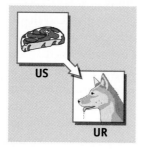

Learning occurs, said Pavlov, when a neutral stimulus is regularly paired with an unconditioned stimulus:

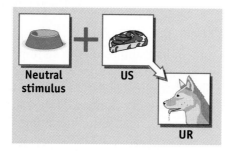

---

unconditioned stimulus (US) The classical-conditioning term for a stimulus that elicits a reflexive response in the absence of learning.

unconditioned response (UR) The classical-conditioning term for a reflexive response elicited by a stimulus in the absence of learning.

The neutral stimulus then becomes a **conditioned stimulus (CS),** which elicits a learned or **conditioned response (CR)** that is usually similar to the original, unlearned one. In Pavlov's laboratory, the sight of the food dish, which had not previously elicited salivation, became a CS for salivation:

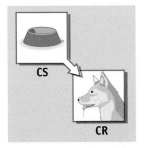

The procedure by which a neutral stimulus becomes a conditioned stimulus became known as **classical conditioning,** also called *Pavlovian* or *respondent conditioning.* Pavlov and his students went on to show that all sorts of things can become conditioned stimuli for salivation if they are paired with food: the ticking of a metronome, the musical tone of a bell or tuning fork, the vibrating sound of a buzzer, a triangle drawn on a large card, even a pinprick or an electric shock. And since Pavlov's day, many automatic, involuntary responses besides salivation have been classically conditioned—for example, heartbeat, stomach secretions, blood pressure, reflexive movements, blinking, and muscle contractions. The optimal interval between the presentation of the neutral stimulus and the presentation of the US depends on the kind of response involved; in the laboratory, the interval is often less than a second.

Principles of Classical Conditioning

Classical conditioning occurs in all species, from worms to *Homo sapiens.* Let us look more closely at how four of the most important classical-conditioning processes work: extinction, higher-order conditioning, and stimulus generalization and discrimination.

Extinction.   Conditioned responses do not necessarily last forever. If, after conditioning, the conditioned stimulus is repeatedly presented without the unconditioned stimulus,

---

conditioned stimulus (CS) The classical-conditioning term for an initially neutral stimulus that comes to elicit a conditioned response after being associated with an unconditioned stimulus.

conditioned response (CR) The classical-conditioning term for a response that is elicited by a conditioned stimulus; it occurs after the conditioned stimulus is associated with an unconditioned stimulus.

classical conditioning The process by which a previously neutral stimulus acquires the capacity to elicit a response through association with a stimulus that already elicits a similar or related response; also called *Pavlovian* or *respondent conditioning.*

the conditioned response eventually disappears, and **extinction** is said to have occurred. Suppose that you train your dog Sophie to salivate to the sound of a bell, but then you ring the bell every five minutes and do *not* follow it with food. Sophie will salivate less and less to the bell and will soon stop salivating altogether; salivation will have been extinguished. However, if you come back the next day and ring the bell, Sophie may salivate again for a few trials. The reappearance of the response, which is called **spontaneous recovery,** explains why completely eliminating a conditioned response usually requires more than one extinction session.

Higher-Order Conditioning.   Sometimes a neutral stimulus can become a conditioned stimulus by being paired with an already established CS, a procedure known as **higher-order conditioning.** Say that Sophie has learned to salivate to the ringing of a bell. Now you flash a bright light before you ring the bell. With repeated pairings of the light and the bell, Sophie may learn to salivate to the light, although the light will probably elicit less salivation than the bell does. This procedure is shown below:

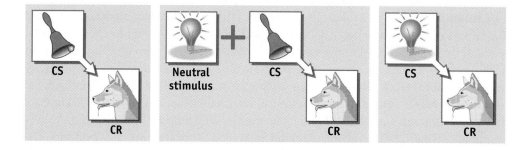

Higher-order conditioning may explain why some words trigger emotional responses in us—why they can inflame us to anger or evoke warm sentimental feelings. When words are paired with objects or other words that already elicit some emotional response, they, too, may come to elicit that response (Chance, 1999; Staats & Staats, 1957). For example, a child may learn a positive response to the word *birthday* because of its association with gifts and attention. Conversely, the child may learn a negative response to ethnic or national labels, such as *Swede, Turk,* or *Jew,* if those words are paired with words that the child has already learned are disagreeable, such as *dumb* or *dirty.* Higher-order conditioning, in other words, may contribute to the formation of prejudices.

---

extinction   The weakening and eventual disappearance of a learned response; in classical conditioning, it occurs when the conditioned stimulus is no longer paired with the unconditioned stimulus.

spontaneous recovery   The reappearance of a learned response after its apparent extinction.

higher-order conditioning   In classical conditioning, a procedure in which a neutral stimulus becomes a conditioned stimulus through association with an already established conditioned stimulus.

Stimulus Generalization and Discrimination.   After a stimulus becomes a conditioned stimulus for some response, other, similar stimuli may produce a similar reaction—a phenomenon known as **stimulus generalization.** For example, if you condition your patient pooch Sophie to salivate to middle C on the piano, she may also salivate to D, which is one tone above C, even though you did not pair D with food. Stimulus generalization is described nicely by an old English proverb: "He who hath been bitten by a snake fears a rope."

The mirror image of stimulus generalization is **stimulus discrimination,** in which *different* responses are made to stimuli that resemble the conditioned stimulus in some way. Suppose that you have conditioned Sophie to salivate to middle C on the piano by repeatedly pairing the sound with food. Now you play middle C on a guitar, *without* following it by food (but you continue to follow C on the piano by food). Eventually, Sophie will learn to salivate to a C on the piano and not to salivate to the same note on the guitar; that is, she will discriminate between the two sounds. If you keep at this long enough, you could train Sophie to be a pretty discriminating drooler.

What Is Actually Learned in Classical Conditioning?

For classical conditioning to be most effective, the stimulus to be conditioned should *precede* the unconditioned stimulus rather than follow it or occur simultaneously with it. This makes sense, because in classical conditioning, the conditioned stimulus becomes a kind of signal for the unconditioned stimulus. It enables the organism to prepare for an event that is about to happen. In Pavlov's studies, for instance, a bell or a buzzer was a signal that meat was coming, and the dog's salivation was preparation for digesting food.

Today, therefore, many psychologists contend that what an animal or person actually learns in classical conditioning is not merely an association between two paired stimuli that occur close together in time, but rather *information* conveyed by one stimulus about another: For instance, "If a tone sounds, food is likely to follow" (Davey, 1992). This view is supported by the research of Robert Rescorla (1988), who showed, in a series of imaginative studies, that the mere pairing of an unconditioned stimulus and a neutral stimulus is not enough to produce learning. To become a conditioned stimulus, the neutral stimulus must reliably signal, or *predict,* the unconditioned stimulus. If food occurs just as often without a preceding tone as with it, the tone is unlikely to become a conditioned stimulus for salivation—because the tone does not provide any information about the probability of getting food.

---

stimulus generalization After conditioning, the tendency to respond to a stimulus that resembles one involved in the original conditioning; in classical conditioning, it occurs when a stimulus that resembles the CS elicits the CR.

stimulus discrimination The tendency to respond differently to two or more similar stimuli; in classical conditioning, it occurs when a stimulus similar to the CS fails to evoke the CR.

In everyday life, too, a potential CS may sometimes predict an unconditioned stimulus and sometimes not, so conditioning is less certain than when the CS and US always occur together in the laboratory. A friend of ours, behaviorist Paul Chance, gave us this example: Suppose you work in an office where you are allowed to receive calls only from other employees; you may take other calls only in emergencies. One day, your lover calls to jilt you; the police call to report that your new car was stolen; and your landlord calls to tell you that a broken water pipe has flooded your apartment. If these were the only calls you got, the next time you heard the phone ring (the CS), you might freak out (the CR). But if they occurred randomly among 50 routine business calls, the phone's ringing would probably not upset you because it would not necessarily signal another disaster.

Rescorla (1988) concluded that "Pavlovian conditioning is not a stupid process by which the organism willy-nilly forms associations between any two stimuli that happen to co-occur. Rather, the organism is better seen as an information seeker using logical and perceptual relations among events, along with its own preconceptions, to form a sophisticated representation of its world." Not all learning theorists agree with this conclusion; an orthodox behaviorist would say that it is silly to talk about the preconceptions of an animal. The important point, however, is that concepts such as "information seeking," "preconceptions," and "representations of the world" open the door to a more cognitive view of classical conditioning.

What Do You Know?

Classical-conditioning terms can be tough to learn, so be sure to take this quiz before going on.

1. Five-year-old Samantha is watching a storm from her window. A huge bolt of lightning is followed by a tremendous thunderclap, and Samantha jumps at the noise. This happens several more times. There is a brief lull and then another lightning bolt. Samantha jumps in response to the bolt.

2. After he is bitten by a German shepherd, Shaun's heart speeds up whenever he sees a dog of that breed—and it also speeds up whenever he sees a Labrador retriever. This is an example of (a) stimulus discrimination, (b) stimulus generalization, (c) higher-order conditioning, (d) extinction.

3. In the view of many learning theorists, pairing a neutral and unconditioned stimulus is not enough to produce classical conditioning; the neutral stimulus must _____ the unconditioned stimulus.

ANSWERS:

1. UC = the thunderclap; UR = jumping elicited by the noise; CS = the sight of the lightning; CR = jumping elicited by the lightning 2. b 3. signal or predict

CLASSICAL CONDITIONING IN REAL LIFE

If a dog can learn to salivate to the ringing of a bell, so can you. In fact, you probably have learned to salivate to the sound of a lunch bell, not to mention the phrase *hot fudge sundae,* "mouth-watering" pictures of food in magazines, and a voice calling out, "Dinner's ready!" But the role of classical conditioning goes far beyond the learning of simple observable reflexes; conditioning affects us every day in many ways.

One of the first psychologists to recognize the real-life implications of Pavlovian theory was John B. Watson, who founded American behaviorism and enthusiastically promoted Pavlov's ideas. Watson believed that the whole rich array of human emotion and behavior could be accounted for by conditioning principles. For example, he argued that learning to love a parent or a lover was no different from learning to salivate to the sound of a bell. It was just a matter of pairing unconditioned stimuli (stroking, cuddling, kissing) with the person doing the stroking and cuddling. (Watson, who was married five times, apparently tried many different pairings.)

Watson turned out to be wrong about love, which is a lot more complicated than he thought. But he was right about the power of classical conditioning to affect our emotions, preferences, and tastes.

Learning to Like

Classical conditioning plays a big role in our emotional responses to objects, symbols, events, and places. It can explain why sentimental feelings sweep over us when we see a school mascot, a national flag, or the logo of the Olympic games. We have learned to experience these emotions because in the past, these objects have been associated with positive feelings.

Many Madison Avenue techniques for getting us to like advertisers' products are also based on the principles first demonstrated by Pavlov, whether advertising executives realize it or not. In one study, college students looked at slides of either a beige pen or a blue pen. During the presentation, half of the students heard a song from a recent American musical film, and half heard a selection of traditional music from India. (The experimenter made the reasonable assumption that the American music would be more appealing to the young Americans in the study.) Later the students were allowed to choose one of the pens. Almost three-fourths of those who heard the popular music chose a pen that was the same color as the one they had seen in the slides. An equal number of those who heard the Indian music chose a pen that *differed* in color from the one they had seen (Gorn, 1982).

In classical-conditioning terms, the music in this study was an unconditioned stimulus for internal responses associated with pleasure or displeasure, and the pens became conditioned stimuli for similar responses. You can see why television commercials often pair their products with music, attractive people, or other appealing sounds and images.

Learning to Fear

Positive emotions are not the only ones that can be classically conditioned; so can dislikes and negative emotions such as fear. A person can learn to fear just about anything if it is paired with something that elicits pain, surprise, or embarrassment. But human beings are biologically primed to acquire some fears more easily than others. It is far easier to establish a conditioned fear of spiders, snakes, and heights than of butterflies, flowers, and toasters. The former can be dangerous to your health, and in the process of evolution, human beings therefore acquired a tendency to be wary of them.

When fear of an object or situation becomes irrational and interferes with normal activities, it qualifies as a *phobia*. To demonstrate how a phobia might be learned, John Watson and Rosalie Rayner (1920) deliberately established a rat phobia in an 11-month-old boy named Albert. For ethical reasons, no psychologist today would do such a thing to a child. Nevertheless, the study remains a classic, and its main conclusion, that fears can be conditioned, is still well accepted.

"Little Albert" was a placid child who rarely cried. When Watson and Rayner gave him a furry white rat to play with (a live one, not a toy), Albert showed no fear; in fact, he was delighted. However, like most children, Albert was afraid of loud noises. When the researchers made a loud noise behind his head by striking a steel bar with a hammer, he would jump and fall sideways onto the mattress he was sitting on. The noise made by the hammer was an unconditioned stimulus for the unconditioned response of fear.

Having established that Albert liked rats, Watson and Rayner set about teaching him to fear them. Again they offered him a rat, but this time, as Albert reached for it, one of the researchers struck the steel bar. Startled, Albert fell onto the mattress. The researchers repeated this procedure several times. Albert began to whimper and tremble. Finally, they held out the rat to him without making the noise. Albert fell over, cried, and crawled away as fast as he could; the rat had become a conditioned stimulus for fear:

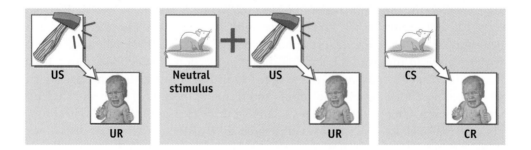

Tests done five days later showed that Albert's fear had generalized to other hairy or furry objects, including white rabbits, cotton wool, a Santa Claus mask, and even John Watson's hair.

Unfortunately, Watson and Rayner lost access to Little Albert and so were unable to reverse the conditioning. A few years later, however, Watson and Mary Cover Jones did reverse a child's conditioned fear—one that was, as Watson put it, "home-grown" rather than psychologist-induced (Jones, 1924). Peter, a 3-year-old, was deathly afraid of rabbits. Watson and Jones eliminated his fear with a method called **counterconditioning,** in which a conditioned stimulus is paired with some other stimulus that elicits a response incompatible with the unwanted response. In this case, the rabbit (the CS) was paired with a snack of milk and crackers, and the snack produced pleasant feelings that were incompatible with the conditioned response of fear. At first, the researchers kept the rabbit some distance from Peter, so that his fear would remain at a low level. Otherwise, Peter might have learned to fear milk and crackers! But gradually, over several days, they brought the rabbit closer and closer. Eventually Peter was able to sit with the rabbit in his lap, playing with it with one hand while he ate with the other. A variation of this procedure, called *systematic desensitization,* was later devised for treating phobias in adults (see Chapter 12).

Accounting for Taste

Classical conditioning can also explain how we learn to like and dislike many foods and odors. In the laboratory, researchers have taught animals to dislike foods or odors by pairing them with drugs that cause nausea or other unpleasant symptoms. One researcher trained slugs to associate the smell of carrots, which slugs normally like, with a bitter-tasting chemical that they detest. Soon the slugs were avoiding the smell of carrots. The researcher then demonstrated higher-order conditioning by pairing the smell of carrots with the smell of potato. Sure enough, the slugs began to avoid the smell of potato as well (Sahley, Rudy, & Gelperin, 1981).

Many people have learned to dislike a food after eating it and then falling ill, even when the two events are unrelated. The food, previously a neutral stimulus, becomes a conditioned stimulus for nausea or other symptoms produced by the illness. Psychologist Martin Seligman once told how he himself was conditioned to hate béarnaise sauce. One night, shortly after he and his wife ate a delicious filet mignon with béarnaise sauce, he came down with the flu. Naturally, he felt wretched. His misery had nothing to do with the béarnaise sauce, of course, yet the next time he tried it, he found he disliked the taste (Seligman & Hager, 1972).

Notice that unlike conditioning in the laboratory, Seligman's aversion to the sauce occurred after only one pairing of the sauce with illness and with a considerable delay between the conditioned and unconditioned stimuli. Further, neither Seligman's wife nor his dinner plate became conditioned stimuli for nausea, even though they, too, had been paired with illness. Apparently many animals (including psychologists) are biologically primed to associate sickness with taste more readily than with sights or sounds (Garcia & Koelling, 1966; Seligman & Hager, 1972). Like the tendency to acquire certain fears, this biological tendency enhances the species' survival: Eating bad food is more likely to be followed by illness than are particular sights or sounds.

---

counterconditioning In classical conditioning, the process of pairing a conditioned stimulus with a stimulus that elicits a response that is incompatible with an unwanted conditioned response.

Reacting to Medical Treatments

Because of classical conditioning, medical treatments can create unexpected misery or relief from symptoms, for reasons that are entirely unrelated to the treatment itself. For example, unpleasant reactions to a treatment may generalize to many other stimuli. In cancer treatment, the nausea and vomiting caused by chemotherapy may generalize to the room where the treatment was given, the smell of rubbing alcohol, or a nurse's uniform. The drug treatment is an unconditioned stimulus for nausea and vomiting, and through association, the other, previously neutral stimuli become conditioned stimuli for these responses. Even *mental images* of the sights and smells of the clinic may become conditioned stimuli for nausea (Dadds et al., 1997; Redd et al., 1993).

Some cancer patients also acquire a classically conditioned anxiety response to anything associated with their chemotherapy. In one study, patients who drank lemon-lime Kool-Aid before their therapy sessions developed an anxiety response to the drink—an example of higher-order conditioning. They continued to feel anxious even when the drink was offered in their homes rather than at the clinic (Jacobsen et al., 1995).

In contrast, patients may have *reduced* pain and anxiety when they take *placebos*—pills and injections with no active ingredients. The bottle containing the drug, the room in which the medication is given, the doctor's white coat, and the pill or injection itself may all become conditioned stimuli for relief from symptoms, because these stimuli have been associated in the past with *real* drugs (Ader, 1997). The real drugs are the unconditioned stimuli, the relief they bring is the unconditioned response, and the placebos acquire the ability to elicit similar reactions (conditioned responses).

In sum, classical conditioning is the invisible mechanism behind many of our likes and dislikes, tastes, and physical and emotional reactions. But to understand behavior, we also need to understand a second type of conditioning, to which we now turn.

What Do You Know?

We hope you haven't acquired a classically conditioned fear of quizzes. See whether you can supply the correct term to describe the outcome in each of these situations:

1. A toddler is afraid of the bath, so her father puts just a little water in the tub and gives the child a lollipop to suck on while she is being washed. Soon, the little girl loses her fear of the bath.

2. A factory worker notices that his mouth waters whenever a bell signals the beginning of his lunch break. One day the bell goes haywire and rings every half hour. By the end of the day, the worker has stopped salivating to the bell.

3. How is the Little Albert study related to our opening story of the dental patient who learned to fear cartoons?

ANSWERS:

1. counterconditioning 2. extinction 3. In both cases, a classically conditioned fear response was learned. Can you identify the US, UR, CS, and CR in the case of the dental patient?

OPERANT CONDITIONING

If you follow tennis, you know that John McEnroe was famous for his on-court antics and spectacular temper tantrums; he was the bad boy of the tennis circuit. Once, when McEnroe noticed a microphone that could pick up what the players were saying, he walked over and hit it with his racquet, breaking a string. He often shouted and cursed at referees and people in the crowd who were booing him. These angry eruptions seemed to work to his advantage: He would get all charged up and revitalized, while his opponent's performance suffered from McEnroe's emotional interruptions. McEnroe also received plenty of attention from fans and the media, who loved him or loved to hate him for his outrageous displays.

In contrast, Bjorn Borg, another tennis champion, was controlled, civilized, and considerate on the court. "Once I was like John [McEnroe]," he told a reporter. "Worse. Swearing and throwing rackets. . . . Then, when I was 13, my club suspended me for six months. My parents locked my racket in a cupboard for six months. Half a year I could not play. It was terrible. But it was a very good lesson. I never opened my mouth on the court again. I still get really mad, but I keep my emotions inside" (quoted in Collins, 1981).

Some people might attribute the opposite emotional styles of these two athletes to their inborn temperaments or to the genetic dispositions underlying specific personality traits—say, for extroversion or agreeableness. But a learning theorist, instead of attributing the men's behavior to their temperaments or personalities, would say that McEnroe's temper and Borg's calm deportment simply illustrate one of the most basic laws of learning—that *behavior becomes more or less likely, depending on its consequences.* McEnroe's outbursts got him what he wanted, so they continued. Borg's outbursts kept him from playing his beloved sport, so they stopped.

An emphasis on environmental consequences is at the heart of **operant conditioning** (also called *instrumental conditioning*), the second type of conditioning studied by behaviorists. In classical conditioning, it does not matter whether an animal's or person's behavior has consequences; in Pavlov's procedure, for example, the dog got food whether it salivated or not. But in operant conditioning, the organism's response (a tantrum by John McEnroe, for example, or a polite gesture by Bjorn Borg) *operates* or produces effects on the environment. These effects, in turn, influence whether the response will occur again.

Classical and operant conditioning also tend to differ in the types of responses they involve. In classical conditioning, the response is a reflex, such as salivation or increased heart rate, and it occurs automatically in reaction to something happening in the environment, such as the delivery of some tasty food or the sound of a clanging bell. Generally, responses in operant conditioning are complex and not reflexive—for instance, riding a bicycle, writing a letter, climbing a mountain, . . . or breaking your tennis racket in a fit of temper.

---

operant conditioning The process by which a response becomes more likely to occur or less so, depending on its consequences.

The Birth of Radical Behaviorism

Operant conditioning has been studied since the start of the twentieth century, although it wasn't called that until later. Edward Thorndike (1898), then a young doctoral candidate, set the stage by observing cats as they tried to escape from a complex "puzzle box" to reach a scrap of fish located just outside the box. At first, the cat would scratch, bite, or swat at parts of the box in an unorganized way. Then, after a few minutes, the animal would chance on the successful response (loosening a bolt, pulling a string, or hitting a button) and rush out to get the reward. Placed in the box again, the cat now took a little less time to escape, and after several trials, the animal immediately made the correct response. According to Thorndike's *law of effect,* the correct response had been "stamped in" by its satisfying results (getting the food). In contrast, annoying or unsatisfying results "stamped out" behavior. Behavior, said Thorndike, is controlled by its consequences.

the neighborhood. Jerry Van Amerongen

An instantaneous learning experience.

This general principle was elaborated and extended to more complex forms of behavior by B. F. (Burrhus Frederic) Skinner (1904–1990). Skinner called his approach "radical behaviorism" to distinguish it from the behaviorism of John Watson, who emphasized classical conditioning. Skinner argued that to understand behavior we should focus on the external causes of an action and the action's consequences. Skinner avoided terms that Thorndike used, such as "satisfying" and "annoying," which reflect assumptions about what an organism feels and wants. Focusing on intentions, values, or states of mind, said Skinner, is "prescientific" and a waste of time. For Skinner, the explanation of behavior was to be found by looking outside the individual rather than within.

One of Skinner's most controversial positions was on the matter of free will. Whereas some other psychologists, notably the humanists, have argued for the existence of free will, Skinner regarded free will as an illusion and steadfastly argued in favor of *determinism.* Environmental consequences may not automatically "stamp in" operant behavior, he said, but they do determine the probability that an action will occur. Skinner refused to credit personality traits (such as curiosity and perseverance) or mental constructs (such as goals and motives) for anyone's accomplishments, including his own. Indeed, he regarded himself not as a "self" but as a "repertoire of behaviors" resulting from an environment that encouraged looking, searching, and investigating (Bjork, 1993). "So far as I know," he wrote in his autobiography (1983), "my behavior at any given moment has been nothing more than the product of my genetic endowment, my personal history, and the current setting."

The Consequences of Behavior

In Skinner's analysis, which has inspired an immense body of research, a response ("operant") can lead to one of three types of consequences.

1 A NEUTRAL CONSEQUENCE DOES NOT ALTER THE RESPONSE. That is, it neither increases nor decreases the probability that the response will recur. If a door handle squeaks each time you turn it, but you ignore the sound and it has no effect on your door-opening behavior, the squeak is considered a neutral consequence. We will not be concerned further with neutral consequences.

2 REINFORCEMENT STRENGTHENS THE RESPONSE OR MAKES IT MORE LIKELY TO RECUR. When your dog begs for food at the table and you give her the lamb chop off your plate, her begging is likely to increase. Reinforcers are roughly equivalent to rewards, and many psychologists have no objection to the use of the words *reward* and *reinforcer* as approximate synonyms. However, strict behaviorists avoid the word *reward* because it is the animal or person, not the response, that is rewarded; the response is *strengthened*. Also, in common usage, a reward is something earned that results in happiness or satisfaction. But to a behaviorist, a stimulus is a reinforcer if it strengthens the preceding behavior, whether or not the organism experiences pleasure or a positive emotion. Conversely, no matter how pleasurable a stimulus is, it is not a reinforcer if it does not increase the likelihood of a response. It is pleasurable to get a paycheck, but if you get paid regardless of the effort you put into your work, the money will not reinforce "hard-work behavior."

3 PUNISHMENT WEAKENS THE RESPONSE OR MAKES IT LESS LIKELY TO RECUR. Any aversive (unpleasant) stimulus or event may be a *punisher*. If your dog begs for food from the table and you shout "No!" in a loud voice, her begging is likely to decrease (as long as you don't feel guilty and then give her the lamb chop anyway).

In a way, operant conditioning is a kind of natural selection applied to the constantly changing behavior of individuals. As we saw in Chapter 3, because of the evolutionary process of natural selection, some genetically influenced characteristics are selected by the environment and become more common in a population over time, whereas others become "deselected" and become less common. Similarly, in operant conditioning, some actions of an individual are "selected" by their environmental consequences and become more frequent in the behavior of the individual, whereas others are deselected and become less frequent.

---

reinforcement The process by which a stimulus or event strengthens or increases the probability of the response that it follows.

punishment The process by which a stimulus or event weakens or reduces the probability of the response that it follows.

Primary and Secondary Reinforcers and Punishers. Food, water, light stroking of the skin, and a comfortable air temperature are naturally reinforcing because they satisfy biological needs. They are therefore known as **primary reinforcers.** Similarly, pain and extreme heat or cold are inherently punishing and are therefore known as **primary punishers.** Primary reinforcers and punishers can be very powerful, but they also have some drawbacks, both in real life and in research. For one thing, a primary reinforcer may be ineffective if an animal or person is not in a deprived state; a glass of water is not much of a reward if you just drank three glasses. Also, for obvious ethical reasons, psychologists cannot go around using primary punishers (say, by hitting their subjects) or taking away primary reinforcers (say, by starving their subjects).

Fortunately, behavior can be controlled just as effectively by **secondary reinforcers** and **secondary punishers,** which are learned. Money, praise, applause, good grades, points, awards, and gold stars are common secondary reinforcers. Criticism, demerits, catcalls, scoldings, fines, and bad grades are common secondary punishers. Most behaviorists believe that secondary reinforcers and punishers acquire their ability to influence behavior by being paired with primary reinforcers and punishers. If that reminds you of classical conditioning, reinforce your excellent thinking with a pat on the head! Indeed, secondary reinforcers and punishers are often called *conditioned* reinforcers and punishers.

Secondary reinforcers and punishers have no real value in and of themselves, but they can be quite potent. Money, for example, has considerable power over most people's behavior because it can be exchanged for primary reinforcers such as food and shelter, and because it is associated with other secondary reinforcers, such as praise and respect.

Positive and Negative Reinforcers and Punishers. The great seventeenth-century English philosopher John Locke wrote that "reward and punishment . . . are the spur and reins whereby all mankind are set on work, and guided." Today we talk about the carrot and the stick as being the two great motivators. But reward and punishment are not quite as simple as they seem. Consider, first, reinforcement. In our example of the begging dog, something pleasant (getting the lamb chop) followed the dog's begging, so the response increased. This kind of process, in which a pleasant consequence makes a response more likely, is known as **positive reinforcement.** But there is another type of reinforcement, **negative reinforcement,** which involves the *removal* of something *unpleasant.* For example, if someone nags you all the time to study, but stops nagging when you comply, your studying is likely to increase—because you will then avoid the nagging.

---

primary reinforcer A stimulus that is inherently reinforcing, typically satisfying a physiological need; an example is food.

primary punisher A stimulus that is inherently punishing; an example is electric shock.

secondary reinforcer A stimulus that has acquired reinforcing properties through association with other reinforcers.

secondary punisher A stimulus that has acquired punishing properties through association with other punishers.

positive reinforcement A reinforcement procedure in which a response is followed by the presentation of, or increase in intensity of, a reinforcing stimulus; as a result, the response becomes stronger or more likely to occur.

negative reinforcement A reinforcement procedure in which a response is followed by the removal, delay, or decrease in intensity of an unpleasant stimulus; as a result, the response becomes stronger or more likely to occur.

The following illustration shows how positive and negative reinforcement can lead to the same result:

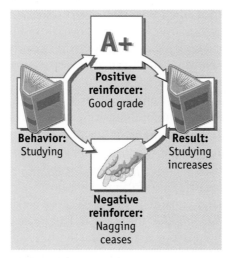

The positive–negative distinction can also be applied to punishment: Something unpleasant may occur following some behavior (positive punishment) or something *pleasant* may be *removed* (negative punishment). For example, if your friends tease you for being an egghead (positive punishment) or if studying makes you lose time with your friends (negative punishment), you may stop studying:

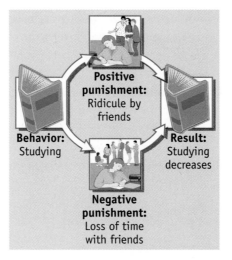

The distinction between positive and negative reinforcement has been a source of confusion and misery for generations of students. If we could spare you having to learn these distinctions, we would. You will master these terms more quickly if you understand that "positive" and "negative" have nothing to do with "good" or "bad." They refer to *procedures*—giving something or taking something away.

In the case of reinforcement, think of a positive reinforcer as something that is added or obtained, and a negative reinforcer as avoidance of, or escape from, something unpleasant. *With either positive or negative reinforcement, a response becomes more likely.* Do you recall what happened after Little Albert learned to fear rats through a process of classical conditioning? Crawling away (an operant behavior) was negatively reinforced by escape from the now-fearsome rodent. Negative reinforcement explains why so many fears are long-lasting. When you avoid a feared object or situation, you also cut off all opportunities for extinguishing your fear.

Understandably, people often confuse negative reinforcement with positive punishment, because both involve an unpleasant stimulus. With punishment, though, you are subjected to the unpleasant stimulus, and with negative reinforcement, it is taken away. To keep these terms straight, remember that *punishment—whether positive or negative—decreases the likelihood of the response it follows, whereas reinforcement—whether positive or negative—increases it.* In real life, positive punishment and negative reinforcement often go hand in hand. If you use a choke collar on your dog to teach it to heel, a yank on the collar *punishes* the act of walking; release of the uncomfortable collar *negatively reinforces* the act of standing still by your side.

You can positively reinforce your studying of this section by taking a snack break. As you master the material, a decrease in your anxiety will negatively reinforce studying. Just don't punish your efforts by telling yourself, "I'll never get it!"

What Do You Know?

Which kind of consequence will follow if you can't answer these questions?

1. A child nags her father for a cookie; he keeps refusing, but finally, unable to stand the nagging any longer, he hands over the cookie. For him, the ending of the child's pleas is a _____. For the child, the cookie is a _____.

2. An able-bodied driver is careful not to park in a handicapped space anymore after paying a large fine for having done so. The loss of money is a _____.

3. Which are secondary reinforcers: quarters spilling from a slot machine, a winner's blue ribbon, a piece of candy, an A on an exam, frequent-flyer miles.

4. During late-afternoon "happy hours" in bars and restaurants, drinks are sold at a reduced price and appetizers are often free. What undesirable behavior may be rewarded by this practice?

ANSWERS:

1. negative reinforcer; positive reinforcer. 2. punisher—or more precisely, a negative punisher (because something desirable was taken away) 3. All but the candy are secondary reinforcers. 4. One possible answer: The reduced prices, free appetizers, and cheerful atmosphere all reinforce heavy alcohol consumption just before the commuter rush hour, thus possibly contributing to drunk driving.

Principles of Operant Conditioning

Thousands of operant-conditioning studies have been done, many using animals. A favorite experimental tool is the *Skinner box,* a cage equipped with a device that delivers food or water into a dish when an animal makes a desired response (see Figure 5.1). Skinner is said to have originally created this apparatus by modifying a Sears, Roebuck ice chest. In the original version, a machine connected to the cage automatically recorded each response and produced a graph on a piece of paper, showing the cumulative number of responses across time. Nowadays, computers are used.

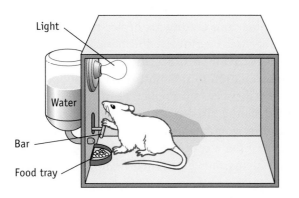

FIGURE 5.1 THE SKINNER BOX *When a rat in a Skinner box presses a bar, a food pellet or drop of water is automatically released.*

Early in his career, Skinner (1938) used the Skinner box for a classic demonstration of operant conditioning. A rat that had previously learned to eat from the pellet-releasing device was placed in the box. Because no food was present, the animal proceeded to do typical ratlike things, scurrying around the box, sniffing here and there, and randomly touching parts of the floor and walls. Quite by accident, it happened to press a lever mounted on one wall, and immediately a pellet of tasty rat food fell into the food dish. The rat continued its movements and again happened to press the bar, causing another pellet to fall into the dish. With additional repetitions of bar pressing followed by food, the animal began to behave less randomly and to press the bar more consistently. Eventually, Skinner had the rat pressing the bar as fast as it could.

A cartoon well known to behaviorists, originally published in a student newspaper, shows two rats in a Skinner box, with one saying to the other, "Boy, do we have this guy conditioned. Every time I press the bar down he drops a pellet in." But, in characteristic fashion, Skinner didn't think it was a joke. To Skinner, the environment was a place where organisms reinforced and punished each other, *reciprocally:* Yes, he conditioned the rat—but the rat also conditioned him (Bjork, 1993).

Skinner's favorite experimental animals were pigeons, which are usually trained to peck at a disk or key, but most behaviorists have worked with rats. By using the Skinner box and similar devices, behavioral researchers have discovered many techniques and applications of operant conditioning.

Extinction. In operant conditioning, as in classical, **extinction** is a procedure that causes a previously learned response to stop. In operant conditioning, extinction takes place when the reinforcer that maintained the response is removed or is no longer available.

---

extinction The weakening and eventual disappearance of a learned response; in operant conditioning, it occurs when a response is no longer followed by a reinforcer.

At first, there may be a spurt of responding, but then the responses gradually taper off and eventually cease. Suppose you put a coin in a vending machine and get nothing back. You may throw in another coin, or perhaps even two, but then you will probably stop trying. The next day you may put in yet another coin, an example of *spontaneous recovery*. Eventually, however, you will probably give up on that machine. Your response will have been extinguished.

The harried mother in our opening story learned, with the help of a sensible therapist, to extinguish the yelling, whining, and arguments of her two daughters. The therapist pointed out that the mother was overinvolved in her children's lives; she was actually rewarding the girls' misbehavior with her attention, which is why the misbehavior continued. His recommendation to the mother was to simply stay out of her daughters' quarrels. As a behaviorist would predict, at first the fighting, shouting, and griping actually escalated, as the girls tried to regain their mother's attention. But she had been warned that this would happen, and she remained steadfast in her new policy of noninvolvement. After a couple of difficult weeks, the girls began to take responsibility for their problems and ceased their fighting and hollering (Seif, 1979).

Immediate Versus Delayed Consequences. In general, the sooner a reinforcer or punisher follows a response, the greater its effect. This principle applies especially to nonhuman animals and children, but human adults also respond more reliably when they don't have to wait too long for a paycheck, a smile, or a grade. When there is a delay, other responses occur in the interval, and the connection between the desired or undesired response and the consequence may not be made.

A delay in punishment explains why pet owners often have trouble teaching their pets to stop misbehaving. The owner comes home, sees that the pooch defecated on the rug or the cat chewed up the sofa pillows, and shouts at or strikes the poor animal. The animal, who is just snoozing happily at the moment, of course hasn't a clue about why this weird human is behaving so oddly. Too much time has elapsed between the misbehavior and the punishment. In operant conditioning, timing is all.

In many situations, immediate rewards tend to outweigh the effects of delayed punishment, so it is hard for people to do what they know they ought to. For example, consider the student in our opening story who resolved to improve his study habits. A behaviorist would say that the immediate pleasures of partying, hanging out with friends, or spending hours in online chat rooms may outweigh the possible chances of getting a D or F on an exam that's two weeks off. Thus, through a process of operant conditioning, "partying behavior" becomes more likely, despite the student's resolve to study harder.

Here's another example. We bet that you already know the basic rules for protecting your health: Get enough sleep, get regular exercise, eat a nutritious diet, and avoid drinking alcohol in excess, overeating, going on starvation diets, and smoking cigarettes. Well, then, why aren't you following all these rules? One obstacle is the fact that smoking, eating rich food, and not exercising bring immediate rewards, whereas their negative effects may not be apparent for years. As a result, many people feel that they are invulnerable and therefore persist in their unhealthy habits. Perhaps you can think of some way to reward yourself—immediately!—for adopting good health practices.

Stimulus Generalization and Discrimination. In operant conditioning, as in classical, **stimulus generalization** may occur. That is, responses may generalize to stimuli that were not present during the original learning situation but that resemble the original stimuli. For example, a pigeon that has been trained to peck at a picture of a circle may also peck at a slightly oval figure. But if you wanted to train the bird to discriminate between the two shapes, you would present both the circle and the oval, giving reinforcers whenever the bird pecked at the circle and withholding reinforcers when it pecked at the oval. Eventually, **stimulus discrimination** would occur.

Sometimes an animal or person learns to respond to a stimulus only when some other stimulus, called a **discriminative stimulus,** is present. The discriminative stimulus signals whether a response, if made, will pay off. For a pigeon in a Skinner box, a light may serve as a discriminative stimulus for pecking at a circle. When the light is on, pecking brings a reward; when it is off, pecking is futile. The light is said to exert **stimulus control** over the pecking by setting the occasion for reinforcement to occur if the response is made. However, the response is not *compelled,* as salivation was compelled by the ringing of the bell in Pavlov's classical-conditioning studies. It merely becomes more probable (or occurs at a greater rate) in the presence of the discriminative stimulus.

Human behavior is controlled by many discriminative stimuli, both verbal ("Store hours are 9 to 5") and nonverbal (traffic lights, doorbells, the ring of a telephone, the facial expressions of others). Learning to respond correctly when these stimuli are present is an essential part of a person's socialization, and failure to make a discrimination can get you in trouble. In a public place, if you have to go to the bathroom, the words *Women* and *Men* are discriminative stimuli for entering one door or the other. One word tells you that the response will be rewarded by an opportunity to empty a full bladder, the other that it will be punished by the jeers or protests of others.

Insufficient generalization also causes problems. For example, "personal growth" workshops provide participants with lots of reinforcement for emotional expressiveness and self-disclosure. Participants often feel that their way of interacting with others has been dramatically transformed. But when they return home and to work, where the environment is full of the same old reinforcers, punishers, and discriminative stimuli, they may be disappointed to find that their new responses have failed to generalize. A grumpy boss or cranky spouse may still be able to "push their buttons," a relapse that is predictable from behavioral principles.

---

stimulus generalization In operant conditioning, the tendency for a response that has been reinforced (or punished) in the presence of one stimulus to occur (or be suppressed) in the presence of other, similar stimuli.

stimulus discrimination In operant conditioning, the tendency of a response to occur in the presence of one stimulus but not in the presence of other, similar stimuli that differ from it on some dimension.

discriminative stimulus A stimulus that signals when a particular response is likely to be followed by a certain type of consequence.

stimulus control Control over the occurrence of a response by a discriminative stimulus.

Learning on Schedule. When a response is first acquired, learning is usually most rapid if the response is reinforced each time it occurs; this procedure is called **continuous reinforcement.** However, once a response has become reliable, it will be more resistant to extinction if it is rewarded on an **intermittent (partial) schedule of reinforcement,** which involves reinforcing only some responses, not all of them. Skinner (1956) happened on this fact when he ran short of food pellets for his rats and was forced to deliver reinforcers less often. (Not all scientific discoveries are planned!) Years later, when he was asked how he could tolerate being misunderstood so often, he replied that he only needed to be understood three or four times a year—his own intermittent schedule of reinforcement.

Many kinds of intermittent schedules have been studied. *Ratio schedules* deliver a reinforcer after a certain number of responses have occurred. *Interval schedules* deliver a reinforcer if a response is made after the passage of a certain amount of time since the last reinforcer. The number of responses that must occur or the amount of time that must pass before the payoff may be *fixed* (constant) or *variable.* Combining the ratio/interval patterns and fixed/variable patterns yields four types of intermittent schedules. These variations in how the reinforcers are delivered have characteristic effects on the rate, form, and timing of behavior—effects that most people are not aware of. The different patterns resulting from these schedules are known as *learning curves.* Figure 5.2 shows typical learning curves for the four basic schedules of reinforcement.

A basic principle of operant conditioning is that if you want a response to persist after it has been learned, you should reinforce it intermittently, not continuously. If you are continuously giving Harry, your hamster, a treat for pushing a ball with his nose, and then you suddenly withdraw the reinforcement, Harry will soon stop pushing that ball. Because the change in reinforcement is large, from continuous to none at all, Harry will easily discern the change. But if you have been reinforcing Harry's behavior only every so often, the change will not be so dramatic, and your hungry hamster will keep responding for quite a while. Pigeons, rats, and people on intermittent schedules of reinforcement have responded in the laboratory thousands of times without reinforcement before throwing in the towel, especially when the timing of the reinforcer varies. Animals will sometimes work so hard for an unpredictable, infrequent bit of food that the energy they expend is greater than that from the reward; theoretically, they could actually work themselves to death!

It follows that if you want to get rid of a response, you should be careful not to reinforce it intermittently. If you are going to extinguish undesirable behavior by ignoring it—a child's tantrums, a friend's midnight phone calls, a parent's unasked-for advice—you must be absolutely consistent in withholding reinforcement (your attention). Otherwise, you will probably only make matters worse. The other person will learn that

---

continuous reinforcement A reinforcement schedule in which a particular response is always reinforced.

intermittent (partial) schedule of reinforcement A reinforcement schedule in which a particular response is sometimes but not always reinforced.

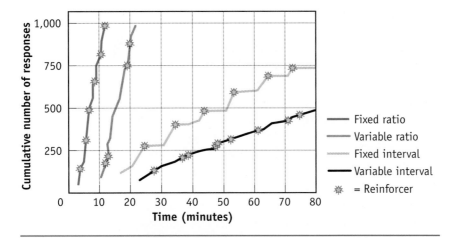

FIGURE 5.2 REINFORCEMENT SCHEDULES AND BEHAVIOR *Different schedules of reinforcement produce different learning curves, or patterns of responding over time. A* fixed-ratio schedule, *which delivers a reinforcer after a fixed number of responses are made, produces a very fast rate of responding. But a* fixed-interval schedule, *which delivers a reinforcer after a fixed amount of time has passed since the last one, results in a scalloped curve, because responses tend to drop off immediately after each reinforcement. (Adapted from Skinner, 1961.)*

if he or she keeps up the screaming, calling, or advice-giving long enough, it will eventually be rewarded. One of the most common errors people make, from a behavioral point of view, is to reward intermittently the responses that they would like to eliminate.

Shaping. For a response to be reinforced, it must first occur. But suppose you want to train Harry the hamster to pick up a marble, a child to use a knife and fork properly, or a friend to play terrific tennis. Such behaviors, and most others in everyday life, have almost no probability of appearing spontaneously. You could grow old and gray waiting for them to occur so that you could reinforce them. The operant solution to this dilemma is a procedure called **shaping.**

In shaping, you start by reinforcing a tendency in the right direction, then gradually require responses that are more and more similar to the final, desired response. The responses that you reinforce on the way to the final one are called **successive approximations.** In the case of Harry and the marble, you might deliver a food pellet if the hamster merely turned toward the marble. Once this response was well established, you might then reward the hamster for taking a step toward the marble. After that, you could reward it for approaching the marble, then for touching the marble,

shaping An operant-conditioning procedure in which successive approximations of a desired response are reinforced.

successive approximations In the operant-conditioning procedure of shaping, behaviors that are ordered in terms of increasing similarity or closeness to the desired response.

Behavioral techniques such as shaping have many practical applications. Monkeys like this one have been trained to assist their paralyzed owners by picking up objects, opening doors, helping with feeding, and turning the pages of books.

then for putting both paws on the marble, and finally for holding it. With the achievement of each approximation, the next one would become more likely, making it available for reinforcement.

Using shaping and other techniques, Skinner was able to train pigeons to play Ping-Pong with their beaks and to "bowl" in a miniature alley, complete with a wooden ball and tiny bowling pins. Animal trainers routinely use shaping to teach dogs to act as the "eyes" of the blind, and to act as the "limbs" of people with spinal cord injuries by turning on light switches, opening refrigerator doors, and reaching for boxes on supermarket shelves.

What Do You Know?

Can you apply the principles of operant conditioning? In each of the following situations, choose the best alternative, and give your reason for choosing it:

1. You want your 2-year-old to ask for water with a word instead of a grunt. Should you give him water when he says "wa-wa" or wait until his pronunciation improves?

2. Your roommate keeps interrupting your studying even though you have asked her to stop. Should you ignore her completely or occasionally respond for the sake of good manners?

3. Your father, who rarely writes to you, has finally sent a letter. Should you reply quickly or wait a while so he will know how it feels to be ignored?

OPERANT CONDITIONING IN REAL LIFE

Over the years, behaviorists have carried operant principles out of the narrow world of the Skinner box and into the wider world of the classroom, athletic field, mental hospital, nursing home, rehabilitation ward, child-care center, factory, and office. The use of operant techniques to help people change unwanted, dangerous, or self-defeating habits in real-world settings is called **behavior modification,** or *applied behavior analysis.*

Behavior modification has had some enormous successes. Behaviorists have taught parents to toilet train their children in only a few sessions (Azrin & Foxx, 1974). They have taught teachers to be "behavioral change agents" (Besalel-Azrin, Azrin, & Armstrong, 1977). They have trained disturbed and mentally retarded adults to communicate, dress themselves, mingle socially with others, and earn a living (Lent, 1968; McLeod, 1985). They have taught brain-damaged patients to control inappropriate behavior, focus attention, and improve their language abilities (McGlynn, 1990). And they have helped ordinary folk eliminate unwanted habits, such as smoking and nail biting, or acquire wanted ones, such as practicing the piano or studying.

Do you remember, from Chapter 2, how false hopes were raised when "facilitated communication" became a popular technique for treating autistic children? Good scientific research has showed that facilitated communication doesn't work at all; it is the adult facilitators who are communicating, not the autistic children. But there are other approaches, based on behavioral principles, that *do* have scientific support and that offer genuine hope in the treatment of this disorder (Green, 1996a, 1996b). A behaviorally trained teacher or therapist often begins by systematically studying the child's behavior and the reinforcers that seem to be maintaining it, such as attention or sensory stimulation. The teacher then uses reinforcers in a consistent, carefully planned manner to increase the child's social, linguistic, academic, and daily-living skills. Extinction, withholding of rewards, and mild punishment may be used to decrease undesirable behaviors, such as spitting or hitting. A child's parents, peers, and siblings are often trained to use these operant techniques at home. Sadly, many therapists and self-appointed experts in autism are unfamiliar with the behavioral approach or have

---

behavior modification   The application of conditioning techniques to teach new responses or reduce or eliminate maladaptive or problematic behavior.

rejected it in favor of unproven fads. The good news is that parents' groups, and an organization called the Association for Science in Autism Treatment, have been spreading the word.

As you can see, behaviorism is more than an academic approach; it can profoundly affect lives. Nonetheless, when people try to apply conditioning principles to common problems, their efforts sometimes miss the mark. Both punishment and reinforcement, useful though they are, also have their pitfalls, as we are about to see.

The Pros and Cons of Punishment

In a perfect world, according to behaviorists, reinforcers would be used so wisely that people would rarely misbehave. Unfortunately, we do not live in a perfect world; bad habits and antisocial acts abound, and we are faced with how to get rid of them.

An obvious approach might seem to be punishment. Most Western countries have banned the physical punishment of schoolchildren by principals and teachers, but in many parts of the United States, schools still permit it for disruptiveness, vandalism, and other misbehaviors. The United States is also far more likely than any other developed country to jail its citizens for nonviolent crimes such as drug use and to enact the ultimate punishment—the death penalty—for violent crimes. And of course in daily life, people punish one another constantly, by yelling, scolding, fining, and sulking. Does all this punishment work?

When Punishment Works. Sometimes punishment is unquestionably effective. Some highly disturbed children have been known to chew their fingers to the bone, stick objects in their eyes, or tear out their hair. You cannot ignore such behavior because the children will seriously injure themselves. You cannot respond with concern and affection because you may unwittingly reward the behavior. But immediately punishing the self-destructive behavior eliminates it (Lovaas, 1977; Lovaas, Schreibman, & Koegel, 1974). Mild punishers, such as a spray of water in the face or even a firm "No!," are often just as effective as strong ones, such as electric shock.

Punishment can also deter some young criminals from repeating their offenses. Patricia Brennan and Sarnoff Mednick (1994) examined data on nearly 29,000 Danish men born between 1944 and 1947, focusing on repeat arrests (recidivism) through age 26. After any given arrest, punishment reduced rates of subsequent arrests for both minor and serious crimes (though recidivism still remained fairly high). Contrary to the researchers' expectations, however, the severity of punishment made no difference: Fines and probation were about as effective as jail time. What mattered most was the *consistency* of the punishment. This is understandable: When punishment is inconsistent—when lawbreakers sometimes get away with their crimes—their behavior is intermittently reinforced and therefore becomes resistant to extinction.

These results show that punishment can reduce recidivism, but they also show why harsh sentencing laws and simplistic efforts to "crack down" on wrongdoers often fail or even backfire. Despite its high incarceration rates, the United States has a far higher rate of violent crime than other developed countries do; and crime rates in the various states show no consistent correlation with rates of incarceration (Currie, 1998). Why? Brennan and Sarnoff point out that in the United States, young offenders are punished far less consistently than they are in Denmark, often because prosecutors, juries, and judges do not want to condemn them to mandatory prison terms. Because the courts have no other options for punishment, they may merely admonish the offenders and set them free. Ironically, then, policies that mandate severe punishment can actually lead to ineffective punishment—or to no punishment at all.

When Punishment Fails. What about punishment that occurs every day, in families, schools, and workplaces? Laboratory and field studies find that it, too, often fails, for several reasons:

1 People often administer punishment inappropriately or mindlessly. They hit or throw things in a blind rage or say things they don't mean, applying punishment so broadly that it covers all sorts of irrelevant behaviors. And even when people are not carried away by anger, they often misunderstand the proper application of punishment. One student told us that his parents used to punish their children before leaving them alone for the evening because of all the naughty things they were *going* to do. Naturally, the children did not bother to behave like angels.

2 The recipient of punishment often responds with anxiety, fear, or rage. Through a process of classical conditioning, these emotional side effects may then generalize to the entire situation in which the punishment occurs—the place, the person delivering the punishment, and the circumstances. These negative emotional reactions can create more problems than the punishment solves. A teenager who has been severely punished may strike back or run away. A spouse who is constantly abused will feel bitter and resentful and is likely to retaliate with acts of hostility. Being physically punished in childhood increases the risk of later depression, low self-esteem, violent behavior, and many other problems (Barrish, 1996; Straus & Kantor, 1994; Weiss et al., 1992).

3 The effectiveness of punishment is often temporary, depending heavily on the presence of the punishing person or circumstances. All of us can probably remember some transgressions of childhood that we never dared commit when our parents were around but that we promptly resumed as soon as they were gone. All we learned was to not get caught.

4 Most misbehavior is hard to punish immediately. Punishment, like reward, works best if it quickly follows a response, as we saw earlier in the example of the misbehaving pets. But outside the laboratory, immediate punishment is often hard to achieve, and during the delay, the behavior may be reinforced many times—the bully gets the treats, the mugger gets the gold watch, the drug addict gets high.

5 Punishment conveys little information. If it immediately follows the misbehavior, punishment may tell the recipient what *not* to do. But it does not communicate what the person (or animal) *should* do. For example, spanking a toddler for messing in his pants will not teach him to use the potty chair, and scolding a student for learning slowly will not teach him to learn more quickly.

6 An action intended to punish may instead be reinforcing because it brings attention. Indeed, in some cases, angry attention may be just what the offender wants. For example, in the schoolroom, teachers who publicly scold children, thus putting them in the limelight, often unwittingly reward the very misbehavior they are trying to eliminate.

Because of these drawbacks, most psychologists believe that punishment, especially severe punishment, is a poor way to eliminate unwanted behavior in most situations. When punishment must be used, these guidelines should be kept in mind: (1) It should not involve physical abuse (e.g., parents can use "time-outs" and loss of privileges instead of hitting); (2) it should be accompanied by information about what kind of behavior would be appropriate; and (3) it should be followed, whenever possible, by the reinforcement of desirable behavior.

Fortunately, a good alternative to punishment exists: extinction of the responses you want to discourage. Of course, the simplest form of extinction—ignoring the behavior—is often hard to carry out. It is not easy to ignore a child nagging for a cookie before dinner, a roommate interrupting your concentration, or a dog barking its lungs out. And ignoring the behavior is not always appropriate. A teacher cannot ignore a child who is hitting a playmate. The dog owner who ignores Fido's backyard barking may soon hear some barking of another sort from the neighbors. A parent whose child is a video-game addict cannot ignore the behavior, because playing the games is rewarding to the child. One solution: Combine extinction of undesirable acts with reinforcement of alternative ones. For example, the parent of a video-game addict might ignore the child's pleas for "just one more game" and at the same time praise the child for doing something else that is incompatible with video-game playing, such as reading or playing basketball.

The Problem with Reward

Researchers have conditioned rats thousands of times, and as far as we know, none of the rats ever refused to cooperate or felt that they were being manipulated. Human beings are different. A little girl we know came home from school one day in a huff after her teacher announced that good performance would be rewarded with play money that could later be exchanged for privileges. "Doesn't she think I can learn without being bribed?" the child asked her mother indignantly.

This child's reaction illustrates a complication in the use of reinforcers. Most of our examples of operant conditioning have involved **extrinsic reinforcers,** which come from an outside source and are not inherently related to the activity being reinforced. Money, praise, gold stars, applause, hugs, and thumbs-up signs are all extrinsic reinforcers. But people (and probably some other animals, too) also work for **intrinsic reinforcers,** such

---

extrinsic reinforcers Reinforcers that are not inherently related to the activity being reinforced, such as money, prizes, and praise.

intrinsic reinforcers Reinforcers that are inherently related to the activity being reinforced, such as enjoyment of the task and the satisfaction of accomplishment.

as enjoyment of the task and the satisfaction of accomplishment. It turns out that if you focus too much on extrinsic reinforcers, they can actually undermine intrinsic ones, destroying the pleasure of doing something for its own sake (Deci, Koestner, & Ryan, 1999; Lepper, Henderlong, & Gingras, 1999).

Consider what happened when psychologists gave nursery-school children the chance to draw with felt-tip pens (Lepper, Greene, & Nisbett, 1973). The children already liked this activity and readily took it up during free play. First, the researchers recorded how long each child spontaneously played with the pens. Then they told some of the children that if they would draw with felt-tip pens for a man who had come "to see what kinds of pictures boys and girls like to draw with Magic Markers," they would get a prize, a "Good Player Award" complete with gold seal and ribbon. After drawing for six minutes, each child got the award, as promised. Other children did not expect a reward and were not given one. A week later, the researchers again observed the children's free play. Those children who had expected and received a reward were spending much less time with the pens than they had before the start of the experiment. In contrast, children who were not given an award continued to show as much interest in the activity as they had shown initially, as you can see in Figure 5.3. Similar results occurred when older children were or were not rewarded for working on academic tasks.

Because promised rewards (otherwise known as bribes) can be effective in the short term and can sometimes increase test scores by boosting students' motivation,

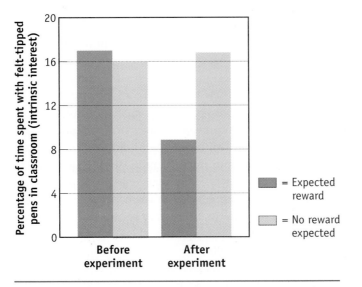

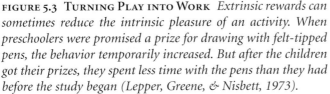

FIGURE 5.3 TURNING PLAY INTO WORK *Extrinsic rewards can sometimes reduce the intrinsic pleasure of an activity. When preschoolers were promised a prize for drawing with felt-tipped pens, the behavior temporarily increased. But after the children got their prizes, they spent less time with the pens than they had before the study began (Lepper, Greene, & Nisbett, 1973).*

"That is the correct answer, Billy, but I'm afraid you don't win anything for it."

some educators advocate using more of them. But motivation to do well on a test is not the same thing as motivation to learn. In a study of 9-year-olds and their mothers, half of the mothers were told to encourage learning for the intrinsic pleasure of it, and half were told to reward high grades and punish low ones. A year later, motivation and school performance had improved in the children in the first group. But extrinsic rewards and punishers actually seemed to impede academic achievement in the second group (Gottfried, Fleming, & Gottfried, 1994).

Why should extrinsic rewards undermine the pleasure of doing something for its own sake? One possibility is that when we are paid for an activity, we interpret it as work. It is as if we say to ourselves, "I'm doing this because I'm being paid for it. Since I'm being paid, it must be something I wouldn't do if I didn't have to." When the reward is withdrawn, we refuse to "work" any longer. Or perhaps, because we regard extrinsic rewards as controlling, they reduce our sense of autonomy and choice ("I guess I should just do what I'm told to do—and *only* what I'm told to do") (Deci & Ryan, 1987). A third, more behavioral explanation is that extrinsic reinforcement sometimes raises the rate of responding above some optimal, enjoyable level. Then the activity really does become work.

The fact that schools rely heavily on grades and other extrinsic incentives may explain why the average college graduate reads few books. Like all extrinsic rewards, grades induce temporary compliance but not necessarily a lifelong disposition to learn. However, we do not want to leave you with the impression that extrinsic rewards *always* weaken the impact of intrinsic ones. If you get money, a high grade, or a trophy for doing a task *well*, rather than for just doing it, your intrinsic motivation is not likely to suffer; in fact, your sense of control and competence, and your enjoyment of the task, may actually increase (Dickinson, 1989; Eisenberger & Cameron, 1996; Eisenberger, Rhoades, & Cameron, 1999). And if you have always been crazy about reading or playing the banjo, you will probably keep reading or playing even when you are not getting a grade or applause for doing so (Mawhinney, 1990).

So, then, what is the take-home message about extrinsic rewards? First, sometimes they are necessary. Few people would trudge off to work every morning if they never got paid; and in the classroom, teachers may need to offer incentives to unmotivated students. Second, we should use extrinsic rewards sparingly, so that intrinsic pleasure in an activity can blossom. As one mother once wrote in a *Newsweek* essay, children need to discover for themselves "the pleasure of health and strength from exercise, the joy of music from songs, the power of mathematics from counting and all of human wisdom from reading" (Skreslet, 1987). And finally, educators and employers can avoid the trap of either-or thinking by recognizing that most people do their best when they get tangible rewards *and* when they have interesting, challenging, and varied kinds of work to do.

Effective behavior modification, as you can see, is not only a science but also an art.

What Do You Know?

Answer these questions and enjoy the intrinsic satisfaction that will follow.

A. According to behavioral principles, what is happening here?

1. An adolescent whose parents have hit him for minor transgressions since he was small runs away from home.

2. A young woman whose parents paid her to clean her room while she was growing up is a slob when she moves to her own apartment.

3. Two parents scold their young daughter every time they catch her sucking her thumb. The thumb sucking continues anyway.

B. In a fee-for-service system of health care, doctors are paid for each visit by a patient or for each service performed—the longer the visit, the higher the fee. In contrast, some health maintenance organizations (HMOs) pay their doctors a fixed amount per patient for the entire year. If the amount spent is less, the physician gets a bonus, and in some systems, if the amount spent is more, the physician must pay a penalty. Given what you know about operant conditioning, what are the advantages and disadvantages of each system?

ANSWERS:

A. 1. The physical punishment was painful, and through a process of classical conditioning, the situation in which it occurred also became unpleasant. Because escape from an unpleasant stimulus is negatively reinforcing, the boy ran away. **2.** Extrinsic reinforcers are no longer available, and room-cleaning behavior has been extinguished. Also, extrinsic rewards may have displaced the intrinsic satisfaction of having a tidy room. **3.** Punishment has failed, possibly because it rewards thumb sucking with attention or because thumb sucking still brings the child pleasure whenever the parents are not around. **B.** In a fee-for-service system, the doctor is likely to provide the attention and tests that ill patients need. However, this system also rewards doctors for unnecessary tests and patient visits, contributing to the explosion in health-care costs. The policies of the HMOs help contain these costs, but because doctors are rewarded for reducing costs and in some cases are penalized for running up charges, some patients may not get the attention or services they need.

THE WORLD AS THE BEHAVIORIST VIEWS IT

In 1913, John Watson's paper "Psychology as the Behaviorist Views It"—sometimes called "the behaviorist manifesto"—transformed American psychology. It immediately appealed to Americans' love of the practical and pragmatic. Today, behavioral concepts continue to offer down-to-earth explanations of events that to others might seem complicated. Let us look at the world as the behaviorist views it by examining two phenomena not usually attributed to conditioning: the persistence of superstitions and the lightning bolt of insight.

Superstition

Do you cross your fingers when you're waiting for good news? Have you ever avoided walking under a ladder because it "brings bad luck"? Do you have a little lucky charm in your car to protect you against accidents? Why do people hold such superstitions?

The answer, say behaviorists, has to do partly with the nature of reinforcement, which can be effective even when it is entirely coincidental. A baseball batter happens to pull on his earlobe, then gets a home run; ever after, he pulls on his earlobe before a pitch. A student uses a purple pen on the first exam of the semester, gets an A, and from then on uses only purple pens for taking tests.

Skinner (1948) once demonstrated how coincidental reinforcement can create superstitions by creating eight "superstitious" pigeons in his laboratory. He rigged their cages so that food was delivered every 15 seconds, even if the birds didn't lift a feather. Pigeons are often in motion, so when the food came, the animals were likely to be doing *something*. That something was then reinforced by delivery of the food. The behavior, of course, was reinforced entirely by chance, but it still became more likely to occur, and thus to be reinforced again. Within a short time, six of the pigeons were practicing some sort of consistent ritual—turning in counterclockwise circles, bobbing their heads up and down, or swinging their heads to and fro. None of these actions had the least effect on the delivery of the reinforcer; the birds were behaving "superstitiously." It was as if they thought their movements were responsible for bringing the food.

Why, though, don't superstitions extinguish? After all, the batter who pulls on his earlobe will not always hit a home run, nor will the student who uses a purple pen always be brilliant on exams. One answer: Intermittent reinforcement makes the response resistant to extinction. As long as these rituals are reinforced occasionally, they may continue indefinitely (Schwartz & Reilly, 1985). Ironically, the fact that our little rituals "work" only some of the time ensures that we will keep using them.

Of course, you don't have to have an accident after walking beneath a ladder or breaking a mirror to believe that these actions bring bad luck. Many superstitions are reinforced by the agreement or attention of others, or by the feeling of control that they provide. And once you have acquired a superstition, you may notice evidence that justifies it but ignore contrary evidence. As long as nothing awful happens when you are carrying a good-luck charm, for example, you can credit it with protective powers;

and if something bad does occur, you can always say that the charm has simply lost its powers (a violation of the principle of falsifiability!). Even when we know the reasons for our superstitions, they can be hard to shake. As Paul Chance (1988) wrote, "A black cat means nothing to me now, nor does a broken mirror. There are no little plastic icons on the dashboard of my car, and I carry no rabbit's foot. I am free of all such nonsense, and I am happy to report no ill effects—knock wood."

Insight

Insight is learning or problem solving that appears to occur in a flash: You suddenly "see" how to solve an equation, assemble a cabinet that came with unintelligible instructions, or finish a puzzle. The human species is not the only one capable of insight. In the 1920s, Wolfgang Köhler (1925) put chimpanzees in situations in which some tempting bananas were just out of reach, then watched to see what the apes would do. Most did nothing, but a few turned out to be quite clever. If the bananas were outside the cage, the animal might pull them in with a stick. If the bananas were hanging overhead, and there were boxes in the cage, the chimpanzee might pile up the boxes and climb on top of them to reach the fruit. Often the solution came after the animal had been sitting quietly for a while. It appeared as though the chimp had been thinking about the problem and suddenly saw the answer.

To most people, insight seems to be an entirely cognitive phenomenon—a new way of perceiving logical and cause-and-effect relationships—in which a person or animal does not simply respond to a stimulus but instead solves a problem. But behaviorists argue that insight can be explained in terms of an organism's reinforcement history, without resorting to cognitive explanations (Windholz & Lamal, 1985). Insight, they say, is just a label for a the combination of previously learned patterns; it does not *explain* the behavior.

Behaviorists point out that even animals not usually credited with higher mental processes seem capable of what looks suspiciously like "insight," under some conditions. In one ingenious study, Robert Epstein and his colleagues (1984) taught four pigeons to perform three separate behaviors, during different training sessions: pushing boxes in a particular direction, climbing onto a box, and pecking at a toy banana in order to obtain grain. The birds were also taught not to fly or jump at the banana; those behaviors were extinguished. Then the pigeons were left alone with the toy banana suspended just out of reach overhead and the box at the edge of the cage.

"At first," the researchers observed, "each pigeon appeared to be 'confused'; it stretched and turned beneath the banana, looked back and forth from banana to box, and so on. Then each subject began rather suddenly to push the box in what was clearly the direction of the banana" (Epstein et al., 1984). Just as Köhler's chimps had

---

insight A form of problem solving that appears to involve the sudden understanding of how elements of a situation are related or can be reorganized to achieve a solution.

FIGURE 5.4 SMART BIRD? *A pigeon looks at a cluster of toy bananas strung overhead (a), pushes a small box beneath the bananas (b), and then climbs onto the box to peck at them (c). The bird had previously learned separate components of this sequence through a process of operant conditioning. Behaviorists view this accomplishment as evidence against the cognitive view of insight.*

done, the birds quickly solved their feeding problem by pushing the box beneath the banana and climbing onto it (see Figure 5.4). Yet few people would want to credit pigeons with complex thought processes.

Most psychologists maintain that although insight may require the use of previously learned responses to solve problems, in human beings (and possibly chimpanzees) it also requires mentally combining these responses in new ways. To behaviorists, however, insight is the *result* of learning, not a way of learning.

BEHAVIORISM: MYTHS AND REALITY

The learning perspective suggests that many behaviors commonly regarded as perplexing, self-defeating, or just plain "natural" may, in fact, be the result of patterns of reinforcement—and that these patterns, once understood, can be manipulated to alter behaviors and improve our lives. But behaviorists and their goals have often been misunderstood.

Skinner, who has often been called the greatest of American psychologists, and is certainly one of the best known, was especially likely to be misinterpreted; many of his ideas were wildly distorted in the popular press and even by other psychologists. For example, many people think that he denied the existence of human consciousness and the value of studying it. It is true that Skinner's predecessor John Watson thought that psychologists should study only public (external) events, not private (internal) ones. But Skinner (1972, 1990) maintained that we *can* study private events—what we call perceptions, emotions, and thoughts—by observing our own sensory responses, the verbal reports of others, and the conditions under which such events occur. Internal events, he said, are as real as any others. He insisted, however, that thoughts and feelings cannot *explain* behavior; these components of "consciousness," he said, are themselves simply behaviors that occur because of reinforcement and punishment.

Another misconception is that Skinner denied the influence of genetics and biology. Skinner knew as well as anyone that genetic dispositions and physical characteristics place limits on what an organism can learn; a fish cannot be trained to climb a ladder, no matter how many years you spend trying to apply shaping techniques. Although he himself did not say much about biological influences, in recent years behaviorists have been paying more attention to the importance of innate tendencies, taking into account that some things are easier for an animal or human being to learn than others.

Because behaviorists believe that the environment can and should be manipulated to alter behavior, some critics have portrayed them as cold-blooded. Again, Skinner was a special target. In the 1970s, after Skinner's book *Beyond Freedom and Dignity* put him on the cover of *Time* magazine, scholars, theologians, and even politicians rushed to attack him. He was called a fascist, and the Chicago *Tribune* ran a picture of a rat with Skinner-like features.

In reality, Skinner was a quiet and mild-mannered person who cared passionately about the wise application of behavioral principles. He adamantly opposed the use of coercion and punishment and was greatly concerned with issues of social justice (Dinsmoor, 1992). Long before the modern feminist movement, he advocated a world of sexual equality in which work is not assigned by gender. Skinner was, in fact, a humanist in the broadest sense of the term, which is why the American Humanist Association once gave him its Humanist of the Year Award. Toward the end of his life, in a book called *Enjoy Old Age,* he offered all sorts of useful tips on how the elderly could make their lives easier (Skinner & Vaughan, 1984). And in 1990, just a week before his death, ailing and frail, he addressed an overflow crowd at the annual meeting of the American Psychological Association, making the case one last time for the approach he was convinced could create a better society.

When you see the world as the behaviorist views it, Skinner was saying, you see the folly of human behavior, but you also see the possibility of improving it. ■

Summary

1. For almost half a century, until the 1960s, *behaviorism* was the dominant approach to the study of learning. Behaviorists have shown that two types of *conditioning* can explain much of human behavior: classical conditioning and operant conditioning.

2. *Classical conditioning* was first studied by Russian physiologist Ivan Pavlov. In this type of learning, when a neutral stimulus is paired with an *unconditioned stimulus (US)* that elicits some reflexive *unconditioned response (UR)*, the neutral stimulus comes to elicit a similar or related response. The neutral stimulus is then called a *conditioned stimulus (CS)*, and the response it elicits, a *conditioned response (CR)*. Nearly any kind of involuntary response can become a CR.

3. In *extinction*, the conditioned stimulus is repeatedly presented without the unconditioned stimulus, and the conditioned response eventually disappears—although later it may reappear (*spontaneous recovery*). In *higher-order conditioning*, a neutral

stimulus becomes a conditioned stimulus by being paired with an already established conditioned stimulus. In *stimulus generalization,* after a stimulus becomes a conditioned stimulus for some response, other, similar stimuli produce a similar reaction. In *stimulus discrimination,* different responses are made to stimuli that resemble the conditioned stimulus in some way.

4. Many theorists believe that what an animal or person learns in classical conditioning is not just an association between the unconditioned and conditioned stimulus, but information conveyed by one stimulus about another. They cite evidence that the neutral stimulus does not become a CS unless it reliably signals or predicts the US.

5. Classical conditioning may help account for positive emotional responses to particular objects and events; fears and phobias; the acquisition of likes and dislikes; and reactions to medical treatments and placebos. John Watson showed how fears may be learned and then may be unlearned through a process of *counterconditioning.*

6. In *operant conditioning,* behavior becomes more likely to occur or less so, depending on its consequences. Responses are generally not reflexive and are more complex than in classical conditioning. Research in this area is closely associated with B. F. Skinner, who called his approach "radical behaviorism."

7. In the Skinnerian analysis, a response ("operant") can lead to neutral, reinforcing, or punishing consequences. *Reinforcement* strengthens or increases the probability of a response. *Punishment* weakens or decreases the probability of a response.

8. Reinforcers are called *primary* when they are naturally reinforcing (e.g., because they satisfy a biological need) and *secondary* when they have acquired their ability to strengthen a response through association with other reinforcers. A similar distinction is made for punishers.

9. Reinforcement and punishment may be positive or negative, depending on whether the consequence involves a stimulus that is presented, or one that is removed or avoided. In *positive reinforcement,* something pleasant follows a response; in *negative reinforcement,* something unpleasant is removed. In *positive punishment,* something unpleasant follows the response; in *negative punishment,* something pleasant is removed.

10. Using the Skinner box and similar devices, behaviorists have shown that *extinction, spontaneous recovery, stimulus generalization,* and *stimulus discrimination* occur in operant as well as in classical conditioning. A *discriminative stimulus* may exert *stimulus control* over a response by signaling that the response is likely to be followed by a certain type of consequence. Immediate consequences usually have a greater effect on a response than do delayed consequences.

11. The pattern of responding in operant conditioning depends in part on the *schedule of reinforcement. Continuous reinforcement* leads to the most rapid learning, but *intermittent (partial) reinforcement* makes a response resistant to extinction. Intermittent schedules deliver a reinforcer after a certain amount of time has passed since the last reinforcer (*interval schedules*) or after a certain number of responses have been made (*ratio schedules*). Such schedules may be *fixed* or *variable.* One of the most common errors people make is to reward intermittently the responses they would like to eliminate.

12. *Shaping* is used to train behaviors that have a low probability of occurring spontaneously. Reinforcers are given for *successive approximations* to the desired response, until the desired response is achieved.

13. *Behavior modification,* the application of operant principles, has been used successfully in many settings and with many people. But reinforcement and punishment both have their pitfalls.

14. Punishment, when used properly, can be effective in discouraging undesirable behavior, including criminal behavior. But it is often misused and may have unintended consequences. It is often administered inappropriately because of the emotion of the moment; it may produce rage and fear; it is hard to administer immediately; its effects are often only temporary; it conveys little information about what kind of behavior is desired; and it may provide attention that is rewarding. Extinction of undesirable behavior, combined with reinforcement of desired behavior, is generally preferable to the use of punishment.

15. In real-world settings, too much reliance on *extrinsic reinforcement* can sometimes undermine the power of *intrinsic reinforcement.* But extrinsic reinforcers such as money and praise do not usually interfere with intrinsic pleasure when a person is rewarded for succeeding or making progress rather than for merely participating in an activity, or when a person is already highly interested in the activity.

16. Behaviorists explain superstitions by noting that accidental or coincidental reinforcement can effectively strengthen a behavior. In this view, when superstitions do not extinguish, the reason is that they are reinforced intermittently, simply by chance. Superstitious behaviors are also reinforced by the agreement or approval of others, and by the illusion of control that they bring.

17. Behaviorists explain *insight* in terms of a person's or animal's history of reinforcement. In their view, insight simply involves the combination of previously learned patterns; it is the result of learning, not a way of learning.

18. Because behaviorists believe that the environment can and should be manipulated to alter behavior, some critics have portrayed them as cold-blooded and have misunderstood or distorted their views. But behaviorists argue that learning principles, if used wisely, can help us improve society and achieve humane goals.

Key Terms

behaviorism   182
conditioning   183
Ivan Pavlov   183
unconditioned stimulus (US)   184
unconditioned response (UR)   184
conditioned stimulus (CS)   185
conditioned response (CR)   185
classical conditioning   185

extinction (in classical conditioning)   186
spontaneous recovery (in classical conditioning)   186
higher-order conditioning   186
stimulus generalization (in classical conditioning)   187
stimulus discrimination (in classical conditioning)   187

CHAPTER SIX

Social and Cognitive Learning

*I*n 1903, an Irish journalist named Frank Skeffington married a young woman named Hanna Sheehy. To demonstrate his commitment to women's rights, he added her name to his, becoming Frank Sheehy-Skeffington; wore a large "Votes for Women" badge; and resigned as registrar of University College, Dublin, when the university refused to grant women equal status with men. Throughout their lives, Frank and Hanna Sheehy-Skeffington never wavered in their commitment to unpopular causes—women's rights, Irish independence, and nonviolence—despite public ridicule, harassment, and even time in jail. In 1915, with World War I raging, Frank wrote to a friend,

> European militarism has drenched Europe in blood; Irish militarism may only crimson the fields of Ireland. . . . I advocate no mere servile lazy acquiescence in injustice. I am, and always will be, a fighter. But I want to see the age-long fight against injustice clothe itself in new forms suited to a new age. I want to see the manhood of Ireland no longer hypnotised by the glamour of "the glory of arms," no longer blind to the horrors of organised murder. (quoted in Levenson, 1983)

Why do individuals like the Sheehy-Skeffingtons care little for the conventional boundaries of masculinity and femininity? What keeps people working for long-term dreams that might never pay off in their lifetimes? How does behavior become so inherently rewarding that it does not depend on the immediate reinforcers offered by society? After all, few of this couple's actions were rewarded; on the contrary, most of their actions were followed by negative consequences. Why did they never lose their commitment to unpopular causes?

To most psychologists, principles of classical and operant conditioning do not offer adequate answers. Even during the early glory years of behaviorism, a few behaviorists were rebelling against explanations that relied solely on conditioning principles. In the 1940s, two social scientists proposed a modification they called "social-learning theory" (Dollard & Miller, 1950). Most human learning, they argued, is acquired by observing other people in social context, rather than through standard conditioning procedures.

By the 1960s and 1970s, social-learning theory was in full bloom, and a new element had been added: the human capacity for higher-level cognitive processes. Its proponents agreed with behaviorists that human beings, along with the rat and the rabbit, are subject to the laws of operant and classical conditioning. But they added that human beings, unlike the rat and the rabbit, are full of attitudes, beliefs, and expectations that affect the way they acquire information, make decisions, reason, and solve problems. These mental processes affect what individuals will do at any given moment and also, more generally, the personality traits they develop.

Today, **social-cognitive learning theories,** as they are now known, differ from behaviorism in their emphasis on the *interaction* between thoughts, beliefs, and expectations, on the one hand, and behavior, on the other (Bandura, 1986; Mischel, 1973). Like behaviorists, social-cognitive learning theorists continue to stress the influence of the immediate environment on a person's actions. Different situational reinforcers are the reason that employees may be honest at work and cheat on their taxes, or that teenagers may behave dutifully and lovingly to their parents but commit thefts and vandalism with their buddies. But social-cognitive learning theorists differ from orthodox behaviorists by arguing that people often choose what situations to get into in the first place, and their behavior in any situation often depends on what they are thinking and feeling about it. Thoughts, behavior, and the situation all affect one another (Mischel, 1984, 1990; Mischel & Shoda, 1995).

In the first half of this chapter, we will consider the distinguishing features of social-cognitive learning approaches. Then we will see how they might help us understand two complex aspects of child development: how children learn the rules of gender and how they become moral and helpful members of society.

BEYOND BEHAVIORISM: THE ROLE OF COGNITIONS

Modern social-cognitive learning theories emphasize four phenomena in particular: (1) latent learning; (2) observational learning; (3) perceptions and interpretations of events; and (4) motivating beliefs, such as enduring expectations of success or failure and confidence or doubt in one's ability to master new skills and achieve goals.

---

social-cognitive learning theories Theories that emphasize how behavior is learned and maintained through the interaction between individuals and their environments, an interaction strongly influenced by such cognitive processes as observations, expectations, perceptions, and motivational beliefs.

Latent Learning

Early behaviorists liked to compare the mind to an engineer's hypothetical "black box," a device whose workings must be inferred because they cannot be observed directly. To them, the box contained irrelevant wiring; it was enough for them to know that pushing a button on the box would produce a predictable response. But even as early as the 1930s, a few behaviorists could not resist peeking into that black box. Edward Tolman (1938) committed virtual heresy at the time by noting that his rats, when pausing at turning points in a maze, seemed to be *deciding* which way to go. Moreover, the animals sometimes seemed to be learning even without any reinforcement. What, he wondered, was going on in their little rat brains that might account for this puzzle?

In a classic experiment, Tolman and C. H. Honzik (1930) placed three groups of rats in mazes and observed their behavior each day for more than two weeks. The rats in Group 1 always found food at the end of the maze. Group 2 never found food. Group 3 found no food for ten days but then received food on the eleventh. The Group 1 rats, which had been reinforced with food, quickly learned to head straight for the end of the maze without going down blind alleys, whereas Group 2 rats did not learn to go to the end. But the Group 3 rats were different. For ten days they appeared to follow no particular route. Then, on the eleventh day, when food was introduced, they quickly learned to run to the end of the maze. By the next day, they were doing as well as those in Group 1, which had been rewarded from the beginning (see Figure 6.1 on the next page).

Group 3 had demonstrated **latent learning,** learning that is not immediately expressed. A great deal of human learning also remains latent until circumstances allow or require it to be expressed. A driver finds her way to Fourth and Kumquat Streets using a new route she has never used before. A little boy observes a parent setting the table or tightening a screw but does not act on this learning for years; then he finds he knows how to do these things, even though he has never done them before.

Latent learning poses problems for behavioral theories. Not only does it occur in the absence of any obvious reinforcer, but it also raises questions about what, exactly, is learned during learning. In the Tolman and Honzik study, the rats that were not given food until the eleventh day had no reason to run toward the end during their first ten days in the maze. Yet clearly they had learned *something*. Tolman (1948) argued that this "something" was information, in this case a mental representation of the spatial layout of the environment. The driver who takes a new route to avoid a traffic jam has similar information; she can take the detour because she already knows how the city is laid out. More generally, according to social-cognitive theories, what we learn in latent learning is not a specific response, but *knowledge* about responses and their consequences. When Tolman opened the "black box" of the mind, many surprises flew out.

---

latent learning A form of learning that is not immediately expressed in an overt response; it occurs without obvious reinforcement.

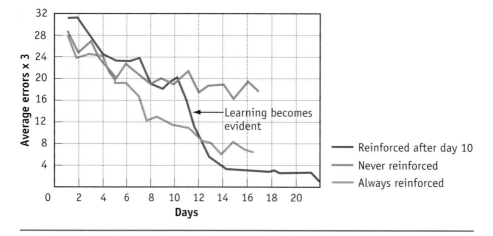

FIGURE 6.1 LATENT LEARNING *In a classic experiment, rats that always found food in a maze made fewer and fewer errors in reaching the food (grey line). Rats that never received food showed little improvement (light blue line). Rats in a third group got no food for ten days, and then were given food on the eleventh. These animals rapidly improved from then on, quickly equaling the performance of the rats that had gotten food from the start (Tolman & Honzik, 1930). Many theorists conclude that learning involves cognitive changes that can occur in the absence of reinforcement and that may not be acted on until a reinforcer becomes available.*

Observational Learning

Late one night, a friend who lives in a rural area was awakened by a loud clattering and banging. Her whole family raced outside to find the source of the commotion. A raccoon had knocked over a "raccoon-proof" garbage can and seemed to be demonstrating to an assembly of other raccoons how to open it: If you jump up and down on the can's side, the lid will pop off.

According to our friend, the observing raccoons learned from this episode how to open stubborn garbage cans, and the observing humans learned how smart raccoons can be. In short, they all benefited from **observational learning:** learning by watching what others do and what happens to them for doing it. Behaviorists have always acknowledged the importance of observational learning, which they call *vicarious conditioning,* and have tried to explain it in stimulus-response terms. But social-cognitive learning theorists believe that in human beings, observational learning cannot be fully understood without taking into account the thought processes of the learner. They emphasize the knowledge that results when a person sees a model—another person—behaving in certain ways and experiencing the consequences (Bandura, 1986).

---

observational learning A process in which an individual learns new responses by observing the behavior of another (a model) rather than through direct experience; in behaviorism, it is called *vicarious conditioning.*

None of us would last long without observational learning. We would have to learn to avoid oncoming cars by walking into traffic and suffering the consequences or to swim by jumping into a deep pool and flailing around. Learning would be not only dangerous but also inefficient. Parents and teachers would be busy 24 hours a day shaping children's behavior. Bosses would have to stand over their employees' desks, rewarding every little link in the complex behavioral chains we call typing, report writing, and accounting.

Many years ago, Albert Bandura and his colleagues showed just how important observational learning is, especially for children who are learning the rules of social behavior (Bandura, Ross, & Ross, 1963). The researchers had nursery-school children watch a short film of two men, Rocky and Johnny, playing with toys. (Apparently the children did not think this behavior was the least bit odd.) In the film, Johnny refuses to share his toys, and Rocky responds by clobbering him. Rocky's actions are rewarded because he winds up with all the toys. Poor Johnny sits dejectedly in the corner, while Rocky marches off with a sack full of his loot and a hobbyhorse under his arm. After viewing the film, each child was left alone for 20 minutes in a playroom full of toys, including some shown in the film. Watching through a one-way mirror, the researchers found that the children were much more aggressive in their play than was a control group that had not seen the film. Some children imitated Rocky almost exactly. At the end of the session, one little girl even asked the experimenter for a sack!

Of course, children imitate positive activities, too. Matt Groening, the creator of the TV cartoon show *The Simpsons,* decided it would be funny if the Simpsons' 8-year-old daughter Lisa played the baritone sax. Sure enough, across the country, little girls began imitating her. Cynthia Sikes, a saxophone teacher in New York, told *The New York Times* (January 14, 1996) that "when the show started, I got an influx of girls coming up to me saying, 'I want to play the saxophone because Lisa Simpson plays the saxophone.'" And Groening said his mail regularly includes photos of girls holding up their saxophones.

Observational learning begins very early. Even children who are too young to speak are natural mimics who learn by observing and imitating the behavior of others. Babies will mimic the facial expressions of adults, and by 1 year of age they are able to learn by watching other babies, too. Elizabeth Hanna and Andrew Meltzoff (1993) designed five puzzle toys that a 1-year-old could not have seen elsewhere. With one toy, the baby had to learn to poke a finger through a hole in a box to activate a buzzer. Another toy was a plastic cup made of rings; the trick was to collapse the cup by pressing it down with the palm of the hand. In one of their experiments, with sixty 14-month-old babies, several babies learned to be "experts" by sitting on their mothers' laps and watching an experimenter demonstrate the toys. The babies then got to play with the toys themselves and were praised for using them correctly. Next, the now-"expert" babies showed three fellow toddlers how the toys worked. When the babies who watched were given a chance to play with the toys, they did so correctly two-thirds of the time, within 20 seconds. This was significantly more often than a control group of toddlers who had not observed the expert, and significantly more often than another control group that had watched a toddler play with the toys without solving the puzzles.

In short, according to social-cognitive learning theories, what we learn in observational learning, as in latent learning, is not a specific response, but knowledge about responses and their consequences. We learn how the world is organized, which paths lead to which places, and which actions can produce which payoffs. This knowledge permits us to be creative and flexible in reaching our goals.

The Power of Perceptions

Social-cognitive learning theories also emphasize the importance of people's perceptions in what they learn and how they behave. Two people may live through the same event and come away with entirely different interpretations of it. All siblings know this. One may regard being grounded by their father as evidence of the father's all-around meanness, and another may see the same behavior as evidence of his care and concern for his children.

Individual differences in perceptions and interpretations help explain why simple solutions to complex social problems often fail. For example, from time to time in the United States, there are public outcries about violence in the media, and solutions range from government censorship to pressuring filmmakers to reduce film mayhem voluntarily. But does violence in television and the movies make the children and adults who observe it more violent themselves? Social-cognitive learning theorists have shown that the answer is yes and no. Because people bring different experiences, knowledge, and assumptions to anything they see, violence in the media does not have the same impact on all viewers.

There is certainly abundant evidence that movies and television programs are powerful shapers of values, attitudes, and beliefs about how we should behave—and what we can get away with. Some children do imitate or are influenced by the incessant aggression they observe on TV, in movies, and in violent video games, just as the Rocky and Johnny findings would predict (Anderson & Dill, 2000). A task force assembled by the American Psychological Association concluded that "there is absolutely no doubt that higher levels of viewing violence on television are correlated with increased acceptance of aggressive attitudes and increased aggressive behavior" (APA Commission on Violence and Youth, 1993).

Leonard Eron (1995), who has been conducting longitudinal research on this issue for many years, has found support for the APA's conclusion in studies of girls and boys in countries as diverse as Australia, Finland, Israel, and Poland. Eron thinks the reason for the link between heavy childhood viewing of TV violence and later aggressive habits is that TV violence teaches children certain attitudes, norms of behavior, and aggressive solutions to problems (yelling, calling people names, hitting, and destroying the enemy in vividly horrible ways). Craig Anderson and Karen Dill (2000), after reviewing the research on violent video games, reach a similar conclusion. The games, they note, provide a complete social-cognitive "learning environment" for aggression: violent models, reinforcement, and the opportunity to rehearse aggressive behavior, a combination that is more potent than any one factor alone. The games do not simply induce automatic, mindless imitation; rather, they simulate and reward aggressive thoughts in the player and aggressive solutions to conflicts.

Eron acknowledges that media violence does not cause all viewers to become aggressive. "The size of the relation [between television violence and aggression]," he said (1995), "is about the same as that between smoking and lung cancer. Not everyone who smokes gets lung cancer and not everybody who has lung cancer ever smoked. But no one outside the tobacco industry would deny that smoking causes cancer. Similarly, not everyone who watches violent TV becomes aggressive and not everyone who is aggressive watched television. But that doesn't mean television violence is not a cause of aggression."

Other psychologists and social critics believe that the relationship between media violence and real violence is not strong enough to worry about, for two reasons (Bushman, 1995; Freedman, 1988). First, children watch many different programs and movies, and they have many models to observe besides those they see in the media; their parents and peers are also influential. For every teenager who is obsessed with playing *Mortal Kombat* and entertains violent fantasies of blowing up the world, dozens more think the game is just plain fun, and then go off to do their homework. One person may learn from seeing people being blown away in a film that violence is cool and masculine; another may conclude that violence is ugly and stupid.

Second, critics of the TV-violence-causes-aggression hypothesis believe that cause and effect work in the opposite direction: aggressive, troubled people are drawn to violent television shows, movies, and video games. Children and adults who are habitually aggressive like to watch violent shows, and are more affected by them, than are nonaggressive people. Given a choice of films to watch, aggressive, hostile individuals prefer the violent ones. When they watch violent films, they feel angrier afterward than nonaggressive people do. And if given the chance to behave aggressively toward others after watching a violent film, they are more likely to do so than nonaggressive people are (Bushman, 1995). According to critics who believe that aggressiveness comes first and media shows are the excuse, a troubled person who is prone to aggression may find the "justification" to behave violently from *anything* he or she sees. Years ago, a German

As social-cognitive learning theory predicts, not everyone admires or imitates the role models that dominate the media!

named Heinrich Pommerencke went to the movies, where, watching women dancing on screen, he became convinced that all women were immoral and deserved to die. He then committed four brutal rape-murders before he was caught. The film that set him off was Cecil B. DeMille's *The Ten Commandments*.

In the social-cognitive view, both explanations for the correlation between media violence and violent behavior have merit. The repeated acts of aggression in the media *do* model behavior and responses to conflict that some people will imitate. But cognitive processes of perception and interpretation, along with other personality dispositions such as aggressiveness (or, in the case of people like Pommerencke, mental illness), are crucial factors that intervene between what we see, what we learn, and how we respond.

What Do You Know?

How latent is your learning?

1. A friend asks you to meet her at a new restaurant across town. You have never been to this specific address, but you find your way there anyway because you have experienced _____ learning.

2. After watching her teenage sister put on some lipstick, a little girl takes a lipstick and applies it to her own lips. She has acquired this behavior through a process of _____.

3. To a social-cognitive theorist, latent learning and observational learning show that we learn not specific responses but rather _____.

4. Although heavy viewing of TV violence by children is associated with later aggression, media violence does not affect everyone in the same way. Give three reasons why.

ANSWERS:

1. latent 2. observational learning 3. knowledge about responses and their consequences 4. Responses to media violence are influenced by individual perceptions and interpretations, personality factors, and the influence of other kinds of models, such as parents and peers.

Motivating Beliefs

Behaviorists would say that we acquire habitual ways of behaving because they have been rewarded over a lifetime. Social-cognitive learning theorists, however, maintain that our learned habits, beliefs, and goals eventually acquire a life of their own, coming to exert their own effects on behavior. In fact, these factors may have more impact on us than external rewards and punishers.

Consider the question of why people work. One obvious answer is survival; people work for food and shelter. Yet survival does not explain what motivates LeRoy to work for caviar on his table and Duane to work for peanut butter on his. It does not explain why some people want to do their work well and others want just to get it done. It does not explain the difference between Aristotle's view ("All paid employments absorb and degrade the mind") and Noël Coward's ("Work is more fun than fun"). According to social-cognitive learning theories, to understand why some people work hard, persisting even when they repeatedly fail, we need to understand their motivating beliefs and the goals they set for themselves.

In psychology, **motivation** refers to any process that causes a person or animal to move *toward* a goal or *away from* an unpleasant situation. The goal may be anything from trying to discover a vaccine for AIDS to escaping a scorpion. With physiological motives, the goal is to satisfy a biological need, as in eating a sandwich to reduce hunger. But psychological motives involve incentives such as becoming the best in a field, earning nine zillion dollars, or becoming famous by rowing across the Atlantic in a dinghy.

According to the learning perspective, no one is born wanting to row across the Atlantic in a dinghy. Behaviorists would say that this ambition, like any other, is a result of a history of reinforcers. When we say, "Pat is motivated to become famous," we are really saying that fame is positively reinforcing to Pat, which is why Pat continues to strive for it. But in the social-cognitive learning view, Pat's motivation eventually becomes internalized and self-directing, even in the absence of external reinforcers (Bandura, 1994).

We turn now to three of the most important internalized beliefs that motivate behavior: how much control people believe they have over their lives; their degree of optimism or pessimism; and their belief in their own competence and abilities.

Locus of Control. Julian Rotter (1966, 1982, 1990) is a psychologist who, in his long career, has demonstrated the benefits of integrating more than one psychological perspective, and of thinking critically about assumptions. When Rotter was first developing his learning approach to personality in the 1950s, he was working as both a psychotherapist and a researcher. He was a behaviorist in the laboratory, but he was also treating clients who weren't behaving according to behavioral principles. They kept having troubling emotions and irrational beliefs (Hunt, 1993). Rotter saw that his clients had formed certain entrenched attitudes as a result of their lifetimes of experience, and that these attitudes were affecting their decisions and actions.

Over time, Rotter concluded, people learn that certain of their acts will be rewarded and others punished, and thus they develop general expectations about whether their efforts will be successful. A child who studies hard and gets good grades, attention from teachers, admiration from friends, and praise from parents will come to expect that hard work in other situations will also pay off. A child who studies hard and gets poor grades, is ignored by teachers and parents, and is rejected by friends for being a grind will come to expect that working hard isn't worth it.

---

motivation A process within a person or animal, which causes movement toward a goal or away from an unpleasant situation.

Once acquired, these expectations often create a **self-fulfilling prophecy:** The person's expectations lead to behavior that makes the prediction come true (Jones, 1977; Merton, 1948). You expect to succeed, so you work hard—and succeed. Or you expect to fail, so you don't do much work, and as a result you do poorly. Self-fulfilling prophecies also occur in love affairs: People who expect to be rejected ("No one could love a schlub like me") often behave in ways that cause their partners to eventually leave them ("OK, you convinced me; you *are* a schlub") (Downey et al., 1998).

One early experiment showed how quickly a self-fulfilling prophecy can be created. Young women were asked to solve 15 anagram puzzles. Before working on each one, they had to estimate their chances of solving it. Half of the women started off with 5 very simple anagrams, but half began with 5 insoluble ones. Sure enough, those who started with the easy ones increased their estimates of success on later ones. Those who began with the impossible ones decided that they would *all* be impossible. These expectations, in turn, affected the young women's ability to solve the last 10 anagrams, which were the same for everyone. The higher the expectation of success, the more anagrams the women solved (Feather, 1966).

Rotter and his colleagues demonstrated the power of expectancies in many experiments. At the same time, both in his private practice and in his research, Rotter met people whose expectations of success never went up even when they were actually successful. "Oh, that was just a fluke," they would say, or "I was lucky; it will never happen again."

"At that point I put together the two sides of my work—as practitioner and as scientist," recalls Rotter, "and hypothesized that some people feel that what happens to them is governed by external forces of one kind or another, while others feel that what happens to them is governed largely by their own efforts and skills" (quoted in Hunt, 1993). Rotter used the term **locus of control** to refer to people's beliefs about whether the results of their actions are under their own control. People who have an *internal locus of control* ("internals") tend to believe that they are responsible for what happens to them, that they control their own destiny. People who have an *external locus of control* ("externals") tend to believe that their lives are controlled by luck, fate, or other people.

To measure these attitudes, Rotter developed an Internal/External (I/E) Scale consisting of pairs of statements. You have to choose the statement in each pair with which you most strongly agree, as in these two items:

1. a. Many of the unhappy things in people's lives are partly due to bad luck.
   b. People's misfortunes result from the mistakes they make.
2. a. Becoming a success is a matter of hard work; luck has little or nothing to do with it.
   b. Getting a good job depends mainly on being in the right place at the right time.

Having an internal locus of control has important advantages. Across cultures and generations, it is strongly related to achievement, especially academic achievement

---

self-fulfilling prophecy An expectation that comes true because of the tendency of the person holding it to act in ways that bring it about.

locus of control A general expectation about whether the results of a person's actions are under his or her control (internal locus) or beyond the person's control (external locus).

(Strickland, 1989). It acts as a buffer against stress (Karasek & Theorell, 1990). And it has many powerful health benefits, helping to reduce chronic pain, speed adjustment to surgery and illness, and hasten recovery from some diseases (Chang, 1998; Shapiro, Schwartz, & Astin, 1996). For example, among patients recovering from heart attacks, those who think the heart attack occurred because they smoked, didn't exercise, or had a stressful job—factors within their control—are more likely to change their bad habits and recover more quickly (Affleck et al., 1987; Ewart, 1995). In contrast, those who think that their illness was due to bad luck or fate—factors outside their control— are less likely to generate active plans for recovery and more likely to resume their old unhealthy habits.

Cultures differ in their degree of fatalism and in their beliefs about whether it is possible to take control of one's health. For example, Germans, who have access to a highly structured social-welfare system, have more psychological control over their health and work than Americans do (Staudinger, Fleeson, & Baltes, 1999). In some other cultures, people feel they have almost no control over their lives, including their health.

Might these cultural attitudes be related to mortality rates? The answer, remarkably, seems to be yes. In traditional Chinese astrology, certain birth years are considered unlucky, and people born in those years often fatalistically expect bad fortune. This expectation can become a self-fulfilling prophecy. In a study of many thousands of people matched by age and cause of death, Chinese-Americans who had been born in a year traditionally considered to be ill-fated died significantly earlier—one to five years earlier!—than whites who had been born in the same year and who had the same disease. The more strongly traditional the Chinese were, the more years of life they lost. These results held for nearly all causes of death studied, even when the researchers controlled for how well the patients took care of themselves and which treatments they were given (Phillips, Ruth, & Wagner, 1993).

Overall, then, having a sense of control is a good thing. But it is not necessarily beneficial to everyone, in all situations. The question must always be asked: control over what? It is surely not beneficial for people to believe they can control absolutely every aspect of their lives; some things, such as death, taxes, or being a random victim of a crime, are out of anyone's control. And some goals ("I'm going to be a movie star!") are not attainable even with the most determined effort, so a person who is unrealistically confident may be devastated by failure. Some psychologists maintain that the very notion of being in control of your destiny reflects a middle-class and Western view of life: Work hard enough and anything is possible (Markus & Kitayama, 1991). For some poor people and minorities, who do not have the resources and opportunities affluent people do, having an external locus of control is one way to preserve self-esteem and cope with objective difficulties. They say, in effect, "I am a good and worthy person; my lot in life is a result of prejudice, fate, or the system" (Crocker & Major, 1989).

Such findings suggest that locus of control is affected by a person's position and experiences in society—and, in turn, that it has the potential to motivate people to make changes in society. During the 1960s, when the American civil-rights movement was gathering steam, civil-rights activists and black student leaders were more likely to score at the internal end of the scale than were their counterparts who were uninvolved in civil-rights efforts (Gore & Rotter, 1963; Strickland, 1965). By the 1970s, however—after the assassinations of Martin Luther King Jr., Malcolm X, and John and Robert Kennedy, and after the United States had become embroiled in the Vietnam War—scores on the locus-of-control scale changed. Civil-rights leaders and college students became less internal—that is, less confident that they, as individuals, could improve social conditions (Strickland, 1989).

Where would you place your own locus of control? How do you think it influences your actions, or apathy, as a student and citizen? How does it affect your beliefs about the possibility of changing yourself or improving the world?

Explanatory Style. When something bad happens to you, what is your first reaction? Do you tell yourself not to panic, that you will somehow come through it okay, or do you gloomily mutter, "More proof that if something can go wrong for me, it will"?

These two responses to bad events reflect *optimistic* and *pessimistic explanatory styles.* People who have a pessimistic explanatory style tend to explain such events as internal ("It's all my fault"), stable ("This misery is going to last forever"), and global ("It affects everything I do"). People who have an optimistic explanatory style regard the same events as external ("I couldn't have done anything"), unstable ("Things will improve"), and limited in impact ("At least the rest of my life is okay").

Like having an internal locus of control, optimism is generally good for you; it is associated with higher achievement, less illness, and faster recovery from defeats and traumas (Carver & Scheier, 1999; Peterson, 2000). If you are a pessimist, you will probably protest that optimism is just a *result,* not a cause, of good health or good fortune; it's easy to think positively when you feel good! But optimism actually seems to produce good health. In one imaginative study of baseball Hall-of-Famers who had played between 1900 and 1950, 30 players were rated according to their explanatory style. A pessimist would attribute a bad performance to a permanent failing in himself, as in, "We didn't win because my arm is shot, and it'll never get better." An optimist would attribute the same performance to external and changing conditions, as in, "We didn't win because we got a couple of lousy calls, just bad luck in this game, but we'll be great tomorrow." The optimists were significantly more likely to have lived well into old age than were the pessimists (Seligman, 1991).

Optimism is also a remarkable predictor of achievement and resilience. For example, studies have found that optimistic life-insurance agents sell more insurance than pessimistic agents; and optimistic Olympic-level swimmers recover from defeat and later swim even faster, whereas pessimistic swimmers, following defeat, get slower (Seligman, 1991). When faced with a serious problem, such as deciding about a risky operation, coping with traumatic events, or overcoming drug abuse, optimists tend to focus on what they can do rather than on how they feel. They keep their senses of humor, plan for the future, and reinterpret the situation in a positive light (Carver & Scheier, 1999). When researchers followed a sample of people in Florida who had suffered devastating losses as a result of Hurricane Andrew, they found that pessimism was a significant predictor of continued distress six months after the disaster, whereas loss of resources was not (Carver et al., 1993). It's not how much you lose, apparently, but how you think about that loss that makes the most difference to your state of mind.

Talk about self-efficacy! Aimee Mullins was born without the bones that connect the knee to the ankle, and her legs were amputated below the knee on her first birthday. Mullins learned to ski and set records at the 1996 Paralympics. In 1998 she became a professional model. "[People] relate to what I'm doing, which is challenging the norm," says Mullins.

Because optimists expect to recover eventually from adversity and to be successful at whatever they do, they work much harder to reach their goals than pessimists do. Thus is another self-fulfilling prophecy created.

Self-efficacy. The third and perhaps most important motivating belief, according to social-cognitive learning theorists, is a person's sense of competence. Albert Bandura (1990, 1994) calls it **self-efficacy,** the conviction that you can successfully accomplish what you set out to do. Some people have an incredible sense of self-efficacy in the face of daunting odds. Jim Abbott became a professional baseball player, his childhood ambition, in spite of having a problem that might have squelched the dreams of most children: He was born without a right hand. Aimee Mullins was born without the bones that connect the knee to the ankle, and her legs had to be amputated below the knee. In adulthood she nonetheless set skiing records for the 100m, 200m, and long jump at the 1996 Paralympics, and she became a professional model in spite of having to use prostheses (artificial legs).

Research in North America, Europe, and Russia has found that self-efficacy has a positive effect on just about every aspect of people's lives: how well they do on a task,

---

self-efficacy A person's belief that he or she is capable of producing desired results, such as mastering new skills and reaching goals.

how persistently they pursue their goals, the kind of career choices they make, their ability to solve complex problems, their health habits, their athletic performance, and how they respond to stress (Ewart, 1995; Maddux, 1995; Stajkovic & Luthans, 1998). According to Bandura (1994), self-efficacy comes from four sources:

1 HAVING EXPERIENCES IN MASTERING NEW SKILLS AND OVERCOMING OBSTACLES. Occasional failures may not be much fun, but they are necessary for self-efficacy. Without them, people learn to expect quick results and tend to be easily discouraged by normal difficulties.

2 HAVING SUCCESSFUL AND COMPETENT ROLE MODELS. By observing the abilities of people you identify with, you learn that a task or occupation is possible. Negative role models, on the other hand, can undermine self-efficacy: If other people in your group have not succeeded, you may come to doubt that you can make it. Role models are usually people of your own culture, gender, or ethnicity, but not always; one young black girl told an educator that her role model for becoming a dancer was the great Russian ballet dancer Mikhail Baryshnikov.

3 GETTING FEEDBACK AND ENCOURAGEMENT FROM OTHERS. Self-efficacy increases when other people give you helpful feedback about your performance, and when they reward your efforts and do not subject you to repeated put-downs and discouragement.

4 LEARNING HOW TO READ AND MANAGE YOUR OWN PHYSIOLOGICAL STATE. You will feel more competent when you are calm and relaxed than when you are tense or under stress. But people with self-efficacy are even able to use nervousness productively. For example, instead of interpreting normal feelings of stage fright as evidence that they are going to make fools of themselves when they give a talk, they regard these jitters as a source of energy that will help them perform better.

Notice that the first entry on Bandura's list includes not only experiences with success but also experiences with failure. This is a very important point. Behaviorists, after all, would predict that failure should cause "achievement behavior" to decline. But to social-cognitive learning theorists, everything depends on how people interpret their failures, which in turn depends on their self-efficacy. Imagine that two people are faced with a difficult problem, and both do poorly. But a person with high self-efficacy interprets failure as an opportunity to learn from mistakes, and a person with low self-efficacy interprets failure as an embarrassing disaster. Thus the one who is low in self-efficacy is likely to give up, whereas the one who is high in self-efficacy keeps striving to master it. These different responses have little to do with their abilities; many talented people lack the self-efficacy to persist in the face of failure, and their talents are lost to history.

Self-efficacy is related, too, to how people think of their goals. People who are motivated by **performance goals** are concerned with doing well, being judged positively, and

---

performance goals Goals framed in terms of performing well in front of others, being judged favorably, and avoiding criticism.

avoiding criticism (Dweck, 1992; Dweck & Sorich, 1999). When such people are focused on how well they are performing and then they do poorly, they often decide the fault is theirs and they stop trying to improve. Because their goal is to demonstrate their abilities, they set themselves up for grief when they temporarily fail—as all of us must if we are to learn anything new. They lack the self-efficacy that would carry them through these occasional failures.

In contrast, those who are motivated by **mastery (learning) goals** are concerned with increasing their competence and skills. Therefore, they regard failure as a source of useful information that will help them improve. Failure and criticism do not discourage them or threaten their self-efficacy because they know that learning takes time. In addition, people who focus on mastery rather than performance usually feel greater intrinsic pleasure in the task they are doing or the goal they are pursuing.

Children acquire performance or mastery goals early. In one study of first-, third-, and fifth-graders, sizable percentages were already showing a pattern of helplessness and giving up when they failed to solve a difficult puzzle. Such children did not see their grades as having much to do with their efforts or abilities (Cain & Dweck, 1995).

Where did these children's attitudes come from? As social-cognitive theory would suggest, reinforcements in the environment are not the whole story. Many parents and teachers lavishly praise a child's intelligence and ability when the child does well ("Wow, Katie, are you smart!") and many parents put boastful bumper stickers on their cars ("My child is an A Student at Tidworthy Middle School"). Yet, as we saw in Chapter 5, such praise can backfire. In several studies, children who were praised for their intelligence and ability later cared more about performance goals and less about mastery goals than did children praised for their *efforts* (see Figure 6.2). And after these "smart" children failed a problem-solving game, they tended to give up on subsequent ones, enjoyed them less, lied to other kids about how well they had done, and actually performed less well than children who had been praised for trying hard (Mueller & Dweck, 1998). The reason seems to be that many American children regard intelligence and ability as fixed traits that you can't do anything about. Therefore, if you fail, you might as well give up. But effort is subject to improvement; you can always try again, and that is the key to mastery. As one learning-oriented child said, "Mistakes are our friends" (Dweck & Sorich, 1999).

Bandura (1994) observes that because ordinary life is "full of impediments, adversities, setbacks, frustrations, and inequities," having an "optimistic sense of personal efficacy" is needed to sustain the effort to persist and succeed. Such a sense lies somewhere between having unrealistic delusions that all things are possible, and cynical beliefs that nothing can ever be done.

The three factors of locus of control, explanatory style, and self-efficacy are, as you might have noticed, closely interrelated. When a team of researchers conducted a factor analysis of many personality inventories and measures of psychological and physical

---

mastery (learning) goals Goals framed in terms of increasing one's competence and skills.

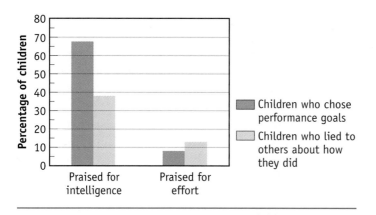

FIGURE 6.2 MASTERY AND MOTIVATION *Children praised for "being smart" rather than for "working hard" tend to lose the pleasure of learning and focus solely on how well they are doing. Nearly 70 percent of fifth-graders who were praised for being intelligent later chose performance goals (doing "problems that aren't too hard, so I don't get many wrong") rather than learning goals (doing "problems that I'll learn a lot from, even if I won't look so smart")—compared to less than 10 percent of children who were praised for their efforts (Mueller & Dweck, 1998).*

health, they found that the first key factor was "optimistic control": a sense of optimism, hope, faith in one's abilities (self-efficacy), self-esteem, and an internal locus of control (Marshall et al., 1994). Together, these concepts take us a long way from strict behaviorism. In the social-cognitive learning view, behavioral principles are important, but they omit the motivating beliefs that keep some people chasing their dreams while others dream their lives away.

What Do You Know?

You can increase your sense of control over the information you just read by answering these questions.

1. Anika usually takes credit for doing well on her work assignments and blames her failures on lack of effort. Benecia attributes her successes to luck and blames her failures on the fact that she is an indecisive Gemini. Anika has an _____ locus of control whereas Benecia has an _____ locus.

2. "I'll never find anyone else to love because I'm not good-looking; that one romance was a fluke" illustrates a(n) _____ explanatory style.

3. You are a schoolteacher and you would like your students to have self-efficacy. You should (a) be sure that they never fail in their efforts, (b) provide competent role models whom the students can relate to, (c) withhold praise so they don't get conceited, (d) avoid all criticism.

4. Ramón and Ramona are learning to ski. Every time Ramona falls down, she says, "This is humiliating! Everyone is watching me behave like a clumsy dolt!" When Ramón falls, he says, "&*!!@*$@! I'll show these dratted skis who's boss!" Why is Ramona more likely than Ramón to give up? (a) She *is* a clumsy dolt; (b) she is less competent at skiing; (c) she is focused on performance; (d) she is focused on learning.

ANSWERS:

1. internal; external 2. pessimistic 3. b 4. c

LEARNING THE RULES OF GENDER

Conversation overheard in the infant department of a large store, between a female clerk and a customer buying a blanket for her friend's newborn baby:

Buyer: I'd like this blanket, please.
Clerk: Is the baby a boy or girl?
Buyer: A boy.
Clerk: In that case, I'd suggest a different pattern. How about this blue one, with the little cowboys?
Buyer: But I like the clowns; they're so colorful and cute.
Clerk: Trust me, honey. I get lots of dads in here, and you can't imagine how much time they spend choosing colors and patterns. They all prefer the cowboys.

A baby's sex is the first thing everyone notices. No parent ever excitedly calls a relative to exclaim, "It's a baby! It's a 7½-pound, black-haired baby!" Most babies, unless they have rare abnormalities, are born unambiguously male or female, an anatomical distinction. But according to psychologists in the learning perspective, children must learn to be masculine or feminine—a psychological distinction. This learning, as the clerk realized, starts at the moment of birth, when the newborn is enveloped in the clothes, colors, and toys the parents think are appropriate for its sex.

To separate what is anatomically given from what is learned, many psychologists distinguish *sex* from *gender* (Deaux, 1985). *Sex* refers to the anatomical and physiological attributes of the sexes; thus we might speak of a "sex difference" in the frequency of baldness or color blindness. *Gender* is used to refer to the cultural and psychological attributes that children learn are appropriate for the sexes; thus we might speak of a "gender difference" in sexual attitudes, dishwashing, and fondness for romance novels. (In Chapter 10 this distinction will turn up again, when we consider from the sociocultural perspective why cultures differ in the gender rules they establish for their members.)

Toddlers can label themselves as boys or girls, but it is not until the age of 4 or 5 that most children develop a secure **gender identity,** a fundamental sense of maleness or femaleness that exists regardless of what they wear or how they behave. Only then do they understand that what boys and girls *do* does not necessarily indicate what sex they are: A girl remains a girl even if she can climb a tree, and a boy remains a boy even if he has long hair. In contrast, **gender typing** reflects society's ideas about which abilities, interests, traits, and behaviors are appropriately "masculine" or "feminine." A person can have a strong gender identity and not be gender typed: A man may be confident in his maleness and not feel threatened by doing "unmasculine" things such as needle-pointing a pillow; a woman may be confident in her femaleness and not feel threatened by doing "unfeminine" things such as serving in combat.

How do children learn the rules of masculinity and femininity, the things that boys do that are supposedly different from what girls do? Why, as one psychologist we know put it, do most preschool children act like the Gender Police, insisting, say, that boys can't be nurses and girls can't be doctors?

Limitations of Early Learning Theories

Early behavioral explanations assumed that the child was a relatively passive participant in his or her own upbringing. They emphasized the rewards and punishments that children get for behaving appropriately or inappropriately for their sex, the adult models they observe, and the lessons they learn from seeing what happens to men and women who break gender rules (Mischel, 1966). In these early formulations, the child absorbed whatever rules and lessons parents and other adults transmitted. Researchers showed that most adults start gender typing as soon as a baby is born, offering dolls to infants they believe are girls and toy footballs or hammers to infants they believe are boys, even when they don't know the infant's true sex (Stern & Karraker, 1989). It followed that if parents wanted to raise children who were free of gender stereotypes, they had only to treat sons and daughters equally and reward the same behaviors in both sexes.

Before long it became apparent that something was wrong with this argument: Children seem to act out masculine and feminine stereotypes no matter what their parents do (Lytton & Romney, 1991). Parents often insist that they treat their sons and daughters equally, yet their toddler sons still prefer trucks while their toddler daughters want tea sets. One couple we know wouldn't let a toy gun, let alone a real one, into their house, yet their 4-year-old son bit his sandwich into the shape of a gun and proceeded to "shoot" his brother. And a female friend who is a physician wondered why her own 3-year-old daughter absolutely, positively "knew" that only boys can be doctors.

Moreover, all over the world, young boys and girls tend to segregate themselves into all-female or all-male groups and play games typical of their sex. They will play

---

gender identity The fundamental sense of being male or female; it is independent of whether the person conforms to the social and cultural rules of gender.

gender typing The process by which children learn the abilities, interests, personality traits, and behaviors associated with being masculine or feminine in their culture.

together if required to, though it is often "side by side" play in which each child does something different. But given their druthers, most children immediately choose to play with friends of their own sex (Lytton & Romney, 1991; Maccoby, 1998).

There were problems with early social-learning approaches too (Jacklin & Reynolds, 1993). One was that children are not passive imitators. They *select* whom they wish to imitate, and they are terribly conformist about this. Children are unlikely to copy an adult of the same sex who is doing something different from other adults, even if the nonconformist is their own parent (hence the physician and her daughter). Another problem was that reinforcement works only when certain people administer it. In nursery and elementary school, for example, girls respond to reinforcers given by teachers but not to those given by boys. Boys, though, respond better to reinforcers given by other boys than to those given by teachers or by girls (Fagot, 1985). A third problem was that parents *respond* to their children's interests and behavior as well as shape them. Children express preferences for what they want to do and play with at a very early age, and parents react to those preferences (Harris, 1998; Snow, Jacklin, & Maccoby, 1983).

Researchers in the biological tradition believe that all this evidence means that young children's gender-typed behavior has a biological basis, perhaps in prenatal hormones, genes, or brain organization. They point out that girls who were exposed to prenatal androgens (masculinizing hormones) in the womb are later more likely than nonexposed girls to prefer "boys' toys" such as cars, fire engines, and Lincoln logs (Berenbaum & Snyder, 1995). And in all primate species, young males are more likely than females to go in for physical roughhousing (Maccoby, 1998). This evidence persuades biological advocates that there is a "biological substrate for toy and play preferences" (Lytton & Romney, 1991).

Social-cognitive learning theorists, as you might expect, do not agree. Most of them have moved away from the oversimplified view that gender typing is entirely a matter of explicit, intentional reinforcements. They believe, instead, that it results largely from three factors: (1) subtle and unintended reinforcers; (2) the development of children's cognitive understanding of gender; and (3) the specific situations the child is in.

Hidden Reinforcers

As we saw, adults often claim that they treat boys and girls equally, and many certainly try to. But social-cognitive learning theorists point out that parents and teachers often communicate subtle gender messages even though they are unaware of doing so (Lott & Maluso, 1993; Yoder, 1999). For example, many adults believe that males are naturally more aggressive and assertive than females and that this difference appears too early to be a result of systematic patterns of reinforcement. But on closer inspection, it turns out that adults respond to boys and girls differently *even when the children are behaving equally aggressively.* In one observational study, 12- to 16-month-old boys and girls did not differ in the frequency of aggressive or assertive acts (such as attempts to get an adult's attention) or in efforts to communicate. Yet teachers responded far more often to assertive boys than to shy ones, and to verbal girls than to less verbal ones. When the researchers observed the same children a year later, a gender difference was now apparent, with boys behaving more assertively and girls talking more to teachers (Fagot et al., 1985).

The hidden reinforcers inherent in the responses of parents, teachers, and other adults affect older children as well. In the early 1980s, Janis Jacobs and Jacquelynne Eccles (1985) were conducting a longitudinal study of seventh- and ninth-grade children's math achievement. At the start of the study, boys and girls were equal in math ability, as determined by test scores and teachers' evaluations. Jacobs and Eccles found that parents who believed that boys had a "natural" superiority in math were unintentionally communicating this message to their children. For instance, parents would say of their sons' good math grades, "You're a natural math whiz, Johnny!" But if their daughters got identically good grades, they would say, "Boy, you really worked hard in math, Janey, and it shows!" The implication, not lost on the children, was clear: When girls do well, it is because of concerted effort; when boys do well, it is because they have a natural gift. Over time, this attitude was related to the reduced likelihood that the girls would take further math courses, remain interested in math, and value math in general. Why should they, if the subject is going to be so hard, takes so much effort, and isn't natural to females anyway?

Parents' stereotypical expectations about boys' and girls' supposedly "natural" abilities in sports and English have a similar influence on their children's performance and feelings of competence in these areas (Eccles, 1993; Eccles, Jacobs, & Harold, 1990; Frome & Eccles, 1998). In the social-cognitive view, these parents have unwittingly transmitted their beliefs and expectations to their children by rewarding different behavior in boys and girls.

Gender Schemas

The second element in modern social-cognitive learning approaches to gender is the role of children's unfolding cognitive abilities. As children mature, they develop a **gender schema,** a mental network of beliefs, metaphors, and expectations about what it means to be male or female (Bem, 1993; Fagot, 1985; Spence, 1985). As soon as children have a

---

gender schema A mental network of knowledge, beliefs, metaphors, and expectations about what it means to be male or female.

gender schema, they change their behavior to conform to it. Thus, once a boy has a concept of himself as male, he automatically values "boy things" and dislikes "girl things," without being taught. In the social-cognitive view, children acquire their beliefs about correct gender-typed behavior from what they observe in their environments, but over time they internalize those beliefs and incorporate them into their gender schemas, which in turn affect their future behavior.

Before you can have a gender schema, of course, you have to recognize that there are two genders. This ability emerges even before children can speak. By the age of 9 months, most babies can discriminate male and female faces (Fagot & Leinbach, 1993), and they can match female faces with female voices (Poulin-Dubois et al., 1994). But it takes a couple of years before children label themselves and others consistently as being boys or girls. Once they can do that, they begin to prefer same-sex playmates and sex-traditional toys, without being explicitly taught to do so. They become more gender typed in their toy play, games, aggressiveness, and verbal skills than children who still cannot consistently label males and females. Most notably, girls stop behaving aggressively (Fagot, 1993). It is as if they go along, behaving like boys, until they know they are girls. At that moment, but not until that moment, they seem to decide, "Girls don't do this; I'm a girl, so I'd better not do it either."

Gender schemas eventually expand to include all sorts of meanings, metaphors, and associations. For example, after age 4, children of both sexes will usually say that rough, spiky, black, or mechanical things are "male" and that soft, pink, fuzzy, or flowery things are "female" (Fagot & Leinbach, 1993). (Crayons, maple trees, cameras, and telephones are neutral.)

One mystery is that virtually all over the world, boys' gender schemas are more rigid than girls' are. That is, boys express stronger preferences for "masculine" toys and activities than girls do for "feminine" ones, and boys are harsher on themselves and other boys who fail to behave in gender-typed ways (Bussey & Bandura, 1992; Maccoby, 1998). One reason may be that most societies value masculine occupations and traits more than feminine ones, and they give males higher status. So when boys behave like (or play with) girls they lose status, and when girls behave like boys they gain status (Serbin, Powlishta, & Gulko, 1993).

With increasing experience and cognitive sophistication, older children construct their own standards of what boys and girls may or may not do. Eventually, they become aware of exceptions to their gender schemas; they understand that women can be engineers and men can be cooks. From middle childhood on, many people become more flexible about gender rules, especially if they have friends of the other sex and if their families, jobs, or cultures encourage such flexibility (Katz & Ksansnak, 1994). Other people retain rigid gender schemas throughout their lives, feeling uncomfortable with or angry about the prospect of a male nurse or female drill sergeant. How flexible are your own gender schemas?

Gender in Social Context

Finally, social-cognitive learning theories emphasize the influence of a person's immediate situation and larger social context in maintaining or reducing gender-typed behavior

(Deaux & Major, 1990). In today's fast-moving world, gender schemas, attitudes, and behavior often shift as people have new experiences and as society changes. Although gender *identity,* the inner sense of being male or female, does not change, gender-typed *behavior* often changes, over time and across situations.

Thus, although most people think of "feminine" and "masculine" qualities as stable aspects of personality, both sexes often behave in feminine ways *and* in masculine ways, depending on the situation and the requirements of their roles (Deaux & Major, 1990; West & Zimmerman, 1991). Some situations, such as a date, evoke gender-typed behavior (or conscious efforts to change it): Which partner pays? Who asks whom out? Who makes the sexual overtures? In other situations, such as working on an assembly line, gender is irrelevant.

Even the salience of a person's gender depends on the situation. If you have ever been the only man in a group of women, or the only woman in a group of men, you know what we mean. You will be seen as a token representative of your sex, and your gender will be what everyone notices and uses to account for your behavior, no matter what your behavior is (Geis, 1993; Kanter, 1977/1993). Thus, the "first woman something" will be criticized for being too feminine or for trying to be "like a man." The "first man something" will be criticized for being "just like a man" or for being "too feminine." (Similarly, if you have ever been the only black, or the only disabled person, or the only young person in a group, you will be familiar with the experience of being treated as a representative of an entire category instead of as an individual.) Only when women (or men) achieve a certain critical density in a group, having enough numbers to be more than tokens or a small minority, are they perceived as having all the diverse qualities and abilities that any category of people contains.

As you can see, the gender rules acquired in childhood are not carved in stone. Gender differences in personality traits and motivations are greatest in early childhood and again in adolescence, but, according to one large meta-analysis of more than 9,000 people, they decline significantly among college-age adults and disappear entirely among older men and women (Cohn, 1991). By middle age, many people report a "gender crossover," as they explore aspects of their personalities and interests they had previously suppressed: Women often become more achievement oriented, men more nurturant and family oriented (Franz, 1997; James & Lewkowicz, 1997; Stewart & Ostrove, 1998).

Three-year-old children may behave like sexist piglets while they are trying to figure out what it means to be male or female; their behavior may be driven by genes, cognitive schemas, parental and social lessons, or a combination of all three factors. But their behavior as toddlers has little to do with how gender typed they will be at 23 or 43. The social-cognitive learning view explains why children can grow up in an extremely gender-typed family yet, as adults, find themselves in careers or relationships they might never have imagined for themselves. If 3-year-olds are the Gender Police, many adults end up breaking the law.

What Do You Know?

Taking a quiz is not a gender-typed activity.

1. Two-year-old Jeremy thinks that if he changed from wearing pants to wearing dresses he could become a girl. He still lacks a stable _____.

2. Many parents say they treat their sons and daughters exactly the same way, yet their children prefer stereotypic "boys' toys" or "girls' toys" anyway. How might a social-cognitive learning theorist explain this phenomenon?

3. Which statement about gender schemas is *false?* (a) They are present in early form by age 1 year; (b) they are permanent conceptualizations of what it means to be masculine or feminine; (c) they eventually expand to include metaphors associated with being male and female.

4. Herb hopes his 4-year-old daughter will be a doctor, but she ignores the toy stethoscope he bought her and insists that only boys can be doctors. What conclusions about gender differences can Herb draw?

Answers:

1. gender identity 2. Adults may be unaware of the hidden gender messages they convey and the influence of subtle reinforcers on children's gender-typed behavior, as when they reward aggressiveness in boys while ignoring it in girls. But even if the parents' claims are true, young children who are developing their own gender schemas can be quite inflexible about the rules and metaphors of gender-typed behavior. 3. b 4. Not many. His daughter's gender-typed behavior is typical when children are acquiring gender schemas, but it does not predict much of anything about what career she will choose as an adult. Gender schemas and notions about gender typing can change as people grow older.

LEARNING TO BE MORAL

What does it mean to be a "moral" human being? This question has been the subject of philosophic and religious debate over the ages, but we like the answer offered by psychologists Michael Schulman and Eva Mekler (1994): A moral person is someone who strives to be kind, fair, and responsible. Helping your friend cheat on a test may be kind to him but it is not fair, and therefore it is not a moral act. Treating all of your siblings in an equally mean and hurtful way may be fair but it is not kind, and therefore it is not a moral act. A moral person takes responsibility for his or her occasional lapses of kindness and fair play; he or she doesn't rely on excuses and lies. Finally, moral behavior rests on good intentions, in that one's goal is primarily the well-being of others. If you visit your 95-year-old aunt only because you hope to inherit her estate, your kindness is not a moral act.

As this definition shows, morality is a complex phenomenon involving empathy for others, intentions, the inner voice of conscience, and behaving in considerate and responsible ways (Kurtines & Gewirtz, 1991). Every perspective in psychology has had something to say about one or another of the facets of morality. Biologically minded researchers believe that empathy, altruism, and cooperation are rooted in our evolutionary heritage. Psychodynamic psychologists explore the unconscious sources of guilt, egotism, and aggression and the mechanisms by which conscience becomes internalized. Cognitive psychologists study the development and nature of moral reasoning. Cultural psychologists investigate how a society's values and traditions affect its definitions of moral behavior. And social psychologists, as we will see in the sociocultural perspective, have identified the external influences that often compel people to behave in unethical ways, in complete contradiction to what they might personally wish to do. In this section, our goal is to show how social-cognitive learning theories, with their multifaceted approach to behavior, extend our understanding of moral development beyond explanations based on biology, behaviorism, or cognition alone.

Behavioral and Cognitive Theories

Moral behavior has always posed a problem for behaviorism. Behaviorists would say that children's moral behavior depends on the rewards and punishments they get as they grow up. Indeed, when children are rewarded for aggressive and competitive acts, such behavior does prevail over cooperation and altruism (Kohn, 1992). But directly rewarding children for being helpful does not necessarily produce helpful children because, for one thing, the point of altruism is to do good with no thought of getting a reward. Moreover, behaviorism overlooks the importance of developing cognitive categories of "right" and "wrong," "good" and "bad," categories that can be applied in new situations where rewards may be absent. Finally, as we saw in the previous chapter, punishment can actually be counterproductive in teaching children or adults how to behave. You can't make people good by causing them to fear being bad.

For many years, the dominant alternative to the behavioral analysis of morality was a cognitive one, based on the child's development of reasoning abilities. The most famous cognitive theory was developed in the 1960s by Lawrence Kohlberg, a charismatic psychologist whose ideas became highly influential (Darley, 1993). Kohlberg outlined a stage theory based on how people reason about moral dilemmas. He did not observe how children or adults actually treat one another; his implicit assumption seemed to be that if people think right, they will do right. Your moral stage, said Kohlberg, can be determined by the answers you give to hypothetical dilemmas. For example, suppose a man's wife is dying and needs a special drug. The man can't afford the drug and the druggist won't lower his price. Should the man steal the drug? What if he no longer loves his wife? If the man is caught, should the judge be lenient? To Kohlberg, the reasoning behind the answers was more important than the decisions themselves.

Kohlberg (1964, 1976, 1984) proposed three universal levels of moral development, each consisting of two stages:

✦ **Preconventional morality.** Very young children obey rules because they fear being punished if they disobey and later because they think it is in their best interest to obey. Their moral reasoning is hedonistic, self-centered, and lacking in empathy; what is "right" is what feels good.

✦ **Conventional morality.** At about ages 10 or 11, according to Kohlberg, children shift to the conventional morality of adult society, which is based at first on conformity and loyalty to others and later on an understanding of the principles of law and justice.

✦ **Postconventional ("principled") morality.** Some adults, said Kohlberg, realize that certain laws—such as those that legitimize the mistreatment of minorities—are immoral. Adults at this level realize that people hold different values and standards, and that laws are important but can be changed. A very few postconventional individuals develop a moral standard based on universal human rights. When faced with a conflict between law and conscience, they follow conscience, even at great personal risk.

Kohlberg's theory of moral reasoning generated much research and discussion. Studies have confirmed the general cognitive shift from preconventional to conventional morality in many cultures (Eckensberger, 1994; Shweder, Mahapatra, & Miller, 1990). However, from a social-cognitive learning view, the theory has three significant limitations:

1 **Kohlberg's theory tends to overlook educational and cultural influences on moral reasoning.** College-educated people tend to give "higher-level" explanations of moral decisions than people who have not attended college, but all that shows, say Kohlberg's critics, is that college-educated people are more verbally sophisticated and have learned to think in legalistic terms (Eckensberger, 1994). Moreover, cultural factors play a major role in how children make moral decisions (Shweder, Mahapatra, & Miller, 1990; Wygant, 1997). In Iceland and Germany, for example, even very young children reveal a moral sense based on concern for others. In countries such as China, moral decisions and values based on social harmony and devotion to parents often conflict with Kohlberg's notion that "higher" moral reasoning is based on analytic, individualistic thinking (Dien, 1982).

"It all depends on how you define 'chop.'"

A child or adult may be verbally sophisticated in moral reasoning, and still do the wrong thing.

2 **PEOPLE'S MORAL REASONING IS OFTEN INCONSISTENT ACROSS SITUATIONS.** The kind of moral reasoning that people express depends on the situation and on the nature of the dilemma (Wygant, 1997). For example, you might show conventional morality by overlooking a racial slur at a dinner party because you do not want to upset anyone, but reveal postconventional reasoning by arguing against a governmental policy you regard as immoral. In one study using Kohlberg's dilemmas, most of the participants gave responses spanning three to six substages; only one young man scored at the same stage for all his moral judgments (Wark & Krebs, 1996).

3 **MORAL REASONING IS OFTEN UNRELATED TO MORAL BEHAVIOR.** Moral–reasoning ability increases during the school years, but so do cheating, lying, cruelty, and the cognitive ability to rationalize these actions (Kagan, 1993). College students usually draw on lofty principles of justice and fair play to justify moral decisions, yet about one-third of American and Canadian college men say they would force a woman into sexual acts if they could get away with it—the lowest form of moral reasoning (Malamuth & Dean, 1990). As Thomas Lickona (1983) wryly summarized, "We can reach high levels of moral reasoning, and still behave like scoundrels."

Another popular approach to moral reasoning was offered in the early 1980s by Carol Gilligan (1982). Gilligan argued that men tend to base their moral choices on abstract principles of law and justice, asking questions such as, "Whose rights should take precedence here?," whereas women tend to base their moral decisions on principles of compassion and caring, asking questions such as "Who will be hurt least?" This was a very appealing theory, and many women found it flattering! But most subsequent studies have found no gender differences, especially when people are allowed to rank all the reasons behind their moral judgments (Clopton & Sorell, 1993; Cohn, 1991; Friedman, Robinson, & Friedman, 1987; Thoma, 1986). Both sexes usually say that they base their moral decisions on compassion *and* on abstract principles of justice, that they worry about feelings *and* fairness.

The main problem with Gilligan's theory, as with Kohlberg's, is that it implies that moral reasoning is fixed and consistent, depending on either your stage or your gender. But moral reasoning at any age depends on what people are reasoning about: abstract dilemmas that have no relevance to their lives or personal dilemmas they care deeply about (Wygant, 1997). Both sexes tend to use justice-based reasoning when they are thinking about highly abstract ethical dilemmas, and both use care-based reasoning when they are thinking about dilemmas in their private lives (Clopton & Sorell, 1993; Walker, de Vries, & Trevethan, 1987).

Moral *behavior,* too, often depends on the situation and the issue, and it may be inconsistent with the way a person reasons about a hypothetical dilemma. A politician may have an excellent record on human rights around the world and yet be unfaithful to his or her spouse; an executive may treat employees ruthlessly, yet be a kind and doting parent. Even those admirable people who reach Kohlberg's sixth stage are not paragons of virtue in all situations. Mohandas Gandhi, for example, reached the highest moral stage because of his commitment to universal principles of peace, justice, and nonviolence. But as Gandhi's biographers have pointed out, he was also aloof from his family and followers, whom he often treated in the harshest and most callous manner.

None of this would surprise a social-cognitive learning theorist. Because the social-cognitive learning approach emphasizes the power of the situation and people's perceptions, values, beliefs, and abilities to rationalize, it accurately predicts that people will not be all good or all bad in their moral reasoning or behavior. Only a few saints can be expected to be fair, just, and responsible in all circumstances; the rest of us are merely human.

What Do You Know?

It is morally appropriate to take this quiz.

1. Margo says you should pay your taxes because it's important to obey the law; Manny says you should pay because otherwise you might get caught. According to Kohlberg, what level of moral reasoning has each of them achieved?

2. Two psychologists noted that in Kohlberg's system, the cruelest lawyer could get a higher moral-reasoning score than the kindest 8-year-old (Schulman & Mekler, 1994). What did the psychologists mean?

ANSWERS:

1. Margo is at a conventional level, Manny at a preconventional level. 2. The lawyer's score reflects verbal sophistication and education and does not indicate whether he or she actually behaves in a kind and moral way; people's moral reasoning and their behavior are often unrelated.

Social-Cognitive Learning Theories

As we have seen, strictly behavioral or cognitive explanations do not explain how children learn to resist the temptations to steal, lie, cheat, and otherwise behave as they might like. Social-cognitive learning theories add some missing ingredients in moral development, such as the power of observational learning. How do celebrities and other role models behave, and what do they get away with? What message is conveyed when a person commits an illegal or unethical act and then earns a fortune from movie deals and a tell-all autobiography? What message is conveyed when sports heroes are allowed to get away with date rape and other acts of violence because their ability to help their teams win is considered too valuable to lose? Social-cognitive learning explanations of moral development also emphasize the processes by which children internalize parental standards of right or wrong and acquire conscience—that inner voice that commends you for doing something kind and makes you feel guilty and miserable when you behave badly.

Moral Emotions. The capacity for moral feeling, like that for language and attachment, seems to be inborn. As Jerome Kagan (1984) said, "Without this fundamental human capacity, which nineteenth-century observers called a *moral sense,* the child could not be socialized." The moral sense develops out of children's attachment to their parents. Because children need to give love to and receive love from their parents, they are motivated to adopt the parents' standards of good and bad behavior. Children who break the parents' rules are afraid not just of being punished, but also of losing their parents' love. Children shift from obeying rules for external reasons, such as fear of punishment, to obeying rules for internal reasons, because they will feel guilty or ashamed of behaving badly or disappointing the loved parent (Bandura, 1991).

The internalization of moral standards begins with *empathy,* the ability to feel bad about another person's unhappiness or pain. The capacity for empathy appears to be innate, though of course it takes different forms and becomes more complex with age (Eisenberg et al., 1996). Even before infants have a sense of themselves as distinct from others, they feel general distress at another person's misery. One 11-month-old girl in a study, seeing an older child fall and cry, behaved as if *she* had been hurt. She looked about to cry, put her thumb in her mouth, and buried her head in her mother's lap (Hoffman, 1989). Parents and societies can encourage or inhibit children's natural empathy. Whether a 4-year-old boy will feel empathy or animosity toward a newborn sister's wails, for instance, depends on the experience he has in taking care of her.

In addition to empathy, other moral emotions—notably shame and guilt—regulate moral behavior. Although people might like a life without shame or guilt, these emotions are essential to the social learning of morality. They help maintain rules and standards, and they encourage moral action. *Shame* is a wound to the self-concept. It comes from perceiving that others have seen you doing something wrong and that they will like you less for having done it. As soon as the toddler has a sense of self, about the age of 2, shame is quick to follow (Lewis, 1992). *Guilt,* in contrast, is the emotion you feel when you have not lived up to your own internal standards; it is remorse for real or imagined wrongdoings, a kind of self-inflicted punishment (Tangney et al., 1996).

Because of their attachment to parents and other family members, their developing feelings of empathy, shame, and guilt, and the development of a sense of self, children by the age of 2 are aware of "right" and "wrong." Even at this tender age they react with anxious concern or distress when a standard has been violated. By the age of 3 or 4, children associate a bad act with being a "bad boy" or "bad girl" and begin to regulate their moral behavior. In every culture around the world, children at this age judge their thoughts, feelings, and behavior against the standards they know are right (Edwards, 1987; Hoffman, 1994; Kagan & Lamb, 1987). In turn, adults begin to treat children differently, expecting them to follow the moral standards they hold appropriate.

Parental Lessons. Children internalize moral standards as much from *how* their parents interact with them as from the content of their parents' lessons. When you did something wrong as a child, what did the adults in your family do about it? Did they shout at you, punish you, or explain the error of your ways? One of the most common methods used by parents to enforce moral standards is **power assertion,** an authoritarian approach in which the adult issues threats, uses physical punishment and ridicule, deprives the child of privileges, and generally takes advantage of being bigger, stronger, and more powerful ("Do it because I say so"). Yet power assertion, which is based on the child's fear of punishment, is associated with a *lack* of moral feeling and behavior in children, poor self-control, and a failure to internalize moral values (Baumrind, 1991).

Perhaps, however, aggressive, disruptive children are hard to discipline consistently, so the parent must respond with efforts to assert power. In many cases this is indeed true (Henry et al., 1996). But longitudinal studies also show that power assertion by parents can lead to aggressiveness and poor impulse control in children. Parents of aggressive children do a lot of shouting, scolding, and spanking, but they fail to clearly connect all that punishment to the child's behavior. They do not state clear rules, require compliance, consistently punish violations, or praise good behavior. Instead, they nag and shout at the child, occasionally and unpredictably tossing in a slap or a loss of privileges. This combination of power assertion with a pattern of intermittent discipline causes the children's aggressiveness to increase and eventually get out of hand. The child becomes withdrawn, manipulative, and difficult to control, which causes the parents to assert their power even more forcefully, which makes the child angrier, . . . and a vicious cycle is generated (Patterson, Reid, & Dishion, 1992; Snyder & Patterson, 1995).

The alternative to power assertion is not total permissiveness. When parents exercise too little control, failing to make clear, strong demands for mature and responsible behavior on the part of their children, their children tend to become impulsive, immature, irresponsible, and unmotivated (Baumrind, 1991). A far more successful method for teaching moral behavior is **induction,** in which the parent states rules clearly and enforces them consistently, but in an authori*tative,* not an authori*tarian* way. The parent *explains* the rules, appealing to the child's own resources, affection for others, and sense of responsibility. For example, a mother may tell her misbehaving child that the child's actions will harm, inconvenience, or disappoint another person ("You made Doug cry; it's not nice to bite"; "You must never poke anyone's eyes because that could hurt them seriously"). Or the parent might appeal to the child's own helpful inclinations ("I know you're a person who likes to be good to others"), which is far more effective than citing external reasons to be good ("You'd better be nice or you won't get dessert") (Eisenberg, 1995). Punishment, when it is used, takes the form of a forceful reprimand or a time-out, accompanied by an explanation ("You can't play with that toy for a while because you hit people with it") (Schulman & Mekler, 1994). Children raised with induction tend to feel guilty if they hurt others. They internalize standards of right and wrong, confess rather than lie if they misbehave, accept responsibility for their misbehavior, and are thoughtful of others (Hoffman, 1994; Radke-Yarrow, Zahn-Waxler, & Chapman, 1983).

---

power assertion A method of correcting a child's behavior in which the parent uses punishment and authority.

induction A method of correcting a child's behavior in which the parent appeals to the child's own abilities, sense of responsibility, and feelings for others.

Of course, there is no single correct way to raise children who are kind, moral, and responsible. Some children do well in authoritarian families, because they interpret their parents' behavior as being in their own best interest (Harris, 1998). And, as we will see in Chapter 9, once children leave home, they are out of their parents' "reach" and become subject to the influences, pressures, and temptations of their peer groups. Nevertheless, certain child-rearing practices have been shown to increase children's immunity to peer pressure and to help them internalize their parents' moral standards: consistent parental discipline and close supervision, parental affection and close parent-child attachment, low levels of aggression in the father, and high parental standards and expectations (McCord, 1992; Patterson et al., 1998; C. Smith et al., 1997).

The Larger Culture. A final influence on children's moral behavior is what adults expect of them, and these expectations vary widely across cultures (Eisenberg, 1995; Segall et al., 1999). In a study of children in Kenya, India, Mexico, the Philippines, the United States, Okinawa, and five other cultures, researchers measured how often children behaved altruistically (offering help, support, or unselfish suggestions) or egoistically (seeking help and attention or wanting to dominate others) (Whiting & Edwards, 1988; Whiting & Whiting, 1975). American children were the least altruistic on all measures and the most egoistic. The most altruistic children came from societies in which children are assigned many tasks, such as caring for younger children and gathering and preparing food. These children knew that their work made a genuine contribution to the well-being or economic survival of the family. In cultures that value individual achievement and self-advancement, taking care of others has less importance.

In summary, in accounting for how children learn to become (or fail to become) kind, helpful, and responsible members of society, social-cognitive learning approaches move beyond simple rewards and punishments or having the sophisticated verbal ability

In many cultures, children are expected to contribute to the family income and to take care of younger siblings. These experiences encourage helpfulness and empathy.

to justify moral decisions. They direct us to the importance of the moral emotions of empathy, shame, and guilt; the role of attachment; the styles of child rearing that foster or inhibit moral standards and behavior; the societal models that children observe and the values of the larger culture; and the importance of the behavior that is expected and required of children in everyday situations.

What Do You Know?

To raise children who are kind and helpful, parents and parents-to-be should be able to answer the following questions.

1. Shame and guilt are (a) unconscious emotions in infancy, (b) necessary for internalizing moral standards, (c) destructive emotions that should be stamped out as soon as possible.

2. Which method of parental discipline tends to create children who have internalized values of helpfulness and empathy? (a) induction, (b) punishment, (c) power assertion, (d) ignoring bad behavior and praising good behavior

3. In the biological perspective you read that many personality traits have a genetic component, are resistant to change, and emerge almost regardless of what parents do. Yet social-cognitive learning theorists offer evidence that what parents do *does* make a difference. How might these two lines of research be reconciled?

ANSWERS:

1. b 2. a 3. We can avoid either-or thinking by asking which qualities may be due largely to temperament (such as timidity and extroversion) and which are strongly affected by parental and societal lessons (such as aggressiveness and empathy). We can also recognize that a child's behavior depends on the interactions between his or her temperament and the parents' reactions, and that the relative impact of temperament and parental technique may change as the child matures.

Principles of social-cognitive learning have much to offer in understanding Frank and Hanna Sheehy-Skeffington, whose story opened this chapter. Their parents were role models of people who practiced what they preached. They held high standards for all of their children and did not require them to conform to gender stereotypes. Frank's father wanted his son to acquire habits of "order, virtue, morality, and feelings of kindliness for others" (quoted in Levenson, 1983). Hanna grew up in a politically active household in which all the daughters were educated and encouraged to develop their own interests. By the time they were young adults, Frank and Hanna had developed a commitment toward others less fortunate than they, as well as a set of motivating beliefs that allowed them to act on that commitment. Like human-rights activists everywhere, they had a strong internal locus of control, optimism, and a sense of self-efficacy about their ability to improve the world, or at least a little part of it, in their lifetimes.

Frank Sheehy-Skeffington died as he had lived, committed to pacifism in violent times. During the Easter Uprising against the British in 1916, Frank, who was thoroughly sympathetic to Ireland's cause, ran to the aid of a British officer who lay bleeding in a crossfire of shells. When Hanna admonished him for risking his life, he said, "I could not let anyone bleed to death while I could help." Later, while posting notices advising the populace not to riot or loot, he was arrested, taken to prison, and there murdered on the whim of a fanatic British captain. Hanna continually assailed the English military and government until the true circumstances of Frank's death were revealed and his murderer was punished. She lived another 30 years as her husband had lived, a tireless campaigner for equality for women and justice for everyone. ◼

Summary

1. Even during the heyday of behaviorism, a few behaviorists were rebelling against explanations that relied solely on conditioning principles. One result was *social-cognitive learning theory,* whose proponents study not only environmental influences on behavior but also the impact of cognitive processes and the interaction between thoughts, behavior, and the environment.

2. Social-cognitive learning theories emphasize latent learning, observational learning, cognitive processes such as perceptions and interpretations of events, and motivating beliefs such as expectations of success or failure.

3. In *latent learning,* no obvious reinforcer may be present during learning, and a response is not expressed until later. In *observational learning,* which begins in infancy, people learn by watching what others (*models*) do and what happens to them for doing it. Social-cognitive learning theories hold that latent and observational learning reflect *knowledge* about responses and their consequences. Because people differ in their perceptions and beliefs, they may learn different lessons from the same event or situation, as in the case of media violence.

4. In contrast to behaviorists, social-cognitive learning theorists maintain that learned habits and beliefs can eventually exert their own effects on behavior and may even supersede the power of external rewards and punishers. In this view, *motivation* depends not simply on one's history of reinforcement but also on internalized beliefs that become self-directing even in the absence of immediate reinforcers. People develop general expectations about which situations and acts will be rewarding, and these expectations often create a *self-fulfilling prophecy.*

5. Self-motivating beliefs concerning locus of control, explanations of events, and self-efficacy are especially important. People who have an *internal locus of control* tend to believe they are responsible for what happens to them; those with an *external locus of control* tend to believe that what happens to them is due to luck, fate, or other people. Having an internal locus of control has important psychological and even physical advantages.

6. People with an *optimistic explanatory style* differ from those with a *pessimistic explanatory style* in how they explain bad events that befall them. Optimism is a predictor of achievement, resilience, and health.

7. *Self-efficacy,* the belief that you are competent and can accomplish your goals, affects health, ambition, and motivation. Self-efficacy comes from experience in mastering new skills, having positive role models, getting encouragement from others, and making constructive interpretations of your own physical or emotional state. A person with high self-efficacy interprets failure as an opportunity to learn from mistakes; a person with low self-efficacy interprets failure as a disaster. Self-efficacy is related to the way people think of their goals. People who set *performance goals* may become discouraged when they temporarily fail and may give up; those who set *mastery (learning) goals,* focusing on learning a task well instead of performing for others, regard failure as a source of useful information, and are less easily discouraged.

8. *Gender identity,* the fundamental sense of maleness or femaleness, is not the same as *gender typing,* the process by which children learn the qualities associated with being masculine or feminine in their culture. Early behavioral explanations of gender typing assumed, mistakenly, that the child was a passive participant in his or her upbringing and that equal treatment of boys and girls would result in children who were not gender typed. But universally, young children tend to choose sextyped toys and prefer to play with children of their own sex. Psychologists in the biological perspective account for these gender differences in terms of genetics, hormones, and brain organization.

9. Social-cognitive learning theorists, in contrast, believe that gender typing occurs because of subtle, hidden reinforcers and societal messages, and also because of the development of *gender schemas,* which help shape a child's gender-typed behavior. Gender schemas tend to be inflexible at first but often become less rigid as the child assimilates new information and matures cognitively. Situations also play a role in fostering or reducing gender-related behavior. Gender typing changes over the life span, depending on people's experiences, social changes, and the gender composition of the situations people are in.

10. For many years, the dominant approach to the study of morality was behavioral or cognitive. Lawrence Kohlberg's cognitive theory of moral development proposed three levels of moral reasoning: *preconventional morality* (based on punishment and self-interest), *conventional morality* (based on conformity, loyalty, and rules of justice and law), and *postconventional ("principled") morality* (based on higher principles of human rights). The shift from preconventional to conventional moral reasoning does occur in many cultures, but from a social-cognitive perspective, Kohlberg's theory has three major limitations: It tends to overlook the influence of culture and education; moral reasoning is often inconsistent across situations; and moral reasoning and moral behavior are often unrelated.

11. Another cognitive theory of moral reasoning was proposed by Carol Gilligan, who argued that women tend to base moral decisions on principles of compassion, whereas men tend to base theirs on abstract principles of justice. Most research,

however, finds no gender differences in moral reasoning; how people reason depends on what they are reasoning about—abstract dilemmas or personal situations.

12. In the social-cognitive learning view, children learn to behave morally by observing other people's behavior and its consequences, and by internalizing moral standards based on their own internal "moral sense" and their attachment to caregivers. Parents and societies can encourage or inhibit children's natural empathy. Other "moral emotions," such as shame and guilt, are also essential to the social learning of morality.

13. Parental methods of discipline have different consequences for a child's moral behavior. The authoritarian practice of *power assertion* is associated with children who are aggressive and impulsive, and who show a lack of empathy and moral behavior. Excessive permissiveness is associated with children who are immature, irresponsible, and unmotivated. *Induction*—in which parents state rules clearly and authoritatively, enforce the rules consistently, and give explanations for rules and punishments—is associated with children who develop empathy and internalized moral standards. Around the world, parents who require children to behave in helpful ways tend to raise altruistic children.

14. In accounting for how people learn to become kind, just, and responsible, social-cognitive learning approaches move beyond explanations based on simple rewards and punishments or on people's verbal ability to justify or rationalize moral decisions.

Key Terms

social-cognitive learning theories   220

latent learning   221

observational learning   222

motivation   227

self-fulfilling prophecy   228

locus of control (internal versus external)   228

explanatory style (optimistic versus pessimistic)   230

self-efficacy   231

performance goals   232

mastery (learning) goals   233

gender identity   236

gender typing   236

gender schema   238

Kohlberg's theory of moral reasoning

   preconventional morality   243

   conventional morality   243

   postconventional ("principled") morality   243

Gilligan's theory of moral reasoning   244

power assertion   247

induction   247

Evaluating the Learning Perspective

B. F. Skinner aroused controversy the way a comedian provokes laughter. One famous controversy occurred when he designed an enclosed "living space" for his younger daughter Deborah when she was an infant. Skinner noticed that when babies cry, it is often because they are wet, hot, cold, or confined by blankets and clothing. To relieve these discomforts, Skinner invented the "baby tender" or "Air-Crib" (the public came to call it the "baby box"). The baby tender had a safety-glass front, a stretched canvas floor, and temperature and humidity controls that maintained a cozy climate so that Deborah could wear just a diaper and move around freely. A long strip of sheeting passed over the canvas, and the Skinners could crank a clean section into place within seconds. The baby box was an example of learning principles in action: If you want to reduce a baby's cries of physical distress and make infant care easier, you should fix the environment.

After writing about his invention in a *Ladies' Home Journal* article, Skinner decided to try marketing it to other parents. Did the world rush to his door in gratitude? Hardly. Although some people did order the Air-Crib, and others built their own using Skinner's plans, in the end the baby box bombed. Many people regarded it as a cage, an oversized "Skinner box" in which Skinner experimented with his own child the way he might with a rat or a pigeon (Skinner, 1978). People imagined, incorrectly, that the Skinners were leaving their child in the Air-Crib all the time without giving her the cuddling and "contact comfort" that are essential to healthy development. For years, rumors circulated that Deborah had gone insane or killed herself. Actually, both of Skinner's daughters turned out to be perfectly normal. Deborah became a successful artist and writer. Julie became a behaviorist and raised her own two daughters in an Air-Crib.

The brouhaha over the baby box illustrates the suspicion with which many people regard the learning perspective, or at least the behavioral part of it. These critics, although they acknowledge the power of the environment, regard deliberate efforts to alter it as coldly manipulative, and they are offended by behaviorism's mechanistic language. Such complaints make learning theorists want to throw up their hands in despair.

CONTRIBUTIONS OF THIS PERSPECTIVE

Defenders of the learning perspective point out that behavioral studies are among the most reliable in all of psychology, and learning principles, when properly understood, have many useful applications. The many contributions of the learning perspective include the following:

1 **THE RECOGNITION THAT WE ALL INFLUENCE OTHERS, AND IN TURN ARE INFLU-ENCED BY OTHERS, EVERY DAY OF OUR LIVES, WHETHER WE KNOW IT OR NOT.** The last time you flirted, had a political argument, or asked someone to do something, you were trying to affect someone's behavior. Even the most easygoing people inevitably influence others by their actions, responses, facial expressions, and silences. We all respond to reinforcers and punishers and produce them in response to the behavior of others; we all observe and imitate models and act as models for the behavior of others. Because we cannot avoid the laws of learning, say psychologists in the learning perspective, we ought to apply them intelligently in order to improve our lives and the lives of others. People are constantly manipulating the environment, whether in a planned or unplanned way. The important question, to a learning theorist, is not whether we should try to influence others but whether society is willing to use learning principles wisely to achieve humane goals.

As early as 1948, in his novel *Walden Two*, B. F. Skinner created his own vision of an ideal society organized and run according to behavioral principles (Skinner, 1948/1976). (He called his society Walden Two because he regarded it as an advance on Henry David Thoreau's 1854 philosophic classic, *Walden*.) Skinner imagined a place where children were reared according to the laws of operant conditioning, music and art flourished, and a modest lifestyle eliminated economic worries. It sounds pretty nice, yet many people disliked Skinner's book for what they regarded as its promotion of a calculated utopia. In response to a particularly vituperative review by the critic Joseph Wood Krutch, Skinner noted that what bothered Krutch was not the particular society Skinner envisioned, but the fact that somebody *planned* it. "Let the accidents of history work out a pattern and it's fine," Skinner said. "Let someone try it as an experimental plan and that's evil" (quoted in Bjork, 1993).

2 **THE UNDERSTANDING THAT MERELY NAMING A BEHAVIOR DOES NOT EXPLAIN IT.** By studying the specific mechanisms that cause behavior to be perpetuated or to become extinguished, behaviorists put pressure on all psychologists to be scientific and focused in their explanations of behavior. Behaviorists continually remind us that labeling someone's behavior does not explain it. What do we learn from saying that a man cannot control his drinking because he is an "alcoholic"? We might as well say that the man drinks too much because he drinks too much! Likewise, learning theorists observe, to say that a boy puts off cleaning his room because of an internal disposition called "laziness" is circular (he's lazy because of laziness) and tells us nothing, certainly not what to do about the behavior. A behaviorist would want to know what is reinforcing

the boy's "laziness": an opportunity to do something that's more fun than cleaning up, perhaps playing video games? A social-cognitive learning theorist would want to know about the boy's models (perhaps his parents are slobs), his attitudes (perhaps he can't think of a single good reason for keeping his room clean), and his gender schemas (perhaps he has learned that real boys don't vacuum). Thus learning approaches break out of circular explanations and offer practical implications for actually changing troubling or self-defeating behaviors.

3 A WIDE RANGE OF PRACTICAL APPLICATIONS. The learning perspective is probably best known for its down-to-earth applicability to people's lives. Other kinds of psychologists might give you pep talks and sermons, analyze your motives, or encourage you to live with the traits you were born with; the learning perspective tells you what to *do.* Learning theorists have sometimes been accused of regarding people as passive pawns of the environment, but that accusation is unfair. Psychologists in this perspective, behaviorists and social-cognitive learning theorists alike, have said again and again that people can and should play an active role in creating new and better environments for themselves and others. If we want emotionally healthy children, we should learn how to rear them in ways that promote emotional health. If we want a peaceful world, we had better not wait around for people's personalities to change; instead, we had better change circumstances so that cooperation is modeled and rewarded, cheaters don't win, and aggressors don't stay in power.

In Chapter 5 we saw that behavior-modification techniques have been applied successfully in homes, schools, offices, and many other settings. Social-cognitive research, too, has contributed significantly to the solution of personal and social problems. One of the most important applications of social-cognitive learning theory has been in the area of motivation. In particular, research suggests ways of helping people *set goals they can achieve.* Goals are most likely to improve performance—whatever the performance is—when three conditions are met (Higgins, 1998; Locke & Latham, 1990; Smither, 1998):

✦ *The goal must be specific.* Defining a goal as "doing your best" is as ineffective as having no goals at all. You need to specify exactly what you are going to do and when you are going to do it: "I will write four pages of this paper today."

✦ *The goal must be challenging but achievable.* You are apt to work harder for tough but realistic goals that make you feel gratified when you reach them, than for easy goals that pose no challenge or impossible goals that can never be attained.

✦ *The goal should be framed in terms of getting what you want rather than avoiding what you do not want.* People who frame their goals in terms of what they are going to accomplish (e.g., "I'm going to lose weight by jogging three times a week") feel better about themselves, feel more competent, are more optimistic and less depressed, and even have fewer colds and other physical symptoms than people who frame the same goals in terms of what they will have to avoid doing (e.g., "I'm going to lose weight by staying away from rich foods"). Can you guess why? Positive goals allow you to focus on what you can actively do to accomplish them, whereas avoidance goals make you focus on what you have to give up (Coats, Janoff-Bulman, & Alpert, 1996; Elliot & Sheldon, 1998).

Social-cognitive research also leads us to think critically about the sources of happiness and well-being. Reaching goals is fine, but what should those goals be? The learning perspective teaches us the importance of having mastery goals and the dangers of ignoring intrinsic reinforcers. In cultures that put a high value on wealth and financial success, many people believe that acquiring money, possessions, and status is the secret of happiness. But the pursuit of material wealth for its own sake has a dark side. According to studies conducted in both America (an affluent nation) and Russia (a struggling nation), people who are primarily motivated to get rich have poorer psychological adjustment and lower well-being than do people whose primary values are self-acceptance, affiliation with others, or wanting to make the world a better place (Kasser & Ryan, 1996; Ryan et al., 1999). This is especially true when the reasons for striving for money are external (something you feel obligated to do, or a way of earning the respect of others) rather than internal (because it is satisfying or a means of assuring the freedom to do what you want) (Carver & Baird, 1998).

Social-cognitive learning theory has also been used to develop programs that will help children and adults acquire self-efficacy, for example, by teaching them skills and providing models and appropriate rewards (Maddux, 1995). In these programs, people learn to alter their environments and their thinking, in order to break out of patterns that are creating a self-fulfilling prophecy. In one study, for example, graduate students in business were taught to perceive ability in making managerial decisions as a skill that can be learned and improved through practice; others were encouraged to believe that managerial ability reflects "basic cognitive processes" that people either have in abundance or don't have (Wood & Bandura, 1989). Learning to see managerial ability as a learned skill, the researchers found, "fostered a highly resilient sense of personal efficacy," which in turn caused students to continue to strive for challenging organizational goals, which in turn improved their performance, which confirmed their self-efficacy.

Finally, social-cognitive techniques can help people learn to change bad habits and take better care of themselves, especially if they have health problems such as diabetes or heart disease, or are at high risk of contracting certain diseases. The usual approaches have been to scare them ("If you do this, you'll *die*") or inundate them with information. But social-cognitive learning approaches have been far more successful: Raise people's self-efficacy and sense of internal control over their health; provide them with models of people who demonstrate how to cope with setbacks and lapses; and teach them new ways of perceiving and coping with their physical symptoms (Meyerowitz & Chaiken, 1987; Taylor, 1998).

Perhaps the clearest evidence of the learning perspective's usefulness is how often advertisers and businesses rely on learning principles to get their customers to change their behavior. Behavioral methods are apparent everywhere: in the free trips we get from frequent-flyer programs, in rebates offered by car companies, in reduced insurance premiums for nonsmokers and good drivers. Ads also draw on social-cognitive learning principles by using attractive models to sell a product, by trying to create favorable perceptions of and feelings about a product, and by encouraging consumers' optimism and self-efficacy (as in Nike's exhortation to "Just do it!").

LIMITATIONS AND MISUSES OF THIS PERSPECTIVE

Of all the perspectives in psychology, the learning perspective probably seems the most intuitively correct. Reward, punishment, observation, values, expectations, self-efficacy—these influences on behavior all seem indisputable and self-evident.

Yet the very success of the learning perspective also highlights one of its inherent limitations. Behavioral and social-cognitive learning researchers tend to study one influence on learning at a time: a parental model, a teacher's reactions, the pattern of reinforcers in a particular situation, media images, self-efficacy, locus of control, and so forth. In real life, as the examples of gender typing and the effects of media violence show, a person is surrounded by hundreds of potential influences, all of them interacting in complicated ways. This fact presents a difficult problem for researchers in the learning perspective: When nearly anything *can* have an influence on a specific behavior, it can be frustratingly difficult to show that any one thing actually *is* having an influence. It's like trying to grab a fistful of fog; you know it's there, but somehow it keeps getting away from you. This is why some learning explanations of complex phenomena, such as gender typing or aggression, can seem so vague. Learning researchers have to say, "Well, your parents play a role, and your attitudes, and unusual experiences you had, and what you observe in your culture, and what your religion teaches, and. . . ."

Of course, the fact that "the environment" consists of many interacting factors isn't a fault of behaviorism or social-cognitive learning theories. (The other perspectives are complex in their own ways, too.) But it does mean we have to be careful to avoid misusing the learning perspective, as is commonly done in the following ways:

1 ENVIRONMENTAL REDUCTIONISM. Some people misinterpret the learning perspective, especially its behavioral branch, and conclude that individuals are as soft as jellyfish, or that with the right environment anyone can become anything. Just as it's a mistake to try to reduce all human behavior to biology, so too it's a mistake to try to reduce everything to environmental influences. Genetic dispositions and biological attributes place definite limits on what individuals and species can learn.

Modern learning theorists, including behaviorists, recognize this fact and have incorporated it into their theories. For example, they recognize that all organisms seem to be biologically prepared to learn some responses more easily than others, and that conditioning procedures work best when they capitalize on these inborn tendencies.

INCONCLUSIVE EXPERIMENT:
PAVLOV'S CAT

Because of biological differences among species, you can't teach all animals the same tricks!

Years ago, two psychologists who became animal trainers, Keller and Marian Breland (1961), described what happens when biological constraints are ignored. The Brelands found that their animals often had trouble learning tasks that should have been easy. For example, a pig was supposed to drop large wooden coins into a box. Instead, the pig would drop the coin, push at it with its snout, throw it into the air, and push at it some more. This odd behavior actually delayed the delivery of the reinforcer (food, which is *very* reinforcing to a pig), so it was hard to explain in terms of operant principles. The Brelands eventually realized that the pig's rooting instinct—its tendency to use its snout to uncover edible roots—was keeping it from learning the task. They called such a reversion to instinctive behavior **instinctive drift.**

In human beings, too, inborn tendencies affect how quickly learning occurs, or even whether it occurs at all. You may remember the psychologist in Chapter 5 who learned, through a process of classical conditioning, to hate béarnaise sauce. Recall that learning took place very rapidly and with a considerable delay between the conditioned and unconditioned stimuli. The reason, as we saw, is that we are biologically predisposed to associate sickness with taste rather than other sensations.

2 **THE ERROR OF ASSUMING THAT IF SOMETHING IS LEARNED, IT CAN EASILY BE CHANGED.** Just as people often wrongly assume that biologically influenced characteristics must be permanent and immutable, so people often wrongly believe that learned behavior must always be flexible and reversible. Actually, as research in the biological perspective shows, even behavior and attributes that are strongly influenced by genetics can change, within limits, over a person's lifetime, because of a person's efforts, attitudes, culture, and experience. Conversely, behavior and attributes that are entirely learned can become deeply ingrained and almost impossible to change, such as people's religious commitments and cultural practices.

Beliefs about the possibility or impossibility of change have important political implications. Throughout history, as we noted in Essay 1 (the evaluation of the biological perspective), people have resorted to "biological politics," using biological arguments

---

instinctive drift   The tendency of an organism to revert to an instinctive behavior over time; it can interfere with learning.

to justify the subordination of women, legitimize racial inequities, and defend the social and political status quo (Fausto-Sterling, 2000; Gould, 1996; Hubbard, 1990). People who advocate egalitarianism and social change, on the other hand, are drawn to the learning perspective. Liberals who wish for a less prejudiced and gender-typed world, for example, can take solace in the idea that human nature is malleable and that what is learned can be unlearned. But just as political motivations underlying a biological view of the world can lead to an incomplete view of human behavior, so can those underlying a learning view.

For example, some psychologists argue that behavioral reductionism has blinded egalitarian-minded people to the persistence of sex differences in certain skills and learning abilities (McGuinness, 1993). Consider again the complex matter of gender typing. Naturally, feminist psychologists and biological psychologists often find themselves on opposite sides of this issue. The former think that virtually all gender differences—in levels of aggression, physical risk taking, preferences for certain toys, occupational interests such as math or nursing, and skills such as flying planes or knitting sweaters—are learned from the lessons and roles of society at large, media images, and adult treatment of boys versus girls. Therefore, in their view, gender differences will eventually fade and disappear if we change sexist images in books, on television, and in popular music; teach parents and teachers to recognize and eliminate the practices that promote gender typing; and instill in children egalitarian values. Biological psychologists, in contrast, argue that many of the persistent differences between the sexes are largely a matter of hormones, genes, and brain lateralization. In this view, parental and societal practices concerning women and men *reflect* gender differences rather than *causing* them. And so the debate over the origins of gender differences goes on, with egalitarians tending to line up on the learning side and traditionalists on the biological side.

But perhaps it is possible to break out of the dichotomous thinking that has characterized this debate for so long. Let's suppose there is a biological component in children's toy preferences. What does that tell us about *adult* occupational interests and gender schemas? The answer: not much—because children grow up and change, and because most adult occupational interests have little or nothing to do with biology and far more to do with what jobs people perceive are available and possible for them (Kanter, 1977/1993). Or suppose that biology contributes to the small *average* difference in certain skills between the sexes; why should that fact have anything to do with an *individual* woman's or man's educational or occupational opportunities? Girls, on the average, do not do as well on spatial–visual tests as boys (Halpern, 2000). Does this finding mean that women who are as good as or better than men in these skills ought to be discouraged from careers in math and science, as so many still are? Are there other ways to teach girls that might help more of them do better? Likewise, boys, on the average, are more likely than girls to have reading disabilities. Shouldn't this finding be used to develop better programs to help boys read? Learning theorists and biological theorists alike can agree that it is only by acknowledging gender differences, and being open-minded about their many possible causes, that we can hope to find the best ways of reducing or eliminating them.

3 Oversimplification in applying learning techniques. By emphasizing the complexity of elements affecting a person's life, social-cognitive learning theories alert us to another misuse of the learning perspective: a tendency to oversimplify. When people try to apply learning principles to problems in the classroom, the workplace, or the home, they often reduce the entire perspective to a simplistic kind of pop behaviorism.

Alfie Kohn (1993) observes that in many institutions, bribes and threats have become the rule: "Do this and you'll get that." American workplaces, Kohn complains, have become "enormous Skinner boxes with parking lots," places where simple-minded, competitive incentive plans have replaced responsible management. The unspoken assumption is that the only way to motivate people is to use the carrot and the stick. The results, says Kohn, often backfire. Children learn to fear their teachers or grow dependent on them, and employees feel the same way about their bosses. Everyone is so worried about failing that no one is willing to take risks. People become mistrustful of one another, demoralized when they "lose," and unwilling to work cooperatively. No one stops to ask what the source of poor performance is in the first place. No one stops to ask whether the behavior that is being rewarded is worth doing.

Learning principles are also misapplied when people give out rewards indiscriminately. For example, some teachers have tried to boost self-esteem in their students by being lavish both with high grades and with praise, in the hope that as children learn to feel good about themselves their academic performance will improve. In one middle school, when teachers tried to use a cutoff of a 3.5 grade-point average for membership in a new academic honor society, they found that *two-thirds* of the school's 600 students were eligible, even though they were not all doing A work (Celis, 1993). Grade inflation has also infiltrated higher education; in some colleges and universities, C's, which once meant average or satisfactory, are nearly nonexistent.

The problem, from a learning-theory point of view, is that to be effective, rewards must be tied to the behavior you are trying to increase. When rewards are dispensed indiscriminately, they become meaningless and are no longer reinforcing; and when teachers praise mediocre work, that is what they are likely to get. Further, an overemphasis on gold stars and happy faces ignores an important finding from social-cognitive learning research: that self-efficacy and high self-esteem come from true accomplishment, not cheap success. When a teacher gushes over work on a task that was actually easy, the hidden message may be that the child isn't very smart ("Gee, Minnie, you certainly did a *fantastic* job . . . of adding two and two"). Well-intended efforts to prop up children's self-esteem with constant praise, therefore, may actually decrease their self-efficacy!

Skinner would have disapproved of pop behaviorism, too. He certainly never advocated the mindless use of extrinsic reinforcers that are bribes in disguise. On the contrary, Skinner (1987) worried about the growing numbers of middle-class people who are bored and depressed. One reason, he said, is that a life based on the pleasures of acquisition—shopping, going to the movies, driving a nice car—can thwart

GABLE
THE GLOBE AND MAIL
Toronto
CANADA

a life of intrinsic satisfaction. "People look at beautiful things, listen to beautiful music, and watch exciting entertainments," said Skinner, "but the only behavior reinforced is looking, listening, and watching." Too rarely, he added, are people reinforced for creativity, risk, participation, taking gambles. Too rarely are they given an opportunity to take pride in the products of their work, or to exercise initiative in their choice of pleasures. Skinner, as you can see, was fully aware of the importance of intrinsic rewards.

Not everyone has shared this awareness, however, and criticisms of how learning principles are misapplied in the everyday world are worth thinking about. As we saw in our discussion of performance versus mastery goals, when people are worried about *how* they are doing, they may never get fully absorbed in *what* they are doing. And they may never develop the ability they need to persist in the face of life's inevitable setbacks and occasional failures.

What Do You Know?

Have you yet discovered the intrinsic pleasure of answering these quizzes?

1. Name three contributions of the learning perspective and three of its potential misuses.

2. An old advertisement for a weight-training program used to promise to transform even a timid, mild-tempered "90-pound weakling" into an aggressive, brave, muscle-bound hunk. What misuse of the learning perspective did this ad illustrate?

3. Now that you are familiar with behavioral and social-cognitive learning principles, what would *you* do as a teacher to design a classroom that fosters achievement, competence, self-efficacy, and an intrinsic love of learning?

ANSWERS:

1. Contributions include making people aware of the ways they influence, and are influenced by, others; the lesson that naming or labeling behavior doesn't explain it; and the practicality of the perspective's findings in solving personal and social problems. Misuses include environmental reductionism; the error of assuming that anything learned can be easily changed; and oversimplification in applying learning techniques. 2. environmental reductionism, because the ad overlooked the possibility of genetic and anatomical constraints on temperament and on body weight and shape 3. There are many possible answers. You might start by eliminating grades on some assignments and having students assess their own interests, strengths, and weaknesses. You might reward students who show improvement in their weakest skills. You might give students free time in each class hour to pursue their own individual projects. You would try to be a role model who demonstrates enthusiasm and love of learning, and who doesn't dispense different rewards to boys and girls for classroom participation. You would help students set individual goals for themselves that were challenging but realistic. You would teach students that criticism of their work is not the same as criticism of *them,* and that honest feedback is necessary for improvement. You would encourage students to regard their failures as "learning experiences" instead of catastrophes. And you would try to get your school system to reward you for teaching this way!

The learning perspective has specific lessons for us and assures us that we are never too old to learn them. In this respect, the learning perspective is, by its nature, an optimistic one. We can change for the better if only we will turn our attention to ways of fashioning better environments for ourselves, our children, and our fellow human beings. In Skinner's *Walden Two,* the main character, Frazier, exclaims, "The one fact that I would cry from every housetop is this: The Good Life is waiting for us—here and now! We have the necessary techniques, both material and psychological, to create a full and satisfying life for everyone."

Frazier was overstating his case, which was his prerogative; he was, after all, a character in a utopian novel. But he was right about one thing: Behavioral and social-cognitive research offers us an armful of "necessary techniques" that can help us improve our lives and make the world a better place.

Summary

1. Behavioral studies are among the most reliable in all of psychology, and learning principles have many useful applications. Major contributions of this perspective include making people aware of the ways they influence, and are influenced by, others; the understanding that naming or labeling behavior does not explain it; and a host of practical techniques for solving a wide range of real-life problems. Behavior modification has been used in many settings. Social-cognitive learning theories have also been helpful because of their emphasis on the interaction of the

person and the environment—for example, in helping people set and achieve goals, increase self-efficacy and motivation, and improve health habits.

2. Rewards, punishment, imitation, values, expectations, and self-efficacy all are indisputable influences on behavior. Yet the learning perspective has an inherent limitation, because in real life there are often so many interacting influences on any given behavior or social problem that it can be difficult to demonstrate the role of any one factor.

3. Misuses of the learning perspective include *environmental reductionism,* the tendency to reduce all behavior to environmental influences and ignore biological ones—such as the tendency of some animals to revert to instinctive behavior (*instinctive drift*); the belief that if something is learned it is easily changeable, which can lead to an incomplete view of a problem and an exaggeration of the possibilities for rapid changes in behavior; and oversimplification in applying learning techniques and principles, as in the mindless use of extrinsic reinforcers that are bribes in disguise.

Key Terms

environmental reductionism   257   instinctive drift   258

PART IV

The Cognitive Perspective

*T*he scene: Japan, long ago. A man is leading a horse down a narrow wooded path. On the horse sits his elegant wife, heavily veiled. Suddenly the couple is attacked by a bandit, who ties up the man and rapes the woman. And then . . . well, and then it depends on who is telling the story.

The thief, when captured, says that the woman tried valiantly to defend herself with a dagger hidden in her clothes. After the assault, he says, she told him that either he or her husband must die, to keep her from being "doubly disgraced." The thief then freed the husband and engaged him in a sword fight, killing him. But when he looked around, the woman was gone.

No, no, that's not what happened at all, says the woman. After the attack, the thief freed the husband and fled. Feeling disgraced and desperate, she ran to her husband, hoping to be comforted. But when she looked into his eyes she saw not sorrow but hatred. She picked up the dagger and begged her husband to kill her, but he sat there unmoved. In despair, she fainted and when she revived, the dagger was in her husband's chest.

Wait, that's not what happened either, says the husband (speaking through a medium, since he is now dead). After the attack, the bandit asked the woman to go away with him. She agreed to do so if the bandit would kill her husband. The bandit was shocked at this request. "What should I do with her?" he asked the husband, at which point the woman ran off, with the bandit in pursuit. Hours later, the bandit returned, cut the husband's bonds, and left. The husband, consumed by grief, used the dagger to kill himself.

Wrong, says a passerby who witnessed the crime. After the assault, the thief begged the woman for forgiveness and offered to marry her. She replied that the men must decide in a duel. Reluctantly, they began to fight. At last, the thief managed to kill the husband, but when he went to claim his prize, the woman had run away.

One incident, four different accounts, and you will find them all in Akira Kurosawa's classic film *Rashomon*. (Rashomon was the south entrance gate to Kyoto, a place where travelers used to meet and tell stories.) Kurosawa's parable teaches that the truth is elusive, that, as one character says, human beings must "create stories" that deceive not only others but also themselves. Our needs, motives, and desire to protect ourselves—all these determine the kinds of narratives we construct about our lives. That is the message of the cognitive perspective as well. As George Gerbner (1988) once observed, we human beings differ from all other species because we tell stories—and live by the stories we tell. In Chapter 7, we will see how the human mind thinks and reasons, sometimes rationally, sometimes not so rationally. In Chapter 8, we will confront the mystery of memory and find out why it is often difficult to know which of our stories are right.

CHAPTER SEVEN

Thinking and Reasoning

Here's a little test for you to try: For 30 seconds or so, look at the calm image on this page and *don't think about anything*. Don't think about what you have to do this week. Don't think about what you ate for breakfast. Don't think about your personal problems. Don't think about the weather. Don't think about reading this chapter. Don't think about psychology and don't think about elephants. *Don't even think about not thinking.* Okay, ready? Begin.

Couldn't do it, could you? Well, this is a test that everyone flunks, with the possible exception of some experienced meditators who have spent years taming the jumpy and restless nature of what Buddhists call the "monkey mind." To be human is to think thoughts from morning until night, and then to keep right on thinking, even during sleep. Descartes' famous declaration "I think, therefore I am" could just as well have been reversed: "I am, therefore I think." Not a day goes by when we don't make plans, solve problems, draw inferences, analyze relationships, concoct explanations, and organize and reorganize the flotsam and jetsam of our mental world. We can't help it.

Our impressive powers of thought and intelligence so inspired our forebears that they gave our species the immodest name *Homo sapiens,* Latin for wise or rational man. But just how "sapiens" are we? The human mind has come up with poetry, penicillin, and pantyhose, but it has also managed to come up with traffic jams, junk mail, and war. To better understand why the same species that figured out how to get to the moon is also capable of breathtaking bumbling here on Earth, this chapter will look at how people reason and solve problems, and also why, too often, they do not.

THE ELEMENTS OF COGNITION

Think about what thinking does for you. It frees you from the confines of the immediate present: You can think about a trip taken three years ago, a party next Saturday, or the French Revolution. It carries you beyond the boundaries of reality: You can imagine unicorns and utopias, Martians and magic. Because you think, you do not need to grope your way blindly through your problems but, with some effort and knowledge, can solve them intelligently and creatively.

To explain these mental abilities, many cognitive psychologists liken the human mind to an information processor, analogous to a computer but far more complex. Information-processing approaches capture the fact that the brain does not passively record information but actively alters and organizes it. When we take action, we physically manipulate the environment; when we think, we *mentally* manipulate internal representations of objects, activities, and situations.

One type of mental representation, or unit of thought, is the **concept,** a mental category that groups objects, relations, activities, abstractions, or qualities having common properties. The instances of a concept are seen as roughly similar. For example, *golden retriever, cocker spaniel,* and *border collie* are instances of the concept *dog;* and *anger, joy,* and *sadness* are instances of the concept *emotion.* Concepts simplify and summarize information about the world so that it is manageable, and so that we can make decisions quickly and efficiently. You may never have seen a *basenji* or eaten *escargot,* but if you know that the first is an instance of *dog* and the second an instance of *food,* you will know, roughly, how to respond (unless you do not like to eat snails, which is what escargot are).

---

concept A mental category that groups objects, relations, activities, abstractions, or qualities having common properties.

Basic concepts have a moderate number of instances and are easier to acquire than those that have either few or many instances (Rosch, 1973). The concept *apple* is more basic than *fruit,* which includes many more instances and is more abstract. It is also more basic than *McIntosh apple,* which is quite specific. Similarly, *book* is more basic than either *printed matter* or *novel.* Children seem to learn basic-level concepts earlier than others, and adults use these concepts more often than others, because basic concepts convey an optimal amount of information in most situations.

The qualities associated with a concept do not necessarily all apply to every instance: Some apples are not red; some dogs do not bark; some birds do not fly or perch on trees. But all instances of a concept do share a family resemblance. When we need to decide whether something belongs to a concept, we are likely to compare it to a **prototype,** a representative example of the concept (Rosch, 1973). For instance, which dog is doggier—a golden retriever or a chihuahua? Which fruit is more fruit-like—an apple or a pineapple? Which activity is more representative of sports—football or weight lifting? Most people within a culture can easily tell you which instances of a concept are most representative, or *prototypical.*

Concepts are the building blocks of thought, but they would be of limited use if we merely stacked them up mentally. We must also represent their relationships to one another. One way we accomplish this may be by storing and using **propositions,** units of meaning that are made up of concepts and that express a unitary idea. A proposition can express nearly any sort of knowledge (*Hortense raises palomino horses*) or belief (*palominos are beautiful*). Propositions, in turn, are linked together in complicated networks of knowledge, associations, beliefs, and expectations. These networks, which psychologists call **cognitive schemas,** serve as mental models of aspects of the world. For example, gender schemas represent a person's beliefs and expectations about what it means to be male or female (see Chapter 6). People also have schemas about cultures, occupations, animals, geographical locations, and many other features of the social and natural environment.

Mental images—especially visual images, pictures in what Shakespeare called "the mind's eye"—are also important in thinking and in the construction of cognitive schemas. Although no one can directly "see" another person's visual images, psychologists are able to study them indirectly. One method is to measure how long it takes people to rotate an image in their imaginations, scan from one point to another in an image, or read off some detail from an image. The results suggest that visual images are much like images on a computer screen: We can manipulate them, they occur in a

---

basic concepts Concepts that have a moderate number of instances and that are easier to acquire than those having few or many instances.

prototype An especially representative example of a concept.

proposition A unit of meaning that is made up of concepts and expresses a single idea.

cognitive schema An integrated mental network of knowledge, beliefs, and expectations concerning a particular topic or aspect of the world.

mental image A mental representation that mirrors or resembles the thing it represents; mental images can occur in many and perhaps all sensory modalities.

mental "space" of a fixed size, and small ones contain less detail than larger ones (Kosslyn, 1980; Shepard & Metzler, 1971).

Most people also report auditory images (for instance, a song, slogan, or poem you can hear in your "mind's ear"), and many report images in other sensory modalities as well—touch, taste, smell, or pain. Some even report kinesthetic images, imagined feelings in the muscles and joints. Athletes often imagine themselves performing a skill, such as diving or sprinting, and this visual and kinesthetic rehearsal seems to improve actual performance (Druckman & Swets, 1988). Brain scans show that mental practice of this sort activates most of the brain circuits involved in the activity itself (Stephan et al., 1995).

Albert Einstein relied heavily on visual and kinesthetic imagery for formulating ideas. The happiest thought of his life, he once recalled, occurred in 1907, when he suddenly imagined a man falling freely from the roof of a house and realized that the man would not experience a gravitational field in his immediate vicinity. This insight led eventually to Einstein's formulation of the principle of general relativity, and physics was never again the same.

HOW CONSCIOUS IS THOUGHT?

When we think about thinking, we usually have in mind those mental activities, such as solving problems or making decisions, that are carried out in a deliberate way, with a conscious goal in mind. However, a great deal of mental processing occurs without conscious awareness.

Subconscious processes lie outside of awareness but can be brought into consciousness when necessary. These processes allow us to handle more information and to perform more complex tasks than if we depended entirely on conscious thought, and they enable us to perform more than one task simultaneously (Kahneman & Treisman, 1984). Consider all the automatic routines performed "without thinking," though they might once have required careful, conscious attention: knitting, typing, driving a car, decoding the letters in a word in order to read it. Because of the capacity for automatic processing, people can, with proper training, even learn to perform simultaneously such complex tasks as reading and taking dictation (Hirst, Neisser, & Spelke, 1978).

Nonconscious processes, in contrast, remain outside of awareness. For example, you have no doubt had the odd experience of having a solution to a problem "pop into mind" after you have given up trying to find one. With sudden insight, you see how to solve an equation, assemble a cabinet, or finish a puzzle, without quite knowing how you managed to find the solution. Similarly, people will often say they rely on "intuition"— hunches and gut feelings—rather than conscious reasoning to make decisions.

---

subconscious processes Mental processes occurring outside of conscious awareness but accessible to consciousness when necessary.

nonconscious processes Mental processes occurring outside of and not available to conscious awareness.

Insight and intuition probably involve two stages of mental processing (Bowers et al., 1990). In the first stage, clues in the problem automatically activate certain memories or knowledge, and you begin to see a pattern or structure in the problem, although you cannot yet say what it is. This nonconscious process guides you toward a hunch or a hypothesis. Then, in the second stage, your thinking becomes conscious, and you become aware of a possible solution. This stage may feel like a sudden revelation ("Aha, I've got it!"), but considerable nonconscious mental work has already occurred.

Imagine that you are given four decks of cards and are told that you will win or lose money, depending on which cards you turn over. Unbeknownst to you, two of the decks are stacked so that they will produce payoffs at first but will make you lose in the long run, whereas the other two pay less at first but cause you to win in the long run. Every so often, someone stops you and asks whether you have figured out the best strategy for winning. Most people, when presented with this problem, start to show physiological signs of anxiety before picking cards from the losing decks, and begin avoiding those decks, *before* they consciously realize which decks are riskier. And some learn to make good choices without *ever* consciously discovering the rules for winning. Interestingly, people with damage in part of the prefrontal cortex have trouble learning that two of the decks are stacked against them; they seem to lack the sort of intuition that most people take for granted (Bechara et al., 1997).

Usually, of course, much of our thinking is conscious, but we may not be thinking very *hard*. Sometimes we act, speak, and make decisions out of habit, without stopping to analyze what we are doing or why we are doing it. Normally such a lack of awareness doesn't cause much trouble, but sometimes it can have devastating consequences. A few years ago, the pilots of an Air Florida flight were going over a pretakeoff checklist. When the de-icer was mentioned, a crew member automatically responded "off." After all, it's always warm in Florida, isn't it? Unfortunately, on this occasion the weather happened to be icy, and the plane crashed, killing 74 people. This sort of mental inertia, which Ellen Langer (1989) has called *mindlessness,* keeps people from recognizing when a change in context requires a change in behavior (Langer & Moldoveanu, 2000).

In one of the first studies by Langer and her associates, a researcher approached people as they were about to use a photocopier and made one of three requests: "Excuse me, may I use the Xerox machine?" "Excuse me, may I use the Xerox machine, because I have to make copies?" or "Excuse me, may I use the Xerox machine, because I'm in a rush?" Normally, people will let someone go before them only if the person has a legitimate reason, as in the third request. In this study, however, people also complied when the reason sounded like an authentic explanation but was actually meaningless ("because I have to make copies"). They heard the form of the request, but not its content, and they mindlessly stepped aside (Langer, Blank, & Chanowitz, 1978).

The mindless processing of information has benefits: If we stopped to think twice about everything we did, we would get nothing done ("I'm reaching for my toothbrush; now I'm putting toothpaste on it; now I'm brushing my upper-right molars"). But mindlessness can also lead to errors and mishaps, ranging from the trivial (putting the butter in the dishwasher or locking yourself out of your apartment) to the serious, as in the case of the Air Florida pilots.

Jerome Kagan (1989) has argued that fully conscious awareness is needed only when we must make a deliberate choice, when events happen that cannot be handled automatically, and when unexpected moods and feelings arise. "Consciousness," he says, "can be likened to the staff of a fire department. Most of the time, it is quietly playing pinochle in the back room; it performs [only] when the alarm sounds." That may be so, but most of us would probably benefit if our mental firefighters paid a little more attention to their jobs. Cognitive psychologists have, therefore, devoted a great deal of study to mindful, conscious thought and the capacity to reason.

What Do You Know?

Think consciously about this quiz.

1. Stuffing your mouth with cotton candy, licking a lollipop, and chewing on a piece of beef jerky are all instances of the _____ *eating.*

2. Which concept is most basic: *furniture, chair,* or *high chair?*

3. Which example of the concept *chair* is most prototypical: *high chair, rocking chair, dining-room chair?*

4. In addition to concepts and images, _____, which express a unitary idea, have been suggested as a basic form of mental representation.

5. Peter's mental representation of *Thanksgiving* includes associations (e.g., with turkeys), attitudes ("It's a time to be with relatives"), and expectations ("I'm going to gain weight from all that food"). They are all part of his _____ for the holiday.

6. Zelda discovers that she has dialed her boyfriend's number instead of her mother's, as she intended. Her error can be attributed to _____.

ANSWERS:

1. concept 2. chair 3. A plain, straight-backed dining-room chair will be prototypical for most people. 4. propositions 5. cognitive schema 6. mindlessness

---

REASONING AND CREATIVITY

Reasoning is purposeful mental activity that involves operating on information in order to reach conclusions. Unlike impulsive or nonconscious responding, reasoning requires us to draw specific inferences from observations, facts, or assumptions. Some forms of reasoning require logical processes, but others require creative leaps of the imagination.

---

reasoning The drawing of conclusions or inferences from observations, facts, or assumptions.

Formal Reasoning

In *formal reasoning problems*—the kind you might find, say, on an intelligence test or a college entrance exam—the information needed for drawing a conclusion or reaching a solution is specified clearly, and there is a single right (or best) answer.

In some formal problems and well-defined tasks, all you have to do is apply an **algorithm,** a set of procedures guaranteed to produce a solution even if you do not really know how it works. To solve a problem in long division, for example, you just apply a series of operations that you learned in elementary school. To make a cake, you apply an algorithm called a recipe.

For other formal problems, the rules of formal logic are crucial tools to have in your mental toolbox. One such tool is **deductive reasoning,** which involves drawing conclusions from a set of observations or propositions (*premises*). In deductive reasoning, if the premises are true, then the conclusion *must* also be true. Deductive reasoning often takes the form of a *syllogism,* a simple argument consisting of two premises and a conclusion:

Premise	*All human beings are mortal.*
Premise	*I am a human being.*
Conclusion	*Therefore I am mortal.*

We all think in syllogisms and use deductive reasoning, although many of our premises are implicit rather than explicitly spelled out: "I never have to work on Saturday. Today is Saturday. Therefore, I don't have to work today." But the ability to apply deductive reasoning to abstract problems that are divorced from everyday life does not come naturally; it depends on experience, culture, and schooling (see Chapter 10). And almost everyone has trouble thinking deductively in some situations.

For example, suppose the premises are "All rich people live in big fancy houses" and "Sheila lives in a big fancy house." Does it follow that Sheila is rich? Many people think so, but they are wrong. Sheila may well be rich, but the conclusion does not follow from the

Zits

---

algorithm A problem-solving strategy guaranteed to produce a solution even if the user does not know how it works.

deductive reasoning A form of reasoning in which a conclusion follows necessarily from certain premises; if the premises are true, the conclusion must be true.

premises. Perhaps she inherited that big, fancy house, or perhaps she bought it 30 years ago when it was inexpensive. Errors of this type occur because people mentally reverse a premise. In this case, they convert "All rich people live in big fancy houses" to "All people who live in big fancy houses are rich." The reversed premise may seem plausible, but it is not the one that was given. Reversed premises can have serious consequences for people's expectations and even their relationships. One of our male students worried about the effects of confusing "All rapists are men" with "All men are rapists."

Another important form of logical thinking is **inductive reasoning,** in which the conclusion *probably* follows from the premises but could conceivably be false. People often mistakenly think of inductive reasoning as the drawing of general conclusions from specific observations, as when you generalize from past experience: "I had three good meals at that restaurant; they sure have great food." But an inductive argument can also have premises that are stated as general statements. Two logicians (Copi & Burgess-Jackson, 1992) give this example:

Premise	*All cows are mammals and have lungs.*
Premise	*All whales are mammals and have lungs.*
Premise	*All humans are mammals and have lungs.*
Conclusion	*Therefore, probably all mammals have lungs.*

Inductive arguments can also have specific conclusions: If your premises are "Most people with season tickets to the New York Mets love baseball," and "Casey has season tickets to the Mets games," you might conclude that Casey loves baseball.

Science depends heavily on inductive reasoning because scientists make careful observations and then draw conclusions that they think are probably true. But in inductive reasoning, no matter how much supporting evidence you gather, it is always possible that new information will turn up to show you are wrong. For example, you might discover that the three good meals you ate at that restaurant were not typical—that, in fact, all the other dishes on the menu are awful. Or you might learn that Casey bought season tickets to the Mets not because he loves baseball but because he wanted to impress his Mets-mad girlfriend. In science, too, new information may show that previous conclusions were faulty and must therefore be revised.

Informal Reasoning

Useful as they are, algorithms and logical reasoning cannot solve every kind of problem. In *informal reasoning problems,* there may be no clearly correct solution. Many approaches, viewpoints, or possible solutions may compete, and you may have to decide which one is most reasonable. Further, the information at your disposal may be incomplete, or you may disagree with others on what the premises should be. Your position on abortion, for example, will depend on your premises about when meaningful human

---

inductive reasoning A form of reasoning in which the premises provide support for a conclusion, but it is still possible for the conclusion to be false.

TABLE 7.1   ✦   Two Kinds of Reasoning

In formal reasoning, we apply rules of logic to solve well-specified problems. In informal, everyday reasoning, we must solve problems that are less clearly defined. Here are some differences between the two modes of thought:

FORMAL	INFORMAL
All premises are supplied.	Some premises are implicit, and some are not supplied at all.
There is typically one correct answer.	There are typically several possible correct answers that vary in quality.
Established methods often exist for solving the problem.	Established procedures of inference that apply to the problem rarely exist.
You usually know when the problem is solved.	It is often unclear whether the current solution is good enough.
The problem often has limited real-world interest.	The problem is often personally relevant.
Problems are often solved as a means of achieving other goals.	Problems are solved for their own sake.

Source: Adapted from Galotti, 1989.

life begins, what rights an embryo or a fetus has, and what rights a woman has to control her own body. People on opposing sides of this issue even disagree on how the premises should be phrased because they have different emotional reactions to terms such as "rights," "meaningful life," and "control over one's body."

Formal and informal reasoning problems typically call for different approaches. (The differences between them are summarized in Table 7.1.) Whereas formal problems can often be solved with an algorithm, informal problems often call for a **heuristic**— a rule of thumb that suggests a course of action without guaranteeing an optimal solution. Anyone who has ever played chess or a card game such as Bridge or Hearts is familiar with heuristics (e.g., "Get rid of high cards first"). In these games, working out all the possible sequences of moves would take too long and be too difficult. Heuristics are also useful to an investor trying to predict the stock market, a renter trying to decide whether to lease an apartment, a doctor trying to determine the best treatment for a patient, and a factory owner trying to boost production. All are faced with incomplete information on which to base a decision and may therefore resort to rules of thumb that have proven effective in the past.

---

heuristic A rule of thumb that suggests a course of action or guides problem solving but does not guarantee an optimal solution.

In thinking about real-life problems, a person must also be able to use **dialectical reasoning,** the process of comparing and evaluating opposing points of view in order to resolve differences. Philosopher Richard Paul (1984) has described dialectical reasoning as movement "up and back between contradictory lines of reasoning, using each to critically cross-examine the other." Dialectical reasoning is what juries are supposed to do to arrive at a verdict: consider arguments for and against the defendant's guilt, point and counterpoint. It is also what voters are supposed to do when thinking about whether the government should raise or lower taxes, encourage or eliminate bilingual classes in elementary schools, or decriminalize marijuana. But on emotional issues such as these, many people reason rationally about only one side of the argument—their own.

Creative Thinking

When certain strategies and rules have been successful in the past, they often become habitual. A person then develops a **mental set,** a tendency to try to solve new problems by using the same heuristics, strategies, and rules that worked in the past on similar problems. Mental sets make human learning and problem solving efficient; because of them, we do not have to keep reinventing the wheel. But they are *not* helpful when a problem calls for fresh insights and methods. They cause us to cling to the same old assumptions and approaches, blinding us to better or more rapid solutions. At such times, mental sets can be a major impediment to effective thinking.

Here's an exercise that illustrates this point. Copy the following figure, and see whether you can connect the dots by using no more than four straight lines, without lifting your pencil or pen from the paper. A line must pass through each point. Can you do it?

Most people have difficulty solving this problem because they have a mental set to interpret the arrangement of dots as a square. Once having done so, they assume that they can't extend a line beyond the "boundaries" of the square. Now that you know this, you might try again if you haven't yet solved the puzzle. (Some possible solutions are given at the end of this chapter.)

One common mental set is the tendency to find meaningful patterns in events. This tendency is adaptive, because it helps us understand and exert some control over what happens in our lives. But it also leads us to see meaningful patterns even when they don't exist. For example, many people with arthritis think that their symptoms follow a

---

dialectical reasoning A process in which opposing facts or ideas are weighed and compared, with a view to determining the best solution or to resolving differences.

mental set A tendency to solve problems using procedures that worked before on similar problems.

pattern dictated by the weather. They suffer more, they say, when the barometric pressure changes, or when it is damp or humid. Yet when researchers followed 18 arthritis patients for 15 months, *no* association whatsoever emerged between weather conditions and the patients' self-reported pain levels, their ability to function in daily life, or a doctor's evaluation of their joint tenderness (Redelmeier & Tversky, 1996). Did the patients say, "Oh, thank you for pointing out that my belief was unfounded! How incredibly interesting"? No, they adamantly refused to believe the results.

Real-world problem solving benefits from the ability to think creatively and with an open mind. People who are uncreative rely on **convergent thinking,** following a particular set of steps that they think will converge on one correct solution. Once they solve a problem, they tend to develop a mental set and approach future problems the same way. People who are creative, however, are able to break free of rigid patterns of perceiving and thinking in order to produce new solutions. They exercise **divergent thinking;** instead of stubbornly sticking to one tried and true path, they explore side alleys and generate several possible solutions. They come up with new hypotheses, imagine other interpretations, and look for connections that may not be immediately obvious. Divergent thinking enhances survival by helping us adapt to constantly changing conditions. It is not confined to traditional creative arts, such as painting or music. It can be found in the auto mechanic who invents a new tool, the mother who designs and makes her children's clothes, or the office manager who devises a clever way to streamline work flow.

Edward de Bono (1971) once illustrated the nature of creative problem solving by asking children ages 4 to 14 to design a "dog-exercising machine." One child came up with the simple idea of having the dog chase a bone held always out of reach by a harness on the dog's back—frustrating for the dog, but effective (see illustration below left). Another child devised a more sophisticated solution (below right): When the dog barks into a "speaking tube," the energy of its barking activates a system of rods and springs, causing the wheels of the cart to turn. An "eye tube" allows the poor pooch to see where it is going, but this is only a courtesy, because a periscope automatically "sees" obstacles and a "transformer box" adjusts the steering accordingly. The more the dog barks, the faster the cart moves.

Source: Edward de Bono, THE DOG EXERCISING MACHINE. www.edwdebono.com

convergent thinking Thinking aimed at finding a single correct answer to a problem.

divergent thinking Mental exploration of unconventional alternatives in solving problems; by breaking mental sets, it tends to enhance creativity.

In the laboratory, psychologists have traditionally studied creativity by using tests that measure fluency, flexibility, and originality in generating solutions to problems (Guilford, 1950). One, the Alternate Uses Test, asks you to think of as many uses as possible for common items, such as a brick or a paper clip. (One friend of ours said a brick could be used as a bug hider: "You leave it alone for a while and then pick it up to see how many bugs are hiding there.") Another, the Remote Associates Test, presents sets of three words and asks you to find an associated word for each set (Mednick, 1962). For example, an appropriate answer for the set *news-clip-wall* is *paper*. Associating elements in new ways by finding a common connection among them is thought to be an important component of creativity. Can you find associates for the following word sets? (The answers are given on page 303.)

1. piggy-green-lash
2. surprise-favors-political
3. mark-shelf-telephone
4. stick-maker-tennis
5. blue-cottage-cloth

Why are some people able to think creatively, whereas others can't climb out of their mental ruts? The answer lies partly in the individual's environment. Creativity tends to flourish when people have control over how to perform a task or solve a problem; are evaluated unobtrusively, instead of being constantly observed and judged; and are given the freedom to work independently (Amabile, 1983). Organizations increase the creativity of employees when they let people take risks, give them plenty of time to think about problems, and welcome innovation. These are the very same working conditions that promote high achievement (see Chapter 9).

Creativity also depends on certain qualities of the individual. Interestingly, having a high IQ does not guarantee creativity. The three personality traits most strongly associated with the ability to think creatively are these (Helson, Roberts, & Agronick, 1995; MacKinnon, 1968; McCrae, 1987; Schank, 1988):

1 **NONCONFORMITY.** Creative individuals are not overly concerned about what others think of them. They are willing to risk ridicule by proposing ideas that may initially appear foolish or off the mark. Geneticist Barbara McClintock's research was ignored and belittled by many of her colleagues for nearly 30 years. But she was sure she could show how genes move around and produce sudden changes in heredity. In 1983, she won the Nobel Prize. The judges called her work the second greatest genetic discovery of its time, after the discovery of the structure of DNA.

2 **CURIOSITY.** Creative people are open to new experiences and are intrigued by everyday puzzles that others would ignore. As Roger Schank (1988) wrote, "They wonder why butterflies have to be caterpillars first. They wonder why the drugstore on the corner always does well and why the one across the street from it seems to be up for sale every two years. . . . They notice things and ask questions about them." Asking questions about things other people ignore or take for granted, you may remember, is the first step in thinking critically.

3 **PERSISTENCE.** This is perhaps the most important attribute of the creative person. After that imaginary lightbulb goes on over your head, you still have to work hard to make the illumination last. Or as Thomas Edison, who invented the real lightbulb, put it, "Genius is one-tenth inspiration and nine-tenths perspiration." No invention or work of art springs forth full-blown from a person's head. There are many false starts, wrong turns, and painful revisions along the way.

These characteristics of creativity are apparent in the biographies of successful artists, writers, scientists, and inventors. Consider the story of Georges de Mestral, a Swiss inventor, who was hunting one day in the late 1940s when he and his dog accidentally brushed up against a bush that left them both covered with burrs. When de Mestral tried to remove the burrs, they clung stubbornly to his clothes. This would be merely a minor annoyance to most of us, but de Mestral was curious about why the burrs were so hard to remove. After he got home, he studied them under a microscope and discovered that hundreds of tiny hooks on each burr had snagged on the threads of his pants. Burrs, he thought, would make great fasteners.

That was the inspiration. There followed several years of perspiration as de Mestral tried to figure out how to attach tiny hooks to pieces of tape so that they would stay lined up (Madigan & Elwood, 1984). He also struggled to find a way of producing equally tiny loops for the hooks to attach to. After testing many methods, he finally succeeded. The result: Velcro fasteners, now used on millions of items, from blood-pressure cuffs to shoes.

What Do You Know?

Put on your thinking cap to answer these questions.

1. Most of the items Mervin bought as holiday gifts this year cost more than they did last year, so he concludes that inflation is increasing. Is he using inductive, deductive, or dialectical reasoning?

2. Yvonne is arguing with Henrietta about whether real estate is a better investment than stocks. "You can't convince me," says Yvonne. "I just know I'm right." Yvonne needs training in _____ reasoning.

3. For many years, if you wanted to avoid carrying a heavy suitcase while traveling, you had to use a collapsible device with wheels on it. Then someone got the brilliant idea of attaching wheels to the case itself. This insight was an example of (convergent/divergent) thinking.

4. Which of the personality traits associated with creativity did Georges de Mestral exemplify?

ANSWERS:

1. inductive 2. dialectical 3. divergent 4. nonconformity, curiosity, and persistence—in other words, all of them

THE DEVELOPMENT OF THOUGHT AND REASONING

The ability to think and reason begins in early infancy. But as anyone who has ever observed a young child knows, children do not think the way adults do. For example, a 4-year-old may protest that a sibling has "more" fruit juice when it is only the shapes of the glasses that differ, not the amount of juice.

In the 1920s, the Swiss psychologist Jean Piaget [Zhan Pee-ah-ZHAY] (1896–1980) proposed a theory of cognitive development to explain such childish mistakes. Piaget was to child development what Sigmund Freud was to psychoanalysis and B. F. Skinner was to behaviorism: a figure of towering influence (Flavell, 1996). His keen observations of children caused a revolution in thinking about how thinking develops, and they inspired thousands of studies by investigators all over the world.

Piaget's great insight was that children's errors are as interesting as their correct responses. Children will say things that seem cute or wildly illogical to adults. But the *strategies* that children use to think and solve problems, said Piaget, are not random or meaningless. They reflect a predictable interaction between the child's maturational stage and the child's experience in the world. In this section we will take a look at Piaget's theory of the cognitive development of children, and then at subsequent research on the cognitive development of adults.

Piaget's Stages: How Children Think

According to Piaget (1929/1960, 1952, 1984), as children develop, they must make constant mental adaptations to new observations and experiences. Adaptation takes two forms: assimilation and accommodation.

Assimilation is what you do when you fit new information into your present knowledge and beliefs or into your mental schemas (networks of associations, beliefs, and expectations about categories of things and people). Suppose that little Harry learns a schema for "dog" by playing with the family spaniel. If he then sees the neighbor's German shepherd and says "doggie!" he has assimilated the new information about the neighbor's pet into his schema for dogs. **Accommodation** is what you do when, as a result of undeniable new information, you must change or modify your existing schemas. If Harry sees the neighbor's Siamese cat and still says "doggie!" his parents are likely to laugh and correct him. Harry will have to modify his schema for *dogs* to exclude cats, and he will have to create a schema for *cats*. In this way, he accommodates the new information that a Siamese cat is not a dog.

---

assimilation In Piaget's theory, the process of absorbing new information into existing cognitive structures.

accommodation In Piaget's theory, the process of modifying existing cognitive structures in response to experience and new information.

Using these concepts, Piaget proposed that all children go through four stages of cognitive development.

1 **THE SENSORIMOTOR STAGE (BIRTH TO AGE 2).** In this stage, the infant learns through concrete actions: looking, touching, hearing, putting things in the mouth, sucking, grasping. "Thinking" consists of coordinating sensory information with bodily movements. Gradually these movements become more purposeful, as the child explores the environment and learns that specific movements will produce specific results. Swatting a cloth away will reveal a hidden toy; letting go of a fuzzy toy duck will cause it to drop out of reach; banging on the table with a spoon will produce dinner (or Mom, taking the spoon away).

A major accomplishment at this stage, said Piaget, is **object permanence,** the understanding that something continues to exist even when you can't see it or touch it. In the first few months, he observed, infants seem to follow the motto "out of sight, out of mind." They will look intently at a little toy, but if you hide it behind a piece of paper they will not look behind the paper or make an effort to get the toy. By about 6 months of age, however, infants begin to grasp the idea that a toy exists and the family cat exists, whether or not they can see the toy or the cat. If a baby of this age drops a toy from her playpen, she will look for it; she also will look under a cloth for a toy that is partially hidden. By 1 year of age, most babies have developed an awareness that even if a toy is covered by a cloth, it must be under there. This is when they love to play peekaboo.

Object permanence, said Piaget, represents the beginning of the child's capacity to use mental imagery and other symbolic systems. The child is able for the first time to hold a concept in mind, to learn that the word *fly* represents an annoying, buzzing creature, and that *Daddy* represents a friendly, playful one.

2 **THE PREOPERATIONAL STAGE (AGES 2 TO 7).** During this stage, the use of symbols and language accelerates. A 2-year-old is able to pretend, for instance, that a large box is a house, table, or train. But Piaget described this stage largely in terms of what (he thought) the child cannot do. Although children can think, said Piaget, they cannot reason, and they lack the mental abilities necessary for understanding abstract principles or cause and effect. Piaget called these missing abilities **operations,** by which he meant reversible actions that the child performs in the mind. An operation is a sort of "train of thought" that can be run backward or forward. Multiplying 2 times 6 to get 12 is an operation; so is the reverse operation, dividing 12 by 6 to get 2.

Piaget also believed (mistakenly, as we will see) that preoperational children cannot take another person's point of view because their thinking is **egocentric.** They see the world only from their own frame of reference and cannot imagine that others see things differently.

---

object permanence The understanding that an object continues to exist even when you cannot see it or touch it.

operations In Piaget's theory, mental actions that are cognitively reversible.

egocentric thinking Seeing the world from only your own point of view; the inability to take another person's perspective.

Further, said Piaget, preoperational children cannot grasp the concept of **conservation,** the notion that physical properties do not change when their forms or appearances change. Children at this age are unable to understand that an amount of liquid, a number of pennies, or a length of rope remains the same even if you pour the liquid from one glass to another, stack the pennies, or coil the rope (see Figure 7.1). If you pour liquid from a short, fat glass into a tall, narrow glass, preoperational children will say that there is more liquid in the second glass. They attend to the appearance of the liquid (its height in the glass) to judge its quantity, and so are misled.

3 THE CONCRETE OPERATIONS STAGE (AGES 7 TO 12). In this stage, Piaget said, children's thinking is still grounded in concrete experiences and concepts, rather than in abstractions or logical deductions. However, the nature and quality of their thought processes change significantly. Children come to understand the principles of conservation, reversibility, and cause and effect. They learn mental operations, such as addition, subtraction, multiplication, and division. They learn to categorize things (e.g., oaks as trees) and to order things serially from smallest to largest, lightest to darkest, and shortest to tallest.

FIGURE 7.1 **PIAGET'S PRINCIPLE OF CONSERVATION** *In a typical test for conservation of number (left), the child must say whether one of the sets of blocks has "more." His answer shows whether he understands that the two sets contain the same number, even though the larger blocks in one set take up more space. In a test for conservation of quantity (right), the child is shown two short, fat glasses with equal amounts of liquid. Then the contents of one glass are poured into a tall, narrow beaker, and the child is asked whether one container now has more. Her answer shows whether she understands that pouring liquid from a short, fat glass into a tall, narrow one leaves the amount of liquid unchanged.*

conservation The understanding that the physical properties of objects—such as the number of items in a cluster or the amount of liquid in a glass—can remain the same even when their forms or appearances change.

And they understand the nature of *identity;* for example, they know that a girl does not turn into a boy by wearing a boy's hat, and that a brother will always be a brother, even if he grows up.

4 THE FORMAL OPERATIONS STAGE (AGE 12 THROUGH ADULTHOOD). In this final stage, teenagers become capable of abstract reasoning. They understand that ideas can be compared and classified, just as objects can. They are able to reason about situations they have not experienced firsthand, and they can think about future possibilities. They are able to search systematically for answers to problems. They are able to draw logical conclusions from premises common to their culture and experience.

Piaget transformed the field of developmental psychology, providing an entirely new vision of the nature of children. (Table 7.2 summarizes Piaget's stages of cognitive development.) However, modern research has challenged certain key aspects of Piaget's theory.

1 THE CHANGES FROM ONE STAGE TO ANOTHER ARE NEITHER AS CLEAR-CUT NOR AS SWEEPING AS PIAGET IMPLIED. Cognitive abilities develop in overlapping waves rather than discrete steps (Siegler, 1996). At any given age, a child may use several different strategies to solve a problem, some more complex or accurate than others. Moreover, children's reasoning ability often depends on the circumstances—who is asking them questions, the specific words used, the materials used, and what they are reasoning *about*—not only on the stage they are in.

2 CHILDREN CAN UNDERSTAND FAR MORE THAN PIAGET GAVE THEM CREDIT FOR. Taking advantage of the fact that infants look longer at novel or surprising stimuli than at familiar ones, psychologists have been able to test what babies know. As we saw in Chapter 3, these methods reveal that babies may be born with a primitive knowledge of number and the physical properties of objects. And infants as young as 2½ to 3½ months are aware that objects continue to exist even when masked by other objects,

TABLE 7.2 ✦ Summary of Piaget's Stages of Cognitive Development	
STAGE	**MAJOR ACCOMPLISHMENTS**
Sensorimotor (0–2)	Object permanence Beginning of capacity to use mental images and symbols
Preoperational (2–7)	Accelerated use of symbols and language
Concrete operations (7–12)	Understanding of conservation Understanding of identity Understanding of serial ordering
Formal operations (12–)	Abstract reasoning Ability to compare and classify ideas

a form of object permanence that Piaget never imagined possible in babies so young (Baillargeon, 1994). Children also advance rapidly in their symbolic abilities earlier than Piaget thought. Between the ages of 2½ and 3, toddlers become able to think of a miniature model of a room in two ways at once: as a room in its own right and as a symbol of the larger room it represents (DeLoache, 1995). This ability is a big step toward adult symbolic thought, in which anything can stand for anything else: a flag for a country, a logo for a company.

3 **PRESCHOOLERS ARE NOT AS EGOCENTRIC AS PIAGET THOUGHT.** Most 3- and 4-year-olds *can* take another person's perspective (Flavell, 1993). When 4-year-olds play with 2-year-olds, for example, they modify and simplify their speech so the younger children will understand (Shatz & Gelman, 1973). By about age 4, children begin to figure out that another person might see things differently than they do. One 5-year-old we know showed her teacher a picture she had drawn of a cat and an unidentifiable blob. "The cat is lovely," said the teacher, "but what is this thing here?" "That has nothing to do with you," said Dara. "That's what the *cat* is looking at."

This shift in perspective-taking is part of a broader change in how the child understands appearance and reality (Flavell, 1993). Two- and 3-year-olds judge by appearance: If you put a dog mask on a cat, they will say it's a dog. By age 5, children know it's still a cat. Even more important, they understand that someone else might be fooled into thinking it's a dog and even act on that false belief. More generally, they understand that you cannot predict what a person will do just by observing a situation or knowing the "facts"; you have to know what the person is feeling and thinking—the person might even lie. They start asking why other people behave as they do ("Why is Johnny so mean?"). In short, they are developing a **theory of mind,** a system of beliefs about how their own and other people's minds work and how people are affected by their beliefs (Flavell, Green, & Flavell, 1990; Jenkins & Astington, 1996; Lillard, 1998).

Most psychologists today accept Piaget's major point, that new reasoning abilities depend on the emergence of previous ones: You cannot learn algebra before you can count, and you cannot learn philosophy before you understand logic. Perhaps the most enduring legacy of Piaget's work is his emphasis on the fact that children are not passive vessels into which education and experience are poured. Children actively interpret their worlds, using their developing schemas and abilities to assimilate new information.

Even young children, however, are capable of forms of logic and inference about other people's behavior that Piaget thought impossible. Moreover, just as Piaget underestimated the cognitive skills of young children, he *overestimated* those of many adults. Not all adolescents and adults develop the ability for formal operational thought and abstract reasoning. Some never develop these capacities, and others think concretely unless a specific problem requires abstract thought. And even the ability to handle formal operations is not the culmination of cognitive development, as we are about to see.

---

theory of mind A system of beliefs about the way your own mind and other people's minds work, and of how people are affected by their beliefs and feelings; it emerges at age 4 or 5.

Beyond Piaget: How Adults Think

Where do you stand on the issue of genetic engineering? How safe do you consider food additives to be? Do you think stories in the news are reported objectively? Over a period of many years, Karen Kitchener and Patricia King asked people of all ages and occupations what they thought about issues like these. They were not interested in how much people knew about such issues; they just wanted to know how their respondents had reached their conclusions. More specifically, they wanted to know whether people use *reflective judgment* in thinking about everyday problems (King & Kitchener, 1994; Kitchener & King, 1990). Reflective judgment is basically what we have called critical thinking: the ability to question assumptions, evaluate evidence, relate that evidence to a theory or opinion, consider alternative interpretations, and reach conclusions that can be defended as reasonable or plausible, while standing ready to reassess those conclusions in the face of new information.

The researchers first provided their interviewees with statements that described opposing viewpoints on various topics. Then the interviewer asked, What do you think about these statements? How did you come to hold that point of view? On what do you base your position? Can you ever know for sure that your position is correct? Why do you suppose disagreement exists about this issue?

Based on the responses, King and Kitchener were able to identify seven cognitive stages on the road to reflective thought, some occurring in childhood and others unfolding throughout adolescence and adulthood. At each stage, people make different assumptions about how things are known and use different ways of justifying or defending their beliefs. Each stage builds on the skills of the prior one and lays a foundation for successive ones.

We will not be concerned here with the details of these stages, but only with their broad outlines. In general, people in the two early, *prereflective* stages assume that a correct answer always exists and that it can be obtained directly through the senses ("I know what I've seen") or from authorities ("They said so on the news"; "That's what I was brought up to believe"). If authorities do not yet have the truth, prereflective thinkers tend to reach conclusions on the basis of what "feels right" at the moment. They do not distinguish between knowledge and belief, or between belief and evidence, and they do not see any reason for justifying a belief (King & Kitchener, 1994):

Interviewer: Can you ever know for sure that your position [on evolution] is correct?

Respondent: Well, some people believe that we evolved from apes and that's the way they want to believe. But I would never believe that way and nobody could talk me out of the way I believe because I believe the way that it's told in the Bible.

During the three *quasi-reflective* stages, people recognize that some things cannot be known with absolute certainty, but they are not sure how to deal with these situations. They realize that judgments should be supported by reasons, but they pay attention only to evidence that fits what they already believe. They know that there are alternative viewpoints, but they seem to think that because knowledge is uncertain, any judgment about the evidence is purely subjective. Quasi-reflective thinkers will defend a position by saying that "We all have a right to our own opinion," as if all opinions are created equal. Here is the response of a college student who uses quasi-reflective reasoning:

Interviewer: Can you say you will ever know for sure that chemicals [in foods] are safe?

Student: No, I don't think so.

Interviewer: Can you tell me why you'll never know for sure?

Student: Because they test them in little animals, and they haven't really tested them in humans, as far as I know. And I don't think anything is for sure.

Interviewer: When people differ about matters such as this, is it the case that one opinion is right and one is wrong?

Student: No. I think it just depends on how you feel personally because people make their decisions based upon how they feel and what research they've seen. So what one person thinks is right, another person might think is wrong. . . . If I feel that chemicals cause cancer and you feel that food is unsafe without it, your opinion might be right to you and my opinion is right to me.

In the last two stages, a person becomes capable of *reflective* judgment. He or she understands that although some things can never be known with certainty, some judgments are more valid than others because of their coherence, their fit with the evidence, their usefulness, and so on. People at these stages are willing to consider evidence from a variety of sources and to reason dialectically. At the very highest stage, they are able to defend their conclusions as representing the most complete, plausible, or compelling understanding of an issue, based on currently available evidence. This interview with a graduate student illustrates reflective thinking:

Interviewer: Can you ever say you know for sure that your point of view on chemical additives is correct?

Student: No, I don't think so. . . . [but] I think that we can usually be reasonably certain, given the information we have now, and considering our methodologies.

Interviewer: Is there anything else that contributes to not being able to be sure?

Student: Yes. . . . it might be that the research wasn't conducted rigorously enough. In other words, we might have flaws in our data or sample, things like that.

Interviewer: How then would you identify the "better opinion"?

Student: One that takes as many factors as possible into consideration. I mean one that uses the higher percentage of the data that we have, and perhaps that uses the methodology that has been most reliable.

Interviewer: And how do you come to a conclusion about what the evidence suggests?

> *Student:* I think you have to take a look at the different opinions and studies that are offered by different groups. Maybe some studies offered by the chemical industry, some studies by the government, some private studies. . . . You wouldn't trust, for instance, a study funded by the tobacco industry that proved that cigarette smoking is not harmful . . . you have to try to interpret people's motives and that makes it a more complex soup to try to strain out.

Most people do not show evidence of reflective judgment until their middle or late twenties, if at all. Most undergraduates tend to score at only Stage 3 during their first year of college. The good news is that when students get support for thinking reflectively and have opportunities to practice, their thinking tends to become more complex, sophisticated, and well-grounded (Kitchener et al., 1993). Moreover, higher education gradually moves people closer to reflective judgment: By their senior year, students typically score at Stage 4; most graduate students score at Stage 4 or 5; and many advanced doctoral students perform consistently at Stage 6 (King & Kitchener, 1994). Longitudinal studies show that these differences do not occur only because lower-level thinkers are more likely to drop out along the way.

The gradual development of thinking skills among college students, said Barry Kroll (1992), represents an abandonment of "ignorant certainty" in favor of "intelligent confusion." It may not seem so, but this is a big step forward! You can see why, in this book, we emphasize thinking about and evaluating the different perspectives in psychology, and not just memorizing their findings.

What Do You Know?

Reflect now on these questions and make your best judgment of the answers.

1. Understanding that two rows of six pennies are equal in number, even if one row is flat and the other is stacked up, is an example of _____.

2. Understanding that a toy exists even after Mom puts it in her purse is an example of _____, which develops during the _____ stage.

3. A 5-year-old who tells his dad that "Sally said she saw a bunny but she was lying" has developed a _____.

4. Research shows that Piaget _____ the cognitive abilities of young children and _____ those of adults.

5. Seymour thinks the media have a liberal political bias, and Serena thinks they are too conservative. "Well," says Seymour, "I have my truth and you have yours. It's purely subjective." Which of King and Kitchener's levels of thinking is Seymour demonstrating?

6. What kind of evidence might resolve the issue that Seymour and Serena are arguing about?

ANSWERS:

expect to perceive.

servative might not be informative because people perceive only what they want or con-

as well. However, subjective ratings of *entire TV* programs or newspapers as liberal or con-

evaluate the editorials as liberal or conservative. You may be able to think of other strategies

raters could read a random sample of newspaper editorials from all over the country and

of TV news shows and measure the time devoted to conservative and liberal viewpoints. Or

overestimated 6. quasi-reflective 5. Researchers might have raters watch a random sample

1. conservation 2. object permanence, sensorimotor 3. theory of mind 4. underestimated;

BARRIERS TO REASONING RATIONALLY

Although most people have the capacity to think logically, reason dialectically, and make judgments reflectively, it is abundantly clear that they don't always do so. One obstacle is the need to be right; if your self-esteem depends on being right all the time, you will find it hard to listen with an open mind to competing views. Another obstacle is mental laziness. Many social critics think such laziness is on the rise because television watching is replacing reading. Reading requires you to sit still and follow extended arguments; it gives you the opportunity to examine connections among statements and to spot contradictions, and you can always go back a page and reread something you missed. When you read a book, therefore, you are usually mindfully engaged in its argument. But television programs often provide sound bites instead of fully developed arguments, encouraging viewers to form quick, impulsive opinions instead of carefully considered ones. As writer Mitchell Stephens (1991) noted, "All television demands is our gaze."

Human thought processes are also tripped up by many predictable biases and errors. Psychologists have studied dozens of these cognitive pitfalls; here we describe just a few of them.

The Hindsight Bias

Would you have predicted, beforehand, that the quirky movie *American Beauty* would win the Oscar in 2000 for best film instead of a more traditional Hollywood blockbuster? When people learn the outcome of an event or the answer to a question, they are often sure that they "knew it all along." Armed with the wisdom of hindsight, they see the outcome that actually occurred as inevitable, and they overestimate the probability that they could have predicted what happened. Compared with judgments made *before* an event takes place, their after-the-fact judgments about their own ability to have predicted the event are inflated (Fischhoff, 1975; Hawkins & Hastie, 1990).

This **hindsight bias** is common in political assessments ("I always knew my candidate would win"), medical judgments ("I could have told you that mole was cancerous"), and military opinions ("The generals should have known that Pearl Harbor would be attacked"). And when investors buy a stock, and then it goes up in price, they are apt to think, in hindsight, that they were more confident about their purchase at the time they made it than they really were (Louie, 1999).

The hindsight bias, like many of our cognitive biases, has adaptive benefits. When we try to predict the future, we consider many possible scenarios, but when we try to make sense of the past, we focus on explaining just one outcome—the one that actually occurred. This strategy is efficient, because explaining outcomes that did *not* take place can be a waste of time. As Scott Hawkins and Reid Hastie (1990) wrote, "Hindsight biases represent the dark side of successful learning and judgment." They are the dark side because when we are sure that we knew something "all along," we are also less willing to find out what we need to know in order to make accurate predictions in the future. In medical conferences, for example, when doctors are told what the postmortem findings were for a patient who died, they tend to think the case was easier to diagnose than it actually was ("I would have known it was a brain tumor"), and so they learn less from the case than they should (Dawson et al., 1988).

Perhaps you feel that we are not telling you anything new because you have always known about the hindsight bias. But then, you may just have a hindsight bias about the hindsight bias!

Avoiding Loss

In general, people have an *aversion to loss*—they are biased to try to avoid or minimize risks and losses when they make decisions. So when a choice is framed in terms of the risk of losing something, they will respond more cautiously than when the *same* choice is framed in terms of gain. They will, for example, choose a ticket that has a 10 percent chance of winning a raffle over one that has a 90 percent chance of losing! Or they will rate a condom as effective when they are told it has a 95 percent success rate in protecting against the AIDS virus, but not when they are told it has a 5 percent failure rate—which is logically the same thing (Linville, Fischer, & Fischhoff, 1992).

Here's another example. Suppose you had to choose between two health programs to combat a disease expected to kill 600 people. Would you prefer a program that will definitely save 200 people, or one with a one-third probability of saving all 600 people and a two-thirds probability of saving none? (Figure 7.2a illustrates this choice.) When asked this question, most people, including physicians, say they would prefer the first program. In other words, they reject the riskier though potentially more rewarding solution in favor of a sure gain. However, people *will* take a risk if they see it as a way to *avoid loss.* Suppose now that you have to choose between a program in which 400 people will definitely die and a program in which there is a one-third probability of nobody dying and a two-thirds probability that all 600 will die. If you think about it, you will see that

---

hindsight bias   The tendency to overestimate one's ability to have predicted an event once the outcome is known; the "I knew it all along" phenomenon.

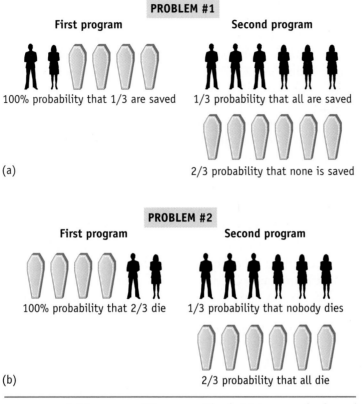

FIGURE 7.2 A MATTER OF WORDING *The decisions we make depend on how the alternatives are framed. When asked to choose between the two programs in choice* a, *which are described in terms of lives saved, most people choose the first program. When asked to choose between the programs in choice* b, *which are described in terms of lives lost, most people choose the second program. Yet the alternatives in* a *are actually identical to those in* b.

the alternatives are exactly the same as in the first problem, just worded differently (see Figure 7.2b). Yet this time, most people choose the second solution. They reject risk when they think of the outcome in terms of lives saved, but they accept risk when they think of the outcome in terms of lives lost (Tversky & Kahneman, 1981).

Few of us will have to face a decision involving hundreds of lives, but we may have to choose between different medical treatments for ourselves or a relative. Our decision may be affected by whether the doctor frames the choice in terms of chances of surviving or chances of dying.

Exaggerating the Improbable

Another common bias is the inclination to exaggerate the probability of very rare events. This is the bias that helps explain why so many people enter lotteries and buy airline disaster insurance.

People are especially likely to exaggerate the likelihood of a rare event if its consequences are catastrophic. They do this because of the **availability heuristic,** the tendency to judge the probability of an event by how easy it is to think of examples or instances (Tversky & Kahneman, 1973). Catastrophes and shocking accidents stand out in our minds and are therefore more "available" mentally than are other kinds of negative events. In one study, people overestimated the frequency of deaths from tornadoes and underestimated the frequency of deaths from asthma, which occur 20 times as often but do not make headlines. These same people estimated deaths from accidents and disease to be equally frequent, even though 16 times as many people die each year from disease as from accidents (Lichtenstein et al., 1978).

People will sometimes work themselves into a froth about unlikely events such as dying in an airplane crash, yet they will irrationally ignore dangers that are harder to visualize, such as the dramatic increase in skin cancer rates due to depletion of the ozone layer in the Earth's atmosphere. Similarly, parents are often more frightened about real but unlikely threats to their children, such as being kidnapped by a stranger or dying from a routine immunization shot (both horrible but extremely rare), than they are about problems more common in children, such as depression, delinquency, and poor grades, or dangers that are far more likely, such as auto accidents or accidental drownings.

The Confirmation Bias

One of the most central cognitive biases in human thinking is the **confirmation bias:** the tendency to notice and accept evidence that confirms what we already believe, and to ignore or reject information that disconfirms our ideas (Edwards & Smith, 1996; Kunda, 1990; Nickerson, 1998). Most of us respond the way people in that arthritis-and-weather study did when confronted with disconfirming evidence. Instead of saying, "Oh, thank you for showing me that I was completely mistaken! I'm so grateful to you!" we usually say, "Oh, buzz off, and take your cockamamie ideas with you."

Here is an example of the confirmation bias. Suppose someone deals out four cards, each with a letter on one side and a number on the other. You can see only one side of each card:

---

availability heuristic The tendency to judge the probability of a type of event by how easy it is to think of examples or instances.

confirmation bias The tendency to look for or pay attention only to information that confirms one's own belief.

Your job is to find out whether the following rule is true: "If a card has a vowel on one side, then it has an even number on the other side." Which two cards do you need to turn over to find out?

The vast majority of people say they would turn over the E and the 6, but they are wrong. You do need to turn over the E (a vowel), because if the number on the other side is even, it confirms the rule, and if it's odd, the rule is false. However, the card with the 6 tells you nothing. The rule does not say that a card with an even number must always have a vowel on the other side. The card you do need to turn over is the 7, because if it has a vowel on the other side, that fact *disconfirms* the rule. People do poorly on this problem because they are biased to look for confirming evidence and ignore the possibility of disconfirming evidence. Don't feel bad if you missed it. Most judges, lawyers, and people with Ph.D.s do, too!

You can see real-life examples of the confirmation bias every day. Politicians routinely accept economic news that confirms their philosophies and dismiss counter-evidence as being inaccurate or unimportant. More seriously, police officers, prosecutors, and jury members who are convinced of a suspect's guilt are likely to take anything the defendant says or does as confirming evidence, and to dismiss evidence that doesn't fit. In one study, people listened to an audiotaped reenactment of an actual murder trial and then said how they would have voted and why. Instead of considering and weighing possible verdicts against the evidence, many people quickly constructed a story about what had happened and considered only the evidence that supported their version of events. These same people were the most confident in their decisions and were most likely to vote for an extreme verdict (Kuhn, Weinstock, & Flaton, 1994).

The confirmation bias can also affect how you react to what you are learning. When students read about scientific findings that dispute one of their own cherished beliefs or that challenge the wisdom of their own actions, they tend to minimize the strengths of the research. In contrast, when a study supports their view, they may acknowledge its flaws but will give them less weight than they would otherwise (Sherman & Kunda, 1989). In thinking critically, it seems, people apply a double standard: They think most critically about results they dislike.

The Need for Cognitive Consistency

Because of the confirmation bias, we don't have to keep changing our minds all the time; we just keep any disconfirming evidence at arm's reach. But what happens when disconfirming evidence finally smacks us in the face, and we cannot ignore or discount it any more? For example, as the twentieth century rolled to an end, predictions of doomsday—the end of the world—escalated. One cult of true believers from Colorado traveled all the way to Israel at the start of 1999, hoping to set up camp with a good view to await Armageddon; the Israelis sent them home. There have been lots of similar doomsday predictions throughout history. What happens to true believers when their prophecy fails?

According to the theory of **cognitive dissonance,** people will resolve such conflicts in predictable, though not always obvious, ways (Festinger, 1957). *Dissonance,* the opposite of consistency (*consonance*), is a state of tension that occurs when you simultaneously hold either two cognitions (beliefs, thoughts, attitudes) that are psychologically inconsistent or a belief that is incongruent with your behavior. This tension is uncomfortable, so you will be motivated to reduce it by rejecting or modifying one of those inconsistent beliefs, changing your behavior, denying the evidence, or rationalizing (Harmon-Jones et al., 1996).

Many years ago, in a famous and clever field study, Leon Festinger and two associates explored people's reactions to failed prophecies by infiltrating a group of people who thought the world would end on December 21 (Festinger, Riecken, & Schachter, 1956). The group's leader, whom the researchers called Marian Keech, promised that the faithful would be picked up by a flying saucer and whisked to safety at midnight on December 20. Many of her followers quit their jobs and spent all their savings, waiting for the end. What would they do or say, Festinger and his colleagues wondered, to reduce the dissonance between "The world is still muddling along on the 21st" and "I predicted the end of the world and sold all my worldly possessions"?

The researchers predicted that believers who had made no public commitment to the prophecy, who awaited the end of the world by themselves at home, would simply lose their faith. But those who had acted on their conviction by selling their property and waiting with Keech for the spaceship would be in a state of dissonance. They would, said the researchers, have to *increase* their religious belief to avoid the intolerable realization that they had behaved foolishly and others knew it. That is just what happened. At 4:45 A.M., long past the appointed hour of the saucer's arrival, the leader had a new vision. The world had been spared, she said, because of the impressive faith of her little band.

Cognitive-dissonance theory predicts that in more ordinary situations, too, people will resist or rationalize information that conflicts with their existing ideas. For example, if you are a cigarette smoker, your behavior is dissonant with your awareness that smoking causes illness. You might try to reduce the dissonance by trying to quit, by rejecting the evidence that smoking is bad, by persuading yourself that you will quit later on ("after these exams"), by emphasizing the benefits of smoking ("A cigarette helps me relax"), or by deciding that you don't want a long life, anyhow ("It will be shorter, but sweeter").

---

cognitive dissonance   A state of tension that occurs when a person simultaneously holds two cognitions that are psychologically inconsistent, or when a person's belief is incongruent with his or her behavior.

Likewise, cigarette manufacturers are good at reducing the dissonance between "this job makes a lot of money for the company and for me" and "cigarette smoking kills 400,000 people a year." When the president of one tobacco company was told that smoking during pregnancy increases the chances of having a low-birthweight baby, he replied, "Some women would prefer having smaller babies" (quoted in Kluger, 1996).

There are three conditions under which people are particularly motivated to reduce dissonance (Aronson, Wilson, & Akert, 1999):

1 WHEN YOU NEED TO JUSTIFY A CHOICE OR DECISION THAT YOU FREELY MADE. All car dealers know about "buyer's remorse": The second that people buy a car, they worry that they made the wrong decision, spent too much, or got a lemon. This is called *post-decision dissonance,* and cognitive-dissonance theory predicts that you will try to resolve it. You will probably decide that the car, toaster, house, or spouse that you chose is really, truly the best in the world. However, if someone else made your decision for you, you will not feel much dissonance if it proves misguided. There is no dissonance between "The Army drafted me; I had no choice about being here" and "I hate basic training."

2 WHEN YOUR ACTIONS VIOLATE YOUR SELF-CONCEPT. If you have a concept of yourself as honest and true to your convictions, you will probably experience dissonance if you are in a situation in which you tell a lie or fail to stand up for something you believe. Westerners are especially likely to feel dissonance in such circumstances, because they regard the "self" as being consistent across situations (see Chapter 10). In countries like Japan, where people think of themselves as being different in different situations, dissonance is less likely to occur.

3 WHEN YOU PUT A LOT OF EFFORT INTO A DECISION, ONLY TO FIND THE RESULTS LESS THAN YOU HOPED FOR. The harder you work to reach a goal, or the more you suffer for it, the more you will try to convince yourself that you value the goal, even if the goal itself is not so great after all (Aronson & Mills, 1959). This explains why hazing, whether in fraternities or the military, turns new recruits into loyal members. You might think that people would hate a group that made them suffer to belong. But the cognition "I went through a lot of awful stuff to join this group" is dissonant with the cognition "and now I find that this group is awful." Therefore people must decide either that the hazing was not so bad or that they really like the group. This mental reevaluation is called the **justification of effort,** and it is one of the most popular methods of reducing dissonance.

Cognitive-dissonance theory has its limitations. Some individuals, like some cultures, do not have a strong need for consistency, and so they are less subject than others to cognitive dissonance (Cialdini, Trost, & Newsom, 1995). And some people are secure enough to own up to their mistakes instead of rationalizing them. Still, under certain conditions the need for cognitive consistency can lead to irrational, self-defeating decisions and actions.

---

justification of effort   The tendency of individuals to increase their liking for something that they have worked hard or suffered to attain; a common form of dissonance reduction.

Overcoming Our Cognitive Biases

The fact that our decisions and judgments are not always logical or rational has enormous implications for the legal system, business, medicine, government—in fact, in all areas. But the situation is not hopeless. For one thing, people are not equally irrational in all situations. When they are doing things they have some expertise in, or are making decisions that have serious consequences, their cognitive biases often diminish. Accountants who audit companies' books, for example, are less subject to the confirmation bias than are undergraduates in psychology experiments, perhaps because auditors can be sued if they overestimate a firm's profitability or economic health (Smith & Kida, 1991).

Further, once we understand a bias, we may be able to reduce or eliminate it. As we have seen, doctors are vulnerable to the hindsight bias if they already know what caused a patient's death. But Hal Arkes and his colleagues (1988) were able to reduce a similar bias in neuropsychologists. The psychologists were given a case study and asked to state one reason why each of three possible diagnoses—alcohol withdrawal, Alzheimer's disease, and brain damage—might have been applicable. This procedure forced the psychologists to consider all the evidence, not just evidence that supported the correct diagnosis. The hindsight bias evaporated when the neuropsychologists realized that the correct diagnosis had not been so obvious at the time the patient was being treated.

What Do You Know?

Think rationally to answer these questions.

1. Stu takes a study break and meets a young woman at the cafeteria. They hit it off, start to see each other regularly, and eventually get married. Says Stu, "I knew that day, when I headed for the cafeteria, that something special was about to happen." What cognitive bias is affecting his thinking, charmingly romantic though it is?

2. In a classic study of cognitive dissonance, students did some boring, repetitive tasks and then had to tell another student, who was waiting to participate in the study, that the work was interesting and fun (Festinger & Carlsmith, 1959). Half of the students were offered $20 for telling this lie and the others only $1. Which students who lied decided later on that the tasks had been fun after all?

ANSWERS:

1. hindsight bias 2. The students who got only $1. They were in a state of dissonance, because "the task was as dull as dishwater" is dissonant with "I said I enjoyed it—and for a mere dollar, at that." Those who got $20 could rationalize that the large sum (which was *really* large in 1956) justified the lie.

ANIMAL MINDS

A green heron swipes some bread from a picnicker's table and scatters the crumbs on a nearby stream. When a minnow rises to the bait, the heron strikes, swallowing its prey before you can say "hook, line, and sinker." A sea otter, floating calmly on its back, bangs a mussel shell against a stone that is resting on its stomach. When the shell cracks apart, the otter devours the tasty morsel inside, tucks the stone under its flipper, and dives for another shell, which it will open in the same way.

Incidents such as these suggest that we are not the only animals with cognitive abilities—that "dumb beasts" are far smarter than we may think. Many best-selling books, such as Elizabeth Marshall Thomas's *The Hidden Life of Dogs* and Jeffrey Masson's *When Elephants Weep,* have described the seemingly humanlike emotions and "thoughts" of animals. But how humanlike are they?

Animal Intelligence

Early in the twentieth century, Wolfgang Köhler (1925) showed that some particularly clever chimpanzees were able to solve problems that appeared to require thought and insight (see Chapter 5). The animals managed to reach bananas that were just beyond their grasp by pulling the fruit into their cages using sticks or by climbing on boxes to reach the fruit. Behaviorists, however, felt that this seemingly impressive behavior could be accounted for perfectly well by the standard principles of operant learning. Because of behaviorism's influence, for years any scientist who claimed that nonhuman animals could think was likely to get laughed at, or worse.

Today, attitudes have changed, and the study of animal intelligence is enjoying a resurgence, especially in the interdisciplinary field of **cognitive ethology** (Gould & Gould, 1995; Hauser, 2000; Ristau, 1991). (*Ethology* is the study of animal behavior, especially in natural environments.) Cognitive ethologists argue that some animals can anticipate future events, make plans, and coordinate their activities with those of their comrades—that they are, indeed, capable of thought. In this view, nonhuman animals may think differently than we do, but that doesn't mean they can't think at all.

When we think about animal cognition, though, we must be cautious, because even complex behavior might be genetically prewired and automatic. The assassin bug of South America catches termites by gluing nest material on its back as camouflage, but it is hard to imagine how the bug's tiny dab of brain tissue could enable it to plan this strategy consciously. Skeptics, including many cognitive ethologists themselves, are cautious about how much cognition they are willing to read into an animal's behavior. An animal could be aware of its environment and know some things, they say, without knowing that it knows and without being able to think about its own thoughts as human beings do (Budiansky, 1998; Hauser, 2000).

---

cognitive ethology The study of cognitive processes in nonhuman animals.

Yet explanations of animal behavior that leave out any sort of consciousness at all and that attribute animals' actions entirely to instinct do not seem to account for some of the amazing things that animals can do. Like the otter who uses a stone to break mussel shells, many animals are capable of using objects in the natural environment as rudimentary tools. For example, mother chimpanzees occasionally show their young how to use stone tools to crack open hard nuts (Boesch, 1991).

In the laboratory, too, nonhuman primates have accomplished some surprising things. In one study, chimpanzees compared two pairs of food wells containing chocolate chips. One pair might contain, say, five chips and three chips, the other four chips and three chips. Allowed to choose which pair they wanted, the chimps almost always chose the one with the higher combined total, showing some sort of summing ability (Rumbaugh, Savage-Rumbaugh, & Pate, 1988). Other chimps have learned to use numerals to label quantities of items and simple sums (Boysen & Berntson, 1989; Washburn & Rumbaugh, 1991). Two rhesus monkeys named Rosencrantz and Macduff learned to order groups of one to four symbols according to the number of symbols in each group (e.g., one square, two trees, three ovals, four flowers). Later, when presented with pairs of groups containing five to nine symbols, they were able to point to the group with more symbols, without any further training (Brannon & Terrace, 1998). This is not exactly algebra, but it does suggest that monkeys have a rudimentary sense of number.

Animal Language

A primary ingredient in human cognition is *language,* the ability to combine elements that are themselves meaningless into an infinite number of utterances that convey meaning. Language is often regarded as the last bastion of human uniqueness, a result of evolutionary forces that produced our species (see Chapter 3). Do animals have anything comparable? Many people have wished they could ask their pet what it's like to be a dog, or a cat, or a horse. If only animals could speak![1]

To qualify as a language, a communication system must meet three criteria (Hockett, 1960):

✦ It must use combinations of sounds, gestures, or symbols that are *meaningful,* not random.

✦ It must permit *displacement,* communication about objects and events that are not present here and now but rather are displaced in time or space; merely pointing to things is not language.

✦ It must have a grammar (syntax) that permits *productivity,* the ability to produce and comprehend an infinite number of new utterances.

---

[1]Philosophers, however, have long debated what the resulting conversations would be like. Ludwig Wittgenstein once said, "If a lion could talk, we would not be able to understand him." And David Premack, who studied ape language for many years, added, "If a chicken had grammar, it wouldn't have anything interesting to say" (quoted in Schuessler, 2000).

By these criteria, no nonhuman species has its own language. Of course, animals do communicate, using gestures, body postures, facial expressions, vocalizations, and odors. And some of these signals have highly specific meanings. For example, vervet monkeys seem to have separate calls to warn about leopards versus eagles versus snakes (Cheney & Seyfarth, 1985). But vervets cannot combine these sounds to produce entirely novel utterances, as in "Look out, Harry, that eagle-eyed leopard is a real snake-in-the-grass."

Perhaps, however, some animals could acquire language if they got a little help from their human friends. Dozens of researchers have tried to provide chimpanzees with just such help. Because the vocal tract of an ape does not permit speech, most of these researchers have tried innovative approaches that rely on gestures or visual symbols. In one project, chimpanzees learned to use as words geometric plastic shapes arranged on a magnetic board (Premack & Premack, 1983). In another, they learned to punch symbols on a computer-monitored keyboard (Rumbaugh, 1977). In yet another, they learned hundreds of signs from American Sign Language (ASL) (Fouts & Rigby, 1977; Gardner & Gardner, 1969).

All of these animals learned to follow instructions, answer questions, and make requests. More important, they combined individual signs or symbols into longer utterances that they had never seen before. Before long, accounts of the apes' abilities were causing quite a stir. The animals were apparently using their newfound skills to apologize for being disobedient, scold their trainers, and even talk to themselves. Koko, a lowland gorilla, reportedly used signs to say that she felt happy or sad, to refer to past and future events, to mourn for her dead pet kitten, and to convey her yearning for a baby. She even lied on occasion, when she did something naughty (Patterson & Linden, 1981).

The animals in these studies were lovable and the findings exciting, so it was easy for emotional reasoning to prevail over critical thinking. But skeptical researchers began to point out serious problems (Seidenberg & Petitto, 1979; Terrace, 1985). In their desire to talk to the animals and their affection for their primate friends, researchers had not always been objective. They had overinterpreted the animal's utterances, reading all sorts of meanings and intentions into a single sign or symbol, and unwittingly giving nonverbal cues that might enable the apes to respond correctly. Further, the animals appeared to be stringing signs and symbols together in no particular order, instead of using grammatical rules to produce novel utterances; "Me eat banana" seemed to be no different for them than "Banana eat me."

These problems still plague some projects. In 1998, America Online sponsored a live chat with Koko. Her trainer, Francine Patterson, used sign language to relay questions from the audience to the gorilla. Critics felt Patterson read much too much into Koko's "replies":

> *Question:* Koko, are you going to have a baby in the future?
>   *Koko:* Pink.
> *Patterson:* Koko was commenting on the color of my shirt. We had an earlier discussion about colors today.
>   *Q:* Do you like to chat with people?
>   *Koko:* Fine nipple.

Patterson:	Nipple rhymes with people, she doesn't sign people per se, she was trying to do a "sounds like . . ."
Q:	Koko, do you feel love from the humans who have raised you?
Koko:	Lips, apple give me.
Patterson:	People give her favorite foods.

Today, however, most researchers have taken the criticisms to heart and have greatly improved their procedures. They have shown that with careful training, chimps can indeed acquire the ability to use symbols to refer to objects. Some animals have even spontaneously used signs to converse with each other, suggesting that they are not merely imitating or trying to get a reward (Van Cantfort & Rimpau, 1982). Bonobos, sometimes mistakenly called pygmy chimps, are even more adept at language. One, named Kanzi, has learned to understand English words, short sentences, and keyboard symbols *without formal training* (Savage-Rumbaugh & Lewin, 1994; Savage-Rumbaugh, Shanker, & Taylor, 1998). Kanzi responds correctly to commands such as "Put the key in the refrigerator" and "Go get the ball that is outdoors," even when he has never heard the words combined in that particular way before. He picked up language as children do—by observing others using it, and through normal social interaction. He has also learned, with training, to manipulate keyboard symbols to request favorite foods or activities (games, TV, visits to friends) and to announce his intentions.

You do not even have to be a primate to acquire some aspects of language. In Hawaii, Louis Herman and his colleagues have taught dolphins to respond to requests made in two artificial languages, one consisting of computer-generated whistles and another of hand and arm gestures (Herman, Kuczaj, & Holder, 1993; Herman & Morrel-Samuels,

Kanzi, a bonobo with the most advanced linguistic skills yet acquired by a nonhuman primate, answers questions and makes requests by punching symbols on a specially designed computer keyboard. He also understands short English sentences. He is shown here with researcher Sue Savage-Rumbaugh.

1996). To interpret a request correctly, the dolphins must take into account both the meaning of the individual symbols in a string of whistles or gestures and the order of the symbols (syntax). For example, they must understand the difference between "To left Frisbee, right surfboard take" and "To right surfboard, left Frisbee take."

In another fascinating project, Irene Pepperberg (2000) has spent over two decades teaching Alex, her African gray parrot, to count, classify, and compare objects by vocalizing English words. When Alex is shown up to six items and is asked how many there are, he responds with spoken (squawked?) English phrases, such as "two cork(s)" or "four key(s)." He can even respond correctly to questions about items specified on two dimensions, as in "How many blue key(s)?" Alex also makes requests ("Want pasta") and answers simple questions about objects ("What color [is this]?" "Which is bigger?"). When presented with a blue cork and a blue key and asked "What's the same?" he will correctly respond "Color." He actually scores slightly better with new objects than with familiar ones, suggesting that he is not merely memorizing a set of stock phrases.

Thinking About the Thinking of Animals

These results on animal language and cognition are impressive, but scientists are still divided over just what the animals in these studies are doing. Do they have true language? Are they "thinking," in human terms?

On one side are those who worry about *anthropomorphism,* the tendency to falsely attribute human qualities to nonhuman beings. They tell the story of Clever Hans, a "wonder horse" at the turn of the century, who was said to possess mathematical and other abilities (Spitz, 1997). For example, Clever Hans would answer math problems by stamping his hoof the appropriate number of times. But a little careful experimentation by a psychologist, Oskar Pfungst (1911/1965), revealed that when Hans was prevented from seeing his questioners, his "powers" left him. It seems that questioners were staring at the horse's feet and leaning forward expectantly after stating the problem, then lifting their eyes and relaxing as soon as he completed the right number of taps. Clever Hans was indeed clever, but not at math or other human skills. He was merely responding to nonverbal signals that people were inadvertently providing.

On the other side are those who warn against *anthropocentrism,* the tendency to think, mistakenly, that human beings have nothing in common with other animals (de Waal, 1997; Fouts, 1997). The need to see our own species as unique, they say, may keep us from recognizing that other species, too, have cognitive abilities, even if not as intricate as our own. Those who take this position point out that most modern researchers have gone to great lengths to avoid the Clever Hans problem.

The outcome of this debate is bound to affect how we view ourselves and our place among other species. Cognitive ethologist Marc Hauser (2000) argues that we can study and respect animal minds and emotions, without assuming sentimentally that they are just like ours. This will not be easy. As Donald Griffin (1992) wrote, "Cognitive ethology presents us with one of the supreme scientific challenges of our times, and it calls for our best efforts of critical and imaginative investigation."

What Do You Know?

Regrettably, your pet beagle can't help you answer this quiz.

1. *True or false:* Many animals use objects in the environment as rudimentary tools.

2. A honeybee performs a little dance that communicates to other bees the direction and distance of food. Because the bee can "talk" about something that is located elsewhere, its communication system shows _____. But because the bee can create only utterances that are genetically wired into its repertoire, its communication system lacks _____.

3. In thinking about animal language and cognition, it is important to avoid both _____ and _____.

ANSWERS:

1. true 2. displacement; productivity 3. anthropomorphism; anthropocentrism

We human beings are used to thinking of ourselves as the smartest species around because of our astounding ability to adapt to change, come up with novel solutions to problems, invent endless new gizmos, and use language to create everything from puns to punditry. This chapter has shown that we are not quite as wise in our thinking as we might think. We can, however, boast of one crowning accomplishment: *We are the only species that tries to understand its own misunderstandings.* We want to know what we don't know; we are motivated (sometimes) to overcome our mental shortcomings. This capacity for self-examination is probably the best reason to remain optimistic about our cognitive capacities.

In the next chapter, we invite you to exercise your own powers of self-examination as we turn to an aspect of human cognition that is widely misunderstood—the mystery of memory. ▢

Summary

1. *Thinking* is the mental manipulation of information. Our mental representations simplify and summarize information from the environment.

2. A *concept* is a mental category that groups objects, relations, activities, abstractions, or qualities that share certain properties. *Basic concepts* have a moderate number of instances and are easier to acquire than concepts with few or many instances. *Prototypical* instances of a concept are more representative than others. *Propositions* are made up of concepts and express a unitary idea. They may be linked together to form *cognitive schemas,* which serve as mental models of aspects of the world. *Mental images* also play a role in thinking.

3. Not all mental processing is conscious. *Subconscious processes* lie outside of awareness but can be brought into consciousness when necessary. *Nonconscious processes* remain outside of awareness but nonetheless affect behavior and are involved in what we call

"intuition" and "insight." Conscious processing may be carried out in a mindless fashion if we overlook changes in context that call for a change in behavior.

4. *Reasoning* is purposeful mental activity that involves drawing inferences and conclusions from observations, facts, or assumptions (premises). *Formal reasoning problems* can often be solved by applying an *algorithm*, a set of procedures guaranteed to produce a solution, or by using logical processes, such as deductive and inductive reasoning. In *deductive reasoning*, which often takes the form of a *syllogism*, if the *premises* are true then the conclusion must be true. In *inductive reasoning*, the premises provide support for a conclusion, but the conclusion could still be false. Science depends heavily on inductive reasoning.

5. In *informal reasoning problems*, there may be no clearly correct solution. Disagreement may exist about basic premises, information may be incomplete, and many viewpoints may compete. Such problems may call for the application of *heuristics*, rules of thumb that suggest a course of action without guaranteeing an optimal solution. The problems may also require *dialectical reasoning* about opposing points of view.

6. Creative problem solving requires us to overcome *mental sets* and to exercise *divergent* as well as *convergent thinking*. Traditional creativity tests measure fluency, flexibility, and originality in generating solutions to problems. Creativity tends to flourish when people have control over how to perform a task or solve a problem; are evaluated unobtrusively, instead of being constantly observed and judged; and are given the freedom to work independently. Personality traits—especially nonconformity, curiosity, and persistence—also play a role in creativity.

7. Children do not think the way adults do. Jean Piaget argued that children's thinking changes and adapts through *assimilation* and *accommodation*. Piaget proposed four stages of cognitive development: *sensorimotor* (birth to age 2), during which the child learns *object permanence; preoperational* (ages 2 to 7), during which language and symbolic thought develop, although the child remains *egocentric* in reasoning; *concrete operations* (ages 7 to 11), during which the child comes to understand *conservation* and *identity;* and *formal operations* (age 12 to adulthood), during which abstract reasoning develops.

8. Researchers have found that the changes from one stage to another are not as clear-cut as Piaget implied; young children have more cognitive abilities, at earlier ages, than Piaget thought; and young children are not always egocentric in their thinking. By the age of 4 or 5 they have developed a *theory of mind* to account for their own and other people's behavior. Cultural practices affect the pace and content of cognitive development, and not all adults develop the ability for formal operations.

9. Studies of *reflective judgment* show that many people have trouble thinking dialectically. People in the *prereflective stages* assume that a correct answer always exists; they do not distinguish between knowledge and belief, or between belief and evidence. Those in the *quasi-reflective stages* think that because knowledge is sometimes uncertain, any judgment about the evidence is purely subjective. Those who think *reflectively* understand that although some things cannot be known with certainty, some judgments are more valid than others, depending on their coherence, usefulness, fit with the evidence, and so on. Higher education moves people gradually closer to reflective judgment.

10. The need to be right can be an obstacle to rational thinking, as can mental laziness, which many commentators think has increased because television watching has replaced reading. But the ability to reason clearly and rationally is also affected by many *cognitive biases*. People have a bias to overestimate their ability to have predicted events (the *hindsight bias*); to be swayed in their choices by the desire to *avoid loss*; to exaggerate the likelihood of improbable events, in part because of the *availability heuristic*; and to attend to evidence that confirms what they want to believe and ignore or reject disconfirming evidence (the *confirmation bias*).

11. The theory of *cognitive dissonance* holds that people are also motivated to reduce the tension that exists when two cognitions are in conflict—by rejecting or changing a belief, changing their behavior, or rationalizing. People are especially likely to try to reduce dissonance when they need to justify a decision, when their actions violate their self-concept, or when they have put hard work into an activity (the *justification of effort*). Once we understand a bias, we may be able to reduce or eliminate it.

12. Researchers in the field of *cognitive ethology* argue that nonhuman animals have greater cognitive abilities than is usually thought. Some animals can use objects as rudimentary tools. Chimpanzees have learned to use numerals to label quantities of items and to use symbols to refer to objects. Several researchers have used visual symbol systems or American Sign Language (ASL) to teach primates language skills, and some animals (even some nonprimates) seem able to use simple grammatical ordering rules to convey or comprehend meaning. However, scientists are still divided as to how to interpret these findings, and they are trying to avoid both *anthropomorphism* and *anthropocentrism*.

Key Terms

Answers to the creativity test on page 277:

back, party, book, match, cheese

Some solutions to the nine-dot problem on page 275 (from Adams, 1986):

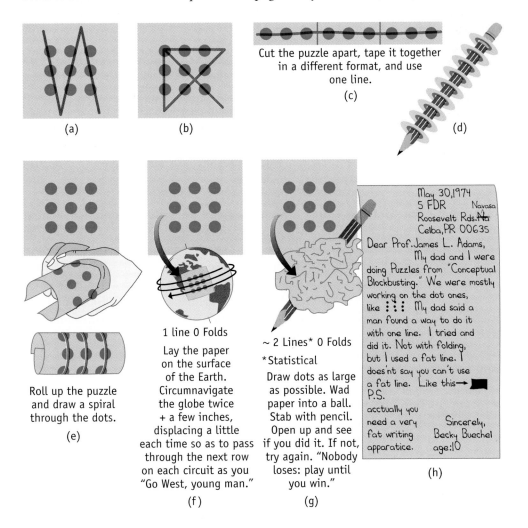

(a)

(b)

Cut the puzzle apart, tape it together in a different format, and use one line.

(c)

(d)

Roll up the puzzle and draw a spiral through the dots.

(e)

1 line 0 Folds

Lay the paper on the surface of the Earth. Circumnavigate the globe twice + a few inches, displacing a little each time so as to pass through the next row on each circuit as you "Go West, young man."

(f)

~ 2 Lines* 0 Folds

*Statistical

Draw dots as large as possible. Wad paper into a ball. Stab with pencil. Open up and see if you did it. If not, try again. "Nobody loses: play until you win."

(g)

May 30, 1974
5 FDR   Navasa
Roosevelt Rds. Na
Ceiba, PR 00635
Dear Prof. James L. Adams,
  My dad and I were doing Puzzles from "Conceptual Blockbusting." We were mostly working on the dot ones, like ⠿ My dad said a man found a way to do it with one line. I tried and did it. Not with folding, but I used a fat line. It does'nt say you can't use a fat line. Like this→ ■
P.S.
acctually you need a very fat writing apparatice.   Sincerely,
   Becky Buechel
   age: 10

(h)

CHAPTER EIGHT

Memory

*I*n 1990, a California jury convicted retired firefighter George Franklin of murder on the basis of his adult daughter's recovered memory. The daughter, Eileen Franklin, testified that while she was playing with her young daughter, a shocking memory had suddenly returned. Her daughter reminded her of a close childhood friend who had been slain 21 years earlier, at the age of 8. The case had never been solved, but in that moment Eileen remembered who had killed her friend because she remembered being there: It was her own father. A few months later, she also remembered that he had molested her for years, starting when she was 3.

Other cases involving recovered memories of sexual abuse in childhood were soon being reported across North America, leading to a wave of criminal charges and lawsuits. In one typical case, a woman named Laura B. sued her father, claiming that he had molested her from the ages of 5 to 23 and had raped her just days before her wedding. Laura B. said she had no memories of these events until they emerged during therapy.

A bitter controversy has raged for years about whether such accusations should be believed, and whether they provide sufficient evidence, in the absence of corroboration, to convict the alleged perpetrators. One side—we'll call it the *recovered-memory school*—believes that false memories are rare, that traumatic memories are commonly blocked from consciousness, and that people who raise doubts about recovered memories of trauma or abuse are inadvertently betraying victims and abetting child molesters (Freyd, 1996; Pope, 1996). The other side—we'll call it the *pseudomemory school*—argues that although real abuse occurs, many false memories of victimization are being encouraged by naïve or uninformed therapists (Lindsay & Read, 1994; Loftus & Ketcham, 1994). Emotions run high because much is at stake: finding justice for true victims by punishing perpetrators of abuse and other crimes, while also protecting adults from false charges that can destroy their lives.

At the end of this chapter we will see what happened in the Franklin case and assess the larger issue of recovered memories. But first, let's consider the reliability of memories in general. Of course, we all forget a great deal: We watch the evening news and half an hour later can't recall the main story; we enjoy a meal and forget what we ate by the next day; we study our heads off for an exam, only to find that some of the information is missing when we need it most. Do we also "remember" things that never happened? Are we likely to forget traumatic events that *did* happen? Are memory malfunctions the exception to the rule, or could they be the norm? And if memory is not always reliable, how can any of us hope to know the story of our own lives? How can we hope to understand the past?

Reconstructing the Past

Memory refers to the capacity to retain and retrieve information, and also to the mental structures that account for this capacity. Human beings are capable of astonishing feats of memory. Most of us can easily remember who fought whom in World War II, the tune of our national anthem, how to use an automated teller machine, the most embarrassing experience we ever had, zillions of details about our favorite sports or films, and countless other bits of information, without hesitation.

Memory confers competence; without it we would be as helpless as newborns, unable to carry out even the most trivial of our daily tasks. Memory also confers a sense of personal identity; each of us is the sum of our recollections, which is why we feel so threatened when others challenge our memories. Individuals and cultures alike rely on a remembered history for a sense of coherence and meaning; memory gives us our past and guides our future.

The Manufacture of Memory

In ancient times, philosophers compared memory to a soft wax tablet that would preserve anything that chanced to make an imprint on it. Then, with the advent of the printing press, they began to think of memory as a gigantic library, storing specific events and facts for later retrieval. Today, in the audiovisual age, many people compare memory to a tape recorder or a movie camera, automatically recording every moment of their lives. One therapist, who apparently never studied introductory psychology, expressed the modern pop-psych vision of memory this way: "The subconscious mind has a memory bank of everything we ever experienced, exactly as we perceived it. Every thought, emotion, sound of music, word, taste and sight. Everything is faithfully recorded somehow in your mind. Your subconscious mind's memory is perfect, infallible" (quoted in Dawes, 1994).

Popular and appealing though this belief about memory is, however, it is utterly wrong. Not everything that happens to us or impinges on our senses is tucked away for later use; memory is selective. If it were not, our minds would be cluttered with mental junk—the temperature at noon Thursday, the price of turnips two years ago, a phone number needed only once. Moreover, recovering a memory is not at all like replaying a videotape of an event; it is more like watching a few unconnected frames and then figuring out what the rest of the scene must have been like.

One of the first scientists to make this point was the British psychologist Sir Frederic Bartlett (1932). Bartlett asked people to read lengthy, unfamiliar stories from other cultures and then tell the stories back to him. As the volunteers tried to recall the stories, they made interesting errors: They often eliminated or changed details that did not make sense to them, and they added other details to make the story coherent, sometimes even adding a moral. Memory, Bartlett concluded, must therefore be largely a *reconstructive process.* We may reproduce some kinds of simple information by rote, said Bartlett, but when we remember complex information, we typically alter it in ways that help us make sense of the material, based on what we already know or think we know. Since Bartlett's time, hundreds of studies have found this to be true for everything from stories to conversations to personal experiences (Schacter, 1996).

In reconstructing their memories, people often draw on many sources. Suppose, for example, that someone asks you to describe one of your early birthday parties. You may have some direct recollection of the event, but you may also incorporate information from family stories, photographs, or home videos, and even from accounts of other people's birthdays and reenactments of birthdays on television. You take all these bits and pieces and build one integrated account. Later, you may not be able to separate your original experience from what you added after the fact—a phenomenon called **source amnesia,** or *source misattribution.*

A dramatic instance of reconstruction once occurred in the sad case of H. M., whom we described briefly in Chapter 4. Ever since 1953, when much of H. M.'s hippocampus and the adjacent cortex were surgically removed, he has been unable to form lasting memories for new events, facts, songs, stories, or faces, and so he does not remember much of anything that has happened since his operation (Hilts, 1995; Ogden & Corkin, 1991). To cope with his devastating condition, H. M. will sometimes resort to reconstruction. On one occasion, after eating a chocolate Valentine's Day heart, H. M. stuck the shiny red wrapping in his shirt pocket. Two hours later, while searching for his handkerchief, he pulled out the paper and looked at it in puzzlement. When a researcher asked why he had the paper in his pocket, he replied, "Well, it could have been wrapped around a big chocolate heart. It must be Valentine's Day!" The researcher could hardly contain her excitement about H. M.'s possible recall of a recent episode. But a short time later, when she asked him to take out the paper again and say why he had it in his pocket, he replied, "Well, it might have been wrapped around a big chocolate rabbit. It must be Easter!"

Sadly, H. M. *had* to reconstruct the past; his damaged brain could not recall it in any other way. But those of us with normal memory abilities also reconstruct, far more often than we realize.

---

source amnesia The inability to distinguish what you originally experienced from what you heard or were told about an event later.

The Fading Flashbulb

Of course, some unusual, shocking, or tragic events, such as earthquakes or accidents, do seem to hold a special place in memory, especially when we were personally involved. Such events seem frozen in time, with all the details intact. Years ago, Roger Brown and James Kulik (1977) labeled these vivid recollections of emotional events "flashbulb memories" because that term captures the surprise, illumination, and seemingly photographic detail that characterize them. They speculated that the capacity for flashbulb memories may have evolved because such memories had survival value. Remembering the details of a surprising or dangerous experience could have helped our ancestors avoid similar situations.

Despite their intensity, however, even flashbulb memories are not always complete or accurate records of the past (Wright, 1993). For example, people who saw the 1986 explosion of the space shuttle *Challenger* often swear that they know exactly where they were and what they were doing when the tragedy occurred. But research done after the explosion has shown that memories like these grow dimmer with time. In one study, college students, on the morning after the *Challenger* tragedy, reported how they had heard the news. Three years later, when they again recalled how they learned of the incident, not one student was entirely correct and a third of them were *completely wrong*, although they felt confident that they were remembering accurately (Neisser & Harsch, 1992). In another study, psychologists interviewed 222 college students in 1995, after the verdict was announced in the O. J. Simpson case. (The popular football hero was found not guilty of murdering his ex–wife and her friend.) Fifteen months later, half of the students' recollections of the case were highly accurate, and only 11 percent contained major errors or distortions. But after 32 months, only 29 percent of the recollections remained accurate, and more than 40 percent contained major distortions (Schmolck, Buffalo, & Squire, 2000).

What about emotionally arousing *positive* events, like a first romantic kiss? These events, too, sometimes have the qualities of a flashbulb memory. Lovers who were highly excited by their first kiss report more details about the experience than people who were not very excited. Some say they can recall what the other person was wearing,

More facts of nature: All forest animals, to this very day, remember exactly where they were and what they were doing when they heard that Bambi's mother had been shot.

the exact hour and day of the kiss, and the first words that were uttered afterward. Yet, alas, time takes a toll on these memories as well, with recall best within two years of the event (Fisher et al., 1999).

Even with flashbulb memories, then, facts tend to get mixed with a little fiction. The conclusion is inescapable: Remembering is an *active* process, one that involves not only dredging up stored information but also putting two and two together to reconstruct the past. Sometimes, though, we put two and two together and get five.

The Conditions of Confabulation

As we saw in Chapter 7, rational cognitive processing is often hampered by the confirmation bias and the need to reduce dissonance. Memory is biased in a similar way: After making a decision, we will remember information that supported the wisdom of our choice and conveniently forget information that might have led us to make an alternative choice (Mather, Shafir, & Johnson, 2000). These predictable memory distortions reduce feelings of regret, but they also make it harder to learn from our mistakes.

Of course, most people don't forget that they made a decision to go to College X rather than College Y, or to marry Mindy rather than Cindy. But because memory is reconstructive, it is subject to *confabulation*—confusing an event that happened to someone else with one that happened to you, or coming to believe that you remember something that never happened. Such confabulations are especially likely to occur under four circumstances (Garry, Manning, & Loftus, 1996; Hyman & Pentland, 1996; Johnson, 1995):

1 You have thought about the imagined event many times. Suppose that at family gatherings you keep hearing about the time that Uncle Sam scared everyone at a New Year's party by pounding a hammer into the wall with such force that the wall collapsed. The story is so colorful that you can practically see Uncle Sam in your mind's eye. The more you think about this event, the more likely you are to believe that you were actually there, even if you were sound asleep in another house.

2 The image of the event contains a lot of details. Ordinarily, we can distinguish an imagined event from a real one by the amount of detail we recall; real events tend to produce more details. However, the longer you think about an imagined event, the more details you are likely to add—what Sam was wearing, the fact that he'd had too much to drink, the crumbling plaster, people standing around in party hats—and these details may in turn persuade you that the event really happened and that you have a direct memory of it.

3 The event is easy to imagine. If forming an image of an event takes little effort (as does visualizing a man pounding a wall with a hammer), then we tend to think that our memory is real. In contrast, when we must make an effort to form an image—for example, of being in a place we have never seen or doing something that is utterly foreign to us—our cognitive efforts apparently serve as a cue that the event did not really take place, or that we were not there when it did.

4 **YOU FOCUS ON YOUR EMOTIONAL REACTIONS TO THE EVENT RATHER THAN ON WHAT ACTUALLY HAPPENED.** Emotional reactions to an imagined event can resemble those that would have occurred in response to a real event, so they can mislead us. This means that your feelings about an event, no matter how strongly you hold them, are no guarantee that the event really happened. Consider again our Sam story, which happens to be true. A woman we know believed for years that she had been present in the room as an 11-year-old child when her uncle destroyed the wall. Because the story was so vivid and upsetting to her, she felt angry at him for what she thought was his mean and violent behavior, and she assumed that she must have been angry at the time as well. Then, as an adult, she learned that she was not at the party at all but had merely heard about it repeatedly over the years; and that Sam had not pounded the wall in anger, but as a joke—to inform the assembled guests that he and his wife were about to remodel their home. Nevertheless, our friend's family has had a hard time convincing her that her memory of this event is entirely wrong, and they are not sure she believes them yet.

As the Sam story illustrates, and as laboratory research verifies, false memories can be as stable over time as true ones (Brainerd, Reyna, & Brandse, 1995; Poole, 1995; Roediger & McDermott, 1995). Yet many people not only believe that memories are permanently stored in the brain with perfect accuracy, but also that there are reliable ways of getting them "out," such as through hypnosis. We will see what is wrong with that assumption next.

What Do You Know?

See whether you can reconstruct what you have read in order to answer these questions.

1. Memory is like (a) a wax tablet, (b) a giant file cabinet, (c) a video recorder, (d) none of these.

2. *True or false:* Like other memories, flashbulb memories are vulnerable to distortion.

3. Which of the following confabulated memories might a person be most inclined to accept as having really happened in the past, and why? (a) being lost in a shopping center at the age of 5, (b) taking a class in astrophysics, (c) visiting a monastery in Tibet as a child, (d) being bullied by another kid in the fourth grade

ANSWERS:

1. d 2. true 3. Because a and d are common emotional experiences that are easy to imagine in vivid detail, they are most likely to be accepted as real. It would be harder to induce someone to believe that he or she had studied astrophysics or visited Tibet, because these are rare events that take an effort to imagine.

MEMORY AND THE POWER OF SUGGESTION

The reconstructive nature of memory helps the mind work efficiently. Instead of cramming our brains with infinite details, we can store the essentials of an experience, then use our knowledge of the world to figure out the specifics when we need them. But precisely because memory is reconstructive, it is also vulnerable to suggestion—to ideas implanted in our minds after the event, which then become associated with it. This normal process raises some thorny problems in legal cases that involve eyewitness testimony or people's memories of what happened, when, and to whom. In this section, we will consider three topics that illustrate the power of suggestion to influence memory: eyewitness testimony, children's testimony, and hypnotic recall of events.

The Eyewitness on Trial

Without the accounts of eyewitnesses, many people who are guilty of crimes would go free. But because memory is reconstructive, eyewitness testimony is not always reliable, even when the witness is dead certain about the accuracy of his or her report (Bothwell, Deffenbacher, & Brigham, 1987; Sporer et al., 1995). As a result, some convictions based solely or mostly on such testimony turn out to be tragic mistakes. According to one estimate, if just half of one percent of all convictions for serious crimes in the United States are in error, each year about 4,500 innocent people go to jail—and some of them go to death row (Cutler & Penrod, 1995). Because of the growing awareness of the problems with eyewitness identification, justice projects in law schools and journalism schools around the country are now successfully challenging many of these convictions.

For example, when researchers looked into 40 cases of wrongful imprisonment in which DNA evidence eventually established the innocence of the accused person, they found that 90 percent of the cases had involved a false identification by one or more eyewitnesses (Wells et al., 1998). Errors by eyewitnesses are especially likely to occur when the suspect's ethnicity differs from that of the witness. Perhaps prejudices or unfamiliarity prevent people from attending to the distinctive features of members of other groups, or perhaps ethnic stereotypes affect people's reconstructions of what happened (Brigham & Malpass, 1985; Chance & Goldstein, 1995; Sherman & Bessenoff, 1999).

Eyewitness accounts are heavily influenced by the way in which questions are put to the witness and by suggestive comments made during an interrogation or interview. In a classic study of *leading questions,* Elizabeth Loftus and John Palmer (1974) showed people short films depicting car collisions. Afterward, the researchers asked some of the viewers, "About how fast were the cars going when they hit each other?" Other viewers were asked the same question, but with the verb changed to *smashed, collided, bumped,* or *contacted.* Estimates of how fast the cars were going varied, depending on which word was used. *Smashed* produced the highest average speed estimates (40.8 mph), followed by *collided* (39.3 mph), *bumped* (38.1 mph), *hit* (34.0 mph), and *contacted* (31.8 mph).

In a similar study, the researchers asked some participants, "Did you see a broken headlight?" but asked of others "Did you see the broken headlight?" (Loftus & Zanni, 1975). The question with *the* presupposes a broken headlight and merely asks whether the witness saw it, whereas the question with *a* makes no such presupposition. People who received questions with *the* were far more likely to report having seen something that had not really appeared in the film than were those who received questions with *a*. If a tiny word like *the* can lead people to "remember" what they never saw, you can imagine how the leading questions of police detectives and lawyers might influence a witness's recall.

Misleading information from any source can profoundly alter what we remember. In one study, students were shown the face of a young man who had straight hair, then heard a description of the face supposedly written by another witness—a description that wrongly said the man had light, curly hair (Loftus & Greene, 1980). When the students reconstructed the face using a kit of facial features, a third of their reconstructions contained the misleading detail, whereas only 5 percent contained it when curly hair was not mentioned. The face on the left below shows one person's (fairly accurate) reconstruction in the absence of the misleading information; on the right is another person's reconstruction of the same face after exposure to the misleading information.

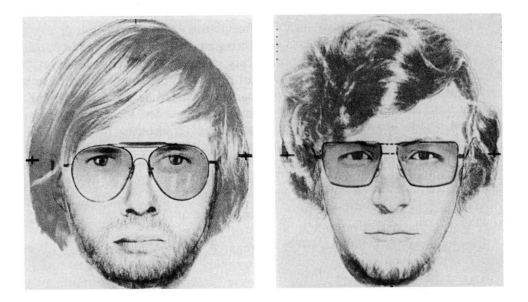

Leading questions, suggestive comments, and misleading information affect people's memories for their own experiences, as well as events they have merely witnessed. In many studies, researchers have induced people to "recall" complicated events from early in life—events that never actually happened at all, such as getting lost in a shopping mall, being hospitalized for a high fever, being harassed by a bully, or even spilling punch all over the mother of the bride at a wedding (Hyman & Pentland, 1996; Loftus & Pickrell, 1995; Mazzoni et al., 1999).

Children's Testimony

The power of suggestion can affect anyone, but many people are especially concerned about its impact on children being questioned about possible sexual abuse. For many decades, most adults believed that children confuse fantasy with reality and tend to say whatever adults expect, and therefore that children's memories could not be trusted. Then, as the issue of child abuse came to public attention in the 1970s and 1980s, some people began to argue that no child would ever lie about or misremember such a traumatic experience.

Resolving this debate became critical as accusations of child abuse in daycare centers across the United States skyrocketed. The first was a case against the McMartin preschool in Los Angeles in the mid-1980s, and it was soon followed by dozens of others. After being interviewed by therapists and police investigators, children in these schools were claiming that their teachers had molested them in terrible ways: hanging them in trees, putting handcuffs on them, raping them, even forcing them to eat feces. Although in no case had parents actually seen the daycare teachers treating the children badly, although none of the children had complained to their parents, and although none of the parents had noticed any symptoms or problems in their children, many of these teachers were sentenced to decades in prison on the basis of what the children were saying (Nathan & Snedeker, 1995). Were these people guilty of unspeakably horrible acts, or had the children been somehow persuaded to make up fanciful stories?

After reviewing the research on this issue, Stephen Ceci and Maggie Bruck (1995) concluded that both extreme positions—"children always lie" and "children never lie"—are wrong. Most young children *do* recollect accurately most of what they have observed or experienced. On the other hand, some children *will* say that something happened when it did not. Like adults, they can be influenced to report an event in a certain way, depending on the frequency of the suggestions and the insistence of the person making them.

Therefore, instead of asking "Are children suggestible?" or "Are children's memories accurate?," Ceci and Bruck (1995) propose asking a more useful question: "Under what conditions are children apt to be suggestible?" One such condition is age. Preschoolers' memories are more vulnerable to suggestive questions than are those of school-age children and adults. Preschoolers are also more likely to have source amnesia, failing to remember whether they actually saw or experienced something themselves or heard about it from an adult. And the boundary between reality and fantasy may blur for very young children, especially in emotionally charged situations, making it more likely that their accounts will include confabulations of imagined events (Poole & Lamb, 1998).

In addition, children's memories, just like adults' memories, can be influenced by pressure to conform to the interviewer's expectations and by the desire to please the interviewer. One team of researchers, having analyzed the transcripts of interrogations of children in the McMartin case, applied the same techniques in an experiment with preschool children (Garven et al., 1998). A young man visited children at their preschool, read them a story, and handed out treats. The man did nothing aggressive, inappropriate, or surprising. A week later the experimenter questioned the children about the man's visit. She asked children in one group leading questions ("Did he

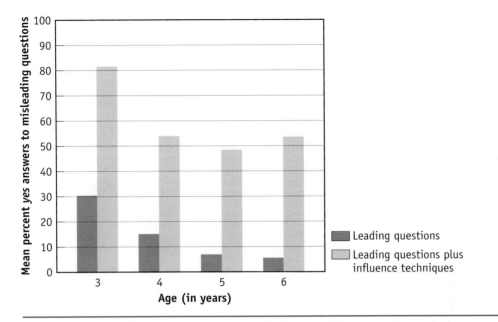

FIGURE 8.1 Social Pressure and Children's Recall *When researchers asked a group of preschoolers whether a visitor to their classroom had committed aggressive acts—acts that had not actually occurred—only a small minority of the 4- to 6-year-olds said that yes, he had (though fully 30 percent of the 3-year-olds said yes). But when the researchers used social-influence techniques taken from real-life child-abuse investigations, most of the children said yes (Garven et al., 1998).*

shove the teacher? Did he throw a crayon at a kid who was talking?"). She asked a second group the same questions but also used influence techniques used by interrogators in the McMartin case and in similar cases: for example, telling the children what "other kids" had supposedly said, expressing disappointment if answers were negative, and praising children for making allegations.

In the first group, children said "yes, it happened" to about 15 percent of the false allegations about the man's visit. This finding alone refutes the notion that children never lie, misremember, or make things up. In the second group, the 3-year-olds, on average, said "yes" to *over 80 percent* of the false allegations suggested to them, and the 4- to 6-year-olds said yes to about half the allegations (see Figure 8.1). Note that the interviews in this study lasted only five to ten minutes, whereas in actual investigations, interviewers often question children repeatedly over many weeks.

In another study of children ages 5 to 7, children who were positively reinforced for reporting something that didn't happen had a false-allegation rate of 35 percent, compared to 12 percent for a control group. Even when questioned about "fantastic" events, such as being taken from school in a helicopter, the children receiving reinforcement made 52 percent false allegations, compared to 5 percent of the controls (Garven, Wood, & Malpass, 2000). False allegations increased even more when the interviewer said that "other kids" reported that something happened:

Interviewer:	Did Paco take you somewhere on a helicopter?
Child:	No.
Interviewer:	You're not doing good. Um-uh. The other kids say that Paco took them to a farm. Did Paco take you to a farm?
Child:	Yes.
Interviewer:	Great. You're doing excellent now.

Some people argue that children cannot be induced to report traumatic experiences that never actually happened to them, but they can be. In one study, schoolchildren were asked for their recollections of an actual incident in which a sniper had terrorized their schoolyard. Many of the children who were not at the school during the shooting, including some who were on vacation at the time, reported memories of hearing shots, seeing someone lying on the ground, and other details they could not possibly have experienced directly. Apparently, they had been influenced by the accounts of the children who had been there (Pynoos & Nader, 1989).

In sum, children, like adults, can be accurate in what they report, and, also like adults, they can distort, forget, fantasize, and be misled. As research shows, their memory processes are only human.

Memory Under Hypnosis

Many people believe that hypnosis can overcome the limitations of ordinary memory and help people relive a long-ago childhood event or recall a seemingly forgotten experience. Stage hypnotists, "past-lives channelers," and some psychotherapists claim that they can "age-regress" hypnotized people to earlier years or even earlier centuries. A few therapists even assert that hypnosis has helped their patients recall alleged abductions by extraterrestrials. In all of these cases, the assumption is that any memory recovered by hypnosis must be accurate, and that total recall is possible. But is that true?

First of all, hypnosis is not a mysterious, trancelike or sleeplike state in which the subject has no control over his or her feelings and behavior. In **hypnosis,** a practitioner suggests changes in the sensations, perceptions, thoughts, feelings, or behavior of the subject (Kirsch & Lynn, 1995). The subject, in turn, tries to alter his or her normal cognitive functioning in accordance with the hypnotist's suggestions (Nash & Nadon, 1997). This is a voluntary effort, although people usually report that it feels involuntary. Hypnosis has been used successfully in the treatment of many psychological and medical problems, for example to alleviate chronic pain; reduce stress and anxiety; anesthetize people undergoing dental work, surgery, or childbirth; and reduce nausea in cancer patients undergoing chemotherapy (Kirsch, Montgomery, & Saperstein, 1995; Nash & Nadon, 1997).

But when it comes to memory, hypnosis is another matter entirely. Overall, hypnosis does *not* increase the accuracy of memory. On the contrary: Under hypnosis, the natural tendency to confuse fact and speculation is increased by a desire to please the hypnotist and by the hypnotist's encouragement of fantasy and the reporting of

---

hypnosis   A procedure in which the practitioner suggests changes in the sensations, perceptions, thoughts, feelings, or behavior of the subject, who cooperates by altering his or her normal cognitive functioning accordingly.

"THE WITNESS HAS BARKED, MEOWED AND GIVEN US FIVE MINUTES OF BABY TALK. I'D SAY HYPNOSIS IS NOT THE ANSWER."

detailed images ("Imagine that you are back in your grandmother's house when you were 7 . . . describe the room and what she is wearing . . ."). Although hypnosis does sometimes boost the amount of information recalled about an actual event, it also increases *errors,* probably because hypnotized people are more willing than non-hypnotized people to guess or because they mistake vividly imagined possibilities for actual memories (Dinges et al., 1992; Kihlstrom, 1994; Nash & Nadon, 1997).

You will remember from the "conditions of confabulation" that the more vivid and imaginable an event is, the more likely people are to believe that it happened to them. In fact, hypnotized people are often supremely confident of the accuracy of their retrieved memories, even when they are completely wrong (Dinges et al., 1992; Kihlstrom, 1994). Because pseudomemories and errors are so common in hypnotically induced recall, the American Psychological Association and the American Medical Association oppose the use of "hypnotically refreshed" testimony in courts of law.

Hypnosis also cannot produce a literal reexperiencing of long-ago events. When Michael Yapko (1994) surveyed nearly 900 family therapists, he discovered that more than half believed that "hypnosis can be used to recover memories as far back as birth." This belief is just plain wrong. When people are regressed to an earlier age, their brain-wave patterns and reflexes do not become childish; they do not show any signs of outgrown emotional disorders; they do not reason as children do or show child-sized IQs (Nash, 1987). They may use baby talk or report that they feel 4 years old, but the reason is not that they *are* 4; they are simply willing to play the role. They will do the same when they are regressed to "past lives." Their belief that they are 7 or 7,000 years old may be sincere and convincing, but it is based on elaborate fantasy and role playing.

In a series of studies that demonstrated how false memories can be constructed under hypnotic suggestion, Nicholas Spanos and his colleagues (1991) directed hypnotized Canadian university students to regress past their own births to previous lives. About a third of the students reported being able to do so. But when they were asked, while supposedly reliving a past life, to name the leader of their country, say whether the country was at peace or war, or describe what currency was in use, the students could not do it. One young man, who thought he was Julius Caesar, said the year was 50 A.D. and he was emperor of Rome. But Caesar died in 44 B.C. and was never crowned emperor, and dating years as A.D. or B.C. did not begin until several centuries later!

In these studies, the students who believed they were reliving a past life were actually weaving events, places, and persons from their present lives into their accounts. Their descriptions and their acceptance of their regression experiences as real were also influenced by the instructions of the hypnotist. A similar process occurs when people under hypnosis report spirit possession or memories of abductions by aliens (Baker, 1992;

Dawes, 1994; Spanos, Burgess, & Burgess, 1994). Often, the hypnotist shapes the person's story by giving subtle and not-so-subtle hints about what the person should say. Here is an exchange between a therapist who believes in alien abductions and a supposed abductee who had been hypnotized (quoted in Newman & Baumeister, 1994):

Dr. Fiore: Now I'm going to ask you a few questions at this point. You will remember everything because you want to remember. When you were being poked everywhere, did they do any kind of vaginal examination?

Sandi: I don't think they did.

Dr. Fiore: Now you're going to let yourself know if they put a needle in any part of your body, other than the rectum.

Sandi: No. They were carrying needles around, big ones, and I was scared for a while they were going to put one in me, but they didn't. [*Body tenses.*]

Dr. Fiore: Now just let yourself relax. At the count of three you're going to remember whether they did put one of those big needles in you. If they did, know that you're safe, and it's all over, isn't it. And if they didn't, you're going to remember that too, at the count of three. One . . . two . . . three.

Sandi: They did.

As cognitive psychologists study hypnosis, they are learning how human suggestibility and the power of imagination affect the way we perceive the present and remember the past.

What Do You Know?

Being hypnotized is unlikely to help you with this quiz.

1. Which statement about hypnosis is correct? (a) It reduces errors in memory; (b) it enables people to relive memories from infancy; (c) it permits people to relive a former life; (d) it demonstrates that memories are permanently and accurately stored in the brain.

2. Under hypnosis, Jim describes the chocolate cake at his fourth birthday and Joan remembers her former life as a twelfth-century French queen. But lemon cake was served at Jim's birthday and Joan can't speak twelfth-century French. What explanation best accounts for their vivid but incorrect memories?

3. Research suggests that the best way to encourage truthful testimony by children is to (a) reassure them that their friends have had the same experience, (b) reward them for telling you that something happened, (c) punish them if you believe they are lying, (d) try to avoid leading questions.

4. In psychotherapy, hundreds of people have claimed to recall long-buried memories of taking part in satanic rituals involving animal and human torture and sacrifice. Yet law-enforcement investigators and psychologists have been unable to confirm any of these reports (Goodman et al., 1995). Based on what you have learned so far, how might you explain such "memories"?

ANSWERS:

1. None of these statements are true. 2. They are using their imaginations to respond to the hypnotist's suggestions and trying to come up with a plausible story. 3. d 4. Therapists who uncritically assume that satanic cults are widespread may ask leading questions, probe for details, and otherwise influence their patients. Patients, who are susceptible to their therapists' interpretations, may then confabulate and "remember" experiences that did not happen, borrowing details from fictionalized accounts or from other troubling experiences in their lives (Ofshe & Watters, 1994). The result may be source amnesia and the patient's mistaken conviction that the memory is real.

IN PURSUIT OF MEMORY

Now that we have seen how memory *doesn't* work—namely, like a tape recorder, an infallible filing system, or a journal written in indelible ink—we turn to studies of how it *does* work. The ability to remember is not an absolute talent; it depends on the type of performance being called for. If you have a preference for essay, multiple-choice, or true-false exams, you already know this.

Measuring Memory

Conscious recollection of an event or an item of information is called **explicit memory.** It is usually measured using one of two methods. The first method tests for **recall,** the ability to retrieve and reproduce information encountered earlier. Essay and fill-in-the-blank exams and memory games such as Trivial Pursuit or Jeopardy require recall. Here's a quick recall test for you, assuming you know the poem *'Twas the Night Before Christmas* or the song *Rudolph the Red-Nosed Reindeer.* Rudolph had eight reindeer friends; name as many of them as you can. (Do this now, before you read further.)

The second method tests for **recognition,** the ability to identify information you have previously observed, read, or heard about. The information is given to you, and all you have to do is say whether it is old or new, or perhaps correct or incorrect, or pick it out of a set of alternatives. The task, in other words, is to compare the information you are given with the information stored in your memory. True-false and multiple-choice tests call for recognition. For example, can you identify Rudolph the Red-Nosed Reindeer's eight reindeer friends from the list on the following page? (The answers are at the end of this chapter—but no fair peeking.)

---

explicit memory Conscious, intentional recollection of an event or of an item of information.
recall The ability to retrieve and reproduce from memory previously encountered material.
recognition The ability to identify previously encountered material.

Blitzen	Dander	Dancer	Masher
Cupid	Dasher	Prancer	Comet
Kumquat	Donder	Flasher	Pixie
Bouncer	Blintzes	Trixie	Vixen

Recognition tests can be tricky, especially when false items closely resemble correct ones. Under most circumstances, however, recognition is easier than recall. Recognition for visual images is particularly impressive. If you show people 2,500 slides of faces and places, and later you ask them to identify which ones they saw out of a larger set, they will be able to identify more than 90 percent of the original slides accurately (Haber, 1970).

The superiority of recognition over recall was once demonstrated in a study of people's memories of their high-school classmates (Bahrick, Bahrick, & Wittlinger, 1975). The participants, ages 17 to 74, first wrote down the names of as many classmates as they could remember. Recall was poor; even when prompted with yearbook pictures, the youngest people failed to name almost a third of their classmates, and the oldest failed to name most of them. Recognition, however, was far better. When asked to look at a series of cards, each of which contained a set of five photographs, and to say which picture in each set showed a former classmate, recent graduates were right 90 percent of the time—and so were people who had graduated 35 years earlier! The ability to recognize names was nearly as impressive.

Sometimes, information encountered in the past affects our thoughts and actions even though we do not consciously or intentionally remember it, a phenomenon known as **implicit memory** (Graf & Schacter, 1985; Schacter, Chiu, & Ochsner, 1993). To get at this subtle sort of knowledge, researchers must rely on indirect methods, instead of the direct ones used to measure explicit memory. One common method, **priming,** asks you to read or listen to some information and then tests you later to see whether the information affects your performance on another type of task.

For example, suppose that you had to read a list of words, some of which began with the letters *def* (such as *define, defend,* or *deform*). Later you might be asked to complete word stems (such as *def-*) with the first word that comes to mind. Even if you could not recognize or recall the original words very well, you would be more likely to complete the word fragments with words from the list than you would be if you had not seen the list. In this procedure, the original words "prime" certain responses on the word-completion task (that is, make them more available), showing that people can retain more knowledge about the past than they realize. They know more than they know that they know.

---

implicit memory Unconscious retention in memory, as evidenced by the effect of a previous experience or previously encountered information on current thoughts or actions.

priming A method for measuring implicit memory in which a person reads or listens to information and is later tested to see whether the information affects performance on another type of task.

Another method of measuring memory, the **relearning method,** or *savings method,* straddles the boundary between implicit and explicit memory tests. Devised by Hermann Ebbinghaus (1885/1913) over a century ago, the relearning method requires you to relearn information or a task that you learned earlier. If you master it more quickly the second time around, you must be remembering something from the first experience. One eminent memory researcher told us that he considers the relearning method to be a test of explicit memory. But another maintained that it can function as a test of implicit memory if the learner is unaware that the material being relearned was ever learned earlier.

Models of Memory

Although people usually refer to memory as a single faculty, as in "I must be losing my memory" or "He has a memory like an elephant's," the term *memory* actually covers a complex collection of abilities and processes. If tape recorders or videocameras are not accurate metaphors for capturing these diverse components of memory, then what metaphor would be better?

As we saw in Chapter 7, many cognitive psychologists liken the mind to an information processor, along the lines of a computer, though more complex. They have constructed *information-processing models* of cognitive processes, liberally borrowing computer programming terms such as *input, output, accessing,* and *information retrieval.* When you type something on your computer's keyboard, the machine encodes the information into an electronic language, stores it on a disk, and retrieves it when you need to use it. Similarly, in information-processing models of memory, we *encode* information (convert it to a form that the brain can process and use), *store* the information (retain it over time), and *retrieve* the information (recover it for use). In storage, the information may be represented as concepts, propositions, images, or *cognitive schemas*—mental networks of knowledge, beliefs, and expectations concerning particular topics or aspects of the world. (If you can't retrieve these terms, see Chapter 7.)

In most information-processing models, storage takes place in three interacting memory systems. *Sensory memory* retains incoming sensory information for a second or two, until it can be processed further. *Short-term memory (STM)* holds a limited amount of information for a brief period of time, perhaps up to 30 seconds or so, unless a conscious effort is made to keep it there longer. *Long-term memory (LTM)* accounts for longer storage—from a few minutes to decades (Atkinson & Shiffrin, 1968, 1971). Information can pass from sensory memory to short-term memory, and in either direction between short-term and long-term memory, as illustrated in Figure 8.2.

---

relearning method A method for measuring retention that compares the time required to relearn material with the time used in the initial learning of the material.

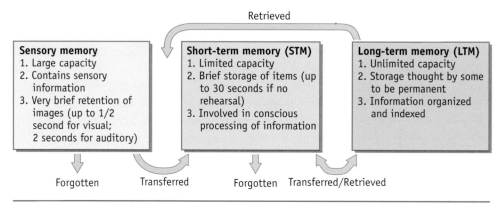

FIGURE 8.2 THREE MEMORY SYSTEMS *In the "three-box model" of memory, information that does not transfer out of sensory memory or short-term memory is assumed to be forgotten forever. Once in long-term memory, information can be retrieved for use in analyzing incoming sensory information or performing mental operations in short-term memory.*

This model, which is often informally called the "three-box model," has dominated research on memory since the late 1960s. However, some psychologists argue that just one system exists, with different mental processes called on for different tasks. Critics of the three-box model also note that the human brain does not operate like your average computer. Most computers process instructions and data sequentially, so the three-box model has emphasized sequential operations; but the human brain performs many operations simultaneously, in parallel. It recognizes patterns all at once rather than as a sequence of information bits, and it perceives new information, produces speech, and searches memory all at the same time. It can do this because millions of neurons are active at once, and each neuron communicates with thousands of others, which in turn communicate with millions more.

Because of these differences between human beings and machines, some cognitive scientists prefer a **parallel distributed processing (PDP),** or *connectionist,* model. Instead of representing information as flowing from one system to another, a PDP model represents the contents of memory as connections among a huge number of interacting processing units, distributed in a vast network and all operating in parallel—just like the neurons of the brain (McClelland, 1994; Rumelhart, McClelland, & the PDP Research Group, 1986). As information enters the system, the ability of these units to excite or inhibit each other is constantly adjusted to reflect new knowledge.

Memory researchers are still arguing about which model of memory is most useful. In this chapter, we emphasize the three-box model, but the computer metaphor that inspired it could one day be as outdated as the metaphor of memory as a camera.

---

parallel distributed processing (PDP) An alternative to the information-processing model of memory, in which knowledge is represented as connections among thousands of interacting processing units, distributed in a vast network, and all operating in parallel.

What Do You Know?

How well have you encoded what you just learned?

1. Alberta solved a crossword puzzle a few days ago. She no longer recalls the words in the puzzle, but while playing a game of Scrabble with her brother, she unconsciously tends to form words that were in the puzzle, showing that she has _____ memories of some of the words.

2. The three basic memory processes are _____, storage, and _____.

3. Do the preceding two questions ask for recall, recognition, or relearning? (And what about *this* question?)

4. If you know the story of Snow White and the Seven Dwarfs, can you remember which of the following are *not* among the seven? Dopey, Dumbo, Sneezy, Sleepy, Surly, Bashful, Horny, Doc, Wheezy, Grumpy, Happy, Mork. How do you know?

5. One objection to traditional information-processing theories of memory is that unlike most computers, the brain performs many independent operations _____.

ANSWERS:

1. implicit 2. encoding, retrieval 3. The first two questions both measure recall; the third question measures recognition. 4. Dumbo, Surly, Horny, Wheezy, Mork. Presumably you know this because you don't recognize these names as belonging to the dwarfs. 5. simultaneously, or in parallel

THE THREE-BOX MODEL OF MEMORY

The information model of three separate memory systems—sensory, short-term, and long-term—remains a leading approach because it offers a convenient way to organize the major findings on memory, does a good job of accounting for these findings, and is consistent with the biological facts about memory described in Chapter 4. Let us now peer into each of the "boxes."

Sensory Memory: Fleeting Impressions

In the three-box model, all incoming sensory information must make a very brief stop in **sensory memory,** the entryway of memory. Sensory memory includes a number of separate subsystems, as many as there are senses. Visual images remain in a visual

---

sensory memory A memory system that momentarily preserves extremely accurate images of sensory information.

subsystem for a maximum of half a second. Auditory images remain in an auditory subsystem for a slightly longer time, by most estimates up to two seconds or so.

Sensory memory acts as a holding bin, retaining information until we can select items for attention from the stream of stimuli bombarding our senses. It gives us a brief time to decide whether information is extraneous or important; not everything detected by our senses warrants our attention. **Pattern recognition,** the identification of a stimulus on the basis of information already contained in long-term memory, occurs during the transfer of information from sensory memory to short-term memory.

Information that does not go on to short-term memory vanishes forever, like a message written in disappearing ink. This is beneficial; if the visual sensory register did not clear quickly, multiple images might interfere with the accurate perception and encoding of information.

Short-term Memory: Memory's Scratch Pad

Like sensory memory, **short-term memory** (STM) retains information only temporarily—for up to about 30 seconds by most estimates, although some researchers think that the maximum interval may extend to a few minutes. In short-term memory, the material is no longer an exact sensory image but is an encoding of one, such as a word or a phrase. This material either transfers into long-term memory or decays and is lost forever.

Individuals with brain injury, such as H. M., demonstrate the importance of transferring new information from short-term memory into long-term memory. H. M., you will recall, can store information on a short-term basis; he can hold a conversation and appears normal when you first meet him. He also retains implicit memories. However, for the most part, H. M. cannot retain explicit information about new facts and events for longer than a few minutes. His terrible memory deficits involve a problem in transferring explicit memories from short-term storage into long-term storage. With a great deal of repetition and drill, H. M. can learn some new visual information, retain it in long-term memory, and recall it normally (McKee & Squire, 1992). But usually information does not get into long-term memory in the first place.

Besides retaining new information for brief periods while we are learning it, short-term memory holds information that has been retrieved from long-term memory for temporary use, providing the mental equivalent of a scratch pad. Thus short-term memory functions in part as a *working memory*. When you do an arithmetic problem, your working memory contains the numbers and the instructions for doing the necessary operations, plus the intermediate results from each step. The ability to bring information from long-term memory into working memory is not disrupted in patients like

---

pattern recognition The identification of a stimulus on the basis of information already contained in long-term memory.

short-term memory (STM) In the three-box model of memory, a limited-capacity memory system involved in the retention of information for brief periods; it is also used to hold information retrieved from long-term memory for temporary use.

H. M. They can do arithmetic, converse, relate events that predate their injury, and do anything else that requires retrieval of information from long-term into short-term memory. Their problem is with the flow of information in the other direction, from short-term memory to long-term.

People such as H. M. fall at the extreme end on a continuum of forgetfulness, but even those of us with normal memories know from personal experience how frustratingly brief short-term retention can be. We look up a telephone number, are distracted for a moment, and find that the number has vanished from our minds. We are introduced to someone and two minutes later find ourselves groping unsuccessfully for the person's name. Is it any wonder that short-term memory has been called a "leaky bucket"?

According to most memory models, if the bucket did not leak it would quickly overflow, because at any given moment, short-term memory can hold only so many items. Years ago, George Miller (1956) estimated its capacity to be "the magical number 7 plus or minus 2." Five-digit zip codes and 7-digit telephone numbers fall conveniently in this range; 16-digit credit card numbers do not. Some researchers have questioned whether Miller's magical number is so magical after all; estimates of STM's capacity have ranged from 2 items to 20. Everyone agrees, however, that the number of items that short-term memory can handle at any one time is small.

If this is so, then how do we remember the beginning of a spoken sentence until the speaker reaches the end? After all, most sentences are longer than just a few words. According to most models of memory, we overcome this problem by grouping small bits of information into larger units, or **chunks.** The real capacity of STM, it turns out, is not a few bits of information but a few chunks. A chunk may be a word, a phrase, a sentence, or even a visual image, and it depends on previous experience. For most Americans, the acronym *FBI* is one chunk, not three, and the date *1492* is one chunk, not four. In contrast, the number *9214* is four chunks and *IBF* is three—unless your address is 9214 or your initials are IBF. To take a more visual example: If you are unfamiliar with football and look at a field full of players, you probably won't be able to remember their positions when you look away. But if you are a fan, you may see a single chunk of information—say, a wishbone formation—and be able to retain it.

Even chunking cannot keep short-term memory from eventually filling up. Fortunately, much of the information we take in during the day is needed for only a few moments. If you are multiplying two numbers, you need to remember them only until you have the answer. If you are talking to someone, you need to keep the person's words in mind only until you have understood them. But some incoming information is needed for longer periods and must be transferred to long-term memory. Items that are particularly meaningful, have an emotional impact, or relate to something already in long-term memory may enter long-term storage easily, with only a brief stay in STM. The destiny of other items depends on how soon new information displaces them in short-term memory. Material in short-term memory is easily displaced unless we do something to keep it there, as we will discuss shortly.

---

chunk A meaningful unit of information; it may be composed of smaller units.

Long-term Memory: Final Destination

The third box in the three-box model of memory is **long-term memory (LTM).** The capacity of long-term memory seems to have no practical limits. The vast amount of information stored there enables us to learn, get around in the environment, and build a sense of identity and a personal history.

Organization in Long-term Memory. Because long-term memory contains so much information, it must be organized in some way, so that we can find the particular items we're looking for. One way to organize words (or the concepts they represent) is by the *semantic categories* to which they belong. *Chair,* for example, belongs to the category *furniture.* In a classic study, people had to memorize 60 words that came from four semantic categories: animals, vegetables, names, and professions. The words were presented in random order, but when people were allowed to recall the items in any order they wished, they tended to recall them in clusters corresponding to the four categories (Bousfield, 1953). This finding has been replicated many times.

Evidence on the storage of information by semantic category also comes from cases of people with brain damage. In one such case, a patient called M. D. appeared to have made a complete recovery after suffering several strokes, with one odd exception: He had trouble remembering the names of fruits and vegetables. M. D. could easily name a picture of an abacus or a sphinx but he drew a blank when he saw a picture of an orange or a carrot. He could sort pictures of animals, vehicles, and other objects into their appropriate categories but did poorly with pictures of fruits and vegetables. On the other hand, when M. D. was *given* the names of fruits and vegetables, he immediately pointed to the corresponding pictures (Hart, Berndt, & Caramazza, 1985). Apparently, M. D. still had information about fruits and vegetables, but his brain lesion prevented him from using their names to get to the information when he needed it, unless the names were provided by someone else. This evidence suggests that information about a particular concept (such as *orange*) is linked in some way to information about the concept's semantic category (such as *fruit*).

Indeed, many models of long-term memory represent its contents as a vast, hierarchically organized network of interrelated concepts and propositions (Anderson, 1990; Collins & Loftus, 1975). In these **network models,** a small part of a conceptual network for *animals* might look something like the one in Figure 8.3. The way people use these networks, however, depends on experience, education, and culture (Tomasello, 1999). For example, studies of rural children in Liberia and Guatemala have shown that the more schooling children have, the more likely they are to use semantic categories in recalling lists of objects. This makes sense, because in school, children must memorize a lot of information in a short time, and semantic grouping can help. Unschooled children,

---

long-term memory (LTM) In the three-box model of memory, the memory system involved in the long-term storage of information.

network models Models of long-term memory that represent its contents as a vast network of interrelated concepts and propositions.

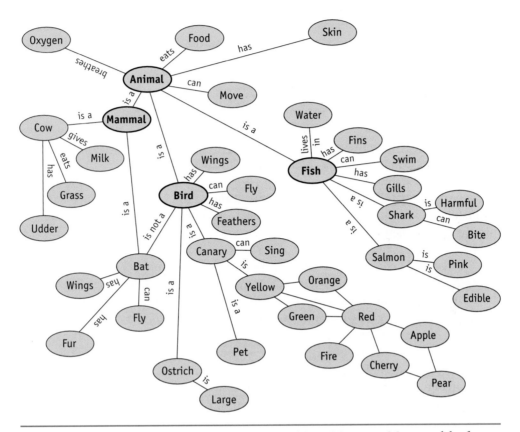

FIGURE 8.3 PART OF A CONCEPTUAL GRID IN LONG-TERM MEMORY *Many models of memory represent the contents of long-term semantic memory as an immense network or grid of concepts and the relationships among them. This illustration shows part of a hypothetical grid for animals.*

having less need to memorize lists, do not cluster items and do not remember them as well. But this does not mean that unschooled children have poor memories. When the task is meaningful to them—say, recalling objects that were in a story or a village scene—they remember extremely well (Mistry & Rogoff, 1994).

We organize information in long-term memory not only by semantic groupings but also in terms of the way words sound or look. Have you ever tried to recall some word that was on the "tip of your tongue"? Nearly everyone experiences such *tip-of-the-tongue (TOT) states,* especially when trying to recall the names of acquaintances or famous persons, the names of objects and places, or the titles of movies or books (Burke et al., 1991). TOT states are reported even by users of sign language, who call them tip-of-the-finger states!

One way to study this frustrating experience is to have people record tip-of-the-tongue episodes in daily diaries. Another is to give people the definitions of uncommon words and ask them to supply the words. When a word is on the tip of the tongue, people tend to come up with words that are similar in meaning to the right one before they finally recall it. For example, for "patronage bestowed on a relative, in business or politics" a person might say "favoritism" rather than the correct response, "nepotism." But verbal information in long-term memory also seems to be indexed by sound and form, and it is retrievable on that basis. Incorrect guesses often have the correct number of syllables, the correct stress pattern, the correct first letter, or the correct prefix or suffix (R. Brown & McNeill, 1966). For example, for the target word *sampan* (an Asian boat), a person might say "Siam" or "sarong."

Information in long-term memory may also be organized by its familiarity, relevance, or association with other information. The method used in any given instance depends on the nature of the memory; you would no doubt store information about the major cities of Europe differently from information about your first date. To understand the organization of long-term memory, then, we must know what kinds of information can be stored there.

The Contents of Long-term Memory.   Most theories of memory distinguish skills or habits ("knowing how") from abstract or representational knowledge ("knowing that"). **Procedural memories** are memories of knowing how to do something—for example, knowing how to comb your hair, use a pencil, solve a jigsaw puzzle, knit a sweater, or swim. Conditioned responses (see Chapter 5) also fall into this category. Many researchers consider procedural memories to be implicit, because once skills and habits are well learned, they do not require much conscious processing. **Declarative memories,** on the other hand, are memories of knowing that something is true, as in knowing that Ottawa is the capital of Canada; they are usually assumed to be explicit.

Declarative memories, in turn, come in two varieties: semantic memories and episodic memories (Tulving, 1985). **Semantic memories** are internal representations of the world, independent of any particular context. They include facts, rules, and concepts—items of general knowledge. On the basis of your semantic memory of the concept *cat,* you can describe a cat as a small, furry mammal that typically spends its time eating, sleeping, prowling, and staring into space, even though a cat may not be present when you give this description, and you probably won't know how or when you first learned it. **Episodic memories** are internal representations of personally experienced events. When you remember how your cat once surprised you in the middle of the night by pouncing on your face as you slept, you are retrieving an episodic memory. Figure 8.4 summarizes these kinds of memories.

As we saw in Chapter 4, patients such as H. M., who cannot form new declarative memories because of damage to the hippocampus, can, with sufficient practice, acquire

---

procedural memories Memories for the performance of actions or skills ("knowing how").

declarative memories Memories of facts, rules, concepts, and events ("knowing that"); they include semantic and episodic memories.

semantic memories Memories of general knowledge, including facts, rules, concepts, and propositions.

episodic memories Memories of personally experienced events and the contexts in which they occurred.

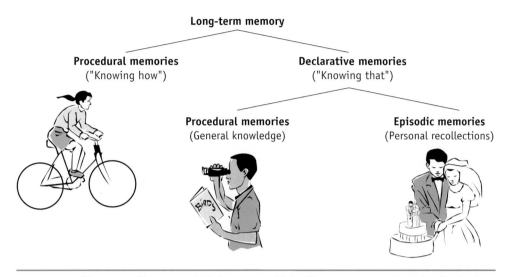

FIGURE 8.4 TYPES OF LONG-TERM MEMORIES *This diagram summarizes the distinctions among long-term memories. Can you come up with other examples of each memory type?*

new procedural memories, including those necessary for manual, perceptual, and problem-solving skills. They can learn to solve a puzzle, read mirror-reversed words, or play tennis—even though they do not remember the training sessions in which they learned these skills. Apparently, the parts of the brain involved in acquiring procedural memories have remained intact.

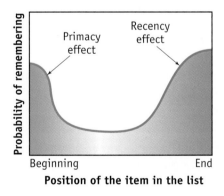

FIGURE 8.5 THE SERIAL-POSITION EFFECT *When people try to recall a list of items, they remember the first and last items best and the middle ones worst.*

From Short-term to Long-term Memory: A Riddle. The three-box model of memory is often invoked to explain an interesting phenomenon called the **serial-position effect.** If you are shown a list of items and are then asked immediately to recall them, your retention of any particular item will depend on its position in the list (Glanzer & Cunitz, 1966). Recall will be best for items at the beginning of the list (the *primacy effect*) and at the end of the list (the *recency effect*). When retention of all the items is plotted, the result is a U-shaped curve, as shown in Figure 8.5 on the left. A serial-position effect occurs when you are introduced to a lot of people at a party and

---

serial-position effect The tendency for recall of the first and last items on a list to surpass recall of items in the middle of the list.

find you can recall the names of the first few people you met and the last, but almost no one in between.

According to the three-box model, the first few items on a list are remembered well because short-term memory was relatively "empty" when they entered, so these items did not have to compete with others to make it into long-term memory. They were thoroughly processed, so they remain memorable. The last few items are remembered for a different reason: At the time of recall, they are still sitting in short-term memory. The items in the middle of a list, however, are not so well retained because by the time they get into short-term memory, it is already crowded. As a result, many of these items drop out of short-term memory before they can be stored in long-term memory.

This explanation makes sense except for one thing: Under some conditions, the last items on a list are well remembered even when the test is delayed past the time when short-term memory has presumably been "emptied" and filled with other information (Greene, 1986). In other words, the recency effect occurs even when, according to the three-box model, it should not. At present, then, the serial-position curve remains something of a puzzle.

What Do You Know?

Find out whether the findings just discussed have transferred from your short-term memory to your long-term memory.

1. _____ memory holds images for a fraction of a second.

2. For most people, the abbreviation *U.S.A.* consists of _____ informational chunk(s).

3. Suppose you must memorize a long list of words that include the following: *desk, pig, gold, dog, chair, silver, table, rooster, bed, copper,* and *horse.* If you can recall the words in any order you wish, how are you likely to group them in recall? Why?

4. When you roller-blade, are you relying on procedural, semantic, or episodic memory? How about when you recall the months of the year? Or when you remember falling while roller-blading on an icy January day?

5. If a child is trying to memorize the alphabet, which sequence should present the greatest difficulty: *abcdefg, klmnopq,* or *tuvwxyz*? Why?

ANSWERS:

1. sensory 2. one 3. *Desk, chair, table,* and *bed* would probably form one cluster; *pig, dog, rooster,* and *horse* a second; and *gold, silver,* and *copper* a third. Concepts tend to be organized in long-term memory in terms of semantic categories, such as *furniture, animals,* and *metals.* 4. procedural; semantic; episodic 5. *klmnopq,* because of the serial-position effect

HOW WE REMEMBER

Once we understand how memory works, we can use that understanding to encode and store information so that it "sticks" and will be there when we need it. What are the best strategies to use?

Effective Encoding

Our memories, as we have seen, are not exact replicas of experience. Sensory information is summarized and encoded—for example, as words or images—almost as soon as it is detected. When you hear a lecture, for example, you may hang on every word (we hope you do), but you do not memorize those words verbatim. You extract the main points and encode them.

To remember information well, you have to encode it accurately in the first place. With some kinds of information, accurate encoding takes place *automatically,* without effort. Think about where you usually sit in your psychology class. When were you last there? You can probably provide this information easily, even though you never made a deliberate effort to encode it. In general, people automatically encode their location in space and time and the frequency with which they do certain things (Hasher & Zacks, 1984). But other kinds of information require *effortful encoding.* To retain such information, you might have to select the main points, label concepts, associate the information with personal experiences or with material you already know, or rehearse it until it is familiar.

Unfortunately, people sometimes count on automatic encoding when effortful encoding is needed. For example, some students wrongly assume that they can encode the material in a textbook as effortlessly as they encode where they sit in the classroom. Or they assume that the ability to remember and perform well on tests is innate and that effort will not make any difference. As a result, they wind up in trouble at test time. Experienced students know that most of the information in a college course requires effortful encoding and often plain hard work.

Rehearsal

An important technique for keeping information in short-term memory and increasing the chances of long-term retention is *rehearsal,* the review or practice of material while you are learning it. When people are prevented from rehearsing, the contents of their short-term memories quickly fade.

In an early study of this phenomenon, people had to memorize meaningless groups of letters. Immediately afterward, they had to start counting backward by threes from an arbitrary number; this counting prevented them from rehearsing the letter groups. Within only 18 seconds, the subjects forgot most of the items. But when they did not have to count backward, their performance was much better, probably because they were rehearsing the items to themselves (Peterson & Peterson, 1959). You are taking advantage of rehearsal when you look up a telephone number and then repeat it over and over in order to keep it in short-term memory until you no longer need it.

A poignant demonstration of the power of rehearsal once occurred during a session with H. M. (Ogden & Corkin, 1991). The experimenter gave H. M. five digits to repeat and remember, but then she was unexpectedly called away. When she returned after more than an hour, H. M. was able to repeat the five digits correctly. He had been rehearsing them the entire time.

Short-term memory holds many kinds of information, including visual information and abstract meanings. But most people—or at least most hearing people—seem to favor speech for encoding and rehearsing the contents of short-term memory. The speech may be spoken aloud or to oneself. When people make errors on short-term memory tests that use letters or words, they often confuse items that sound the same or similar, such as *d* and *t,* or *bear* and *bare.* These errors suggest that they have been rehearsing verbally.

Some strategies for rehearsing are more effective than others. **Maintenance rehearsal** involves merely the rote repetition of the material. This kind of rehearsal is fine for keeping information in STM, but it will not always lead to long-term retention. A better strategy if you want to remember for the long haul is **elaborative rehearsal,** also called *elaboration of encoding.* Elaboration involves associating new items of information with material that has already been stored or with other new facts. It can also involve analyzing the physical, sensory, or semantic features of an item.

Suppose, for example, that you are studying the hypothalamus in Chapter 4. Impoverished encoding of the concept might look something like this:

In contrast, elaborative encoding, which would promote better retention, might look like this:

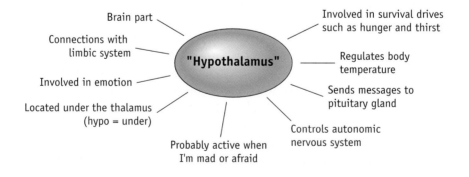

---

maintenance rehearsal Rote repetition of material in order to maintain its availability in memory.

elaborative rehearsal The association of new information with already stored knowledge and the analysis of the new information to make it memorable.

The more you elaborate the concept of the hypothalamus while you are studying, the better you will remember it.

A related strategy for prolonging retention is **deep processing,** or the processing of meaning (Cermak & Craik, 1979). If you process only the physical or sensory features of a stimulus, such as how the word *hypothalamus* is spelled and how it sounds, your processing will be shallow even if it is elaborated. If you recognize patterns and assign labels to objects or events ("The *hypo*thalamus is *below* the thalamus"), your processing will be somewhat deeper. If you fully analyze the meaning of what you want to remember (for example, by encoding the functions and importance of the hypothalamus), your processing will be deeper yet.

Shallow processing is sometimes useful; when you memorize a poem, for instance, you will want to pay attention to (and elaboratively encode) the sounds of the words and the patterns of rhythm in the poem, not just the poem's meaning. Usually, however, deep processing is more effective. Unfortunately, students often try to memorize information that has little or no meaning for them, which explains why the information doesn't stick.

Mnemonics

In addition to using elaborative rehearsal and deep processing, people who want to give their powers of memory a boost sometimes use **mnemonics** [neh-MON-iks], formal strategies and tricks for encoding, storing, and retaining information. (Mnemosyne, pronounced neh-MOZ-eh-nee, was the ancient Greek goddess of memory. Can you remember her?) Some mnemonics take the form of easily memorized rhymes (e.g., "Thirty days hath September / April, June, and November . . . "). Others use formulas (e.g., "**E**very **g**ood **b**oy **d**oes **f**ine" for remembering which notes are on the lines of the treble clef in musical notation). Still others use visual images or word associations.

The best mnemonics force you to encode material actively and thoroughly. They may also reduce the amount of information by chunking it, which is why so many companies now use words for their phone numbers instead of unmemorable numbers ("Dial GET RICH" or some such gimmick). Many mnemonics make the material meaningful and thus easier to store and retrieve, as in the weaving of unrelated facts and words into a coherent story (Bower & Clark, 1969). If you needed to remember the parts of the digestive system for a physiology course, you could construct a narrative about what happens to a piece of food from the moment it enters a person's mouth until it finishes its journey through the stomach and intestines, then repeat the narrative aloud to yourself or to a study partner.

Some stage performers with amazing recall rely on more complicated mnemonics. These tricks can be a lot of fun at parties! But we are not going to spend time on them

---

deep processing In the encoding of information, the processing of meaning, rather than simply the physical or sensory features of a stimulus.

mnemonics Strategies and tricks for improving memory, such as the use of a verse or a formula.

MEMORY SCHOOL

MNEMONICS

"YOU SIMPLY ASSOCIATE EACH NUMBER WITH A WORD, SUCH AS 'TABLE' AND 3,476,029."

here, because for ordinary memory tasks, such tricks are often no more effective than rote rehearsal, and sometimes they are actually worse (Wang, Thomas, & Ouellette, 1992). Most memory researchers do not use such mnemonics themselves. After all, why bother to memorize a grocery list using a fancy mnemonic when you can write down what you need to buy?

The fastest route to a good memory is to follow the principles suggested by the findings in this section and by other research on memory. Encode elaboratively and try to make the material as meaningful as possible. Relate new information to previous knowledge or to your previous experiences. Create visual images, and don't be afraid to make them strange, silly, or otherwise memorable. Take your time: Leisurely learning, spread out over several sessions, usually produces better results than harried cramming (although *reviewing* material just before a test can be helpful). In terms of hours spent, "distributed" (spaced) learning sessions are more efficient than "massed" ones. Thus you may find that you retain information better after three separate one-hour sessions than after one session of three hours. But don't wait until the night before a test to start learning material for the first time. Just as concrete takes times to set, the brain changes that underlie long-term memory take time to develop. This is why memories require a period of *consolidation,* or stabilization, before they "solidify" and become resistant to disruption.

It is also helpful to keep monitoring your learning. By testing yourself frequently, rehearsing thoroughly, and reviewing periodically, you will have a better idea of how you are doing. Don't just evaluate your learning immediately after reading the material, though; because the information is still in short-term memory, you are likely to feel a false sense of confidence about your ability to recall it later. If you delay making a judgment for at least a few minutes, your evaluation will probably be more accurate (Nelson & Dunlosky, 1991). Finally, try to *overlearn* the material. You can't remember something you never learned well in the first place. Overlearning—studying even after you think you know the material—is one of the best ways to ensure that you will remember it.

Whatever strategies you use, you will find that active learning produces more comprehension and therefore more retention than passive reading or listening. As the great philosopher Confucius said, "I hear and I forget. I see and I remember. I do and I understand." But no matter what strategies you use, be wary of popular books and tapes that promise you a "perfect," "photographic" memory, or "instant recall." They fly in the face of what psychologists know about how the mind operates. Our advice: Forget them.

What Do You Know?

Camille is furious with her history professor. "I read the chapter three times, but I still failed the exam," she fumes. "The test must have been unfair." What's wrong with Camille's reasoning, and what are some other possible explanations for her poor performance, based on principles of critical thinking and what you have learned so far about memory?

ANSWERS:

Camille is reasoning emotionally and is not examining the assumptions underlying her explanations. Perhaps she relied on automatic rather than effortful encoding, used maintenance instead of elaborative rehearsal, and used shallow instead of deep processing when she studied. She may also have tried to encode everything, instead of being selective.

WHY WE FORGET

Have you ever, in the heat of some deliriously happy moment, said to yourself, "I'll never forget this, never, *never*, NEVER"? Do you find that you can more clearly remember saying those words than the deliriously happy moment itself? Sometimes you encode an event, you rehearse it, you analyze its meaning, you tuck it away in long-term storage—and still you forget it. Is it any wonder that most of us have wished, at one time or another, that memory really were as accurate as a videocamera?

Actually, having a perfect memory is not the blessing that you might suppose. The Russian psychologist Alexander Luria (1968) once told of a journalist, S., who could reproduce giant grids of numbers both forward and backward, even after the passage of 15 years. S. also remembered the exact circumstances under which he had originally learned the material. To accomplish his astonishing feats, he used mnemonics, especially the formation of visual images. But you should not envy him, for he had a serious problem: He could not forget even when he wanted to. Along with the diamonds of experience, he kept dredging up the pebbles. Images he had formed in order to remember kept creeping into consciousness, distracting him and interfering with his ability to concentrate. At times he even had trouble holding a conversation because the other person's words would set off a jumble of associations. In fact, Luria called him "rather dull-witted." Eventually, S. took to supporting himself by traveling from place to place, demonstrating his mnemonic abilities for audiences.

Like remembering, then, a certain degree of forgetting contributes to our survival and our sanity. Think back; would you want to recall every angry argument, every embarrassing episode, every painful moment in your life? Could it be that self-confidence and optimism depend on locking some follies and grievances in a back drawer of memory? Nonetheless, most of us forget more than we would like to, and we would like to know why.

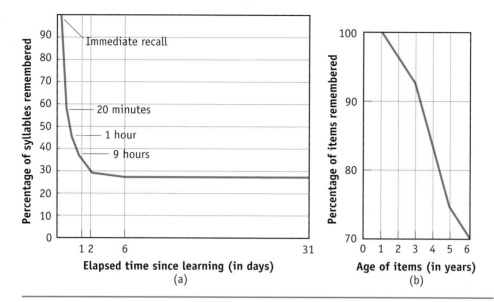

FIGURE 8.6 TWO KINDS OF FORGETTING CURVES *When Hermann Ebbinghaus tested his own memory for nonsense syllables, his forgetting was rapid at first and then tapered off (a). In contrast, when Marigold Linton tested her own memory for personal events over several years, her retention was excellent at first, but then it declined at a gradual but steady rate (b).*

Over a century ago, in an effort to measure pure memory loss independent of personal experience, Hermann Ebbinghaus (1885/1913) memorized long lists of nonsense syllables—such as *bok, waf,* or *ged*—and then tested his retention over a period of several weeks. Most of his forgetting occurred soon after the initial learning and then leveled off (see Figure 8.6a). Ebbinghaus's method of studying memory was adopted by generations of psychologists, even though it did not tell them much about the kinds of memories that people care about most.

Nearly a century later, Marigold Linton decided to find out how people forget real events rather than nonsense syllables. Like Ebbinghaus, she used herself as a subject, but she charted the curve of forgetting over years rather than days. Every day for 12 years she recorded on a 4- × 6-inch card two or more things that had happened to her that day. Eventually, she accumulated a catalogue of thousands of discrete events, both trivial ("I have dinner at the Canton Kitchen: delicious lobster dish") and significant ("I land at Orly Airport in Paris"). Once a month, she took a random sampling of all the cards accumulated to that point, noted whether she could remember the events on them, and tried to date the events. Linton (1978) later told how she had expected the kind of rapid forgetting reported by Ebbinghaus. Instead, as you can see in Figure 8.6b, she found that long-term forgetting was slower and proceeded at a much more constant pace, as details gradually dropped out of her memories.

Of course, some memories, especially those that mark important transitions, are more memorable than others. But why did Marigold Linton, like the rest of us, forget so many details? Psychologists have proposed five mechanisms to account for forgetting:

decay, replacement of old memories by new ones, interference, motivated forgetting, and cue-dependent forgetting.

Decay

One commonsense view, the **decay theory,** holds that memory traces fade with time if they are not "accessed" now and then. We have already seen that decay occurs in sensory memory and that it occurs in short-term memory as well, unless we rehearse the material. However, the mere passage of time does not account so well for forgetting in long-term memory. People commonly forget things that happened only yesterday while remembering events from many years ago. Indeed, some memories, both procedural and declarative, remain accessible for a lifetime. If you learned to swim as a child, you will still know how to swim at age 30, even if you have not been in a pool or lake for 22 years. We are also happy to report that some school lessons have great staying power. In one study, people did well on a Spanish test some 50 years after taking Spanish in high school, even though most had hardly used Spanish at all in the intervening years (Bahrick, 1984). Decay alone, although it may play some role, cannot entirely explain lapses in long-term memory.

Replacement

Another theory holds that new information entering memory can replace old information, just as rerecording on an audiotape or videotape will obliterate the original material. In one study supporting this view, researchers showed people slides of a traffic accident and used leading questions to get them to think that they had seen a stop sign when they had really seen a yield sign, or vice versa. People in a control group who were not misled in this way were able to identify the sign they had actually seen. Later, all the participants were told the purpose of the study and were asked to guess whether they had been misled. Almost all of those who had been misled continued to insist that they had *really, truly* seen the sign whose existence had been planted in their minds (Loftus, Miller, & Burns, 1978). The researchers interpreted these findings to mean that the subjects had not just been trying to please them, and that people's original perceptions had in fact been erased by the misleading information.

Interference

A third theory holds that forgetting occurs because similar items of information interfere with one another in either storage or retrieval. The information is not erased; it may get into memory and remain there, but it becomes confused with other information. Such interference, which occurs in both short- and long-term memory, is especially

---

decay theory The theory that information in memory eventually disappears if it is not accessed; it applies more to short-term than to long-term memory.

common when you have to recall isolated facts—names, addresses, personal identification numbers, area codes, and the like.

Suppose you are at a party and you meet someone named Julie. A little later you meet someone named Judy. You go on to talk to other people, and after an hour, you again bump into Julie, but by mistake you call her Judy. The second name has interfered with the first. This type of interference, in which new information interferes with the ability to remember old information, is called **retroactive interference.**

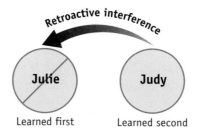

Retroactive interference is illustrated by the story of an absent-minded professor of ichthyology (the study of fish) who complained that whenever he learned the name of a new student, he forgot the name of a fish.

Because new information is constantly entering memory, we are all vulnerable to the effects of retroactive interference—or at least most of us are. H. M. is an exception. Despite his terrible memory deficits, his recollections of childhood and adolescence are unusually detailed, clear, and unchanging. H. M. can remember actors who were famous when he was a child, the films they were in, and who their costars were. He also knows the names of friends from the second grade. Presumably, these early declarative memories were not subject to interference from memories acquired since the operation because H. M. could not acquire any new memories.

Interference also works in the opposite direction. Old information (such as the Spanish you learned in high school) may interfere with the ability to remember new information (such as the French you are trying to learn now). This type of interference is called **proactive interference.**

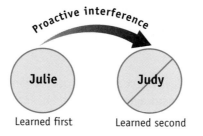

---

retroactive interference Forgetting that occurs when recently learned material interferes with the ability to remember similar material stored previously.

proactive interference Forgetting that occurs when previously stored material interferes with the ability to remember similar, more recently learned material.

Over a period of weeks, months, and years, proactive interference may cause more forgetting than retroactive interference does, because we have stored up so much information that can potentially interfere with anything new.

Cue-dependent Forgetting

Often, when we need to remember, we rely on *retrieval cues,* items of information that can help us find the specific information we're looking for. For example, if you are trying to remember the last name of an actor, it might help to know the person's first name or the name of a recent movie the actor starred in.

When we lack retrieval cues, we may feel as if we are lost among the stacks in the mind's library. In long-term memory, this type of memory failure, called **cue-dependent forgetting,** may be the most common type of all. Willem Wagenaar (1986), who, like Marigold Linton, recorded critical details about events in his life, found that within a year, he had forgotten 20 percent of those details, and after five years, he had forgotten 60 percent. However, when he gathered cues from witnesses about ten events that he thought he had forgotten, he was able to recall something about all ten, which suggests that some of his forgetting was cue dependent.

Cues that were present when you learned a new fact or had an experience are apt to be especially useful later as retrieval aids. That may explain why remembering is often easier when you are in the same physical environment as you were when an event occurred: Cues in the present context match those from the past. Some people have suggested that the overlap between present and past cues may also lead to a *false* sense of having been in exactly the same situation before; this is the eerie phenomenon of *déjà vu* (which means "already seen" in French). Ordinarily, however, contextual cues help us remember the past more accurately.

Your mental or physical state may also act as a retrieval cue, evoking a **state-dependent memory.** For example, if you are intoxicated when something happens, you may remember it better when you once again have had a few drinks than when you are sober. (This is not an endorsement of drunkenness! Your memory will be best if you are sober during both encoding and recall.) Likewise, if your emotional arousal is especially high or low at the time of an event, you may remember that event best when you are once again in the same emotional state. When victims of violent crimes have trouble recalling details of the experience, it may be in part because they are far less emotionally aroused than they were at the time of the crime (Clark, Milberg, & Erber, 1987).

You may also be better able to retrieve a memory when your current mood matches the *kind of material* you are trying to remember. You are likely to remember happy events better when you are feeling happy than when you are sad. Similarly, you are likely to remember unhappy events better and remember more of them when you are feeling

---

cue-dependent forgetting The inability to retrieve information stored in memory because of insufficient cues for recall.

state-dependent memory The tendency to remember something when the rememberer is in the same physical or mental state as during the original learning or experience.

unhappy (Mayer, McCormick & Strong, 1995; Rusting & DeHart, 2000). This "mood-congruent memory effect" can in turn create a vicious cycle. The more unhappy memories you recall, the more depressed you feel, and the more depressed you feel, the more unhappy memories you recall . . . so you stay stuck in your depression and make it even worse (Lyubomirsky, Caldwell, & Nolen-Hoeksema, 1998). You can break out of this trap by purposely focusing on memories of happy events instead of unpleasant ones.

Psychogenic Amnesia

Amnesia is an inability to remember important personal information, usually of a traumatic or stressful nature. Amnesia can result from organic conditions such as brain disease or head injury. When no physical causes are apparent, however, **psychogenic amnesia** is said to occur (meaning it is psychological in origin). Psychogenic amnesia can often be traced to embarrassment, guilt, a desire to protect self-esteem, or, more typically, extreme emotional shock. For example, a woman who has been raped or a man who has been in a horrible car accident may have temporary amnesia for the experience. Generally, however, the memory returns within a fairly short period of time (Schacter, 1996).

The mechanisms that might account for psychogenic amnesia have aroused great controversy among psychologists in recent years because of the debate over recovered memories of sexual abuse. In the psychodynamic view, the mechanism is *repression*—the selective, involuntary forgetting of information that causes the individual pain (see Chapter 11). The repressed material is not lost, but is allegedly stored in the brain, where it can be retrieved when the anxiety associated with the memory is removed. The recovered-memory school believes repression explains cases such as those of Eileen Franklin (said to have repressed the single traumatic experience of observing her friend being murdered by her father) and Laura B. (said to have repressed years of repeated sexual abuse by her father).

However, most cognitive psychologists are skeptical of the psychodynamic concept of repression (Holmes, 1990; Schacter, 1996). They think it is too vague, too ill-defined, and too easy to apply indiscriminately. They point out that repeated experiences—even of traumatic events such as battles, torture, or childhood beatings—are more likely to be remembered than forgotten (Schacter, 1996). Indeed, victims of trauma often *cannot* forget even when they want to, suffering from persistently intrusive, unwanted memories; why aren't these people "repressing"? Critics also note that accounts of repression are based mostly on clinical reports of people in psychotherapy who appear to recall long-buried memories. Only rarely have such retrieved memories been corroborated by objective evidence, so it is difficult and often impossible to determine their accuracy (Holmes, 1990).

In sum, while psychologists agree that people can and do forget experiences for psychological reasons, most cognitive scientists are skeptical that "repression" is the cause, or

---

psychogenic amnesia The partial or complete loss of memory (due to nonorganic causes) for threatening information or traumatic experiences.

that repression is a unique phenomenon that differs from other mechanisms of forgetting. Perhaps people with psychogenic amnesia are intentionally keeping themselves from retrieving their painful memories, say by distracting themselves when a memory is awakened. Perhaps, understandably, they are not rehearsing these memories (by thinking and talking about them), which makes the memories more likely to fade. Perhaps they avoid any of the retrieval cues that would evoke the memories again. Psychogenic amnesia may occur for any or all of these reasons, or for others that remain to be discovered.

What Do You Know?

If you have not repressed what you just read, try these questions.

1. After reading *Even Cowgirls Get the Blues* many years ago, Wilma fell in love with the novels of Tom Robbins. Later, she developed a crush on actor Tim Robbins, but every time she tried to recall his name she called him "Tom." Why?

2. When a man at his twentieth high-school reunion sees his old friends, he recalls incidents he thought were long forgotten. Why?

ANSWERS:

1. proactive interference 2. The sight of his friends provides retrieval cues for the incidents.

AUTOBIOGRAPHICAL MEMORIES

For most of us, our autobiographical memories—our memories of our own lives—are by far the most fascinating. We use them as entertainment ("Did I ever tell you about the time . . .?"); we manipulate them—some people even publish them—to create an image of ourselves; and we analyze them to learn more about who we are.

Childhood Amnesia: The Missing Years

A curious aspect of autobiographical memory is that most adults cannot recall any events from earlier than the third or fourth year of life. A few people apparently can recall momentous experiences that occurred when they were as young as 2 years old, such as the birth of a sibling, but not earlier (Newcombe et al., 2000; Usher & Neisser, 1993). As adults, we cannot remember being fed in infancy by our parents, taking our first steps, or uttering our first halting sentences. We are victims of **childhood amnesia** (sometimes called *infantile amnesia*).

---

childhood (infantile) amnesia The inability to remember events and experiences that occurred during the first two or three years of life.

There is something disturbing about childhood amnesia—so disturbing that some people adamantly deny it, claiming to remember events from their second or even first year. But like other confabulated memories, these are merely reconstructions based on photographs, family stories, and imagination. The remembered event may not even have taken place. Swiss psychologist Jean Piaget (1952b) once reported a memory of nearly being kidnapped at the age of 2. Piaget remembered sitting in his pram, watching his nurse as she bravely defended him from the kidnapper. He remembered the scratches she received on her face. He remembered a police officer with a short cloak and white baton who finally chased the kidnapper away. But when Piaget was 15, his nurse wrote to his parents confessing that she had made up the entire story. Piaget noted, "I therefore must have heard, as a child, the account of this story . . . and projected it into the past in the form of a visual memory, which was a memory of a memory, but false."

Of course, we all retain procedural memories from the toddler stage, when we first learned to use a fork, drink from a cup, and pull a wagon. We also retain semantic memories acquired early in life: the rules of counting, the names of people and things, knowledge about objects in the world. Further, toddlers who are only 1 to 2 years old can often remember past experiences, and some 4-year-olds can remember experiences that occurred before age 2½ (Bauer & Dow, 1994; McDonough & Mandler, 1994). What young children do not do well is carry their early episodic memories—memories of particular events—into later childhood or adulthood.

Sigmund Freud thought that childhood amnesia was another case of repression, but most memory researchers today think that repression has nothing to do with it. Biological psychologists believe that childhood amnesia occurs because brain areas involved in the formation or storage of events, and other areas involved in working memory (such as the prefrontal cortex), are not well developed until a few years after birth (McKee & Squire, 1993; Newcombe et al., 2000). Cognitive psychologists have proposed other explanations, which include the following:

1. **LACK OF A SENSE OF SELF.** In one view, we cannot have an autobiographical memory of our*selves* until we have a self to remember. Indeed, autobiographical memories do not begin until the emergence of a self-concept, an event that occurs at somewhat different ages for different children, but not before the age of 2 (Howe, Courage, & Peterson, 1994).

2. **IMPOVERISHED ENCODING.** Preschoolers probably encode experiences far less elaborately than adults. Young children have not yet mastered the social conventions for reporting events; they do not know what is important and interesting to others. Instead, they tend to rely on adults' questions to provide retrieval cues ("Where did we go for breakfast?" "Who did you go trick-or-treating with?"), and this dependency on adults may prevent them from building up a stable core of remembered material that will be available when they are older (Fivush & Hamond, 1991).

3. **A FOCUS ON THE ROUTINE.** Preschoolers tend to focus on the routine, familiar aspects of an experience, such as eating lunch or playing with toys, rather than the distinctive aspects that will provide retrieval cues and make an event memorable in the long run (Fivush & Hamond, 1991).

4. **Different ways of thinking about the world.** The cognitive schemas used by preschoolers are very different from those used by older children and adults. Only after acquiring language and starting school do children learn to think like adults do. Their new, adultlike schemas are not useful for recalling earlier experiences, so memories of those experiences are lost (Howe & Courage, 1993).

Whatever the explanation for childhood amnesia, our first memories, even when they are not accurate, may provide some useful insights into our personalities, current concerns, ambitions, and attitudes toward life (Kihlstrom & Harackiewicz, 1982). Do you think your earliest memories reveal anything important about you? The psychologist Lloyd Morgan once wrote that an autobiography "is a story of oneself in the past, read in the light of one's present self." That is just what our private memories are.

Memory and Narrative: The Stories of Our Lives

In the introduction to the cognitive perspective, we noted George Gerbner's observation that our species is unique because we tell stories and live by the stories we tell. This view of human beings as the "storytelling animal" has had a huge impact in cognitive psychology. The *narratives* we compose to simplify and make sense of our lives have a profound influence on our plans, memories, love affairs, hatreds, ambitions, and dreams.

Thus we say, "I am this way because, as a small child, this happened to me, and then my parents . . . " We say, "Let me tell you the story of how we fell in love." We say, "When you hear what happened, you'll understand why I felt entitled to take such coldhearted revenge." These stories are not necessarily fictions, as in the child's meaning of "tell me a story." Rather, they are attempts to provide a unifying theme that organizes and gives meaning to the events of our lives. But because these narratives rely heavily on memory, and because memories are reconstructed and are constantly shifting in response to present needs, beliefs, and experiences, our stories are also, to some degree, works of interpretation and imagination. Adult memories thus reveal as much about the present as they do about the past (Ross, 1989).

Once we have formulated a story's central theme or gist ("My parents opposed my plans," "My lover was domineering"), that theme may then serve as a cognitive schema that guides what we remember and what we forget (Schank & Abelson, 1995). The story's theme may also influence our judgments of events and people in the present. If you have a fight with your lover, for example, the central theme in your story about the fight might be negative ("He was a jerk") or neutral ("It was a mutual misunderstanding"). This theme may bias you to blame or forgive your partner long after you have forgotten what the conflict was all about or who said what (McGregor & Holmes, 1999). You can see that the "spin" you give a story is critical—so be careful about the stories you tell!

As we age, certain periods of our lives tend to stand out. Old people remember more from adolescence and early adulthood than from midlife, a phenomenon known as the *reminiscence bump* (MacKavey, Malley, & Stewart, 1991). Perhaps the younger years are especially memorable because they are full of significant milestones and transitions: going off to college, graduating, getting a first job, falling in love, marrying or forming a committed relationship. Or perhaps people are especially likely to weave events from their youth into a coherent story and thus remember them better ("After I graduated from college I met the love of my life, who dumped me in the most cruel and heartless fashion, and before I knew it . . .").

Yet, as we have seen throughout this chapter, many details about events, even those landmarks we are sure we remember clearly, are probably distorted, forgotten, or added after the fact. (Table 8.1 summarizes the seven basic memory problems we have discussed.) By now, you should not be surprised that memory can be as fickle as it can be accurate. As cognitive psychologists have shown repeatedly, we are not merely actors in our personal life dramas; we also write the scripts.

TABLE 8.1   ✦   Memory's Seven Basic Sins

The problems of memory discussed in this chapter can be summarized by the following categories, which Daniel Schacter (1999) calls memory's "seven basic sins." The first three problems involve forgetting, the second three involve distortion, and the last involves unwanted remembering.

PROBLEM	DESCRIPTION	EXAMPLE
Transience	Information becomes less accessible over time.	You forget a phone number you just looked up.
Poor encoding	Inattention or shallow processing results in weak storage.	You do poorly on an exam because you didn't concentrate while studying.
Blocking	Retrieval problems cause temporary inaccessibility.	You have a name you know on the tip of your tongue.
Misattribution	A recollection or idea is attributed to the wrong source (source amnesia).	Your memory of your first day in kindergarten is really based on what your mother told you.
Suggestibility	Leading questions or comments implant a memory that did not previously exist.	A witness "remembers" a suspect's face after being questioned in a leading manner.
Bias	Current knowledge and beliefs distort memory of the past.	Current resentments toward a parent cause you to overestimate the parent's past harshness toward you.
Persistence	A person is unable to forget information or events despite wanting to do so.	An assault victim has persistent "flashbacks" to the event.

MEMORIES AND MYTHS

We are now ready to reconsider the story that opened this chapter. Eileen Franklin claimed that a long-buried memory had returned in a flash, with perfect accuracy: her friend's murder at the hands of George Franklin. But as we have seen, research disputes the belief that memories, even of shocking experiences, can be preserved for years in a pristine, uncontaminated state of repression; all memories are vulnerable to distortion, error, and influence by others. Leading questions and suggestive interrogation methods can encourage memories for events that never happened. And, unfortunately, a person's confidence in his or her memory is not a reliable guide to its accuracy.

The recovered-memory school argues that these findings do not apply to memories of something as horrible as murder or incest. Yet the Franklin case, which launched the recovered-memory phenomenon, eventually fell apart. George Franklin's conviction was reversed on the grounds that Eileen's testimony could have been based on information she read in the newspapers rather than on her own memories, which provided no new details or incriminating evidence. It also turned out that Eileen's "memories" had emerged under hypnosis during psychotherapy, not spontaneously as she had initially claimed. And her accusations escalated: After accusing her father of murdering her friend, she "remembered" that he murdered two other girls. An investigation completely exonerated him.

Of course, all psychologists realize that people can and do forget troubling, embarrassing, and painful experiences, and that with the right cues, these memories may return. One clinician reported a case of a client who became upset when he saw several men reading X-rated magazines at a newsstand. Eventually he remembered that when he was 11, he had been sexually molested by his cousin and several other older boys—who had been reading the same kind of magazine (Nash, 1994). Obviously, therefore, not all recovered memories are false. How, then, should we respond to an individual's claim to have recovered memories of abuse?

Based on the research in this chapter, we should be skeptical if the person says that, thanks to therapy, he or she now has memories from the first year or two of life. We should be skeptical if, over time, the person's memories become more and more implausible—for instance, the person says that sexual abuse continued day and night for 15 years without ever being remembered and without anyone else in the household noticing anything amiss. And we should hear alarm bells go off if a therapist used suggestive techniques, such as hypnosis and leading questions, to "help" a patient recall the alleged abuse (Loftus, 1996). In contrast, a person's recollections are more likely to be trustworthy if there is corroborating evidence from medical records or from the recollections of other family members; if the person reacted emotionally at the time; and if the person spontaneously recalled the event without pressure from others or the use of suggestive techniques in therapy.

In many ways, we are our memories: What we remember, and what we forget, are the hallmarks of our personalities. Shared memories, real or distorted, bind families—and sometimes destroy them. Private memories, real or distorted, make up the narratives that guide our lives. Psychological research on this hugely complex and fascinating topic can give us greater respect for our ability to remember, and greater humility when we fail to remember accurately. ■

Summary

1. Unlike a tape recorder or videocamera, human memory is highly selective and is *reconstructive:* People add, delete, and change elements in ways that help them make sense of information and events. They often have *source amnesia,* the inability to distinguish information stored during an event from information added later. Even *flashbulb memories,* emotionally powerful memories that seem particularly vivid, are often embellished or distorted and tend to become less accurate over time.

2. Because memory is reconstructive, it is subject to *confabulation,* the confusion of imagined events with actual ones. Confabulaton is more likely when people have thought about the imagined event many times, the image of the event contains many details, the event is easy to imagine, and the focus of attention is on emotional reactions to the event.

3. The reconstructive nature of memory makes memory vulnerable to suggestion. Eyewitness testimony is especially vulnerable to error when the suspect's ethnicity differs from that of the witness, when *leading questions* are put to witnesses, or when the witnesses are given misleading information.

4. Findings on memory help clarify the issues in the debate about whether children are capable of making up accounts of sexual abuse. Children, like adults, are often able to remember accurately the essential aspects of an important event. However, like adults, they can also be suggestible, especially when they are very young, are in emotionally charged situations that blur the line between fantasy and reality, are asked leading questions, or wish to please the interviewer or conform to what they believe that other children have said.

5. In *hypnosis,* the practitioner suggests changes in the subject's feelings or behavior, and the subject in turn cooperates with the suggestions. There is nothing magical or trancelike about hypnosis. It has been used successfully for medical and psychological purposes, but it does not produce special abilities, permit people to regress to their childhoods, or increase the accuracy of memory. Because hypnosis encourages people to confuse facts and vividly imagined possibilities, "hypnotically refreshed" memories are often full of errors and pseudomemories.

6. The ability to remember depends in part on the type of performance called for. In tests of *explicit memory* (conscious recollection), *recognition* is usually better than *recall.* In tests of *implicit memory,* which is measured by indirect methods such as *priming,* past experiences may affect current thoughts or actions, even when these experiences are not consciously and intentionally remembered. The *relearning method* seems to straddle the boundary between explicit and implicit tests of memory.

7. In *information-processing models,* memory involves the *encoding, storage,* and *retrieval* of information. In the *three-box model,* there are three interacting systems: sensory memory, short-term memory, and long-term memory. Some cognitive scientists prefer a *parallel distributed processing (PDP)* or *connectionist model,* which represents knowledge as connections among numerous interacting processing units, distributed in a vast network and all operating in parallel. But the three-box model continues to offer a convenient way to organize the major findings on memory.

8. In the three-box model, incoming sensory information makes a brief stop in *sensory memory,* which momentarily retains it in the form of literal sensory images. *Pattern recognition* occurs during the transfer of information from sensory memory to short-term memory. Sensory memory gives us a little time to decide whether information is important enough to warrant further attention.

9. *Short-term memory (STM)* retains new information for up to 30 seconds by most estimates (unless rehearsal takes place) and also serves as a *working memory* for the processing of information retrieved from long-term memory for temporary use. The capacity of STM is extremely limited but can be extended if information is organized into larger units by *chunking.* Items that are meaningful, have an emotional impact, or link up to something already in long-term memory may enter long-term storage easily, with only a brief stay in STM.

10. *Long-term memory (LTM)* contains an enormous amount of information that must be organized to make it manageable. For example, words (or the concepts they represent) seem to be organized by *semantic categories. Network models* of LTM represent its contents as a network of interrelated concepts. The way people use these networks depends on experience, education, and culture. Research on *tip-of-the-tongue states* shows that words are also indexed in LTM in terms of sound and form.

11. *Procedural memories* ("knowing how") are memories for how to perform specific actions; *declarative memories* ("knowing that") are memories for abstract or representational knowledge. Declarative memories include *semantic memories* (general knowledge) and *episodic memories* (memories for personally experienced events).

12. The three-box model is often invoked to explain the *serial-position effect* in memory, but although it can explain the *primacy effect*, it cannot explain why a *recency effect* sometimes occurs even when the model predicts that it should not.

13. In order to remember material well, we must encode it accurately in the first place. Some kinds of information, such as material in a college course, require *effortful*, as opposed to *automatic, encoding*. Rehearsal of information keeps it in short-term memory and increases the chances of long-term retention. *Elaborative rehearsal* is more likely to result in transfer to long-term memory than is *maintenance rehearsal*, and *deep processing* is usually a more effective retention strategy than *shallow processing*.

14. *Mnemonics* can also enhance retention by promoting elaborative encoding and making material meaningful, but for ordinary memory tasks, complex memory tricks are often ineffective or even counterproductive. Distributed (spaced) learning sessions are more efficient than a single intensive session because memories require a period of *consolidation*, or stabilization, before they "solidify" and become resistant to disruption.

15. Forgetting can occur for several reasons. Information in sensory and short-term memory appears to *decay* if it does not receive further processing. New information may "erase" old information in long-term memory. *Proactive* and *retroactive interference* may take place. Most significantly, *cue-dependent forgetting* may occur when *retrieval cues* are inadequate. The most effective retrieval cues are those that were present at the time of the initial experience. A person's mood or physical state may also act as a retrieval cue, evoking a *state-dependent memory*.

16. Some lapses in memory may be due to *psychogenic amnesia*, the forgetting of psychologically disturbing or shocking events, but psychologists are divided about whether this amnesia is due to the psychodynamic notion of *repression*, as the recovered-memory school claims. Critics argue that the concept of repression is too vague, that the problem for most trauma victims is an inability to forget the trauma, and that most clinical accounts of repression have not been objectively verified.

17. Most people cannot recall any events from earlier than their third or fourth year. The reason for such *childhood amnesia* may be partly biological. Cognitive explanations include the lack of a sense of self until at least age 2, young children's impoverished encoding of their experiences, their focus on routine rather than distinctive aspects of an experience, and their immature cognitive schemas.

18. A person's *narrative* or "life story" organizes the events of his or her life and gives them meaning. Narratives change as people build up a store of episodic memories, and because memories are reconstructive, life stories are, to some degree, works of interpretation and imagination. The central themes of our stories can guide recall and influence our judgments of people and events. Older people remember more from adolescence and young adulthood than from midlife (the *reminiscence bump*).

19. Findings on memory suggest caution in evaluating claims of recovered memories of past sexual trauma, especially when such memories emerge after suggestive techniques have been used in therapy, when the memories involve events from the first year or two of life, and when the memories become increasingly implausible.

Key Terms

memory   305

reconstructive memory   306

source amnesia   306

"flashbulb memories"   307

confabulation   308

leading questions   310

hypnosis   314

explicit memory   317

recall   317

recognition   317

implicit memory   318

priming   318

relearning method   319

information-processing models   319

encoding, storage, and retrieval   319

cognitive schemas   319

"three-box model"   320

parallel distributed processing (PDP) models   320

sensory memory   321

pattern recognition   322

short-term memory (STM)   322

working memory   322

chunks   323

long-term memory (LTM)   324

semantic categories   324

network models   324

tip-of-the-tongue state   325

procedural memories   326

declarative memories   326

semantic memories   326

episodic memories   326

serial-position effect   327

primacy and recency effects   327

effortful versus automatic encoding   329

maintenance versus elaborative rehearsal   330

deep versus shallow processing   331

mnemonics   331

consolidation   332

decay theory   335

retroactive versus proactive interference   336

retrieval cues   337

cue-dependent forgetting   337

state-dependent memory   337

psychogenic amnesia   338

repression   338

childhood (infantile) amnesia   339

narratives   341

reminiscence bump   341

Answers to the recall and recognition tests on pages 317 and 318: Rudolph's eight friends were Dasher, Dancer, Prancer, Vixen, Comet, Cupid, Donder, and Blitzen.

Evaluating the Cognitive Perspective

♦ A student recalled a wonderful trip to Ireland with his father when he was a pre-schooler; he has vivid visual memories of their travels together—the green hills, the meandering roads. There is only one problem: He was blind for the first few years of his life, and his father died before the son gained his sight.

♦ United States law-enforcement officials developed a list of "drug-courier profiles" to help them decide when to stop and question air travelers who might be smuggling drugs. The "profiles" include these suspicious behaviors: having no luggage, having brand-new luggage; carrying a small bag, carrying a medium-sized bag, carrying two heavy suitcases; traveling alone, traveling with a companion; acting too calm, acting too nervous; dressing casually, wearing expensive clothing and gold jewelry; walking quickly through the airport, walking slowly through the airport, walking aimlessly through the airport (Cole, 1999).

♦ Two teenage couples in North Carolina decided to rob a convenience store. While one pair went in to rob the store, the other waited in the getaway car. When the robbers came out with the loot, the other couple had locked the car doors and were engaging in steamy, non-robber-like behavior. They told the robber couple to "be patient." The delay was long enough for witnesses to get the car's license number, and all four were arrested (Cassingham, 1998).

The cognitive perspective shows us why and how our mental abilities can go awry. In these cases, a young man, loving and missing his father, re-creates a "memory" of an event that he could never have seen. Government officials, obsessed with winning the war on drugs and catching smugglers, fall victim to the confirmation bias—seeing "evidence" of suspect behavior in *anything* a suspect does. And two young couples, acting mindlessly and impulsively, fail to think through the procedures and consequences of a hasty decision to rob a store; one of the couples apparently stops thinking altogether.

One of the most important lessons from the cognitive perspective is the value of intellectual humility and the danger of arrogance. As cognitive research has shown so clearly, we are far from being rational creatures; our reasoning can go awry, we may get mired in mental ruts, our memories are frighteningly fallible. Yet even as this perspective makes us aware of our mental limitations, it offers techniques for overcoming them. We can immunize ourselves against biases; we can create the conditions that allow creativity to blossom; we can learn to reason dialectically and make judgments reflectively; we can adopt strategies that make our memories more accurate.

CONTRIBUTIONS OF THIS PERSPECTIVE

Since the turn toward cognitive explanations of behavior in the 1960s, the cognitive perspective has dramatically transformed the study of psychology and generated many findings of great social and psychological relevance. Here are just a few of this perspective's major contributions to the field.

1 INNOVATIVE METHODS FOR EXPLORING THE "BLACK BOX" OF THE MIND. As we saw in Chapter 5, behaviorists have sometimes compared the mind to an engineer's hypothetical "black box"; the processes within the box, they argue, are irrelevant for understanding human behavior, and in any case, they cannot be known. Cognitive psychologists, however, have challenged that claim by devising ingenious methods for peering into the black box, as we have seen in the previous two chapters. Jean Piaget asked children to compare different quantities, and from their performance he was able to draw inferences about the mental processes necessary for understanding conservation. Karen Kitchener and Patricia King asked adolescents and adults to explain their positions on a variety of issues, and from the responses were able to discern differences in the reasoning processes of prereflective, quasi-reflective, and reflective thinkers. Leon Festinger and his associates infiltrated a doomsday group and found out how people respond to new information when it conflicts with their existing beliefs. Nicholas Spanos and his colleagues hypnotized college students and discovered that the students' accounts of "past lives" were affected by their knowledge (or ignorance) of history. Elizabeth Loftus and her associates asked people leading questions and showed that the mind incorporates misinformation into its reconstructions of events. Other memory researchers have used the subtle method of priming to uncover implicit memories that cannot be consciously retrieved but that nonetheless continue to affect behavior. And these are only a few of the many creative strategies devised by researchers in the cognitive perspective.

2 AN UNDERSTANDING OF HOW COGNITION AFFECTS BEHAVIOR AND EMOTION. Behaviorists have never denied that people think, remember, and have strong feelings, but they have denied that these internal events *explain* behavior. In the behaviorist view, cognitions are themselves simply behaviors that can be accounted for in terms of reinforcement and punishment. Psychologists who take a cognitive perspective, however, have produced convincing evidence that cognitions often do, in fact, explain the way people act and the emotions they feel.

According to the cognitive perspective, how we think about events makes all the difference.

Think of all the examples you read in the previous two chapters of how biases and normal processes in thinking and memory affect—for better or worse—our decisions and actions. The confirmation bias may lead us in one direction rather than another: A district attorney may proceed with a case, a physician may pursue only one diagnosis, a teacher may interpret a child's disruptive behavior in only one way—all of them failing to consider disconfirming evidence. We may try to resolve cognitive dissonance by making one decision rather than another, in order to stop feeling uncomfortable or stupid. And we all behave in ways that accord with our memories, which may be accurate or totally wrong. For example, many of the women who came to "remember" in therapy that their parents sexually abused them then severed relations entirely with their parents. Some sued their parents and some filed criminal charges against them—appropriate restitution if the memories were accurate, a tragedy if they were not.

So it is abundantly clear that our thoughts, biases, and memories affect behavior. What many people don't realize is that our cognitions also affect our emotions. Although each of the basic emotions is associated with a somewhat different pattern of activity in the brain and autonomic nervous system (Davidson, 1995; Levenson, 1992), physical changes alone cannot explain the full experience of most emotions. In the 1960s, Stanley Schachter and Jerome Singer (1962) argued that emotions also depend on our *cognitive interpretations* of events and of our own bodily states.

For example, suppose you have had a crush for weeks on a fellow student in your English class. Heart pounding, palms sweating, you cheerfully say, "Hi, there!" Before you can add another word, the student has walked right past you without even a nod. Do you feel angry? sad? embarrassed? Your answer will depend on how you explain the student's behavior:

Angry: "What a rude thing to do, to ignore me like that!"
Sad: "I knew it; I'm no good. No one will ever like me."
Embarrassed: "Oh, no! Everyone saw how I was humiliated!"

Notice that your emotion in this situation depends as much on your interpretation of the event as the event itself. Here's another example. Most people assume that an A on an exam brings happiness and failure brings unhappiness, but the emotions you feel will depend more on how you *explain* your grade than on what you actually get. Do you attribute your grade to your own efforts or to the teacher, fate, or luck? In one series of experiments, students who believed they did well because of their own efforts tended to feel proud, happy, and satisfied. Those who believed they did well because of a lucky fluke or chance tended to feel gratitude, surprise, or guilt ("I don't deserve this"). Those who believed their failures were their own fault tended to feel regretful, guilty, or resigned. And those who blamed others tended to feel—no surprise—angry (Weiner, 1986).

Or consider this fascinating example of how thoughts affect emotions: Of two Olympic finalists, one who wins a second-place silver medal and one who wins a third-place bronze medal, which will feel happier? Won't it be the silver medalist? Nope. In a study of athletes' reactions to placing second and third in the 1992 Olympics and the 1994 Empire State games, the bronze medalists were happier than the silver medalists (Medvec, Madey, & Gilovich, 1995). Apparently, the athletes were comparing their performance to "what might have been." The second-place winners, comparing themselves to the gold medalists, were unhappy that they didn't get the gold. But the third-place winners, comparing themselves to those who did worse than they, were happy that they had earned a medal at all! Over a century ago, William James commented on the paradox of an athlete who is "shamed to death" because he is merely the second best in the whole world: "That he is able to beat the whole population of the globe minus one is nothing; he has 'pitted' himself to beat that one; and as long as he doesn't do that nothing else counts."

The cognitions that are involved in emotion range from your immediate perceptions of an event to your general philosophy of life (Lazarus, 1991; Oatley & Jenkins, 1996). If your guiding philosophy is that winning is everything and that trying your best counts for nothing, you may feel depressed rather than happy if you "only" come in second (like those silver medalists). If you believe that anger is healthy and normal, you may be quicker to give vent to this emotion than if you believe that anger is dangerous and destructive. As the cognitive perspective has shown, our emotions cannot be separated from our mental lives.

3 Findings of tremendous social and legal relevance. The cognitive perspective has generated empirical findings of great importance for social work, legal issues, and the justice system. For example, research on memory and eyewitness testimony has contributed to better identification techniques in criminal cases. The traditional method, asking witnesses to look at individuals in a lineup and pick out the perpetrator, has a serious drawback: Sometimes witnesses pick the one most like the person they saw, even when *all* the participants in the lineup are innocent (Wells, 1993). Cognitive research has found a better approach: The witness views the lineup members one at a time, without being told how many will be viewed, and must respond to each one individually, without ever going back to an earlier lineup member. That way, the witness compares each person with his or her memory of the offender and not with the other lineup members. This procedure reduces false identifications without reducing correct identifications (Wells et al., 1998).

Similarly, research on the limitations of hypnosis, children's testimony, and recovered memories of abuse has produced many benefits: the exoneration of people falsely convicted of crimes they did not commit, better ways of interviewing children in sex-abuse cases, a ban on "hypnotically refreshed" testimony in court, and a better understanding of how the use of suggestive methods in therapy can create memories of events that never happened (Poole & Lamb, 1998). For example, in the case of Laura B., the woman who said she had repressed the memory of 18 years of molestation by her father (see the beginning of Chapter 8), the judge wrote that her recovered memories would not be admissible because "the phenomenon of memory repression, and the process of therapy used in these cases to recover the memories, have not gained general acceptance in the field of psychology; and are not scientifically reliable" (*State of New Hampshire v. Joel Hungerford,* May 23, 1995). Many other courts across the country have reached similar decisions.

4 UNDERSTANDING AND IMPROVING MENTAL ABILITIES FROM INFANCY TO OLD AGE. One of the most heartening findings from cognitive research is that our cognitive abilities are not fixed or frozen at some critical period; the brain, as we saw in Essay 1, is capable of learning and changing throughout life, in response to stimulation and experience.

For example, children's mental abilities improve when parents *talk* to their children about many topics and describe things accurately and fully, encourage them to think things through, read to them, and expect them to do well (Ramey & Ramey, 1998). These parenting skills can be taught. In one study, 30 middle-class parents learned to ask open-ended questions when reading to their toddlers ("What is the cat doing?") instead of merely asking the children to point out objects or answer yes–no types of questions ("Is the cat asleep?"). The parents also learned to expand on the children's answers, provide alternative responses, and correct inaccurate responses. Parents in a control group read just as often to their children but did not get the special instruction. After only a month, the children in the experimental group were eight and a half months ahead of those in the control group in their expressive language skills and six months ahead of them in vocabulary skills (Whitehurst et al., 1988). A similar study, in which parents and teachers read interactively with low-income children, also produced highly significant vocabulary gains (Whitehurst et al., 1994). The implications are enormous when you consider that by one estimate, the average low-income child enters first grade with only 25 hours of one-on-one picture-book reading, compared to 1,000 to 1,700 hours for middle-class children (Adams, 1990).

At the other end of the lifespan, some cognitive abilities typically decline with age. It takes older people longer to retrieve names, dates, and other information; the speed of cognitive processing in general slows down (Bashore, Ridderinkhoff, & van der Molen, 1997; Verhaeghen & Salthouse, 1997). *Fluid intelligence,* the capacity for deductive reasoning and the ability to use new information to solve problems, also diminishes, regardless of a person's experience and education. Fluid intelligence, which reflects an inherited predisposition, parallels other biological capacities in its rise and, in later years, decline (Baltes & Graf, 1996; Bosworth & Schaie, 1999).

Now for the good news. *Crystallized intelligence* consists of the knowledge and skills that are built up over a lifetime—the kind of intelligence that gives us the ability to solve math problems, define words, or summarize the President's policy on the environment. Crystallized intelligence depends heavily on culture, education, and experience, and it tends to remain stable or even improve over the life span. This is why physicians, lawyers, teachers, farmers, musicians, insurance agents, politicians, psychologists, and people in many other occupations can continue working well into old age (Baltes & Graf, 1996).

Cognitive research has shown that other problems once thought inevitable in old age, such as depression and passivity, typically result from the loss of meaningful activity, intellectual stimulation, and control over events (Langer, 1989; Schaie, 1994). The strongest predictors of a vigorous and healthy old age are remaining intellectually active and mentally stimulated, getting exercise, and cultivating resilience—the ability to bounce back after losses and stresses (Rowe & Kahn, 1998). A longitudinal Canadian study of 250 middle-aged and older adults found that those who remained involved in intellectually challenging activities did *not* show declines in cognitive ability (Hultsch et al., 1999).

Just as training programs can enhance children's cognitive abilities, so can training programs for older people slow or reverse the loss of certain cognitive abilities. Older adults can do as well on memory tests as people in their 20s when given guidance and cues for retrieving memories—for example, when they are taught to use effective encoding strategies rather than making lists (Loewen, Shaw, & Craik, 1990). Short-term training programs for people between 60 and 80 produce gains in mental test scores that are as large as the losses typical for that age group (Baltes, Sowarka, & Kliegl, 1989; Willis, 1987).

Some cognitive psychologists who study aging are worried about the growing numbers of people living into their 90s and 100s, when rates of cognitive impairment and dementia rise dramatically (Baltes & Graf, 1996; Thomassen, van Schaick, & Blansjaar, 1998). However, other researchers observe that when people are healthy and have challenging occupations and interests, they are likely to function just fine (Kolb & Whishaw, 1998). The challenge for cognitive scientists, and for society, is to make sure that the many people who will be living into their 90s can keep using their cognitive abilities instead of losing them.

"Too soon old," goes an old Yiddish lament, "and too late smart." The cognitive perspective, however, is more encouraging. It shows us that if we apply the lessons of the perspective, it is never too late to get smart—or at least a little smarter.

MISUSES AND MISINTERPRETATIONS OF THIS PERSPECTIVE

Despite its many contributions, the cognitive perspective, like every other, has its limitations. Perhaps the most common criticism of the cognitive approach is that its models of the mind are based on metaphors, a problem that behaviorists have been pointing out for years. Are there really three "boxes" for sensory, short-term, and long-term memory? Does the mind work like a computer? Are mental concepts really arranged in our minds in a giant "grid"? At present, many competing models seem equally convincing. Cognitive psychologist Howard Gardner (1995) once noted that without a decisive way to distinguish one information-processing model from another, cognitive psychology might end up with as many convincing diagrams of the mind as there are ingenious researchers to think them up!

Further, the cognitive perspective, like all others, can be misused when its findings are poorly understood or incorrectly applied. Misuse of this perspective results in three common errors:

1 COGNITIVE REDUCTIONISM. Enthusiasm about the cognitive revolution has caused some people to reduce all human behavior to what goes on in people's minds. Those who are inclined to think in a reductionist fashion may infer that to solve personal problems or the world's problems, all we need to do is think a little differently about things. ("Think rich and get rich in 60 days!") Many self-help and transformational programs preach just this kind of simplistic message, which can lead people to feel responsible for bad experiences that are entirely beyond their control (Becker, 1993).

Some pop-psych writers even claim that "no one gets sick unless they want to be sick" and conversely that "the power of positive thinking can always get you well." It is true that cognitive factors—such as being optimistic, feeling in control of events, and having high self-efficacy—have a powerful effect on behavior, mental and physical health, and the speed of recovery from illness, as we saw in Chapter 6. Yet the fact that cognition plays an important role in health does not mean that cognitive factors are the *only* factors of importance. Serious diseases, poverty, unemployment, and injustice are not caused by negative thinking and cannot be treated with positive thinking alone (Angell & Kassirer, 1998). Mind does matter, but it is not all that matters.

2 ERRORS OF CAUSE AND EFFECT. In their understandable excitement about the power of attitudes, reasoning, and beliefs to influence behavior, some people overlook the fact that the relationship between mind and body, or between thoughts and circumstances, is a two-way street. Believing that you have control over your life may affect your health, but being suddenly stricken with an illness or physical disability may affect how much control you think you have. High motivation and the "right attitude" can help people get out of miserable circumstances, but miserable circumstances—such as living with chronic poverty, violence, or unemployment—can also suppress motivation and optimism. Negative thinking can make people feel sad and gloomy, but feeling sad and gloomy also makes people more likely to have negative thoughts. Cognitive psychologists have shown how our life stories or narratives influence our memories, decisions, and goals, but actual events and experiences also shape the stories we tell about our lives (Howard, 1991).

3 COGNITIVE RELATIVISM. Another misreading of the cognitive perspective leads to cognitive relativism: the assumption that all ideas, thoughts, or memories

Cognitive relativism can lead to an inability to distinguish unfounded beliefs from well-supported ones.

have an equal claim to be taken seriously. This belief is the very *opposite* of what cognitive research shows. As we have seen, some thinking is rational and reflective, and some is not; some beliefs are based on objective evidence, and some are not; some memories are accurate, and some are not; some ways of managing problems are creative and fruitful, and some are not. However, as findings from the cognitive perspective make their way into the popular media, people sometimes draw the erroneous conclusion that if cognitions are important, they must also be valid. They assume that if your interpretation of events is true for you, that is all that matters; never mind what the evidence shows. This is an example of the quasi-reflective thinking described in Chapter 7.

Cognitive relativism leads to the belief that there are at least two sides to every issue, and that all sides must have equal merit. For example, as we noted in Chapter 1, some people claim that the Holocaust never happened; a recent revision of that piece of revisionism is that Jews were in concentration camps but were not gassed to death but merely died of natural causes. These assertions are not equally valid alternatives to the amply documented, grisly evidence of the systematic Nazi effort to exterminate Jews, any more than there are two sides to whether the United States had a civil war or the French had a revolution. Similarly, some religious fundamentalists believe that the Earth and all its species were created in six days, just a few thousand years ago. They argue that "creation science" should get equal time with evolution in biology and geology classes; indeed, "equal treatment" laws have been passed in several states. But from a scientific point of view, there are not two sides to this issue, because creationist doctrine is refuted by all known facts about the development of the Earth and its species (Shermer, 1997). Most religious people, including scientists, know this; they accept evolution because of the overwhelming empirical support behind it.

If we take the cognitive perspective seriously, we must be prepared to analyze not only the beliefs, biases, memories, and reasoning processes of others but also our own. The cognitive perspective teaches us to reject mindless acceptance of ideas and to become more aware of why we think and behave as we do.

What Do You Know?

1. Name four contributions of the cognitive perspective.

2. Suppose that you go to a party with a date. When you see your date talking animatedly with someone else, you become irrationally jealous. How would a psychologist in the cognitive perspective explain your jealousy, and what might he or she suggest for overcoming it?

3. Name three common errors resulting from the misuse of this perspective.

 4. A motivational speaker exhorts his audience to think positively about being wealthy. Getting rich, he says, is all a matter of having the right attitude. What error discussed in the previous section is the speaker making?

ANSWERS:

1. Contributions include innovative methods for exploring the "black box" of the mind, an understanding of how cognition affects behavior and emotions, research findings that have crucial implications for social and legal issues, and strategies for improving mental abilities throughout life. 2. You might be feeling jealous because of thoughts such as "My date finds other people more attractive" or "My date's behavior is humiliating me." A cognitive psychologist would observe that your thoughts are not necessarily accurate. Instead, you could be saying to yourself, "It's a compliment to me that other people find my date attractive." 3. Errors include cognitive reductionism, confusion of cause and effect, and cognitive relativism. 4. The speaker is committing the error of cognitive reductionism. Attitudes are important to financial success, but they alone cannot guarantee wealth. Amassing wealth also depends on an individual's opportunities, the general state of the economy, the needs of the marketplace—and, most of all, how much money the person has to begin with.

The findings of the cognitive perspective, as we have seen, have consequences for intellectual development, emotional well-being, social policy, and the justice system. Much remains to be learned, however, about how people think, deliberate, entertain ideas, make decisions, recall the past, and convey the results of all this mental effort to others. We can draw the "boxes" of memory, and we can reach for ever more sophisticated metaphors of the mind, but there is much we still do not understand about consciousness and reasoning, which make human thought so different from the "cognition" of a computer (Damasio, 1999). Cognitive scientist Daniel Dennett (1991) wrote that "no mere machine, no matter how accurately it mimicked the brain processes of the human wine taster, would be capable of appreciating a wine, or a Beethoven sonata, or a basketball game. For appreciation, you need consciousness—something no mere machine has."

Ultimately, many cognitive scientists believe, the mystery of the mind will fall to science. Some people would rather it did not; like love, they say, the mind will become a duller, less magnificent thing if we ever truly comprehend it. But the demystification of the mind need not diminish our wonder at its workings. "Fiery gods driving golden chariots across the skies are simpleminded comic-book fare compared to the ravishing strangeness of contemporary cosmology," wrote Dennett. "When we understand consciousness—when there is no more mystery—consciousness will be different, but there will still be beauty, and more room than ever for awe." ▪

Summary

1. The cognitive perspective teaches the value of intellectual humility and the danger of intellectual arrogance. It shows that overcoming the barriers to clear and effective thought is a lifelong process, and it offers many techniques and strategies for doing so.

2. The cognitive perspective has contributed innovative methods for exploring the "black box" of the mind; has shown how cognitive processes—such as beliefs, interpretations of events, and expectations—can affect behavior and emotions; has generated much research with important social and legal implications (for example, for eyewitness identification and children's testimony); and has produced many programs and strategies for improving mental abilities from infancy and childhood to old age. For example, cognitive psychologists distinguish *fluid intelligence,* which typically declines, from *crystallized intelligence,* which tends to remain stable or even improve over the life span, and they have been able to develop training programs in cognitive skills, which can slow or overturn some of the cognitive decline associated with aging.

3. Misunderstanding or misapplication of cognitive findings can lead to *cognitive reductionism,* the tendency to reduce all human behavior to what goes on in people's minds; errors of cause and effect, when people forget that the relationship between mind and body, or between thoughts and circumstances, is a two-way street; and *cognitive relativism,* the mistaken notion that all ideas, thoughts, or memories are equally valid or have an equal claim to be taken seriously.

Key Terms

fluid intelligence   352

crystallized intelligence   352

cognitive reductionism   354

cognitive relativism   354

PART V

The
Sociocultural
Perspective

A professor we know told us this story, which occurred in his English class for foreign students. An Egyptian student was describing a tradition of his home country. Something he said embarrassed a Japanese student, who did what was customary in his culture to disguise his shame: He smiled. The Egyptian demanded to know what was so funny about his customs. The Japanese, now feeling publicly humiliated, giggled. This made the first student angry because he felt he wasn't being taken seriously. What went wrong here?

During the Nazi occupation of France, people living in the impoverished Protestant village of Le Chambon, led by their pastor André Trocmé and his wife, Magda, rescued some 5,000 Jewish children from being sent to their deaths. In Los Angeles in 1992, Terri Barnett and Gregory Alan Williams, along with other African-Americans, rescued whites during the violence and looting that followed the acquittal of several police officers who had beaten black motorist Rodney King. In both Le Chambon and Los Angeles, the rescuers rose above the temptation to play it safe and do nothing, choosing instead to save fellow human beings in trouble. Why did they do it?

In Waco, Texas, in 1993, a charismatic cult leader named David Koresh, believing that Armageddon was at hand, led dozens of his followers to their deaths rather than surrender to FBI agents, who had warrants for the arrest of group members for arms violations and other felonies. The members of the cult had come from all walks of life, and some were highly educated professionals. Why did so many adults hand over their minds and lives, and those of their children, to such a leader?

Psychologists working in the sociocultural perspective explore these and many other questions by examining the individual in a social context. They focus on all the possible things outside the person that affect how we think, perceive, feel, and act—for example, the rules and roles of society, the impact of groups and situations, and the subtle yet dramatic power of culture. In Chapter 9 we will discuss the social side of the sociocultural perspective, including the processes of obedience, conformity, and dissent; in Chapter 10 we will explore the cultural influences on behavior and attitudes.

The basic assumption of researchers in the sociocultural perspective is that as human beings we are constantly being influenced by other people and by the requirements of society, even when we believe we are acting independently. Without a social context, a person is like a Rockette without her chorus line or a quarterback having a huddle by himself. We all depend on others of our kind, and we constantly adjust our behavior to what others are doing. It's hard to find true loners. Even Batman has Robin.

CHAPTER NINE

The Social Context

A man was on trial for murder, although he personally had never killed anyone. Six psychiatrists examined him and found him sane. His family life was normal, and he had deep feelings of love for his wife, children, and parents. Two observers, after reviewing transcripts of his 275-hour interrogation, described him as "an average man of middle class origins and normal middle class upbringing, a man without identifiable criminal tendencies" (Von Lang & Sibyll, 1984).

The man was Adolf Eichmann, a high-ranking officer of the Nazi SS, an elite military unit of storm troopers. Eichmann supervised the deportation and deaths of millions of Jews during World War II. He was proud of his efficiency at his work and his ability to resist feeling pity for his victims (though he found actual visits to the concentration camps "upsetting"). But when the Israelis captured him and put him on trial in 1961, he insisted that he was not anti-Semitic: He had had a Jewish mistress, and he had personally arranged for the protection of his Jewish half-cousin—two dangerous crimes for an SS officer. Shortly before his execution by hanging, Eichmann said, "I am not the monster I am made out to be. I am the victim of a fallacy."

The fallacy to which Eichmann referred was the widespread belief that a person who does monstrous deeds must be a monster, someone sick and evil. The Nazis, who used technology to carry mass slaughter to horrendous new extremes, have understandably come to symbolize the most monstrous of human beings. Perhaps for this reason, some people today regard them as an aberration, a story safely buried in the past. But the Nazis were not a strange historical oddity; torture, genocide, and massacres are all too common in history. Americans and Canadians slaughtered native peoples in North America, Turks slaughtered Armenians, the Khmer Rouge slaughtered millions of fellow Cambodians, the Spanish conquistadors slaughtered native peoples in Mexico and South America, Idi Amin waged a reign of terror against his own people in Uganda, the Japanese slaughtered Koreans and Chinese, Iraqis slaughtered Kurds, despotic political regimes in Argentina and Chile killed thousands of dissidents and rebels. In Rwanda in the 1990s, hundreds of thousands of Tutsis were shot or hacked to death with machetes by members of the rival Hutu tribe; and in the former Yugoslavia, Bosnian Serbs massacred Bosnian Muslims in the name of "ethnic cleansing."

Of course, human history is also marked by acts of bravery and self-sacrifice. In Nazi Germany, some people risked their lives to aid and shelter victims or to disobey orders in other ways. A German physician, known to history only as Dr. Marie L., refused Nazi requests that she participate in sadistic experiments on prisoners in concentration camps. One Nazi doctor, Eduard Wirths, tried to persuade her by pointing out that the Jews to be operated on were subhuman beings. "Can you not see," he asked, "that these people are different from you?" She replied that many people were different from her, starting with Dr. Wirths (Lifton, 1986).

What gave Dr. L. and others like her their courage? Why, in contrast, do most people do what they are told without thinking twice about it? Why do most people go along with the crowd, even when the crowd is committing morally reprehensible acts? Why do some people behave in helpful and cooperative ways, and others in hurtful or destructive ones?

Psychologists who take one of the other perspectives discussed in this book would answer in terms of the qualities of each individual. Aggressive behavior might result from a genetic predisposition to be violent; it might be a learned response to provocation; it might be an unconscious defense against anxiety. However, researchers working in the social side of the sociocultural perspective—particularly those in the specialties of *social psychology* and *industrial/organizational psychology*—are interested in the social and situational forces that influence behavior, thoughts, and feelings. In this chapter we will see what they have found about the importance of the roles we play and the groups we belong to, and the social influences on our attitudes and motivations.

ROLES AND RULES

"We are all fragile creatures entwined in a cobweb of social constraints," social psychologist Stanley Milgram once said. The constraints he referred to are social **norms,** rules about how we are supposed to act, enforced by threats of punishment if we violate them and promises of reward if we follow them (Kerr, 1995). Norms are the conventions of everyday life that make interactions with other people predictable and orderly; like a cobweb, they are often as invisible as they are strong. Some norms are enshrined in law, such as, "A person may not beat up another person, except in self-defense." Some are unspoken cultural understandings, such as, "A man may beat up another man who insults his masculinity." And some are tiny, unspoken regulations

---

norms (social) Rules that regulate human life, including social conventions, explicit laws, and implicit cultural standards.

that people learn to follow unconsciously, such as, "You may not sing at the top of your lungs on a public bus."

In every society, people also fill a variety of social **roles,** positions that are regulated by norms about how people in those positions should behave. Gender roles define the proper behavior for a man and a woman. Occupational roles determine the correct behavior for a manager and an employee, a professor and a student. Family roles set tasks for parent and child, husband and wife. Certain aspects of every role must be carried out or there will be penalties—emotional, financial, professional. As a student, for instance, you know just what you have to do to pass your psychology course—or you should by now!

How might you identify a role requirement? One way is simply by violating it. For instance, in your family, whose job is it to buy gifts for parents, send greeting cards to friends, organize parties and prepare the food, remember an elderly aunt's birthday, and call friends to see how they're doing? Chances are you are thinking of a woman. These activities are considered part of the woman's role in most cultures, and women, not men, are usually criticized if they do not carry them out (di Leonardo, 1987; Lott & Maluso, 1993).

Likewise, what are the role requirements of a "real man"? According to studies conducted with a test called the Male Role Norms Scale, traditional male norms require a man to be strong (e.g., "A man should never back down in the face of trouble"), reject qualities associated with women (e.g., "It bothers me when a man does something that I consider 'feminine'"), keep his problems to himself (e.g., "Nobody respects a man very much who frequently talks about his worries, fears, and problems"), and behave aggressively if threatened (e.g., "Fists are sometimes the only way to get out of a bad situation") (Fischer et al., 1998). When men violate these norms, for example by revealing their fears and worries, they are frequently regarded by both sexes as being "too feminine" and poorly adjusted (Peplau & Gordon, 1985; Taffel, 1990).

However, the requirements of any social role can change with changing social and economic conditions. As we will discuss further in Chapter 10, norms for both the female role and the male role are changing rapidly in industrialized societies. Today many women are working outside the home, and many men are doing more inside the home. Even the old norm of the "stoic, silent" male is fading, as increasing numbers of men think it is normal and beneficial to express their feelings; many male politicians and athletes even cry in public!

Of course, people bring their individual personalities and interests to the roles they play. Just as two actors will play James Bond differently although they are reading from the same script, you will have your own "reading" of the role of student, friend, parent, or employer. Nonetheless, the requirements of a social role can be quite strong. In some cases they can be strong enough to cause you to behave in ways that shatter your fundamental sense of the kind of person you are, as we will see next.

---

role A given social position that is governed by a set of norms for proper behavior.

The Obedience Study

In the early 1960s, Stanley Milgram (1963, 1974) designed a study that was to become world famous. It was, in effect, a test of Eichmann's claim that he was just a normal guy following orders, not a "monster."

Milgram wanted to know how many people would obey an authority figure when directly ordered to violate their own ethical standards. Participants in the study thought they were part of an experiment on the effects of punishment on learning. Each was assigned, apparently at random, to the role of "teacher." Another person, introduced as a fellow volunteer, was to be the "learner." Whenever the learner, seated in an adjoining room, made an error in reciting a list of word pairs he was supposed to have memorized, the teacher had to give him an electric shock by depressing a lever on a machine (see Figure 9.1). With each error, the voltage (marked from 0 to 450) was to be increased by another 15 volts. The shock levels on the machine were labeled from SLIGHT SHOCK to DANGER—SEVERE SHOCK and, finally, ominously, XXX. In reality, the learners were confederates of Milgram and did not receive any shocks, but none of the teachers ever realized this during the study. The actor-victims played their parts convincingly: As the study continued, they shouted in pain and pleaded to be released, all according to a prearranged script.

Before doing this study, Milgram asked a number of psychiatrists, students, and middle-class adults how many people they thought would "go all the way" to XXX on orders from the researcher. The psychiatrists predicted that most people would refuse to go beyond 150 volts, when the learner first demanded to be freed, and that only one person in a thousand, someone who was disturbed and sadistic, would administer the highest voltage. The nonprofessionals agreed with this prediction, and all of them said that they personally would disobey early in the procedure.

However, that is not the way the results turned out. Every single person administered some shock to the learner, and about two-thirds of the participants, of all ages and from

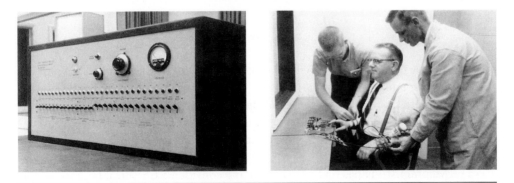

FIGURE 9.1 THE MILGRAM OBEDIENCE EXPERIMENT *On the left is Milgram's original shock machine; in 1963, it looked pretty ominous. On the right, the "learner" is being strapped into his chair by the experimenter and the "teacher."*

all walks of life, obeyed to the fullest extent. Many protested to the experimenter, but they backed down when he calmly asserted, "The experiment requires that you continue." They obeyed no matter how much the victim shouted for them to stop and no matter how painful the shocks seemed to be. They obeyed even when they themselves were anguished about the pain they believed they were causing. As Milgram (1974) noted, participants would "sweat, tremble, stutter, bite their lips, groan, and dig their fingernails into their flesh"—but still they obeyed.

More than 1,000 people at several American universities eventually went through replications of the Milgram study. Most of them, men and women equally, inflicted what they thought were dangerous amounts of shock to another person (Blass, 1993). Researchers in other countries have also found high percentages of obedience, ranging to more than 90 percent in Spain and the Netherlands (Meeus & Raaijmakers, 1995; Smith & Bond, 1994).

Milgram and his team subsequently set up several variations of the study to determine the circumstances under which people might disobey the experimenter. They found that virtually nothing the victim did or said changed the likelihood of compliance—even when the victim said he had a heart condition, screamed in agony, or stopped responding entirely, as if he had collapsed. However, people *were* more likely to disobey under the following conditions:

◆ **WHEN THE EXPERIMENTER LEFT THE ROOM.** Many people then subverted authority by giving low levels of shock but reporting that they had followed orders.

◆ **WHEN THE VICTIM WAS RIGHT THERE IN THE ROOM,** and the teacher had to administer the shock directly to the victim's body.

◆ **WHEN TWO EXPERIMENTERS ISSUED CONFLICTING DEMANDS** to continue the experiment or to stop at once. In this case, no one kept inflicting shock.

◆ **WHEN THE PERSON ORDERING THEM TO CONTINUE WAS AN ORDINARY MAN,** apparently another volunteer, instead of the authoritative experimenter.

◆ **WHEN THE SUBJECT WORKED WITH PEERS WHO REFUSED TO GO FURTHER.** Seeing someone else rebel gave subjects the courage to disobey.

Obedience, Milgram concluded, was more a function of the situation than of the particular personalities of the participants. "The key to [their] behavior," Milgram (1974) summarized, "lies not in pent-up anger or aggression but in the nature of their relationship to authority. They have given themselves to the authority; they see themselves as instruments for the execution of his wishes; once so defined, they are unable to break free."

The Milgram study has had its critics. Some consider it unethical because people were kept in the dark about what was really happening until the session was over (of course, telling them in advance would have invalidated the study) and because many suffered emotional pain (Milgram countered that they would not have felt pain if they had simply disobeyed instructions). Others question the conclusion that personality traits always have less influence on behavior than the demands of the situation; certain traits, such as hostility and rigidity, do increase obedience to authority in real life (Blass, 1993, 2000).

Some psychologists also object to the parallel Milgram drew between the behavior of the study's participants and the brutality of the Nazis and others who commit acts of barbarism in the name of duty (Berkowitz, 1999; Darley, 1995). The people in Milgram's study obeyed only when the experimenter was hovering right there, and many of them felt enormous discomfort and conflict. In contrast, the Nazis acted without direct supervision by authorities, without external pressure, and without feelings of anguish. There is a big difference, critics note, between people who initiate sadistic, barbarous policies and those who follow orders (Berkowitz, 1999).

Nevertheless, this study has had a tremendous influence on public awareness of the dangers of uncritical obedience (Blass, 2000). As John Darley (1995) observed, "Milgram shows us the beginning of a path by means of which ordinary people, in the grip of social forces, become the origins of atrocities in the real world."

The Prison Study

Imagine that one day, as you are walking home from school, a police car pulls up. Two uniformed officers get out, arrest you, and take you to a prison cell. There you are stripped of your clothes, sprayed with a delousing fluid, assigned a prison uniform, photographed with your prison number, and put behind bars. You feel a little queasy but you are not panicked; you have agreed to play the part of prisoner for a two-week study and your arrest is merely part of the script. Your prison cell, while apparently authentic, is located in the basement of a university building.

So began an effort to discover what happens when ordinary college students take on the roles of prisoners and guards (Haney, Banks, & Zimbardo, 1973). The young men who volunteered for this experience were paid a nice daily fee. They were randomly assigned to be prisoners or guards, but other than that, they were given no instructions about how to behave. The results were dramatic. Within a short time, the prisoners became distressed, helpless, and panicky. They developed emotional symptoms and physical ailments. Some became apathetic; others became rebellious. After a few days, half of the prisoners begged to be let out. They were more than willing to forfeit their pay to gain an early release.

Within an equally short time, the guards had adjusted to their new power. Some tried to be nice, helping the prisoners and doing little favors for them. Some were "tough but fair," holding strictly to "the rules." But about a third became tyrannical. Although they were free to use any method to maintain order, they almost always chose to be harsh and abusive, even when the prisoners were not resisting in any way. One guard, unaware that he was being observed by the researchers, paced the corridor while the prisoners were sleeping, pounding his nightstick into his hand. Another put a prisoner in solitary confinement (a small closet) and tried to keep him there all night. He concealed this information from the researchers, who, he thought, were "too soft" on the prisoners. Not one of the less actively cruel guards ever intervened or complained about the behavior of their more abusive peers.

The researchers, who had not expected such a speedy and terrifying transformation of healthy students, ended this study after only six days. The prisoners were relieved by this decision, but most of the guards were disappointed. They had enjoyed their short-lived authority.

Critics of the prison study maintain that you cannot learn much from such an artificial setup. They argue that the volunteers already knew, from movies, TV, and games, how they were supposed to behave. The guards acted their parts to the hilt in order to have fun and please the researchers. Their behavior was no more surprising than if they had been dressed in football gear and had then been found to be willing to bruise each other. The prison study made a great story, say some critics, but it wasn't *research.* That is, the researchers did not carefully investigate relationships between factors; for all the study's drama, it provided no new information (Festinger, 1980).

Craig Haney and Philip Zimbardo, who designed the prison study, responded that this dramatization illustrated the power of roles in a way that no ordinary lab experiment ever could. Moreover, if the guards were just having fun, why did they lose sight of the "game" and behave as if it were a real job? Twenty-five years after the prison study was done, Haney and Zimbardo (1998) noted how much it contributed to understanding the behavior of real prisoners and guards in prisons, and also to increasing public awareness of how situations can outweigh personality and private values in influencing behavior.

The Power of Roles

The two imaginative studies we have described vividly demonstrate the power of social roles to influence the behavior of individuals. When people in the Milgram study believed they had to follow the legitimate orders of authority, most of them put their private values aside. The behavior of the prisoners and guards varied—some prisoners were more rebellious than others, some guards were more abusive than others—but ultimately what the students did depended on the roles they were assigned.

Obedience, of course, is not always harmful or bad. A certain amount of routine compliance with rules is necessary in any group, and obedience to authority has many benefits for individuals and society. A nation could not operate if all its citizens ignored traffic signals, cheated on their taxes, dumped garbage wherever they chose, or assaulted each other. An organization could not function if its members came to work only when they felt like it. But obedience also has a darker aspect. Throughout history, the plea "I was only following orders" has been offered to excuse actions carried out on behalf of orders that were foolish, destructive, or illegal. The writer C. P. Snow once observed that "more hideous crimes have been committed in the name of obedience than in the name of rebellion."

Most people follow orders because of the obvious consequences of disobedience: They can be suspended from school, fired from their jobs, or arrested. They may also obey because of what they hope to gain: being liked, getting certain advantages or promotions from the authority; learning from the authority's greater knowledge or experience. Primarily, though, people obey because they are deeply convinced of the authority's legitimacy—that is, they obey not in hopes of gaining some tangible benefit, but because they like and respect the authority (Tyler, 1997).

But what about all those obedient people in Milgram's study who felt they were doing wrong and who wished they were free, yet who could not untangle themselves from the cobweb of social constraints? Why do people obey when it is not in their interests, or when obedience requires them to ignore their own values or even commit a crime? How do they become morally disengaged from the consequences of their actions? Researchers looking at the social context of behavior draw our attention to several factors that cause people to obey when they would rather not (Bandura, 1999; Gourevich, 1998; Kelman & Hamilton, 1989; Staub, 1999):

1 **HAVING A STRONG RESPECT FOR AUTHORITY.** In situations in which people have an exceptionally strong respect for authority, they hand over responsibility to the authority and thereby absolve themselves of accountability for their actions. In Milgram's study, many of those who administered the highest levels of shock relinquished responsibility to the white-coated experimenter, adopting an attitude of "It's his problem; I'm just following orders." In contrast, individuals who refused to give high levels of shock took responsibility for their actions and refused to grant the authority legitimacy. "One of the things I think is very cowardly," said a 32-year-old engineer, "is to try to shove the responsibility onto someone else. See, if I now turned around and said, 'It's your fault . . . it's not mine,' I would call that cowardly" (Milgram, 1974).

2 **ROUTINIZING THE TASK.** When people define their actions in terms of routine duties and roles, their behavior starts to feel normal, just a job to be done. Becoming absorbed in busywork distracts them from raising doubts or ethical questions, and it fosters an uncritical, mindless attention to details rather than the larger picture. In the Milgram study, some people became so fixated on the "learning task" that they shut out any moral concerns about the learner's demands to be let out. Routinization is typically the mechanism by which governments enlist citizens to aid and abet programs of genocide. Nazi bureaucrats (like Adolph Eichmann) kept meticulous records of every victim, and in Cambodia the Khmer Rouge recorded the names and histories of the millions of victims they tortured and killed. "I am not a violent man," said Sous Thy, one of the clerks who recorded these names, to a reporter from *The New York Times*. "I was just making lists."

3 **WANTING TO BE POLITE.** Good manners protect people's feelings and make relationships and civilization possible. But once people are caught in what they perceive to be legitimate roles and are obeying a legitimate authority, good manners ensnare them into further obedience. They do not want to rock the boat, appear to doubt the experts, or be rude, because they know they will be disliked for doing so (Collins & Brief, 1995).

Most people learn the language of manners ("please," "thank you," "I'm sorry for missing your birthday"), but they literally lack the words to justify disobedience and rudeness toward an authority they respect. In the Milgram study, many people could not find the words to justify walking out, so they stayed. One woman kept apologizing to the experimenter, trying not to offend him with her worries for the victim: "Do I go right to the end, sir? I hope there's nothing wrong with him there." (She did go right to the end.) A man repeatedly protested and questioned the experimenter, but he too obeyed, even when the victim had apparently collapsed in pain. "He thinks he is killing someone," Milgram (1974) commented, "yet he uses the language of the tea table."

4 **Becoming entrapped. Entrapment** is a process in which individuals escalate their commitment to a course of action in order to justify their investment in it (Brockner & Rubin, 1985). The first steps of entrapment pose no difficult choices, but one step leads to another, and before you realize it, you have become committed to a course of action that poses problems. In Milgram's study, once subjects had given a 15-volt shock, they had committed themselves to the experiment. The next level was "only" 30 volts. Because each increment was small, before they knew it most people were administering what they believed were dangerously strong shocks. At that point, it was difficult to explain a sudden decision to quit. Participants who resisted early in the study, questioning the procedure, were less likely to become entrapped and more likely to eventually disobey (Modigliani & Rochat, 1995).

Everyone, individuals and nations alike, is vulnerable to the sneaky process of entrapment. You start dating someone you like moderately; before you know it, you have been together so long that you can't break up, although you don't want to become committed, either. Government leaders start a war they think will end quickly. Years later, the nation has lost so many soldiers and so much money that the leaders believe they cannot retreat without losing face.

A chilling study of entrapment was conducted with 25 men who had served in the Greek military police during the authoritarian regime that ended in 1974 (Haritos-Fatouros, 1988). A psychologist who interviewed the men identified the steps used in training them to use torture in questioning prisoners. First the men were ordered to stand guard outside the interrogation and torture cells. Then they stood guard in the detention rooms, where they observed the torture of prisoners. Then they "helped" beat up prisoners. Once they had obediently followed these orders and became actively involved, the torturers found their actions easier to carry out.

Many people expect solutions to moral problems to fall into two clear categories, with right on one side and wrong on the other. Yet in everyday life, as in the Milgram study, people often set out on a path that is morally ambiguous, only to find that they have traveled a long way toward violating their own principles. From Greece's torturers to the Khmer Rouge's dutiful clerks, from Milgram's well-meaning volunteers to all of us in our everyday lives, people face the difficult task of drawing a line beyond which they will not go. For many, the demands of the external role defeat the inner voice of conscience.

---

entrapment A gradual process in which individuals escalate their commitment to a course of action to justify their investment of time, money, or effort.

What Do You Know?

Step into your role as student to answer these questions.

1. About what percentage of the people in Milgram's obedience study administered the highest levels of shock? (a) two-thirds, (b) one-half, (c) one-third, (d) one-tenth

2. Which of the following actions by the "learner" reduced the likelihood of being shocked by the "teacher" in Milgram's study? (a) protesting noisily, (b) screaming in pain, (c) complaining of having a heart ailment, (d) nothing he did made a difference

3. A friend of yours, who is moving, asks you to bring over a few boxes. Since you are there anyway, he asks you to fill them with books. Before you know it, you have packed up his entire kitchen, living room, and bedroom. What social-psychological process is at work here?

ANSWERS:

1. a 2. d 3. entrapment

INDIVIDUALS IN GROUPS

Something happens to individuals when they collect in groups. They act differently than they would on their own, regardless of whether the group has gathered to solve problems, make decisions, or have fun, and regardless of whether the members know each other or are just a loose collection of individuals waiting around in a room. Research in the sociocultural perspective suggests that a group's actions depend less on the personalities of its members than on the structure and dynamics of the group itself.

Group Pressures

One thing people in groups do is conform, taking action or adopting attitudes as a result of real or imagined group pressure.

Conformity. Suppose that you are required to appear at your professor's laboratory for an experiment on perception. You join seven other students already seated in a room. You are shown a 10-inch line and asked which of three other lines is identical to it:

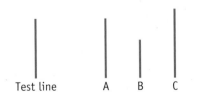

Test line   A   B   C

The correct answer, line A, is obvious, so you are amused when the first person in the group chooses line B. "Bad eyesight," you say to yourself. "He's off by 2 whole inches!" The second person also chooses line B. "What a dope," you think. But by the time the fifth person has chosen line B you are beginning to doubt yourself. The sixth and seventh students also choose line B, and now you are worried about *your* eyesight. The experimenter looks at you. "Your turn," he says. Do you follow the evidence of your own eyes or the collective judgment of the group?

This was the design for a series of classic studies of conformity conducted by Solomon Asch (1952, 1965). The seven "nearsighted" students were actually Asch's confederates. Asch wanted to know what people would do when a group unanimously contradicted an obvious fact. He found that when people made the line comparisons on their own, they were almost always accurate. But in the group, only 20 percent of the students remained completely independent on every trial, and they were often apologetic for not agreeing with the group. One-third conformed to the group's incorrect decision more than half the time, and the rest conformed at least some of the time. Conformers and independents often felt uncertain regardless of their decision. As one participant later said, "I felt disturbed, puzzled, separated, like an outcast from the rest."

Asch's experiment has been replicated many times over the years, in the United States and other countries. According to a meta-analysis of 133 studies in 17 countries, conformity in America has declined since the 1950s, when Asch first did his work, suggesting that conformity rises or falls according to changing social norms. Conformity also reflects cultural norms. People in individual-oriented nations, such as the United States, are less conformist than are people in group-oriented cultures, where social harmony is considered more important than individual assertiveness (a cultural difference we will consider further in Chapter 10). But regardless of culture, we are all more likely to conform when the group consists of people who are like us—in age, sex, and ethnicity—and as the group's size increases (Bond & Smith, 1996).

People conform for all sorts of reasons. Some do so because they identify with group members and want to be like them in dress, attitudes, or behavior. Some want to be liked and know that disagreeing with a group can make them unpopular. Some believe the group has knowledge that is superior to their own. And some conform out of pure self-interest, to keep their jobs, win promotions, or win votes. For their part, groups are often uncomfortable with nonconformists, and their members will try to persuade a deviant to conform. If pleasant persuasion fails, the group may punish, isolate, or reject the deviant altogether (Moscovici, 1985).

Like obedience, conformity has both its positive and its negative sides. Society runs more smoothly when people know how to behave in a given situation and when they share the same attitudes. But conformity can also suppress critical thinking and creativity. In a group, many people will deny their private beliefs, agree with silly notions, and violate their own values (Cialdini, 1993).

Groupthink. Close, friendly groups usually work well together. But they face the problem of getting the best ideas and efforts of their members while avoiding an extreme form of conformity called **groupthink,** the tendency to think alike and suppress dissent. According to Irving Janis (1982, 1989), groupthink occurs when a group's need for total agreement overwhelms its need to make the wisest decision. The symptoms of groupthink include:

✦ **An illusion of invulnerability.** The group believes it can do no wrong and is 100 percent correct in its decisions.

✦ **Self-censorship.** Dissenters decide to keep quiet rather than make trouble, offend their friends, or risk being ridiculed.

✦ **Direct pressure on dissenters to conform.** The leader teases or humiliates dissenters or otherwise pressures them to go along.

✦ **An illusion of unanimity.** By discouraging dissent, leaders and group members create an illusion of consensus. They may even explicitly deny suspected dissenters the chance to say what they think.

Janis examined the records of historical military decisions and identified typical features of groups that are vulnerable to groupthink: Their members feel that they are part of a tightly connected team; they are isolated from other viewpoints; they feel under pressure from outside forces; and they have a strong, directive leader.

Throughout history, groupthink has led to disastrous decisions in military and civilian life. One example occurred in 1961, when President John F. Kennedy, after meeting with his advisers, approved a CIA plan to invade Cuba at the Bay of Pigs and overthrow the government of Fidel Castro; the invasion was a humiliating defeat. Another occurred in the mid-1960s, when President Lyndon Johnson and his cabinet escalated the war in Vietnam in spite of obvious signs that further bombing and increased troops were not bringing the war to an end. And a third example occurred

---

groupthink In close-knit groups, the tendency for all members to think alike for the sake of harmony and to suppress dissent.

in 1986, when NASA officials made the fatal decision to launch the space shuttle *Challenger,* which exploded shortly after takeoff. Apparently they insulated themselves from the objections of dissenting engineers who tried to warn them that the rocket was unsafe (Moorhead, Ference, & Neck, 1991).

Groupthink can occur in any setting, including hospitals. For example, throughout the 1990s, psychiatrists at mental hospitals in Texas, Illinois, and elsewhere persuaded many patients that they were victims of ritual abuse by satanic cults, despite a complete absence of evidence that the cults even existed (Kaczynski, 1997). The psychiatrists favoring this interpretation of their patients' problems refused to consider alternative explanations from "outsiders" and suppressed dissent from staff nurses and other physicians. It took a wave of successful malpractice suits to break this epidemic of psychiatric groupthink.

Groupthink can be counteracted by creating conditions that explicitly encourage and reward the expression of doubt and dissent and by basing decisions on majority rule instead of unanimity (Kameda & Sugimori, 1993). President Kennedy apparently learned this lesson from the Bay of Pigs decision. In his next political crisis, provoked by missiles placed in Cuba by the then–Soviet Union in 1962, Kennedy brought in outside experts to advise his inner circle, often absented himself from the group so as not to influence their discussions, and encouraged free debate between the "hawks" and the "doves" (Aronson, Wilson, & Akert, 1999). The crisis, one of the most dangerous in post-World War II history, was resolved peacefully.

Of course, it is easy to see after the fact how conformity contributed to a bad decision, as Janis did. Predicting whether a group will make good or bad decisions *in the future* is far more complicated; you have to know a lot more about the history, structure, and purpose of the group (Aldag & Fuller, 1993). Nevertheless, according to many laboratory studies and analyses of historical events, Janis put his finger on a phenomenon that many of us have experienced: individual members of a group suppressing their real opinions and doubts so as to be good team players.

Peers. Of all the social groups that people belong to and feel a need to conform to, peers—our agemates, friends, and fellow employees—have the greatest influence. This influence begins early. In her book *The Nurture Assumption,* Judith Rich Harris (1998) argued that a child's peers, along with the child's own temperament, are far more powerful influences on the child's personality than the child's parents are. Harris was harshly criticized by many developmental psychologists (and parents!), but in fact she was simply reporting a basic principle of social psychology: Children's behavior, like that of adults, often depends on the situation they are in and the influences of the groups they belong to. This is why children and adolescents who are competitive with their siblings may be cooperative with friends, or honest at home and deceitful at school, or vice versa. At home, children learn how their parents want them to behave and what they can get away with; as soon as they leave home, they conform to the dress, habits, language, and rules of their peers. Children who were law-abiding in the fifth grade may start breaking the law in high school, if that is what it takes—or what they think it takes—to win the respect of their peers.

Adolescent culture often consists of many different peer groups, organized by interests (e.g., jocks, nerds, musicians, artists), ethnicity, or status and popularity. Children and teenagers who are temperamentally fearful and shy, have few or no friends, or are physically unattractive or weak are more likely than other kids to be bullied, victimized, and rejected by their peers (Hodges & Perry, 1999). Peer acceptance is so important to children and adolescents that these experiences are often far more traumatic and memorable than is punitive treatment by parents. In one Canadian study, college students were asked, "What made you most unhappy when you were a child?" Only 9 percent mentioned their parents; 37 percent described humiliation or rejection by peers (Ambert, 1997).

Consider the tragic example of Eric Harris and Dylan Klebold, who, in 1999, shot 12 of their fellow students and one teacher at Columbine High School in Littleton, Colorado. Everyone wondered what made them do it. What kind of horrible parents did they have? Had the teenagers been beaten or emotionally abused? In a videotape the killers made before carrying out their attack, they inadvertently answered these questions. The one thing they were sorry for, they said, was that their parents would be blamed for their actions. They loved their parents, they said. "I wish I was a sociopath," said Harris, "so I didn't have any remorse for this. But I do. They are going to go through hell for this." Still, they said, they "had" to proceed with their murderous plans. They wanted to "get paybacks" against the peers who, they felt, had rejected and humiliated them.

Harris and Klebold are, of course, extreme examples of adolescent anguish caused by peers. But peers can supersede parental values in countless other, far more common, ways. When the values of parents and peers conflict, adolescents' mental health and motivation may suffer. For example, in a study of 15,000 students at nine different American high schools, researchers sought reasons for the average difference in test scores of Asian-Americans, African-Americans, Latinos, and whites (Steinberg, Dornbusch, & Brown, 1992). Asian-American students, who had the highest grades on the average, reported having the highest level of peer support for academic achievement. They studied together in groups, cheered one another on, and praised one another's success. But many African-American students feel a sharp conflict between the values of their peers and those of the larger culture, regarding academic success as a sign of selling out to the white establishment. High-achieving black students often said they had few black friends for this reason; they felt they had to choose between doing well in school and being popular with their friends. This dilemma affects students of *any* ethnicity or gender whose peer group thinks that academic success is only for nerds (Arroyo & Zigler, 1995). And it can be emotionally stressful. Among African-American students, academic achievement is often correlated with high feelings of self-efficacy, but also with feelings of anxiety and depression (Arroyo & Zigler, 1995; Fordham, 1991).

According to Harris, the attachment of children and adolescents to their peer groups is not irrational (as parents think), but essential. Identification with the peer group, not identification with the parent, is the key to survival of the next generation, because peers are going to travel through life together. That is why children have their own traditions, words, rules, and games, and why their culture often operates in opposition to adult rules. In adolescence, the peer group becomes even more important, because it represents the values and style of the adolescent's generation. The ages of 16 to 24 appear to be critical for the formation of a *generational identity* that persists throughout adulthood. The major political events and social changes that occur during these years—an economic depression or economic boom, war, a social movement, an invention like the birth-control pill—make deep impressions and exert a lasting influence (Inglehart, 1990; Schuman & Scott, 1989).

Of course, some children and adults have the resources, because of their temperaments or close family bonds, to resist peer pressure. But exceptions should not detract from the rule: Most of us are oriented to our peers and thus feel a need to conform to our agemates' attitudes, dress, and behavior. Do *you* dress, think, speak, and behave more like others of your generation or more like your parents? What do you think might be the critical events affecting your own "generational identity"?

The Anonymous Crowd

Suppose you were in trouble on a city street or in another public place—say, being mugged or having a sudden appendicitis attack. Do you think you would be most likely to get help if (1) one other person was passing by, (2) several other people were in the area, or (3) dozens of people were in the area? Most people would choose the third answer. But that is not how human beings operate. On the contrary, the more people there are around you, the *less* likely it is that one of them will come to your aid. The reason has to do with a group process called the **diffusion of responsibility,** in which responsibility for an outcome is diffused, or spread, among many people. In crowds, individuals often fail to take action because they believe that someone else will do so.

The many news reports of *bystander apathy* reflect the diffusion of responsibility. When others are near, people fail to call the police when they see a woman being attacked on the street, or they fail to report that a child in their neighborhood is being neglected and beaten by a parent. People are more likely to come to a stranger's aid if they are the only ones around to help, because responsibility cannot be diffused.

In work groups, the diffusion of responsibility sometimes takes the form of *social loafing:* Each member of a team slows down, letting others work harder (Karau & Williams, 1993; Latané, Williams, & Harkins, 1979). Social loafing occurs when individual group members are not accountable for the work they do; when people feel that working harder would only duplicate their colleagues' efforts; when workers feel that others are getting a "free ride"; or when the work itself is uninteresting (Shepperd, 1995). When the challenge of the job is increased or when each member of the group has a different, important job to do, the sense of individual responsibility rises and social loafing declines (Harkins & Szymanski, 1989; Williams & Karau, 1991).

The most extreme instances of the diffusion of responsibility occur in large, anonymous mobs or crowds—whether they are cheerful ones, such as sports spectators, or

---

diffusion of responsibility In organized or anonymous groups, the tendency of members to avoid taking responsibility for actions or decisions because they assume that others will do so.

angry ones, such as rioters. In crowds like these, people often lose all awareness of their individuality and seem to "hand themselves over" to the mood and actions of the crowd, a state called **deindividuation** (Festinger, Pepitone, & Newcomb, 1952). You are more likely to feel deindividuated in a large city, where no one recognizes you, than a small town, where it is hard to hide. Sometimes organizations actively promote the deindividuation of their members in order to enhance conformity and allegiance to the group. This is an important function of uniforms or masks, which eliminate each member's distinctive identity.

Deindividuation has long been considered a prime reason for mob violence. Because deindividuated people in crowds "forget themselves" and do not feel accountable for their actions, they are more likely to violate social norms and laws than they would on their own: breaking store windows, looting, getting into fights, rioting at a sports event. Their usual inhibitions against aggressiveness are weakened. Indeed, deindividuation increases a person's willingness to harm a stranger, cheat, or break the law (Aronson, Wilson, & Akert, 1999). Deindividuation even eliminates gender differences in aggressiveness, in spite of the belief that women are "naturally" less aggressive than men. In two studies, men behaved more aggressively than women in a competitive video war game when they were individuated—that is, when their names and background information about them were spoken aloud, heard by all participants, and recorded publicly by the experimenter. But when the men and women believed they were anonymous to their fellow students and to the experimenter—that is, when they were deindividuated—they did not differ in how aggressively they played the game (Lightdale & Prentice, 1994).

But deindividuation does not always make people more combative. Sometimes it makes them more friendly; think of all the chatty, anonymous people on buses and planes who reveal things to their seatmates they would never tell anyone they knew. What really seems to be happening when people are in large crowds or anonymous situations is not that they become "mindless" or "uninhibited," but that they become more likely to conform to the norms of the *specific situation* (Postmes & Spears, 1998). College students who go on wild sprees during spring break may be violating the local laws and norms of Palm Springs or Key West, not because their "aggressiveness" has been released but because they are conforming to the "let's party!" norms of their fellow students.

Two classic experiments illustrate the power of the situation to influence what deindividuated people will do. In one, women who wore Ku Klux Klan–like disguises that completely covered their faces and bodies (see photo on the next page) delivered twice as much apparent electric shock to another woman as did women who were undisguised and also wore large name tags (Zimbardo, 1970). In a second experiment, women who were wearing nurses' uniforms gave *less* shock than did women in regular dress (Johnson & Downing, 1979). Evidently, the KKK disguise was a signal to behave aggressively; the nurses' uniforms were a signal to behave nurturantly.

---

deindividuation In groups or crowds, the loss of awareness of one's own individuality and the abdication of mindful action.

Women who were "deindividuated" by being covered in Ku Klux Klan-like disguises gave more shocks to another woman than did women who were not disguised or who were identified with name tags (Zimbardo, 1970).

In real life, too, members of crowds, conforming to the goals and norms of the situation, can be induced to take part in either collective violence or collective kindness. Conformity to an angry mob can induce people to commit hate crimes, such as violence against gay men or lesbians, attacks on black people or Jews, and the rape of women by gangs of civilians or soldiers (Franklin, 1998; Green, Glaser, & Rich, 1998). On the other hand, when collective norms are positive, members of a community will behave in constructive ways. When Swissair Flight 111 crashed over Halifax, Nova Scotia, in 1998, killing 229 people, the entire community—which holds a group norm about the importance of helping one another in that tough terrain—turned out to join in the rescue effort and comfort families in distress.

Deindividuation has important legal implications. Should individuals in a crowd be held accountable for their harmful "deindividuated" behavior? Consider a trial held in South Africa in the late 1980s, in which six black residents of an impoverished township were accused of murdering an 18-year-old black woman who was having an affair with a hated black police officer. The woman was "necklaced"—a tire was placed around her neck and set afire—during a community protest against the police. The crowd danced and sang as she burned to ashes.

The six men were convicted of murder, but their sentence was commuted to 20 months of prison when a British social psychologist, Andrew Colman (1991), testified that deindividuation should reduce the "moral blameworthiness" of their behavior. The young men were swept up in the mindless behavior of the crowd, he argued, and hence were not fully responsible for their actions. Do you agree? An African social scientist, Pumla Gobodo-Madikizela (1994), did not. She interviewed some of the men accused of the necklacing and found they were not so mindless after all. Some were tremendously upset, were well aware of their actions, had debated the woman's guilt, had thought about running away, and consciously tried to rationalize their behavior. Moreover, she argued, we must remember that in every crowd, some people do not go along; they remain mindful of their own values and norms.

From a sociocultural perspective, mob violence, bystander apathy, groupthink, and deindividuation cannot be easily reduced by appeals to reason and individual responsibility. Because these persistent problems in social life stem from the structure of groups, solutions must involve restructuring groups and situations rather than just fixing individuals. And so, should the deindividuation excuse, like the "I was only following orders" excuse, exonerate a person of responsibility for looting, rape, or murder? If so, to what degree?

The Conditions of Independent Action

In 1942, Wladyslaw Misiuna, a young man from Radom, Poland, was ordered by the Germans to supervise inmates at a concentration camp. Misiuna stuffed his pockets with bread, milk, and potatoes and smuggled the food to the 30 women in his charge. One day one of his workers, Devora Salzberg, came to see him about an infection that had covered her arms with open lesions. Misiuna knew that if the Germans discovered her illness, they would kill her; but there was no way he could get a doctor to the camp to treat her. So Misiuna did the only thing he could think of: He infected himself with her blood, contracted the lesions himself, and went to a doctor. Then he shared with Devora the medication he was given. Both were cured, and both survived the war (Fogelman, 1994).

Rosa Parks being fingerprinted on the day she was arrested.

Throughout history, men and women have not always obeyed orders or conformed to ideas that they believed to be misguided or immoral; sometimes they have resisted them, and their actions have changed the course of history. In 1956 in Montgomery, Alabama, Rosa Parks refused to give up her seat and move to the back of a bus, as the segregation laws of the time required. She was arrested and convicted of violating the law. Her calm defiance touched off a boycott in which the black citizens of Montgomery refused to ride city buses until they were integrated. It took them over a year, but they won, and the civil-rights movement began.

Dissent and *altruism*, the willingness to take selfless or dangerous action on behalf of others, are in part a matter of deeply held moral values and conscience (Fogelman, 1994; Oliner & Oliner, 1988). However, just as there are situational reasons for obedience, conformity, and diffusion of responsibility, so there are situational influences on your decision to speak up for an unpopular opinion, choose conscience over conformity, or help a stranger in trouble (Aronson, Wilson, & Akert, 1999):

1 THE SITUATION INCREASES THE CHANCES THAT YOU WILL PERCEIVE THE NEED FOR INTERVENTION OR HELP. It may seem obvious, but before you can take independent action, you must realize that such action is necessary. Sometimes people willfully blind themselves to wrongdoing to justify their own inaction ("I'm just minding my business here"; "I never had any idea what they were doing over there at Dachau"). But blindness to the need for action also occurs when a situation imposes too many demands on people's attention. Workers who must juggle many pressures from work and family cannot stop to make a fuss about every problem or bureaucratic misdeed they notice. Likewise, residents of densely populated cities cannot take notice of everyone who seems to need help; they would never do anything else (Levine et al., 1994).

2 THE SITUATION MAKES IT MORE LIKELY THAT YOU WILL TAKE RESPONSIBILITY. When you are in a large crowd of observers or in a large organization, it is easy to avoid action because of the diffusion of responsibility. Even when you might like to help a stranger in trouble, in some places it is impossible to help everyone who needs it, as in cities where homeless persons number in the thousands. The decision to take responsibility also depends on the degree of risk involved. It is easier to be a whistle-blower or to protest a company policy when you know you can find another job, but what if jobs in your field are scarce and you have a family to support? People are less likely to take an independent position if situational risks are high.

3 THE COST-BENEFIT RATIO SUPPORTS YOUR DECISION TO GET INVOLVED. The cost of helping or protesting might be embarrassment and wasted time or, more seriously, lost income, loss of friends, and even physical danger. The cost of not helping or remaining silent might be guilt, blame from others, loss of honor, or, in some tragic cases, the injury or death of others. Three employees of Rockwell International weighed these two sets of costs and ended up trying to convince NASA that the space shuttle *Challenger* was unsafe. The NASA authorities (perhaps influenced by groupthink, as we noted earlier) weighed the costs differently and refused to postpone the launch. The price of their decision was an explosion that caused the deaths of the entire crew.

4 YOU HAVE AN ALLY. In Asch's conformity experiment, the presence of one other person who gave the correct answer was enough to overcome agreement with the majority. In Milgram's experiment, the presence of a peer who disobeyed the experimenter's instruction to shock the learner sharply increased the number of people who also disobeyed. One dissenting member of a group may be viewed as a troublemaker and two dissenting members as a conspiracy, but several are a coalition. An ally reassures a person of the rightness of the protest, and their combined efforts may eventually persuade the majority (Wood et al., 1994).

5 **YOU BECOME ENTRAPPED.** Once having taken the initial step of getting involved, most people will increase their commitment. In one study, nearly 9,000 federal employees were asked whether they had observed wrongdoing at work, whether they had told anyone about it, and what happened if they had told. Nearly half of the sample had observed some serious cases of wrongdoing, such as stealing federal funds, accepting bribes, or creating a situation that was dangerous to public safety. Of that half, 72 percent had done nothing at all, but the other 28 percent reported the problem to their immediate supervisors. Once they had taken that step, a majority of the whistle-blowers eventually took the matter to higher authorities (Graham, 1986).

As you can see, certain social factors make altruism, disobedience, and dissent more likely to occur, just as other factors suppress them. This is why people often behave inconsistently across situations: A woman may be forthright about her opinions on her job, yet conform to the opinions of others when she serves on a jury; a man may leap into a frozen river on Tuesday to rescue a child, yet keep silent on Wednesday when his employer orders him to ignore worker-safety precautions at a factory. To social psychologists, these inconsistencies are not lapses of personality, but predictable responses to different situations.

What Do You Know?

On your own, take responsibility for answering these questions.

   A. Which phenomenon discussed in the previous section is illustrated in the following situations?

   1. The president's closest advisers are afraid to disagree with his views on arms negotiations.

   2. You are at a Halloween party wearing a silly gorilla suit. When you see a chance to play a practical joke on the host, you do it.

   3. Walking down a busy street, you see that fire has broken out in a store window. "Someone must have called the fire department," you say.

   B. Imagine that you are chief executive officer of a new electric-car company. To improve productivity and satisfaction, you want your employees to feel free to offer their suggestions and criticisms, and to inform managers if they find any evidence that the cars are unsafe. Using concepts from this chapter, how should you encourage your employees to do this?

ANSWERS:

A. 1. groupthink 2. deindividuation 3. diffusion of responsibility **B.** *Some possibilities:* Encourage and acknowledge deviant ideas, and do not require unanimous group decisions (to avoid groupthink); reward individual innovation and suggestions by paying attention to them and implementing the best ones (to avoid social loafing and deindividuation); establish a written policy to protect and reward whistle-blowers. Can you think of other ideas?

SOCIAL INFLUENCES ON BELIEFS

Social psychologists are interested not only in what people do in social situations, but also in what goes on in their heads while they are doing it. Researchers in the area of **social cognition** examine how the social environment influences people's thoughts, beliefs, and memories, and how people's perceptions of themselves and others affect their relationships (A. Fiske & Haslam, 1996). We will consider two important topics in this area: how people explain their own behavior and that of others, and the nature of social influence and persuasion.

Attributions

People read detective stories to find out *who* did the dirty deed, but in real life we also want to know *why* people do things—was it because of a terrible childhood, a mental illness, possession by a demon, or what? According to **attribution theory,** the explanations we make of our behavior and the behavior of others generally fall into two categories. When we make a *situational attribution,* we are identifying the cause of an action as something in the situation or environment: "Joe stole the money because his family is starving." When we make a *dispositional attribution,* we are identifying the cause of an action as something in the person, such as a trait or a motive: "Joe stole the money because he is a born thief."

When people are trying to find reasons for someone else's behavior, they reveal a common bias: They tend to overestimate the influence of personality traits and underestimate the influence of the situation (Nisbett & Ross, 1980). In terms of attribution theory, they tend to ignore situational attributions in favor of dispositional ones. This tendency has been called the **fundamental attribution error** (sometimes called the *correspondence bias,* because of the underlying assumption that people's dispositions correspond to their behavior) (Jones, 1990; Van Boven, Kamada, & Gilovich, 1999). Were the hundreds of people who obeyed Milgram's experimenters sadistic by nature? Were the student guards in the prison study sadistic and the prisoners cowardly? Do people conform simply because they are gullible or conventional? Those who think so are committing the fundamental attribution error.

People are especially likely to overlook situational attributions when they are in a good mood and not inclined to think about other people's motives critically, or when they are distracted and preoccupied and don't have time to stop and ask themselves, "Why, exactly, *is* Aurelia behaving like a dork today?" (Forgas, 1998). Instead, they leap to the easiest attribution, which is dispositional: Aurelia simply has a dorky personality.

---

social cognition An area in social psychology concerned with social influences on thought, memory, perception, and other cognitive processes.

attribution theory The theory that people are motivated to explain their own and others' behavior by attributing causes of that behavior to a situation or a disposition.

fundamental attribution error The tendency, in explaining other people's behavior, to overestimate the influence of personality factors and underestimate the influence of the situation.

The fundamental attribution error is fairly ingrained in Western countries, where middle-class people tend to believe that individuals are responsible for their own actions and that, therefore, a person's behavior must reflect his or her personality traits. In countries such as India, where everyone is embedded in caste and family networks, and in Japan, China, and Hong Kong, where people are more group oriented than in the West, people are more likely to be aware of situational constraints on behavior (Choi, Nisbett, & Norenzayan, 1999; Morris & Peng, 1994). Thus, if an athlete plays badly in a soccer match, if a member of an organization commits a crime, or if a team member can't get along with the team, a person from India or China, unlike a Westerner, is more likely to attribute the reason to something amiss in the team or organization (e.g., "He wasn't being supervised properly") than to the individual's own dispositions ("He's incompetent" or "He's a crook") (Menon et al., 1999).

Westerners do not always prefer dispositional attributions, however. When it comes to explaining their *own* behavior, they often reveal a **self-serving bias:** They tend to choose attributions that are favorable to them, taking credit for their good actions (a dispositional attribution) but letting the situation account for their failures, embarrassing mistakes, or harmful actions (Campbell & Sedikides, 1999). For instance, most North Americans, when angry, will say, "I am furious for good reason; this situation is intolerable." They are less likely to say, "I am furious because I am an ill-tempered grinch." On the other hand, if they do something admirable, such as donating to charity, they are likely to attribute their motives to a personal disposition ("I'm so generous") instead of the situation ("That guy on the phone pressured me into it").

According to the **just-world hypothesis,** attributions are also affected by the need to believe that the world is fair and that justice prevails, and particularly that good people are rewarded and bad guys punished. This belief, which is especially prevalent in North America, helps people make sense out of senseless events and feel safe in the presence of threatening events (Lerner, 1980). Unfortunately, it also leads to a dispositional attribution called *blaming the victim*. If a friend is fired, if a woman is raped, if an innocent bystander is shot 41 times by the police, it is reassuring to think that they all must have done something to deserve what happened or to provoke it. Blaming the victim is virtually universal when people are ordered or entrapped into harming others (Bandura, 1999). It was apparent in the Milgram study, when some "teachers" made comments such as, "[The learner] was so stupid and stubborn he deserved to get shocked" (Milgram, 1974).

Of course, sometimes dispositional (personality) attributions *do* explain a person's behavior. The point to remember is that attributions, whether they are accurate or not, have tremendously important consequences. Here's an example that will apply to your own relationships: Happy couples tend to attribute their partners' occasional lapses to something in the situation ("Poor Harold is under a lot of stress at work"), and his or

---

self-serving bias The tendency, in explaining one's own behavior, to take credit for one's good actions and rationalize one's mistakes.

just-world hypothesis The notion that many people need to believe that the world is fair and justice is served; that bad people are punished and good people rewarded.

her positive actions to stable, internal dispositions ("Harold has the sweetest nature"). But unhappy couples do just the reverse, attributing lapses to their partners' personalities and good behavior to the situation. These attributional habits aren't permanent; they can change over time. But they are strongly related to satisfaction with the partner (Karney & Bradbury, 2000). Thus the attributions you make about your partner, your parents, and your friends will make a big difference in how you get along with them—and how long you will put up with their failings.

What Do You Know?

To what do you attribute your success in answering these questions?

1. What kind of attribution is being made in each case, situational or dispositional? (a) A man says, "My wife has sure become a grouchy person." (b) The same man says, "I'm grouchy because I've had a bad day at the office." (c) A woman reads that unemployment is high in inner-city communities. "Well, if those people weren't so lazy, they would find work," she says.
2. What attributional biases are suggested by the items in the preceding question?

ANSWERS:

1. a. dispositional b. situational c. dispositional 2. Item *a* illustrates the fundamental attribution error; *b*, the self-serving bias; and *c*, blaming the victim.

Processes of Persuasion

Most people think that their opinions and beliefs are based on thinking, a reasoned conclusion about how things work. Sometimes, of course, that's true. But some of our beliefs are a result of not thinking at all. They are a result of conformity, habit, rationalization, economic self-interest, and the efforts of other people to get us to agree with them. Sometimes people persuade us to change our minds using reasoned argument; sometimes they use subtle manipulation; and sometimes they use outright coercion. The best defense against manipulation and coercion is not rigid thinking and the refusal to accept new ideas; it is critical thinking and the ability to identify some of the social forces that influence the formation of attitudes—and their change.

Friendly Techniques. All around you, every day, advertisers and politicians try to get you to change your opinions of their products or policies. One powerful weapon they use is the drip, drip, drip of a repeated idea until it is as familiar as an old shoe. Familiarity is the reason that advertisements are repeated so often, and the reason that many people spend four times as much for a familiar brand of aspirin as for an unfamiliar one, even though the cheaper but unfamiliar product is just as good. Repeated

New State TV Ads Link Smoking to Impotence in Men

By DAN MORAIN
TIMES STAFF WRITER

SACRAMENTO—What Viagra may give, tobacco taketh away. So says the California Department of Health Services.

State health officials, trying to pound their anti-tobacco message through to young men, unveiled new television commercials Monday making the point that smoking is a leading cause of impotence.

Associated Press
Ad portrays smoking's effect on sexual potency.

Ads are always trying to persuade us to change our behavior—but some techniques are more effective than others, as the text describes. Do you think this antismoking ad will get results?

exposure even to a nonsense syllable like *zug* is enough to make a person feel more positive toward it (Zajonc, 1968).

The effectiveness of familiarity has long been known to politicians, too: Repeat something often enough, even the basest lie, and eventually the public will believe it. Hitler's propaganda minister, Joseph Goebbels, called this technique the "Big Lie." Its formal name is the **validity effect**. In a series of experiments, Hal Arkes and his associates demonstrated how the validity effect operates (Arkes, 1993; Arkes, Boehm, & Xu, 1991). In a typical study, people read a list of statements, such as "Mercury has a higher boiling point than copper" or "Over 400 Hollywood films were produced in 1948." They had to rate each statement for its validity, on a scale of 1 (definitely false) to 7 (definitely true). A week or two later, they again rated the validity of some of these statements and also rated others that they had not seen previously. The result: Mere repetition increased the perception that the familiar statements were true. The same effect also occurred for other kinds of statements, including unverifiable opinions (e.g., "At least 75 percent of all politicians are basically dishonest"), opinions that subjects initially felt were true, and even opinions they initially felt were false. "Note that no attempt has been made to persuade," said Arkes (1993). "No supporting arguments are offered. We just have subjects rate the statements. Mere repetition seems to increase rated validity. This is scary."

Another effective technique for influencing people is to have arguments presented by someone who is considered admirable, knowledgeable, or beautiful; this is why advertisements are full of sports heroes, experts, and models (Cialdini, 1993). Persuaders may also try to link their message with a good feeling. In one classic study, students who were given peanuts and Pepsi while listening to a speaker's point of view were more likely to be convinced by it than were students who listened to the same words without the pleasant munchies and soft drinks (Janis, Kaye, & Kirschner, 1965).

---

validity effect The tendency of people to believe that a statement is true or valid simply because it has been repeated many times.

This finding, which has been replicated many times, may explain why so much business is conducted over lunch, and so many courtships over dinner!

In contrast, the emotion of fear can cause people to resist arguments that are in their own best interest (Pratkanis & Aronson, 1992). Fear tactics are often used to try to persuade people to quit smoking or abusing other drugs, drive only when sober, use condoms, check for signs of cancer, and prepare for earthquakes. Fear tactics can be effective if the message also provides information about how to avoid the danger and if people feel competent to take advantage of this information (Aronson, 1999b). But when messages about a future disaster are too terrifying and when people believe that they can do nothing to avoid it, they tend to deny the danger. (This finding makes us curious about antismoking ads that inform men that smoking is a leading cause of impotence. Do you think they will work?)

Coercive Techniques. Some manipulators use harsher tactics, not just hoping that people will change their minds but attempting to force them to. These tactics are sometimes referred to as *brainwashing,* a term first used during the Korean War to describe techniques used on American prisoners of war (POWs) to get them to collaborate with their Chinese Communist captors and to endorse anti-American propaganda. Most psychologists, however, prefer the phrase *coercive persuasion.* "Brainwashing" implies that a person has a sudden change of mind and is unaware of what is happening; it sounds mysterious and strange. In fact, the methods involved are neither mysterious nor unusual. The difference between "persuasion" and "brainwashing" is often only a matter of degree and the observer's bias, just as a group that is a crazy cult to one person may be a group of devoutly religious people to another.

How, then, might we distinguish coercive persuasion from its more benign form? Persuasion techniques become coercive when they suppress an individual's ability to reason, think critically, and make choices in his or her own best interests. Studies of religious, political, and other cults have identified some of the key processes of coercive persuasion (Galanter, 1989; Mithers, 1994; Ofshe & Watters, 1994; Singer, Temerlin, & Langone, 1990; Zimbardo & Leippe, 1991):

1 THE PERSON IS PUT UNDER PHYSICAL OR EMOTIONAL DISTRESS. The individual may not be allowed to eat, sleep, or exercise; may be isolated in a dark room with no stimulation or food; or may be induced into a trancelike state through repetitive chanting or fatigue.

2 THE PERSON'S PROBLEMS ARE REDUCED TO ONE SIMPLE EXPLANATION, WHICH IS REPEATEDLY EMPHASIZED. There are as many of these simplistic explanations as there are cults, but here are some real examples: Are you afraid or unhappy? It all stems from the pain of being born. Are you worried about homeless earthquake victims? It's not your problem; victims are responsible for everything that happens to them. Are you struggling financially? It's your fault for not fervently wanting to be rich. Members may also be taught to blame their problems on particular enemies: Jews, blacks, whites, nonbelievers.

3 THE LEADER OFFERS UNCONDITIONAL LOVE, ACCEPTANCE, AND ATTENTION. The new recruit may be given a "love bath" from the group—constant praise, support, applause, and affection. Euphoria and well-being are generated, which are especially intense because they typically follow exhaustion and fatigue. In exchange, the leader demands everyone's adoration and obedience.

4 A NEW IDENTITY BASED ON THE GROUP IS CREATED. The recruit is told that he or she is part of the chosen, the elite, or the saved. To foster this new identity, many cults require their members to wear special clothes or eat special diets, and they assign each member a new name.

5 THE PERSON IS SUBJECTED TO ENTRAPMENT. At first, the new member agrees only to do small things, but gradually the demands increase: for example, to spend a weekend with the group, then another weekend, then take weekly seminars, then advanced courses. During the Korean War, the Chinese first got the American POWs to agree with mild remarks, such as "The United States is not perfect." Then the POWs had to add their own examples of American imperfections. At the end, they were signing their names to anti-American broadcasts (Schein, Schneier, & Barker, 1961).

6 THE PERSON'S ACCESS TO INFORMATION IS SEVERELY CONTROLLED. As soon as a person is a committed believer or follower, the group limits the person's choices, denigrates critical thinking, makes fun of doubts, and insists that any private distress is due to lack of belief in the group. Total conformity is demanded. The person may be physically isolated from the outside world and thus from antidotes to the leader's ideas. In many groups, members are encouraged or required to break all ties with their families, who are the most powerful link to the members' former world and thus the greatest threat to the leader's control.

You could see these strategies in operation in the Heaven's Gate cult, which made the news a few years ago when its leader, Marshall Applewhite, and all 38 of his followers committed suicide. Applewhite had offered members a new identity (extraterrestrials in human bodies) and a simplistic solution to their problems (suicide would free them to travel to heaven in a spaceship hiding in the tail of a comet). He encouraged members to sever their relationships with friends and relatives, had them dress alike, and censored all dissenting opinions. Applewhite entrapped his followers in an escalating series of obligations and commitments. He never said to new recruits, "If you follow me, you will eventually give up your marriages, your homes, your children, and your lives"; but by the end, that is just what they did.

Some people may be more vulnerable than others to coercive tactics. But these techniques are powerful enough to overwhelm even strong individuals; by all accounts, Applewhite's followers were pleasant people without serious mental disorders, and many were well educated. The first step in increasing people's resistance to coercive persuasion, therefore, is to dispel their illusion of invulnerability to these tactics (Sagarin, Cialdini, & Rice, 1998).

What Do You Know?

Now, how can we persuade you to take this quiz without using coercive tactics?

1. Candidate Carson spends 3 million dollars to make sure his name is seen and heard frequently, and to repeat unverified charges that his opponent is a thief. What psychological process is he relying on to win?

2. *True or false:* Strong, educated people can fall victim to cults.

3. Your best friend urges you to join a "life-renewal" group called "The Feeling Life." Your friend has been spending increasing amounts of time with her fellow Feelies, and you have some doubts about them. What questions would you want to have answered before joining up?

ANSWERS:

1. the validity effect 2. true 3. A few things to consider: Is there an autocratic leader who tolerates no dissent or criticism, while rationalizing this practice as a benefit for members? ("Doubt and disbelief are signs that your feeling side is being repressed.") Have long-standing members cut off ties with their families and given up their interests and ambitions for this group? Does the leader offer simple but unrealistic promises to repair your life and all that troubles you? Are members required to make extreme personal sacrifices and donate large amounts of money to the group?

SOCIAL INFLUENCES ON MOTIVATION

Imagine that you live in a town that has one famous company, Boopsie's Biscuits & Buns. Everyone in the town is grateful for the 3B company and goes to work there with high hopes. Soon, however, an odd thing starts happening to many employees. They complain of fatigue and irritability. They are taking lots of sick leave. Productivity declines. What's going on at Boopsie's Biscuits & Buns? Is everybody suffering from sheer laziness?

When people contemplate why some individuals are motivated to achieve and others seem not to care, they usually think of qualities within the person. In the early 1950s, David McClelland and his associates (1953) speculated that some people have a **need for achievement** (abbreviated *nAch*) that motivates them as much as hunger motivates people to eat. To measure the strength of this motive, McClelland used the **Thematic Apperception Test (TAT),** which requires the test-taker to make up a story about each scene in a set of ambiguous pictures. A standardized scoring system permits the test to

---

need for achievement A learned motive to meet personal standards of success and excellence in a chosen area (abbreviated *nAch*).

Thematic Apperception Test (TAT) A personality test that asks respondents to interpret a series of drawings showing ambiguous scenes of people; scored for various motives such as the needs for achievement, affiliation, or power.

be scored for the need for achievement, power, affiliation, and other motives. The strength of these internal motives, said McClelland (1961), is captured in the fantasies the test-taker reveals. "In fantasy anything is at least symbolically possible," he explained. "A person may rise to great heights, sink to great depths, kill his grandmother, or take off for the South Sea Islands on a pogo stick."

Needless to say, people with high achievement motivation do not fantasize about taking off for the South Seas or sinking to great depths. They tell stories about working hard, becoming rich and famous, and clobbering the opposition with their wit and brilliance; if they don't succeed, they foresee devastation. When high achievers are in situations that arouse their competitiveness and desire to succeed—when, for example, they are told that the TAT measures their intelligence and leadership ability—their achievement-related themes shoot up (Atkinson, 1958). In the laboratory and real life, people who score high on the need for achievement consistently differ from those who score low. High scorers are more likely, for example, to start their own businesses. They set high personal standards. They prefer to work with capable colleagues who can help them succeed rather than with co-workers who are merely friendly (McClelland, 1987).

However, many psychologists have criticized the idea that achievement depends entirely on having an "achievement motive," an enduring, unchanging quality. This notion, they say, leads to the incorrect inference that people who don't "make it" have only themselves to blame (Morrison & Von Glinow, 1990). Some people undoubtedly do lack motivation, but research in the sociocultural perspective finds that accomplishment does not depend on internal motives alone. Social psychologists and industrial/organizational psychologists find that it can be nurtured or reduced by the work you do and the conditions under which you do it.

The Conditions of Work

Several specific aspects of the work environment are known to increase job involvement, work motivation, and job satisfaction (S. Brown, 1996; Kohn & Schooler, 1983):

+ The work provides a sense of meaningfulness.

+ Employees have control over many aspects of their work—for example, they can set their own hours and make decisions.

+ Tasks are varied rather than repetitive.

+ The company maintains clear and consistent rules for its workers.

+ Employees have supportive relationships with their superiors and co-workers.

+ Employees receive useful feedback about their work, so they know what they have accomplished and what they need to do to improve.

+ The company offers opportunities for its employees' growth and development.

Companies that foster these conditions tend to have more productive and satisfied employees, and this is true in countries as diverse as the Netherlands, Hungary, and

Bulgaria (Roe et al., 1998). In contrast, workers tend to become less creative in their thinking, and feel worse about themselves and their work, when they feel stuck in routine, boring jobs that give them no control or flexibility over their daily tasks (Karasek & Theorell, 1990; Locke & Latham, 1990). Conversely, when people with high achievement motivation are put in situations that frustrate their desire and ability to express this motive, they become dissatisfied and stressed, and their achievement motive declines (Jenkins, 1994).

Did you notice anything missing from that list of beneficial working conditions? Where is money, supposedly the great motivator? Actually, work motivation is related not to the amount of money you get, but to how and when you get it. The strongest motivator is *incentive pay*, bonuses that are given upon completion of a goal rather than as an automatic raise (Locke et al., 1981). Incentive pay increases people's feelings of competence and accomplishment ("I got this raise because I deserved it"). (This doesn't mean that people should accept low pay so they will like their jobs better, or that they should never demand cost-of-living raises!)

One of the most important working conditions that affects achievement is, simply, having the *opportunity* to achieve. At one time, for example, women were said to be less successful than men in the workplace because women had an internalized "fear of success." Yet as opportunities for women improved and sex discrimination was made illegal, this apparent "motive" vanished.

Similarly, when the proportion of men and women in an occupation changes, so does people's motivation to work in that field (Kanter, 1977/1993). Many occupations are still highly segregated by gender; there are few male secretaries or female auto mechanics. As a result, many people form gender stereotypes of the requirements of such careers: "Female" jobs require kindness and nurturance, "male" jobs require strength and smarts. These assumptions, in turn, stifle people's aspirations to enter a nontraditional career (Cejka & Eagly, 1999). As job segregation breaks down, however, people's motivations change. When law and bartending were almost entirely male professions, few women aspired to become lawyers or bartenders. Now that women make up a large percentage of both occupations, their motivation to become lawyers or bartenders has changed rapidly.

Once in a career, people may become more or less motivated to advance up the ladder, depending on how many rungs they are permitted to climb. Men and women who work in dead-end jobs with no prospect of promotion tend to play down the importance of achievement, fantasize about quitting, and emphasize the social benefits of their jobs instead of the intellectual or financial benefits (Kanter, 1977/1993). Consider the comments of a man who realized in his mid-30s that he was never going to be promoted to top management and who scaled down his ambitions accordingly (Scofield, 1993). As organizational psychologists would predict, he began to emphasize the benefits of not achieving: "I'm freer to speak my mind," "I can choose not to play office politics," and "I don't volunteer for lousy assignments." He had time for coaching Little League and could stay home when the kids were sick. "Of course," he wrote, "if I ever had any chance for upward corporate mobility it's gone now. I couldn't take the grind. Whether real or imagined, that 'glass ceiling' has become an invisible shield."

Women and members of minority groups are especially likely to encounter a "glass ceiling" in management—a barrier to promotion that is so subtle as to be transparent, yet strong enough to prevent advancement. For example, in a study of the banking industry, the three most significant problems that African-Americans reported were not being "in the network," and therefore not being told what was going on; racism; and an inability to find a mentor (Irons & Moore, 1985). When a company has a glass ceiling, a minority person's educational level, work experience, and professional accomplishments do not predict advancement as they do for white men (Cabezas et al., 1989; Graham, 1994; Valian, 1998).

The U.S. Department of Labor launched a Glass Ceiling Initiative to determine how various industries fill their middle- and upper-management positions. It found that most companies have a level beyond which few women or minorities advance, although white women often get farther than minorities of either sex do (Smither, 1998). Male managers typically believe that women and minorities quit or fail to be promoted because of their lack of ambition or commitment to the company, but research does not confirm this belief (Snyder, 1993; Valian, 1998). When minorities reach the glass ceiling, many leave for better jobs or to find more congenial environments.

Competition and Cooperation

If you want to make some money, play the dollar auction with a few friends. Everyone must bid for your dollar in 5-cent increases, and the auction is over when there is no new bid for 30 seconds. The catch is this: The second-highest bidder must also pay you, although he or she will get nothing in return. Usually, the bidding starts quickly and soon narrows to two competitors. After one of them has bid $1, the other decides to bid $1.05, because she would rather pay $1.05 for your dollar than give you 95 cents for nothing. Following the same logic, the person who bid $1 decides to go to $1.10. By the time they quit, you may have won $5 or $6. Your bidders will have been trapped by the nature of competition. Both will want to win; both will fear losing; both will try to save face. Had they thought of cooperation, however, they would both have won. The bidders could have agreed to set a limit on the bidding (say, 45 cents) and split the profits.

During a competitive game, participants and spectators are involved and energized and have a good time. Competition in business can lead to better services and products and new inventions. Yet there are some psychological hazards to competition. When winning is everything, competitors may find no joy in being second or even being in the activity at all.

After reviewing the huge number of studies on the effects of competition, Alfie Kohn (1992) concluded that "the phrase *healthy competition* is a contradiction in terms." Competition, research shows, often decreases work motivation. It can make people feel insecure and anxious, even if they win; it fosters jealousy and hostility; and it can stifle achievement. Cooperation, in contrast, often promotes higher achievement, greater self-esteem, and warmer feelings toward partners (Stanne, Johnson, & Johnson, 1999).

Years ago, Muzafer Sherif and his colleagues used a natural setting, a Boy Scout camp called Robbers Cave, to demonstrate how competition can inflame hostility and conflict between groups (Sherif, 1958; Sherif et al., 1961). Sherif randomly assigned 11- and 12-year-old boys to two groups, the Eagles and the Rattlers. To build team spirit, he had each group work together on projects such as making a rope bridge and building a diving board. Sherif then put the teams in competition for prizes. During fierce games of football, baseball, and tug-of-war, the boys whipped up a competitive fever that soon spilled off the playing fields. They began to raid each other's cabins, call each other names, and start fistfights. No one dared to have a friend from the rival group. Before long, the Rattlers and Eagles were as hostile toward each other as any two gangs fighting for turf or any two nations fighting for dominance. Their hostility continued even when they were just sitting around together watching movies.

Then Sherif came up with a plan to undo the hostility he had created and make peace between the Eagles and Rattlers. He and his associates created a series of predicaments in which both groups needed to work together. The boys had to cooperate to get the water supply system working. They had to pool their resources to get a movie they all wanted to see. When the staff truck "accidentally" broke down on a camping trip, they all had to join forces to pull the truck up a steep hill and get it started again.

This policy of *interdependence in reaching mutual goals* was highly successful in reducing the boys' hostility and competitiveness. The boys eventually made friends with their former enemies (see Figure 9.2). Interdependence has a similar effect in adult groups. When adults work together in a cooperative group in which teamwork is rewarded, they often like one another better and are less hostile than when they are competing for individual success (Deutsch, 1949, 1980). Organizational psychologists have found that in many companies, employees do better, and their motivation is higher, when they work in cohesive work teams than when they work competitively or alone. For example, an alternative to the standard assembly line is to have factory employees work in groups and handle different aspects of assembling the product instead of one repeated routine. This approach has been tried successfully by Volvo, General Foods, Sherwin-Williams, and Saab (Sundstrom, De Meuse, & Futrell, 1990).

Teamwork produces many benefits, including better problem solving, greater satisfaction, and increased participation. Of course, as we saw, teams must be careful to avoid groupthink and to reward individual innovation. Certain conditions of the

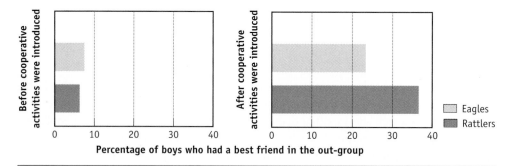

Percentage of boys who had a best friend in the out-group

Eagles
Rattlers

FIGURE 9.2 THE EXPERIMENT AT ROBBERS CAVE *In this study, competitive games such as tug-of-war fostered hostility between the Rattlers and the Eagles; few boys had a best friend from the other group (left). But after the boys had to cooperate to solve various problems, such as repairing the camp's water-supply system, the percentage who made friends across "enemy lines" shot up (right) (Sherif et al., 1961).*

group raise members' motivation and reduce the risk of groupthink: clarity of purpose, autonomy for each member, prompt feedback on performance, a physical environment that permits informal face-to-face meetings, and a system of rewards and recognition in which the benefits to individual members depend on the whole team's performance (Sundstrom, De Meuse, & Futrell, 1990).

The sociocultural perspective shows that what appears to be a simple question— "Why is Alfred knocking himself out at his new job when he used to be such a slug at his old one?"—has many answers, and not all of them are in Alfred. Work motivation and satisfaction depend on the right fit between qualities of the individual and conditions of the work. Companies face the challenge of how best to structure the work environment so that employees will be productive and satisfied, striving to do their best rather than feeling apathetic, resentful, or burned out.

What Do You Know?

Work on your understanding of work motivation.

1. Which of these factors significantly increase work motivation? (a) incentive pay, (b) regular pay, (c) feedback, (d) job predictability, (e) being told what to do, (f) being able to make decisions, (g) having a chance of promotion, (h) having routine work

2. The manager of Boopsie's Biscuits & Buns thinks that worker productivity and satisfaction are low because the employees are lazy and have low achievement motivation. What guidelines of critical thinking, and factors described in the preceding section, is the manager overlooking?

ANSWERS:

1. a, c, f, g   2. The manager should consider other explanations and examine the evidence. Perhaps the working conditions are unsatisfactory—the work provides little interest, challenge, or flexibility. Perhaps employees receive no feedback, support, or incentive pay. There may be few opportunities for promotion. Workers might feel competitive with one another rather than part of a team. The company might have an entrenched glass ceiling and discriminate against minorities. What other possible explanations come to mind?

THE QUESTION OF HUMAN NATURE

Psychologists, like everyone else, like to debate whether human beings are, at heart, good, helpful, cooperative, and hardworking, or selfish, cruel, aggressive, and lazy. Those who believe that people are basically decent and kind often rely on moral persuasion as a tactic for making the world less hostile and more cooperative. Those who believe that people are governed by aggressive, competitive instincts hope that we can find constructive ways of displacing or channeling our violent energies and our need to compete.

Psychologists working in the sociocultural perspective would say that it is in our "nature" to behave both generously and savagely, to be selfish and altruistic, to be lazy and to work hard, to be mindless and to be mindful, to conform and to behave independently, to compete and to cooperate. The task is to identify the conditions that make these reactions likely to occur. To do this, we must understand such normal psychological processes and circumstances as roles, obedience to authority, conformity, entrapment, deindividuation, and working conditions.

At the beginning of this chapter, we reported Adolf Eichmann's claim that he was "not the monster I am made out to be." Philosopher Hannah Arendt (1963), who observed his trial and later wrote about it, agreed with him, describing his actions as evidence of "the banality of evil." (*Banal* means "commonplace" or "unoriginal.") Eichmann and his fellow Nazis were ordinary men, Arendt wrote, just doing their jobs. The compelling evidence for the banality of evil is, perhaps, the hardest lesson in psychology. Most people want to believe that only evil people, who are bad down to their bones, do harm to others; it is reassuring to divide the world into those who are good or bad, kind or cruel, moral or immoral.

Of course, some people do stand out as being unusually heroic or unusually sadistic; roles and situations do not account entirely for the prevalence of altruism or of genocide (Berkowitz, 1999; Staub, 1999). Yet the sociocultural perspective shows us that good people can do terribly disturbing things when norms and roles encourage or require them to do so, or when the situation takes over and they do not stop to think critically. Otherwise healthy people may join self-destructive cults, inflict pain on others if ordered to, or go along mindlessly with a violent crowd.

And so the bad news is that cruelty cannot be eliminated by getting rid of a few "bad" people or nations, because cruelty and cowardice are often a result of normal, everyday social processes. The good news, from the sociocultural perspective, is that all that human nature gives us is potential. It's up to us to create conditions that will foster the "banality of virtue"—everyday acts of kindness, selflessness, and generosity. ■

Summary

1. Psychologists working in the sociocultural perspective explore psychological questions by examining the individual in a social context. The social side of this perspective, which includes the specialties of *social psychology* and *industrial/organizational psychology,* focuses on the social and situational influences on behavior, thoughts, and feelings. *Norms* and *roles* place powerful constraints on human behavior, and role requirements can cause a person to behave in ways that violate his or her feelings, personal wishes, and sense of self.

2. Two classic studies illustrate the power of roles to affect individual actions. In Milgram's obedience study, most people in the role of "teacher" inflicted what they thought was extreme shock on another person because of the authority of the

experimenter. In Zimbardo's prison study, college students quickly fell into the role of "prisoner" or "guard."

3. Obedience to authority contributes to the smooth running of society, but obedience can also lead to actions that are deadly, foolish, or illegal. People obey orders to avoid being punished, to show respect for authority, and to gain advantages. Even when they would rather not obey, they may do so because they have a strong respect for authority and regard its decisions as legitimate, thereby absolving themselves of responsibility for their actions; because the role is *routinized* into duties that are performed mindlessly; because they are embarrassed to break the rules of good manners and lack the words to protest; or because they have been *entrapped*.

4. Individuals act differently in groups than they would on their own. A group's actions depend less on the personalities of its members than on the nature of the group itself. In groups, individuals often conform to social pressure because they identify with a group, trust the group's judgment or knowledge, hope for personal gain, or wish to be liked. But they also may conform mindlessly and self-destructively, violating their own preferences and values because "everyone else is doing it."

5. Groups that are strongly cohesive, are isolated from other views, are under outside pressure, and have strong leaders are vulnerable to *groupthink,* the tendency of group members to think alike, censor themselves, actively suppress disagreement, and feel that their decisions are invulnerable. Groupthink often produces faulty decisions because group members fail to seek disconfirming evidence for their ideas. However, groups can be structured to counteract groupthink.

6. Children, adolescents, and adults are especially likely to conform to their peers—their agemates, friends, and fellow employees—in attitudes, dress, preferences, and behavior. The need for peer acceptance and approval can supersede parental values, as the example of academic achievement illustrates. The shared experiences of a young adult's age group or generation are the basis of a *generational identity* that is influential all through life.

7. *Diffusion of responsibility* in a group can lead to inaction on the part of individuals, such as *bystander apathy* or, in work groups, *social loafing.* The diffusion of responsibility is especially likely to occur under conditions that promote *deindividuation,* the loss of awareness of one's individuality. Deindividuation increases when people feel anonymous, as in a large group or crowd, or when they are wearing masks or uniforms. In some situations, crowd norms lead deindividuated people to behave aggressively, but in others, crowd norms foster helpfulness.

8. The willingness to speak up for an unpopular opinion, blow the whistle on illegal or immoral practices, or help someone in trouble (*altruism*) is partly a matter of personal belief and conscience. But several social and situational factors are also important. These include seeing a need for help, which increases when there are few environmental stimuli to attend to; deciding to take responsibility, which increases when there are few situational risks of independent action; deciding that the costs of not doing anything are greater than the costs of getting involved; having an ally; and becoming entrapped in a commitment to help or dissent.

9. Social psychologists who study *social cognition* examine how the social environment affects people's thoughts and beliefs. According to *attribution theory,* people are motivated to search for causes to which they can attribute their own and other people's behavior. Their attributions may be *situational* or *dispositional.* The *fundamental attribution error* occurs when people overestimate personality traits as a cause of behavior and underestimate the influence of the situation. A *self-serving bias* allows people to excuse their mistakes by blaming the situation yet take credit for their good deeds. The belief that the world is fair and that people get what they deserve (the *just-world hypothesis*) often leads to *blaming the victims* for provoking or deserving bad things that happen to them, instead of blaming the perpetrators.

10. People's beliefs and opinions are subject to many tactics of social influence. One is the *validity effect:* Simply repeating a statement over and over again makes it seem more believable. Other persuasion techniques include associating a product or message with someone who is famous, attractive, or expert, and linking the product with good feelings. Fear tactics tend to backfire.

11. Some methods of persuasion are intentionally manipulative. Techniques of *coercive persuasion* include putting a person under extreme distress, defining problems simplistically, offering the appearance of unconditional love and acceptance in exchange for unquestioning loyalty, creating a new identity for the person, using entrapment, and controlling access to outside information.

12. The motivation to work depends partly on a person's ambitions and energy; people who are motivated by a high *need for achievement,* often measured by the *Thematic Apperception Test (TAT),* set their own standards for success and excellence.

13. Work motivation also depends on working conditions and opportunities to achieve. Key working conditions that promote motivation and satisfaction are those that provide workers with a sense of meaningfulness, control, variation in tasks, clear rules, supportive relationships, feedback, and opportunities for advancement and learning. *Incentive pay* is more effective than predictable raises in elevating work motivation. An important factor in the motivation to enter a career is its gender ratio. The motivation to achieve also depends on having the opportunity to be promoted, in contrast to hitting a "glass ceiling."

14. Competition in business can lead to better services and products and new inventions, but it can also decrease work motivation, make people feel insecure, and foster hostility. Conflict and hostility between groups can be reduced by promoting interdependence in reaching mutual goals. In business, cooperative teamwork can produce better problem solving, worker satisfaction, and increased performance, as long as groupthink is avoided and individual innovation is also rewarded.

15. Psychologists working in the sociocultural perspective argue that it is "human nature" to behave both generously and savagely, to be selfish and altruistic, to be lazy and to work hard, to be mindless and to be mindful, to conform and to behave independently. The task is to identify the conditions that make these reactions likely to occur.

Key Terms

CHAPTER TEN

The Cultural Context

*I*n a suburb of Baton Rouge, Louisiana, Yoshihiro Hattori, a 16-year-old Japanese exchange student, went along with his friend Webb Haymaker to a Halloween party. They mistakenly stopped in front of a house covered in Halloween decorations and rang the bell. Hearing no answer, Yoshihiro went around the side of the house to see if the party might be in the backyard. The home owner, Bonnie Peairs, opened the front door, saw Webb in a Halloween costume, and then saw Yoshihiro running back toward her waving an object (which turned out to be a camera). She panicked and called for her husband to get his gun. Rodney Peairs grabbed a loaded .44 Magnum and shouted at Yoshihiro to "freeze." Yoshihiro, not understanding the word, did not stop. Peairs shot him in the heart, killing him instantly. Little more than a minute had passed between the time that Yoshihiro Hattori rang the doorbell and the time that Rodney Peairs shot him to death.

When the case came to trial, the jury acquitted Rodney Peairs of manslaughter after only three hours of deliberation.

If ever a tragic misunderstanding illustrated the power of cultural differences, this one is it. To the Japanese news media, the story illustrated everything that is wrong with America. It is a nation rife with guns and violence—a "developing nation," as one commentator put it, that is still growing out of its Wild West past. Japanese television reporters, in amazement, showed their viewers American gun stores, restaurants that display guns on the walls, and racks of gun magazines. The Japanese cannot imagine a nation in which private individuals are allowed to keep guns. In the entire nation of Japan each year, only about 70 people are killed by guns, almost all of them members of organized crime; in the United States, a person is fatally shot every 16 minutes.

"I think for Japanese the most remarkable thing is that you could get a jury of Americans together, and they could conclude that shooting someone before you even talked to him was reasonable behavior," Masako Notoji, a professor of American cultural studies in Tokyo, told *The New York Times.* "We are more civilized. We rely on words." Yet the citizens of Baton Rouge were surprised that the case came to trial at all. What is more right and natural, they said, than protecting yourself and your family from intruders? "A man's home is his castle," said one potential juror, expressing puzzlement that Peairs had even been arrested. A local man, joining the many sympathizers of Rodney Peairs, said, "It would be to me what a normal person would do under those circumstances."

Bonnie Peairs wept on the witness stand. "There was no thinking involved," she said. "I wish I could have thought. If I could have just thought."

The clash of American and Japanese cultures, which is so clear in this sad case, shows why it is important to understand what culture means and how it influences us. Defining culture is easier said than done, however. As cross-cultural psychologist Walter Lonner (1995) observed, "It ranks right up there with truth, beauty, justice, and intelligence as abstract and fuzzy constructs whose precise definitions challenge even the most insightful thinkers." But, in general, he and most other researchers agree that **culture** can be defined as a program of shared rules and customs that govern the behavior of members of a community or society, and a set of values, beliefs, and attitudes shared by most members of that community. Every culture includes a system of rules, passed from one generation to another, for just about everything in the human-made environment: for getting along with other people, for raising children, for making decisions, for organizing work and family life, and for making love or war (Lonner, 1995; Segall et al., 1999).

Cultural psychologists study the many ways in which people are affected by the culture in which they live; for example, they might study how the American cultural values of independence and youthfulness affect Americans' behavior, beliefs, and self-esteem. *Cross-cultural psychologists* compare members of different societies, searching for both their commonalities and their distinctive differences. For example, they might study several cultures to determine whether the stages of children's cognitive development are universal. Both of these fields overlap somewhat with *cultural anthropology,* the study of customs within and across human cultures, and indeed we will be reporting some research from anthropologists. But anthropologists tend to study the economy and customs of a cultural unit as a whole, whereas cultural psychologists are more interested in how culture affects individual psychological processes such as reasoning abilities or the motivation to achieve.

Until recently, most Western psychologists were uninterested in the influence of culture on individuals. In contrast to physiology, which they treated as real and tangible, they regarded culture as merely a light veneer on human behavior, or perhaps a source of information for tourist travel ("Did you know that in Spain, people eat dinner at midnight?"). As a result, students and teachers knew little about the psychological characteristics of people living in other societies and assumed they could safely generalize from studies of people in their own culture to people everywhere (Betancourt & López, 1993; Matsumoto, 1996).

---

culture A program of shared rules that govern the behavior of members of a community or society, and a set of values, beliefs, and attitudes shared by most members of that community.

Researchers in the sociocultural perspective, however, are demonstrating that culture is just as powerful an influence on human behavior as any biological process. In fact, culture affects biological processes. Everyone needs to eat, for instance, but culture affects how often people eat, what they eat, and with whom they eat. Depending on your culture, you might eat lots of little meals throughout the day or only one large meal. You will eat food that your culture calls delicious—whale meat in Inuit communities, lizards in South America, locusts in Africa, horses in France, dogs in Asia—and you are likely to find unfamiliar food preferences disgusting. You won't eat foods that your culture calls taboo: pigs among Muslims and Orthodox Jews, cows in India, horses in America, deer among the Tapirapé (Harris, 1985). And your culture affects your choice of dining companions. People generally don't eat with those they consider their social inferiors, which in various cultures includes servants, employees, women, or children. These cultural influences on a process as essential as eating can cause people to eat when they are not hungry (to be sociable) or not to eat when they *are* hungry (because the company or food is culturally unappetizing).

Sometimes, cultural pressures directly conflict with biological dispositions. Evolution has programmed women to maintain a reserve of fat necessary for healthy childbearing, nursing, and, after menopause, the production and storage of the hormone estrogen. And, as we saw in Chapter 3, genes influence body shape and weight. Yet the contemporary cultural ideal for many North American white women is a boyishly slim body, an ideal that is by no means universal across cultures or historical epochs. The result of the battle between biological design and cultural standards is that many women are obsessed with weight, continually dieting, excessively exercising, or suffering from eating disorders such as bulimia (bingeing and vomiting) (Silverstein & Perlick, 1995).

We begin with a discussion of some unique difficulties that the study of culture poses for psychologists. We will then consider the influence of culture on a diverse assortment of psychological processes and behaviors, ranging from the gestures you make to support your favorite football team to your very identity. However, although describing individual cultural customs is a fascinating project on its own, cultural psychologists want to do more than just tote up examples of different practices as if they were a stack of potato chips. As we will see, they also try to explain these practices—where they come from, why they change, and what purpose they serve for the society as a whole.

THE STUDY OF CULTURE

The study of culture poses a distinct set of challenges for researchers, both in designing methods and interpreting results.

1 METHODOLOGICAL PROBLEMS. Devising good procedures and getting good samples is difficult enough when you are studying just one culture; these tasks are even more daunting when you are comparing two or more. Right off the bat, you have to worry about whether your questionnaires, interviews, or instructions convey the same meanings in every language. This is hard to do because sometimes a concept that is tremendously important in one culture cannot easily be translated into an equivalent term in another culture. The Chinese Value Survey, for instance, contains items that seem strange to many Westerners, such as "filial piety," defined as "honoring of ancestors and obedience to, respect for, and financial support of parents" (Hofstede & Bond, 1988). You also have to be sure that the people you interview or observe are truly matched across cultures—that is, that your samples are similar in all aspects of their lives (including age, economic status, and education) except for their nationality.

2 **PROBLEMS IN INTERPRETING RESULTS.** Once you have findings from two or more cultures, you then have to think about how to interpret them. A custom in one culture might not have the same meaning or purpose as the same practice elsewhere. For example, the circumcision of male babies has a religious purpose among Jews and serves to strengthen identification with the group, but the same practice became widespread in Europe and America during the Victorian era for a very different reason: It was (mistakenly) believed that circumcised boys wouldn't masturbate and thus succumb to "masturbatory insanity" (Paige & Paige, 1981). In addition, a custom may persist long after its original function or intention has been abandoned. Circumcision continued in North America, but not in Europe, decades after masturbatory insanity was forgotten as its rationale, because the medical establishment endorsed the procedure in the name of hygiene.

3 **THE PROBLEM OF STEREOTYPING.** A third problem in studying culture is how to identify and describe average differences across societies without stereotyping. As one student of ours put it, "How come when we students speak of 'the' Japanese

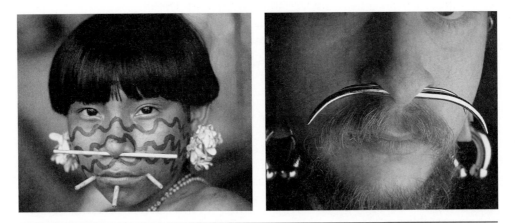

The same behavior may have different functions in different cultures. For the Yanomamo Indians (left), nose piercing is a part of normal facial decoration and display, but a Westerner (right) might do it to be unusual, rebellious, or shocking.

or 'the' blacks or 'the' whites or 'the' Latinos, it's called stereotyping, and when you do it, it's called 'cross-cultural psychology'?" This question shows excellent critical thinking! The study of culture does not rest on the assumption, implicit in stereotypes, that *all* members of a culture behave the same way. As the other psychological perspectives have shown, individuals vary according to their temperaments, beliefs, and learning histories, and this variation occurs within every culture. Cultural researchers know that just as people play their social roles differently, they read their cultural scripts differently. But the fact that individuals vary within a culture does not negate the existence of cultural rules that, *on the average,* make Swedes different from Bedouins or Cambodians different from Italians. Figure 10.1 illustrates the challenge facing cultural psychologists: how to describe average differences without ignoring the overlap among individuals.

As if these difficulties were not enough, we then have to deal with the political and emotional sensitivity of many cross-cultural findings. It is often hard for people to talk about cultural differences when they feel uncomfortable with other groups and defensive about their own. Emotions run high. Many people read a study that finds a difference between groups and jump to the conclusion that one group is "superior" to the other. Or they read something about their own ethnic group and complain that the researcher is insulting them or stereotyping—*they* are not like that. These reactions are common. Social and cultural psychologists have, in fact, studied why discussions of culture so often deteriorate into judgmental, emotional language; why people assume that *differences* between groups imply *deficiencies* in one; and why so many people assume that their own culture is the best.

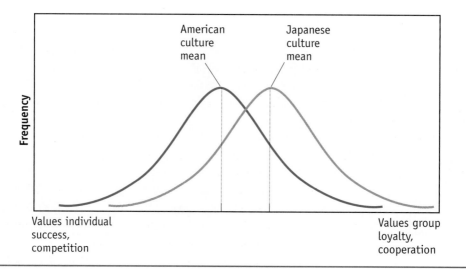

FIGURE 10.1 HYPOTHETICAL DISTRIBUTIONS OF VALUES IN TWO CULTURES *Whenever cultural psychologists speak of differences between two cultures, they are really describing average differences. There is always overlap among individuals.*

What Do You Know?

Students from all cultures should be able to answer this quiz.

1. Dr. Livingston does research on Americans' habit of making frequent moves and how it affects their attitudes toward friendship and sociability. Dr. Livingston can best be described as a (cultural/cross-cultural) psychologist.

2. Like eating, sleeping is a biological process that is influenced in many ways by culture. Can you think of some of those ways?

3. Several decades ago, a study compared arranged marriages in Japan with marriages for love in the United States. After 10 years of married life, the groups did not differ in their self-rankings of marital satisfaction and love. What might be a problem in interpreting these findings?

ANSWERS:

1. cultural 2. Culture affects what time people go to sleep and get up in the morning; the kind of bed, cot, or mat they sleep on; what they wear, if anything; whether they rely on an artificial signal (e.g., an alarm clock) to wake them up; whether they permit their infants or older children to sleep with them; and whether (and when) they take naps. (This list is not exhaustive.) 3. One problem is that "satisfaction" and "love" might have had different meanings in the two cultures or might have been measured in different ways.

THE RULES OF CULTURE

A young wife leaves her house one morning to draw water from the local well as her husband watches from the porch. On her way back from the well, a male stranger stops her and asks for some water. She gives him a cupful and then invites him home to dinner. The husband, wife, and guest have a pleasant meal together. The husband, in a gesture of hospitality, invites the guest to spend the night—with his wife. In the morning, the husband leaves early to bring home breakfast. When he returns, he discovers his wife again in bed with the visitor.

Question: At what point in this story does the husband feel angry? *Answer:* It depends on his culture (Hupka, 1981, 1991). A North American husband would feel rather angry at a wife who had an extramarital affair, and a wife would feel rather angry at being offered to a guest as if she were a lamb chop. But these reactions are not universal. A Pawnee husband of the nineteenth century would be enraged at any man who dared ask his wife even for water. An Ammassalik Inuit husband finds it perfectly honorable to offer his wife to a stranger, but only once. He would be angry to find his wife and the guest having a second encounter. A Toda husband in turn-of-the-century India would not be angry at all, because the Toda allowed both husband and wife to take lovers. Both spouses might feel angry, though, if one of them had a *sneaky* affair, without announcing it publicly.

People learn their culture's rules as effortlessly as they learn its language. Just as they can speak without being able to state the rules of grammar, most people follow their culture's prescriptions without being aware of them. In this section, we will consider some of those invisible rules.

Nonverbal Communication

Fiorello La Guardia, who was mayor of New York from 1933 to 1945, was fluent in English, Italian, and Yiddish. La Guardia knew more than the words of those languages; he also knew the gestures that went along with each one. Researchers who studied films of his speeches could tell which language he was speaking with the sound turned off! They could do so by reading his *body language,* the nonverbal signals of body movement, posture, gesture, and gaze that people constantly express (Birdwhistell, 1970). Many Italians and Jews embellish their speech with circular movements of their arms and hands, and by measuring the radius of those movements you can actually predict whether a speaker is of Italian or Jewish descent: The larger the radius, the more likely the speaker is Italian (Keating, 1994).

Some signals of body language, like some facial expressions, seem to be "spoken" universally. Across cultures, people generally recognize body movements that reveal pleasure or displeasure, liking or dislike, high status or low status, depression or anger (Buck, 1984; Matsumoto, 1996). However, most aspects of body language are specific

Be careful where you make this gesture.

to particular spoken languages and cultures, which makes even the simplest gesture subject to misunderstanding and offense. The sign of the University of Texas football team, the Longhorns, is to extend the index finger and the pinkie. In Italy and other parts of Europe this gesture means a man's wife has been unfaithful to him—a serious insult!

Even the smile, which is universally recognized as a sign of friendliness, has many culture-specific meanings. Americans smile more often than Germans. This does not mean that Americans are friendlier than Germans; it means that they differ in their notions of when a smile is appropriate. After a German-American business session, Americans often complain that their German counterparts are cold and aloof. In turn, Germans often complain that the Americans are excessively cheerful, hiding their real feelings under the mask of a smile (Hall & Hall, 1990). The Japanese smile even more than the Americans, to disguise anger, embarrassment, or other negative emotions whose public display is considered rude and improper. Smiling for this reason is what got the Japanese student of our introductory story (on page 359) in hot water with his Egyptian classmate.

Another important nonverbal rule governs *conversational distance:* how close people normally stand to one another when they are speaking (Hall, 1959, 1976). Arabs like to stand close enough to feel your breath, touch your arm, and look into your eyes—a distance that makes most white Americans, Canadians, and northern Europeans uneasy, unless they are talking intimately with a lover. The English and the Swedes stand farthest apart when they converse; southern Europeans stand closer; and Latin Americans and Arabs stand the closest (Keating, 1994; Sommer, 1969).

When a nonverbal rule is broken, you are likely to feel extremely uncomfortable without knowing why. And even if you know why, it is not always easy to change your own rules. Caroline Keating (1994), an American cross-cultural psychologist, tells of walking with a Pakistani colleague: "I found myself clumsily stepping off the sidewalk. Without realizing it, the closer my Muslim colleague moved toward me (seeking the interpersonal closeness he was comfortable with) the more I moved over streetside (seeking the interpersonal distance I was comfortable with). . . . I would suddenly disappear from his view, having fallen into the street; perhaps not 'the ugly American,' but a clumsy one!"

People from different cultures also differ in how attentive they are to body language and nonverbal signals, and in how much they rely on these sources of information in contrast to direct verbal expression (Ambady et al., 1996; Goldman, 1994; Gudykunst & Ting-Toomey, 1988; Hall, 1983). In Japan, for example, people pay close attention to nonverbal signs such as posture, tone of voice, and distance between speakers. They assume a shared knowledge and history, so things don't have to be spelled out directly. Thus, people will rarely say "No, I can't do that" right to your face; it would be considered too direct and too insulting. They are more likely to say, "That is difficult" or "We will see." This response seems inexplicable to many North Americans, who rely more on direct verbal expression than on nonverbal signals.

The misunderstandings that can arise between these two forms of communication cannot be overestimated: They can even lead to war (Triandis, 1994). On January 9, 1991, the foreign minister of Iraq, Tariq Aziz, met with the American secretary of state, James Baker, to discuss Iraq's invasion of Kuwait. Seated next to Aziz was the half-brother of Iraq's president, Saddam Hussein. Baker said, "If you do not move out of Kuwait we will attack you." An unmistakable statement, right? But his *nonverbal* language was that of an American diplomat, moderate and polite. He didn't roar, stamp his feet, or wave his hands. Saddam Hussein's brother, for his part, behaved like a normal Iraqi: He paid attention to Baker's nonverbal language, which he considered the important form of communication. He reported to Saddam Hussein that Baker was "not at all angry. The Americans are just talking, and they will not attack." Saddam therefore instructed Aziz to be inflexible and yield nothing. This misunderstanding contributed to the outbreak of a bloody war in which untold thousands of adults and children died.

The Organization of Time

Imagine that you have arranged to meet a friend for lunch at noon. The friend has not arrived at 12:15, 12:30, or even 12:45. Please answer these questions: What time would *you* have arrived? Would you have been "on time"? How long would you wait for your friend before you started to feel worried or annoyed? When would you leave?

In most parts of North America, the answers are obvious. You would have been there pretty close to noon and would not have waited much past 12:30. That is because

Canada and the United States, along with northern European nations, are **monochronic cultures:** Time is organized into linear segments in which people do one thing "at a time" (Hall, 1983; Hall & Hall, 1990). The day is divided into appointments, schedules, and routines, and because time is a precious commodity, people don't like to "waste" time or "spend" too much time on any one activity. In such cultures, therefore, it is considered the height of rudeness (or high status) to keep someone waiting. But the farther south you go in Europe, South America, and Africa, the more likely you are to find **polychronic cultures.** Here, time is organized along parallel lines. People do many things at once, and the needs of friends and family supersede those of the appointment book. People in Latin America and the Middle East think nothing of waiting all day, or even a week, to see someone. The idea of having to be somewhere "on time," as if time were more important than a person, is unthinkable. Table 10.1 summarizes the differences between these two cultural styles.

The Japanese have one of the few cultures to combine elements of both systems. With the American occupation that followed World War II, they started being monochronic as a way of creating harmony with the *gaijin* (foreigners). Today, they are extremely monochronic about schedules, but in every other way they are polychronic. For instance, they are loyal to long-term business relationships, and employees and managers share office space and information freely (Hall & Hall, 1990).

In culturally diverse North America, the two time systems keep bumping into each other. An Anglo judge in Miami got into hot water when he observed that "Cubans always show up two hours late for weddings"—late in his culture's terms, that is. The judge was accurate in his observation; the problem was his implication that there was something wrong with Cubans for being "late." And "late" compared with what, by the way? The Cubans were perfectly on time for Cubans.

A culture's way of organizing time is not arbitrary. It stems from the culture's economic system, social organization, political history, and ecology. The monochronic structure of time emerged as a result of the Industrial Revolution in England (Hall, 1983). That makes sense; when thousands of people began working in factories and assembly lines, their efforts had to become coordinated. Moreover, factories have no intrinsic rhythms; people can and do work day or night in them. But in rural economies, where work is based on the rhythms of nature, people think of time differently. When Edward Hall (1983) worked with the Hopi many years ago, he found that they were amused by the "white" government's compulsive schedules for building roads and houses. Unlike the maturing of a sheep or the ripening of corn, said the Hopi, building a house has no inherent timetable. The Hopi *did* care about completing their planting and religious ceremonies, activities that indeed had to be done "on time"—nature's time, not human time.

---

monochronic cultures Cultures in which time is organized sequentially; schedules and deadlines are valued over people.

polychronic cultures Cultures in which time is organized horizontally; people tend to do several things at once and value relationships over schedules.

TABLE 10.1 ✦ Cross-cultural Differences in the Uses and Structure of Time	
MONOCHRONIC PEOPLE	**POLYCHRONIC PEOPLE**
Do one thing at a time.	Do many things at once.
Concentrate on the job.	Are highly distractible and subject to interruptions.
Take time commitments seriously.	Consider time commitments secondary to relationships.
Give the job first priority.	Give people first priority.
Adhere closely to plans.	Change plans often and easily.
Are concerned about not disturbing others; value privacy.	Are more concerned with relationships than with privacy.
Like "own space" or private office to work in.	Freely share working space, which increases flow of information.
Place high value on private property; seldom borrow or lend.	Borrow and lend things often.
Emphasize promptness.	Care less about own promptness than about other people's needs; are almost never "on time."
Develop many short-term relationships.	Build lifetime relationships.

Source: Hall & Hall, 1990.

The Self and Self-identity

Who are you? Take as much time as you like to complete this sentence: "I am _____." Your response to this question will be influenced by your cultural background.

Individualism and Collectivism. One of the most important ways in which cultures differ has to do with whether the individual or the group is given the greater emphasis (Hofstede & Bond, 1988; Markus & Kitayama, 1991; Triandis, 1996). In **individualist cultures,** the independence of the individual often takes precedence over the needs

---

individualist cultures Cultures in which the self is regarded as autonomous, and individual goals and wishes are prized above duty and relations with others.

of the group, and the self is often defined as a collection of personality traits ("I am outgoing, agreeable, and ambitious") or in occupational terms ("I am a psychologist"). In **collectivist cultures,** group harmony takes precedence over the wishes of the individual, and the self is defined in the context of relationships and the community ("I am the son of a farmer, descended from three generations of storytellers on my mother's side . . .").

In collectivist cultures, typical of Asian nations, the boundaries between the self and other people are more flexible and shifting than they are in individualist cultures; people feel that they change across situations more than Westerners do (Markus & Kitayama, 1991). In a study comparing Japanese and Americans, the Americans reported that their sense of self changes only 5 to 10 percent in different situations, whereas the Japanese said that 90 to 99 percent of their sense of self changes (de Rivera, 1989). For the Japanese, it is important to enact *tachiba,* to perform one's social roles correctly so that there will be harmony with others. (As we just noted, this was one reason they adopted the American monochronic system of time after World War II.) Americans, in contrast, tend to value "being true to yourself" and having a "core identity."

The way that people define the self affects many aspects of individual psychology, including which personality traits are encouraged, how emotions are expressed, and whether relationships or individual freedom are valued more (Campbell et al., 1996; Kashima et al., 1995). For instance, in the individualist United States, where mobility is prized and people move many times in their lives, the ability to make friends quickly and develop a surface sociability is adaptive and valuable. In collectivist cultures, where people rarely change homes and neighborhoods, friendship develops slowly; it takes a long time to flower, but then it blooms for life. The difference between these two styles is revealed in reactions to the proverb "A rolling stone gathers no moss." In America, it means keep moving; don't let anything cling to you. In Japan, it means stay where you are; if you keep moving you will never experience the beauty of stability.

In collectivist cultures, the strongest human bond is usually not between husband and wife but between parent and child or siblings (Triandis, 1995). Child rearing is a communal matter; everyone has a say in correcting the child's behavior. The idea of privacy for children is unknown, and the goal is to raise children who are obedient, hardworking, and dutiful toward their parents. Can you predict what will happen if a collectivist man marries an individualist woman? The chances are high that the husband will regard his relationship with one or both of his parents as most important, whereas his wife will expect his relationship to her to be most important. And they are likely to disagree intensely, without knowing why, about such matters as letting their children have their own rooms, speak their minds, make their own choices, talk back, and become independent.

In the spirit of practicing what we preach about not stereotyping, however, we want to emphasize that the East-West, collectivism-individualism distinction is an *average* one, not absolute. There is great overlap: Many Asians are highly individualistic, and many

---

collectivist cultures Cultures in which the self is regarded as embedded in relationships, and harmony with one's group is prized above individual goals and wishes.

Westerners are very "groupy!" Moreover, there are differences within these orientations. In America, the most collectivist region is the Deep South, with its history of strong regional identity, whereas the West, with its history of rugged frontier individualism, is the least (Vandello & Cohen, 1999). The Chinese and the Japanese both value group harmony, but the Chinese are more likely to promote individual achievement, whereas the Japanese strive for group consensus (Dien, 1999).

Ethnic Identity and Acculturation.   Everyone develops a personal identity based on his or her traits and unique history. But people also develop **social identities** based on their nationality, ethnicity, religion, and social roles (Brewer & Gardner, 1996; Tajfel & Turner, 1986). Social identities—"I am French; I am a Buddhist; I am an engineer"— give us a feeling of place and position in the world. Without them, most of us would feel like loose marbles rolling around in a chaotic universe. Because of the importance of social identities, most people feel that their group is distinctive and special. This is one reason that they tend to dislike and quarrel with groups that, to outsiders, seem so similar to themselves: Fraternities dislike other fraternities, Communists quarrel with socialists, feminists with other feminists, born-again Christians with other conservative Christians. The other group is "too close for comfort" and thus threatens their feeling of distinctiveness and rightness (White & Langer, 1999).

In modern societies, many social identities are possible. People often face the dilemma of balancing their **ethnic identity,** a close identification with their religious or ethnic group, with **acculturation,** an identification with the dominant culture (Cross, 1971; Phinney, 1996; Segall et al., 1999). As Table 10.2 shows, there are four ways of balancing ethnic identity and acculturation, depending on whether each is strong or weak (Berry, 1994; Phinney, 1990). People who are *bicultural* have strong ties both to their ethnicity and to the larger culture: They say, "I am proud of my ethnic heritage, but I identify just as much with my country." They can alternate easily between their culture of origin and the majority culture, slipping into the customs and language of each as circumstances dictate (LaFromboise, Coleman, & Gerton, 1993). People who choose *assimilation* have weak feelings of ethnicity but a strong sense of acculturation: Their attitude, for example, might be, "I'm an American, period." *Ethnic separatists* have a strong sense of ethnic identity but weak feelings of acculturation: They may say, "My ethnicity comes first; if I join the mainstream, I'm betraying my origins." And some people feel *marginal*, connected to neither their ethnicity nor the dominant culture.

The way a person balances ethnic identity and acculturation often changes in response to personal experiences and larger social and historical events (Berry, 1998). Thus, many immigrants arrive in North America with every intention of becoming "true"

---

social identity The part of a person's self-concept that is based on his or her identification with a nation, culture, or ethnic group or with a gender role or other roles in society.

ethnic identity A person's identification with a religious or ethnic group.

acculturation The process by which members of groups that are minorities in a given society come to identify with and feel part of the mainstream culture.

TABLE 10.2 ✦ Patterns of Ethnic Identity and Acculturation

		ETHNIC IDENTITY IS	
		STRONG	WEAK
ACCULTURATION IS	STRONG	Bicultural	Assimilated
	WEAK	Separatist	Marginal

Canadians or Americans. If they encounter discrimination or setbacks, however, they may decide that acculturation is harder than they anticipated or that ethnic separatism offers greater solace. Moreover, acculturation is rarely a complete accommodation to mainstream culture. Most people pick and choose among customs of their own ethnicity and those of the dominant culture, or set limits on how far they want acculturation to go (Segall et al., 1999). You might become acculturated to another ethnic group's food and customs, but believe in the importance of marrying within your own group.

As groups develop a strong ethnic identity, they often reject the name that was imposed on them by the majority culture and choose their own. The Eskimos of Canada are now called the Inuit, their own name for themselves, and the Sioux are now the Lakota. A group's name reflects its history, status, and self-concept. The shift from Negro (a label based on racial categories) to black (based on skin color) to African-American (based on geographical origin) reflects the evolution of ethnic identity, self-concept, and political strength (Cross, 1971, 1991; Fairchild, 1985; Sellers et al., 1998).

To add to the confusion, not all members of each ethnic group agree on a group label. Some—blacks?—feel no special kinship to Africa; the social critic Henry Louis Gates, Jr., called his autobiography *Colored People*, the term he prefers, and the writer Stanley Crouch prefers *Negro*. The American Indian Movement and the National Congress of American Indians continue to use the term *American Indian* even though the "correct" term is supposed to be *Native American* (Trimble & Medicine, 1993). *Hispanic* is a label used by the U.S. government to include all Spanish-speaking groups; but many "Hispanics" dislike the term, pointing out that Spaniards, Mexican-Americans (Chicanos), Latin Americans (Latinos), Cubans, and Puerto Ricans differ in their cultures and histories, and therefore in their ethnic identity. And not all "white" Americans want to be called Anglos, which refers to a British heritage, or European-American, as if all European countries from Greece to Norway were the same.

These tensions over group names are likely to continue, as ethnic groups struggle to define their place, raise their status, and secure their identity in a medley of cultures.

What Do You Know?

Are you acculturated yet to student culture?

1. Cultures whose members do things one at a time and put schedules over relationships are called _____; cultures whose members do many things at once and put relationships ahead of schedules are called _____.

2. Cultures whose members regard the "self" as a collection of stable personality traits are called _____.

3. Frank, an African-American college student, finds himself caught between two philosophies on his campus. One holds that blacks should move toward full integration into mainstream culture. The other holds that blacks should immerse themselves in the history, values, and contributions of African culture. The first group values _____, whereas the second emphasizes _____.

ANSWERS:

1. monochronic; polychronic; 2. individualist 3. acculturation, ethnic identity

---

CULTURE AND INTELLIGENCE

What does it mean to be smart? Cultural psychologists answer that it is not enough to assess a person's cognitive abilities. You have to understand the cultural environment in which that person lives.

The Meanings of Intelligence

Years ago, in a study of the Kpelle tribe in Africa (Scribner, 1977), researchers gave an unschooled farmer this reasoning problem, a standard Western syllogism: "All Kpelle men are rice farmers. Mr. Smith is not a rice farmer. Is he a Kpelle man?" The farmer insisted that the information provided did not allow a conclusion. "If I know him in person," the farmer said, "I can answer that question, but since I do not know him in person I cannot answer that question." The interviewer concluded that because the farmer was accustomed to drawing on personal knowledge alone to reach conclusions, he could not reason deductively (see Chapter 7). Yet the Kpelle farmer *was* reasoning deductively:

premise	If I do not know a person, I cannot draw any conclusions about that person.
premise	I do not know Mr. Smith.
conclusion	Therefore I cannot draw any conclusions about Mr. Smith.

"You can't build a hut, you don't know how to find edible roots and you know nothing about predicting the weather. In other words, you do terribly on our IQ test."

The answer that the Kpelle farmer gave was not what his interviewer expected, but it was perfectly smart in *his* culture's terms. Basic cognitive capacities are universal, but because cultures differ in which of these abilities they foster and which they regard as unnecessary, the very meaning of "intelligence" is culturally determined. Thus, like the Kpelle, people everywhere are able to learn to reason deductively, but the areas in which they apply such reasoning will depend on their experiences and needs.

The development of cognitive abilities likewise reveals human commonalities and cultural differences. Cross-cultural studies have supported Jean Piaget's theory of the hierarchical sequence of cognitive stages, which we discussed in Chapter 7. Children everywhere are able to progress from the sensorimotor stage to the preoperational stage, and on to concrete operations and formal operations such as deductive reasoning. But cultural differences may occur in the rate of development of these stages, because cultures differ in which cognitive skills are needed and nurtured in their members (J. Miller, 1999; Rogoff & Chavajay, 1995). For example, children in Zambia get a lot of experience making models out of wire and sticks, but they do not get the chance to do much drawing, as children in industrialized cultures do. If you measure these children's visual skills and spatial intelligence, you will find cultural differences, reflecting the children's different experiences in modeling and making things (Serpell, 1994).

Pierre Dasen (1994), who studied with Piaget, spent years testing Piaget's theory in different cultural contexts: among the Aborigines in Australia, the Inuit in Canada, the Ebri and the Baoulé of the Ivory Coast, and the Kikuyu in Kenya. Dasen found that traditional nomadic hunting peoples, such as the Inuit and the Aborigines, do not quantify things and do not need to. The Aborigines have number words only up to five; after that, all quantities are described as "many." In such cultures, the cognitive ability to understand the conservation of quantity or number (for example, that an amount of water remains the same whether it is in a tall, narrow glass or a short, fat one) develops late, if at all. But nomadic hunting tribes rely on their spatial orientation, because they need to know where water holes and successful hunting routes are, and so spatial abilities develop rapidly. In contrast, children who live in settled agricultural communities, such as the Baoulé, develop rapidly in the domain of quantification and much more slowly in spatial reasoning.

Culture and the Measurement of Intelligence

Understanding how culture defines and shapes intelligence has had enormous implications, as you might expect, for educational policy and for the industry of intelligence testing. The sociocultural perspective has highlighted two important issues: First, is it possible to design a test of intelligence that applies to everyone across all cultures? Second, if there are many kinds of intelligence, is it wrong to use a test that accurately measures only the kind of intelligence valued by the dominant culture?

A bit of history is instructive. Intelligence testing began in 1904, when the French Ministry of Education asked psychologist Alfred Binet to design a test that would identify individual children who were slow learners and who would therefore benefit from remedial work. The ministry was reluctant to let teachers identify such children, because the teachers might have prejudices about the low-income children who were being admitted to public schools for the first time. They wanted a more objective approach. (The method Binet developed for measuring IQ is described in Chapter 3.)

Binet emphasized that his test merely *sampled* a kind of mental ability and should not be confused with intelligence itself. He intended the test to be given to each child individually, so the test-giver could see whether a child was ill or nervous, had poor vision, or was not trying. The purpose was to identify and help children with learning problems, not to rank them. But when Binet's test crossed the Atlantic to the United States, his original intentions were lost at sea. Stanford psychologist Lewis Terman revised Binet's test and established norms for American children. (Terman's version, the Stanford-Binet Intelligence Scale, was first published in 1916 and has been updated several times since.) Unlike the French, Americans assumed that IQ tests revealed a permanent, inherited trait, and they used the test not to bring slow learners up to the average but to track people according to their presumed "natural" abilities or failings (Gould, 1996).

The original intelligence tests developed for use in American schools favored city children over rural ones, middle-class children over poor ones, and white children over nonwhite children. One item, for example, asked whether the Emperor Concerto was written by Beethoven, Mozart, Bach, Brahms, or Mahler. (The answer is Beethoven.) The tests also favored the problem-solving strategies emphasized in Western cultures (Serpell, 1994). In the West, white, middle-class children typically learn to classify things by category—to say that an apple and a peach are similar because they are both fruits, and that a saw and a rake are similar because they are both tools. But children who are not trained in middle-class ways of sorting things may classify objects according to their function. They will say that an apple and a peach are similar because they taste good. That's a charming and innovative answer, but it is one that test-givers interpret as less intelligent (Miller-Jones, 1989).

Throughout the 1960s and 1970s, criticisms of the inherent cultural biases in the IQ test became noisier. Test-makers responded by trying to construct tests that were *culture free*. Such tests were usually nonverbal; in some, instructions were even pantomimed. Psychologists also tried to design tests that were *culture fair*. Their aim was not to eliminate the influence of culture, but to find items that incorporate knowledge and skills common to many different cultures. But both approaches were less successful than originally hoped for because cultural values affect just about *everything* to do with taking a test: a person's attitude toward tests, comfort in the settings required for testing, motivation, rapport with the test-giver, competitiveness, and experience in solving problems independently rather than with others (Anastasi & Urbina, 1997; López, 1995).

In theory, it should be possible to establish test norms that are not based on white urban children, by throwing out items on which such children get higher scores than others. A similar strategy was actually used years ago to eliminate gender differences in IQ. On early tests, girls scored higher than boys at every age (Samelson, 1979). No one was willing to conclude that males were intellectually inferior, so in the 1937 revision of the Stanford-Binet test, Lewis Terman simply deleted the items on which boys had done poorly. Poof! No sex differences.

But few people seem willing to do for cultural differences what Terman did for gender differences, and the reason reveals a dilemma at the heart of intelligence testing. Intelligence tests put some groups of children at a disadvantage, yet they also measure skills and knowledge useful in the classroom. How can educators recognize and accept cultural differences and, at the same time, require students to demonstrate mastery of the skills, knowledge, and attitudes that will help them succeed in school and in the larger society? How can they eliminate cultural biases from tests, while recognizing that cultural differences exist?

Many scientists believe that it is important for society to keep using IQ tests. The tests predict school performance fairly well, and they identify not only the mentally retarded but also gifted students who have not previously considered higher education. To these scientists, concealing the effects of cultural disadvantage by rejecting conventional tests is "equivalent to breaking a thermometer because it registers a body temperature of 101" (Anastasi, 1988). When the tests reveal group differences, the pro-test camp maintains, the solution is to give special help to children who need it so they can do better. But other social scientists feel that conventional mental tests do more harm than good. Sociologist Jane Mercer (1988) tried for years to get testers to understand that children can be *ignorant* of information required by IQ tests without being *stupid,* but she finally gave up, resolving instead to "kill the IQ test."

The resolution of the IQ debate may ultimately depend on whether test-users can learn to use intelligence tests more intelligently—by keeping a person's background in mind, interpreting the results cautiously, and using results to benefit individual children. But the sociocultural perspective reminds us that no psychological test exists in a cultural vacuum, and its use will depend on the culture's politics, prejudices, racial and gender ideologies, and educational goals. One ironic lesson of a sociocultural analysis is that the IQ controversy might never have occurred if the United States had imported Binet's cultural values along with his test of intelligence.

Culture and Academic Performance

Cross-cultural findings also shed light on why cultures and ethnic groups may differ, on the average, in their academic performance. (The biological perspective, as we saw in Chapter 3, can account for some of the individual variation in mental abilities within a group, but not for average differences *between* groups.) One factor has to do with cultural beliefs about the origins of intelligence and the reasons for achievement.

For many years, Harold Stevenson and his colleagues have been studying attitudes toward academic achievement in Japan, China, and the United States. The researchers began in 1980 by comparing large samples of first- and fifth-grade children, their parents, and their teachers in Minneapolis, Sendai (Japan), and Taipei (Taiwan). In another project, they compared children from 20 schools in Chicago and 11 schools in Beijing (Stevenson & Stigler, 1992). In 1990, Stevenson, along with Chuansheng Chen and Shin-ying Lee (1993), revisited the original schools to collect new data on fifth-graders, and they also retested many of the children who had been in the 1980 study and who were now in the eleventh grade.

In 1980, the Asian children far outperformed the American children on a broad battery of mathematical tests. On computations and word problems, there was virtually no overlap between schools, with the lowest-scoring Beijing schools doing better than the highest-scoring Chicago schools. By 1990, the gap between the Asian and American children had grown even greater. Only 4 percent of the Chinese children and 10 percent of the Japanese children had scores as low as those of the *average* American child.

These differences could not be accounted for by educational resources: The Chinese had worse facilities and larger classes than the Americans, and on average, the Chinese parents were poorer and less educated than the American parents. Nor did it have anything to do with intellectual ability in general, because the American children were just as knowledgeable and capable as the Asian children on tests of general information. But the Asians and Americans were worlds apart, so to speak, in their attitudes, expectations, and efforts:

✦ **Beliefs about intelligence.** American parents, teachers, and children are far and away more likely than Asians to believe that mathematical ability is innate. They think that if you "have it," you don't have to work hard, and if you don't have it, there is no point in trying (see Figure 10.2 on the next page).

✦ **Standards.** American parents have far lower standards for their children's performance; they are satisfied with scores barely above average on a 100-point test. The Chinese and Japanese parents are happy only with very high scores.

✦ **Values.** American students do not value education as much as Asian students do and are more complacent about doing mediocre work. When asked what they would wish for if a wizard could give them anything they wanted, more than 60 percent of the Chinese fifth-graders named something related to their education. Can you guess what the American children wanted? A majority said money or possessions.

Culturally influenced ideas about the nature of intelligence often become internalized, affecting how well children and adults within a society do on tests of mental abilities. Stereotypes that portray members of certain ethnicities, women, old people,

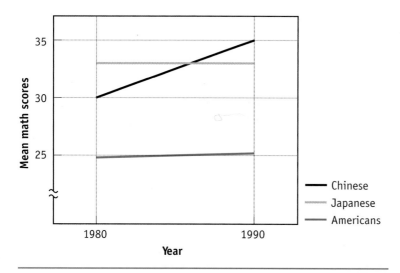

FIGURE 10.2 MATH PERFORMANCE OF ASIAN AND AMERICAN CHILDREN *In 1980 and again in 1990, the math performance of fifth-graders in Taiwan and Japan far outstripped that of children in the United States (Stevenson, Chen, & Lee, 1993). This performance gap was associated with differences in attitudes, standards, and effort.*

or working-class people as being "unintelligent" can actually depress the test performance of people in these groups. You might think that a woman would say, "So sexists think women are dumb at math? I'll show *them*" or that an African-American would say, "So racists believe that blacks aren't as smart as whites? Just give me that exam." But often that is not what happens.

On the contrary, such individuals commonly feel a burden of doubt about their abilities that Claude Steele (1992, 1997) has labeled **stereotype threat.** The threat occurs because they believe that if they do not do well, they will confirm the stereotypes about their group. Their anxiety may then worsen their performance. Or they may cope by "disidentifying" with the test, saying to themselves, in effect, "The outcome of this test has no bearing on how I feel about myself" (Major et al., 1998). As a result, they may not be motivated to do well.

Stereotype threat has been shown to affect the test performance of many African-Americans, low-income people, women, and elderly people—all of whom perform better on tests when they are not feeling self-conscious about themselves as members of negatively stereotyped groups (Brown & Josephs, 1999; Croizen & Claire, 1998; Levy, 1996; Steele & Aronson, 1995). But white men, too, can be affected by stereotype threat. White male athletes who are self-conscious about the stereotype that "white

stereotype threat A burden of doubt a person feels about his or her performance, due to negative stereotypes about his or her group's abilities.

men can't jump" actually do *not* jump as high in the presence of a black experimenter as in the presence of a white one (Garcia, Helms, & Garcia, undated)!

Positive stereotypes, in contrast, can *improve* performance. When Asian-American women answered a questionnaire about their ethnicity, they then performed better on a math test than did Asian-American women who did not answer the questionnaire. Apparently, the positive stereotype—"Asians are good at math"—had been activated, and the women tried to live up to it. But when the women answered a questionnaire about their *gender* and then took the test, they did worse than the control group! In this case, a negative stereotype—"women are bad at math"—had been activated (Shih, Pittinsky, & Ambady, 1999).

When it comes to intelligence, therefore, the lesson is clear: Cultural attitudes and values about achievement, about what intelligence is and whether it is innate or a result of effort, and about which groups have "natural" ability, play a big role in how "intelligent" people become.

What Do You Know?

Are you feeling smart about intelligence?

1. *True or false:* Culture-fair tests have eliminated group differences that show up on traditional IQ tests.

2. When Alfred Binet designed the first IQ test, his goal was to (a) label and categorize children, (b) identify children who could benefit from individualized programs, (c) study intellectual differences among ethnic groups.

3. From the sociocultural view, what is the "dilemma at the heart of IQ testing"?

4. Hilda, who is 66, is about to take an IQ test, but she is worried because she knows that older people are often assumed to have diminished mental abilities. Hilda is being affected by _____.

5. A researcher studying ethnic differences in children's mental abilities focuses on one group's lower performance in school. What factors might cultural psychologists investigate to explain this difference?

ANSWERS:

1. false 2. b 3. How can educators accept the existence of cultural differences that put some children at a disadvantage on IQ tests, and at the same time require students to demonstrate mastery of the skills need for success in school and in the larger society; skills measured by standard IQ tests? 4. stereotype threat 5. Some factors include cultural experiences in each group, which foster or deemphasize particular abilities; how the groups define "intelligence"; each group's values and attitudes toward academic success; and whether parents, teachers, and children believe that mental abilities are innate or the result of hard work.

THE ORIGINS OF CULTURE

When most people read about the customs of other cultures, they are inclined to say, "Oh, boy, I like the attitudes of the Gorks but I hate the habits of the Zorks." Yet a culture's practices cannot easily be exported elsewhere, like cheese, or surgically removed, like a tumor. The reason is that a culture's attitudes and practices are deeply embedded in its history, environment, economy, and survival needs (Diamond, 1997).

To explain the origins of cultural customs, researchers working from a sociocultural perspective study a culture's political system and its economy, and how that economy is affected by geography, natural resources, and even the weather. They find out who controls and distributes the resources, and how safe a society is from interlopers. They study the kinds of work that people do. They observe whether there is environmental pressure on a group to produce more children or to have fewer of them. To illustrate this approach, we will take a look at sociocultural explanations of the origins of gender roles and why those roles vary across cultures.

Let's start with a story. A young boy notices, at an early age, that he seems different from other boys. He prefers playing with girls. He is attracted to the work adult women do, such as cooking and sewing. He often dreams of being a girl, and he even likes to put on girls' clothes. As he enters adolescence, people begin to whisper that he's "different," that he seems feminine in his movements, posture, and language. One day the boy can hide his secret feelings no longer and reveals them to his parents.

How will his parents respond? By now you will not be surprised to know that the answer depends on their culture. In the United States, many parents would react with tears, anger, or guilt. They might haul their son off to a psychiatrist, who would diagnose him as having a "gender identity disorder" and begin intensive treatment. But these reactions are not universal. Until the late 1800s, in a number of Plains Indians and western American Indian tribes, parents and other elders reacted with sympathy and understanding when a young man wanted to live the life of a woman. A man in this role (whom whites called a *berdache*) was often given an honored status as a shaman, a person with the power to cure illness and act as an intermediary between the natural and the spiritual worlds, and he was permitted to dress as and perform the duties of a woman. In some tribes, he was even permitted to marry another man (Williams, 1986).

In the Sambian society of Papua New Guinea, parents would react still differently (Herdt, 1984). In Sambia, all adolescent boys are *required* to engage in oral sex with older males as part of their initiation into manhood. Sambians believe that a boy cannot mature unless he ingests another man's semen over a period of several years. However, Sambian parents would react with shock and disbelief if a son said he wanted to live as a woman. Every man and woman in Sambian society marries someone of the other sex and performs the work assigned to his or her own sex.

These diverse reactions support the view of most cultural psychologists that anatomical *sex* does not determine *gender*—the duties, rights, and behaviors a culture considers appropriate or inappropriate for males and females. (As we saw in discussing gender typing in Chapter 6, social-cognitive learning theorists also make this

Mary Read op Jamaica in de Gevangenisse overleden

A person's anatomical sex and the culturally assigned duties of gender do not always correspond. Throughout history, some men have chosen the roles and dress of women, sometimes with the approval of their communities. In the photo on the left, taken about 1885, We-Wha, a Zuni Indian man, wears the traditional dress and decoration of a woman. Likewise, some women have worn the dress and taken on the roles of men, as did the eighteenth-century pirate Mary Read (right).

point.) Sociobiologists and evolutionary psychologists believe that sex heavily influences gender—that the biological fact of being male or female plays a major role in determining what work the sexes do and the roles they play. But social and cultural psychologists are more interested in how the rules and roles of gender vary around the world, changing when necessary. By comparing different cultures, cross-cultural psychologists hope to identify which aspects of gender roles are universal and which are culturally specific.

Gender and Culture: Themes and Variations

First, let's consider the commonalities. In general, men have had, and continue to have, more status and more power than women, especially in public affairs. Men have fought the wars and they commit more acts of physical aggression and violence than women do. If a society's economy includes hunting large game, traveling a long way from home, or making weapons, men typically handle these activities. Women have had the primary responsibility for cooking, cleaning, and taking care of children. Corresponding with this division of tasks, in many cultures around the world, masculinity is regarded as something that boys must achieve through strenuous effort. Males must pass physical tests, endure pain, confront danger, suppress their emotions, and separate themselves psychologically and even physically from their mothers and the world of women. Sometimes they have to prove their self-reliance and courage in harsh initiation rites. Femininity, in contrast, is generally associated with responsibility, obedience, and child care, and it is seen as something that develops without any special intervention from others (Archer, 1996).

Those are the common themes. But the status of women varies dramatically around the world, being highest in Scandinavian countries and lowest in Bangladesh and Afghanistan. (Women's status has been assessed by measures of economic security, educational opportunities, access to birth control and medical care, degree of self-determination, participation in public and political life, power to make decisions in the family, and physical safety.) In some places, women are completely under the rule of men. Women in Saudi Arabia are not allowed to drive a car; many girls in India submit to arranged marriages as early as age 9. Yet elsewhere, women are attaining greater power and independence. In the twentieth century, women were elected heads of state in Israel, India, Norway, England, Iceland, Pakistan, Nicaragua, Bangladesh (where most women have extremely low status), Poland, Ireland, Turkey, . . . the list keeps growing. And there are many other variations in men's and women's roles:

◆ **WORK.** The content of what is considered "men's work" and "women's work" varies from culture to culture. In some places, dentistry and teaching are men's work; in others, these are considered female jobs.

◆ **EMOTIONS.** In the United States and Canada, women are considered the "emotional" sex and express their emotions more often and more freely than most men (Kring & Gordon, 1998). But in cultures throughout the Middle East and South America, men are expected to be as emotionally expressive as women, or even more so, and many Asian cultures expect *both* sexes to control their emotions (Buck & Teng, 1987).

◆ **DEGREE OF CONTACT.** In many farm communities and in most modern occupations in North America and Europe, men and women work together. At the other end of the continuum, men and women are forbidden to work, pray, or socialize together. Some Middle Eastern societies practice *purdah*, the custom of veiling women and secluding them from all male eyes except those of their close relatives.

◆ **SEXUALITY.** In some cultures, particularly those of East Asia, Southeast Asia, and Muslim societies, female chastity is highly prized. Women are expected to suppress all sexual feeling until marriage, and premarital or extramarital sex is cause for the woman's ostracism from the community or even her death. Yet in other cultures, such as those of Polynesia, Scandinavia, and northern Europe, female chastity is considered unimportant (Buss, 1995; Hatfield & Rapson, 1996). Women are expected to have sex before marriage, and even extramarital sex is not necessarily cause for alarm.

✦ NOTIONS OF DIFFERENCE. Some cultures exaggerate differences between the sexes; others minimize them. Among the Ifaluk, the Tahitians, and the people of Sudest Island near New Guinea, men and women do not regard each other as the "opposite" sex or even as being very different (Lepowsky, 1994; Lutz, 1988). Tahitian men are not more aggressive than women, nor are women gentler or more nurturant than men (Levy, 1984). To Tahitians, gender is no big deal.

Gender and Culture: Explaining the Differences

Cultural researchers argue that biological differences cannot account for the wide variation in gender roles around the world. They have examined instead two other fundamental factors that exaggerate or reduce gender differences: *production* (matters pertaining to the economy and the creation of food, clothing, and shelter) and *reproduction* (matters pertaining to the bearing, raising, and nurturing of children).

One important finding is that strict concepts of manhood tend to exist wherever there is a great deal of competition for resources—which is to say, in most places (Gilmore, 1990). For the human species, life has usually been harsh. Consider a group trying to survive in the wilds of a South American forest; or in the dry and unforgiving landscape of the desert; or in an icy Arctic terrain that imposes limits on the number of people who can survive by fishing. When conditions like these exist, men are the sex that is taught to hunt for large game, compete with one another for resources, and fight off enemies. Men are socialized to face confrontation and to resist the impulse to retreat from danger. They are "toughened up" and pushed to take risks, even with their lives. (This division of labor may originally have occurred because of men's relatively greater upper-body muscular strength and the fact that they do not become pregnant or nurse children.)

How do you get men to wage war and risk death, go off on long treks for food, and be willing to get bloodied defending the homestead? Far from being natural to men, some cultural researchers argue, aggressiveness has to be constantly rewarded. To persuade men to wage war and risk death, societies have to give them something; and the something is prestige, power—and women (Harris, 1997). That in turn means you have to raise obedient women; if the king is going to offer his daughter in marriage to the bravest warrior, she has to agree to be handed over. In contrast, in societies such as Tahiti and Sudest Island, where resources are abundant and there are

no serious hazards or enemies to worry about, men do not feel they have to prove themselves or set themselves apart from women (Lepowsky, 1994).

Honor, Economics, and Male Aggression. To researchers in the biological perspective, male aggression is largely a matter of genetic predispositions and testosterone. To researchers in the learning perspective, it is largely a result of a man's learning history—the rewards or punishments that follow aggressive behavior. But to researchers in the sociocultural perspective, a culture's economy and social structure best explain the worldwide variations in the degree of aggression required and expected of men.

In a fascinating analysis of the rates of violence in different regional cultures of the United States, Richard Nisbett (1993) set out to explain why the American South, and some western regions of the country originally settled by southerners, have much higher rates of white homicide than the rest of the country has. Southerners are more likely to endorse the use of violence for protection (recall the reactions to Rodney Peairs's shooting of the Japanese exchange student) and as the proper response to perceived insults. "Violence has been associated with the South since the time of the American Revolution," begins an essay in the *Encyclopedia of Southern Culture,* and it goes on to devote 39 pages to bloodcurdling accounts of feuds, duels, lynchings, violent sports, and murder.

Nisbett ruled out explanations based on poverty and racial tensions. Although both factors are associated with violence, "southernness" remained a predictor of homicide even when he controlled for regional differences in poverty and the percentage of blacks in the population, by county. Nisbett also ruled out a history of slavery as an explanation; regions of the South that had the highest concentrations of slaves in the past have the lowest white homicide rates today.

Nisbett argues that rates of violence in the South derive ultimately from economic causes. The New England and middle Atlantic states were settled by Puritans, Quakers, and Dutch farmers and artisans who had an advanced agricultural economy. For them, the best policy was one of cooperation for the common good. In contrast, the South was settled largely by immigrants from Scotland and Ireland, whose economies were based on herding and hunting, activities that provided their economic base in America.

Why should herding, as opposed to farming, make such a difference in rates of violence? People who depend economically on their herds are extremely vulnerable; their livelihoods can be lost in an instant by the theft of their animals. To reduce the likelihood of theft, says Nisbett, herders "cultivate a posture of extreme vigilance toward any act that might be perceived as threatening in any way, and respond with sufficient force to frighten the offender and the community into recognizing that they are not to be trifled with." This is why cattle rustling and horse thievery were capital crimes in the Old West, and why Mediterranean and Middle Eastern herding cultures also place a high value on male aggressiveness. When Nisbett examined agricultural practices within the South, he found that homicide rates were more than twice as high in the hills and dry plains regions (where herding occurs) as in farming regions.

The emphasis on aggressiveness and vigilance in herding cultures, in turn, fosters a *culture of honor,* in which even apparently small disputes and trivial insults (trivial to people from other cultures, that is) put a man's reputation for toughness on the line, requiring him to respond with violence to restore his status (Cohen, 1998). Although the herding economy has become less important in the South and West, the legacy of its culture of honor remains. Nisbett and his colleagues conducted three experiments with male students who had grown up in the North or the South. In each, students were insulted by a confederate and called an offensive name. Northerners were relatively unaffected by the insult—they shrugged it off—but southerners went ballistic! They felt that their masculine reputation was threatened, and they were more upset (as shown by a rise in their stress hormones), more physiologically primed for aggression (as shown by a rise in testosterone levels), and more likely to retaliate aggressively than northerners were (Cohen et al., 1996).

Because of research like this, cultural psychologists conclude that male biology does not inevitably dictate aggressive behavior. Males are raised to behave aggressively in cultures of honor, which promote violence as a way to restore a man's reputation and protect society's economic interests.

Industrialization and Equality. In terms of the kinds of gender roles they promote, cultures fall along a continuum from *traditional* to *modern (egalitarian)*. In a cross-cultural study of 100 men and women from each of 14 countries in North and South America, Europe, and Asia, people filled out an inventory describing ideal role relationships between women and men (Best & Williams, 1993). Sample items included, "The husband should be regarded as the legal representative of the family group in all matters of law" (a traditional attitude) and "A woman should have exactly the same freedom of action as a man" (a modern attitude). The results showed that as countries become industrialized and urban, their gender roles also become more modern. Why might this be so?

One answer is that industrialization eliminates the traditional reasons for a sexual division of labor. Most jobs in industrial nations, including military jobs, now involve service skills and brainwork that both sexes can do—a situation that has never existed before in human history. Another profound change also occurred in the twentieth century for the first time: Reproduction was revolutionized. Although women in many countries still lack access to safe and affordable contraceptives, it is now technologically possible for women to limit reliably the number of children they will have and to plan when to have them.

Along with these changes, ideas about the "natural" qualities of men and women are being transformed. It is no longer news that a woman can be an astronaut or run a country. And it is no longer news that many men, whose own fathers would no more have diapered a baby than jumped into a vat of boiling oil, now want to be involved fathers and are spending nearly twice as many hours a day with their kids as their own fathers did (Barnett & Rivers, 1996; Bianchi & Robinson, 2000; Gerson, 1993). In England in May 2000, the whole country got involved in the question of whether the Prime Minister, Tony Blair, would take paternity leave when his fourth baby was born. (He did.)

What cross-cultural research shows, then, is that many of our gender arrangements, and the qualities associated with being male and female, are affected by practical conditions, such as a culture's economy and the kind of labor force it needs. These conditions have a strong influence in determining whether men are expected to be fierce or gentle, and whether women are expected to be passive or ambitious. This perspective also suggests that no matter how entrenched our own cultural habits are, they can change depending on the kind of work we do, technological advances, and the needs of society.

What Do You Know?

Your gender is unlikely to affect your answers to these questions.

1. Which of the following is most common in cultures around the world? (a) Women do the weaving, marketing, and teaching; (b) men have more status and power in public affairs than women do; (c) men and women are physically separated while working.

2. What two general factors do cultural researchers emphasize in explaining variations in gender roles around the world?

3. Studies of regional differences in violence suggest that an important cause of male aggressiveness is (a) how people earn their livings, (b) racial tensions, (c) poverty, (d) hormones.

ANSWERS:

1. b. 2. production and reproduction 3. a

CROSS-CULTURAL RELATIONS

By now, you should be persuaded that cultures differ in countless ways and that a culture's customs do not arise for some arbitrary or foolish reason. But it has probably also been difficult for you to turn off your mental moral evaluator, the little voice that says, "Boy, a culture that does *that* must really be dumb." That little voice, which everyone hears to one degree or another, is the echo of **ethnocentrism,** the belief that your own cultural, social, or ethnic group is superior to all others. Ethnocentric thinking is especially common during war, when enemies regard each other as inhuman and deserving of destruction. But you can see everyday examples of it at football games, during elections, or in discussions of controversial issues.

Ethnocentrism is so pervasive that it is even embedded in some languages: The Chinese word for China means "the center of the world" and both the Navajo and the Inuit call themselves simply "The People." Ethnocentrism is probably universal because it aids survival by making people feel attached to their own group and willing to work

---

ethnocentrism The belief that one's own ethnic group, nation, or religion is superior to all others.

on the group's behalf, even dying for the group when necessary. But does the fact that people feel good about their own culture or nationality (or gender, or school) mean that prejudice toward other groups is inevitable? Does it mean we are destined to live in a world of ethnic separatism? Can't people say, "Well, I'm happy being a Burgendian, and I love our customs, but I also am grateful to the people who invented jazz, television, paper, pizza, the tango, democracy, antibiotics . . ."?

Ethnocentrism and Stereotypes

Ethnocentrism rests on a basic social identity: Us. As soon as people have created a category called "us," however, they invariably perceive everybody else as "not us." The experiment at Robbers Cave (described in Chapter 9) showed how easy it is to activate *us-them thinking* when any two groups perceive themselves to be in competition. Although competition is sufficient to stimulate ethnocentrism, however, it isn't necessary. Just being a member of an in-group will do it.

In fact, feelings of in-group superiority can be manufactured in a minute in a laboratory, as Henri Tajfel and his colleagues (1971) first demonstrated in a classic experiment with British schoolboys. Tajfel showed the boys slides with varying numbers of dots on them and asked the boys to guess how many dots there were. The boys were arbitrarily told they were "overestimators" or "underestimators" and were then asked to work on another task. In this phase, they had the chance to allocate points to other boys who were known to be overestimators or underestimators. Although each boy worked alone in a private cubicle, almost every single one assigned far more points to other boys he thought were like him, an overestimator or an underestimator. As the boys emerged from their rooms, they were asked, "Which were you?"—and the answer received a mix of cheers and boos from the others.

Even the collective pronouns that apply to *us* and *them* are powerful emotional signals. In one experiment, which students believed was testing their verbal skills, nonsense syllables such as *xeh, yof, laj,* or *wuh* were randomly paired with either an in-group word (*us, we,* or *ours*), an out-group word (*them, they,* or *theirs*), or, for a control measure, another pronoun (such as *he, hers,* or *yours*). The students then had to rate the syllables on how pleasant or unpleasant they were. Why, you might ask, would anyone have an emotional reaction to the nonsense word *yof*? Yet students liked the nonsense syllables significantly more when they had been paired with in-group words. Not one student guessed why; none was aware of how the words had been paired (Perdue et al., 1990).

Us-them thinking both creates and reflects stereotyping. A **stereotype** is a summary impression of a group of people in which a person believes that all members of that group share a common trait or traits. Stereotypes may be negative ("Artists are crazy"), positive ("My school produces the best athletes"), or neutral. There are stereotypes of people who drive SUVs or BMWs, of men who wear earrings and of

---

stereotype A summary impression of a group, in which a person believes that all members of the group share a common trait or traits (positive, negative, or neutral).

women who wear business suits, of engineering students and art students, of feminists and fraternity members.

Stereotypes play an important role in human thinking. They help us quickly process new information and retrieve memories. They allow us to organize experience, make sense of differences among groups, and predict how people will behave (Garcia-Marques & Mackie, 1999). They are useful "tools in the mental toolbox"—energy-saving devices that allow us to make efficient decisions (Macrae, Milne, & Bodenhausen, 1994). The problem with stereotypes is not that they are always wrong; many have a grain of truth, capturing with some accuracy something about a group. The problems occur when people assume that the grain of truth is the whole seashore. Stereotypes reflect reality but also distort it in three ways (Judd et al., 1995):

1. *Stereotypes accentuate differences between groups.* They emphasize the ways in which groups are different and overlook the common features. So the stereotyped group may seem odd, unfamiliar, or dangerous—"not like us."

2. *Stereotypes produce selective perception.* People tend to see only the evidence that fits the stereotype and reject any perceptions that do not fit.

3. *Stereotypes underestimate differences within other groups.* People realize that their own groups are made up of all kinds of individuals: Fred is stingy, Fatima is generous. But stereotypes create the impression that all members of other groups are the same: One rude French waiter means that all French people are rude; one Greek thief means that all Greeks are thieves. If someone in their own group is rude or steals, however, most people draw no such conclusions.[1]

Some stereotypes stem from cultural values about whether a particular behavior is desirable or unacceptable, which is why people from different cultures may evaluate the same event differently (Taylor & Porter, 1994). For example, Chinese students in Hong Kong, where communalism and respect for elders are valued, think that a student who comes late to class or argues with a parent about grades is being selfish and disrespectful of adults. But Australian students, who value individualism, think that the same behavior is perfectly appropriate (Forgas & Bond, 1985). You can see how the Chinese might form negative stereotypes of "rude, disrespectful Australians," and how the Australians might form negative stereotypes of the "mindlessly obedient" Chinese. And it is a small step from negative stereotypes to prejudice.

Prejudice

A *prejudice* consists of a negative stereotype and a strong, unreasonable dislike or hatred of a group or its individual members. Feelings of prejudice violate the spirit of

---

[1]This cognitive habit of perceiving diversity in your own group but not in others starts early. Social psychologist Marilynn Brewer (1993) reported that her daughter returned from kindergarten one day announcing that "Boys are crybabies." The child's evidence was that she had seen two boys crying on their first day away from home. Brewer asked whether there hadn't been little girls who cried also. Oh yes, said her daughter, "But only some girls cry; I didn't cry."

critical thinking because they resist rational argument and evidence. In his classic book *The Nature of Prejudice,* social psychologist Gordon Allport (1954/1979) described the responses characteristic of a prejudiced person when confronted with evidence contradicting his or her beliefs:

> Mr. X: The trouble with Jews is that they only take care of their own group.
>
> Mr. Y: But the record of the Community Chest campaign shows that they give more generously, in proportion to their numbers, to the general charities of the community, than do non-Jews.
>
> Mr. X: That shows they are always trying to buy favor and intrude into Christian affairs. They think of nothing but money; that is why there are so many Jewish bankers.
>
> Mr. Y: But a recent study shows that the percentage of Jews in the banking business is negligible, far smaller than the percentage of non-Jews.
>
> Mr. X: That's just it; they don't go in for respectable business; they are only in the movie business or run night clubs.

Notice that Mr. X does not respond to Mr. Y's evidence; he just uses it to slide along to another reason for his dislike of Jews. That is the slippery nature of prejudice. Elliot Aronson (1999b) gives another example: Suppose someone tried to persuade you to eat broiled insects. "Ugh," you might say, "they are so ugly." "But so are lobsters," he says, "and lots of people love lobsters." "Well, insects have no food value," you say. "Actually, they are a good source of protein," he answers. He might try other arguments, but the fact is that you have a food prejudice against eating insects, a reaction that exists in some cultures but by no means all. Prejudices can persist in the complete absence of experience: Mr. X may never have met a Jewish person; you may never have eaten broiled locusts. And, unlike misconceptions that can be corrected with information, prejudices are often stubbornly resistant to change.

The Origins of Prejudice.   Prejudice is a universal human experience because it has so many sources: evolutionary, psychological, social, and cultural. An evolutionary explanation is that prejudice bonds people to their groups, making them willing to fight and die for "their own kind" and thereby increasing the chances of the group's survival. This explanation accounts for the fact that prejudices toward unfamiliar "outsiders" are virtually universal and relatively easy to instill in children (Fishbein, 1996). In this respect, prejudice is the partner of ethnocentrism; it is not only that we are good, but also that they are bad, lazy, or dumb (Brewer, 1999).

Psychologically, prejudice often serves to ward off feelings of uncertainty and fear. Prejudiced persons may transfer their worries onto the target group; thus a person who has doubts or anxieties about his own sexuality may develop a hatred of gay people. Prejudice also allows people to use the target group as a scapegoat: "Those people are the source of all my troubles." And, as research from many nations has confirmed, prejudice is a tonic for low self-esteem: People puff up their own low self-worth by disliking or hating groups they see as inferior (Islam & Hewstone, 1993; Stephan et al., 1994; Tajfel & Turner, 1986).

In a demonstration of the link between low self-esteem and prejudice, 60 students participated in what they believed were two separate studies (Fein & Spencer, 1997). In the first, they got positive or negative feedback about their performance on a test of "social perceptiveness" and verbal skills. In the second, they were asked to evaluate the résumé of a woman who had applied for a job as personnel manager. All the subjects were shown the same résumé and photograph of the candidate, but half were told her name was Julie Goldberg and that she did volunteer work for a Jewish organization, and half were told her name was Maria D'Agostino and that she volunteered at a Catholic organization. (Data from the few Jewish students in the sample were excluded.) The students who were feeling good about their test scores did not evaluate the "Jewish" woman differently from the "Italian" woman. But those who had received a blow to their self-esteem evaluated the woman they believed to be Jewish more harshly than the Italian candidate. Their denigration of her, in turn, had the effect of raising their own self-esteem. The same results occurred when heterosexual students evaluated a man they believed to be gay. Their evaluations of him were harsher when their self-esteem had been threatened (Fein & Spencer, 1997).

Not all prejudices have psychological roots, however. From a social-psychological point of view, many prejudices are a result of factors *outside* the individual. For example, as a result of groupthink and conformity, many people go along with the biased views of friends, relatives, or associates rather than risk losing these relationships or being called troublemakers. Some prejudices are acquired mindlessly as children grow up, as when parents let them know, subtly or explicitly, that "we don't associate with people like that." And some prejudices are acquired from advertising, movies, and other media that perpetuate derogatory images of certain groups, such as old people or fat people.

From a cultural perspective, one of the most important external factors in maintaining prejudice is its economic function: Prejudice often pays off. Prejudice makes official forms of discrimination seem legitimate, by justifying the majority group's dominance, status, or greater wealth (Sidanius, Pratto, & Bobo, 1996). Historically, white men in positions of power have justified their exclusion of women, blacks, and other minorities from the workplace and politics by claiming that those groups were inferior, irrational, or incompetent (Gould, 1996). But it is not just powerful white men who do this. *Any* majority group—of any ethnicity, gender, or nationality—that benefits by discriminating against a minority will call upon prejudice to legitimize its actions. For example, in a series of experiments in Bangladesh, Muslims (who are the majority there) and Hindus (a minority) both revealed strong in-group favoritism, but only the Muslims also felt the need to denigrate the minority Hindus (Islam & Hewstone, 1993).

Just as prejudice legitimizes discrimination, it rationalizes conflict and war. Although it is widely believed that prejudice is the primary cause of fighting between groups, prejudice is actually more often a *result* of conflict. When any two groups are in direct competition for jobs, or when people are worried about their incomes and the safety of their communities, prejudice between them increases (Aronson, 1999b; Doty, Peterson, & Winter, 1991). Consider the rise and fall of attitudes toward Chinese immigrants in the United States in the nineteenth century, as reported in newspapers of the time. When the Chinese were working in the gold mines and potentially taking jobs from white laborers, whites described them as "depraved and vicious . . . gross gluttons . . . bloodthirsty and inhuman" (quoted in Aronson, 1999b). Just a decade later, when the Chinese began working on the transcontinental railroad—doing difficult and dangerous jobs that few white men wanted—prejudice against them declined. Whites described them as hardworking, intelligent, and trustworthy. Then, after the railroad was finished and the Chinese had to compete with Civil War veterans for scarce jobs, white attitudes changed again. Whites now considered the Chinese to be "criminal," "crafty," "conniving," and "stupid." (The white newspapers did not report the attitudes of the Chinese.) Today too, during times of economic recession and high unemployment, or when people are feeling economically vulnerable, prejudice increases significantly—in the forms of negative attitudes toward minorities and also hate crimes against Jews, blacks, gay men, and other targeted minorities (Doty, Peterson, & Winter, 1991; Herek, 1998).

Similarly, when two nations are at war, prejudice toward the enemy allows each side to continue feeling righteous about its cause. Each side portrays people on the other side in stereotyped ways—calling them traitors, heathens, vermin, inhuman, baby-killers, or monsters—to demonize and dehumanize the enemy, making it seem that the enemy deserves to be killed.

The Varieties of Prejudice. One problem in studying prejudice is that not all prejudiced people are prejudiced in the same way or to the same extent. Gordon Allport (1954/1979) astutely observed that "defeated intellectually, prejudice lingers emotionally." That is, a person might realize that a prejudice is unwarranted, yet still feel uncomfortable with members of certain groups. Should we put this person in the same category as one who is an outspoken bigot or who actively discriminates against others because of their sex, culture, sexual orientation, weight, disability, or skin color? Do good intentions mitigate stupid or ignorant remarks? What if a person knows nothing about another culture and mindlessly blurts out a dopy remark that reflects that ignorance? Does that count as prejudice or mere thoughtlessness? These questions complicate the measurement of prejudice.

If you ask people directly about their attitudes, you might conclude that prejudice in the United States and Canada is declining. White attitudes toward integration have become steadily more favorable, and the belief that whites are superior to blacks has become much less prevalent (Plant & Devine, 1998). The number of men openly expressing prejudice toward women executives declined from 41 percent in 1965 to only 5 percent in 1985 (Tougas et al., 1995), and between 1970 and 1995, antiwoman attitudes in general dropped sharply (Twenge, 1997).

However, many social scientists believe that these statistics are misleading. Overt attitudes, they say, are not necessarily an accurate measure of prejudice, because people know they should not admit their prejudices. For example, when white students fill out a prejudice questionnaire in the presence of a black experimenter, they have lower prejudice scores than they do when the experimenter is white (Fazio et al., 1995). So researchers have turned to other ways of measuring prejudice. Some argue that prejudice toward blacks lurks behind a mask of *symbolic racism,* in which whites focus not on dislike of black individuals but on issues such as "reverse discrimination," "hard-core criminals," or "welfare abuse." In this view, such issues have become code words for the continuing animosity that many whites feel toward blacks (Bell, 1992; Jones, 1997). So instead of asking respondents about blacks as individuals or about feelings of prejudice in general, researchers might probe for hostile feelings that lie beneath surface attitudes. The same whites who will not admit to disliking blacks, for example, might agree that "blacks are getting too demanding in their push for equal rights" (Brauer, Wasel, & Niedenthal, 2000).

Another method of measuring prejudice is to observe how people who say they are unprejudiced actually behave when they are angry or stressed or have been insulted (Jones, 1991; Sinclair & Kunda, 1999). In one experiment, students thought they were giving shock to other students as a measure of biofeedback. White students initially showed *less* aggression toward blacks than toward whites. But as soon as the white students were angered by overhearing derogatory remarks about themselves, they showed *more* aggression toward blacks than toward whites (Rogers & Prentice-Dunn, 1981). (See Figure 10.3.) In another study, English-speaking Canadians who had been put through a frustrating experience with failure rated members of the out-group (French-

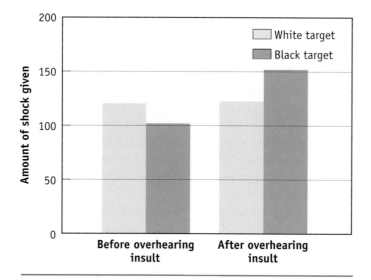

FIGURE 10.3 Provocation and Prejudice *White students, whether angered by the experimenter or not, gave the same amount of shock to other whites. But when they had been insulted, whites gave much higher levels of shock to blacks than they did when not angry (Rogers & Prentice-Dunn, 1981). Studies of the majority's behavior toward other minorities, such as Jews, gays, and French Canadians, find the same results.*

speaking Canadians) more negatively than did those who had not been frustrated (Meindl & Lerner, 1985). Findings like these imply that people are willing to control negative feelings toward their customary targets of prejudice under normal conditions. But as soon as they are angry, frustrated, or provoked, or suffer a loss of self-esteem, their real prejudice reveals itself.

A third approach to measuring prejudice relies on unobtrusive, *implicit* measures rather than direct, *explicit* attitude questionnaires or behavioral indicators (Fazio et al., 1995; Guglielmi, 1999). These methods were derived from studies of implicit memory in cognitive psychology (see Chapter 8). Implicit processes are assumed to be nonconscious, automatic, and unintentional, and hence a truer measure of a person's "real" prejudice. One example of an implicit measure is the *Implicit Association Test* (IAT), which taps people's unconscious associations between a stimulus and its degree of pleasantness or unpleasantness (Greenwald, McGhee, & Schwartz, 1998). On the IAT, people everywhere implicitly associate flowers and musical instruments with pleasant words (*happy, peace, family*) and weapons and insects with unpleasant ones (*crash, rotten, ugly*). Given these implicit links, it takes them longer to process discrepant associations, such as "insect + [pleasant word]."

Applying this approach to the measure of prejudice, researchers have found that many people who describe themselves as being unprejudiced nonetheless have unconscious prejudiced associations for certain groups. For example, the Japanese and the Koreans have a long history of mutual antagonism. In one experiment, ethnically Korean students found it more difficult to process Japanese names associated with pleasant words than Korean names with pleasant associations, and the reverse was true for the Japanese (Greenwald, McGhee, & Schwartz, 1998). The IAT has also been used to identify allegedly unconscious prejudices against blacks, women, and the elderly.

However, it is difficult to know what these implicit measures actually measure: "real" prejudice, unfamiliarity with the target stimulus, or activation of a stereotype. In one experiment with white and Asian-American students, those who were shown photos of highly admired blacks (Martin Luther King, Jr., Denzel Washington, and Michael Jordan) and admired elderly people (Mother Teresa and former television anchorman Walter Cronkite) showed a sharp drop in "unconscious prejudice" toward blacks and the elderly as measured by the IAT (Dasgupta, 1999). If unconscious prejudice can be manipulated simply by reminding people that not all members of a negatively stereotyped group are the same, is it really prejudice? If the IAT shows that people in any given group unconsciously prefer their own group to any other, is that a measure of prejudice or of social identity? And remember that, as we saw in Chapter 9, people find familiar names, products, and even nonsense syllables to be more pleasant than unfamiliar ones. So is the IAT measuring true prejudice toward a particular target or merely unfamiliarity with it?

As you can see, defining and measuring prejudice are not easy tasks. They involve distinguishing explicit attitudes from unconscious hostility, active dislike from simple discomfort, and what people say from how they actually behave. One review of the implicit-prejudice research concluded that prejudice is not a single thing, but a process that involves automatic activation of stereotypes upon thinking about a member of the target group; the decision to apply those stereotypes to a particular individual; and conscious beliefs and ways of behaving toward members of the target group. These three components may be strongly related for extremely prejudiced people but weakly related for others (Brauer, Wasel, & Niedenthal, 2000).

Efforts to Reduce Prejudice

Given the many sources and definitions of prejudice, no one method of reducing it is likely to work in all situations. That is why social and cultural psychologists have designed different programs to try to reduce cultural misunderstandings and prejudice, depending on the origins of a given conflict and the factors that are supporting it.

For example, according to Patricia Devine (1995), different strategies should be used with people who are trying to break their "prejudice habit" than with people who are perfectly comfortable with their bigotry. In the former situation, a "cycle of distrust" and animosity can emerge even when the majority and minority members of a group start off with the best intentions to get along. Some majority-group members may be self-conscious and anxious about doing the wrong thing. Their anxiety makes them behave awkwardly, for instance by blurting out dumb remarks and avoiding eye contact with minority-group members. The minority members, based on their own history of discrimination, may interpret the majority-group members' behavior as evidence of hostility and respond with withdrawal, aloofness, or anger. The majority members, not understanding that their anxieties have been interpreted as evidence of prejudice, regard the minority members' behavior as unreasonable or mysterious, so they reciprocate the hostility or withdraw. This behavior confirms the minority members' suspicions about the majority's true feelings and prejudices (Devine, Evett, & Vasquez-Suson, 1996). By understanding this cycle, Devine argues, people can learn to break it. Both sides can learn the difference between prejudice and discomfort and start seeing each other's behavior from several points of view. Both sides, Devine (1995) emphasizes, should remember that reducing prejudice is a *process* and does not happen overnight.

What happens, however, when two groups really do bear enormous animosity toward each other? How then might their conflicts be reduced? Sociocultural researchers emphasize the importance of changing people's circumstances, rather than waiting around for individuals to undergo a moral conversion. They have identified four conditions that must be met before conflict and prejudice between groups can be lessened (Allport, 1954/1979; Dovidio, Gaertner, & Validzic, 1998; Fisher, 1994; Pettigrew, 1998; Rubin, 1994; Slavin & Cooper, 1999; Staub, 1996; Stephan, 1999; Wittig & Grant-Thompson, 1998):

1 Both sides must have equal legal status, economic opportunities, and power. This requirement is the spur behind efforts to change laws that permit discrimination. Integration of public facilities in the American South would never have occurred if civil-rights advocates had waited for segregationists to have a change of

heart. Women would never have gotten the right to vote, attend college, or do "men's work" without persistent challenges to the laws that permitted gender discrimination. Laws, however, do not necessarily change attitudes if all they do is produce unequal contact between groups or if competition for jobs continues.

2 AUTHORITIES AND COMMUNITY INSTITUTIONS MUST ENDORSE EGALITARIAN NORMS AND PROVIDE MORAL SUPPORT AND LEGITIMACY FOR BOTH SIDES. Society must establish norms of equality and support them in the actions of its officials—teachers, employers, the judicial system, government officials, and the police.

3 BOTH SIDES MUST HAVE OPPORTUNITIES TO WORK AND SOCIALIZE TOGETHER, FORMALLY AND INFORMALLY. According to the *contact hypothesis*, prejudice declines when people have the chance to get used to one another's rules, food, music, customs, and attitudes. By making friends with one another, people of different groups and cultures can discover their shared interests and shared humanity, and stereotypes are shattered (Pettigrew, 1998). The contact hypothesis has been supported by many studies in the laboratory and in the "real world": studies of newly integrated housing projects in the American South during the 1950s and 1960s; relationships between German and immigrant Turkish children in German schools; young people's attitudes toward the elderly; healthy people's attitudes toward the mentally ill; nondisabled children's attitudes toward the disabled; and straight people's prejudices toward gay men and lesbians (Fishbein, 1996; Herek, 1999; Herek & Capitanio, 1996; Pettigrew, 1997; Wilner, Walkley, & Cook, 1955). When people make friends with members of another group, they do tend to become less prejudiced toward the group as a whole. Nevertheless, contact and friendship alone are not enough to reduce prejudice and achieve harmony between groups. This is sadly apparent at multiethnic schools, where students often form ethnic cliques, fighting other groups and defending their own ways.

4 BOTH SIDES MUST COOPERATE, WORKING TOGETHER FOR A COMMON GOAL. Cooperation often reduces us-them thinking and prejudice by creating an encompassing social identity ("We're all in this together"). Many successful cooperative situations have been established in schools, businesses, and communities, requiring formerly antagonistic groups to work together for a common goal—the Eagles and the Rattlers solution (see Chapter 9). For example, some elementary schools have experimented with having children from different ethnic groups work together on a task that is broken up like a jigsaw puzzle; each child needs the cooperation of the others to put the assignment together. Children in such "jigsaw" classes do better, like their classmates more, and show less stereotyping and prejudice than children in regular competitive classrooms (Aronson & Patnoe, 1997; Slavin & Cooper, 1999). However, cooperation does not work when members of a group have unequal status, blame one another for loafing or "dropping the ball," or believe that their teachers or employers are playing favorites.

Each of these four approaches to reducing prejudice is important, but none is sufficient on its own. Perhaps one reason that group conflicts and prejudice are so persistent is that all four conditions are rarely met at the same time.

What Do You Know?

Are you prejudiced against quizzes?

  A. Identify which concept—ethnocentrism, stereotyping, or prejudice—is illustrated by the following three statements.

   1. Juan believes that all Anglos are uptight and cold, and he won't listen to any evidence that contradicts his belief.

   2. John knows and likes the Mexican minority in his town but he privately believes that Anglo culture is superior to all others.

   3. Jane believes that Honda owners are thrifty and practical. June believes that Honda owners are stingy and dull.

  B. What are the four conditions necessary for the reduction of conflict and prejudice between two groups?

  C. Millicent believes that prejudice is wrong. But when her sorority votes to reject an Iranian applicant, she goes along. In the sociocultural view, why has she done this? (a) She really is prejudiced; (b) her prejudice fulfills certain psychological needs; (c) conformity to the group is stronger than her own personal preferences; (d) she hasn't had enough contact with Iranians.

   D. Large percentages of blacks, Asian-Americans, and Latinos hold negative stereotypes of one another and are often as prejudiced as whites toward other minorities (White & Langer, 1999). What are some reasons that people who have been victims of stereotyping and prejudice would be prejudiced toward others?

ANSWERS:

A. 1. prejudice 2. ethnocentrism 3. stereotypes **B.** Both sides must have equal status and power; have the moral, legal, and economic support of authorities; have opportunities to socialize formally and informally; and cooperate for a common goal. **C.** c **D.** low self-esteem; conformity with friends and relatives who share these prejudices; parental lessons and messages conveyed by the media; and economic competition for jobs and resources

---

CAN CULTURES GET ALONG?

Sometimes the possibility of harmonious relations between cultures looks bleak indeed. All over the world, ancient animosities erupt in bloody battles, and new wars emerge even where groups had been living together companionably. When cultures with different customs, values, and nonverbal languages collide, misunderstandings are no joke; they can be fatal. In Stockton, California, a driver used a hand signal to alert a car behind him that his headlights were off. The driver of the second car, taking this gesture as a sign of disrespect, shot at the first car, killing a passenger.

Cultural psychology, which has identified many of the causes of international and multicultural conflict, also gives us hope for reducing it. The knowledge of how cultures differ, even in the smallest rules of time management and hand gestures, benefits everyone who has to deal with another culture—which, on this shrinking planet, is all of us: neighbor, tourist, diplomat, business executive. In the sociocultural view, conflict and war are not inherent in human biology, but in our circumstances. Therefore, as circumstances change, so does the need for violence and confrontation. Indeed, throughout history, societies have changed from being warlike to being peaceful, and vice versa. Scandinavians were once the most warlike of cultures, but today they are among the most pacifistic (Groebel & Hinde, 1989).

When people think about resolving conflicts between cultures, they often hold one of two unrealistic goals. At one extreme, some people dream of persuading or forcing every other group and religion to become just like them. At the other extreme, some people dream of getting all cultures to live together in perfect harmony, respecting their differences. The sociocultural perspective teaches that we would do better to accept the fact that cultures will always differ in countless ways, from small nonverbal habits to larger philosophies of how the world works and how people should behave; and that conflicts between cultures will always occur because of economic inequities and because of cultural misunderstandings. Given this knowledge, the sociocultural perspective suggests, we can turn our attention to finding nonviolent ways of resolving conflicts and of getting along with cultures that differ from ours. ▣

Summary

1. *Culture* is a program of shared rules that govern the behavior of members of a community or society, and a set of values, beliefs, and attitudes shared by most members of that community. *Cultural psychologists* study how people are affected by the culture in which they live; *cross-cultural psychologists* compare members of different cultures, searching for commonalities and differences. The study of culture is challenging because of difficulties in devising good methods and getting samples from many societies in order to make valid cultural comparisons, the difficulty of interpreting results when the same custom may have different meanings and functions across cultures, the risk of stereotyping, and the political sensitivity of many findings.

2. Some aspects of *body language* seem to be universal, but most, such as rules governing *conversational distance* and notions of when a smile is appropriate, are specific to particular cultures. In some cultures, people pay close attention to nonverbal signs; in others, people pay more attention to words than to nonverbal cues.

3. People from *monochronic cultures* are more concerned with punctuality and doing things "one at a time" than are people from *polychronic cultures,* who value relationships above time schedules. People from *individualist cultures* tend to define the "self" as a collection of stable personality traits and to value individual freedom over relationships; people from *collectivist cultures* tend to see the "self" as embedded in relationships and to value group harmony over individual freedom.

In collectivist cultures, the strongest human bond is usually not between husband and wife but between parent and child, and child rearing is communal.

4. People develop *social identities* based on their nationality, ethnicity, religion, and social roles. One important social identity is an *ethnic identity.* In ethnically diverse societies, many people face the problem of balancing ethnic identity with *acculturation* into the mainstream culture. Depending on whether ethnic identity and identification with the larger culture are strong or weak, a person may become *bicultural,* choose *assimilation,* become an *ethnic separatist,* or feel *marginal.* Ethnic labels have great symbolic and emotional significance, which is why they are so politically sensitive.

5. Culture influences which mental abilities are fostered and encouraged and what it means to be "intelligent." Although most people everywhere can learn to reason deductively, the situations in which they apply deductive reasoning will depend on their circumstances. Cultural differences occur in the pacing of the stages described by Piaget, because cultures differ in which cognitive skills are needed and nurtured in their members.

6. Alfred Binet designed the first widely used intelligence test for the purpose of identifying children who could benefit from remedial work. But in the United States, people assumed that intelligence tests revealed "natural ability," and they used the tests to categorize students rather than to help slow students do better. IQ tests have been criticized for being biased in favor of white, middle-class people. However, efforts to construct *culture-free* and *culture-fair tests* have been disappointing. Culture affects nearly everything to do with taking a test, including attitudes about achievement, expectations, and experience in solving problems independently. Many social scientists consider IQ tests useful for predicting school performance and identifying children who are gifted or who have learning difficulties, as long as test scores are combined with other information and used "intelligently." Some critics would like to dispense with IQ tests because they are so often misused or misinterpreted.

7. Beliefs about the origins of mental abilities, parental standards, and attitudes about the value of education help account for average group differences in academic performance, such as those between Asians and Americans. Negative stereotypes about a person's ethnicity, gender, or age may cause the person to feel *stereotype threat,* a burden of doubt about his or her own abilities, which can lead to anxiety and "disidentification" with the test.

8. In the sociocultural view, a culture's attitudes and practices are embedded in its history, environment, economy, and survival needs. Although some gender differences appear to be universal, there are many variations in women's status, the work that men and women do, the degree of male-female contact, the value placed on female chastity, and the salience of gender differences. Factors pertaining to *production* (the economy and ecology) and *reproduction* (availability of birth control and the need for many or few children) help explain these variations.

9. Economic and social factors are also involved in the variations in male aggressiveness and in the status of women. High rates of male violence and white homicide

in the American South and West are related to a history of reliance on herding rather than farming. Herding economies tend to foster a *culture of honor,* in which males are raised to be sensitive to perceived insults and respond aggressively to defend their honor. As countries become industrialized and urban, their gender roles become more egalitarian. Access to reliable birth control and the growth of jobs involving service skills and brainwork are eliminating the traditional reasons for a sexual division of labor.

10. *Ethnocentrism,* the belief that one's own group or nation is superior to all others, promotes "us-them" thinking. *Stereotypes* help people process new information, retrieve old memories, organize experience, make sense of the differences among individuals and groups, and predict how others will behave. But stereotypes distort reality by exaggerating differences between groups, underestimating the differences within groups, and producing selective perception. Cultural values influence stereotypes and therefore how people from different cultures interpret the same event.

11. A *prejudice* is an unreasonable negative feeling toward a category of people. Prejudice wards off feelings of anxiety and doubt, provides a simple explanation of complex problems, and bolsters self-esteem when a person feels threatened. People acquire prejudices through parental lessons, conformity and groupthink, and media messages. An important function of prejudice is to justify a majority group's economic interests and dominance, or, in extreme cases, to legitimize war. During times of economic insecurity and competition for jobs, prejudice rises significantly.

12. Prejudice occurs in many varieties and degrees, a fact that causes debates about how to define racism, sexism, and other prejudices. People often disagree on whether racism and other prejudices are declining or have merely taken new forms. Because many people are unwilling to admit their prejudices openly, some researchers measure *symbolic racism* (prejudice disguised in opinions about race-related social issues); people's actual behavior toward a target group when they are stressed, provoked, or insulted; or nonconscious, *implicit* prejudice. The *Implicit Association Test* assesses nonconscious attitudes, though the measure may be assessing a person's unfamiliarity with a target or stereotypes rather than actual prejudice.

13. Efforts to reduce prejudice and group conflict must take into account the origins of the conflict and the factors that support it. In groups where members of majority and minority groups are unfamiliar with one another's ways, it is important to break the "cycle of distrust," by not inferring prejudice or hostility when none is intended.

14. Four conditions are required for reducing prejudice and conflict between groups: Both sides must have equal legal status, economic standing, and power; both sides must have the legal and moral support of authorities and the larger culture; both sides must have opportunities to work and socialize together (the *contact hypothesis*); and both sides must work together for a common goal.

15. Cultural psychologists have identified many reasons for cultural conflicts and solutions for reducing them. In the sociocultural view, conflict and aggression are not inherent in human biology, but in our circumstances. Therefore, as circumstances change, so does the need for conflict and aggression.

Key Terms

Evaluating the Sociocultural Perspective

Social psychologist Roger Brown (1986), who was born and raised in Indiana, went to a Big Ten university in the Midwest. There he encountered a young woman from New York, who seemed to him to have "the most extraordinarily original personality." But after he had met half a dozen other young women from New York, he realized that the personality he thought was unique was in fact "99 percent New York generic." In turn, he admits, the young women were learning that he was "99 percent Indiana standard."

Roger Brown had discovered the importance of culture—the cultures of New York and Indiana. In this respect, his story is a metaphor for what has happened to the whole discipline of psychology, because the sociocultural perspective has transformed the way psychologists think and do research. Indeed, it is safe to say that it caused as much of an upheaval in the 1990s as the cognitive revolution did in the 1960s and 1970s, when behaviorism was challenged by the rediscovery of the mind.

CONTRIBUTIONS OF THIS PERSPECTIVE

The sociocultural perspective has made significant contributions to the field of psychology in four major ways:

1 **MAKING PSYCHOLOGY MORE REPRESENTATIVE AND SCIENTIFIC.** Psychologists used to joke that their field was based on the study of the white male rat. Then others said no, it was actually the study of the white, male, *sophomore* rat. Then friends of ours pointed out that because rats are nocturnal and most psychologists aren't, psychology was really the study of the white, male, sophomore, *sleepy* rat. All of these jokes, though, reflected the realization that you don't have much of a "science" of psychology if your findings are based on a tiny, narrow, limited segment of the population—samples limited by their age, gender, or culture. The inclusion of diverse groups in research has made psychology more representative and scientific.

By making research more representative of all humanity, the sociocultural perspective has also strengthened psychology's original goal of identifying basic principles of behavior that affect people all over the world. Social psychology has identified such universal processes as conformity, obedience to authority, peer pressure, deindividuation, and persuasion. Cross-cultural psychology has identified such universal experiences as attachment and love; the emotions of happiness, grief, anger, and fear; the enjoyment of humor; the pleasures of music; and the impulse to stereotype and dehumanize our enemies. As Pierre Dasen (1994) observed, "Universality and cultural diversity are not opposites, but are complementary aspects of all human behavior and development."

2 EMPHASIZING THE IMPORTANCE OF THE INDIVIDUAL'S SOCIAL CONTEXT. For much of the twentieth century, psychologists tended to focus solely on the individual, paying little or no attention to what was going on in the world around the person (Gergen, 1973; Unger, 1990). They assumed that the laws of behavior were fairly independent of a person's generation, peer group, or working conditions. The sociocultural perspective, however, causes us to question this assumption. When researchers study individuals without regard for how the social and historical context might be affecting their behavior, the findings, far from being universal, are often only narrowly applicable.

For example, when psychologists first began to follow people's lives from childhood to adulthood, in the 1950s and 1960s, they found that most middle-class people's lives were consistent and predictable (Kagan & Moss, 1962). Theories of adult development therefore often spoke of "universal" stages and experiences (psychodynamic theories still do, as we will see in Chapter 11). However, these theories turned out to be describing a life sequence that was true only for some people at a particular time and place. Today, because of changes in the economy and in social roles, adult development in North America and Europe is marked by inconsistency. Most people no longer have one job or career for their whole lives. The timing and length of marriage are no longer predictable, if people marry at all, and neither is parenthood: Some people have their first baby at 15, and others have their first baby at 45. Because of these changes, theories of adult development had to be reconsidered, and the idea of universal stages or passages of development was scrapped.

3 EMPHASIZING THE IMPORTANCE OF CULTURE IN EVERY ASPECT OF HUMAN DEVELOPMENT. We have seen that nearly every topic in psychology, from thinking to emotion, has been affected by the growing awareness of the influence of culture on human behavior (Lonner & Malpass, 1994; Segall et al., 1999). But nowhere has the study of culture had greater impact than in the field of human development. For instance, in Western psychology a supposed milestone of infant development occurs when babies sleep for eight uninterrupted hours by the age of 4 or 5 months. This is a big milestone for North American parents! But it is also considered a sign of the infant's neurological maturity, although many babies wail when the parent puts them in the crib at night and leaves the room. But among Mayan Indians, rural Italians, the Kipsigis of Kenya, and urban Japanese, this nightly clash of wills never occurs because the infant sleeps with the

mother for the first few years of life, waking and nursing about every four hours. Although many North American mothers constantly worry about the "right" or "wrong" way of caring for an infant, neither custom is better than the other. These differences in babies' sleep arrangements reflect cultural values. Mayan mothers believe it is important to sleep with the baby in order to forge a close bond with the child; many North American and German parents believe it is important to foster the child's independence as soon as possible (Kagan, 1998b; Morelli et al., 1992; Super & Harkness, 1994).

Similarly, *adolescence* is a cultural concept, not a biological one. It describes the period of development between *puberty,* the age at which a person becomes capable of sexual reproduction, and adulthood. In some cultures, the time span between puberty and adulthood is only a few months; a sexually mature boy or girl is expected to marry and assume adult tasks. In modern Western societies, however, teenagers are not considered emotionally mature enough to be full-fledged adults with all the rights, responsibilities, and roles of adulthood.

In psychology, the "turmoil theory" of adolescent development, popular for many years, held that anguish and rebellion are necessary and inevitable, the means by which teenagers separate themselves psychologically from their parents and form their own identities (Blos, 1962). The theory assumed that a child who maintains a close bond with the parents is immature; this was said to be especially true of young men. But cross-cultural research has found that separation is an issue primarily in societies that value male independence. Most other cultures place a high value on continued love and connection between child and parent (Apter, 1990). Once American researchers could see beyond the cultural assumption that "separation" is the main theme of adolescence, they found that even in Western cultures attachment to parents is neither rare nor an indication of a young person's immaturity or dependence. Although adolescents in Western cultures are indeed more likely than those elsewhere to report conflict with parents and to have higher rates of reckless, rule-breaking behavior, extreme turmoil and emotional disorder are the exception, not the rule (Arnett, 1999; Steinberg, 1990).

4 INCREASING PSYCHOLOGY'S RELEVANCE TO SOCIAL LIFE. By making psychology more encompassing of cultural differences, and by identifying the universal social forces that affect behavior, the sociocultural perspective also increases our ability to understand and resolve individual conflicts and social problems. It shows us that well-meaning efforts to persuade people to behave well toward others will have little effect if we overlook people's circumstances, group pressures, social roles, and cultural obligations. To improve work motivation, we need to consider a person's working conditions. To improve race relations, we need to consider disparities between groups in income, power, status, and opportunity. To make better decisions and wiser purchases, we need to consider the powerful but often invisible influences of conformity, advertising, and tactics of persuasion.

Understanding cultural influences, too, has immediate benefits and relevance, especially for anyone who works as a diplomat or conducts business across cultures. For example, when monochronic and polychronic people try to do business with one another, they often make unintentional mistakes because they are unaware that they hold different attitudes toward time—and they make the wrong attributions about why the other person is behaving so oddly. Consider the plight of a French sales-man who had worked for a company that was bought by Americans. When the new American manager ordered him to step up his sales within the next three months, the employee quit in a huff, taking his customers with him. Why? In polychronic France, it takes years to develop customers; in family-owned businesses, relationships with customers may span generations. The monochronic American manager wanted instant results, as Americans do, but the French salesman knew this was impossible and quit. The American view was, "He wasn't up to the job; he's lazy and disloyal, so he stole my customers." The French view was, "There is no point in explaining anything to a person who is so stupid as to think you can acquire loyal customers in three months" (Tavris, 1987).

The sociocultural perspective poses many challenges for research, because cross-cultural and cross-situational studies are difficult and costly to do. Yet its findings continually remind us that when we overlook this perspective, our ability to explain and predict behavior is seriously diminished.

MISUSES AND MISINTERPRETATIONS OF THIS PERSPECTIVE

Despite these contributions, the sociocultural perspective also raises concerns because of the potential for misinterpreting and misusing its findings.

1 SOCIOCULTURAL REDUCTIONISM AND REIFICATION. Reducing human behavior to the single factor of culture or society is no improvement over biological reduction-ism, behavioral reductionism, or cognitive reductionism. Any one-factor explanation can lead to an abdication of individual responsibility, which is why "The system made me do it" or "Peer pressure made me do it" or "My culture made me do it" is no more valid than "My hormones made me do it" or "My upbringing made me do it." This perspec-tive teaches us to appreciate the power of circumstances, situations, roles, and working conditions in influencing behavior, but we should not forget that there is an individual person rattling around in there. The writer Jane O'Reilly (1980) said that she shifted from taking 100 percent responsibility for everything that happened to her to blaming "the system" 100 percent. "Nowadays," she said, "I divide the blame more equitably: half for me and half for societal arrangements." We think most sociocultural researchers would agree with that assessment.

Some people reduce behavior to culture in a literal way, speaking as if there were "culture genes" that make people behave a certain way, just as genes cause eye color. When people talk as though culture were something permanent residing inside the indi-vidual, they are making an error called *reification*. To *reify* means to regard an intangible

"I used to hate my body. Now, instead, I hate the forces that conspire to make me hate my body."

Sometimes, blaming the system is appropriate.

process as if it were a literal object. For example, when people say, "I have a lot of anger buried in me," they are reifying anger. They are treating it as a thing that sits inside them like a kidney, instead of as a complex cluster of mental and physical reactions that come and go.

People often reify culture and social roles when they cite these factors as explanations without identifying the specific mechanisms that are operating. In doing so, they ignore the fact that culture and social roles are not static; these concepts describe customs and conventions that can and do change. Moreover, to say, "The Japanese work hard because of their culture," "Americans are violent because of their culture," or "Men are violent because of their gender role" shows circular reasoning. Using a label as an explanation in this way, observed Walter Lonner and Roy Malpass (1994), is like telling a man with a leg injury that he can't walk because he is lame. If we observe that Culture A behaves more aggressively than Culture B, it explains nothing to say that Culture A does so because it is "warlike." Instead, we need to ask what is going on in Culture A that makes it different from Culture B. "To say that the difference is cultural," say Lonner and Malpass, "just means that we have to look for the explanation in the details of how people live."

2 **STEREOTYPING.** A woman we know, originally from England, married a Lebanese man. They were happy together but had the usual number of marital misunderstandings and squabbles. After a few years, they visited his home town in Lebanon, where she had never been before. "I was stunned," she told us. "All the things I thought he did because of his *personality* turned out to be because he's *Lebanese*! Everyone there was just like him!"

Our friend's reaction illustrates both the contributions and the limitations of cultural research. She was right in recognizing that some of her husband's behavior was attributable to his culture; for example, his Lebanese notions of time were very different from her English notions. But she would be wrong to infer that the Lebanese are all "like him." Individuals are affected by their culture, but they vary within it.

The danger in focusing on how cultural groups differ, therefore, is that people may begin to exaggerate the differences and overlook variations within groups. Researchers themselves can succumb to this tendency. When she was doing fieldwork with Bedouin women, anthropologist Lila Abu-Lughod (1992) found considerable divergence among them. The scientist who strives for general descriptions of a culture, she said, "risks smoothing over contradictions, conflicts of interest, doubts and arguments, not to mention changing motivations and historical circumstances." Smoothing over contradictions within groups is the essence of stereotyping, and all of us need to resist the temptation to do so.

When we stereotype groups, our expectations and beliefs affect what we perceive about them (Geis, 1993). In the case of gender, the belief that "men are aggressive" and "women are nurturant" has caused many people, including psychologists, to overlook the many worldwide examples of male nurturance and female aggression. When David Gilmore (1990) examined how cultures define manhood, he expected to find masculinity equated with selfishness and hardness. Yet by resisting this stereotype, he was able to see that masculinity frequently entails selfless generosity and sacrifice. Men nurture their families and society, he observed, by "bringing home food for both child and mother . . . and by dying if necessary in faraway places to provide a safe haven for their people."

Likewise, people who have a stereotype of women as kind and compassionate may miss the abundant evidence of female aggressiveness. It depends on how you define your terms. If you define "aggressiveness" as committing physical violence, then men are indeed more aggressive than women. But if you define it as "the intention to harm another," the gender difference vanishes. Little boys are more likely than girls to display overt aggression, by hitting, pushing, and kicking. But little girls are more likely than boys to display "relational aggression" by excluding others from a play group, spreading rumors, or being verbally mean (Crick et al., 1999). Many adult women behave aggressively by saying cruel and hurtful things; slapping, kicking, biting, or throwing objects during arguments; humiliating and abusing their children; holding vengeful attitudes toward their perceived enemies; and supporting and participating in war, in whatever ways their societies permit (Campbell, 1993; Elshtain, 1987).

From the sociocultural perspective, the moral is that we can study and talk about average differences between groups, the sexes, or nationalities, but we should do so without implying that these groups are as different as chocolate and cheese—or, as the best-selling pop-psych book grandiosely asserted, that *Men Are from Mars, Women Are from Venus.* That's stereotyping.

3 EXTREME CULTURAL RELATIVISM. Cultural psychologists have described problems with both "absolutist" and "relativist" attitudes toward cultural differences (Adamopolouos & Lonner, 1994). The *absolutist* assumptions of traditional psychology hold that there are universal truths and a common human nature; murder is murder, torture is torture, and violations of human rights are to be condemned wherever they occur. *Relativists,* sensitive to differences among cultural and ethnic groups, believe that the customs and practices of a group can be judged only on its own terms. Extreme relativists take a nonjudgmental view of all cultural or ethnic practices, even those that cause suffering and death, or that violate what others regard as universal human rights.

But perhaps there is a route between extreme relativism and extreme absolutism. The sociocultural perspective directs our attention to why certain cultural practices have survived and what their adaptive consequences might be. This does not necessarily mean that any custom that survives must therefore be proper and good, or that we must accept it as permanent and inevitable.

For example, in more than 25 countries throughout Africa, the Middle East, and Indonesia, girls are subjected to genital mutilation. Performed on an estimated 2 million female children a year, ranging in age from infancy to adolescence, the operation takes one of three forms: in *circumcision,* part of the clitoris is removed; in *excision,* the entire clitoris and all or part of the vaginal lips (labia) are removed; and in *infibulation,* the clitoris and the inner and outer labia are removed and the sides of the vaginal opening are stitched together, leaving only a small hole for urination and menstruation. These operations, usually done without anesthesia or even an antiseptic, are excruciatingly painful and hazardous; some girls bleed to death. Most women who have been excised or infibulated develop lifelong medical problems and, according to some estimates, 20 percent die in childbirth (Bardach, 1993).

The people who practice female genital mutilation believe that it will ensure a girl's chastity at marriage and her fidelity afterward. Most Westerners, and many members of these cultures as well, find this practice barbaric, which is why they call it "genital mutilation" (Burstyn, 1995). This cultural conflict is not just an intellectual matter in countries such as France, England, and the United States, which have growing numbers of immigrants who subject their daughters to the surgery. In these countries, the law of the majority, which forbids the practice, clashes with the immigrants' desire to continue their tradition.

An absolutist would simply condemn genital mutilation and call for its immediate abolition. An extreme relativist might feel personal revulsion at the custom but, as did the Australian feminist Germaine Greer, defend the right of those who practice it to preserve their traditions without interference from "cultural imperialists." A third position might begin with the realization that you can condemn a practice such as genital mutilation *and* study the reasons for its existence, understanding that it will not be eradicated until the reasons for it have vanished. The sociocultural perspective reminds us that because most cultural customs are embedded in the larger structure of society, they cannot simply be yanked out like a bad tooth.

In cultures where it is practiced, female genital mutilation works something like a marriage contract, guaranteeing a woman a place in society (Paige & Paige, 1981). Outsiders who want to barge in and make the custom illegal, ignoring the system of kinship and economic arrangements that support the practice, might actually condemn countless women to even more hardship—because, unmarried, they would have no family to support them. African women who are working to eliminate female genital mutilation know this (Burstyn, 1995). They know that although passing laws to prohibit the practice are an essential first step, the custom will not cease without other changes that raise the status and security of women.

The sociocultural perspective thus does not lead automatically to extreme relativism. But it also cautions us about extreme absolutism, the dangers of climbing up on an ethnocentric high horse and galloping off in the certainty that our own ways are always right and normal and everyone else's are wrong. Writer Alice Walker, whose novel *Possessing the Secret of Joy* is a haunting condemnation of female genital mutilation, pointed out in a television interview that while genital mutilation might be cruel, plenty of American women also mutilate themselves—with breast implants, plastic surgery, and liposuction—to achieve their culture's standards of beauty. How would we like it, she asked, if outsiders pressured the United States government to make plastic surgery for cosmetic purposes illegal? Or consider this: Among the developed nations of the world, only the United States continues to execute criminals in increasing numbers. To other nations, the death penalty is barbaric, a violation of human rights, and unjust because it is disproportionately applied to minorities, the poor, and the mentally ill. Across Europe and Canada, many people are publicly protesting the American "cultural practice" of the death penalty. But many Americans would counter that it's our tradition and no one has the right to interfere.

The sociocultural perspective urges us to avoid the pitfalls of both extreme absolutism and extreme relativism. It teaches us to find stronger criteria than emotional reasoning ("I hate that custom") by which to decide when to let other cultures alone, when and how to try to influence them, and even—imagine this!—when we would be wise to let them influence us.

4 **HEIGHTENED ETHNOCENTRISM.** It is both ironic and tragic that the sociocultural perspective, which has done so much to make people aware of the dangers of ethnocentrism, is sometimes misused to inflame it. Research from this perspective was never meant to be twisted to foster ethnic, societal, and gender separatism, in which people celebrate only their own group and regard other cultures or the other sex as inherently inferior—or so hopelessly different that there is no point in trying to get along with them.

It is understandable that many minority groups that were once (or still are) targets of discrimination and prejudice would jump at the chance to replace theories biased against them with theories biased in their favor. In popular culture, you can find many examples of this impulse: Women are the nurturant sex that will save the world; Native Americans were and are the peaceful, planet-loving people, living in environmental harmony with the Earth; Africans are the "sun people" who have a "humanistic, spiritualistic value system," whereas Europeans are the "ice people" who are "egoistic, individualistic, and exploitative" (Traub, 1993). There seems to be a great longing to find the one culture in human history in which all members live in peace, harmony, and kindness.

But a correct reading of the sociocultural perspective teaches us, to be blunt, to forget it. No culture has ever been entirely wise and compassionate—or entirely greedy and brutal. For example, many African-Americans understandably regard slavery as an invention of European whites, because white Europeans and Americans were responsible for slavery in the United States. In fact, however, the ancient Romans, Aztecs, and Egyptians all had slaves—people they conquered, of whatever skin color. So did Muslim Arabs for many centuries, and so did some Native American tribes (Davis,

1984; Oliver, 1992). Nor were Africans always virtuous and "humanistic"; many of them sold their fellow Africans into slavery. Indeed, as Robert Hughes (1993) wrote, "The *African* slave trade as such, the black traffic, was a Muslim invention, developed by Arab traders with the enthusiastic collaboration of black African ones, institutionalized with the most unrelenting brutality centuries before the white man appeared on the African continent, and continuing long after the slave market in North America was finally crushed."

Does this information detract one whit from the moral condemnation of American slavery? Not at all. But it does give us insight into the long nightmare of slavery in history and confirms what sociocultural research finds repeatedly: No cultural group has always and everywhere been superior to every other in its dealings with the rest of humanity. All cultures and individuals are subject to the factors identified by the sociocultural perspective, along with the forces of history that shape behavior (Diamond, 1997). As Kwame Appiah (1994), a professor of Afro-American studies who is originally from Ghana, wrote, "Cruelty and kindness are not Western prerogatives, any more than intelligence and creativity. . . . The proper response to Eurocentrism is surely not a reactive Afrocentrism, but a new understanding that humanizes all of us by learning to think beyond race."

What Do You Know?

1. Name four contributions of the sociocultural perspective.
2. What are four potential misuses of this perspective?
3. When a chief of the Miranhas was asked why his people practiced cannibalism, he said, "It is all a matter of habit. When I have killed an enemy it is better to eat him than let him go to waste" (Askenasy, 1994). Colin and Carin are arguing about the Miranhas' custom. "If that's their tradition, there's nothing wrong with it," says Colin. "They are barbaric and stupid," says Carin. What positions are Colin and Carin taking in regard to cultural findings, and what other approach might they consider?

Answers:

1. The contributions include making psychology more representative and scientific, placing the individual in social context, emphasizing the importance of culture in every domain of human development, and making psychology a more socially relevant field. 2. The misuses include sociocultural reductionism, stereotyping, extreme cultural relativism, and heightened ethnocentrism. 3. Colin is being extremely relativistic and Carin is being absolutist. A more useful middle course might be to ask how this custom evolved among the Miranhas, what purpose it served, and the functions it might have had in different cultures, from religious ritual to survival. (Taking this approach doesn't mean Colin and Carin have to become tolerant of cannibalism!)

Making Peace

The sociocultural perspective is making a difference in hundreds of ways, large and small. Because of research on the ways in which organizational structure affects workers' motivation, companies are experimenting with new forms of teamwork and incentive pay. Because of research on cross-cultural differences in nonverbal language, individualism and collectivism, communication, and notions of time, some businesses are hiring cultural advisers to help them make the best use of their own employees' diversity and do better business with people in other countries. Research on bystander apathy, conformity, and diffusion of responsibility is being used to create situations that may permit more people to speak up and help others. And social psychologists are working on programs to reduce stereotyping and prejudice in schools, businesses, and nations (Aronson & Patnoe, 1997; Staub, 1999; Wittig & Grant-Thompson, 1998).

The sociocultural perspective illuminates the social and cultural forces that lie beyond individual choice or even awareness. Yet we must not forget the remarkable capacity of human beings to wriggle out of the confines of role and culture and, with impressive leaps of imagination and empathy, bridge the chasms of difference. Individuals are able to do this even when war has created animosities and ethnocentric self-justifications that might be expected to last forever.

And so we will end with a story of how one man finally put his animosities toward another culture to rest. People do not need to forget what has happened to them, he reasoned, but they can begin to forgive; and for that, they need to break out of their habitual patterns of assuming their own group is superior and of stereotyping the enemy. They need to see their enemies as human beings and recognize the common humanity beneath people's cultural differences.

Many years after the Vietnam War, veteran William Broyles Jr. traveled to Vietnam to try to resolve his feelings about the horrors he had seen there. In a PBS documentary called "Faces of the Enemy," he explained that he wanted to meet his former enemies "as people, not abstractions." In a small village that had been a Marine base camp, he met a woman who had been with the Viet Cong. As they talked, Broyles realized that her husband had been killed at exactly the time that he and his men had been patrolling. "My men and I might have killed your husband," he said. She looked at him steadily and replied, "But that was during the war. The war is over now. Life goes on." Broyles said this about his healing visit to Vietnam:

> I used to have nightmares. Since I've been back from that trip, I haven't had any. Maybe that sounds too personal to support any larger conclusions, but it tells me that to end a war you have to return to the same personal relationships you would have had with people before it. You do make peace. Nothing is constant in history. ■

Summary

1. The sociocultural perspective challenges the traditional assumption that psychological research automatically generalizes to all human beings everywhere, regardless of their history, situation, or culture. This perspective has made psychology more scientific by pressing the field to become more representative of all humanity.

2. Other contributions of this perspective include emphasizing the individual in social and historical context, making psychologists aware of the importance of culture in every domain of psychology, especially human development, and making psychology more socially relevant.

3. One misinterpretation of the sociocultural perspective is *sociocultural reductionism*, the tendency to reduce the complexities of human behavior to the single factor of culture or society. Reductionism often leads to the common tendency to *reify* "culture" or "society" as an explanation, without identifying the mechanisms or aspects of a group that influence behavior.

4. Other misuses of this perspective include stereotyping (exaggerating differences between groups and overlooking variation within them); taking an entirely *relativist*, nonjudgmental view of all cultural practices, even when such practices cause suffering and violate what most people regard as universal human rights; and using cultural findings to foster greater ethnocentrism and ethnic, societal, and gender separatism.

5. Perhaps the most important contribution of the sociocultural perspective is the understanding that although groups and cultures differ, all human beings are subject to the same basic needs, psychological processes, and social forces.

Key Terms

sociocultural reductionism   440

reification   441

cultural absolutism   442

cultural relativism   442

PART VI

The Psychodynamic Perspective

*I*magine this scene: Three hundred strangers in a room are told to pair up and ask their partner a single question, "What do you want?" When psychiatrist Irvin Yalom (1989) conducts this exercise, he is always stunned by the reaction it unleashes:

> Often, within minutes, the room rocks with emotion. Men and women . . . are stirred to their depths. They call out to those who are forever lost—dead or absent parents, spouses, children, friends: "I want to see you again." "I want your love." "I want to know you're proud of me." "I want you to know I love you and how sorry I am I never told you." "I want you back—I am so lonely." "I want the childhood I never had." "I want to be healthy—to be young again." "I want to be loved, to be respected." "I want my life to mean something." "I want to accomplish something." "I want to matter, to be important, to be remembered."

"So much wanting," writes Yalom. "So much longing. And so much pain, so close to the surface, only minutes deep."

The psychodynamic perspective in psychology holds that other perspectives—biological, learning, cognitive, and sociocultural—cannot begin to account for the emotional pain and longing that are "only minutes deep" in human experience. To understand the full mystery of human behavior, say psychodynamic psychologists, we must understand the inner life: the unconscious conflicts hidden from awareness that nonetheless drive our actions; the anxieties about death and loss that we try to suppress; the insecurities and fears originating in childhood that we reexperience in adulthood; and the symbols and themes that invade our uniquely human imaginations.

In Chapter 1 we described the psychodynamic perspective as the thumb on the hand of psychology—connected to the other fingers, yet set apart from them. Now you'll see why.

CHAPTER ELEVEN

The Inner Life

*R*obert Hobson (1985), a psychodynamic therapist, spent many weeks trying to communicate with Stephen, a troubled 15-year-old boy who refused to speak or to look at him. One day, in frustration, Hobson took an envelope and drew a squiggly line. Then Hobson invited Stephen to add to the picture. Stephen drew a ship, thereby turning Hobson's meaningless line into a tidal wave:

Was Stephen, Hobson wondered, afraid of being emotionally "drowned"? Hobson next drew a landing pier, representing safety. Stephen was not interested in safety. On his boat, he put a person waving goodbye:

Hobson, suspecting that Stephen's problem might stem from emotional separation from his mother, drew a woman waving goodbye from the landing pier. Ignoring the figure of the woman, Stephen added a creature caught in the wave, and spoke for the first time: "A flying fish." Hobson added an octopus in the water.

Stephen, shoulders drooping in sadness, marked up the entire sketch with lines, adding, "It's raining." Hobson, hoping to convey optimism, drew the sun, adding rays that conflicted with the rain:

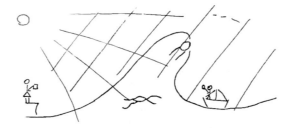

Stephen paused and looked at Hobson intently for the first time. He drew large arcs embracing the whole illustration. "A rainbow," said Stephen. He smiled.

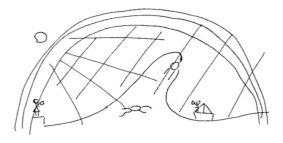

Biological, learning, cognitive, and sociocultural psychologists would have trouble accounting for this touching emotional exchange. The interaction between Stephen and his therapist is almost entirely nonverbal, yet it is filled with meaningful symbols and deeply felt emotion. To a psychodynamic psychologist, the other perspectives offer only the most superficial ways of understanding, let alone reaching, a boy like Stephen—or any of the rest of us.

More than any other psychological perspective, the psychodynamic approach to human behavior is embedded in popular culture, particularly in people's ways of talking and thinking about their problems and everyday actions. A man apologizes for "displacing" his frustrations at work onto his family. A woman suspects that she is "repressing" a childhood trauma. An alcoholic reveals that he is no longer "in denial" about his dependence on drinking. A newspaper columnist advises readers to vent their anger or risk becoming physically ill. A wife speculates about the unconscious conflicts that might have caused her husband to lapse into depression. A teacher informs a divorcing couple that their 8-year-old child, formerly well behaved, is "regressing" to immature behavior on the playground. A husband tells his wife that her headaches and allergies are "psychosomatic." And everyone ponders the hidden meanings of dreams.

All of this language—about displacing, repressing, denying, venting, and regressing; about the unconscious; about the significance of dreams—derives from the first psychodynamic theory of personality, Sigmund Freud's theory of **psychoanalysis.** Today many other psychodynamic approaches exist, differing in various ways from classical psychoanalysis and from one another. But they generally share five elements:

1. *An emphasis on unconscious* **intrapsychic** *dynamics,* the movement of mental (psychic) energy within the mind.
2. *A belief in the primacy of the first five years*—that is, an assumption that adult personality and ongoing problems are formed primarily by experiences in early childhood.
3. *A belief that psychological development occurs in fixed stages,* during which predictable mental events occur and unconscious issues or crises must be resolved.
4. *A focus on a person's "psychic reality"—his or her fantasies and the symbolic meanings of events—rather than actual experiences* as the main influence on behavior.
5. *A reliance on subjective rather than objective methods of getting at the truth of a person's life:* for example, through analysis of dreams, myths, folklore, symbols, and, most of all, the revelations uncovered in psychotherapy.

In this chapter, we will introduce you to the fundamental concepts of Freudian theory and to some contemporary psychodynamic approaches that have arisen from it. In the evaluation that follows, we will discuss why the psychodynamic perspective has been in such conflict with other psychological perspectives, and whether it is possible to find common ground among them.

FREUD AND PSYCHOANALYSIS

No one disputes the worldwide influence of Sigmund Freud. But there is plenty of dispute about the lasting significance of his work, reflected in three current attitudes toward Freud and his ideas. The first, held by Freud himself and by his most devoted followers to this day, is that Freud was one of the geniuses of history, an intellectual revolutionary like Copernicus, Darwin, and Newton (Gay, 1988). The second view, held by

---

psychoanalysis A theory of personality and a method of psychotherapy developed by Sigmund Freud; it emphasizes unconscious motives and conflicts.

intrapsychic Within the mind (psyche) or self.

many psychiatrists and clinical psychologists, is that although some of Freud's ideas have proved faulty, the overall framework and insights of his theories are timeless and brilliant (Westen, 1998). The third view, held by many scientists and by psychologists in other perspectives, is that psychoanalytic theory is sheer nonsense (Cioffi, 1998). One critic, the British scientist and Nobel laureate Peter Medawar (1982), called psychoanalysis "the most stupendous intellectual confidence trick of the twentieth century."

What kind of theory could produce such passionately different reactions? To answer, let us enter the world of Freud, a realm beneath our daily thoughts and conscious actions. Freud believed that the most important impulses and motives affecting behavior are sexual and aggressive. Because these primitive urges are threatening, we push them out of consciousness, deep into our unconscious minds. Yet, said Freud, they make themselves known in hundreds of ways: in dreams, apparent accidents, jokes, myths, art, and fantasy. Even a slip of the tongue was no random flub to Freud. The British member of Parliament who referred to the "honourable member from Hell" when he meant to say "Hull," said Freud (1920/1960), was revealing his true, unconscious appraisal of his colleague.

To chart the byways of the unconscious, Freud developed the methods of psychoanalysis. And as he listened to his patients unburden themselves in therapy, he formulated a sweeping theory of the structure and dynamics of personality.

The Structure of Personality

According to Freud, the personality is made up of three major systems: the *id*, the *ego*, and the *superego*. Although each system has its own functions and elements, human behavior is nearly always a result of the interaction among all three (Freud, 1905b, 1920/1960, 1923/1962).

The **id**, which is present at birth, is the reservoir of unconscious psychological energies and the motives to avoid pain and obtain pleasure. The id contains two competing instincts: the life, or sexual, instinct (fueled by psychic energy called the **libido**) and the death, or aggressive, instinct. As energy builds up in the id, tension results. The id may discharge this tension in the form of reflex actions, physical symptoms, or uncensored mental images and unbidden thoughts.

The **ego**, the second system to emerge, is a referee between the needs of instinct and the demands of society. It bows to the realities of life, putting a rein on the id's desire for sex and aggression until a suitable, socially appropriate outlet for them can be found. The ego, said Freud, is both conscious and unconscious, and it represents "reason and good sense."

The **superego**, the last system of personality to develop, represents morality, the rules of parents and society, and the power of authority; it includes the conscience,

---

id In psychoanalysis, the part of the mind containing inherited psychic energy, particularly sexual and aggressive instincts.

libido [li-BEE-do] In psychoanalysis, the psychic energy that fuels the life or sexual instincts of the id.

ego In psychoanalysis, the part of the mind that represents reason, good sense, and rational self-control; it mediates between id and superego.

superego In psychoanalysis, the part of the mind that represents conscience, morality, and social standards.

TABLE 11.1 ✦ Summary of Freud's Model of the Mind

Id	Ego	Superego
Location of sexual and aggressive instincts	Location of reason; mediates between desires of the id and demands of the superego; uses defense mechanisms to protect against unconscious anxiety	Location of conscience and society's standards
"I'm so mad I could kill you" (felt unconsciously)	Might make a conscious choice ("Let's talk about this") or resort to unconscious defense mechanism, such as denial ("I am *not* angry at you")	"Thou shalt not kill"

the inner voice that says you did something wrong. The superego, which is partly conscious but largely unconscious, judges the activities of the id, handing out good feelings of pride and satisfaction when you do something well and handing out miserable feelings of guilt or shame when you break the rules.

An old joke summarizes the role of the id, ego, and superego this way: The id says, "I want it, and I want it now"; the superego says, "You can't have it; it's bad for you"; and the ego, the rational mediator, says, "Well, maybe you can have some of it—later." According to Freud, the healthy personality must keep all three systems in balance. (For a summary of Freud's model of the mind, see Table 11.1.) Someone who is too controlled by the id is governed by impulse and selfish desires. Someone who is too controlled by the superego is rigid, moralistic, and bossy. Someone who has a weak ego is unable to balance personal needs and wishes with social duties and realistic limitations.

If a person feels anxious or threatened when the wishes of the id conflict with the demands of conscience and social rules, the ego has certain weapons at its command to relieve the tension. These unconscious strategies, called **defense mechanisms,** deny or distort reality, but according to Freud, they are necessary for normal functioning because they protect us from uncomfortable conflict and anxiety. They become unhealthy only when they cause emotional problems and self-defeating behavior. Freud described 17 defense mechanisms; later, other psychoanalysts expanded and modified his list. Here are some of the primary defenses identified by Freud's daughter Anna Freud (1967), who became a psychoanalyst herself, and by most contemporary psychodynamic psychologists (Vaillant, 1992):

1 **REPRESSION** occurs when a threatening idea, memory, or emotion is blocked from consciousness. A woman who had a frightening experience in childhood that she

---

defense mechanisms Methods used by the ego to prevent unconscious anxiety or threatening thoughts from entering consciousness.

*"I'm sorry, I'm not speaking to anyone tonight.
My defense mechanisms seem to be out of order."*

cannot remember, for example, is said to be repressing her memory of it. Repression does not mean that you consciously bite your tongue rather than reveal a guilty secret. It refers to the mind's effort to keep a lid on unacceptable feelings and thoughts in the unconscious, so that you aren't even aware of them.

2 **PROJECTION** occurs when one's own unacceptable or threatening feelings are repressed and then attributed to someone else. A person who is embarrassed about having sexual feelings toward members of a different ethnic group, for example, may project this discomfort onto them, saying, "Those people are dirty-minded and oversexed."

One target of projection is the *scapegoat,* a powerless person or group that is blamed for a problem by individuals who feel insecure or threatened. (For the ancient Hebrews, a scapegoat was literally a goat. During the days of repentance at the start of the new year, a religious leader would place his hands on the head of a goat as he recited the sins of the community. The goat was then allowed to escape into the wilds, symbolically taking the people's sins with it.) You can see examples of scapegoating in many contexts. Some families make one weak child the scapegoat for their emotional conflicts. Some nations make a minority the scapegoat for their economic difficulties, as the early Romans did with the Christians and as modern white supremacists do with the Jews.

3 **REACTION FORMATION** occurs when a feeling that produces unconscious anxiety is transformed into its opposite in consciousness. A woman who is afraid to admit to herself that she fears her husband may cling to the belief that she loves him deeply. A person who is aroused by erotic images may angrily claim that pornography is disgusting. How does such a transformed emotion differ from a true emotion? In reaction formation the professed feeling is excessive, and the person is extravagant and vehement in demonstrating it ("Of course I love him! I *never* have any bad thoughts about him! He's perfect!").

4 **REGRESSION** occurs when a person reverts to a previous phase of psychological development. A child who is anxious about his parents' increasingly abusive quarreling may regress to earlier habits of thumb sucking or clinging. Adults, too, may regress

to immature behavior when they are under pressure—for example, by having sudden, unpredictable temper tantrums.

5 DENIAL occurs when people refuse to face up to an unpleasant realization, such as the fact that they need surgery or that their partner is abusing them; that they are drinking too much; or that they are feeling a forbidden emotion, such as anger. Denial protects a person's self-image and preserves the illusion of invulnerability ("It can't happen to me").

6 DISPLACEMENT occurs when people direct their emotions (especially anger) toward things, animals, or other people that are not the real object of their feelings. People use displacement when they perceive the real target as being too threatening to confront directly. A boy who is forbidden to express anger at his father, for example, may "take it out" on his toys or his younger sister. When displacement serves a higher cultural or socially useful purpose, it is called *sublimation.* Freud believed that the price of civilization is the displacement or sublimation of sexual and aggressive energies into socially constructive forms. Sexual passion may be sublimated into the creation of art; aggressive energy may be displaced into competitive sports.

7 ACTING OUT consists of impulsive actions in which the person fails to consider the consequences of his or her behavior. A young girl who suddenly starts stealing money and small items from her friends might be acting out her sadness over her grandmother's death. Boys who become disruptive or even violent may be acting out their anger and loneliness.

8 HUMOR is a way of defending against fear, awareness of aging and death, sexual desires, aggressive impulses, and anxiety about sexual performance, which is why so many jokes are about these themes.

According to Freud, these defense mechanisms protect the ego from anxiety and allow the person to cope with the demands of the real world. People differ in the defenses they use, in how rigid their defenses are, and in whether their defenses lead to healthy or disturbed functioning (Bernstein & Warner, 1993; Vaillant, 1992). Unhealthy efforts to defend against anxiety may produce a *neurosis,* characterized by self-punishing behavior (e.g., drinking too much), emotional symptoms (e.g., anxiety), or physical symptoms (e.g., stomachaches). Freud thus promoted the idea that many physical problems have a psychological, "neurotic" cause.

Freud was aware of the ways in which culture, custom, and law shape human behavior and desires. Indeed, he wrote sympathetically and poignantly of the psychological impact on women of the sexual sublimation that society requires of them (Freud, 1908), and in his great book *Civilization and Its Discontents* (1930/1962) he examined the inevitable tensions between individual desires and the needs of society. At the same time, Freud believed that the unconscious was primary and universal. Cultures come and go, societies differ and change, but the unconscious goes on forever. Out of the internal battle between the forces of order and anarchy, said Freud, civilization emerges. "Where id is," he wrote (1933), "there must ego come to be."

What Do You Know?

A. A Freudian would say that a man who is concerned only with his own pleasure, even at the expense of hurting others, is ruled by his _____ and has too little _____.

B. Which Freudian defense mechanisms do these events suggest?

1. A celibate priest writes poetry about sexual passion.

2. A man who is angry at his boss shouts at his kids for making noise.

3. A racist justifies segregation by saying that black men are only interested in sex with white women.

4. A 9-year-old boy who moves to a new city starts having tantrums.

5. A man ignores obvious signs that his lover is unfaithful.

C. A psychoanalyst and a social-cognitive learning theorist are arguing about the displacement of aggression in sports. What positions are they likely to take, and what kind of evidence would you need to decide who is right?

ANSWERS:

A. id, superego **B.** 1. sublimation 2. displacement 3. projection 4. regression 5. denial **C.** The Freudian would assume that aggression would decrease for participants and observers of aggressive sports, because their violent instincts are being displaced. The social-cognitive learning theorist would argue that people are likely to imitate aggressive behavior, especially that of sports heroes who are role models, and that playing aggressively increases the behavior because it gets reinforced. One way to test these notions is to measure people's aggressive behavior before and after they watch or participate in aggressive sports, in contrast to nonaggressive sports. Another way is to find out whether nations that encourage aggressive sports have fewer wars (the Freudian view) or more wars (the learning view) than nations that promote nonaggressive sports. Such studies uniformly favor the social-learning explanation (Tavris, 1989).

The Development of Personality

Freud maintained that personality develops during childhood in a fixed series of five stages. He called these stages *psychosexual* because he believed that psychological development depends on the changing expression of sexual energy in different parts of the body as the child matures. Each new step, however, produces a certain amount of frustration, conflict, and worry. If these become too great, normal development may be halted, and the child may remain *fixated*, or stuck, at the current stage.

For example, said Freud, people who remain fixated at the *oral stage*, the first year of life (when babies experience the world through their mouths), may seek oral gratification in smoking, overeating, nail biting, or chewing on pencils; or they may become clinging and dependent, like a nursing child. Those who remain fixated at the *anal stage*, ages 2 to 3 (when toilet training and control of bodily wastes are the key issues), may become "anal retentive," holding everything in, obsessive about neatness and cleanliness. Or they may become just the opposite, "anal expulsive"—messy and disorganized.

For Freud, however, the most crucial stage for the formation of personality was the *phallic (Oedipal) stage,* which lasts roughly from age 3 to age 5 or 6. During this stage, said Freud, the child unconsciously wishes to possess the parent of the other sex and to get rid of the parent of the same sex. Children will often announce proudly, "I'm going to marry Daddy (or Mommy) when I grow up," and they reject the same-sex "rival." Freud (1924a, 1924b) labeled this phenomenon the **Oedipus complex,** after the Greek legend of King Oedipus, who unwittingly killed his father and married his mother.

Boys and girls, Freud believed, go through the Oedipal stage differently. Boys are discovering the pleasure and pride of having a penis, so when they see a naked girl for the first time, they are horrified. Their unconscious exclaims (in effect), "Her penis has been cut off! Who could have done such a thing to her? Why, it must have been her powerful father. And if he could do it to her, my father could do it to me!" This **castration anxiety,** said Freud, causes the boy to repress his desire for his mother, accept the authority of his father, and identify with him.[1] Identification is the process by which boys take in, as their own, the father's standards of conscience and morality. The superego has emerged.

Freud admitted that he didn't quite know what to make of females, who, lacking the penis, obviously couldn't go through the same steps. He speculated that a girl, upon discovering male anatomy, would panic that she had only a puny clitoris instead of a stately penis. She would conclude, said Freud, that she already *had* been castrated. As Freud (1924b) described it, "When she makes a comparison with a playfellow of the other sex, she perceives that she has 'come off badly' and she feels this is a wrong done to her and a ground for inferiority." As a result, girls don't have the motivating fear of castration anxiety that boys do to enable them to give up their Oedipal feelings. Girls have only a lingering sense of "penis envy," which lasts until they grow up and have children. "Her Oedipus complex culminates in a desire, which is long retained, to receive a baby from her father as a gift—to bear him a child," wrote Freud (1924b). "The two wishes—to possess a penis and a child—remain strongly cathected [emotionally linked] in the unconscious and help to prepare the female creature for her later sex role." The neurotic female, in contrast, resolves penis envy by trying to be like men, perhaps by having a career. In either case, Freud concluded, women do not develop the strong moral superegos that men do.

By about age 5 or 6, when the Oedipus complex is resolved, said Freud, the child's personality patterns are fundamentally formed. The child settles into a supposedly nonsexual *latency* stage in later childhood, in preparation for the stage of mature *genital sexuality* in adulthood. (Modern research, however, shows that most "latency"-age children

[1]Freud used the term *castration* to mean loss of the penis, but in modern medical terms it means removal of the testes.

Oedipus complex In psychoanalysis, a conflict in which a child desires the parent of the other sex and views the same-sex parent as a rival; it is the key issue in the phallic stage of development.

castration anxiety In psychoanalysis, the boy's unconscious fear of castration by the powerful father; this anxiety motivates the resolution of the Oedipus complex.

are far from being nonsexual. They are curious about sex, masturbate, and experiment with sexual play [Friedrich, 1998; Reynolds, 1998].)

Now, perhaps you can imagine why these ideas were not exactly received with yawns. Sexual feelings in infants and children! Repressed longings in the most respectable adults! Unconscious meanings in dreams! Penis envy! Sexual sublimation! This was strong stuff, and before long, psychoanalysis had captured the public imagination in Europe and America (Hornstein, 1992).

To his supporters, Freud was a brilliant explorer of the mind, the man who discovered and charted the mysterious pathways of the unconscious and revealed those pathways through the techniques of psychoanalysis. They regard him as a man who bravely battled public censure and ridicule in his unwavering pursuit of scientific truth (Gay, 1988). Yet to his critics, Freud was not so much an innovator as a self-promoter, a clever packager and marketer of other people's ideas. Citing evidence from Freud's letters and those of his colleagues, along with reviews of his work at the time, they argue that Freud actually manufactured a myth that he was a poor, misunderstood genius in order to gain sympathy and credibility (Crews, 1998; Sulloway, 1992).

Moreover, new scholarship, based on papers that had been suppressed by Freud or left unpublished for most of the twentieth century, has seriously, perhaps fatally, wounded Freud's claim that he was an impartial scientist who simply reported what his patients told him and deduced his theories from those accounts. Freud's own writings reveal that he often formulated his theories and then pressed his patients to accept them (Crews, 1998; Esterson, 1993; Powell & Boer, 1994; Webster, 1995). Early in his career, for example, Freud believed that traumatic early experiences, usually of sexual molestation, caused adult neuroses. When patients fail to report a traumatic memory, Freud wrote, "We must not believe what they say, we must always assume, and tell them, too, that they have kept something back because they thought it unimportant or found it distressing. We must insist on this, we must . . . represent ourselves as infallible, till at last we are really told something" (Breuer & Freud, 1895, cited in Powell & Boer, 1994).

A few years later, however, Freud made a critical shift of emphasis: He decided that his patients were reporting fantasies of sexual molestation rather than real events, and that all children fantasize about having sexual relations with the parent of the other sex. It is people's unconscious guilt about wanting sex with the parent, he said, not the actual experience of sexual abuse, that causes most adult emotional problems. With this turnaround, the cornerstone of psychoanalytic theory, the Oedipus complex, was established. Now Freud began to press his patients into accepting this revised theory, and he put greater weight on discovering their supposed sexual fantasies than on considering the effects of their actual sexual experiences (Powell & Boer, 1995).

A particularly chilling example is the famous case of "Dora," whose real name was Ida Bauer (Lakoff & Coyne, 1993). Eighteen-year-old Dora had been spurning the explicit sexual advances made by her father's friend, "Herr K," since she was 14, and she finally complained to her father. But her father wanted her to accept Herr K's overtures, perhaps because he himself was having an affair with Herr K's wife; so he sent her off to Freud, who attempted to "cure" Dora of her "hysterical" refusal to have sex with her father's friend. Freud tried to convince Dora that it was not the ugly situation involving her father and Herr K that was distressing her, but her own repressed desires for sex. "I should without question consider a person hysterical," Freud (1905a) wrote, "in whom an occasion for sexual excitement elicited feelings that were preponderantly or exclusively unpleasurable." Dora angrily left treatment after three months, and Freud was unable to accept her "obstinate" refusals to go along with his analysis of her symptoms. If only Herr K had learned, said Freud, "that the slap Dora gave him by no means signified a final 'No' on her part," and if he had resolved "to press his suit with a passion which left room for no doubts, the result might very well have been a triumph of the girl's affection for him over all her internal difficulties."

Sigmund Freud, the great analyst, advising another man not to take no for an answer, incapable of hearing what Dora was telling him? Yet this was the same man who encouraged women, including his own daughter Anna, to become psychoanalysts, and who wrote sensitively about the ways that the sexual double standard often trapped women in loveless, sexless marriages. Freud was thus a man of contradictions, a mix of vision and blindness, sensitivity and arrogance. Freud left a powerful legacy to psychology, and it was one that others began to tinker with immediately.

What Do You Know?

Find out whether Freudian terms have registered in the conscious part of your mind by giving the term a psychoanalyst might use to describe each of the following situations.

1. A toddler immediately puts every new toy he gets into his mouth.

2. A 4-year-old girl wants to snuggle on Daddy's lap but refuses to kiss her mother.

3. In Neil Simon's play *The Odd Couple,* two roommates drive each other crazy because one is a slob and the other a compulsive neatnik.

ANSWERS:

1. oral stage 2. Oedipal stage 3. fixation (of both characters) at the anal stage

DISSENTERS AND DESCENDANTS

"Few theories in science," said Frank Sulloway (1992), a historian of science, "have spawned a following that can compare with the psychoanalytic movement in its cult-like manifestations, in its militancy, and in the aura of religion that has permeated it." Even the movement's own adherents recognized the religious zeal they brought to their "conversion." One said that he accepted psychoanalysis "as a revealed religion," and another follower wrote that he became "the apostle of Freud who was my Christ!" (quoted in Sulloway, 1992). For his part, Freud punished the heretics who questioned his ideas by "excommunicating" them, literally excluding them from the inner circle of analysts (Crews, 1998).

One such heretic was Alfred Adler (1870–1937), who, along with others, took issue with Freud's emphasis on sexual and aggressive motivations. Adler instead emphasized the individual's need for other people and the desire for self-improvement. The impulse for improvement stems from the natural feelings of inferiority that we all have, first as children, when we are weak and powerless as compared with adults, and then later, when we must recognize the limitations on our abilities. Some individuals, wrote Adler, react to these uncomfortable feelings by developing an **inferiority complex,** because they are raised by parents who fail to encourage their abilities. They become overly concerned with protecting their self-esteem and they try to mask their feelings by pretending to be strong and capable. Human beings, however, are creators of their own destinies, and so people may be able to overcome such problems. Development does not stop with the resolution of the Oedipal complex, said Adler; we can grow and change throughout life. In 1911, Adler was banished by Freud from the Vienna Psychoanalytic Society, and he and his followers formed their own organization.

Other dissenters, however, were able to remain in the psychoanalytic circle. They included some female analysts who were not too pleased (as you might imagine) with the Freudian concept of "penis envy." Female psychology altogether was deeply puzzling to Freud, who once famously asked: "What do women want?" (Generations of women have answered him, starting with: "Ask them!") One thing all the dissenters agreed on was that women do *not* want a penis. One contemporary of Freud's, Karen Horney [HORN-eye] (1926/1973), argued that it was insulting philosophy and bad science to claim that half the human race is dissatisfied with its anatomy. When women feel inferior to men, Horney said, we should look for explanations in the "actual social subordination of women." She worried that Freudian theory would justify continued discrimination against women by making it seem that female inferiority was in their nature and not in the conditions of their lives.

Horney went on to chastise her male colleagues for their one-sided point of view. "If we try to free our minds from this masculine mode of thought," she wrote (1926/1973), "nearly all the problems of feminine psychology take on a different appearance." The first thing we notice, she said, is a woman's "indisputable and by no means negligible physiological superiority." In fact, said Horney, if anyone has an envy problem, it is men. Men have "womb envy": They envy the female ability to bear and nurse children. Men glorify their own genitals, she said, because they are unable to give birth themselves and because they unconsciously fear women's sexual power over them. Horney agreed with Freud that men suffer from castration anxiety. But whereas Freud thought the reason was the little boy's unconscious fear that his father could castrate him, Horney (1967) thought the reason was the adult man's unconscious fear that his own female lover could castrate him. The origin of men's fear of women, she wrote, "lies in the fact that during intercourse the male has to entrust his genitals to the female body, that he presents her with his semen and interprets this as a surrender of vital strength to the woman."

---

inferiority complex To Alfred Adler, an inability to accept one's natural limitations; it occurs when the need for self-improvement is blocked or inhibited.

For Horney (1945), the driving force in personality was not the aggressive and sexual instincts of the id, but **basic anxiety,** the feeling of being isolated and helpless in a hostile world. Because people are dependent on one another, she said, they often end up in a state of anxious conflict when others don't treat them well. Insecure, anxious children develop personality patterns that help them cope with their feelings of isolation and helplessness. They may become aggressive as a way of protecting what little security they do have. Or they may become overly submissive, or selfish and self-pitying as a way of gaining attention or sympathy.

Adler's and Horney's ideas influenced later researchers, who empirically investigated many of the topics they had raised. Other theorists, too, parted company with Freud by emphasizing the social conditions that influence human behavior, downplaying the role of instincts, and emphasizing the possibility of self-improvement. We turn now to three schools of psychodynamic thought that continue to be influential today.

Jungian Theory

Carl Jung [Yoong] (1875–1961) was originally one of Freud's closest friends; in fact, Jung accompanied Freud on his only visit to the United States. But Jung began to differ with Freud on the nature of the unconscious, and by 1914 Jung had left Freud's inner circle.

Jung's greatest difference with Freud concerned the nature of the unconscious. In addition to the individual's personal unconscious, said Jung (1967), there is a **collective unconscious** shared by all human beings, containing universal memories, symbols, and images that are the legacy of human history. In his studies of myths, art, and folklore in cultures all over the world, Jung identified a number of these common themes, which he called **archetypes.** An archetype can be a picture, such as the "magic circle," called a *mandala* in Eastern religions, which Jung thought symbolizes the unity of life and "the totality of the self." Or it can be a mythical figure found in fairy tales and legends, such as the Hero, the Nurturing Mother, the Powerful Father, or the Wicked Witch. It can even be an aspect of the self. For example, said Jung, the *shadow* archetype reflects the prehistoric fear of wild animals and represents the bestial, evil side of human nature.

Jung distinguished the conscious self from the unconscious archetypes that govern our behavior. According to Jung, the *persona* is the public personality, the aspects of yourself that you reveal to others, the role that society expects you to play. The *anima* is your unconscious inner self, consisting of "all those common human qualities which the conscious attitude lacks. The tyrant tormented by bad dreams, gloomy forebodings, and inner fears is a typical figure. . . . Thus his anima contains all those fallible human qualities his persona lacks. If the persona is intellectual, the anima will quite certainly be sentimental." Sometimes Jung used the term *anima* to mean the feminine quality

---

basic anxiety To Karen Horney, the feeling of being isolated and helpless in a hostile world; it is the motivating emotion in social relations.

collective unconscious To Carl Jung, the universal memories and experiences of humankind, represented in the symbols, stories, and images (archetypes) that occur across all cultures.

archetypes [AR-ki-tipes] Universal, symbolic images that appear in myths, art, stories, and dreams; to Carl Jung, they reflect the collective unconscious.

within a man. Later he added the corresponding archetype of the *animus,* the masculine quality within a woman.

Like Freud, Jung had a rather disdainful view of women, whom he regarded as being more emotional and less intellectual than men, better suited to relationships than to thinking: "In men, Eros, the function of relationship, is usually less developed than Logos [the intellect]," he said. "In women, on the other hand, Eros is an expression of their true nature, while their Logos is often only a regrettable accident." But also like Freud, Jung recognized that "masculine" and "feminine" qualities are to be found in both sexes. Problems can arise, Jung said, if a person tries to repress the internal archetype of the Other—that is, if a man totally denies his softer, "feminine" side or if a woman denies her "masculine" aspects. People also create problems in relationships when they expect a partner to behave like the ideal archetypal man or woman, instead of a real human being who has both sides.

Although Jung shared with Freud a fascination with the darker aspects of the personality, he also, like Adler and other dissenters, had confidence in the positive, forward-moving strengths of the ego. He believed that people are motivated not only by past conflicts, as Freud thought, but also by their goals and by the desire to fulfill themselves. And Jung was among the first to identify extroversion/introversion as a basic dimension of personality, as indeed it is (see Chapter 3).

Jung's theory of archetypes remains popular today. Although most psychologists regard Jung's idea of the collective unconscious as a mystical concept rather than a scientific one, they recognize that some basic archetypes, such as the Hero and the Villain, reflect universal human experiences and thus appear in virtually every society in different forms (Campbell, 1949/1968; Neher, 1996). Modern Jungians have used archetypes to explain recurring images in the films, books, and comics of popular culture, such as the endless versions of Dracula (Iaccino, 1994). "Shadow" archetypes like Dracula, Darth Vader, and the dragons and demons of literature can never be killed, Jungians would say, because we can never eradicate the evil side of human nature.

Other Jungians, drawing on contemporary research on the cognitive concepts of schema and narrative (see Chapters 7 and 8), are interested in how universal images and stories affect the way people see their own lives. When Dan McAdams (1988) asked 50 people to tell their life stories in a two-hour session, he found that they tended to report a common archetype, a mythic character, at the heart

In The Wizard of Oz, *the Wicked Witch of the West became a beloved example of the archetype of evil.*

of their life narratives. For example, many individuals told stories that could be symbolized by the myth of the Greek god Dionysus, the pleasure seeker who escapes responsibility. Archetypes, says McAdams, represent "the main characters in the life stories we construct as our identities."

Erikson's Psychosocial Theory

Freud believed that personality development is completed by age 5 or 6, when the Oedipal complex is resolved. A fuller theory of adult development, stretching from birth to death, was proposed by psychoanalyst Erik H. Erikson (1902–1994). Erikson (1950/1963, 1982) argued that everyone passes through eight developmental stages on the way to wisdom and maturity. Erikson called his theory *psychosocial*, instead of "psychosexual" as Freud had, because he believed that people are propelled by many kinds of psychological and social forces, not just by sexual motives. Each stage, said Erikson, is the result of a combination of biological drives and societal demands. At each one, a "crisis" must be resolved if healthy development is to proceed:

1 TRUST VERSUS MISTRUST is the crisis that occurs during the baby's first year, when the baby depends on others to provide food, comfort, cuddling, and warmth. If these needs are not met, the child may never develop the essential trust necessary to get along in the world, especially in relationships.

2 AUTONOMY (INDEPENDENCE) VERSUS SHAME AND DOUBT is the crisis that occurs when the child is a toddler. The young child is learning to be independent and must do so without feeling too ashamed or doubtful of his or her actions.

3 INITIATIVE VERSUS GUILT is the crisis that occurs as the preschooler develops. The child is acquiring new physical and mental skills, setting goals, and enjoying newfound talents, but must also learn to control impulses and energies. The danger lies in developing too strong a sense of guilt over his or her fantasies, growing abilities, and childish instincts.

4 COMPETENCE VERSUS INFERIORITY is the crisis for school-age children, who are learning to make things, use tools, and acquire the skills for adult life. Children who fail these lessons of mastery and competence risk feeling inadequate and inferior.

5 IDENTITY VERSUS ROLE CONFUSION is the crisis of adolescence, when teenagers must decide what they are going to be and what they hope to make of their lives. The term *identity crisis* describes what Erikson considered to be the primary conflict of this stage. Those who resolve this crisis will come out of this stage with a strong identity, ready to plan for the future. Those who do not will sink into confusion, unable to make decisions.

6 INTIMACY VERSUS ISOLATION is the crisis of young adulthood. Once you have decided who you are, said Erikson, you must share yourself with another and learn to make commitments. No matter how successful you are in work, you are not complete until you are capable of intimacy.

7 GENERATIVITY VERSUS STAGNATION is the crisis of the middle years. Now that you know who you are and have an intimate relationship, will you sink into complacency and selfishness, or will you experience generativity, the pleasure of creativity and renewal? Parenthood is the most common means for the successful resolution of this stage, but people can be productive, creative, and nurturant in other ways, in their work or their relationships with the younger generation.

8 EGO INTEGRITY VERSUS DESPAIR is the crisis of old age. As people age, they strive to reach the ultimate goal—wisdom, spiritual tranquility, an acceptance of their lives. Just as the healthy child will not fear life, said Erikson, the healthy adult will not fear death.

Erikson recognized that cultural and economic factors affect these stages of psychological development. Some societies, for example, make the transition from one stage to another relatively easy. If you know you are going to be a farmer like your mother and father and you have no alternative, then moving from adolescence into young adulthood is not a terribly painful step (unless you hate farming). If you have many choices, however, as adolescents in urban societies often do, the transition can become prolonged. Some people put off making choices indefinitely and never resolve their "identity crisis." Similarly, cultures that place a high premium on independence and individualism will make it difficult for many of their members to resolve Erikson's sixth crisis, that of intimacy versus isolation.

Erikson's work was important because he showed that development is never finished; it is an ongoing process, and the unconscious crises or issues of one stage may be reawakened during another. Erikson placed adult development in the context of family and society, and he identified the essential concerns of adulthood: trust, competence, identity, love and generativity, the ability to enjoy life and accept death.

However, researchers have shown that Erikson's stages are far from universal, and the psychological concerns he identified do not necessarily occur at only one stage of life. Although in Western societies adolescence *is* often a time of confusion about identity and aspirations, an identity crisis is not limited to the teen years. A man who has worked in one job all his adult life, and then is laid off and must find an entirely new career, may have an identity crisis, too. Likewise, competence is not mastered once and for all in childhood. People learn new skills and lose old ones throughout their lives, and their sense of competence rises and falls accordingly. Individuals who are highly generative (in terms of being committed to helping the next generation) tend to be so *throughout* their lives, doing volunteer work or choosing occupations that allow them to help others (Mansfield & McAdams, 1996). And women (who were omitted from Erikson's original work) have often done things "out of order," for example by entering the stage of "generativity" and having families before they faced the matter of professional "identity" (Helson & McCabe, 1993).

For all these reasons, modern theories of adult development emphasize the transitions and milestones that mark adult life in all its variation, instead of a rigid developmental sequence that applies to everyone.

Object-Relations Theory

In the late 1950s, John Bowlby (1958), a British psychoanalyst, contested the Freudian view that an infant's attachment to the mother could be explained solely in terms of her ability to gratify the baby's oral needs. As we saw in Chapter 3, Bowlby had found that infants who were deprived of normal contact with parents and other adults suffered terribly, and he argued for the primacy of attachment needs: the baby's need for social stimulation, warmth, and contact. Bowlby's work influenced other psychoanalysts to acknowledge the fundamentally social nature of human development. Although the need for social contact now seems obvious, this change in emphasis was a significant departure from the classic Freudian view, for Freud essentially regarded the baby as if it were an independent, greedy little organism ruled by its own instinctive desires.

Today, an emphasis on relationships as the foundation of unconscious dynamics and psychological development is associated most closely with **object-relations theory,** developed in Great Britain by Melanie Klein, W. Ronald Fairbairn, and D. W. Winnicott (Hughes, 1989). In contrast to Freud's emphasis on the Oedipal period, object-relations theorists hold that the infant's first two years are the most critical for development of the inner core of personality. Freud emphasized the child's fear of the father; object-relations analysts emphasize the child's need for the powerful mother, who is usually the baby's main caregiver during the first critical years. Freud's theory was based on the dynamics of inner drives and impulses; object-relations theory holds that the basic human drive is not impulse gratification but the need to be in relationships (Horner, 1991; Hughes, 1989; Kernberg, 1976).

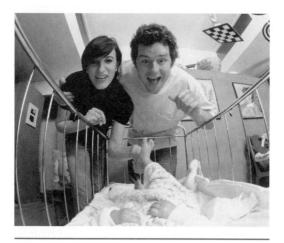

According to object-relations theory, a baby constructs unconscious representations of his or her parents, which will influence the child's relations with others throughout life.

The reason for the clunky word *object* in object-relations theory (instead of the warmer word *human* or even *parent*) is that the infant's attachment is not only to a real person (usually the mother), but also to the infant's evolving perception of her. The child "takes in" a representation of the mother—someone who is kind or fierce, protective or rejecting—that is not literally the same as the woman herself. A *representation* is a complex cognitive schema that is constructed by the child. The child's representations of important adults, whether realistic or distorted, unconsciously affect personality throughout life, influencing

---

object-relations theory A psychodynamic approach that emphasizes the importance of the infant's first two years and the baby's formative relationships, especially with the mother.

how the person relates to others: with trust or suspicion, acceptance or criticism (Westen, 1998).

In Freudian theory, the central psychodynamic problem is the displacement of psychic energy—sexual and aggressive drives in particular—onto other people. Other people are relevant only insofar as they gratify our drives or block them. But to object-relations theorists, other people are important as *sources of attachment.* Therefore the central dynamic tension, the key issue in life, is the constantly changing balance between independence and connection to others. This balance requires constant adjustment to separations and losses, from small ones that occur during quarrels and spats, to moderate ones such as leaving home for the first time, to major ones such as divorce or death. Our reactions to these separations as adults is largely determined by our experiences in our first two years (and some object-relations theorists would say in the first few months). The relationship with the first caregiver, usually the mother, forms a model for all later ones.

Other people, of course, can never treat us perfectly. Even the most loving and attentive mother will occasionally fail to be perfectly attuned to her infant. Thus infants learn virtually right away that Mom will occasionally let them down. As two object-relations therapists put it, "The unsatisfying experiences that occur in relation to mother then find their expressions in a particular reflection of her in the infant's inner world. Mother becomes a disappointing person who has to be split in two: the known and longed-for giving mother and the known and deeply disappointing mother" (Eichenbaum & Orbach, 1983).

This concept of **splitting** is important in object-relations theory (Kernberg, 1976; Ogden, 1989). It means the separating of opposites: good and bad, right and wrong, weak and strong, pleasure and pain. Infants cannot comprehend that all of these opposites can be mixed together in one person, so "Mom" is split into two versions: the Terrific Mother and the Terrible Mother. Then, between about 1½ and 3 years of age, children begin to accept ambivalent feelings about themselves and others (Young-Eisendrath, 1993). They understand that the "good" mother who comforts them is the same as the "bad" mother who went away for a weekend. By adulthood, healthy individuals can recognize and accept ambivalence. But unhealthy individuals cannot understand that every relationship is a mix of good and bad, pleasure and unhappiness. They resort to the childish defense mechanism of splitting: The minute a partner reveals a normal human flaw, he or she becomes a completely terrible person who must be rejected. Even emotionally healthy adults, when threatened or overwhelmed, succumb to splitting. The kind of "us-them" stereotyping that occurs during group conflict and war is an example of splitting. Few people can acknowledge the good qualities of their worst enemies.

The object-relations school also departs from classic Freudian theory on the nature of male and female psychological development. Whereas Freud thought that female development was the problem, many proponents of the object-relations school regard male development as the problem (Chodorow, 1978; Dinnerstein, 1976; Sagan, 1988; Winnicott, 1957/1990). In their view, children of both sexes identify first with the mother. Girls, who are the same sex as the mother, do not need to separate from

---

splitting In object-relations theory, the division of qualities into their opposites, as in the Good Mother versus the Bad Mother; it reflects an inability to understand that people are made up of good and bad qualities.

her; the mother treats a daughter as an extension of herself. But boys, if they are to develop a male identity, must break away from the mother. Often, individual mothers encourage this emotional separation. When they don't, some cultures see to it that young boys separate physically and emotionally from the "women's world"—for example, by going through severe male initiation rites.

However male identity is attained, according to object-relations theorists, it is more precarious and insecure than female identity, because it is based on not being like women. In this view, the reason that many men fear intimacy and disdain "women's qualities" such as softness and nurturance is that they fear losing their masculinity. As D. W. Winnicott (1957/1990) wrote, "Traced to its root in the history of each individual, this fear of *women* turns out to be a fear of recognizing the fact of dependence." As a result of this fear, men develop more rigid *ego boundaries* between themselves and other people than women do. Later in life, the typical problem for women is how to increase their independence, so they can assert their own abilities and not be used as doormats in their close relationships. In contrast, the typical problem for men is how to permit close attachments (Gilligan, 1982).

In Freud's theory, as you may recall, a boy's superego and moral conscience emerge after the Oedipal phase and develop because of his identification with the father's authority; girls, lacking this clear-cut resolution of the Oedipal conflict, develop a more limited moral capacity. But to some object-relations analysts, the real origin of moral values lies in the infant's early relationship to the mother, long before the emergence of the superego, and it is men who have the more limited moral capacity. Because men must defend themselves so thoroughly against the memory of the nurturing mother, in this view, and because they learn to regard women as a threat to their masculinity, they feel psychically bound to disparage the moral virtues associated with females: nurturance, pity, compassion, and love (Sagan, 1988).

What Do You Know?

Can you match each idea (right) with the analyst or school who proposed it (left)?

1. Sigmund Freud	a. collective unconscious
2. Karen Horney	b. splitting
3. Alfred Adler	c. superego
4. Erik Erikson	d. womb envy
5. Carl Jung	e. Oedipus complex
6. object-relations theory	f. identity crisis
	g. archetype
	h. representation of mother
	i. inferiority complex
	j. psychosocial stages
	k. basic anxiety

ANSWERS:

1. c,e 2. d,k 3. i 4. f,j 5. a,g 6. b,h

HUMANIST AND EXISTENTIAL PSYCHOLOGY

As we have seen, psychodynamic psychologists seek the unconscious motivations that they believe are the keys to personality and behavior, which is why we called this chapter "The Inner Life." Other approaches also emphasize the inner life—not by emphasizing unconscious motives, however, but by concentrating on a person's own sense of self, which exists beneath the external masks we present to the world.

Psychologists who adopt this view—humanists and existentialists—differ from traditional psychodynamic theorists by focusing on the qualities that separate human beings from other animals: freedom of choice and free will. We include these theorists in our discussion of the psychodynamic perspective because they share a reliance on subjective methods, the therapeutic goals of insight and helping people find meaning in their experiences, and an emphasis on a person's psychic reality.

In the early 1960s, as we saw in Chapter 1, **humanist psychology** was launched as a distinctive movement within psychology. Its chief leaders were Abraham Maslow (1908–1970), Rollo May (1909–1994), and Carl Rogers (1902–1987). These men rejected the psychoanalytic emphasis on hostility, biological instincts, and repressed conflicts. The trouble with psychology, said Maslow (1971), was that it had forgotten that human nature includes some good things, such as joy, laughter, love, happiness, and *peak experiences,* rare moments of rapture caused by the attainment of excellence or the experience of beauty. The qualities that Maslow emphasized were those of what he called the *self-actualized person,* the person who strives for a life that is meaningful, challenging, and satisfying.

Carl Rogers, like Freud, derived many of his ideas from observing his clients in therapy. As a clinician, Rogers (1951, 1961) was interested not only in why some people cannot function well, but also in what he called the "fully functioning" individual. Rogers' theory of personality is based on the relationship between your conscious view of yourself and the cumulative effect of all of your experiences, including unconscious feelings, perceptions, and wishes. These experiences are known only to you, through

For humanist and existential psychologists, the central issue for us all is the meaning of life—though we'll all come up with different answers.

---

humanist psychology A psychological approach that emphasizes personal growth and the achievement of human potential rather than the scientific understanding and assessment of behavior.

your own frame of reference. How you behave depends on your own subjective reality, Rogers said, not on the external reality around you. Fully functioning people have a *congruence,* or harmony, between their conscious and unconscious selves. They are trusting, warm, and open; they are not defensive or intolerant; they are realistic about themselves. People in a state of incongruence are at war with parts of themselves, "out of sync" with their unconscious needs or wishes.

To become fully functioning people, Rogers believed, we all need **unconditional positive regard,** love and support for the people we are, without strings (conditions) attached. This doesn't mean that Winifred gets to kick her brother when she is angry with him or that Wilbur may throw his dinner out the window because he doesn't like pot roast. In these cases, a parent can correct the child's behavior without withdrawing love from the child. The child can learn that the behavior, not the child, is what is bad. "House rules are 'no violence,' kids," is a very different message from "You are a horrible person for kicking your brother, Winifred."

Unfortunately, said Rogers, many children are raised with *conditional* positive regard: "I'll love you if you behave well and I won't love you if you behave badly." Adults often treat each other this way, too. But people treated with conditional regard, Rogers believed, begin to suppress or deny feelings or actions that they believe are unacceptable to those they love. The result is incongruence, the sensation of being "out of touch with your feelings," of not being true to your "real self." The suppression of feelings and parts of oneself produces low self-regard, defensiveness, and bitterness. (In Chapter 12 we will consider Rogers' contributions to psychotherapy.)

Not all humanists have focused, as Maslow and Rogers did, on joy, love, peak experiences, and other cheerful aspects of human nature. Rollo May (1994), for example, emphasized some of the inherently difficult and tragic aspects of the human condition, including loneliness, anxiety, and alienation. In books such as *The Meaning of Anxiety, Existential Psychology,* and *Love and Will,* May brought to American psychology elements of the European philosophy of *existentialism.* This doctrine holds that free will and freedom of choice confer on us responsibility for our actions. The price is often anxiety and despair, which is why many people try to escape from freedom into narrow certainties and blame others for their misfortunes. We can choose to make the best of ourselves, but we can never escape the brutal realities of life and death.

Like May, **existential psychologists** emphasize the universal struggle to find meaning in life, to decide what is right and moral and then to live by that decision, to come to an understanding and acceptance of suffering and death—and, in accord with our final guideline of critical thinking, to live with uncertainty about some of the choices we make (Becker, 1973; Yalom, 1980).

According to Irvin Yalom (1989), a contemporary existential analyst, the primal conflicts and concerns of life do not stem, as Freud thought, from repressed instinctual desires

---

unconditional positive regard To Carl Rogers, love or support given to another person, with no conditions attached.

existential psychology An approach to psychology that emphasizes free will and responsibility for one's actions, and the importance of struggling with the harsh realities of existence, such as the need to find meaning in life and to accept suffering and death.

or traumatic childhood experiences. Rather, he argues, anxiety emerges from a person's efforts, conscious and unconscious, to cope with the harsh realities of life, what he calls "the 'givens' of existence." Those "givens" are "the inevitability of death for each of us and those we love; the freedom to make our lives as we will; our ultimate aloneness; and, finally, the absence of any obvious meaning or sense to life. However grim these givens may seem, they contain the seeds of wisdom and redemption." Perhaps the most remarkable example of a man able to find seeds of wisdom in a barren landscape was Victor Frankl (1955), who developed a form of existential therapy after surviving a Nazi concentration camp. In that pit of horror, he observed, some people maintained their dignity and sanity because they were able to find meaning in the experience, shattering though it was.

Existential and humanist psychologists maintain that our lives are not inevitably determined by our parents, our pasts, or our present circumstances; we have the power to choose our own destinies, even when fate delivers us into tragedy. We can choose to make the best of ourselves, using our inner resources of love, intelligence, and courage. This approach has added richness and depth to the study of psychology by acknowledging the importance of meaning, suffering, and narrative in how people construct their experiences and make decisions about their lives.

What Do You Know?

It's time to struggle with the inevitable realities of quizzes.

1. Abraham Maslow thought that the most important qualities to understand were those of the (a) fully functioning individual, (b) anxious individual, (c) self-actualized individual.

2. According to Carl Rogers, a man who loves his wife only when she is looking her best is giving her (a) conditional or (b) unconditional positive regard.

3. List three things that humanist and existential psychologists share with traditional psychodynamic theorists.

4. An existentialist psychologist and a psychoanalyst are arguing about whether people are basically good or bad, the nature of free will, and the main motives of human life. What different assumptions are they likely to bring to their discussion?

ANSWERS:

1. c 2. a 3. A reliance on subjective methods, the therapeutic goals of insight and helping people find meaning in their experiences, and an emphasis on a person's psychic reality. 4. The psychoanalyst may assume that people are inherently selfish and destructive; that "free will" is an illusion because we are all governed by unconscious processes stemming from early relations with our parents; and that the most important motives in human behavior are sex and aggression. The existentialist is likely to assume that people are inherently capable of generosity and courage; that people do have free will and responsibility for their actions; and that the most important human motives are the struggles to find meaning, cope with loneliness and alienation, and accept loss and death.

THE PSYCHODYNAMIC PARADOX

Reflect for a moment on some of the conflicting views you have encountered in this chapter:

✦ Freud thought that because women lack the prized penis, they fear and envy men and therefore come to accept their inferior status. Horney thought that because men lack the wonderful womb, they fear and envy women and must therefore force women into an inferior status.

✦ Freud considered the Oedipal phase the most important in the development of personality; object-relations theorists think the first two years are the most important; and Erikson believed that development continues all through life.

✦ Freud assumed that sex and aggression are the driving forces in human development; Adler assumed that the most important motive is a need for self-improvement and accomplishment; existentialists assume it is the need for meaning.

✦ Freud thought that women have the greater problem in psychic development and end up morally deficient; many object-relations adherents think that men have the greater problem in psychic development and end up morally deficient.

✦ Freud, observing his patients and the flow of events in history, saw conflict, destructive drives, selfishness, and lust. Other analysts and humanists, also observing their patients and the flow of events in history, have seen cooperation, creativity, altruism, love, and hope.

Of course, psychologists within every perspective disagree about certain concepts and assumptions; disagreement is not the problem. The difference between other psychologists and psychodynamic theorists, however, is that the latter rely almost entirely on inference and subjective interpretation to draw their conclusions about what a baby feels or desires, about whether or why men and women unconsciously envy and fear each other, and about the central motivation of human behavior. Most psychodynamic and humanist assumptions are untestable by the usual methods of psychological research. And that is ultimately the most interesting and exasperating thing about them: How are we supposed to evaluate these ideas? Which have merit? Should we endorse one theorist over another on the basis of intuitive "rightness," or in some other way?

And yet, the psychodynamic perspective stands alone in trying to describe personality and behavior in a coherent framework. Biological research accounts for certain human qualities, trait by trait; learning principles account for some acquired habits and expectations, piece by piece; cognitive research focuses on thoughts and beliefs, one by one; and sociocultural research identifies the influential elements of our social worlds, situation by situation. But psychodynamic, humanist, and existential psychologists attempt to put all of these components together in terms of each person's lived experience.

Thus, it's one thing to say that the mind is designed for cognitive consistency; the psychodynamic perspective tries to explain why people bring so much heat and passion—indeed, *defensiveness*—to protecting their beliefs. For example, the psychodynamic perspective confronts the depths of emotional loathing and panic that often characterize prejudice toward gay men and lesbians in America. Freud (1961) believed that homosexuality was "no vice, no degradation" but "a variation of the sexual function." Indeed, Freud said, everyone has at least an unconscious attraction to members of the same sex, although awareness of this "latent homosexuality" is highly threatening to most people. So Freud would not have been surprised to read a letter we saw in a magazine, written in response to an article about homosexuality on campus:

> [Homosexuality] ranks as an odious sex crime on the level of bestiality, rape and incest. It is a behavior that is a perversion of nature, and it is a sin that is repugnant to man and to society. It is the activity that is responsible for the degradation and the mutilation of human lives and beautiful people. By publishing articles not only condoning this aberration, but brazenly, shamelessly and audaciously promoting it, you . . . undermine the very core and foundation of this great educational institution so that it will ultimately crumble and be destroyed.

Why is the man who wrote this letter so emotional, so overwrought? Psychodynamic theorists would say that something is going on in his unconscious that involves far more than an objective appraisal of homosexuality or even mere discomfort. Something is impeding his ability to reason objectively about the issue. They would point out that it is possible for heterosexuals to be uncomfortable about homosexuality without sharing this man's wholesale condemnation of homosexuals or the *ferocity* he brings to the discussion. A Freudian might say the man is repressing his own homosexual impulses, which frighten him; a Jungian might speak of his inability to accept his *anima;* an object-relations analyst might suspect that he had difficulty separating from his mother and defining his own masculinity. But they are all on a similar track in addressing the unconscious fears, needs, and hostility that certainly seem to be motivating this man's attitudes.

And so the psychodynamic perspective leaves us with a paradox: Many of its ideas and analyses are intuitively appealing; yet, as scientists in psychology and other fields have repeatedly shown, intuition is often a pretty shaky ground to stand on. When put to objective test, many psychodynamic intuitions have turned out to be dead wrong. Perhaps the sex researcher Havelock Ellis said it best. In 1910, Ellis was called upon to write a review of one of Freud's early works. "Even when Freud selects a very thin thread" in tying together his theories, Ellis concluded, "he seldom fails to string pearls on it, and these have their value whether the thread snaps or not." We turn now to an examination of the weak points in the psychodynamic thread, and to the beauty of the pearls. ■

Summary

1. The psychodynamic perspective holds that the key to understanding human behavior is the inner, unconscious life. The first psychodynamic theory of personality was Sigmund Freud's theory of *psychoanalysis.* Today there are many others that differ from classical psychoanalysis and from one another, but they generally share five elements: an emphasis on unconscious *intrapsychic* dynamics; an assumption that adult behavior and problems are determined primarily by experiences in early childhood; a belief that psychological development occurs in fixed stages; a focus on a person's *psychic reality* rather than actual experiences as the main influence on behavior; and a reliance on subjective rather than objective methods of getting at the truth of a person's life.

2. Freud believed that the most important motives affecting behavior are sexual and aggressive. According to Freud, the personality consists of the *id,* the source of unconscious instincts and the *libido;* the *ego,* the source of reason; and the *super-ego,* the source of conscience. The healthy personality must keep all three systems in balance.

3. The ego, in Freud's view, uses unconscious *defense mechanisms* to ward off the anxiety and tension that occur when the wishes of the id conflict with the demands of conscience and social rules. They include *repression, projection, reaction formation, regression, denial, displacement* and *sublimation, acting out,* and *humor.* Different personalities emerge because people differ in the defenses they use, in how rigid their defenses are, and in whether their defenses lead to healthy or disturbed functioning. Unhealthy efforts to defend against anxiety may produce a *neurosis.*

4. Freud believed that personality develops in a series of *psychosexual stages:* oral, anal, phallic (Oedipal), latency, and genital. During the phallic stage, Freud believed, the *Oedipus complex* occurs, in which the child desires the parent of the other sex and feels rivalry with the same-sex parent. When the complex is resolved, the child identifies with the same-sex parent. Freud thought that boys and girls resolve the Oedipal stage differently; boys resolve it when they experience *castration anxiety,* but girls are left with a lingering sense of "penis envy." Women, Freud believed, do not develop the strong moral superegos that men do.

5. Freud's theory still has many admirers and supporters, but new research calls into question Freud's ethics and methods. For example, Freud often formulated his theories first, and then pressed his patients to accept and confirm them.

6. Many early dissenters within psychoanalysis went on to formulate their own psychodynamic theories and schools. For example, Alfred Adler argued that the central motive in life is a desire for self-improvement, stemming from feelings of inferiority in childhood; these feelings can result in an *inferiority complex.* Karen Horney criticized Freud's notion of penis envy, countering that men envy women's reproductive ability ("womb envy") and fear women's sexual power. She argued that *basic anxiety* was the central human motive. Other theorists, too, parted company with Freud by emphasizing social influences on behavior, downplaying the role of instincts, and emphasizing the possibility of self-improvement.

7. Carl Jung believed that people share a *collective unconscious* that contains universal human memories and *archetypes.* Individuals are governed by the *persona* (the public self), the *shadow* (the evil, bestial side of human nature), and the *anima* (in men) or *animus* (in women). Jung's notion of archetypes remains popular today.

8. Erik Erikson proposed a *psychosocial theory* of development, which holds that life consists of eight stages, each with a unique psychological crisis that must be resolved, such as competence in childhood and an *identity crisis* in adolescence. Modern research has found that these psychological concerns are not confined to any particular age or stage, but occur throughout life, and that the sequence of stages is not universal. But Erikson made important contributions by considering the individual in the context of society and by identifying the important concerns of adulthood.

9. *Object-relations theory* puts relationships at the center of psychological development. It differs from classical Freudian theory in emphasizing the importance of the first two years of life, rather than the Oedipal phase; the infant's relationships to important figures, especially the mother, rather than sexual needs and drives; and the problem in male development of breaking away from the mother. The central dynamic tension in life, in this view, is the constantly changing balance between independence and connection to others.

10. Object-relations theory stresses the importance of the child's unconscious *representations* of important adults, which affect how the child will relate to others throughout life. The healthy child will grow beyond the defense mechanism of *splitting* and recognize that all human beings combine good and bad qualities. Some object-relations theorists believe that men's distance from and fear of women causes them to disparage the moral virtues associated with females, such as nurturance and compassion.

11. *Humanist* and *existential psychologists* focus on a person's subjective perceptions of self and free will to change. Humanist psychologists emphasize human potential and the strengths of human nature, as in Abraham Maslow's concepts of *peak experiences* and *self-actualization.* Carl Rogers stressed the role of *congruence* for a "fully functioning person," and the importance of *unconditional positive regard* in creating such healthy individuals.

12. Rollo May helped bring existentialism to American psychology. Existential psychologists emphasize the inherent dilemmas of the human condition, including loneliness and anxiety; the search for meaning and moral standards; and the quest to understand and accept suffering and death. They depart from many psychodynamic theorists in maintaining that people are not determined by their parents, pasts, or unconscious drives but by their power to choose their own destinies.

13. Psychodynamic, humanist, and existential theories rely almost entirely on inference and subjective interpretations, and most of their assumptions are untestable by the usual methods of psychological research. But this perspective stands alone in trying to describe personality and behavior in a coherent framework and in terms of each person's lived, subjective experience.

Key Terms

Evaluating the Psychodynamic Perspective

Throughout this century, the psychodynamic perspective and scientific psychology—the kind represented by the previous four perspectives in this book—have been at war, fighting over fundamental assumptions about the meaning of science and truth. What is science? How do we know what is true? What kind of evidence is required to support a hypothesis?

As far as the early psychoanalysts were concerned, science had nothing to do with controlled experiments, interviews, statistics, or counting the frequency of some behavior. "Constructing a science of the mind could mean only one thing," Gail Hornstein wrote (1992), "—finding some way to peer through the watery murk of consciousness to the subaquean reality that lay beyond. The efforts of [research] psychologists, with their bulky equipment and piles of charts and graphs, seemed superficial and largely irrelevant to this goal." Psychoanalysts rejected all this paraphernalia and relied solely on their own interpretations of cases they saw in therapy, of myths and literature, and of people's behavior in everyday life.

But to research psychologists, the idea that analysts could claim to be doing science while chucking out the cardinal rules of the scientific method—replicable findings, publicly verifiable data, objective confirmation of evidence, and the concerted effort to control prejudices and any other possible sources of bias—was enough to make them break out in hives. When psychoanalysis first became popular in the United States in the 1920s, many scientific psychologists regarded it as a popular craze, something on a par with mind reading or phrenology, that would blow over. John Watson called it "voodooism." "Psychoanalysis attempts to creep in wearing the uniform of science," wrote another critic at the time, "and to strangle it from the inside" (quoted in Hornstein, 1992).

These two opposite notions of what science meant, and how a psychologist could discover the "truth" of a person's life, put the psychodynamic perspective and empirical psychology on a collision course that continues to this day. "Psychoanalysis is a pseudoscience, with which we have been associated too long," complained Hans Eysenck (1993), representing the view of many researchers. "The Freudian empire has been found wanting

477

in every detail, including truthful accounts of its origins, its effectiveness, and its theoretical cogency. If we do not make it clear that modern scientific psychology has nothing to do with Freudian psychoanalysis, we will forever be tarred with the same brush." But to those in the psychodynamic tradition, their perspective alone captures the inner life that eludes behavioral observations and questionnaires. Nancy Chodorow (1992), explaining why she fell "intellectually in love" with psychoanalysis, said, "I have learned from psychoanalysis that we cannot measure human life solely in socially determinist terms. In the integration of their conscious and unconscious lives, in the quality of their primary emotional relationships with others, as in social organization and politics, people can help to create for themselves a more meaningful life."

CONTRIBUTIONS OF THIS PERSPECTIVE

Psychodynamic psychologists argue that scientific psychology, in contrast to their own approach, misses the essence and intensity of people's mental lives. In aiming to pin down small pieces of the personality, they add, scientific psychologists fail to see the whole person (Westen, 1998). As for their methods, psychodynamic psychologists observe that the fact that they don't use traditional methods doesn't mean that they have none at all. Let's look more closely, then, at this perspective's contributions.

1 A WILLINGNESS TO ADDRESS "BIG PICTURE" QUESTIONS. Psychologists in the psychodynamic perspective are not only willing but eager to take on large, important concerns in human life that are often difficult to study empirically. They have speculated about the reasons for universal symbols and images, folktales and myths. They have theorized about the consequences of the unique human awareness of mortality and the need to find meaning in life. They have grappled with the irrational energy that people often bring to matters of sexuality and gender, trying to explain why so many women and men regard one another as exotic, mysterious creatures—the "Other."

2 AN IMAGINATIVE USE OF QUALITATIVE INFORMATION. Psychodynamic theorists are willing to look everywhere for evidence, creatively drawing on cultural rituals, literature, fairy tales, jokes, or any other source of information they find useful. Such an approach, they argue, allows them to explore questions that are difficult and perhaps impossible to study by the usual methods of scientific psychology. Consider the common, apparently worldwide, fascination with horror stories and fairy tales about ghosts and evil witches. Specific psychodynamic explanations of these phenomena vary, but they share a view that such stories both reflect and exorcise unconscious anxieties about danger and death.

These explanations are appealing because they make sense of behavior that seems irrational. For example, why do so many people like going to movies in order to be scared out of their wits? In his cultural history of modern horror movies, David Skal (1993) used psychodynamic concepts to make the argument that the themes in these films reflect unconscious anxieties caused by specific economic and social conditions.

In the psychodynamic view, Dracula will never die—and neither will Dracula movies.

The ultimate appeal of all fictitious monsters, says Skal, is that they allow audiences to displace their anxieties (about the economy, about strangers, about death) and also transcend them. Horror movies were born after the unprecedented slaughter of soldiers and civilians in World War I, with *The Cabinet of Dr. Caligari* and *Nosferatu*. In the 1920s, the prevalence of mutilated and maimed war veterans prompted an outpouring of films with disfigured heroes, such as *The Phantom of the Opera* and *The Hunchback of Notre Dame.* During the Great Depression of the 1930s, films such as *Frankenstein* and *Dracula* captured the national anxiety and despair about the economy. After World War II, horror movies took a new shape, reflecting people's fears of the atomic bomb and the new enemy, communists. The popular horror films of this era were about giant, mutated monsters (*Godzilla*) or about invasions of aliens (*Invasion of the Body Snatchers*).

In the 1960s and 1970s, horror films featured monstrous babies and unnatural births—this time, Skal believes, reflecting national insecurities about the sexual revolution and changing gender roles. And in the 1990s, horror movies seemed to reflect anxiety about the power of technology over our lives: Films were suddenly full of menacing androids, "machine-men," computers that go crazy, and the like.

Notice the difference between this analysis and that, say, of the social-cognitive learning approach. A learning theorist would say that the public should worry about violent horror films because they model behavior that children might imitate and because they desensitize viewers to cruelty. Psychodynamic theorists would reply that we have about as much chance of getting rid of horror films and stories as we do of actually killing Dracula. Because these creatures serve our unconscious needs, they will always return in one form or another.

3 **AN EMPHASIS ON SELF-KNOWLEDGE, ESPECIALLY THE FACTORS BELOW CONSCIOUS AWARENESS THAT INFLUENCE OUR BEHAVIOR.** On a more personal level, the psychodynamic perspective reminds us that because of unconscious patterns and needs, individuals are often the last to know the reasons for their own behavior. Explanations based on unconscious dynamics try to account for the unpredictable ways that people react to one another, unwanted negative moods that seem to arrive for no reason, and emotional overreactions to innocent remarks. To illustrate this point, psychoanalyst Mardi Horowitz (1988) described the reactions of a man he treated, whom he called Tom. One day when Tom was under a lot of pressure at work, he got a call from his father telling him that his mother had died suddenly. Tom's reaction was to laugh harshly and say "Damn it!" in a bitter tone. His father, startled and hurt, hung up, and Tom went home to get ready to fly across the country for the funeral. He felt dull and unresponsive as he packed his clothes, and his 5-year-old daughter tried to joke with him. Tom suddenly snarled angrily at her. When she fled the room in tears, he was overcome by remorse and began to cry.

"It is not surprising that Tom cried," observed Horowitz, "but *when* he cried was— as also were his laughter and abrupt anger at the unexpected news of his mother's death, and his explosive rage at his beloved daughter. More important, these reactions were inappropriate, distressing to others, and followed by his own remorse." In the psychodynamic view, many unconscious mechanisms caused Tom's inappropriate reactions: denial of the reality of his mother's death; projection of his anger at fate onto his father, who was only the messenger of bad news; and regression to feeling like a "needy child" himself, which prevented him from being able to respond maturely to his daughter's demands for attention.

A contribution of the object-relations school, in particular, has been to show how unconscious expectations and habits, established in early relations with important family members, reproduce themselves in adult relationships. "Experiences with our mother, father, siblings, and others form powerful impressions, like engravings on some inner wall of our psyche, which become the standards against which all other relationships are measured," wrote Barry Dym and Michael Glenn (1993). They observed that a boy who learns that he can trust his mother with his secrets and worries will, as an adult, continue to trust women. But a boy whose mother changes the subject every time he confesses a problem, or who tells him that "real boys" don't have silly worries, may feel betrayed and inadequate; later in life, he is likely to be reluctant to share his confidences with women.

Of course, the learning and cognitive perspectives also recognize the importance of learned patterns in affecting adult behavior, but the psychodynamic perspective emphasizes their *unconscious* aspects. Imagine a woman who finds, much to her own puzzlement, that she keeps sabotaging close relationships. An object-relations analyst would suspect that she had suffered repeated losses of, or separations from, one or both parents, experiencing these losses as personal rejections and thus growing up to expect further rejections. The reason she sabotages her current relationships, according to object-relations theory, is that she is projecting her image of a rejecting parent onto her friends and lovers, inducing them to fulfill her expectation. Dym and Glenn (1993) put it this way: "If, for example, I cast the image of a rejecting person onto you and then act as if you were indeed rejecting me, you might pull away, be critical, or otherwise treat me rejectingly. The closer your actions mirror my projections, the more my beliefs about who you are [are] confirmed." Again, this process is mostly unconscious.

MISUSES AND LIMITATIONS OF THIS PERSPECTIVE

The contributions of psychodynamic theorists have been important to the study of psychology. Critics, however, are concerned about some inherent problems and misuses of the psychodynamic perspective.

1 **PSYCHODYNAMIC REDUCTIONISM.** Every perspective in psychology, as we have seen throughout this book, suffers from the risk of reductionism, and the psychodynamic perspective is no exception. Psychodynamic psychologists tend to emphasize a person's psychic reality over the actual circumstances of the person's life. However, psychic reality isn't everything; it is a mistake to reduce all behavior to unconscious processes and thereby overlook the importance of biology, conscious thoughts, experiences, culture, and circumstance. Yet psychoanalysts and some other psychodynamic therapists often regard a patient's conflicts with children, financial problems, job stresses, or relationships with family not as potential *sources of distress* but solely as *results of unconscious dynamics* (Fancher, 1995).

The practice of explaining a person's behavior entirely in terms of intrapsychic dynamics was not invented by psychoanalysts. In the early years of the nineteenth century, a physician named Samuel Cartwright argued that many slaves were suffering from the mental illness of "drapetomania," an uncontrollable urge to escape from slavery (from the Latin word *drapetes,* "runaway slave," and *mania,* meaning "mad" or "crazy"). The so-called symptoms included being disobedient, talking back, refusing to work, and fighting back when beaten (Kutchins & Kirk, 1997; Landrine, 1988). Thus doctors could assure slave owners that a mental illness, not the intolerable condition of slavery, made slaves seek freedom. Today drapetomania sounds foolish and cruel, but it reflects a way of thinking that is still prevalent: attributing a person's behavior to internal, unconscious dynamics and failing to consider external circumstances.

Psychodynamic reductionism is often apparent in literary psychobiographies, in which an author (who may or may not be a psychologist) relies on psychodynamic ideas to explain the behavior of some famous person. You get arguments such as "Adolf Hitler hated his mother and had sexual insecurities, so he caused World War II"; never mind the historical, cultural, and economic events that created him and allowed him to attain power.

At least a biography can't hurt anyone, except perhaps the reputation of its subject. But other examples of psychodynamic reductionism have had disastrous, even fatal, results, as when people with brain tumors or diseases have been diagnosed entirely in terms of unconscious dynamics and the real cause of their illness left untreated (Crews, 1998; Thornton, 1984). In spite of the fact that most North American psychoanalysts have been psychiatrists, and therefore trained as medical doctors, they have committed this error for the past hundred years. They have maintained that autism, rheumatoid arthritis, ulcers, migraines, and other physical disorders were caused by neurotic personality patterns, unconscious anger, suppressed hatred of parents, and other such factors. This error still occurs. In California, a psychiatrist was convicted of malpractice because he failed to diagnose a patient who was suffering from myasthenia gravis, a progressive but treatable muscle disease.[1] For 12 years the poor woman got steadily worse, until she couldn't even lift her hand to brush her teeth. The reason, he said, was her "repressed rage" at her parents. One of our own students was told by a psychotherapist

---

[1]You may recall the similar misdiagnosis of Sheila Allen, whose story opened Part II, the biological perspective.

that her abdominal pain was a sign of "repressed memories" of sexual abuse; the pain turned out to be caused by a tumor.

With any diagnosis of physical symptoms or emotional problems, therefore, it is essential to avoid reductionism. Many possibilities should be considered, and the evidence for each should be reviewed, before drawing conclusions.

But apart from its inherent inclination toward reductionism (seeing complex behavior and physical symptoms as evidence of unconscious dynamics), the psychodynamic perspective also contains several weaknesses that set it apart from empirical psychology, limitations described in the rest of this list.

2 **VIOLATING THE PRINCIPLE OF FALSIFIABILITY.** As we saw in Chapter 2, a theory that is impossible to disconfirm in principle is not a scientific theory. Many psychodynamic ideas about unconscious motivations are, in fact, impossible to confirm or disconfirm. If your experience seems to support these ideas, it is taken as evidence of their correctness; but if you doubt them, you must be "revealing defensiveness," lack observational skills, or (a favorite accusation) be "in denial."

This way of responding to criticism started with Freud (1924a), who once remarked, "One hears of analysts who boast that, though they have worked for dozens of years, they have never found a sign of the existence of a castration complex. We must bow our heads in recognition of . . . [this] piece of virtuosity in the art of overlooking and mistaking." So if analysts see castration anxiety in their patients, Freud was right; and if they fail to see it, they are "overlooking" it, and Freud was still right. This is why arguing with some psychodynamic theorists can be exasperating: If you agree with them, fine; but if you don't agree and you offer counterevidence, there must be something wrong with *you*. This kind of reasoning is neither scientific nor fair!

The inherent subjectivity of psychodynamic explanations and the fact that they often violate the principle of falsifiability may be why this perspective, more than any other, is full of names: Freud, Adler, Horney, Jung, Erikson, ... When theories cannot be disconfirmed, their appeal depends more on the popularity and charisma of their proponents than on the accuracy of their content. Researchers in other perspectives call themselves "neuropsychologists," "cognitive scientists," "social-cognitive learning theorists," "cross-cultural psychologists," and the like; even most radical behaviorists no longer call themselves "Skinnerians." But psychodynamic psychologists go around calling themselves "Freudians," "Jungians," "Adlerians," and so forth. Their critics believe that this allegiance to individuals rather than to verifiable concepts is one of the perspective's problems. Robert Fancher (1995), who was trained as a psychoanalyst but became disenchanted with many aspects of the profession, observes that because psychoanalysis lacks scientifically reliable methods by which differences of opinion can be resolved, it "is always ripe for schism"—for people breaking away from established doctrine to form their own schools.

3 **DRAWING UNIVERSAL PRINCIPLES FROM THE EXPERIENCES OF A FEW, ATYPICAL PATIENTS.** Freud and most of his followers generalized from a very few individuals, often patients in therapy, to all human beings. Of course, the problem of overgeneralizing from small samples occurs in other perspectives too, and insights about human

behavior may sometimes be obtained from observations of limited numbers of people. Jean Piaget, for one, originally developed his theories of cognitive development from closely observing a very small sample: his own children. The problem occurs when the observer fails to confirm these observations by studying other samples, incorrectly inferring that what applies to one group applies to all.

For instance, if a gay man goes into therapy for help with emotional problems, a therapist cannot logically conclude that all gay men have emotional problems; gay men who are not in therapy would have to be studied. Indeed, when such research was finally done, it disproved the belief—once common among many psychoanalysts as well as the public—that gay men and lesbians are more emotionally disturbed than heterosexuals (Hooker, 1957; Kurdek, 1987). Similarly, Freud did not seek to confirm his ideas about penis envy by actually observing or talking to young children. However, when researchers interview preschool-age children, they typically find that many children of *both* sexes envy one another. In one charming study of 65 preschool-age boys and girls, 45 percent of the girls had fantasized about having a penis or being male in other ways, and 44 percent of the boys had fantasized about being pregnant (Linday, 1994).

The problem of small samples is compounded when those samples come from one culture or socioeconomic class, as has usually been the case. Traditional psychoanalysts still tend to ignore the importance of culture and history and elevate this oversight into something of a virtue. As psychoanalyst Stephen Mitchell (1993) observed, members of his profession "see themselves as dealing with universal, timeless dimensions of human experience, currents that run deeper than the surface ripples of cultural change and intellectual or social fashion." As the sociocultural perspective shows, however, culture is not a "surface ripple"; it exerts a profound influence on every aspect of human behavior.

4 **BASING THEORIES OF DEVELOPMENT ON THE RETROSPECTIVE ACCOUNTS AND FALLIBLE MEMORIES OF PATIENTS.** Most psychodynamic theorists have not observed random samples of children at different ages, as modern cognitive and child psychologists do, to construct their theories of development. Instead they have worked backward, creating theories based on themes in adults' recollections of childhood. From Freud to the present, nearly all have concluded that children develop according to a series of fixed psychological stages, at which key "issues" or "crises" occur. The seeds of adult pathology are said to be planted when a child has a traumatic experience, becomes fixated at a specific stage, and then carries the unresolved emotional problem into the next stage. The corollary is that adults must look backward to their childhoods to find the origins of their current emotional problems.

Analysis of memories can be a useful and illuminating way to achieve insights about our lives; in fact, it is the only way we can think about our own lives! But as we saw in Chapter 8, memory is often inaccurate, influenced as much by what is going on in our lives now as by what happened in the past. If you are currently not getting along with your mother, you may remember all the times in your childhood when she was hard on you and forget the counterexamples of her kindness.

Retrospective analysis has another problem: It creates an *illusion of causality* between events. People often assume that if A came before B, then A must have caused B. For example, if your mother spent three months in the hospital when you were 5 years old and today you feel shy and insecure in college, an object-relations analyst would probably draw a connection between the two facts. But a lot of other things could be causing your shyness and insecurity, such as your temperament, your learning history, or the fact that your college is large and impersonal.

Because looking backward at our lives creates, as Freud (1920/1963) himself acknowledged, "the impression of an inevitable sequence of events," *retrospective* studies, in which people tell interviewers or therapists about their pasts, often find what seem to be consistent patterns of development. But *longitudinal* studies, in which people are followed from childhood to adulthood, often do not. For example, one of the most entrenched assumptions in psychodynamic theory is that childhood traumas inevitably produce long-lasting psychological symptoms into adulthood. Yet studies that follow people from childhood to adulthood challenge the widespread assumption that childhood traumas always have specific, inescapably harmful effects:

◆ *Recovery from war.* After World War II, many European children, made homeless by the war, were adopted by American families. About 20 percent of the children had problems at first, but over the years they all made good progress in school; none had psychiatric problems; and all established happy, affectionate relationships with their new parents (Rathbun, DiVirgilio, & Waldfogel, 1958).

◆ *Recovery from abusive or alcoholic parents.* Compared to children of healthy parents, more children of abusive or alcoholic parents become abusive or alcoholic themselves, but the majority do not (Cohen, 1999; Kaufman & Zigler, 1987; West & Prinz, 1987).

◆ *Recovery from sexual abuse.* Children who have been sexually abused do have more emotional and behavioral symptoms than nonabused children, especially if the abuse is severe, repeated, and part of other chronically stressful experiences in a child's life. Yet the research shows, much to people's surprise, that by adulthood, most victims are as well adjusted as people in the general population. Meta-analyses of studies of nearly 37,000 college students and of more than 12,000 other adults found no overall link between childhood sexual abuse and later emotional disorders or unusual psychological problems (Rind & Tromovitch, 1997; Rind, Tromovitch, & Bauserman, 1998). And researchers who reviewed 45 other longitudinal studies concluded, "No one symptom characterized a majority of sexually abused children. . . . The findings suggest the absence of any specific syndrome in children who have been sexually abused and no single traumatizing process" (Kendall-Tackett, Williams, & Finkelhor, 1993).

Of course, none of this means that *all* children are able to survive terrible childhood experiences. Longitudinal studies also confirm that children who have been beaten or neglected, who have been constantly subjected to verbal and physical abuse by their parents, or who live in violent communities are more likely than other children to have emotional problems, become delinquent and violent themselves, commit crimes, have low IQs, drop out of school, or attempt suicide (Malinosky-Rummell & Hansen, 1993; Maxfield & Widom, 1996; Moore & Pepler, 1998). But *most* children recover, particularly if they have good support systems, a resilient temperament that allows them to cope with adversity, and positive experiences (Cowen et al., 1990; Garmezy, 1991; Masten & Coatsworth, 1998; Thomas & Chess, 1984; Werner & Smith, 1992).

Many psychodynamic clinicians have found these results difficult to accept because, by virtue of the work they do, they see the people who are having trouble coping with the effects of difficult or traumatic childhoods (Spiegel, 2000). They do not see the people in the general population who have overcome their pasts or vow not to repeat their parents' mistakes. But as Daniel Stern (1985), a psychiatrist who examined psychodynamic assumptions about child development in the light of empirical evidence, concluded, "Psychological insults and trauma at a specific age or stage should result in predictably specific types of clinical problems later on. No such evidence exists."

5 RELYING ON SUBJECTIVE METHODS THAT ARE OFTEN UNVALIDATED AND UNRELIABLE. Some psychologists have used psychodynamic concepts to design tests of personality and unconscious motivation. They have developed **projective tests,** which are based on the psychodynamic assumption that when people are asked to make up a story about a neutral or ambiguous picture or statement, they will project their own unconscious feelings and beliefs onto it. The test is administered to an individual patient by a psychologist, and the psychologist alone interprets the responses.

Many clinicians love projective tests and swear by their accuracy in helping them understand their clients. They maintain that projective techniques are a rich source of information because test-takers cannot fake or lie as easily as they can on objective tests. The tests can help a clinician establish rapport with a client and encourage a person to open up about anxieties, conflicts, and problems. And projective tests may help clinicians determine when someone is defensively attempting to hide worries or mental problems (Shedler, Mayman, & Manis, 1993).

However, when projective tests are used for other purposes—most commonly, to diagnose mental disorders or personality problems, determine whether a child has been sexually abused, or determine whether a parent is fit to have custody of a child—they have repeatedly been shown to be unreliable. That is, different clinicians often interpret the same test responses differently; they themselves may be "projecting" when they decide what a specific response means (Anastasi & Urbina, 1997; Lilienfeld, 1999).

In addition, many projective tests lack validity. For example, during the 1980s, some therapists began using projective methods to determine whether a child had been sexually abused. They claimed they could identify a child who had been abused by observing how the child played with "anatomically detailed" dolls (dolls with prominent genitals), and that is how many of them testified in hundreds of court cases (Ceci & Bruck, 1995). Unfortunately, these therapists did not test their beliefs by using a fundamental scientific procedure: a control group. They did not ask, "How do *nonabused* children play with these dolls?" When psychological scientists did ask this question and conducted controlled research to answer it, they found that most children, abused or

---

projective tests Psychological tests used to infer a person's motives, conflicts, and unconscious dynamics on the basis of the person's interpretations of ambiguous stimuli.

not, are fascinated with the dolls' genitals. Abused children do not play any differently with the dolls than nonabused children do, and hence you cannot diagnose abuse on the basis of children's doll play (Koocher et al., 1995; Poole & Lamb, 1998).

A Rorschach inkblot.

Problems with reliability and validity also plague the widely used **Rorschach Inkblot Test,** which was devised by Swiss psychiatrist Hermann Rorschach in 1921. The Rorschach consists of ten cards with symmetrical abstract patterns, originally formed by spilling ink on paper and folding the paper in half (you can see an example here). You report what you see in the inkblots, and the clinician interprets your answers according to the symbolic meanings emphasized by psychodynamic theories.

Although the Rorschach is enormously popular among many clinicians, efforts to confirm its reliability and validity have repeatedly failed (Garb, Florio, & Grove, 1998; Lilienfeld, 1999; Wood et al., 2000). The clinicians who score the tests repeatedly show poor agreement with one another on what various answers mean, and test–retest reliability is also low. The Rorschach cannot be reliably used to diagnose depression, posttraumatic stress reactions, personality disorders, or psychopathology (Wood et al., 2000). One testing expert, Raymond McCall, concluded, "Though tens of thousands of Rorschach tests have been administered . . . and while many relationships to personality dynamics and behavior have been hypothesized, the vast majority of these relationships *have never been validated empirically,* despite the appearance of more than 2,000 publications about the test" (emphasis in original; quoted in Dawes, 1994).

In recent years, a different scoring method, called the Comprehensive System, has become widely used (Exner, 1993). But there are significant problems with this method too. Many scores are of questionable validity; they do not measure the personality traits they claim to measure, particularly in contrast to the objective tests described in Chapter 2. Claims of the system's success come from Rorschach workshops where clinicians are taught how to use the method, which is not an impartial way of assessing it (Wood, Nezworski, & Stejskal, 1996). Positive findings for Rorschach scores have rarely been independently replicated by impartial investigators with no vested interest in the use of the test (Garb, 1999). Some supporters of the Rorschach have published their significant results but not their insignificant results, biasing the overall picture. One researcher (West, 1998) claimed that her meta-analysis of 12 studies showed that the Rorschach can be used reliably to detect child sexual abuse. But when other researchers examined those original studies, they found that she had excluded data from 9 of them—the 9 that found that the Rorschach was unreliable (Garb, Wood, & Nezworski, 2000).

Rorschach Inkblot Test A projective personality test that asks respondents to interpret abstract, symmetrical inkblots.

The reverse error, failing to identify abusers, has also occurred because of misuses of the Rorschach. James Wood, who is both a clinician and a researcher, told us about a woman who reported to Child Protection Services (CPS) that her ex-husband was molesting their 4-year-old son. CPS thought that the mother was perhaps "deranged" in making this accusation, so they had her tested by a psychologist who administered the Rorschach. The mother said that one blot looked like "a Thanksgiving turkey already eaten"—and the psychologist, ignoring the fact that the test was being given shortly after Thanksgiving, scored this "food response" as evidence of the woman's dependency. CPS, accepting the psychologist's conclusion that the mother had emotional problems, refused to investigate her claims. A year later the boy was brought to the emergency room after a visit with his father. This time, semen was found in the boy's rectum.

Because of the vast potential for misuse and misdiagnosis that the Rorschach has, some clinicians and researchers are calling for a moratorium on its use in clinical and forensic settings, until impartial research settles the matter (Garb, 1999).

And so we come back to the theme that most divides psychodynamic psychologists and scientific psychologists: the failure of many psychodynamic assumptions to survive the scrutiny of scientific methods, and the disagreement as to whether that failure matters. Increasingly, however, some psychodynamic psychologists are using empirical methods and research findings from other perspectives to test and refine their theories (Westen, 1998). They draw on cognitive findings on schemas, narratives, consciousness, and infant mental abilities; social-cognitive learning and sociocultural findings on gender roles and the impact of culture; and biological findings on the genetic aspects of personality traits and the physiology of emotions.

For their part, some research psychologists trained in other perspectives are studying ideas spawned by psychodynamic theories. Cognitive psychologists are investigating nonconscious processes in thought and memory and the influence of mental representations (Blatt, Auerbach, & Levy, 1997; Epstein, 1994). Some have developed empirical tests of defense mechanisms, studying the ways in which defenses protect self-esteem and reduce anxiety (Cramer, 2000; Plutchik et al., 1988). Other researchers are empirically investigating the psychodynamic emphasis on how people unconsciously relive past relationships in their present ones (Andersen & Berk, 1998). And some social and learning psychologists are identifying the situations and conditions under which people "displace" aggressive feelings onto innocent bystanders (Marcus-Newhall et al., 2000).

What Do You Know?

1. List three contributions of the psychodynamic perspective.
2. Describe this perspective's major misuse and four of its inherent limitations.
3. Name one clinical benefit of projective tests and two scientific limitations.

Answers:

when interpreting people's answers. Another is that the tests have poor validity. projective tests are unreliable, because clinicians show low agreement with one another and tell when the client seems defensive and anxious. One major limitation is that many and unreliable. 3. One benefit is that they help the clinician establish rapport with a client than on longitudinal studies; and relying on subjective methods that are often unvalidated individuals in therapy; basing theories on retrospective accounts and fallible memories rather include violating the principle of falsifiability; drawing universal principles from atypical and unconscious motives. 2. A common misuse is psychodynamic reductionism; limitations qualitative information, such as folktales and symbols; and an emphasis on self-knowledge 1. Contributions include a willingness to look at " big picture" topics; an imaginative use of

In the final analysis (so to speak), there may be no resolution of many of the fundamental tensions between the psychodynamic perspective and the empirical branches of psychology. The people who work in this perspective do so for the framework of meaning it provides, knowing that many of its tenets will never be confirmed with scientific methods. In the coming years, it will be interesting to see what happens to this perspective in relation to the rest of psychology. Will it continue on a separate, parallel track? Will it break off from the discipline entirely and become allied with literary criticism, the humanities, and therapy? Will it turn out to be, as Peter Medawar (1982) predicted, a dinosaur in the history of ideas? Or will its best concepts become woven into scientific psychology, forming a seamless vision of human behavior? ■

Summary

1. To most research psychologists in the other four perspectives of psychology, the psychodynamic perspective is unscientific. But psychodynamically minded people believe that this perspective alone captures the inner life that eludes questionnaires and behavioral observations and that it alone best describes the whole person in all of his or her emotional complexity.

2. The main contributions of the psychodynamic perspective are a willingness to raise "big picture" questions; an imaginative use of qualitative information, such as analysis of movies, folktales, and symbols; and the emphasis on self-knowledge, especially of our unconscious motives. The object-relations school in particular emphasizes how unconscious expectations and patterns established early in life with important family members can reproduce themselves in adult relationships.

3. As with all of the previous perspectives, one misuse of this perspective is reductionism. *Psychodynamic reductionism* is the tendency to overemphasize a person's psychic reality and ignore biological factors, learning, culture, and the actual circumstances of the person's life. Critics have identified four other practices that they believe are inherent limitations of the psychodynamic perspective: violating the

principle of falsifiability; drawing universal principles from the experiences of only a few, atypical patients in a particular culture; basing theories of development on the retrospective accounts and fallible memories of patients, which may create an *illusion of causality* and which has often led to beliefs that are not supported by longitudinal research; and relying on subjective methods that are often unvalidated and unreliable, such as *projective tests*.

4. Projective tests can be useful to help people open up in therapy. But when they are used to diagnose disorders or personality problems, determine whether a child has been sexually abused, or determine whether a parent is fit to have custody of a child, projective tests such as the *Rorschach Inkblot Test* and doll play tend to have low reliability and validity. Clinicians do not agree with one another on how to interpret them, and the tests do not always measure what they claim to measure.

5. Some psychodynamic psychologists are using empirical research methods and drawing on findings from other perspectives to formulate their theories. For their part, some research psychologists are studying issues raised by psychodynamic theories, such as the nature of defenses and unconscious processes. But the relationship between the psychodynamic perspective and the rest of psychology remains conflicted, uneasy, and uncertain.

Key Terms

psychodynamic reductionism   481

illusion of causality   483

projective test   485

Rorschach Inkblot Test   486

PART VII

*Putting the
Perspectives
Together*

A friend of ours attended a conference in which psychologists were discussing the case of a troubled girl. The girl was disruptive and belligerent, and this behavior made her mother angry. The father, who worked long hours, came home tired most nights and didn't want to deal with the situation.

The first psychologist thought the problem was that the child was temperamentally difficult from birth—a biological matter that could be treated with drugs. The second psychologist thought the problem was that the child had learned to behave inappropriately and aggressively in order to get the attention of her father; this pattern could be treated with behavior therapy. The third psychologist thought the problem was the mother, who was misinterpreting her daughter's behavior as an intentional effort to provoke her; the mother could be helped with cognitive therapy. The fourth psychologist saw the situation as stemming from traditional gender roles within this family's culture (the "absent" father, the "overprotective" mother) and the role of each individual in a family network; all of them would benefit from family therapy. The fifth psychologist thought that the problem was the child's unresolved Oedipal feelings, the mother's displacement of affectional needs for her husband onto the child, and the father's unconscious anxieties about being a father; the child and the parents could be helped with psychodynamic therapy.

Like the blind men and the elephant in the poem that began this book, each of these psychologists "was partly in the right, and all of them were wrong." Fortunately for this family, the psychologists handling the child's case decided on a team approach. Instead of blaming the child, the mother, or the father for causing the problem, they treated it as an interaction of many different factors. The child learned to control her outbursts; the father faced the fears and unspoken reasons in his own past for avoiding his wife and daughter; the mother, feeling undervalued as a homemaker, took steps to develop her own interests. As each individual changed, so did the family.

We don't want to imply that the contributions of all five psychological perspectives carry equal weight in explaining every human problem or experience. As we have seen, some problems, such as autism, are due to biology; some issues, such as concepts of time, are primarily cultural; and some behaviors, such as a child's whining, are learned. But most topics can be best understood with a "team approach." In this final chapter we will consider what psychologists from each of the perspectives have contributed to the diagnosis and treatment of everyday problems in life as well as serious mental disorders. And in Essay 6, we will show what each perspective contributes to understanding two wonderful, universal experiences—music and sex— and what we might learn, in an ideal world, by studying the whole elephant.

CHAPTER TWELVE

Mental Disorders and Their Treatment

Margaret Mary Ray believed with all her heart that late-night talk show host David Letterman was in love with her. Caught up in this delusion, she stalked Letterman day and night for a decade, writing him letters and repeatedly breaking into his house. She camped out on his tennis court and once stole his car. Her exploits were routinely reported in the tabloids, which treated her delusions as a running joke. Finally, she gave up. She wrote to her mother, "I'm all traveled out," and put herself in front of a coal train. She was killed instantly.

You don't have to be a psychologist to know that something was terribly wrong with Margaret Mary Ray. When people think of "mental illness," they usually think of individuals like her—people with delusions, people who behave in bizarre ways, or people who, like the Unabomber Theodore Kaczynski, plant bombs or commit random murders. But most psychological problems are far less dramatic and far more common. Some people function adequately every day, yet suffer chronic feelings of melancholy, always feeling below par in happiness. Some have bad habits, like procrastination, that keep them from accomplishing their goals. Some feel painfully shy in groups. Some people have panic attacks that come on suddenly, apparently out of the blue, and make them feel that they are dying. Many people who have survived a traumatic experience, such as a hurricane or a crime, have recurring anxiety symptoms for months, even years. And all of us on occasion have difficulties that seem too much to handle, that make us feel we cannot cope.

In this chapter, we will show how psychologists working in the five major psychological perspectives study and treat a range of psychological problems, including normal life stresses, emotional conflicts, and severe mental illnesses like the one that tormented Margaret Mary Ray.

DIAGNOSING MENTAL DISORDER

To begin with, we need to define our terms. In the law, the definition of mental disorder rests primarily on whether a person is aware of the consequences of his or her actions and can control his or her behavior. If not, the person may be declared insane and therefore incompetent to stand trial. But *insanity* is a legal term only; psychologists and psychiatrists do not use the terms *sanity* or *insanity* in either research or diagnosis. Most psychologists define **mental disorder** broadly: any behavior or emotional state that causes an individual great suffering or worry; is self-defeating or self-destructive; or is maladaptive and disrupts either the person's relationships or the larger community.

The standard reference for diagnosing mental disorders is the *Diagnostic and Statistical Manual of Mental Disorders* (DSM), published by the American Psychiatric Association. The DSM's primary aim is descriptive: to provide clear diagnostic categories for purposes of study and treatment. It gives the symptoms of each disorder, predisposing factors, course of the disorder, prevalence of the disorder, and other information. (For a list of the DSM's major categories, see Table 12.1.)

However, even armed with the DSM, psychologists have found that agreeing on specific diagnoses is often easier said than done. One reason is that cultural consensus plays a role in deciding what is and is not a mental disorder. As George Albee (1985), a past president of the American Psychological Association, put it, "Appendicitis, a brain tumor and chicken pox are the same everywhere, regardless of culture or class; mental conditions, it seems, are not." For example, in most North American cultural groups, having hallucinations of a departed loved one (though not at all uncommon) is considered abnormal; but the Chinese, the Hopi, and members of many other cultures regard such visions as perfectly normal. Similarly, in many cultures, painting your forehead and chin red might be taken as a sign of mental disturbance; but to the Samburu of Kenya it is a normal form of self-adornment.

For this reason, critics of the DSM's efforts to categorize and label mental disorder argue that diagnosis is more a matter of subjective agreement, reflecting prevailing attitudes and biases, than of objective classification (Kutchins & Kirk, 1997; Maddux, 1996; Tiefer, 1995). Physicians do not vote on whether cancer or diabetes are diseases, but psychiatrists are often asked to vote on what conditions should be included in the manual—or removed. "Narcissism" was voted out in the 1968 edition of the DSM, and then voted back in the 1980 edition. "Self-defeating personality disorder"—which would have applied mainly to women who have the extreme self-sacrificing qualities required by the traditional female role—was adopted in 1987, and voted out in 1994. The latest edition of the DSM contains many everyday problems that were not considered to be mental disorders in previous versions, including "disorder of written expression" (having trouble writing clearly), "mathematics disorder" (not doing well in math), and "caffeine-induced sleep disorder" (which at least is easy to treat; just switch to decaf!).

---

mental disorder Any behavior or emotional state that causes an individual great suffering or worry, is self-defeating or self-destructive, or is maladaptive and disrupts the person's relationships or the larger community.

TABLE 12.1 ✦ Major Diagnostic Categories in the DSM-IV

Disorders usually first diagnosed in infancy, childhood, or adolescence include mental retardation, attention deficit disorders (such as hyperactivity or an inability to concentrate), and developmental problems.

Delirium, dementia, amnesia, and other cognitive disorders are those resulting from brain damage, degenerative diseases such as syphilis or Alzheimer's, toxic substances, or drugs.

Substance-related disorders are problems associated with excessive use of or withdrawal from alcohol, amphetamines, caffeine, cocaine, hallucinogens, nicotine, opiates, or other drugs.

Schizophrenia and other psychotic disorders are disorders characterized by delusions, hallucinations, and severe disturbances in thinking and emotion.

Mood disorders include major depression, bipolar disorder (manic depression), and dysthymia (chronic depressed mood).

Anxiety disorders include generalized anxiety disorder, phobias, panic attacks with or without agoraphobia, posttraumatic stress disorder, and obsessive thoughts or compulsive rituals.

Eating disorders include anorexia nervosa (self-starvation because of an irrational fear of being or becoming fat) and bulimia nervosa (episodes of binge eating and vomiting).

Somatoform disorders involve physical symptoms (e.g., paralysis, heart palpitations, fatigue) for which no organic cause can be found. This category includes hypochondria (an extreme preoccupation with health and the unfounded conviction that one is ill) and conversion disorder (in which a physical symptom, such as a paralyzed arm or blindness, serves a psychological function).

Dissociative disorders include dissociative amnesia (in which important events cannot be remembered after a traumatic event) and dissociative identity disorder (formerly "multiple personality disorder"), characterized by the presence of two or more distinct identities or personalities.

Sexual and gender identity disorders include problems of sexual (gender) identity, such as transsexualism (wanting to be the other gender), problems of sexual performance (such as premature ejaculation or lack of orgasm), and paraphilias (unusual or bizarre imagery or acts that are necessary for sexual arousal, as in sadomasochism or exhibitionism).

Impulse control disorders involve an inability to resist an impulse to perform some act that is harmful to the individual or to others, such as pathological gambling, stealing (kleptomania), setting fires (pyromania), or having violent rages.

Personality disorders are inflexible and maladaptive patterns that cause distress to the individual or impair the ability to function; they include paranoid, narcissistic, and antisocial personality disorders.

Additional conditions that may be a focus of clinical attention include "problems in living" such as bereavement, academic difficulties, spiritual problems, and acculturation problems.

Nymphomania (wanting to have sex "too often") is no longer considered a disorder, but not wanting to have sex often "enough" is (Groneman, 2000; Tiefer, 1995). As these examples show, as times change, so does the cultural consensus about what is normal and what is not.

In response to these criticisms, the DSM's defenders point out that empirical support for many of its categories is improving, and that the manual does include information on how culture influences the experience and expression of certain emotional problems. Without careful descriptions such as those in the DSM, say its defenders, clinicians could not identify the correct problem in order to provide proper treatment (Kessler et al., 1994; Wittchen et al., 1995). Thus it is important to know whether a person has a true anxiety disorder or a medical condition that mimics it, or whether a person has schizophrenia or bipolar (manic-depressive) disorder, which often respond to different medications. Moreover, while some diagnoses are clearly specific to certain cultures, others appear to be universal. In societies around the world, from the Inuit of Alaska to the Yorubas of Nigeria, some individuals have delusions, are severely depressed, or cannot control their behavior; and in every culture, such individuals are considered to have mental illnesses (Butcher, Lim, & Nezami, 1998; Kleinman, 1988).

SOME MAJOR DISORDERS

We turn now to a consideration of four categories of disorders that have been the attention of researchers all over the world: problems with anxiety and panic; mood disorders, including depression; personality disorders; and schizophrenia. In our discussion, we will look at what each psychological perspective has contributed to the understanding of these problems. Then we will turn to the kinds of treatment that each perspective has developed.

Anxiety Disorders

Anyone who is waiting for important news, or living in a situation that is unpredictable and uncontrollable, quite sensibly feels *anxiety,* a general state of apprehension or psychological tension. And anyone who is in a dangerous or unfamiliar situation quite sensibly feels flat-out fear. In the short run, these emotions are adaptive because they energize us to cope with danger or threat.

But in some individuals, fear and anxiety become detached from any actual danger, or these feelings linger even when danger and uncertainty are past. Such individuals may be suffering from *generalized anxiety disorder,* marked by long-lasting feelings of apprehension and doom; *panic attacks,* short-lived but intense feelings of spontaneous anxiety; *phobias,* excessive fears of specific things or situations; or *obsessive-compulsive disorder,* in which repeated thoughts and rituals are used to ward off anxious feelings.

Anxiety States. The chief characteristic of **generalized anxiety disorder** is continuous, uncontrollable anxiety or worry that occurs on a majority of days during a six-month period and that is not brought on by physical causes such as disease, drugs, or drinking too much coffee. Symptoms include feeling restless and keyed up, difficulty concentrating and sleeping, irritability, muscle tension and jitteriness, and feelings of impending doom.

According to researchers in the biological perspective, some people suffer from generalized anxiety disorder because of a physiological tendency to experience anxiety symptoms when they are in challenging or uncontrollable situations. Others may be temperamentally shy, predisposed to react with anxiety in novel situations. Researchers who hold a learning view, in contrast, focus on the fact that some chronically anxious people have a history, starting in childhood, of being unable to control or predict their environments (Chorpita & Barlow, 1998). Learning psychologists also consider the *precipitating factors* that may set off an episode of anxiety, such as living in a state of chronic uncertainly about one's job, relationship, or health.

People who survive uncontrollable and unpredictable dangers—such as war, rape, torture, or natural disasters—may suffer from **posttraumatic stress disorder (PTSD).** Typical anxiety symptoms in PTSD include reliving the trauma in recurrent, intrusive thoughts or dreams; "psychic numbing," a sense of detachment from others and an inability to feel happy or loving; and increased physiological arousal, which causes insomnia, irritability, and difficulty concentrating. These symptoms can occur either immediately after a trauma or after a delay of weeks or months, and episodes may recur for months, years, or even decades (Kessler et al., 1995). In long-term sufferers of PTSD, chronically high levels of stress hormones may be literally toxic to parts of the brain. Biological research finds that recovered Vietnam vets and those who still have PTSD differ significantly in the size of the hippocampus and in memory function (Shin et al., 1997).

Another anxiety disorder is **panic disorder,** in which a person has sudden attacks of intense fear or panic, with feelings of impending doom (Clark & Ehlers, 1993; McNally, 1998). Panic attacks, which may last from a few minutes to (more rarely) several hours, are scary because the person feels that he or she is losing control and may even die. Symptoms include trembling and shaking, dizziness, chest pain, heart palpitations, feelings of unreality, hot and cold flashes, and sweating.

Although panic attacks seem to occur out of nowhere, they are often related to stress, prolonged emotion, exercise, specific worries, high consumption of caffeine or

---

generalized anxiety disorder A continuous state of anxiety marked by feelings of worry and dread, apprehension, difficulties in concentration, and signs of motor tension.

posttraumatic stress disorder (PTSD) An anxiety disorder in which a person who has experienced a traumatic or life-threatening event has symptoms such as psychic numbing, reliving of the trauma, and increased physiological arousal.

panic disorder An anxiety disorder in which a person experiences recurring *panic attacks,* periods of intense fear and feelings of impending doom or death, accompanied by physiological symptoms such as rapid breathing and pulse, and dizziness.

nicotine, or the aftermath of a traumatic experience (Beck, 1988; McNally, 1998). For example, a friend of ours was on a plane that was a target of a bomb threat while airborne at 33,000 feet. He coped beautifully at the time, but two weeks later, seemingly out of nowhere, he had a panic attack. Such delayed attacks after life-threatening scares are common. Researchers in the cognitive perspective, however, have identified the essential difference between people who go on to develop panic disorder and those who do not: The difference lies in *how they interpret their bodily reactions* (Clark & Ehlers, 1993; McNally, 1998). Healthy people who have occasional panic attacks see them correctly as a result of a passing crisis or period of stress, comparable to another person's migraines. But people who develop a full-fledged panic disorder regard the attack as a sign of impending death or disaster, and they begin to live their lives in restrictive ways, trying to avoid future attacks.

Findings from the sociocultural perspective show that while people who have panic disorder are found throughout the world, culture influences the particular symptoms they experience (Barlow, Chorpita, & Turovsky, 1996). Feelings of choking or being smothered, numbness, and fear of dying are most common in Latin America and southern Europe; fear of public places is most common in northern Europe and America; and a fear of going crazy is more common in the Americas than in Europe. In Greenland, some fishermen suffer from "kayak-angst": a sudden attack of dizziness and fear that occurs while they are fishing in small, one-person kayaks (Amering & Katschnig, 1990).

Fears and Phobias.   Are you afraid of bugs, snakes, or dogs? Are you so afraid that you can't stand to be around one, or are you just vaguely uncomfortable? A **phobia** is an exaggerated fear of a specific situation, activity, or thing. A phobia is truly frightening and often incapacitating for its sufferer. It is not just a tendency to say "ugh" at tarantulas or skip the snake display at the zoo. Some common phobias—such as fear of snakes, heights (acrophobia), thunder (brontophobia), or closed spaces (claustrophobia)—may have evolved in human beings because these fears were adaptive. Other, more idiosyncratic phobias, such as of the color purple (porphyrophobia), may be acquired through classical conditioning. Still other phobias, such as fear of dirt and germs (mysophobia) or of the number 13 (triskaidekaphobia), reflect personality differences or cultural norms.

By far the most disabling fear disorder is **agoraphobia,** which accounts for more than half of the phobia cases for which people seek treatment. In ancient Greece, the *agora* was the social, political, business, and religious center of town, the public meeting place away from home. The fundamental fear in agoraphobia is of being alone in a public place, where escape might be difficult or where help might be unavailable. Individuals with agoraphobia report many specific fears—of public

phobia An exaggerated, unrealistic fear of a specific situation, activity, or object.

agoraphobia A set of phobias, often set off by a panic attack, involving the basic fear of being away from a safe place or person.

buses, driving in traffic or tunnels, eating in restaurants, or going to parties—but the underlying fear is of being away from a safe place, usually home, or a safe person, usually a parent or spouse.

Agoraphobia usually begins with a panic attack that seems to come from nowhere. The attack is so unexpected and so scary that the agoraphobic-to-be begins to avoid situations that he or she thinks may provoke another one. For example, a woman we know had a panic attack while driving on a freeway. This was a perfectly normal post-traumatic response to the suicide of her husband a few weeks earlier, but thereafter she avoided freeways—as if the freeway, and not the suicide, had caused the attack. In extreme agoraphobia, the sufferer retreats to one safe haven, such as the home. But because the actions associated with this phobia are designed to help the person avoid a panic attack, cognitive psychologists regard agoraphobia as a "fear of fear" rather than a fear of places.

Obsessions and Compulsions.   **Obsessive-compulsive disorder** (OCD) is character-ized by recurrent, persistent, unwished-for thoughts or images (*obsessions*) and by repetitive, ritualized, stereotyped behaviors that the person feels must be carried out to avoid disaster (*compulsions*). Of course, many people have trivial compulsions and practice superstitious rituals; baseball players are famous for them. Obsessions and compulsions become a disorder when they become uncontrollable and interfere with a person's life, and when they are frightening or repugnant. For example, the person may have repetitive thoughts of killing a child or of becoming contaminated by shak-ing hands. Obsessive thoughts take many forms, but they are alike in reflecting mal-adaptive ways of reasoning and processing information.

The most common compulsions are hand washing, counting, touching, and check-ing. A woman *must* check the furnace, lights, locks, oven, and fireplace three times before she can sleep; or a man *must* wash his hands and face precisely eight times before he leaves the house. Most sufferers of OCD do not enjoy such rituals and realize that the behavior is senseless. But if they try to forgo the ritual, they feel mounting anxiety that is relieved only by giving in to it.

What causes OCD? Some cases may involve a brain abnormality; PET scans find that several parts of the brain are hyperactive in people with OCD. One area of the frontal lobes, the *orbital cortex* (which lies just above the eye sockets), apparently sends messages of impending danger to an area involved in controlling the movement of the limbs and to other structures involved in preparing the body to feel afraid and respond to external threats. Normally, once danger is past or a person realizes that there is no cause for fear, the alarm signals are switched off. In people with OCD, however, the orbital cortex sends out repeated false alarms and mistaken "fear!" messages. The suf-ferer feels in a constant state of danger and tries repeatedly to reduce the resulting anx-iety (Schwartz et al., 1996). However, it is not known whether psychological, learned, or genetic factors cause this "brain glitch" in the first place.

---

obsessive-compulsive disorder (OCD) An anxiety disorder in which a person feels trapped in repetitive, persis-tent thoughts (obsessions) and repetitive, ritualized behaviors (compulsions) designed to reduce anxiety.

Mood Disorders

In the DSM, "mood disorders" include disturbances in mood ranging from extreme depression to extreme mania. Of course, most people feel sad from time to time, and also joyful. And most people, at some time in their lives, will know the wild grief that accompanies tragedy and bereavement. These feelings, however, are a far cry from the clinical disorders described by the DSM.

Depression and Bipolar Disorder. The most widespread serious mood disorder is **major depression,** which involves emotional, behavioral, cognitive, and physical changes severe enough to disrupt a person's ordinary functioning for six months or longer. The writer William Styron, who fought and recovered from it, used the beginning of Dante's classic poem, *The Divine Comedy,* to convey his suffering:

> In the middle of the journey of our life
> I found myself in a dark wood.
> For I had lost the right path.

"For those who have dwelt in depression's dark wood," wrote Styron in *Darkness Visible,* "and known its inexplicable agony," recovery feels like "trudging upward and upward out of hell's black depths and at last emerging into . . . 'the shining world.'" People with major depression, like Styron, feel despairing and hopeless. They may think often of death or suicide. They lose interest or pleasure in their usual activities; it takes an enormous effort just to get up and get dressed. Their thinking patterns feed their bleak moods. They exaggerate minor failings, ignore or discount positive events ("She didn't mean that compliment; she was only being polite"), and interpret any little thing that goes wrong as evidence that nothing will ever go right. Unlike emotionally healthy people who are grieving, depressed people interpret losses as signs of personal failure and conclude that they will never be happy again. Depression is accompanied by physical changes as well. The depressed person may overeat or stop eating, have difficulty falling asleep or sleeping through the night, have trouble concentrating, and feel tired all the time. Some sufferers have other physical reactions, such as headaches or inexplicable pain in the joints or muscles.

At the opposite pole from depression is *mania,* an abnormally high state of exhilaration. You might think it's impossible to feel too good, but mania is not the normal joy of being in love or winning the Pulitzer Prize. Someone in a manic state is expansive, energetic, and "hyper" to an extent that is out of character, bubbling over with plans and ambitions that are unrealistic and irrational.

When people experience episodes of both depression and mania, they are said to have **bipolar disorder** (formerly called *manic-depressive disorder*), a much rarer problem than depression. The great humorist Mark Twain had bipolar disorder, which he

---

major depression A mood disorder involving disturbances in emotion (excessive sadness), behavior (loss of interest in one's usual activities), cognition (thoughts of hopelessness), and body function (fatigue and loss of appetite).

bipolar disorder A mood disorder in which episodes of both depression and mania (excessive euphoria) occur.

described as "periodical and sudden changes of mood . . . from deep melancholy to half-insane tempests and cyclones." Other writers, artists, musicians, and scientists have suffered from this disorder. During the highs, many of these artists create their best work, but the price of the lows is broken relationships, bankruptcy, and sometimes suicide (Barondes, 1998).

Although bipolar disorder occurs equally in both sexes, major depression occurs two or three times as often among women as among men, all over the world (Culbertson, 1997; McGrath et al., 1990). Some psychologists think that women are truly more likely to become depressed than men are, but others think the difference is more apparent than real. Because women are more likely than men to *express* negative emotions like depression and fear, and because women are much more likely than men to seek help for depression, depression in males may be overlooked or misdiagnosed. Men who are depressed often try to mask the feeling by denying their unhappiness, abusing drugs, or committing acts of violence (Canetto, 1992; Kessler et al., 1994).

Theories of Depression.   Each perspective has contributed to our understanding of the multiple causes of depression: biological predispositions, learned habits, negative ways of thinking, social conditions, and problems with close attachments.

1 BIOLOGICAL EXPLANATIONS EMPHASIZE GENETICS AND BRAIN CHEMISTRY. Studies of adopted children and twins support the belief that depression and bipolar disorder have a genetic component, although the precise gene or genes have yet to be identified (DiLalla et al., 1996). Genes may exert their influence by creating biochemical imbalances in neurotransmitters, which permit messages to be transmitted from one neuron to another in the brain. Two neurotransmitters that may be implicated in depressive disorders are serotonin and norepinephrine. In the view of some researchers, depression is caused by a deficient production of one or both of these neurotransmitters, and manic moods are caused by an excessive production. In addition, brain-scan studies find that the brains of depressed people seem less active, especially the left frontal lobes, which are involved in positive emotions (Davidson, 1995). However, brain scans alone do not tell us whether low activation in the brain causes depression, or whether depression changes the brain. It may work both ways, of course.

2 LEARNING EXPLANATIONS EMPHASIZE HOW REPEATED EXPERIENCES WITH FAILURE AND PAIN CAN "EXTINGUISH" THE ENERGY TO COPE AND OVERCOME SETBACKS. In the 1970s, the theory of *learned helplessness* held that people become depressed when their efforts to avoid pain or to control the environment consistently fail (Seligman, 1975). Research with dogs and other animals that were repeatedly subjected to inescapable shocks found that the animals eventually stopped trying to escape the pain, even when escape became possible; the parallels to depressed human beings seemed obvious. However, a serious limitation of this theory was that not all depressed people have actually failed in their lives or have been trapped in painful, inescapable relationships, and even living in painful or difficult situations does not make everyone depressed.

3 COGNITIVE EXPLANATIONS EMPHASIZE PARTICULAR HABITS OF THINKING AND WAYS OF INTERPRETING EVENTS. The real problem for depressed people, research shows, is not their past experiences but rather their *beliefs* about those experiences and the way they explain them (Seligman, 1991). Depressed people have three characteristically pessimistic habits of thinking:

✦ *Internality.* Depressed people tend to believe that the reason for their misery is internal, an entrenched aspect of their personality. They will say, for example, "I'm unattractive and awkward; no wonder I'm not making friends" instead of considering external explanations, such as "This school is so big and impersonal that it's hard to meet new people" (Anderson et al., 1994).

✦ *Stability.* Depressed people tend to believe that their situation is permanent ("Nothing good will ever happen to me"; "I'll never fall in love"). Expecting nothing to get better, they do nothing to improve their lives, and therefore they remain unhappy.

✦ *Lack of control.* Depressed people tend to believe that they have no control over their emotions or the situations that caused those emotions ("I'm depressed because I'm ugly and horrible and I can't do anything about it").

Of course, when you are already feeling sad, gloomy thoughts come more easily. But negative, pessimistic thinking is also an independent cause of depression (Alloy, Abramson, & Francis, 1999).

Another cognitive bad habit that is strongly associated with depression is brooding. People who ruminate endlessly about their unhappiness tend to prolong it, in contrast to those who are able to distract themselves, look outward, and seek solutions to their problems. Women are more likely than men to develop the kind of ruminating, introspective style that fosters depression. This mental habit may contribute both to longer-lasting depressions in women and to the sex difference in reported rates (Bromberger & Matthews, 1996; Nolen-Hoeksema & Girgus, 1994).

4 SOCIAL EXPLANATIONS EMPHASIZE THE STRESSFUL CIRCUMSTANCES OF PEOPLE'S LIVES. From a social perspective, women are more likely than men to suffer from depression because they have less satisfying work and family lives, lower status than men in work and society, and higher rates of poverty and sexual victimization. Mothers are especially vulnerable to depression: The more children a woman has, the more likely she is to become depressed, especially if she is unemployed (McGrath et al., 1990). In contrast, men are more likely than women to be both married and working full time, a combination of activities that is strongly associated with mental health and low rates of depression (G. Brown, 1993; Culbertson, 1997). Violence is also a risk factor for depression: Inner-city adolescents of both sexes who are exposed to high rates of violence report higher levels of depression and more attempts to commit suicide than those who are not subjected to constant violence in their lives or communities (Mazza, Reynolds, & Grover, 1995). Social analyses, however, fail to explain why *most* victims of violence, let alone most mothers and poor people, do not become clinically depressed. Nor do they explain why some people become depressed even though their lives are comfortable and safe.

5 ATTACHMENT AND OBJECT-RELATIONS EXPLANATIONS EMPHASIZE PROBLEMS WITH CLOSE RELATIONSHIPS. In this view, depression results from disturbed relationships; separations and losses, both past and present; and a history of insecure attachments (Klerman et al., 1984; Roberts, Gotlib, & Kassel, 1996). This explanation is supported by the fact that depressive episodes are frequently set off by disruption of a primary relationship. However, it is not always clear whether a broken relationship causes depression, or the relationship dissolves because one partner is chronically depressed. Depressed people often seem demanding and "depressing" to family and friends, who in turn feel angry or sad when they cannot help the sufferer, and eventually break away (Alloy et al., 1998). One longitudinal study found that the direction of cause and effect may be different for husbands and wives: In general, for wives, marital problems made them depressed; for husbands, being depressed caused the marital problems (Fincham et al., 1997).

Increasingly, researchers and psychotherapists are integrating all of these explanations into what they call a *"vulnerability-stress"* approach. They hold that depression and other disorders result from an *interaction* between individual vulnerabilities—in personality traits, habits of thinking, or genetic predispositions—and environmental stresses or unhappy events (Alloy, Abramson, & Francis, 1999). By understanding the causes of depression as an interaction among an individual's biology, ways of thinking, and experiences, we can see why the same precipitating event, such as a minor setback or even the loss of a loved one, might produce normal sadness in one person and extreme depression in another.

What Do You Know?

We hope you won't feel anxious or sad about taking this quiz.

A. Match the anxiety disorder on the left with its description on the right.

1. generalized anxiety disorder	a. need to perform a ritual
	b fear of fear, of being trapped in public
2. posttraumatic stress disorder	c. continuing sense of doom and worry
3. agoraphobia	
4. compulsion	d. repeated, unwanted thoughts
5. obsession	e. anxiety following severe shock

B. In the view of some biological researchers, depression involves a deficit in the neurotransmitters _____ and/or _____ .

C. Depressed people tend to believe that the reasons for their unhappiness are (a) internal, (b) temporary, (c) controllable, (d) caused by the situation.

D. A newspaper headline announces that a single gene has been identified as the cause of depression, but when you read the fine print you learn that other studies have failed to support this finding. What explanations can you think of to explain these contradictory results?

Personality Disorders

Personality disorders involve rigid, maladaptive traits that cause great distress or an inability to get along with others. The DSM describes such a disorder as "an enduring pattern of inner experience and behavior that deviates markedly from the expectations of the individual's culture [and] is pervasive and inflexible." That means it is not caused by depression, drugs, or a situation that temporarily induces a person to behave in ways that are out of character.

For example, **paranoid personality disorder** involves pervasive, unfounded suspiciousness and mistrust of other people; irrational jealousy; secretiveness; and doubt about the loyalty of others. People with paranoid personalities have delusions of being persecuted by everyone from their closest relatives to government agencies, and their beliefs are immune to disconfirming evidence. **Narcissistic personality disorder** involves an exaggerated sense of self-importance and self-absorption. (Narcissism gets its name from the Greek myth of Narcissus, a beautiful young man who fell in love with his own image.) Individuals who are narcissistic are preoccupied with fantasies of unlimited success, power, brilliance, or ideal love. They demand constant attention and admiration and feel entitled to special favors, without being willing to reciprocate. They fall in love quickly and out of love just as fast, when the beloved proves to have some human flaw.

Notice that although these descriptions evoke flashes of recognition ("I know that type!"), it is hard to know where value judgments end and a clear disorder begins (Maddux & Mundell, 1997). Cultures draw the line differently. For example, American society often encourages people to pursue dreams of unlimited success and ideal love, but such dreams might be considered signs of serious disturbance in a more group-oriented society. Where would you draw the line between having a "narcissistic personality disorder" and being a normal member of a group or culture that encourages you to put your own needs ahead of those of your family and friends, and that puts a premium on youth and beauty?

---

personality disorders   Rigid, maladaptive personality patterns that cause personal distress or an inability to get along with others.

paranoid personality disorder   A disorder characterized by habitually unreasonable and excessive suspiciousness or jealousy.

narcissistic personality disorder   A disorder characterized by an exaggerated sense of self-importance and self-absorption.

Antisocial Personality Disorder. Throughout history, most societies have recognized and feared the few members in their midst who lack all human connection to anyone else—who can cheat, con, and kill without flinching. In the 1830s these individuals were said to be afflicted with "moral insanity," and in the twentieth century they came to be called "psychopaths" or "sociopaths." The DSM, trying to avoid such emotionally charged terms, refers to **antisocial personality disorder (APD).** By any name, this condition is fascinating and frightening because of the great harm these people inflict on their victims and on society.

According to the DSM, people diagnosed with APD must meet at least three of seven criteria: (1) They repeatedly break the law; (2) they are deceitful, using aliases and lies to con others; (3) they are impulsive and unable to plan ahead; (4) they repeatedly get into physical fights or assaults; (5) they show reckless disregard for their own safety or that of others; (6) they are constantly irresponsible, failing to meet obligations to others; and (7) they lack remorse for actions that harm others.

Lacking conscience and remorse, people with APD can lie, seduce, and manipulate others without a twinge of feeling or regret. If caught in a lie or a crime, they may seem sincerely sorry and promise to make amends, but it is all an act. Some are sadistic, able to kill a pet, a child, or a random adult. Others direct their energies into con games or career advancement, abusing other people emotionally or economically rather than physically. Antisocial personality disorder occurs in only about 3 percent of all males and less than 1 percent of all females. Yet people with APD may account for more than half of all serious crimes committed in the United States (Hare, 1993).

Causes of APD. Researchers who are studying APD, like those studying other mental disorders, think that biological, social, and cultural factors, in interaction, contribute to antisocial personalities.

People with APD do seem to be wired differently from others. Normally, when a person is anticipating danger, pain, or punishment, the electrical conductance of the skin changes—a classically conditioned response that indicates anxiety or fear. But people with APD are slow to develop such responses, which suggests that they are unable to feel the anxiety necessary for learning that their actions will have unpleasant consequences (see Figure 12.1). Their inability to feel emotional arousal—empathy, guilt, fear of punishment, anxiety under stress—suggests some abnormality in the brain and central nervous system (Hare, 1965, 1993; Raine, 1996).

Some researchers believe that people who are antisocial, hyperactive, addicted, or impulsive may share a common inherited disorder: an inability to control responses to frustration and provocation or to inhibit a pleasurable action that may have unpleasant consequences (Luengo et al., 1994; Raine, 1996). The biological children of parents with APD, substance-abuse problems, or impulsivity disorders are at higher risk of

---

antisocial personality disorder A disorder characterized by antisocial behavior such as lying, stealing, manipulating others, and sometimes violence; and a lack of guilt, shame, and empathy. (Sometimes called *psychopathy* or *sociopathy*.)

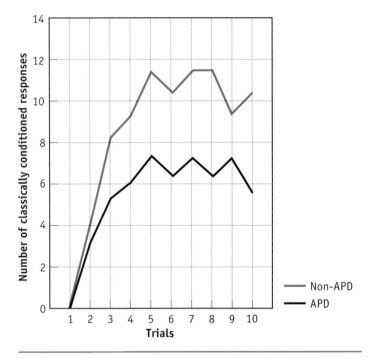

FIGURE 12.1 EMOTIONS AND ANTISOCIAL PERSONALITY DISORDER
In several experiments, people with antisocial personality disorder (APD) were slow to develop classically conditioned responses to anticipated danger, pain, or shock—responses that indicate normal anxiety (Hare, 1965). This deficit may be related to the ability of people with APD to behave in destructive ways, without remorse or regard for the consequences (Hare, 1993).

developing these disorders themselves, even when these children are reared by others (Nigg & Goldsmith, 1994).

Many children who become violent and antisocial have suffered neurological impairments, a result not of genetics but of physical battering and subsequent brain injury (Lewis, 1992; Milner & McCanne, 1991; Moffitt, 1993; Raine et al., 1998). Consider the chilling results of a study that compared two groups of delinquent boys: violent boys who had been arrested for vicious assault, rape, or murder, and boys whose violence was limited to fistfights. More than three-fourths of the extremely violent boys had suffered head injuries as children, had a history of serious medical problems, or had been beaten savagely by their parents, compared with one-third of the other boys (Lewis, 1981).

Nevertheless, brain damage or genetic predispositions alone are rarely enough to create a violent or antisocial individual. According to the *vulnerability-stress model* of APD, it takes an interaction among several factors. As we saw in Chapter 4, when biological vulnerability is combined with physical abuse, parental neglect, lack of love and contact comfort, or other environmental stresses, individuals are far more likely to become impulsively uncontrolled and violent, often ending up in prison (Raine, Brennan, & Mednick, 1994). As sociocultural psychologists remind us, cultures and environments can also make antisocial behavior more likely or less so. Societies and subcultures that place a premium on success at all costs and on individual achievement may cultivate qualities of selfishness, professional ruthlessness, and emotional hard-heartedness. In contrast, small, close-knit cultures that depend on each member's cooperation and consideration for others would find selfishness and coldness intolerable.

It seems, then, that several routes lead to the development of antisocial personality disorder: neurological abnormalities; having a genetic disposition toward impulsivity, addiction, or hyperactivity, which leads to rule breaking and crime; being neglected or rejected by parents; having brain damage as a result of birth complications or physical abuse in childhood; and living in a culture or environment that rewards and fosters antisocial traits. These multiple origins may explain why rates of antisocial personality disorder vary across societies and history.

Schizophrenia

In 1911, Swiss psychiatrist Eugen Bleuler coined the term **schizophrenia** to describe cases in which the personality loses its unity. People with schizophrenia do not have a "split" or "multiple personality," however. Rather, schizophrenia is a fragmented condition in which words are split from meaning, actions from motives, perceptions from reality. It is an example of a **psychosis,** a mental condition that involves distorted perceptions of reality and an inability to function in most aspects of life.

Symptoms of Schizophrenia. If depression is the common cold of psychological disorder, said psychiatrist Donald Klein (1980), schizophrenia is its cancer: elusive, complicated, varying in form and duration, and difficult to treat. In general, schizophrenia produces two categories of symptoms. *Active* or *positive symptoms* involve an exaggeration or distortion of normal thinking processes and behavior. These symptoms are called "positive" because they are *additions* to normal behavior; healthy people do not have delusions that their brains are receiving Martian signals. In contrast, *negative symptoms* involve the *loss* of normal traits and abilities, such as the ability to speak intelligibly and feel warm emotions.

The most common active symptoms include the following:

1 BIZARRE DELUSIONS (false beliefs), such as the belief that dogs are extraterrestrials disguised as pets. Some people with schizophrenia have paranoid delusions, taking innocent events—a stranger's cough, a helicopter overhead—as evidence that the world is plotting against them. Some have delusions of identity, believing that they are

---

schizophrenia A psychotic disorder or group of disorders marked by positive symptoms (e.g., delusions, hallucinations, disorganized and incoherent speech, and inappropriate behavior) and negative symptoms (e.g., emotional flatness and loss of motivation).

psychosis An extreme mental disturbance involving distorted perceptions and irrational behavior; it may have psychological or organic causes. (Plural: *psychoses.*)

Moses, Jesus, Joan of Arc, or some other famous person. Some, like Margaret Mary Ray, whose story opened this chapter, have delusions that a celebrity loves them.

2 HALLUCINATIONS AND HEIGHTENED SENSORY AWARENESS. Schizophrenic hallucinations, which feel intensely real to the sufferer, usually take the form of voices speaking odd, garbled words; a running conversation in the head; or two or more voices conversing with each other. But some hallucinations are tactile (e.g., feeling insects crawling over the body) or visual (e.g., seeing a famous actress in the mirror). People with schizophrenia also have difficulty in filtering out sensory stimulation and distracting sounds, making it difficult and sometimes impossible for them to concentrate.

3 DISORGANIZED, INCOHERENT SPEECH consisting of an illogical jumble of ideas and symbols, linked by meaningless rhyming words or by remote associations called *word salads*. A patient of Bleuler's wrote, "Olive oil is an Arabian liquor-sauce which the Afghans, Moors and Moslems use in ostrich farming. The Indian plantain tree is the whiskey of the Parsees and Arabs. Barley, rice and sugar cane called artichoke, grow remarkably well in India. The Brahmins live as castes in Baluchistan. The Circassians occupy Manchuria and China. China is the Eldorado of the Pawnees" (Bleuler, 1911/1950).

4 GROSSLY DISORGANIZED AND INAPPROPRIATE BEHAVIOR that may range from child-like silliness to unpredictable and violent agitation. The person may wear three overcoats and gloves on a hot day, start collecting garbage, or hoard scraps of food.

In contrast to these positive symptoms, negative symptoms include loss of motivation; poverty of speech (making only brief, empty replies in conversation, because of diminished thought rather than an unwillingness to speak); and, most notably, emotional flatness—unresponsive facial expressions, poor eye contact, and diminished emotionality. Some people with schizophrenia withdraw completely, sitting for hours without moving, a condition called *catatonic stupor*. These negative symptoms may appear months before active ones do, and they often persist when the active symptoms are in remission.

In some individuals, schizophrenic symptoms appear abruptly, often in response to a stressful situation; in such cases, the prognosis for recovery is relatively good. In other individuals, the onset is more gradual; negative symptoms slowly emerge, and friends and family report a slow change in personality. The person may stop working or bathing, become isolated and withdrawn, and start behaving in peculiar ways. In these cases, the outlook is less predictable. The more breakdowns and relapses the individual has had, the poorer the chances for complete recovery (Eaton et al., 1992a, 1992b). Yet many people suffering from this illness learn to control the symptoms, while working and having good family relationships (Harding, Zubin, & Strauss, 1992).

Theories of Schizophrenia. Obviously, any disorder that has so many variations and symptoms will pose many problems for diagnosis and explanation. Early theories from the psychodynamic and learning perspectives—that schizophrenia results from being raised by an erratic, cold, rejecting mother or from living in an unpredictable environment—have not been supported. The leading theories today come primarily from the biological perspective, although biological explanations are, as usual, not the whole story. Biological researchers are searching for genetic factors, abnormalities in the brain and neurotransmitters, and abnormalities in prenatal development. Here are some of their major findings:

1 GENETIC PREDISPOSITIONS. A person has a considerably greater risk of developing schizophrenia if an identical twin does, and this is true even if the person is reared apart from the affected sibling (Gottesman, 1991, 1994). Moreover, children with one schizophrenic parent have a lifetime risk of 12 percent, and children with two schizophrenic parents have a lifetime risk of 35–46 percent, compared to a risk in the general population of only 1–2 percent (Goldstein, 1987). (See Figure 12.2.)

These and similar findings indicate the existence of a genetic contribution to the disorder or to some of its specific symptoms, such as hallucinations and hypersensitivity to sounds (Blouin et al., 1998; Leonard et al., 1998). To date, however, researchers have been unsuccessful in pinpointing any particular gene; some believe the quest itself is hopeless, given all the different forms that schizophrenia can take (Levinson et al., 1998). Further, genes alone cannot predict who will develop the disorder. Even among identical twins, when one develops schizophrenia, the chances that the other will do so are slightly less than half (Torrey et al., 1994). And remember that even if 12 percent of all children with one schizophrenic parent develop the disorder, that means that 88 percent of them do not.

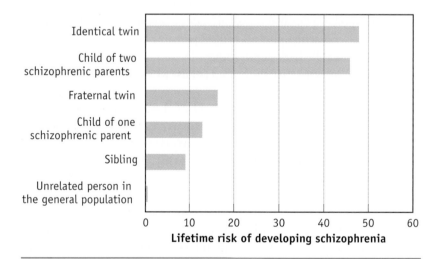

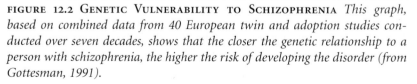

FIGURE 12.2 GENETIC VULNERABILITY TO SCHIZOPHRENIA *This graph, based on combined data from 40 European twin and adoption studies conducted over seven decades, shows that the closer the genetic relationship to a person with schizophrenia, the higher the risk of developing the disorder (from Gottesman, 1991).*

2 STRUCTURAL BRAIN ABNORMALITIES. Some individuals with schizophrenia show signs of cerebral damage: decreased brain weight, a decrease in the volume of the temporal lobe or limbic regions, reduced numbers of neurons in the prefrontal cortex, or enlargement of the *ventricles,* spaces in the brain that are filled with cerebrospinal fluid (Akbarian et al., 1996; Heinrichs, 1993; Zorrilla et al., 1997). Schizophrenics are also more likely than healthy individuals to have abnormalities in the thalamus, the traffic-control center that filters sensations and focuses attention (Andreasen et al., 1994; Gur et al., 1998).

3 NEUROTRANSMITTER ABNORMALITIES. Abnormalities in several neurotransmitters, including serotonin, glutamate, and most notably dopamine, have been associated with schizophrenia. For example, many schizophrenics have high levels of activity in brain areas served by dopamine, and a particular kind of dopamine receptor is more common in their brains than in those of healthy people (Seeman, Guan, & Van Tol, 1993). However, similar neurotransmitter abnormalities are also found in many other mental disorders, such as depression and alcoholism, making it difficult to know whether these abnormalities play a specific role in schizophrenia.

4 PRENATAL ABNORMALITIES. Damage to the fetal brain increases the likelihood of schizophrenia (and, again, of other mental disorders). In some cases, the damage may occur because of malnutrition: Babies conceived during times of famine have twice the schizophrenia rate as babies whose mothers ate normal diets during pregnancy (Susser et al., 1996). Another culprit may be an infectious virus during prenatal development (Hooper, 1999; Torrey et al., 1994). There is a significant association between a mother's exposure to the influenza virus during her second trimester of pregnancy, when the fetal brain is forming crucial connections, and the onset of schizophrenia in the child 20 to 30 years later (Mednick, Huttunen, & Machón, 1994).

Although the evidence for brain abnormalities in schizophrenia is compelling, many researchers believe that the onset and course of this disorder are best explained, as other disorders are, by a *vulnerability-stress model.* They observe that genes or brain damage alone will not inevitably produce schizophrenia, and a vulnerable person who lives in a good environment may never show full-fledged signs of the disorder. For many years, the Copenhagen High-Risk Project has followed 207 children at risk for schizophrenia (because they had a schizophrenic parent) and a control group of 104 low-risk children. The project has identified several factors that, in combination, increase the likelihood of schizophrenia: the existence of schizophrenia in the family; physical trauma during childbirth, which might damage the brain; exposure to the flu virus or other prenatal trauma during the second trimester of gestation; and unstable, stressful environments (Olin & Mednick, 1996).

The interaction of individual vulnerabilities and environmental stresses shows how several factors may combine to produce any given case of schizophrenia. Perhaps schizophrenia will turn out to be not one disorder, but several, each with a different primary cause. The riddle of schizophrenia remains to be unraveled.

What Do You Know?

The following quiz is not a hallucination.

1. Biological research suggests that people with APD differ from others in their physiological responses to _____, but according to the _____ explanation, this disorder results from an interaction of biology and environmental stresses.

2. A patient with schizophrenia hears voices in her head when no one is around. Is this an example of a positive symptom or a negative one?

3. Abnormally high levels of which neurotransmitter are thought to be involved in schizophrenia?

4. *True or false:* Most people with schizophrenia have a schizophrenic parent.

ANSWERS:

1. danger, pain, or punishment; vulnerability-stress 2. positive 3. dopamine 4. false

We turn now to the contributions of each psychological perspective to the treatment of the emotional problems just discussed, as well as other problems that people have. We begin with biological approaches, which include direct intervention in brain function and, more commonly, the use of drugs. We will then turn to the major schools of psychotherapy arising from the learning, cognitive, sociocultural, and psychodynamic perspectives. Each of these approaches is successful with some problems or individuals but not others. As we go along, we will report the evidence showing which therapies might be best for which particular problems and individuals.

THE BIOLOGICAL PERSPECTIVE

For centuries, physicians trained in the biological approach treated mental illness by trying to change brain function directly. In the seventeenth century, for example, they tried to release the "psychic pressures" they believed were causing a person's symptoms by drilling holes in the person's skull—a method called *trepanning*. **Psychosurgery,** surgery designed to destroy selected areas of the brain thought to be responsible for emotional disorders or disturbed behavior, continues to be performed to the present day.

The most famous form of modern psychosurgery was invented in 1935, when a Portuguese neurologist, Egas Moniz, drilled two holes into the skull of a mental patient and used a specially designed instrument to cut or crush nerve fibers running from the

---

psychosurgery Any surgical procedure that destroys selected areas of the brain believed to be involved in emotional disorders or violent, impulsive behavior.

prefrontal lobes to other areas. This operation, called a *prefrontal lobotomy,* was supposed to reduce the patient's emotional symptoms without impairing intellectual ability. The procedure—which, incredibly, was never assessed or validated scientifically—was performed on tens of thousands of people. Tragically, lobotomies left many patients apathetic, withdrawn, and unable to care for themselves (Valenstein, 1986). Yet Moniz won a Nobel Prize for his work.

Today, psychosurgery is rare, but some neurosurgeons have not given up on the effort to cure mental illness by operating on the brains of severely depressed or anxious patients whose symptoms have not responded to other treatments (Marino & Cosgrove, 1997). Although the physicians usually claim success, these reports are anecdotal and, to date, the procedures have no greater scientific support than lobotomy did (Vertosick, 1997). Sometimes the criterion for "success" is only the psychiatrist's report, not even the patient's!

Another controversial procedure is **electroconvulsive therapy (ECT),** or "shock therapy," which is used for the treatment of severe depression. An electrode is placed on one or both sides of the head, and a current of between 70 and 130 volts is turned on. The current triggers a seizure that typically lasts one minute, causing the body to convulse. Today, unlike in the past, patients are given muscle relaxants and anesthesia, so they can sleep through the procedure and their convulsions are minimized. ECT is sometimes used effectively on people who are at immediate risk of committing suicide, although no one knows how or why it works (Sarason & Sarason, 1999). However, ECT is *ineffective* with other disorders, such as schizophrenia or alcoholism, though it is occasionally misused for these conditions.

ECT's supporters argue that when ECT is used properly, it is safe and effective and causes no long-term cognitive impairment or brain damage (Coffey, 1993; Devanand et al., 1994). One psychologist, Norman Endler (1990), used ECT successfully to treat his own severe depression, later diagnosed as bipolar disorder; in contrast, we know a woman whose brain function was severely and permanently impaired as a result of a series of ECT treatments. Critics argue that ECT is too often used improperly, and that it can indeed damage the brain (Breggin, 1991). One psychiatrist said that using ECT was "like hitting [someone] with a two-by-four" (Fisher, 1985). The ECT controversy promises to continue.

Medicating the Mind

By far the most widely used biological intervention in mental disorders is medication. Because drugs are so widely prescribed these days, both for severe disorders such as schizophrenia and for more common problems such as anxiety and depression, the public needs to understand what these drugs are, how they can best be used, and what their limitations are.

---

electroconvulsive therapy (ECT) A procedure used in cases of prolonged and severe major depression, in which a brief brain seizure is induced.

The main classes of drugs used in the treatment of mental and emotional disorders are these:

1 **Antipsychotic drugs,** also called *neuroleptics*—older ones such as chlorpromazine and haloperidol and newer, "second-generation" ones such as clozapine and risperidone—are used in the treatment of schizophrenia and other psychoses. Many antipsychotic drugs block or reduce the sensitivity of brain receptors that respond to dopamine. Some also increase levels of serotonin, a neurotransmitter that inhibits dopamine activity. Antipsychotic drugs can reduce a patient's agitation, delusions, and hallucinations, and they can shorten schizophrenic episodes. However, they offer little relief from other symptoms of schizophrenia, such as jumbled thoughts, difficulty concentrating, or inability to interact with others. And, according to one estimate, drugs help only about 60 percent of all schizophrenics (Valenstein, 1998).

Even when medication works, many schizophrenics stop taking it because of its unpleasant side effects, which can be dangerous if the drug is taken over many years. About one-fourth of all adults who take these drugs, and fully one-third of elderly patients who do so, develop a neurological disorder called *tardive* (late appearing) *dyskinesia,* which is characterized by hand tremors and other involuntary muscle movements (Masand, 2000). Some evidence suggests that second-generation antipsychotic drugs, such as clozapine and risperidone, are more effective than older antipsychotics—they treat more symptoms of schizophrenia and have fewer side effects (Feltus & Gardner, 1999; Schulz, 2000). But other studies find that these drugs, too, taken over time, increase the risk of tardive dyskinesia and disorders of the white blood cells (Modestin et al., 2000). These cautions are important, because the newer antipsychotics are increasingly being used to treat depression, bipolar disorder, impulsive aggression, and other disorders.

2 **Antidepressant drugs** are used primarily in the treatment of depression, anxiety, phobias, and obsessive-compulsive disorder. *Monoamine oxidase (MAO) inhibitors,* such as Nardil, elevate the level of norepinephrine and serotonin in the brain by blocking or inhibiting an enzyme that deactivates these neurotransmitters. *Tricyclic antidepressants,* such as Elavil, boost norepinephrine and serotonin levels by preventing the normal reabsorption, or "reuptake," of these substances by the cells that have released them. *Selective serotonin reuptake inhibitors (SSRIs),* such as Prozac, work on the same principle as the tricyclics but specifically target serotonin. Antidepressants are nonaddictive, but they can produce some unpleasant physical reactions, including dry mouth, headaches, constipation, nausea, gastrointestinal problems, weight gain, and, in as many as one-third of all patients, decreased sexual desire and blocked or delayed orgasm.

3 **Tranquilizers,** such as Valium and Xanax, increase the activity of the neurotransmitter gamma-aminobutyric acid (GABA). They are the drugs most often prescribed by physicians in general practice for patients who complain of depressed mood, panic, or

---

antipsychotic drugs Drugs used primarily in the treatment of schizophrenia and other psychotic disorders.

antidepressant drugs Drugs used primarily in the treatment of mood disorders, especially depression and anxiety.

tranquilizers Drugs commonly but often inappropriately prescribed for patients who complain of unhappiness, anxiety, or worry.

anxiety—but they are the wrong drugs for such problems. They are not effective for depression or panic disorder, and while they may help an anxious person temporarily feel calmer during an acute experience of anxiety, they are not considered the treatment of choice over a long period of time. One reason is that a significant percentage of people who take tranquilizers overuse the drugs and develop problems with withdrawal and tolerance (i.e., they need larger and larger doses). Xanax can also result in rebound panic attacks if it is not taken exactly on schedule.

4 A special category of drug, a salt called **lithium carbonate,** often helps people who suffer from bipolar disorder. It may produce its effects by moderating levels of norepinephrine or by protecting brain cells from being overstimulated by another neurotransmitter, glutamate (Nonaka, Hough, & Chuang, 1998). Lithium must be given in exactly the right dose, and bloodstream levels of the drug must be carefully monitored, because too little will not help and too much is toxic.

Evaluating Medical Treatments

Unfortunately, many psychiatrists and drug companies are trumpeting the benefits of medication without informing the public of the drugs' limitations and potential risks. Here are some of them:

1 THE PLACEBO EFFECT. New drugs, like new psychotherapies, often promise quick and effective cures. But the **placebo effect** (see Chapter 2) ensures that some people will respond positively to new drugs just because of the enthusiasm surrounding them and their own expectations that the drug will make them feel much better. After a while, when placebo effects decline, many drugs turn out to be neither as effective as promised nor as widely applicable. This has happened repeatedly with each new generation of tranquilizer and is happening again with antidepressants.

The belief that antidepressants are the treatment of choice for depression is widespread, so we were as surprised as anyone to discover the large amount of evidence questioning that belief (Antonuccio et al., 1999; Valenstein, 1998). One meta-analysis found that although clinicians considered antidepressants helpful, the patients' ratings showed no advantage for the drugs beyond the placebo effect (Greenberg et al., 1992). Another meta-analysis, of 19 double-blind studies involving more than 2,000 depressed patients, found that 75 percent of the drugs' effectiveness was due to the placebo effect or other nonchemical factors, and only 25 percent to the chemical properties of the drug (Kirsch & Sapirstein, 1998). Even Prozac, which arrived with much fanfare and enthusiasm, is generally no more effective than the older generation of antidepressants (Greenberg et al., 1994).

2 HIGH RELAPSE AND DROPOUT RATES. A person may have short-term success with antipsychotic or antidepressant drugs. However, in part because of their negative

---

lithium carbonate A drug frequently given to people suffering from bipolar disorder.

placebo effect The apparent success of a medication or treatment that is due to the patient's expectations or hopes rather than to the drug or treatment itself.

side effects, half to two-thirds of people stop taking them (McGrath et al., 1990; Torrey, 1988). Individuals who take antidepressants without also learning how to cope with their problems are also more likely to relapse in the future (Antonuccio et al., 1999).

3 DOSAGE PROBLEMS. The challenge with drugs is to find the *therapeutic window,* the amount that is enough but not too much. This problem is compounded by the fact that the same dose of a drug may be metabolized differently in men and women, old people and young people, and different ethnic groups (Willie et al., 1995). When psychiatrist Keh-Ming Lin moved from Taiwan to the United States, he was amazed to learn that the dosage of antipsychotic drugs given to American patients with schizophrenia was often 10 times higher than the dose for Chinese patients. In subsequent studies, Lin and his colleagues confirmed that Asian patients require significantly lower doses of the medication for optimal treatment (Lin, Poland, & Chien, 1990). Similarly, African-Americans suffering from depression or bipolar disorder seem to need lower dosages of tricyclic antidepressants and lithium than other ethnic groups do (Strickland et al., 1991, 1995). Groups may differ in the dosages they can tolerate because of variations in metabolic rates, amount of body fat, the number or type of drug receptors in the brain, or cultural practices such as smoking and eating habits.

4 LONG-TERM RISKS. We noted that antipsychotic drugs can have dangerous consequences if taken for many years. Antidepressants, in contrast, are assumed to be quite safe, but the effects of taking them for many years are still unknown. The general public and even many physicians do not realize that new drugs are often tested on only a few hundred people for only a few weeks or months, even when the drug is one that patients might take for many years. For example, clozapine was tested in controlled trials that lasted only six weeks (*FDA Drug Bulletin,* 1990). And none of the other second-generation antipsychotic drugs have been used long enough to determine

their long-term risk of producing tardive dyskinesia (Gupta et al., 1999). Many physicians and the public, feeling reassured if a drug is effective in the short run, overlook the possibility of long-term dangers.

Without question, drugs have rescued some people from emotional despair, suicide, or years in a mental hospital. They have enabled severely depressed or disturbed people to function and respond to psychotherapy. Although medication cannot magically eliminate people's problems, it can be a useful first step in treatment.

Nevertheless, it is important to think critically about the popularity of an exclusively biological approach to mental disorders. For one thing, many American doctors prescribe drugs routinely, often without accompanying psychotherapy for the person's problems. The overprescription of drugs in the United States is partly a result of pressure from managed-care organizations, which prefer to pay for one patient visit for a prescription rather than ten visits for psychotherapy. But it is also a result of advertising by drug companies, which are spending fortunes to study and market these highly profitable products. (In 1997 the Food and Drug Administration [FDA] permitted pharmaceutical companies to advertise directly to consumers, a practice still forbidden in Canada and Europe.) Most consumers do not realize that once a drug is approved by the FDA, doctors are then permitted to prescribe it for other conditions and to other populations than those on which it was originally tested. That is why antidepressants are now being marketed for "social phobias," Ritalin, the drug widely prescribed for hyperactive children, is being prescribed for 2- and 3-year-olds, and antipsychotics are being used for nonpsychotic disorders.

Most worrisome for the future of impartial research, many if not most of the researchers who are studying the effectiveness of medication have strong financial ties to the pharmaceutical industry, in the form of lucrative consulting fees, funding for studies, stock investments, and patents (Bodenheimer, 2000; Critser, 1996). The former editor of *The New England Journal of Medicine*, Marcia Angell (2000), reported that the authors of a paper on antidepressant drugs versus cognitive-behavior therapy (Keller et al., 2000) had such extensive ties to companies that make antidepressant drugs that the journal could not even list them all, for space reasons. Disclosure of a researcher's ties to a drug company, Angell cautioned readers, is not enough to ensure honest research. When a judge discloses that she has financial interests in a particular case, after all, she is expected to remove herself from the trial.

The overprescription of drugs for mood disorders in North America also occurs because of a common but mistaken assumption: that if a disorder appears to have biological origins or involve biochemical abnormalities, then biological treatments must be most appropriate. But, as we will see in our discussion of cognitive and behavioral therapies, changing behavior and thoughts can also change the way the brain functions. This point was dramatically illustrated in a PET-scan study of people with obsessive-compulsive disorder. Among those who were taking Prozac, the metabolism of glucose in the brain improved, suggesting that the drug was having a beneficial effect. But two studies found exactly the *same* brain changes in patients who were getting cognitive-behavior therapy and no medication (Baxter et al., 1992; Schwartz et al., 1996).

In sum, consumers need to be aware of the danger of the misuses and over-prescription of drugs. The drugs used for treating psychological problems are neither totally miraculous nor totally worthless. Their effectiveness depends on the individual, the problem, and whether medication is combined with psychotherapy.

What Do You Know?

A. Match these treatments with the problems for which they are typically used.

1. antipsychotic drugs
2. antidepressant drugs
3. lithium carbonate
4. electroconvulsive therapy

   a. suicidal depression
   b. obsessive-compulsive disorder
   c. bipolar disorder
   d. schizophrenia
   e. depression and anxiety

B. Give four reasons why the public should be cautious about concluding that drugs for emotional disorders are miracle cures.

 C. Jezebel has had occasional episodes of depression, which seem to be getting worse. Her physician prescribes an antidepressant. Before taking it, what questions should Jezebel ask herself—and the doctor?

ANSWERS:

A. 1. d 2. b 3. c 4. a **B.** Placebo effects are common; dropout and relapse rates are high; appropriate dosages can be difficult to determine and can vary by sex, age, and ethnicity; and some drugs have known or unknown long-term risks. **C.** Jezebel might want to ask, Has the physician considered possible medical reasons for her depression, and given her a complete physical exam? Has the physician explored with her the possible emotional and psychological reasons for her depression, or referred her to a mental-health professional who will do so? Would psychotherapy be appropriate, either with or without medication? Does the medication have any unpleasant physical effects or long-term risks? Will the doctor monitor her reactions to the drug on a regular basis?

THE LEARNING AND COGNITIVE PERSPECTIVES

Psychotherapies derived from the learning perspective focus on helping people change the behavioral patterns that are causing them grief and difficulty, patterns acquired in the lifelong process of being rewarded and punished by others. Psychotherapies derived from the cognitive perspective focus on ways of helping people change the beliefs, expectations, and attitudes that are creating negative emotions and self-defeating habits. We combine these two approaches under one heading here because behavioral and cognitive techniques are so often combined in therapeutic practice.

Behavior Therapy

Behavior therapists draw on techniques derived from the behavioral principles of classical and operant conditioning discussed in Chapter 5. Here are some of their most commonly used methods:

1 SYSTEMATIC DESENSITIZATION is a step-by-step process of desensitizing a client to a feared object or experience. It is based on the classical-conditioning procedure of *counterconditioning,* in which a stimulus for an unwanted response (such as fear) is paired with some other stimulus or situation that elicits a response incompatible with the undesirable one. In this case, the incompatible response is usually relaxation. The client learns to relax deeply while imagining or looking at a sequence of feared stimuli, arranged in a hierarchy ranging from the least frightening to the most frightening. The sequence for a person who is terrified of flying might be to read about airplane safety, look at pictures or models of airplanes, visit an airport and watch planes taking off, sit in a plane while it is on the ground, take a short flight, and then take a long flight. At each step the person must become relaxed and comfortable before going on. Eventually, the fear responses are extinguished.

2 AVERSIVE CONDITIONING substitutes punishment for the reinforcement that has perpetuated a bad habit. Suppose a woman who bites her nails is reinforced each time she does so by relief from her anxiety and a brief good feeling. A behavior therapist might have her wear a rubber band around her wrist and ask her to snap it (hard!) each time she bites her nails or feels the desire to do so. The goal is to make sure that she receives no continuing rewards for the undesirable behavior.

3 EXPOSURE TREATMENTS, sometimes called "flooding," have clients who are suffering from specific anxieties confront the feared situation or memory directly. (Normally, people who are afraid of some situation or traumatic memory do everything they can to *avoid* confronting or thinking of it. This only makes the fear worse.) For example, a person who is trying to avoid thinking of a traumatic event might be asked to imagine the event over and over, until it no longer evokes the same degree of panic. Likewise, a person suffering from agoraphobia might be taken into the very situation that he or she fears most—a department store, say, or a subway—and would remain there, with the therapist, until the panic and anxiety declined.

4 BEHAVIORAL RECORDS AND CONTRACTS help clients identify the reinforcers (rewarding consequences) that are keeping their unwanted habits going. For example, a man who wants to curb his overeating may not be aware of how much he eats throughout the day to relieve tension; a behavioral record might show that he eats more junk food than

---

systematic desensitization In behavior therapy, a step-by-step process of desensitizing a client to a feared object or experience; based on the classical-conditioning procedure of counterconditioning.

aversive conditioning In behavior therapy, a method in which punishment is substituted for the reinforcement that is perpetuating a bad habit.

exposure treatment In behavior therapy, a method in which a person suffering from an anxiety disorder, such as a phobia or panic attacks, is taken directly into the feared situation until the anxiety subsides.

In this "virtual reality" version of systematic desensitization, people with spider phobias are gradually exposed to computerized but extremely life-like images of spiders in a realistic, three-dimensional environment.

he realized in the late afternoon. Once the unwanted behavior is identified, along with the reinforcers that have been maintaining it, a treatment program can be designed to change it; the man might find other ways to reduce stress and make sure that he is nowhere near junk food in the late afternoon. The therapist also helps people set *behavioral goals,* small step by small step. A husband and wife who fight over housework, for instance, might be asked to draw up a contract indicating who will do what, with specified rewards for carrying out their duties. With such a contract, they can't fall back on accusations such as "You never do anything around here."

5 Skills training provides practice in behaviors that are necessary for achieving the person's goals. It is not enough to tell someone "Don't be shy" if the person does not know how to make small talk with others; skills training would teach the shy person how to converse in social settings (for example, by focusing on other people rather than on his or her own insecurity). Countless skills-training programs are available for parents who don't know how to discipline children, for people who don't know how to manage anger, for children and adults who don't know how to express their wishes clearly, and so on.

Cognitive Therapy

As psychologists in the cognitive perspective have amply demonstrated, people's thoughts, feelings, and motivations can influence their behavior. *Cognitive therapy* helps clients identify the beliefs and expectations that might be unnecessarily prolonging their unhappiness, conflicts, and other problems. To a cognitive therapist, expressing emotions is not the way to get rid of them, if the thoughts behind the emotions remain (Greenberger & Padesky, 1995). So cognitive therapists require clients to examine the evidence for their beliefs—say, that everyone is mean and selfish, that ambition is hopeless, or that love is doomed. Cognitive therapy, you can see, teaches critical thinking!

For example, anger typically results from the perception that you have been insulted or treated unfairly. A cognitive therapist would therefore help an angry person consider other interpretations for a person's irritating behavior and become more empathic about other people's possible motives. Perhaps that dope on the freeway who cut in front of you was not really trying to kill you; perhaps your father's strict discipline was intended not to control you but to protect you.

One of the oldest and best-known schools of cognitive therapy is Albert Ellis's *rational emotive behavior therapy* (Ellis, 1993; Ellis & Blau, 1998). In this approach, the therapist uses rational arguments to directly challenge a client's unrealistic beliefs or expectations. For example, people who are emotionally upset often overgeneralize: They decide that one annoying act by someone means that person is totally bad in every way. Or they interpret their own normal failings and mistakes as evidence that they are totally incompetent and worthless individuals. The rational emotive behavior therapist directly challenges these thoughts and interpretations, showing the client why they are irrational and misguided. In contrast, another popular approach, devised by Aaron Beck (1976, 1991), avoids direct challenges to the client's beliefs. Instead, the therapist encourages the person to test those beliefs against the evidence, to stop trying to read other people's minds ("I *know* he's out to get me"), and to avoid turning normal upsets and setbacks into catastrophes—a common mistake in thinking that cognitive therapists call "catastrophizing."

A cognitive therapist might treat a student who procrastinates by asking the student to write down his or her thoughts about work, read the thoughts as if someone else had said them, and then write a rational response to each one. This technique would encourage the student to examine the validity of his or her assumptions and beliefs. Many procrastinators are perfectionists; if they cannot do something perfectly, they will not do it at all. Unable to accept their limitations, they set impossible standards and catastrophize:

NEGATIVE THOUGHT	RATIONAL RESPONSE
This paper isn't good enough; I'd better rewrite it for the twentieth time.	Good enough for what? It won't win a Pulitzer Prize, but it is a pretty good paper.
If I don't get an A+ on this paper, my life will be ruined.	My life will be a lot worse if I keep getting incompletes. It's better to get a B or even a C than to do nothing at all.

Strict behaviorists consider thoughts to be "behaviors" that are modifiable by learning principles; they do not regard thoughts as causes of behavior. But most psychologists believe that thoughts and behavior influence each other, which is why cognitive-behavior therapy is more common than either form alone.

Evaluating Behavior and Cognitive Therapies

To test the effectiveness of different kinds of therapy, clinical researchers have conducted hundreds of controlled clinical trials, in which people with a given problem or disorder are randomly assigned to one or more treatment groups or to a control group. The APA's Division of Clinical Psychology convened a task force to assess the empirical research evaluating specific methods for specific problems (Barlow, 1996; Chambless et al., 1996, 1998). Although the task force could not assess every therapy in existence, one key finding emerged clearly: For many problems and most emotional disorders, cognitive and behavior therapies are the preferred methods. These therapies are particularly effective for the following problems:

◆ *Depression.* Cognitive therapy's greatest success has been in the treatment of mood disorders, especially depression. It is often more effective than antidepressant drugs alone, and people in cognitive therapy are also less likely than those on drugs to relapse when the treatment is over. The reason may be that the lessons learned in cognitive therapy last a long time, according to follow-ups done from 15 months to many years after treatment (Antonuccio et al., 1999; McNally, 1996; Seligman et al., 1998; Whisman, 1993).

◆ *Anxiety disorders.* Exposure techniques are more effective than any other treatment for posttraumatic stress disorder, simple phobias, and agoraphobia. Systematic desensitization is usually all that is necessary to treat phobias such as a fear of dogs or public speaking. Cognitive-behavior therapy is also more effective than medication for panic disorder, generalized anxiety disorder, and obsessive-compulsive disorder (Kozak, Liebowitz, & Foa, 2000; Schwartz et al., 1996).

◆ *Anger and impulsive violence.* Cognitive therapy is extremely successful in reducing hotheadedness, chronic anger, abusiveness, and hostility; it also teaches people how to express anger more calmly and constructively (Deffenbacher et al., 1998). It has been used to help young male athletes learn to control angry outbursts that lead to physical and verbal abuse (Abrams & Feindler, 1998).

◆ *Health problems.* Cognitive and behavior therapies are highly successful in helping people cope with pain, chronic fatigue syndrome, headaches, and irritable bowel syndrome; quit smoking or overcome cocaine and alcohol dependence; recover from eating disorders such as bulimia and binge eating; and manage other health problems (Butler et al., 1991; J. Skinner et al., 1990; Wilson & Fairburn, 1993).

◆ *Childhood and adolescent behavior problems.* Behavior therapy is the most effective treatment for behavior problems that range from bed-wetting to defiant rebelliousness, and even for problems that have a large biological component, such as autism (see Chapter 5). A meta-analysis of more than 100 studies of children and adolescents found that behavioral treatments worked better than others regardless of the child's age, the therapist's experience, or the specific problem (Weisz et al., 1987, 1995).

Cognitive therapy can also prevent mood disorders from developing in the first place. One intervention program targeted 69 fifth- and sixth-grade children who were considered at risk of depression because they scored high on a children's depression inventory, came from homes with high levels of parental conflict, or both. The children were taught to identify pessimistic beliefs, examine the evidence for and against those beliefs, and generate positive ways of coping. A control group of children who were also at risk of depression did not get this training. As you can see in Figure 12.3, after the training, children in the intervention group had lower depression scores than did those in the control group at all four follow-up sessions. The differences still held two years later, when the children were entering adolescence and when depression rates in the control group shot up steeply (Gillham et al., 1995).

Of course, as the APA task force acknowledged, these important findings do not mean that no other therapy is useful. Cognitive-behavior therapies are designed for specific, identifiable problems, but sometimes people seek therapy for less clearly defined reasons. They may wish to introspect about their feelings and lives, find solace and courage, or explore moral issues. Moreover, behavior and cognitive therapies have had their failures, especially with people who are unmotivated to carry out the program or who have entrenched personality problems (Brody, 1990; Foa & Emmelkamp, 1983). To date, for example, no therapy, including cognitive-behavior therapy, has been successful in treating antisocial personality disorder.

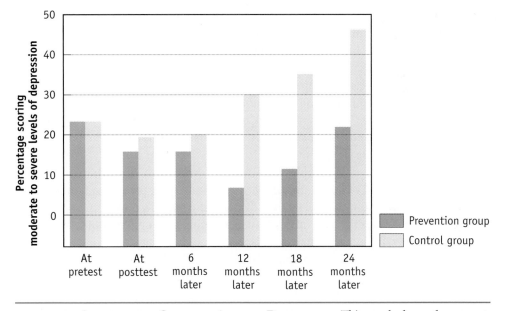

FIGURE 12.3 INOCULATING CHILDREN AGAINST DEPRESSION *This graph shows the percentage of children who were at moderate to high risk of depression (pretest), and their depression scores after a cognitive intervention (posttest) and during four follow-up assessments. Notice that the effects of the intervention were still strong two years later, as the children entered adolescence (Gillham et al., 1995).*

The Sociocultural Perspective

The sociocultural perspective has contributed not only to the development of specific kinds of psychotherapy, but also to a clearer understanding of the social interactions that go on within any therapy and of the larger cultural setting in which therapy takes place. This perspective warns us to beware of books, programs, or therapies that promise to "liberate the self," as if the "self" existed apart from a social and cultural world of influences, obligations, and values.

Therapy in Social Context

The social side of the sociocultural perspective emphasizes the power of social roles, relationships with others, and the processes of conformity and persuasion to affect our feelings and behavior (see Chapter 9). As applied to therapy, an understanding of these social processes is important for two reasons: Clients need to realize how their behavior is constantly being affected by other people who are important in their lives (family members, friends, or co-workers), and also how the very success of therapy depends on their relationship with the therapist.

Family therapy is based on fundamental principles of social psychology. In the view of family therapists, when people have family conflicts or have developed angry, abusive, or unproductive patterns of dealing with each other, it is important to try to work with the whole family together. Family members are usually unaware of how they influence one another, but every family member affects every other, and each has his or her own perceptions about the others, which may be entirely wrong. Many couples, for example, fall into classic "approach-withdraw" patterns: The wife prods the husband for more attention, help, or expressions of affection, but the more she does so, the more he withdraws. "Why won't he talk to me?" she complains. "Why does she keep nagging me?" he responds. Soon they are in a little dance; he retreats, she pursues, and then he retreats because she pursues (Christensen & Jacobson, 2000).

Family therapists help couples and families break out of such patterns and renegotiate their ways of communicating. By working with the entire family (or, in the case of couples, both partners), they discover the family's power imbalances and help its members identify and correct misperceptions (Luepnitz, 1988; Minuchin, 1984). A teenager, for instance, may see his mother as crabby and nagging when actually she is tired and worried. A parent may see a child as rebellious when in fact the child is lonely and craving attention. When one member of a family is schizophrenic or otherwise ill, family therapy actually reduces the chances of the sick person's relapse by teaching all family members how to cope with the problem constructively (Goldstein & Miklowitz, 1995).

Even when it is not possible to work with the whole family, some therapists will treat individuals from a *family-systems* perspective, showing the client how family patterns create a system of behavior (Bowen, 1978; Lerner, 1989). If one member's behavior changes, the whole system will be affected. That is why, clients learn, if they change in any way, even for the better, their families may protest noisily or send subtle messages that read, "Change back!" Why? Because when one family member changes, each of the others must change too. But most people do not like change. They are comfortable with old patterns and habits, even those that cause them trouble. Family-systems therapists teach clients to understand and prepare for this reaction. For example, one student of ours told us that to her dismay, her family was not as happy with her success in college and her new goal to be a pharmacist as she had expected them to be. They kept undermining her enthusiasm—for example, by telling her she would never make it. Her therapist helped her see how frightened her family was by her ambition and by the changes in the old family patterns they knew it would create.

Some therapists also take advantage of another lesson from social psychology— namely, that the influence of other people may accomplish what a single therapist cannot. In *group therapy,* people with the same or different problems are put together to find solutions. Members learn that their problems are not unique. They also learn that they cannot get away with their usual excuses because others in the group have tried them all (Yalom, 1995). Group therapies are commonly used in institutions, such as prisons and mental hospitals. They are also popular among people who repeatedly get into bad relationships, or who are too shy to meet people, or who share a traumatic experience, such as sexual assault (Becker et al., 1984).

Finally, the social perspective on psychotherapy reminds us that the success of therapy, as of all relationships, depends in part on the bond that the client and therapist establish between them. This bond is called the **therapeutic alliance.** In a good therapeutic alliance, the two parties feel connected, respecting and understanding one another. They agree on the goals of treatment and thus are more likely to meet them. In a study of people being treated for alcohol abuse or dependence, those who had a strong therapeutic alliance with their therapists (as measured by a questionnaire filled out by both parties) were drinking much less alcohol a year after therapy ended. This was true regardless of which of three different treatment programs they had been in (Connors et al., 1997).

Therapy in Cultural Context

From the cultural side of the sociocultural perspective, researchers have demonstrated how important it is for therapists to understand any cultural differences that might exist between themselves and their clients. As we saw in Chapter 10, cultures differ in many things, from body language to basic beliefs to rules of behavior. So therapists must be sure that they do not misinterpret a client's actions, transforming a cultural norm into a pathological problem (Betancourt & López, 1993).

Many Latino and Asian clients, for example, are likely to react to a formal interview with a therapist with relative shyness, deference, and inhibited silence, but these reactions are in no way signs of emotional disorder. Latinos may respond to catastrophic stress

---

therapeutic alliance The bond of confidence and mutual understanding established between therapist and client, which allows them to work together to solve the client's problems.

with an *ataque nervioso,* a nervous attack of screaming, crying, fainting, and agitation. It is a culturally determined response, but an uninformed clinician might label it as a sign of pathology. Similarly, *susto,* or "loss of the soul," is a syndrome common in Latin American cultures as a response to extreme grief or fright. The person suffering from *susto* believes that his or her soul has departed along with that of the deceased relative. A therapist who was unfamiliar with this culturally determined response might conclude that the sufferer was delusional or psychotic.

For their part, clients may withhold feelings or beliefs that they feel a therapist would not understand or accept. For example, a lifetime of experience with racism may keep some African-American clients from being wholly candid with a white therapist. Misunderstandings and prejudice may be a major reason that Asian-, Mexican-, and African-American psychotherapy clients are more likely to stay in therapy, and thus benefit from it, when their therapists have the same ethnic background (Sue, 1998). (If such clients stay in therapy and do not drop out early, however, most are as likely to do as well with an "unmatched" therapist.)

Sensitivity to cultural issues is not the same as stereotyping. The therapist must not assume that all clients from a particular culture are alike or tailor the therapy to fit some abstract notion of cultural rules. Some Asians, after all, do have problems with excessive shyness and some Latinos do have emotional disorders! However, therapists must do what is necessary to ensure that the client will find the therapist to be trustworthy and effective, and clients must be aware of their prejudices too (Sue, 1998).

As a result of the growing understanding of the importance of culture, the American Psychiatric Association (1994) now recommends that all therapists take a patient's cultural background into consideration in diagnosis and treatment. For example, one New York psychiatrist, originally from Peru, treated a woman suffering from *susto* by "prescribing" a tradition important in her culture: a mourning ritual to help her assimilate the loss of her uncle. This wake had a powerful effect, the psychiatrist told *The New York Times* (December 5, 1995): "She didn't need any antidepressants, and within a few meetings, including two with her family, her symptoms lifted and she was back participating fully in life once again."

As cultural psychologists would emphasize, the goals of psychotherapy itself reflect values of the larger culture. In his book *The Shrinking of America,* Bernie Zilbergeld (1983) argued that American psychotherapy, while often very helpful, promotes the myths that people should always be happy and competent, that almost any change is possible, and that change is relatively easy. People who accept these myths, said Zilbergeld, set themselves up for disappointment if their efforts fail. Yet these myths reflect a philosophy embedded in American and many other Western cultures: If you don't like something about yourself or the world, change it, fix it, or fight it.

In contrast, Eastern cultures have a less optimistic view of change; they are more tolerant of events they regard as being outside of human control. If you don't like something about yourself or the world, well, learn to live with it or go on doing your best in spite of it (Weisz, Rothbaum, & Blackburn, 1984). A Japanese psychologist offered examples of Japanese proverbs that illustrate this philosophy (Azuma, 1984): *Willow trees do not get broken by piled up snow* (no matter how many problems come your way, flexibility will allow you to survive them), and *The true tolerance is to tolerate the intolerable* (some

THE SEVEN DWARFS AFTER THERAPY

How much can therapy change a person? Cultures differ in how much change they think is possible—or desirable.

situations that seem unbearable are facts of life that no amount of protest will change). Perhaps you can imagine how many burdens most Americans would be prepared to carry without protesting, or how long they would be prepared to tolerate the intolerable!

Some Western psychotherapists have been borrowing ideas from the Japanese, attempting to teach greater self-acceptance instead of constant self-improvement. In the Japanese practice of Morita therapy, for example, clients are taught how to live with their most troubling emotions, instead of trying to eradicate them. The point is not that one cultural approach is better or healthier than the other, but rather that both have their place. A "fighting back" strategy encourages self-expression, independent thinking, and protest for change; but the price may be anger, isolation, and unrealistic goals. A "live with it" strategy leads to acceptance of the inevitable and greater serenity; but the price may be self-denial, stagnation, and unnecessary acceptance of misery.

Evaluating the Sociocultural Contribution

One of the greatest contributions of this perspective has been to highlight the fact that therapy is a social exchange, in which the therapist influences and inspires the client. This influence is normal and necessary; after all, the client goes to therapy in the first place in order to be influenced by the therapist's ideas!

But the therapist's influence, if it is not used wisely to promote validated methods and ideas, has the potential to be harmful. Some therapists have abused their clients' trust, pressuring them, in subtle or overt ways, to engage in sexual intimacies with them or behave in other ways that are unethical and against the client's interests (Peterson, 1992). Some therapy groups have even acquired the cultlike attributes described in Chapter 9, persuading their members that their mental health depends on staying in the group and severing their connections to their "toxic" or "evil" families (Mithers, 1994; Watters &

Ofshe, 1999). Some therapists are ignorant about cultural issues, or biased against clients who are of a different ethnicity from their own, and this bias can adversely affect the course of therapy (Comas-Díaz & Greene, 1994; Cross & Fhagen-Smith, 1996; Franklin, 1993; Sue, 1998). And sometimes the therapist's prejudices have led to inappropriate or even harmful techniques (Brodsky, 1982; López, 1989). For example, for many years gay men and lesbians who entered therapy were told that homosexuality was a mental illness that could be "cured." Some of the so-called treatments were horribly harsh, such as shock applied to the genitals for "inappropriate" arousal. Although the American Psychological Association and the American Psychiatric Association have gone on record opposing therapies that claim to turn gay men and lesbians into heterosexuals, these therapies still surface from time to time, most recently promoted in a campaign by Christian fundamentalists who believe homosexuality is a sin.

Research from the sociocultural perspective has raised awareness of another source of potential harm in therapy: The therapist's influence can in some cases produce a disorder that the patient did not have upon entering treatment. Some therapists so zealously believe in the prevalence of certain problems or the meaning of certain symptoms that they induce the client to produce the very symptoms they are looking for. This process seems to account for the rise of *multiple personality disorder (MPD)* (called, in the DSM-IV, **dissociative identity disorder**), which involves the appearance, within one person, of two or more distinct identities.

Some clinicians believe that MPD originates in childhood, as a means of coping with unspeakable, repeated traumas, such as torture (Gleaves, 1996; Kluft, 1993; Ross, 1995). In this view, the trauma produces a mental dissociation or split: One personality emerges to handle everyday experiences and another emerges to cope with the bad ones. Skeptics, however, believe that the disorder has been wildly overdiagnosed and that clinicians may actually be creating the symptoms in their clients through the power of suggestion, sometimes bordering on coercion (McHugh, 1993a, 1993b; Merskey, 1995; Spanos, 1996; Watters & Ofshe, 1999). It is no accident, say the critics, that before 1980, fewer than 200 cases of MPD had ever been diagnosed anywhere in the world, and since 1980, some *40,000* cases have been reported, virtually all of them in North America (see Table 12.2) (Acocella, 1999). When Canadian psychiatrist Harold Merskey (1992) reviewed the published cases of MPD, he was unable to find a single one in which a patient developed MPD without being influenced by the therapist's suggestions or reports about the disorder in books and the media.

It may seem unlikely, even preposterous, that a clinician could induce a client to reveal a dissociated personality, but the mechanisms are perfectly normal. They are the same processes that explain how kind people can become entrapped into self-defeating or cruel behavior, obey unethical orders given by an authority, conform to the mindless actions of a mob, or become seduced by the allure of a charismatic leader (see Chapter 9). For example, one prominent believer in MPD, Richard Kluft (1987), described how he goes about "discovering" multiple personalities in a client.

---

dissociative identity disorder A controversial disorder marked by the appearance within one person of two or more distinct personalities, each with its own name and traits; commonly known as *multiple personality disorder (MPD)*.

TABLE 12.2 ✦ The Rise of Multiple Personality Disorder

1789	Early case of young German woman with several "personalities" (including a French woman and a little boy).
1816	First recorded case of "multiple personality" in America (Mary Reynolds).
1875	Condition renamed "multiple personality" in France.
1886	Robert Louis Stevenson's *Dr. Jekyll and Mr. Hyde* popularizes notion of "two personalities" in one body.
1800s–1960	**Scattered cases reported worldwide.**
1957	*The Three Faces of Eve* published.
1960–1970	**8 cases reported.**
1976	*Sybil* (movie) released.
1980	**DSM includes MPD diagnosis for first time.**
1980	The book *Michelle Remembers* claims "Satanic ritual abuse" as cause of MPD.
1980–1991	Media coverage escalates in popular books and talk shows (*Oprah, Geraldo*) that feature MPD "victims."
1985	Psychiatrist Richard Kluft claims to have treated 250 MPD patients.
By 1986	**6,000 cases reported in North America.**
1987	First MPD inpatient treatment unit established at Rush Presbyterian Hospital in Chicago; others follow across the country.
By 1994	**40,000 cases reported in North America.**
1995	Diane Humenansky becomes first psychiatrist found guilty of malpractice for inducing multiple personalities in a vulnerable patient.
1996–present	Other successful lawsuits won against major proponents of MPD diagnosis and treatment units in hospitals.

Sources: Acocella, 1999; Kenny, 1986; Loftus, 1996; Nathan, 1994; Pendergrast, 1995; Piper, 1997.

Efforts to determine the presence of MPD may require, he wrote, "between 2½ and 4 hours of continuous interviewing. Interviewees must be prevented from taking breaks to regain composure. . . . In one recent case of singular difficulty, the first sign of dissociation was noted in the 6th hour, and a definitive spontaneous switching of personalities occurred in the 8th hour." But think about it: After eight hours of "continuous interviewing" without a single break, how many of us wouldn't do what the interviewer wanted?

No one disputes that some troubled, highly imaginative individuals can produce many different "personalities" when asked to, just as healthy, imaginative students in a hypnosis study may "remember" a past life as Julius Caesar or Queen Elizabeth I (Spanos et al., 1991; see Chapter 8). The *sociocognitive* explanation of this phenomenon, however, disputes the belief that people who reveal other personalities are suffering from a disorder over which they have no control. It is, rather, that these vulnerable individuals go along with the clinician's diagnosis and expectations, motivated by a need to make sense of their problems (Acocella, 1999; Showalter, 1997; Spanos, 1996). By the mid-1990s, many people who had been led to believe they were "multiples" had successfully sued their psychiatrists for malpractice. Many of the medical centers that had promoted treatments for MPD were closed, and the epidemic of multiple personality disorder began to wane.

The story of the rise and fall of MPD shows the importance of understanding how sociocultural variables can create, maintain, or extinguish some "mental disorders." In this case, North American cultural practices—such as the media's promotion of sensational stories and big rewards of money, fame, and attention both for patients and therapists—supported and perpetuated this trendy diagnosis. During therapy, the processes of social influence, conformity, and coercion affected how vulnerable patients came to interpret and label their problems (Showalter, 1997). The sociocultural perspective urges us, when considering any mental disorder and its treatment, to think about the social and cultural factors that might be involved, and not just the internal psychological ones.

What Do You Know?

You don't need a therapist to help you with this quiz.

1. If you had an extreme fear of snakes, a behavior therapist would probably use _____ to treat your phobia; if you were agoraphobic and afraid to leave the house, a behavior therapist would most likely use the technique of _____.

2. If you were feeling lonely and depressed and had decided that you would never feel happy again, how might a cognitive therapist help you?

3. Which of the following aspects of the therapist–client relationship is most important for a successful outcome? (a) Both parties have a strong therapeutic alliance; (b) both parties share the same cultural background; (c) both parties are the same sex; (d) both parties realize that cultural factors are less important than the techniques used.

4. Suppose you are on a jury in which the defendant, who killed six prostitutes, claims that he suffers from multiple personality disorder. He has no memory of murdering anybody, he says, and his psychiatrist, who interviewed the defendant for the first time only after the crimes were committed, testifies that the man is a true case of MPD. As a critical thinker, what questions would you want to ask about this defense? (By the way, this is a real case.)

THE PSYCHODYNAMIC PERSPECTIVE

Sigmund Freud was the father of what one of his patients called the "talking cure." Psychoanalysis and its many psychodynamic offshoots became the most popular kind of "depth" therapy throughout most of the twentieth century. Their proponents refer to them as depth therapies because the goal is to delve into unconscious conflicts and defenses rather than concentrate on "superficial" symptoms and conscious beliefs. Other therapies, based on humanist and existential psychology, share with psychoanalysis an appreciation of the client's own subjective and experiential views of the world, and so we will include them in this section, even though their approaches differ from psychodynamic ones.

Therapies for the "Inner Life"

In Freud's method of *psychoanalysis,* the guiding assumption is that intensive analysis of a patient's past and unconscious motives will help the patient achieve insight into the reasons for his or her symptoms and unhappiness. With insight and emotional release, in this view, the symptoms will disappear. Psychoanalysis has evolved into many different forms of psychodynamic therapy, the most popular today being approaches based on object-relations theory (see Chapter 11). To bring unconscious conflicts into awareness, psychodynamic therapists often ask the client to talk about his or her dreams, fantasies, and memories. They encourage the person to *free associate,* saying whatever comes to mind.

A major element of psychodynamic therapy is **transference,** the client's transfer (displacement) of emotional elements of his or her inner life—usually feelings about the client's parents—outward onto the analyst. Have you ever found yourself responding to a new acquaintance with unusually quick affection or dislike, and later realized it was because the person reminded you of a relative that you loved or loathed? That experience

---

transference In psychodynamic therapies, a critical step in which the client transfers unconscious emotions or reactions, such as emotional feelings about his or her parents, onto the therapist.

"HAVE A COUPLE OF DREAMS, AND CALL ME IN THE MORNING."

is similar to transference. In therapy, a woman who failed to resolve her Oedipal love for her father might believe she has fallen in love with the analyst. A man who is unconsciously angry at his mother for rejecting him might become furious with his analyst for going on vacation. Through analysis of transference, psychodynamic therapists believe, clients eventually resolve their emotional conflicts.

In orthodox psychoanalysis, the client meets with the therapist as often as several times a week, for a period of years. The analyst listens to the client's free associations and dreams but rarely comments. There is no rush to solve the problem that brought the client into therapy. In fact, a person may come in complaining of a symptom such as anxiety or headaches, and the therapist may not get around to that symptom for months or even years. The analyst views the symptom as only the tip of the mental iceberg. Some traditional analysts do not attempt cures at all. The goal, they say, is understanding, not change.

Today, however, most psychodynamic therapists reject the orthodox approach, while retaining the key techniques of transference, free association, and probing for unconscious motives (Westen, 1998). They sit facing the client; they participate more actively; and they are more goal-directed. Many practice time-limited therapy, consisting of 15 to 25 sessions, focusing on self-defeating patterns and recurring problems that are troubling the client.

Humanist therapies, like their parent philosophy humanism, start from the assumption that people seek self-actualization and self-fulfillment. The therapist generally does not dig into past conflicts, aiming instead to help clients feel better about themselves and free themselves from self-imposed limits. Humanist therapists want to know how clients perceive their own situations, so they can help them develop the will and confidence to bring about change. That is why, unlike psychoanalysts, humanists explore what is going on "here and now," not the issues of "why and how." For example, in *client-centered* or nondirective therapy, developed by Carl Rogers, the therapist's role is to listen to the client's needs in an accepting, nonjudgmental way and offer what Rogers called *unconditional positive regard* (see Chapter 11). Whatever the client's specific complaint, the goal is to build the client's self-esteem and help the person feel that he or she is accepted and respected. Rogers (1961) believed that effective therapists must be warm, genuine, and honest in expressing their feelings, and must show an empathic understanding of the client's problems.

Existential therapy helps clients explore the meaning of existence and confront the great questions of death, freedom, free will, alienation from oneself and others, loneliness, and meaninglessness. Existential therapists, like humanist therapists, believe that our lives are not inevitably determined by our pasts or our circumstances and that we have the power to choose our own destinies. As Irvin Yalom (1989) explained, "The crucial first step in therapy is the patient's assumption of responsibility for his or her life predicament. As long as one believes that one's problems are caused by some force or agency outside oneself, there is no leverage in therapy."

The Scientist–Practitioner Gap

As we noted in Essay 5, where we evaluated the psychodynamic perspective, there has long been a major divide between psychodynamic assumptions and methods and those of the other, research-based perspectives—one that many psychologists now refer to candidly as the *scientist–practitioner gap.* Many psychodynamic therapists believe that trying to evaluate psychotherapy using standard empirical methods is an exercise in futility. Psychotherapy is an art, they say, not a science. Other kinds of clinicians, too, believe that empirical research can capture only a small and shadowy image of the complex exchange between a therapist and a client, and that clinical experience is more valuable than the methods of traditional research (Edelson, 1994). A survey of 400 clinical psychologists found that the great majority paid little attention to empirical research at all, stating that they gained their most useful information from clinical work with clients (Elliott & Morrow-Bradley, 1994).

Scientific psychologists agree that research has little to say about the existential aims of therapy, such as helping people come to terms with illness and death or helping them choose which values to live by. But scientists, and many clinicians themselves, are concerned that when therapists fail to keep up with empirical findings in the field or understand the contributions of other perspectives, their clients may pay the price, as occurred during the epidemic of multiple personality diagnoses. Clinical insight and experience, while valuable within the course of therapy, have repeatedly been shown to be unreliable bases for predicting behavior, determining the best therapeutic approach, or making objectively better decisions (Dawes, Faust, & Meehl, 1989; Grove & Meehl, 1996).

Psychological scientists believe that all therapists should be aware of research on the most beneficial methods for particular psychological problems; on topics relevant to their practice, such as memory, hypnosis, and child development; and on ineffective or potentially harmful techniques or ideas. As social critic Frederick Crews (1995) observed, "Incorrect but widely dispersed ideas about the mind inevitably end by causing social damage. Thanks to the once imposing prestige of psychoanalysis, people harboring diseases or genetic conditions have deferred effective treatment while scouring their infantile past for the sources of their troubles. Parents have agonized about having caused their children's homosexuality. Women have accepted a view of themselves as inherently envious, passive, and amoral."

"Depth" therapies such as psychodynamic, humanist, and existential approaches are most helpful for people who want to explore philosophic questions about themselves, the dilemmas of life, or moral choices on which science is silent. But for people who have the specific emotional problems described in this chapter, such as panic disorder, depression, or obsessive-compulsive disorder, beginning with an empirically validated approach would seem to be the wisest course of action.

What Do You Know?

"Depth" studying should help you answer this quiz.

A. Match each method with the therapy most likely to use it.

1. free association	a. cognitive therapy
2. systematic desensitization	b. psychoanalysis
3. facing the fear of death	c. humanist therapy
4. reappraisal of thoughts	d. behavior therapy
5. unconditional positive regard	e. family therapy
6. contract specifying duties	f. existential therapy
7. systems approach to relationships	

B. What does the "scientist–practitioner gap" refer to?

ANSWERS:

A. 1. b 2. d 3. f 4. a 5. c 6. d 7. e **B.** The widening split between many psychological scientists and clinical practitioners in how much they rely on empirical methods and research findings.

THERAPY IN PERSPECTIVE

The varied approaches to treatment generated by the different psychological perspectives may seem quite different from one another, and in theory they are. Yet in practice, many psychotherapists avoid the reductionism of depending on only one approach, and instead draw on methods and ideas from cognitive, behavioral, family, and psychodynamic approaches. Some team up with psychiatrists so that their patients can receive both medication and psychotherapy. (Currently, many clinical psychologists are lobbying for the right to prescribe medication.) Some problems, and some clients, respond best to these combined methods. For example, people who have severe depression often respond better to a combination of antidepressants and psychotherapy than to either method alone (Keller et al., 2000; Thase et al., 1997). A promising treatment for sex offenders, whose behavior is very difficult to change, combines cognitive therapy, aversive conditioning, sex education, group therapy, reconditioning of sexual fantasies, and social-skills training (Abel et al., 1988; Kaplan, Morales, & Becker, 1993).

The primary questions for consumers who are thinking critically about any form of psychotherapy should be: Does it work any better than a placebo? Does its rationale make sense, or is it just a fancy form of psychobabble? Is it successful because of its promoters' ability to inspire and persuade, or because it uses techniques known to be effective? Will the therapist be flexible in selecting treatment strategies, or is the therapist wedded to just one approach, no matter what the nature of the problem?

Consumers also need to be cautious about therapies that have no grounding in *any* of psychology's major perspectives. New therapies are often started by a charismatic leader, who may or may not have professional training in psychology. They are then endorsed by enthusiastic practitioners who have been "certified" in the method, usually by attending a weekend workshop promoted by the therapy's founder. Some of these therapies are packaged and promoted with virtually no scientific support at all (Beyerstein, 1999). For example, Thought Field Therapy (TFT), originated by Roger Callahan, assumes that emotional problems are caused by "perturbations" (disturbances) in "a subtle energy field" rather than by cognitions, environmental events, or chemical imbalances. Callahan claims he can successfully cure people on the phone, using his special patented Voice Technology™ method to assess their perturbations (Gallo, 1998).

Today most therapists, across all perspectives, are realistic about what psychotherapy can and cannot do. In the hands of an empathic and knowledgeable practitioner, cognitive-behavioral techniques can teach you new skills and new ways of thinking and can help you clarify your values and goals. Family therapy can help you get along better with your family and break out of destructive family patterns, and group therapy can provide insights from people who share your situation. Medications, if prescribed and monitored carefully, may help alleviate depression, panic attacks, or other anxiety disorders, especially if combined with psychotherapy. "Depth" therapies may give you insights into your life and into motives of which you are unaware. And many forms of therapy can get you through bad times when no one seems to care or understand.

But psychotherapy, no matter which part of "the elephant" it focuses on, cannot transform you into someone you're not. It cannot cure a disorder overnight. It cannot provide a life without problems. And it cannot substitute for experience—for work that is satisfying, relationships that are sustaining, activities that are enjoyable. As Socrates said, the unexamined life is not worth living. But, we might add, the unlived life is not worth examining. ◪

Summary

1. Broadly defined, a *mental disorder* is any behavior or emotional state that causes an individual great suffering or worry, is self-defeating or self-destructive, or is maladaptive and disrupts the person's relationships or the larger community.

2. The *Diagnostic and Statistical Manual of Mental Disorders* (DSM) is designed to provide objective criteria and categories for diagnosing mental disorder. Critics argue that the diagnosis of mental disorders, unlike those of medical diseases, is inherently a subjective process that can never be entirely free of cultural values and biases. Supporters of the DSM believe that when the DSM criteria are used correctly, reliability in diagnosis improves; and that although some diagnoses are indeed subjective and culture-specific, other disorders are universal.

3. *Generalized anxiety disorder* involves continuous, chronic anxiety, with signs of nervousness, worry, and irritability. When anxiety results from exposure to an

unexpected traumatic event, it can lead to *posttraumatic stress disorder,* which involves mental reliving of the trauma and increased physiological arousal. In some long-term sufferers of PTSD, high levels of stress hormones may be toxic to the hippocampus and other parts of the brain. *Panic disorder* involves sudden, intense attacks of profound fear, with feelings of impending doom. Panic attacks are common in the aftermath of stress or frightening experiences; those who go on to develop a disorder tend to interpret the attacks as a sign of impending disaster rather than as a normal stress reaction.

4. *Phobias* are unrealistic fears of specific situations, activities, or things. Some phobias may have evolved because they were adaptive for the species; others are learned, reflecting quirks of personality or cultural practices. *Agoraphobia,* the fear of being away from a particular place or person, is the most disabling phobia. It often begins with a panic attack, which the person tries to avoid in the future by staying close to "safe" places.

5. *Obsessive-compulsive disorder* (OCD) involves recurrent, unwished-for thoughts or images (obsessions) and repetitive, ritualized behaviors (compulsions) that a person feels unable to control. Several parts of the brain having to do with fear and response to threat are especially active in people with OCD.

6. Symptoms of *major depression* include distorted thinking patterns, low self-esteem, physical ailments such as fatigue and loss of appetite, and prolonged grief and despair. In *bipolar disorder,* a person experiences episodes of both depression and *mania* (excessive euphoria). Women are more likely than men to be treated for major depression, but psychologists disagree on whether the difference is real or due to misdiagnosis of men's symptoms.

7. *Biological* explanations of depression emphasize low levels of the neurotransmitters serotonin and norepinephrine, and the role of genetic predispositions. *Learning* explanations emphasize experiences that make people feel trapped and unable to escape from painful environments. *Cognitive* explanations attribute depression to particular ways of thinking that foster hopelessness (believing that the origin of one's unhappiness is internal, stable, and uncontrollable) and habits of brooding or rumination. *Social and cultural* explanations emphasize the circumstances of people's lives, such as troubles at work, family problems, motherhood, and experiences with violence. *Attachment and object-relations* theories hold that depression results from a history of insecure attachment or from broken or conflicted relationships. *Vulnerability-stress models* look at interactions between individual vulnerabilities (genetic dispositions, cognitive habits, and personality traits) and environmental stress.

8. *Personality disorders* are characterized by rigid, self-destructive traits that cause distress or an inability to get along with others. They include *paranoid, narcissistic,* and *antisocial personality disorders.*

9. A person with antisocial personality disorder (APD) lacks empathy and remorse, is unafraid of punishment, and is impulsive and lacks self-control. The disorder may involve a neurological condition that is genetic or is caused by damage to

the brain and central nervous system at birth or during childhood, parental rejection and abuse, or a combination of biological vulnerability and stressful or violent environments. (Not all persons with APD are violent, however; some are deceitful and heartless con artists.)

10. *Schizophrenia* is a *psychotic* disorder involving *positive* or *active symptoms* (including delusions, hallucinations, disorganized speech called *word salads,* and inappropriate behavior), and *negative symptoms* (including loss of motivation, poverty of speech, *catatonic stupor,* and emotional flatness). Cases of schizophrenia vary in severity, duration, and prognosis.

11. The leading theories of schizophrenia are biological, focusing on genetic predispositions; structural brain abnormalities; neurotransmitter abnormalities; and abnormalities of prenatal development resulting from maternal malnutrition, viral infection, or other trauma during the second trimester. According to the *vulnerability-stress model,* these biological vulnerabilities are not enough to produce the disorder unless they interact with stressful experiences in a person's childhood or young adulthood.

12. Throughout history, there have been efforts to root out mental illness literally, by intervening directly in the brain. *Psychosurgery,* which destroys selected areas of the brain thought to be responsible for a psychological problem, is rarely done today, although some surgeons continue to experiment with it. *Electroconvulsive therapy* (ECT), in which a brief current is sent through the brain, has been used successfully to treat suicidal depression. However, controversy exists about its effects on the brain and the appropriateness of its use.

13. Medications commonly prescribed for mental disorders include *antipsychotic drugs,* used in treating schizophrenia and other psychotic disorders; *antidepressants,* used in treating depression, anxiety disorders, and obsessive-compulsive disorder; *tranquilizers,* often prescribed inappropriately for emotional problems; and *lithium carbonate,* used to treat bipolar disorder.

14. Drawbacks of drug treatment include the *placebo effect;* high dropout and relapse rates among people who take medications without also learning how to cope with their problems; the difficulty of finding the correct dose (the *therapeutic window*) for each individual, compounded by the fact that a person's ethnicity, sex, and age can influence a drug's effectiveness; and the long-term risks of medication, known and unknown. Medication can be helpful and can even save lives, but it should not be prescribed mindlessly and routinely, especially when nondrug therapies can work as well as drugs for many mood and behavioral problems.

15. *Behavior therapists* draw on principles of learning to correct problematic behavior. Their methods include systematic desensitization, aversive conditioning, flooding or exposure, behavioral contracts, and skills training. *Cognitive therapists* aim to change the irrational thoughts that generate negative emotions and self-defeating actions. Controlled clinical trials show that behavior and cognitive-behavior therapies are the most effective for depression, anxiety disorders, anger and impulsive violence, certain health problems, eating disorders, and childhood and adolescent behavior problems.

16. The sociocultural perspective focuses on the nature of the social interactions that go on in any form of therapy and draws attention to the cultural context in which therapy occurs. *Family therapy* treats individual problems in the context of the whole family network. The *family-systems* approach makes clients aware of how family members create a system or pattern of behavior; if one member changes, the others must protest or change, too. Some therapists also treat individuals in *group therapy,* hoping that the influence of other people with similar psychological problems will help the participants improve. The social contributions to therapy include an understanding of the *therapeutic alliance* between therapist and client and of the processes of influence in therapy.

17. Cultural analyses of psychotherapy highlight the importance of understanding ethnic differences in values, body language, and the expression of distress, as well as the larger culture's beliefs about the possibility of change and individual control over events.

18. The sociocultural perspective has raised concerns about the potential for harming clients in therapy when the therapist is coercive or unethical; holds biases about the client's gender, ethnicity, or sexual orientation; or actually creates a mental disorder in a vulnerable patient through undue influence or suggestion. Many social critics believe that the rise in diagnoses of *multiple personality disorder* (MPD) reflects therapist influence and sometimes coercion, combined with a cultural environment that has rewarded and promoted the reporting of sensational cases.

19. *Psychodynamic ("depth") therapies* include Freudian psychoanalysis and its modern variations, such as object-relations therapy, which explore unconscious dynamics through the processes of *free association* and *transference. Humanist* and *existential therapies* attempt to help people by focusing on here-and-now issues of self-fulfillment and philosophical dilemmas, such as the meaning of life and the fear of death. Depth therapies may be most effective for people who want to introspect about their lives. But a *scientist–practitioner gap* has developed because of the different assumptions held by researchers and many psychodynamic and humanist clinicians regarding the value of empirical research in doing psychotherapy and assessing its effectiveness.

20. Although each perspective has contributed a different approach to treating everyday problems and serious mental disorders, many therapists try to avoid reductionism, drawing on methods and ideas from different schools. Some problems and some clients respond best to therapies that combine several methods, such as medication and psychotherapy, or cognitive and group therapies.

21. Consumers should be cautious about the many new therapies that have no grounding in any of the empirical perspectives and should choose an approach that has been validated for the problem they have. Consumers also need to be realistic about what they expect of psychotherapy. Therapy can help people in many ways, but it cannot transform them into something they are not, and it cannot substitute for the family, friends, and work that everyone needs.

Key Terms

insanity 493

mental disorder 493

Diagnostic and Statistical Manual of Mental Disorders (DSM) 493

generalized anxiety disorder 496

posttraumatic stress disorder (PTSD) 496

panic disorder (panic attack) 496

phobia 497

agoraphobia 498

obsessive-compulsive disorder (OCD) 499

major depression 499

mania 499

bipolar disorder 499

vulnerability-stress model of depression 502

personality disorders 503

paranoid personality disorder 503

narcissistic personality disorder 503

antisocial personality disorder (APD) 504

vulnerability-stress model of APD 505

schizophrenia 506

psychosis 506

positive symptoms and negative symptoms 506

word salads 507

catatonic stupor 507

vulnerability-stress model of schizophrenia 509

psychosurgery 510

prefrontal lobotomy 511

electroconvulsive therapy (ECT) 511

antipsychotic drugs (neuroleptics) 512

tardive dyskinesia 512

antidepressant drugs 512

monoamine oxidase (MAO) inhibitors 512

tricyclic antidepressants 512

selective serotonin reuptake inhibitors (SSRIs) 512

tranquilizers 512

lithium carbonate 513

placebo effect 513

therapeutic window 514

behavior therapy 517

systematic desensitization 517

aversive conditioning 517

exposure (flooding) 517

behavioral records and contracts 517

behavioral goals 518

skills training 518

cognitive therapy 518

rational emotive behavior therapy 519

family therapy 522

family-systems approach 522

group therapy 523

therapeutic alliance 523

multiple personality disorder (MPD) (dissociative identity disorder) 526

sociocognitive explanation of MPD 528

psychoanalysis 529

free association 529

transference 529

humanist therapies 530

client-centered therapy 530

unconditional positive regard 530

existential therapy 530

scientist-practitioner gap 531

The Whole Elephant

Why are some people musical geniuses, and others musical lunkheads who can't carry a tune in a bucket? Why is sex a source not only of pleasure and connection but also of manipulation and misery? Why is violence, from domestic battles to international wars, so prevalent? When most people think of answers, they tend to think in one-dimensional terms: "You're born musical or tone deaf"; "sex is just a matter of doing what comes naturally, except for a few people who are 'unnatural'"; "some people and countries are inherently brutal."

As we hope we have persuaded you by now, no single perspective in psychology has all the answers, though each offers important contributions to the understanding of these and other puzzles of human behavior. In the last chapter of this book, we described the contributions of the five perspectives to treating mental and emotional problems. In this concluding essay, we want to take two other topics—music and sex—and show what we might learn by seeing them from many perspectives rather than only one. Then we will consider how you might apply a "whole-elephant" approach to solving problems in your own life.

THE JOY OF MUSIC

If music be the food of love, play on.

WILLIAM SHAKESPEARE, *TWELFTH NIGHT*

Every society on earth has discovered the pleasures of music. Why is this so, when music does not have any obvious survival value? Where does musical genius come from? Why are there so many differences in the kinds of music that people like, and why are these differences related to the social class, culture, ethnicity, and age group they belong to?

Music consists of three basic elements: pitch (melody), rhythm (sounds grouped according to a prescribed system), and timbre (the qualities of a tone that make a C-sharp sound different on a tuba than on a guitar). From these building blocks, human beings have created rock and roll, rap, string quartets, blues, folk songs, chants, ragas, symphonies, jazz, opera, . . . the variations are endless. Where there are human beings, there is music.

Howard Gardner (1983) has brought findings from diverse perspectives to the study of what he calls "musical intelligence." His ability to weave together research on the brain, culture, learning, and perception and other cognitive processes is a model of the kind of multiperspective approach we have been advocating, so we want to give you a look at how he went about it.[1]

Gardner first distinguishes the qualities that might be responsible for musical *genius* in contrast to the "core musical abilities" that everyone shares to one degree or another. Biographies of musical prodigies suggest that musical genius is in part heritable. Mozart played the harpsichord at age 3 and wrote his first composition before he was 7. And, as Gardner notes, other brilliant composers have described how natural creating music always felt to them; Wagner said he produced music like a cow producing milk, and Saint-Saëns compared the process to an apple tree producing apples.

As Gardner shows, however, even those of us who are not musical geniuses are born with an ability to recognize and appreciate music's basic structure, which suggests that it is a biologically based phenomenon. Babies sing as well as babble, and before long they can imitate tones sung by others. Infants only 2 months old can match the pitch, loudness, and melodic line of their mother's songs, and at 4 months they can match the rhythmic structure of a song as well.

Using brain scans, biological researchers have found that the mechanisms by which pitch is apprehended and stored are different from the mechanisms that process other sounds, particularly those of language. Studies of people whose brains have been damaged by stroke or other trauma also confirm that music and language are localized in different places in the brain: Linguistic abilities are located primarily in the left hemisphere, musical abilities in the right hemisphere. This means that people can suffer impaired verbal ability but retain their musical ability, and vice versa. A few rare individuals suffer from a condition called *amusia,* complete tone deafness. They cannot recognize a melody, distinguish one melody from another, repeat a tune, or tell the difference between harmony and dissonance. If you hum "happy birthday" to them, they won't know what it is—until you speak the lyrics.

Except in amusics, the abilities to experience and react to music are wired into the nervous system in complex ways. Within the right hemisphere, different sets of neurons are activated when people are listening to music than when they are playing an instrument. And musical practice literally changes the brain. For example, the left

---

[1]Gardner has nothing to say about the psychodynamic approach, whose contributions he believes are more literary and philosophic than scientific (Gardner, 1992).

hands of string musicians, especially those who began training before age 12, are represented by larger brain areas than are the left hands of nonmusicians. Moreover, the amount of cortical reorganization in those brain areas is correlated with the age at which the person began to play, suggesting that years of music practice in childhood actually affect the brain (Elbert et al., 1995; Jancke, Schlaug, & Steinmetz, 1997). On the other hand (so to speak), perfect pitch—the ability to identify a note just by hearing it—appears very early in life and seems to be innate. Curiously, it is relatively independent of any other musical or mental ability, and has a high incidence among individuals with autism (Sacks, 1995).

Of course, all babies are born into specific cultures, and cultures differ in which of the fundamental components of music they emphasize: pitch, rhythm, or timbre. In most Asian societies, pitch gets the musical emphasis; music consists of small quarter-tone intervals without great rhythmic variation. In sub-Saharan Africa, in contrast, rhythmic patterns of dazzling complexity are the main form of musical expression.

Cultures also differ widely in their attitudes and expectations about musical ability. In the United States, many people seem to think you're either born with musical ability or you're not, so most children fail to develop their musical abilities unless they are exceptionally gifted. But the Anang of Nigeria believe that everyone is capable of making music. Infants only a week old are introduced to music and dancing by their mothers, and fathers make drums for their children as soon as the babies can pound them. At age 2, children join groups where they learn to sing, dance, and play instruments. By age 5, Anang children can sing hundreds of songs, play several percussion instruments, and dance complicated steps. In Japan, China, and Hungary, children are expected to become proficient in singing and if possible also an instrument.

Between the contributions of biology and culture fall those of cognition and learning. By school age, most children have developed a cognitive schema of what a song should be like and they can imitate the tunes they commonly hear. Culture imposes these schemas when children are very young, which is why it is often hard for people to respond emotionally to songs outside their cultural experience. It is also often hard for people to respond emotionally to music outside their generation's experience. Each generation defines itself, in part, by its favorite songs and kind of music, which the preceding generation usually detests!

Cognitive psychologists are studying how rhythm and pitch are perceived and remembered, from small musical units (a tune) to large-scale musical forms like a symphony (Krumhansl, 2000). And learning affects all aspects of musical intelligence. Even children born with musical potential in a culture that values musical ability need something more if they are to succeed as musicians. As behavioral and social-learning research predicts, they need motivation, persistence, drive, social support, rewards and encouragement, teachers and role models.

As you can see, research from all of these perspectives is necessary if we are to understand the incredible emotional power of music on all of us, and the incredible musical abilities of some of us.

THE JOY OF SEX

Sex is by no means everything. It varies, as a matter of fact, from only as high as 78 per cent of everything to as low as 3.10 per cent.

JAMES THURBER & E. B. WHITE, *IS SEX NECESSARY?*

Most people believe that sex is a matter of doing what comes naturally, that it is a relatively simple biological drive. But researchers have found that sex is neither simple nor simply biological. Why do people have sex, and why do they have sex with the particular partners they have sex with? Why do people differ in what they find sexy and whether they feel sexy? Let's consider how psychologists in the five perspectives would answer these questions.

The Biological Perspective

Biologically oriented researchers study the physiology of sexual desire, arousal, and behavior. For example, by studying individuals with unusually low levels of testosterone, they have found that having a minimum level of the hormone testosterone seems to promote sexual desire in both sexes (Sherwin, 1988, 1998a). However, hormones don't "cause" sexual behavior in a simple, direct way, even though some pop-psych books claim they do. Testosterone treatments may be of benefit to women who have unusually low levels of the hormone, as might occur if their ovaries were removed, but for most women, psychological factors influence sexual desire far more than hormone levels do (Bancroft et al., 1991). Further, sex offenders who are chemically castrated when they take a medication that suppresses production of testosterone do not always lose their sexual desires. And in all cases, hormones and behavior travel a two-way street: Testosterone contributes to sexual arousal, but sexual activity also produces higher levels of testosterone (Sapolsky, 1997).

Physiological research has also dispelled a lot of nonsense written about female sexuality. Freud, for example, claimed that when women reach puberty their locus of sexual sensation shifts from the "childish" clitoris to the "mature" vagina, and women can then have healthy "vaginal" orgasms instead of immature "clitoral" ones. (Freud's theory was at least an improvement on the notion, still held in some cultures, that normal or "good" women don't have orgasms at all.) Freudian ideas caused countless women to worry that they were mentally disturbed or sexually repressed if they were not having the correct kind of orgasm (Ehrenreich, 1978).

Today we know that male and female arousal and orgasms are remarkably similar and that all orgasms are physiologically the same, regardless of the source of stimulation (Masters & Johnson, 1966). Although many people continue to believe that the sexes are "opposite," in fact male and female genitals evolve from the same embryonic tissues and are therefore similar in structure and even parallel in many of their functions. For example, the penis and clitoris develop from the same tissue; they differ in size, of course, but not in sensitivity.

Biological researchers have made a major contribution to our understanding of sexuality by sweeping away the cobwebs of superstition and ignorance about how the body functions. They have dispelled once and for all the pervasive myth that there is a "right" kind of orgasm for women to have, and they have documented the physiological capacity for sexual arousal, orgasm, and pleasure in both sexes.

The Learning Perspective

Merely having the physical equipment to perform a sexual act, however, is not the whole story. According to behaviorists and social-cognitive learning theorists, men and women learn their ideas about "proper" sexual behavior from parental lessons, from observation, and from patterns of reinforcement (direct and vicarious). They learn what to consider sexy. They learn whether sex itself is supposed to be good or bad, healthy or sinful. Even the physiological responses of sexual arousal and orgasm are profoundly affected by learning.

In studying sexual desire and behavior, learning psychologists ask questions like these: Did your parents teach you, in word or example, that sex is dirty or delightful, a source of disgust or of pleasure? Or did they say nothing at all, conveying a message by their very silence? Have your own personal experiences been enjoyable or miserable, guilty or pleasurable, forced or desired? How knowledgeable are you about your genitals, and do you regard your sexual anatomy with pleasure or disgust? Even in supposedly liberated North America, many women have not examined their genitals and cannot accurately label the clitoris or the vulva (Lerner, 1989). Men have many words for their genitals and rarely confuse their penises with anything else in the vicinity. What message about sexuality is thereby imparted to boys and girls?

In the influential learning theory of John Gagnon and William Simon (1973; Laumann & Gagnon, 1995), sexual behavior depends on the *sexual scripts* that people learn to follow. These scripts are scenarios that specify proper sexual behavior for a person in a given situation. They are heavily influenced by a society's gender roles, the collections of rules that determine the proper attitudes and behavior for men and women. Just as an actor in the role of Hamlet needs a script to learn his part, a person following a gender role needs a sexual script that teaches men and women how to behave during dating and sex. Are women, for example, supposed to be sexually adventurous and assertive or sexually modest and passive? The answers vary from culture to culture, from one ethnic group to another within a culture, and from one individual to another.

According to Gagnon and Simon, in many parts of North America, boys acquire their attitudes about sex in a competitive atmosphere where the goal is to impress other males, talking and joking about masturbation and other sexual experiences with their friends. While boys are learning to value physical sex, however, girls are learning to value relationships and to make themselves attractive. They learn that their role is to be sexually desirable (which is "good"), but not to indulge in their own sexual pleasures (which would be "bad"). As one psychologist, summarizing the different sexual scripts that boys and girls learn, put it, "'Nice women' don't say yes and 'real men' don't say no" (Muehlenhard, 1988). Does this describe the script your own culture has written for you? If not, what are your culture's sexual rules?

The Cognitive Perspective

People's values, expectations, fantasies, and beliefs profoundly affect their sexual desire and responsiveness. This is why a touch on the knee by an exciting new date feels terrifically sexy, but the same touch by a creepy stranger on a bus feels disgusting.

Erotic fantasies and expectations can create sexual desire, but distracting thoughts can interfere with it. Most men know what it feels like to lose an erection, and women to lose an imminent orgasm, when their partner says something to break the mood or when a distracting worry crosses their minds. And people who are "thinking too much" during sex play—for example, who are worrying about how they look or whether they are doing the wrong thing—may have difficulty letting go and yielding to sexual sensations.

Interestingly, people's perceptions and beliefs may also lead them to misinterpret their own physical arousal, which can be caused by many things other than sexual desire. In women, vaginal lubrication is not always a sign of arousal; it is sometimes a response to nervousness, excitement, disgust, or fear. Similarly, a man's erection is not always due to sexual stimulation; a man can also have an erection as a response to fear, anger, or exercise. This information has important implications for relationships. For instance, if a man learns to interpret arousal that is actually due to anger as evidence of sexual desire, he may associate sexuality with aggression. And if a woman is embarrassed to acknowledge that she is sexually aroused because she thinks such a revelation will mark her as a bad woman, she may learn to interpret such arousal as evidence of love.

In the cognitive perspective, therefore, sexual arousal and orgasm are matters as much of the mind as of the genitals. In this view, the sexiest sex organ is the brain, where perceptions begin.

The Sociocultural Perspective

Sociocultural researchers examine how cultures vary and change in their sexual norms and gender roles; how group pressure affects people's sexual behavior; and the importance of cultural norms in determining what qualities people find exciting in a sexual partner. They have investigated the power of sexuality to create and sustain love and intimacy. But they have also explored some of the darker social motives of sexuality: to exact revenge on a partner, get money or other benefits, dominate the other person, or fulfill a perceived obligation.

The social perspective on sexuality, for instance, has identified the many external pressures on people to have sex even when they don't want to. In numerous studies of

North American college students, large numbers of women *and* men say they have had unwanted sex because of social pressures—to appease the partner, to impress one's friends, or to conform to what "everyone else" seems to be doing (Cooper, Shapiro, & Powers, 1998). Some women say they give in because it is easier than having an argument; because they don't want to lose the relationship; because they feel obligated, once the partner has spent time and money on them; or because the partner makes them feel guilty or inhibited. For their part, many men feel obliged to "make a move" when they don't want to. Some do so to "prove their masculinity" by "scoring." Others do so because of peer pressure, inexperience, a desire for popularity, or a fear of seeming homosexual or unmasculine (Muehlenhard & Cook, 1988).

The two sexes differ in the reasons they give for having unwanted sex, but nowhere do they differ more dramatically than in their perceptions of outright sexual coercion. In a nationally representative survey of more than 3,000 Americans ages 18 to 59, nearly one-fourth of the women said that a man (usually a husband or boyfriend) had forced them to do something sexually that they did not want to do (Laumann et al., 1994). But only about 3 percent of the men said they had ever forced a woman into a sexual act. Obviously, what many women regard as coercion is not always seen as such by men.

Researchers in the cultural side of this perspective remind us that sexual customs, like all human customs, are varied, depending on the larger network of roles, norms, and economic and social concerns in which they occur (Hatfield & Rapson, 1996). Cultures differ in what parts of the body and what style of clothing (if any) are defined as erotic or repulsive. In some cultures, such as on Pentacost Island in the South Pacific, nudity is not considered particularly arousing or sexy. In some cultures, female breasts are erotic symbols; elsewhere, they are about as erotic as the elbow. And cultures differ in the specific sexual acts and positions that are considered erotic or repulsive. In some societies, for example, oral sex is considered a bizarre deviation; in others, oral sex is considered not only normal but supremely desirable.

The cultural standards that affect sexual desire and response are deeply ingrained; just because they are learned doesn't mean they are easy to change. To see what we mean, contemplate for a moment the sexual norms of your own culture and peer group. Do you think you could be attracted to someone of another culture? Are you attracted only to partners who fit your culture's standard of ideal beauty—and what is that standard, anyway? What are the values, beliefs about sexual normalcy, and standards of erotic beauty that you have internalized in your own sexual history?

The Psychodynamic Perspective

Finally, psychodynamic psychologists focus on the inner dynamics of sexual attraction, conflict, guilt, and fear; the unconscious fears and angers that perpetuate the "battle of the sexes"; and the psychic dilemmas originating in childhood that may affect adult sexual choices and responses to a partner. For example, a psychodynamic therapist would try to identify the unconscious meanings and motives that many people bring to a sexual encounter: Perhaps a woman is withholding orgasm out of an inability to trust her partner; perhaps a man is coercing a woman into sex in order to displace his feelings of rage at his mother or to disguise his feelings of sexual inadequacy (Glenmullen, 1993).

Because, in this view, unconscious sexual drives are always competing with the socializing forces of society, sexuality is particularly susceptible to defense mechanisms such as denial, projection, and displacement. Sex, to psychodynamic psychologists, is never only about sex. It is also about the paradoxical need for closeness and fear of closeness. It is about the playing out of childish insecurities and fears, which repeat themselves in adult relationships (Stoller, 1985). According to object-relations theory, for example, men are more likely than women to have casual sexual relationships because men unconsciously retain from their earliest years a fear of emotional intimacy. Because they associate intimacy with their early attachment to their mothers and hence with femininity, intimacy can threaten their masculine identity (see Chapter 11).

The psychodynamic perspective holds that women and men have different kinds of unconscious sexual fears and vulnerabilities, which affect their sexual desire and performance. These unconscious processes begin with the anatomical differences between the sexes. For women, sexual anxieties are connected to fears of being overwhelmed, violated, raped, or impregnated (Benjamin, 1988). For men, sexual anxieties are related to fear of the inability to perform sexually, which represents to them a loss of power. The psychodynamic perspective puts more emphasis than any other approach on the unconscious emotions evoked by sexuality, including the distrust, anger, fear, envy, and insecurities that are often part of many relationships. But it, like the others, also recognizes that sexuality can be a life-affirming link between two otherwise alienated souls.

Each of the five perspectives thus contributes important knowledge to our understanding of sexuality. Together, they show us that the answer to the question "Why do people have sex?" is not just "Because it's natural" or "Because it feels good." In addition to the pleasure and intimacy of sex, the range of motives that are involved include intimidation, conformity, revenge, anger, and unconscious fears. Sexuality reflects physiology and learning, individual preferences and cultural rules, conscious and unconscious motives.

REFLECTIONS ON PSYCHOLOGY

As our discussions of music and sexuality illustrate, no single perspective in psychology has a monopoly on insights into human behavior. This means that in trying to solve a personal problem, understand the puzzling behavior of a friend, or choose the wisest position on a matter of social policy, we would do well to try to see the whole elephant from different angles. For instance, if you are having a problem, you might start with questions like these:

✦ *Biological influences.* What is going on in your body? Do you have a physical condition that might be affecting your behavior? Do you have a temperamental tendency to be easily aroused or to be calm? Are alcohol or other drugs altering your ability to make decisions or behave as you would like? Might an irregular schedule be impairing your efficiency?

✦ *Learning influences.* As you further analyze the situation, you would want to ask, What are the contingencies and consequences governing your behavior and that of others? What rewards are maintaining your behavior? Of the many messages being aimed at you by television, books, parents, and teachers, which have the greatest influence? Who are the people you most admire and wish to emulate?

✦ *Cognitive influences.* To solve your problem, you would also need to ask yourself how you are framing the situation you are in. Are your explanations of what is causing the problem reasonable? Have you tested them? Are you wallowing in negative thoughts? Do you attribute your successes to luck but take all the blame for your failures, or vice versa? Do you assume the worst about others? Do you make external attributions or internal ones? Are you responding to other people's behavior in a mindless way?

✦ *Sociocultural influences.* Everyone conforms, to one extent or another, to the expectations and demands of others. Who are the people who affect your attitudes and behavior? Do your friends and relatives support or hinder you in achieving your goals? Which situations make you feel ambitious, confident, or content, and which ones make you feel helpless, pessimistic, or angry? How do your ethnicity and nationality affect your beliefs, values, roles, and behavior? What gender roles do they specify for you in close relationships? Are conflicts you might be having with other people a result of cultural misunderstandings?

✦ *Psychodynamic influences.* If you find that you are repeating self-defeating patterns, expectations, and emotional reactions that you acquired in childhood, you might want to consider unconscious motivations. Do other people "push your buttons" for reasons you cannot explain? Are you displacing feelings about your parents onto your friends or intimates? Are you carrying around "unfinished business" from childhood losses and hurts?

It may seem daunting to keep all these factors in mind. But once you get into the habit of seeing a situation from many points of view, relying on any one approach will feel as if you are wearing blinders. Cultivating the ability to see the world and your part in it from different angles will also make you wary of anyone who offers simplistic solutions. And it will inoculate you against ideas that are unsupported by evidence, even when those ideas are promoted by experts and authorities who ought to know better.

Psychobabble, with its promise of quick fixes and simple solutions, narrows our vision; good psychology, with its demands for critical thinking and evidence, expands it. Psychobabble is popular because it creates mirages—oases of hope that tend to evaporate under close scrutiny. In contrast, serious psychology creates a wealth of useful information, the kind that contributes to a rich and lasting understanding of the human spirit and its capacity for self-delusion and self-awareness, cowardice and compassion, hatred and love.

Empirical findings from each of the perspectives in psychology have made enormous contributions not only to understanding human behavior, but also to applying this knowledge to the resolution of social problems and to the alleviation of individual distress. The study of psychology will never free us from emotional crises, the pain of loss, or anger at injustice. But it can illuminate some pathways out of the blind alleys and dark corners that, as human beings, we all will encounter on the journey of life. ▉

"I still don't have all the answers, but I'm beginning to ask the right questions."

GLOSSARY

accommodation   In Piaget's theory, the process of modifying existing cognitive structures in response to experience and new information.

acculturation   The process by which members of groups that are minorities in a given society come to identify with and feel part of the mainstream culture.

activation-synthesis theory   The theory that dreaming results from the cortical synthesis and interpretation of neural signals triggered by activity in the lower part of the brain.

adrenal hormones   Hormones that are produced by the adrenal glands and that are involved in emotion and stress; they include cortisol, epinephrine, and norepinephrine.

agoraphobia   A set of phobias, often set off by a panic attack, involving the basic fear of being away from a safe place or person.

algorithm   A problem-solving strategy guaranteed to produce a solution even if the user does not know how it works.

amnesia   *See* childhood amnesia, psychogenic amnesia.

amygdala [uh-MIG-dul-uh]   A brain structure involved in the arousal and regulation of emotion, particularly fear, and the initial emotional response to sensory information.

antidepressant drugs   Drugs used primarily in the treatment of mood disorders, especially depression and anxiety.

antipsychotic drugs   Drugs used primarily in the treatment of schizophrenia and other psychotic disorders.

antisocial personality disorder   A disorder characterized by antisocial behavior such as lying, stealing, manipulating others, and sometimes violence; and a lack of guilt, shame, and empathy. (Sometimes called *psychopathy* or *sociopathy*.)

applied psychology   The study of psychological issues that have direct practical significance and the application of psychological findings.

archetypes [AR-ki-tipes]   Universal, symbolic images that appear in myths, art, stories, and dreams; to Carl Jung, they reflect the collective unconscious.

arithmetic mean   An average that is calculated by adding up a set of quantities and dividing the sum by the total number of quantities in the set.

assimilation   In Piaget's theory, the process of absorbing new information into existing cognitive structures.

attribution theory   The theory that people are motivated to explain their own and others' behavior by attributing causes of that behavior to a situation or a disposition.

autonomic nervous system   The subdivision of the peripheral nervous system that regulates the internal organs and glands.

availability heuristic   The tendency to judge the probability of a type of event by how easy it is to think of examples or instances.

aversive conditioning   In behavior therapy, a method in which punishment is substituted for the reinforcement that is perpetuating a bad habit.

axon   A neuron's extending fiber that conducts impulses away from the cell body and transmits them to other neurons.

basic anxiety   To Karen Horney, the feeling of being isolated and helpless in a hostile world; it is the motivating emotion in social relations.

basic concepts   Concepts that have a moderate number of instances and that are easier to acquire than those having few or many instances.

basic psychology   The study of psychological issues in order to seek knowledge for its own sake rather than for its practical application.

behavior modification   The application of conditioning techniques to teach new responses or reduce or eliminate maladaptive or problematic behavior.

behavioral genetics   An interdisciplinary field of study concerned with the genetic bases of behavior and personality.

behaviorism   An approach to psychology that emphasizes the study of observable behavior and the role of the environment as a determinant of behavior.

biofeedback   A method for learning to control bodily functions, including ones usually thought to be involuntary, by attending to feedback from an instrument that monitors the function and that signals changes in it.

biological perspective   A psychological approach that emphasizes bodily events and changes associated with actions, feelings, and thoughts.

biological rhythm   A periodic, more or less regular fluctuation in a biological system; it may or may not have psychological implications.

bipolar disorder   A mood disorder in which episodes of both depression and mania (excessive euphoria) occur.

brain stem   The part of the brain at the top of the spinal cord, consisting of the medulla and the pons.

case study   A detailed description of a particular individual being studied or treated.

castration anxiety   In psychoanalysis, the boy's unconscious fear of castration by the powerful father; this anxiety motivates the resolution of the Oedipus complex.

cell body   The part of the neuron that keeps it alive and determines whether it will fire.

central nervous system (CNS)   The portion of the nervous system consisting of the brain and spinal cord.

cerebellum   A brain structure that regulates movement and balance, and that is involved in the learning of certain kinds of simple responses.

cerebral cortex   A collection of several thin layers of cells covering the cerebrum; it is largely responsible for higher mental functions. (*Cortex* is Latin for "bark" or "rind.")

cerebral hemispheres   The two halves of the cerebrum.

cerebrum [suh-REE-brum]   The largest brain structure, consisting of the upper part of the brain; it is in charge of most sensory, motor, and cognitive processes. (From the Latin for "brain.")

childhood (infantile) amnesia   The inability to remember events and experiences that occurred during the first two or three years of life.

chromosomes   Within every body cell, rod-shaped structures that carry the genes.

chunk   A meaningful unit of information; it may be composed of smaller units.

circadian [sur-CAY-dee-un] rhythm   A biological rhythm with a period (from peak to peak or trough to trough) of about 24 hours; from the Latin *circa*, "about," and *dies*, "a day."

classical conditioning   The process by which a previously neutral stimulus acquires the capacity to elicit a response through association with a stimulus that already elicits a similar or related response; also called *Pavlovian* or *respondent conditioning*.

coefficient of correlation   A measure of correlation that ranges in value from −1.00 to +1.00.

cognitive dissonance   A state of tension that occurs when a person simultaneously holds two cognitions that are psychologically inconsistent, or when a person's belief is incongruent with his or her behavior.

cognitive ethology   The study of cognitive processes in nonhuman animals.

cognitive perspective   A psychological approach that emphasizes mental processes in perception, memory, language, problem solving, and other areas of behavior.

cognitive schema   An integrated mental network of knowledge, beliefs, and expectations concerning a particular topic or aspect of the world.

collective unconscious   To Carl Jung, the universal memories and experiences of humankind, represented in the symbols, stories, and images (archetypes) that occur across all cultures.

collectivist cultures   Cultures in which the self is regarded as embedded in relationships, and harmony with one's group is prized above individual goals and wishes.

concept   A mental category that groups objects, relations, activities, abstractions, or qualities having common properties.

conditioned response (CR)   The classical-conditioning term for a response that is elicited by a conditioned stimulus; it occurs after the conditioned stimulus is associated with an unconditioned stimulus.

conditioned stimulus (CS)   The classical-conditioning term for an initially neutral stimulus that comes to elicit a conditioned response after being associated with an unconditioned stimulus.

conditioning   A basic kind of learning that involves associations between environmental stimuli and the organism's responses.

confirmation bias   The tendency to look for or pay attention only to information that confirms one's own belief.

conservation   The understanding that the physical properties of objects—such as the number of items in a cluster or the amount of liquid in a glass—can remain the same even when their forms or appearances change.

contact comfort   The innate pleasure derived from close physical contact; it is the basis of an infant's first attachment.

continuous reinforcement   A reinforcement schedule in which a particular response is always reinforced.

control condition   In an experiment, a comparison condition in which subjects are not exposed to the same treatment as in the experimental condition.

convergent thinking   Thinking aimed at finding a single correct answer to a problem.

corpus callosum [CORE-puhss cah-LOW-suhm]   The bundle of nerve fibers connecting the two cerebral hemispheres.

correlation   A measure of how strongly two variables are related to one another.

correlational study   A descriptive study that looks for a consistent relationship between two phenomena.

counterconditioning   In classical conditioning, the process of pairing a conditioned stimulus with a stimulus that elicits a response that is incompatible with an unwanted conditioned response.

critical thinking   The ability and willingness to assess claims and make judgments on the basis of well-supported reasons and evidence, rather than emotion or anecdote.

cross-sectional study   A study in which subjects of different ages are compared at a given time.

cue-dependent forgetting   The inability to retrieve information stored in memory because of insufficient cues for recall.

culture   A program of shared rules that govern the behavior of members of a community or society, and a set of values, beliefs, and attitudes shared by most members of that community.

decay theory   The theory that information in memory eventually disappears if it is not accessed; it applies more to short-term than to long-term memory.

declarative memories   Memories of facts, rules, concepts, and events ("knowing that"); they include semantic and episodic memories.

deductive reasoning   A form of reasoning in which a conclusion follows necessarily from certain premises; if the premises are true, the conclusion must be true.

deep processing   In the encoding of information, the processing of meaning, rather than simply the physical or sensory features of a stimulus.

defense mechanisms   Methods used by the ego to prevent unconscious anxiety or threatening thoughts from entering consciousness.

deindividuation   In groups or crowds, the loss of awareness of one's own individuality and the abdication of mindful action.

dendrites   A neuron's branches that receive information from other neurons and transmit it toward the cell body.

dependent variable   A variable that an experimenter predicts will be affected by manipulations of the independent variable.

descriptive methods Methods that yield descriptions of behavior but not necessarily causal explanations.

descriptive statistics Statistical procedures that organize and summarize a body of data.

dialectical reasoning A process in which opposing facts or ideas are weighed and compared, with a view to determining the best solution or to resolving differences.

diffusion of responsibility In organized or anonymous groups, the tendency of members to avoid taking responsibility for actions or decisions because they assume that others will do so.

discriminative stimulus A stimulus that signals when a particular response is likely to be followed by a certain type of consequence.

dissociative identity disorder A controversial disorder marked by the appearance within one person of two or more distinct personalities, each with its own name and traits; commonly known as *multiple personality disorder (MPD)*.

divergent thinking Mental exploration of unconventional alternatives in solving problems; by breaking mental sets, it tends to enhance creativity.

dizygotic twins *See* identical twins.

DNA (deoxyribonucleic acid) The chromosomal molecule that transfers genetic characteristics by way of coded instructions for the structure of proteins.

double-blind study An experiment in which neither the subjects nor the individuals running the study know which subjects are in the control group and which are in the experimental group until after the results are tallied.

effect size In an experiment, the amount of variance in the data accounted for by the independent variable.

ego In psychoanalysis, the part of the mind that represents reason, good sense, and rational self-control; it mediates between id and superego.

egocentric thinking Seeing the world from only your own point of view; the inability to take another person's perspective.

elaborative rehearsal The association of new information with already stored knowledge and the analysis of the new information to make it memorable.

electroconvulsive therapy (ECT) A procedure used in cases of prolonged and severe major depression, in which a brief brain seizure is induced.

electroencephalogram (EEG) A recording of neural activity detected by electrodes.

empirical Relying on or derived from observation, experimentation, or measurement.

endocrine glands Internal organs that produce hormones and release them into the bloodstream.

endorphins [en-DOR-fins] Chemical substances in the nervous system that are similar in structure and action to opiates; they are involved in pain reduction, pleasure, and memory, and are known technically as *endogenous opioid peptides*.

entrapment A gradual process in which individuals escalate their commitment to a course of action to justify their investment of time, money, or effort.

episodic memories Memories of personally experienced events and the contexts in which they occurred.

ethnic identity A person's identification with a religious or ethnic group.

ethnocentrism The belief that one's own ethnic group, nation, or religion is superior to all others.

evolution A change in gene frequencies within a population over many generations; a mechanism by which genetically influenced characteristics of a population may change.

evolutionary psychology A field of psychology emphasizing evolutionary mechanisms that may help explain human commonalities in cognition, development, emotion, social practices, and other areas of behavior.

existential psychology An approach to psychology that emphasizes free will and responsibility for one's actions, and the importance of struggling with the harsh realities of existence, such as the need to find meaning in life and to accept suffering and death.

experiment   A controlled test of a hypothesis in which the researcher manipulates one variable to discover its effect on another.

experimenter effects   Unintended changes in subjects' behavior due to cues inadvertently given by the experimenter.

explicit memory   Conscious, intentional recollection of an event or of an item of information.

exposure treatment   In behavior therapy, a method in which a person suffering from an anxiety disorder, such as a phobia or panic attacks, is taken directly into the feared situation until the anxiety subsides.

extinction   The weakening and eventual disappearance of a learned response. In classical conditioning, it occurs when the conditioned stimulus is no longer paired with the unconditioned stimulus; in operant conditioning, it occurs when a response is no longer followed by a reinforcer.

extrinsic reinforcers   Reinforcers that are not inherently related to the activity being reinforced, such as money, prizes, and praise.

factor analysis   A statistical method for analyzing the intercorrelations among different measures or test scores; clusters of measures or scores that are highly correlated are assumed to measure the same underlying trait or ability (factor).

feminist psychology   A psychological approach that analyzes the influence of social inequities on gender relations and on the behavior of the two sexes.

field research   Descriptive or experimental research conducted in a natural setting outside the laboratory.

fraternal (dizygotic) twins   Twins that develop from two separate eggs fertilized by different sperm; they are no more alike genetically than are any other pair of siblings.

frontal lobes   Lobes at the front of the brain's cerebral cortex; they contain areas involved in short-term memory, higher-order thinking, initiative, social judgment, and (in the left lobe, typically) speech production.

functionalism   An early psychological approach that emphasized the function or purpose of behavior and consciousness.

fundamental attribution error   The tendency, in explaining other people's behavior, to overestimate the influence of personality factors and underestimate the influence of the situation.

gender identity   The fundamental sense of being male or female; it is independent of whether the person conforms to the social and cultural rules of gender.

gender schema   A mental network of knowledge, beliefs, metaphors, and expectations about what it means to be male or female.

gender typing   The process by which children learn the abilities, interests, personality traits, and behaviors associated with being masculine or feminine in their culture.

generalized anxiety disorder   A continuous state of anxiety marked by feelings of worry and dread, apprehension, difficulties in concentration, and signs of motor tension.

genes   The functional units of heredity; they are composed of DNA and specify the structure of proteins.

genetic marker   A segment of DNA that varies among individuals, has a known location on a chromosome, and can function as a genetic landmark for a gene involved in a physical or mental condition.

genome   The full set of genes in each cell of an organism (with the exception of sperm and egg cells).

glial cells   Nervous system cells that aid the neurons by providing them with nutrients, insulating them, and removing cellular debris when they die.

groupthink   In close-knit groups, the tendency for all members to think alike for the sake of harmony and to suppress dissent.

heritability   A statistical estimate of the proportion of the total variance in some trait that is attributable to genetic differences among individuals within a group.

heuristic   A rule of thumb that suggests a course of action or guides problem solving but does not guarantee an optimal solution.

higher-order conditioning   In classical conditioning, a procedure in which a neutral stimulus becomes a conditioned stimulus through association with an already established conditioned stimulus.

hindsight bias   The tendency to overestimate one's ability to have predicted an event once the outcome is known; the "I knew it all along" phenomenon.

hippocampus   A brain structure involved in the storage of new information in memory.

hormones   Chemical substances, secreted by organs called *glands,* that affect the functioning of other organs.

humanist psychology   A psychological approach that emphasizes personal growth and the achievement of human potential rather than the scientific understanding and assessment of behavior.

hypnosis   A procedure in which the practitioner suggests changes in the sensations, perceptions, thoughts, feelings, or behavior of the subject, who cooperates by altering his or her normal cognitive functioning accordingly.

hypothalamus   A brain structure involved in emotions and drives vital to survival, such as fear, hunger, thirst, and reproduction; it regulates the autonomic nervous system.

hypothesis   A statement that attempts to predict or to account for a set of phenomena; scientific hypotheses specify relationships among events or variables and are empirically tested.

id   In psychoanalysis, the part of the mind containing inherited psychic energy, particularly sexual and aggressive instincts.

identical (monozygotic) twins   Twins that develop when a fertilized egg divides into two parts that develop into separate embryos.

implicit memory   Unconscious retention in memory, as evidenced by the effect of a previous experience or previously encountered information on current thoughts or actions.

independent variable   A variable that an experimenter manipulates.

individualist cultures   Cultures in which the self is regarded as autonomous, and individual goals and wishes are prized above duty and relations with others.

induction   A method of correcting a child's behavior in which the parent appeals to the child's own abilities, sense of responsibility, and feelings for others.

inductive reasoning   A form of reasoning in which the premises provide support for a conclusion, but it is still possible for the conclusion to be false.

infantile amnesia   *See* childhood amnesia.

inferential statistics   Statistical procedures that allow researchers to draw inferences about how statistically meaningful a study's results are.

inferiority complex   To Alfred Adler, an inability to accept one's natural limitations; it occurs when the need for self-improvement is blocked or inhibited.

insight   A form of problem solving that appears to involve the sudden understanding of how elements of a situation are related or can be reorganized to achieve a solution.

instinctive drift   The tendency of an organism to revert to an instinctive behavior over time; it can interfere with learning.

intelligence quotient (IQ)   A measure of intelligence originally computed by dividing a person's mental age by his or her chronological age and multiplying the result by 100; it is now derived from norms provided for standardized intelligence tests.

intermittent (partial) schedule of reinforcement   A reinforcement schedule in which a particular response is sometimes but not always reinforced.

intrapsychic   Within the mind (psyche) or self.

intrinsic reinforcers   Reinforcers that are inherently related to the activity being reinforced, such as enjoyment of the task and the satisfaction of accomplishment.

just-world hypothesis   The notion that many people need to believe that the world is fair and justice is served; that bad people are punished and good people rewarded.

justification of effort   The tendency of individuals to increase their liking for something that they have worked hard or suffered to attain; a common form of dissonance reduction.

language   A system that combines meaningless elements such as sounds or gestures to form structured utterances that convey meaning.

language acquisition device   According to many psycholinguists, an innate mental module that facilitates the young child's development of language.

latent learning   A form of learning that is not immediately expressed in an overt response; it occurs without obvious reinforcement.

lateralization   Specialization of the two cerebral hemispheres for particular operations.

learning perspective   A psychological approach that emphasizes how the environment and experience affect a person's or animal's actions; it includes *behaviorism* and *social-cognitive learning theories.*

libido [li-BEE-do]   In psychoanalysis, the psychic energy that fuels the life or sexual instincts of the id.

limbic system   A group of brain areas involved in emotional reactions and motivated behavior.

linkage studies   Studies that look for patterns of inheritance of genetic markers in large families in which a particular condition is common.

lithium carbonate   A drug frequently given to people suffering from bipolar disorder.

localization of function   Specialization of particular brain areas for particular functions.

locus of control   A general expectation about whether the results of a person's actions are under his or her control (internal locus) or beyond the person's control (external locus).

long-term memory (LTM)   In the three-box model of memory, the memory system involved in the long-term storage of information.

long-term potentiation   A long-lasting increase in the strength of synaptic responsiveness, thought to be a biological mechanism of long-term memory.

longitudinal study   A study in which subjects are followed and periodically reassessed over time.

magnetic resonance imaging   *See* MRI.

maintenance rehearsal   Rote repetition of material in order to maintain its availability in memory.

major depression   A mood disorder involving disturbances in emotion (excessive sadness), behavior (loss of interest in one's usual activities), cognition (thoughts of hopelessness), and body function (fatigue and loss of appetite).

mastery (learning) goals   Goals framed in terms of increasing one's competence and skills.

mean   *See* arithmetic mean.

medulla [muh-DUL-uh]   A structure in the brain stem responsible for certain automatic functions, such as breathing and heart rate.

melatonin   A hormone, secreted by the pineal gland, that is involved in the regulation of daily biological rhythms.

mental disorder   Any behavior or emotional state that causes an individual great suffering or worry, is self-defeating or self-destructive, or is maladaptive and disrupts the person's relationships or the larger community.

mental image   A mental representation that mirrors or resembles the thing it represents; mental images can occur in many and perhaps all sensory modalities.

mental set   A tendency to solve problems using procedures that worked before on similar problems.

meta-analysis   A procedure for combining and analyzing data from many studies; it determines how much of the variance in scores across all studies can be explained by a particular variable.

mnemonics   Strategies and tricks for improving memory, such as the use of a verse or a formula.

monochronic cultures   Cultures in which time is organized sequentially; schedules and deadlines are valued over people.

motivation   A process within a person or animal, which causes movement toward a goal or away from an unpleasant situation.

MRI (magnetic resonance imaging)   A method for studying body and brain tissue, using magnetic fields and special radio receivers.

multiple personality disorder   *See* dissociative identity disorder.

myelin sheath   A fatty insulation that may surround the axon of a neuron.

narcissistic personality disorder   A disorder characterized by an exaggerated sense of self-importance and self-absorption.

natural selection   The evolutionary process in which individuals with genetically influenced traits that are adaptive in a particular environment tend to survive and to reproduce in greater numbers than other individuals; as a result, their traits become more common in the population.

need for achievement   A learned motive to meet personal standards of success and excellence in a chosen area (abbreviated *nAch*).

negative correlation   An association between increases in one variable and decreases in another.

negative reinforcement   A reinforcement procedure in which a response is followed by the removal, delay, or decrease in intensity of an unpleasant stimulus; as a result, the response becomes stronger or more likely to occur.

nerve   A bundle of nerve fibers (axons and sometimes dendrites) in the peripheral nervous system.

network models   Models of long-term memory that represent its contents as a vast network of interrelated concepts and propositions.

neuron   A cell that conducts electrochemical signals; the basic unit of the nervous system; also called a *nerve cell.*

neurotransmitter   A chemical substance that is released by a transmitting neuron at the synapse and that alters the activity of a receiving neuron.

nonconscious processes   Mental processes occurring outside of and not available to conscious awareness.

norms   In test construction, established standards of performance.

norms (social)   Rules that regulate human life, including social conventions, explicit laws, and implicit cultural standards.

object permanence   The understanding that an object continues to exist even when you cannot see it or touch it.

object-relations theory   A psychodynamic approach that emphasizes the importance of the infant's first two years and the baby's formative relationships, especially with the mother.

observational learning   A process in which an individual learns new responses by observing the behavior of another (a model) rather than through direct experience; in behaviorism, it is called *vicarious conditioning.*

observational study   A study in which the researcher carefully and systematically observes and records behavior without interfering with the behavior; it may involve either naturalistic or laboratory observation.

obsessive-compulsive disorder (OCD)   An anxiety disorder in which a person feels trapped in repetitive, persistent thoughts (obsessions) and repetitive, ritualized behaviors (compulsions) designed to reduce anxiety.

occipital [ahk-SIP-uh-tuhl] lobes   Lobes at the lower back part of the brain's cerebral cortex; they contain areas that receive visual information.

Oedipus complex   In psychoanalysis, a conflict in which a child desires the parent of the other sex and views the same-sex parent as a rival; it is the key issue in the phallic stage of development.

operant conditioning   The process by which a response becomes more likely to occur or less so, depending on its consequences.

operational definition   A precise definition of a term in a hypothesis, which specifies the operations for observing and measuring the process or phenomenon being defined.

operations   In Piaget's theory, mental actions that are cognitively reversible.

panic disorder   An anxiety disorder in which a person experiences recurring *panic attacks,* periods of intense fear and feelings of impending doom or death, accompanied by physiological symptoms such as rapid breathing and pulse, and dizziness.

parallel distributed processing (PDP)   An alternative to the information-processing model of memory, in which knowledge is represented as connections among thousands of interacting processing units, distributed in a vast network, and all operating in parallel.

paranoid personality disorder   A disorder characterized by habitually unreasonable and excessive suspiciousness or jealousy.

parasympathetic nervous system   The subdivision of the autonomic nervous system that operates during relaxed states and that conserves energy.

parietal [puh-RYE-uh-tuhl] lobes   Lobes at the top of the brain's cerebral cortex; they contain areas that receive information on pressure, pain, touch, and temperature.

pattern recognition   The identification of a stimulus on the basis of information already contained in long-term memory.

perception   The process by which the brain organizes and interprets sensory information.

performance goals   Goals framed in terms of performing well in front of others, being judged favorably, and avoiding criticism.

peripheral nervous system (PNS)   All portions of the nervous system outside the brain and spinal cord; it includes sensory and motor nerves.

personality disorders   Rigid, maladaptive personality patterns that cause personal distress or an inability to get along with others.

PET scan (positron-emission tomography)   A method for analyzing biochemical activity in the brain, using injections of a glucoselike substance containing a radioactive element.

phobia   An exaggerated, unrealistic fear of a specific situation, activity, or object.

pituitary gland   A small endocrine gland at the base of the brain, which releases many hormones and regulates other endocrine glands.

placebo   An inactive substance or fake treatment used as a control in an experiment or given by a medical practitioner to a patient.

placebo effect   The apparent success of a medication or treatment that is due to the patient's expectations or hopes rather than to the drug or treatment itself.

polychronic cultures   Cultures in which time is organized horizontally; people tend to do several things at once and value relationships over schedules.

pons   A structure in the brain stem involved in, among other things, sleeping, waking, and dreaming.

positive correlation   An association between increases in one variable and increases in another.

positive reinforcement   A reinforcement procedure in which a response is followed by the presentation of, or increase in intensity of, a reinforcing stimulus; as a result, the response becomes stronger or more likely to occur.

positive-emission tomography   *See* PET scan.

postmodernism   A school of thought holding that an observer's values, culture, worldview, and status in society inevitably affect the person's observations and explanations.

posttraumatic stress disorder (PTSD)   An anxiety disorder in which a person who has experienced a traumatic or life-threatening event has symptoms such as psychic numbing, reliving of the trauma, and increased physiological arousal.

power assertion   A method of correcting a child's behavior in which the parent uses punishment and authority.

primary punisher   A stimulus that is inherently punishing; an example is electric shock.

primary reinforcer   A stimulus that is inherently reinforcing, typically satisfying a physiological need; an example is food.

priming   A method for measuring implicit memory in which a person reads or listens to information and is later tested to see whether the information affects performance on another type of task.

principle of falsifiability   The principle that a scientific theory must make predictions that are specific enough to expose the theory to the possibility of disconfirmation; that is, the theory must predict not only what will happen, but also what will not happen.

proactive interference   Forgetting that occurs when previously stored material interferes with the ability to remember similar, more recently learned material.

procedural memories   Memories for the performance of actions or skills ("knowing how").

projective tests   Psychological tests used to infer a person's motives, conflicts, and unconscious dynamics on the basis of the person's interpretations of ambiguous stimuli.

proposition   A unit of meaning that is made up of concepts and expresses a single idea.

prototype   An especially representative example of a concept.

psychoanalysis   A theory of personality and a method of psychotherapy originally developed by Sigmund Freud which emphasizes unconscious motives and conflicts.

psychodynamic perspective   A psychological approach that emphasizes unconscious dynamics within the individual, such as inner forces, conflicts, or the movement of instinctual energy.

psychogenic amnesia   The partial or complete loss of memory for threatening information or traumatic experiences due to nonorganic causes.

psychological tests   Procedures used to measure and evaluate personality traits, emotional states, aptitudes, interests, abilities, and values.

psychology   The discipline concerned with behavior and mental processes and how they are affected by an organism's physical state, mental state, and external environment; often represented by Ψ, the Greek letter psi (usually pronounced "sy").

psychosis   An extreme mental disturbance involving distorted perceptions and irrational behavior; it may have psychological or organic causes. (Plural: *psychoses.*)

psychosurgery   Any surgical procedure that destroys selected areas of the brain believed to be involved in emotional disorders or violent, impulsive behavior.

punishment   The process by which a stimulus or event weakens or reduces the probability of the response that it follows.

random assignment   A procedure for assigning people to experimental and control groups in which each individual has the same probability as any other of being assigned to a given group.

rapid eye movement (REM) sleep   Sleep periods characterized by quick eye movements, loss of muscle tone, and dreaming.

reasoning   The drawing of conclusions or inferences from observations, facts, or assumptions.

recall   The ability to retrieve and reproduce from memory previously encountered material.

recognition   The ability to identify previously encountered material.

reductionism   The process of reducing a phenomenon to a single type of explanation or to a limited set of elements of a particular type (for example, biological or cognitive).

reinforcement   The process by which a stimulus or event strengthens or increases the probability of the response that it follows.

relearning method   A method for measuring retention that compares the time required to relearn material with the time used in the initial learning of the material.

reliability   In test construction, the consistency of scores derived from a test, from one time and place to another.

REM sleep   *See* rapid eye movement sleep.

representative sample   A group of subjects, selected from a population for study, which matches the population on important characteristics such as age and sex.

reticular activating system (RAS)   A dense network of neurons found in the core of the brain stem; it arouses the cortex and screens incoming information.

retroactive interference   Forgetting that occurs when recently learned material interferes with the ability to remember similar material stored previously.

role   A given social position that is governed by a set of norms for proper behavior.

Rorschach Inkblot Test   A projective personality test that asks respondents to interpret abstract, symmetrical inkblots.

schizophrenia   A psychotic disorder or group of disorders marked by positive symptoms (e.g., delusions, hallucinations, disorganized and incoherent speech, and inappropriate behavior) and negative symptoms (e.g., emotional flatness and loss of motivation).

secondary punisher   A stimulus that has acquired punishing properties through association with other punishers.

secondary reinforcer   A stimulus that has acquired reinforcing properties through association with other reinforcers.

self-efficacy   A person's belief that he or she is capable of producing desired results, such as mastering new skills and reaching goals.

self-fulfilling prophecy   An expectation that comes true because of the tendency of the person holding it to act in ways that bring it about.

self-serving bias   The tendency, in explaining one's own behavior, to take credit for one's good actions and rationalize one's mistakes.

semantic memories   Memories of general knowledge, including facts, rules, concepts, and propositions.

sensation   The detection of physical energy emitted or reflected by physical objects; it occurs when energy in the external environment or the body stimulates receptors in the sense organs.

sensory memory   A memory system that momentarily preserves extremely accurate images of sensory information.

serial-position effect   The tendency for recall of the first and last items on a list to surpass recall of items in the middle of the list.

set point   The genetically influenced weight range for an individual, thought to be maintained by a biological mechanism that regulates food intake, fat reserves, and metabolism.

sex hormones   Hormones that regulate the development and functioning of reproductive organs and that stimulate the development of male and female sexual characteristics; they include androgens, estrogens, and progesterone.

sex typing   *See* gender typing.

shaping   An operant-conditioning procedure in which successive approximations of a desired response are reinforced.

short-term memory (STM)   In the three-box model of memory, a limited-capacity memory system involved in the retention of information for brief periods; it is also used to hold information retrieved from long-term memory for temporary use.

significance tests   Statistical tests that show how likely it is that a study's results occurred merely by chance.

single-blind study   An experiment in which subjects do not know whether they are in an experimental or a control group.

social cognition   An area in social psychology concerned with social influences on thought, memory, perception, and other cognitive processes.

social identity   The part of a person's self-concept that is based on his or her identification with a nation, culture, or ethnic group or with a gender role or other roles in society.

social-cognitive learning theories   Theories that emphasize how behavior is learned and maintained through the interaction between individuals and their environments, an interaction strongly influenced by such cognitive processes as observations, expectations, perceptions, and motivational beliefs.

sociobiology   An interdisciplinary field that emphasizes evolutionary explanations of social behavior in animals, including human beings.

sociocultural perspective   A psychological approach that emphasizes social and cultural influences on behavior.

somatic nervous system   The subdivision of the peripheral nervous system that connects to sensory receptors and to skeletal muscles; sometimes called the *skeletal nervous system.*

source amnesia   The inability to distinguish what you originally experienced from what you heard or were told about an event later.

spinal cord   A collection of neurons and supportive tissue running from the base of the brain down the center of the back, protected by a column of bones (the spinal column).

splitting   In object-relations theory, the division of qualities into their opposites, as in the Good Mother versus the Bad Mother; it reflects an inability to understand that people are made up of good and bad qualities.

spontaneous recovery   The reappearance of a learned response after its apparent extinction.

standard deviation   A commonly used measure of variability that indicates the average difference between scores in a distribution and their mean.

standardize   In test construction, to develop uniform procedures for giving and scoring a test.

state-dependent memory   The tendency to remember something when the rememberer is in the same physical or mental state as during the original learning or experience.

stereotype   A summary impression of a group, in which a person believes that all members of the group share a common trait or traits (positive, negative, or neutral).

stereotype threat   A burden of doubt a person feels about his or her performance, due to negative stereotypes about his or her group's abilities.

stimulus control   Control over the occurrence of a response by a discriminative stimulus.

stimulus discrimination   The tendency to respond differently to two or more similar stimuli. In classical conditioning, it occurs when the conditioned stimulus similar to the conditioned stimulus fails to evoke the conditioned response; in operant conditioning, it occurs when an organism learns to make a response in the presence of other, similar stimuli that differ from it on some dimension.

stimulus generalization   After conditioning, the tendency to respond to a stimulus that resembles one involved in the original conditioning. In classical conditioning, it occurs when a stimulus that resembles the conditioned stimulus elicits the conditioned response; in operant conditioning, it occurs when a response that has been reinforced (or punished) in the presence of one stimulus occurs (or is surpressed) in the presence of other, similar stimuli.

subconscious processes   Mental processes occurring outside of conscious awareness but accessible to consciousness when necessary.

successive approximations   In the operant-conditioning procedure of shaping, behaviors that are ordered in terms of increasing similarity or closeness to the desired response.

superego   In psychoanalysis, the part of the mind that represents conscience, morality, and social standards.

suprachiasmatic [soo-pruh-KIE-az-MAT-ick] nucleus (SCN)   An area of the brain containing a biological clock that governs circadian rhythms.

surveys   Questionnaires and interviews that ask people directly about their experiences, attitudes, or opinions.

sympathetic nervous system   The subdivision of the autonomic nervous system that mobilizes bodily resources and increases the output of energy during emotion and stress.

synapse   The site where a nerve impulse is transmitted from one nerve cell to another; it includes the axon terminal, the synaptic cleft, and receptor sites in the membrane of the receiving cell.

systematic desensitization   In behavior therapy, a step-by-step process of desensitizing a client to a feared object or experience; based on the classical-conditioning procedure of counterconditioning.

temperaments   Physiological dispositions to respond to the environment in certain ways; they are present in infancy and are assumed to be innate.

temporal lobes   Lobes at the sides of the brain's cerebral cortex, just above the ears; they contain areas involved in hearing, memory, perception, emotion, and (in the left lobe, typically) language comprehension.

thalamus   A brain structure that relays motor impulses to the spinal cord and sensory messages to the cerebral cortex.

Thematic Apperception Test (TAT)   A personality test that asks respondents to interpret a series of drawings showing ambiguous scenes of people; scored for various motives such as the needs for achievement, affiliation, or power.

theory   An organized system of assumptions and principles that purports to explain a specified set of phenomena and their interrelationships.

theory of mind   A system of beliefs about the way your own mind and other people's minds work, and of how people are affected by their beliefs and feelings; it emerges at age 4 or 5.

therapeutic alliance   The bond of confidence and mutual understanding established between therapist and client, which allows them to work together to solve the client's problems.

trait   A characteristic of an individual, describing a habitual way of behaving, thinking, and feeling.

tranquilizers   Drugs commonly but often inappropriately prescribed for patients who complain of unhappiness, anxiety, or worry.

transference   In psychodynamic therapies, a critical step in which the client transfers unconscious emotions or reactions, such as emotional feelings about his or her parents, onto the therapist.

unconditional positive regard   To Carl Rogers, love or support given to another person, with no conditions attached.

unconditioned response (UR)   The classical-conditioning term for a reflexive response elicited by a stimulus in the absence of learning.

unconditioned stimulus (US)   The classical-conditioning term for a stimulus that elicits a reflexive response in the absence of learning.

validity   The ability of a test to measure what it was designed to measure.

validity effect   The tendency of people to believe that a statement is true or valid simply because it has been repeated many times.

variables   Characteristics of behavior or experience that can be measured or described by a numeric scale; variables are manipulated and assessed in scientific studies.

volunteer bias   A shortcoming of findings derived from a sample of volunteers instead of a representative sample; the volunteers may differ from those who did not volunteer.

BIBLIOGRAPHY

AAAS Project 2061 (1989). *Science for all Americans.* New York: Oxford University Press.

Abel, Gene G.; Mittelman, Mary; Becker, Judith V.; et al. (1988). Predicting child molesters' response to treatment. *Annals of the New York Academy of Sciences, 528,* 223–234.

Abrams, Mitchell, & Feindler, Eva (1998). Violence reduction via anger management for male athletes. Paper presented at the annual meeting of the American Psychological Association, San Francisco.

Abu-Lughod, Lila (1992). *Writing women's worlds: Bedouin stories.* Berkeley: University of California Press.

Acocella, Joan (1999). *Creating hysteria: Women and multiple personality disorder.* San Francisco: Jossey-Bass.

Adamopoulos, John, & Lonner, Walter J. (1994). Absolutism, relativism, and universalism in the study of human behavior. In W. J. Lonner & R. S. Malpass (eds.), *Psychology and culture.* Needham Heights, MA: Allyn & Bacon.

Adams, James L. (1986). *Conceptual blockbusting: A guide to better ideas* (3rd ed.). Boston: Addison-Wesley.

Adams, M. J. (1990). *Learning to read: Thinking and learning about print.* Cambridge, MA: MIT Press.

Ader, Robert (1997). The role of conditioning. In A. Harrington (ed.), *The placebo effect: An interdisciplinary exploration.* Cambridge, MA: Harvard University Press.

Affleck, Glenn; Tennen, Howard; Croog, Sydney; & Levine, Sol (1987). Causal attribution, perceived control, and recovery from a heart attack. *Journal of Social and Clinical Psychology, 5,* 339–355.

Ainsworth, Mary D. S. (1979). Infant-mother attachment. *American Psychologist, 34,* 932–937.

Akbarian, Schahram; Kim, J. J.; Potkin, Steven G.; et al. (1996). Maldistribution of interstitial neurons in prefrontal white matter of the brains of schizophrenic patients. *Archives of General Psychiatry, 53,* 425–436.

Albee, George W. (1985, February). The answer is prevention. *Psychology Today,* 60–64.

Aldag, Ramon J., & Fuller, Sally R. (1993). Beyond fiasco: A reappraisal of the groupthink phenomenon and a new model of group decision processes. *Psychological Bulletin, 113,* 533–552.

Alkon, Daniel L. (1989). Memory storage and neural systems. *Scientific American, 261,* 42–50.

Allen, Laura S., & Gorski, Robert A. (1992). Sexual orientation and the size of the anterior commissure in the human brain. *Proceedings of the National Academy of Sciences, 89,* 7199–7202.

Alloy, Lauren; Abramson, Lyn Y.; & Francis, Erika L. (1999). Do negative cognitive styles confer vulnerabil-ity to depression? *Current Directions in Psychological Science, 8,* 128–132.

Alloy, Lauren B.; Fedderly, Sharon S.; Kennedy-Moore, Eileen; & Cohan, Catherine L. (1998). Dysphoria and social interaction: An integration of behavioral confirmation and interpersonal perspectives. *Journal of Personality and Social Psychology, 74,* 1566–1579.

Allport, Gordon W. (1954/1979). *The nature of prejudice.* Reading, MA: Addison-Wesley.

Alpert, Bené; Field, Tiffany; Goldstein, Sheri; & Perry, Susan (1990). Aerobics enhances cardiovascular fitness and agility in preschoolers. *Health Psychology, 9,* 48–56.

Amabile, Teresa M. (1983). *The social psychology of creativity.* New York: Springer-Verlag.

Ambady, Nalini; Koo, Jasook; Lee, Fiona; & Rosenthal, Robert (1996). More than words: Linguistic and nonlinguistic politeness in two cultures. *Journal of Personality and Social Psychology, 70,* 996–1011.

Ambert, Anne-Marie (1997). *Parents, children, and adolescents: Interactive relationships and development in context.* New York: Haworth Press.

American Psychiatric Association (1994). *The diagnostic and statistical manual of mental disorders* (4th ed.). Washington, DC: American Psychiatric Association.

Amering, Michaela, & Katschnig, Heinz (1990). Panic attacks and panic disorder in cross-cultural perspective. *Psychiatric Annals, 20,* 511–516.

Anastasi, Anne (1988). *Psychological testing* (6th ed.). New York: Macmillan.

Anastasi, Anne, & Urbina, Susana (1997). *Psychological testing* (7th ed.). Upper Saddle River, NJ: Prentice-Hall.

Andersen, Barbara L.; Kiecolt-Glaser, Janice K.; & Glaser, Ronald (1994). A biobehavioral model of cancer stress and disease course. *American Psychologist, 49,* 389–404.

Andersen, Susan M., & Berk, Michele S. (1998). The social-cognitive model of transference: Experiencing past relationships in the present. *Current Directions in Psychological Science, 7,* 109–115.

Anderson, Craig A., & Dill, Karen E. (2000). Video games and aggressive thoughts, feelings, and behavior in the laboratory and in life. *Journal of Personality and Social Psychology, 78,* 772–790.

Anderson, Craig A.; Miller, Rowland S.; Riger, Alice L.; et al. (1994). Behavioral and characterological attributional styles as predictors of depression and loneliness: Review, refinement, and test. *Journal of Personality and Social Psychology, 66,* 549–558.

Anderson, John R. (1990). *The adaptive nature of thought.* Hillsdale, NJ: Erlbaum.

Andreasen, Nancy C.; Arndt, Stephan; Swayze, Victor, II; et al. (1994). Thalamic abnormalities in schizophrenia visualized through magnetic resonance image averaging. *Science, 266,* 294–298.

Angell, Marcia (2000, May 18). Is academic medicine for sale? [Editorial]. *New England Journal of Medicine, 342,* 1516–1518.

Angell, Marcia, & Kassirer, Jerome P. (1998, September 17). Alternative medicine: The risks of untested and unregulated remedies. *New England Journal of Medicine, 339,* 839–841.

Antonuccio, David O.; Danton, William G.; & DeNelsky, Garland Y.; et al. (1999). Raising questions about antidepressants. *Psychotherapy and Psychosomatics, 68,* 3–14.

APA Commission on Violence and Youth (1993). *Violence and youth: Psychology's response.* Washington, DC: American Psychological Association.

APA Research Office (1998). *APA doctorate employment survey, 1996.* Washington, DC: American Psychological Association.

Appiah, Kwame A. (1994). Beyond race: Fallacies of reactive Afrocentrism. *Skeptic, 2*(4), 104–107.

Appley, Mortimer, & Maher, Winifred B. (1989). *Social and behavioral sciences: Report of the Project 2061 Phase I social and behavioral sciences panel.* Available from the American Association for the Advancement of Science. 1333 H Street NW, Washington, DC, 20005.

Apter, Terri (1990). *Altered loves: Mothers and daughters during adolescence.* New York: St. Martin's Press.

Archer, John (1996). Sex differences in social behavior: Are the social role and evolutionary explanations compatible? *American Psychologist, 51,* 909–917.

Arendt, Hannah (1963). *Eichmann in Jerusalem: A report on the banality of evil.* New York: Viking.

Arkes, Hal R. (1993). Some practical judgment and decision-making research. In N. J. Castellan, Jr., et al. (eds.), *Individual and group decision making: Current issues.* Hillsdale, NJ: Erlbaum.

Arkes, Hal R.; Boehm, Lawrence E.; & Xu, Gang (1991). The determinants of judged validity. *Journal of Experimental Social Psychology, 27,* 576–605.

Arkes, Hal R.; Faust, David; Guilmette, Thomas J.; & Hart, Kathleen (1988). Eliminating the hindsight bias. *Journal of Applied Psychology, 73,* 305–307.

Arnett, Jeffrey J. (1999). Adolescent storm and stress, reconsidered. *American Psychologist, 54,* 317–326.

Aronson, Elliot (1999a). Dissonance, hypocrisy, and the self concept. In J. E. Harmon-Jones & J. Mills (eds.), *Cognitive dissonance: Progress on a pivotal theory in social psychology.* Washington: American Psychological Association.

Aronson, Elliot (1999b). *The social animal* (8th ed.). New York: W. H. Freeman.

Aronson, Elliot, & Mills, Judson (1959). The effect of severity of initiation on liking for a group. *Journal of Abnormal and Social Psychology, 59,* 177–181.

Aronson, Elliot, & Patnoe, Shelley (1997). *Cooperation in the classroom: The jigsaw method.* New York: Longman.

Aronson, Elliot; Wilson, Timothy D.; & Akert, Robin A. (1999). *Social psychology: The heart and the mind* (3rd ed.). New York: Longman.

Arroyo, Carmen G., & Zigler, Edward (1995). Racial identity, academic achievement, and the psychological well-being of economically disadvantaged adolescents. *Journal of Personality and Social Psychology, 69,* 903–914.

Asch, Solomon E. (1952). *Social psychology.* Englewood Cliffs, NJ: Prentice-Hall.

Asch, Solomon E. (1965). Effects of group pressure upon the modification and distortion of judgments. In H. Proshansky & B. Seidenberg (eds.), *Basic studies in social psychology.* New York: Holt, Rinehart and Winston.

Aserinsky, Eugene, & Kleitman, Nathaniel (1955). Two types of ocular motility occurring in sleep. *Journal of Applied Physiology, 8,* 1–10.

Askenasy, Hans (1994). *Cannibalism: From sacrifice to survival.* Amherst, NY: Prometheus.

Atkinson, John W. (ed.) (1958). *Motives in fantasy, action, and society.* Princeton, NJ: Van Nostrand.

Atkinson, Richard C., & Shiffrin, Richard M. (1968). Human memory: A proposed system and its control processes. In K. W. Spence & J. T. Spence (eds.), *The psychology of learning and motivation* (Vol. 2): *Advances in research and theory.* New York: Academic Press.

Atkinson, Richard C., & Shiffrin, Richard M. (1971, August). The control of short-term memory. *Scientific American, 225*(2), 82–90.

Azrin, Nathan H., & Foxx, Richard M. (1974). *Toilet training in less than a day.* New York: Simon & Schuster.

Azuma, Hiroshi (1984). Secondary control as a heterogeneous category. *American Psychologist, 39,* 970–971.

Bahrick, Harry P. (1984). Semantic memory content in permastore: Fifty years of memory for Spanish learned in school. *Journal of Experimental Psychology: General, 113,* 1–29.

Bahrick, Harry P.; Bahrick, Phyllis O.; & Wittlinger, Roy P. (1975). Fifty years of memory for names and faces: A cross-sectional approach. *Journal of Experimental Psychology: General, 104,* 54–75.

Bailey, J. Michael (1993, March 25). Science and the fear of knowledge. *Chicago Tribune,* opinion page.

Bailey, J. Michael; Gaulin, Steven; Agyei, Yvonne; & Gladue, Brian A. (1994). Effects of gender and sexual orientation on evolutionarily relevant aspects of human mating psychology. *Journal of Personality and Social Psychology, 66,* 1081–1093.

Bailey, J. Michael, & Pillard, Richard C. (1995). Genetics of human sexual orientation. *Annual Review of Sex Research, 6,* 126–150.

Bailey, J. Michael, & Zucker, Kenneth J. (1995). Childhood sex-typed behavior and sexual orientation: A conceptual analysis and quantitative review. *Developmental Psychology, 31,* 43–55.

Baillargeon, Renée (1994). How do infants learn about the physical world? *Current Directions in Psychological Science, 5,* 133–140.

Baker, Mark C. (1999). Innateness and the universality of universal grammar: Evidence from Mohawk. Paper presented at the annual meeting of the American Association for the Advancement of Science, Anaheim.

Baker, Robert A. (1992). *Hidden memories: Voices and visions from within.* Buffalo, NY: Prometheus.

Baltes, Paul B., & Graf, Peter (1996). Psychological aspects of aging: Facts and frontiers. In D. Magnusson (ed.), *The lifespan development of individuals.* Cambridge, England: Cambridge University Press.

Baltes, Paul B.; Sowarka, Doris; & Kliegl, Reinhold (1989). Cognitive training research on fluid intelligence in old age: What can older adults achieve by themselves? *Psychology and Aging, 4,* 217–221.

Bancroft, John; Sherwin, Barbara B.; Alexander, G. M.; et al. (1991). Oral contraceptives, androgens, and the sexuality of young women: II. The role of androgens. *Archives of Sexual Behavior, 20,* 121–135.

Bandura, Albert (1986). *Social foundations of thought and action: A social cognitive theory.* Englewood Cliffs, NJ: Prentice-Hall.

Bandura, Albert (1990). Self-regulation of motivation through goal systems. In R. A. Dienstbier (ed.), *Nebraska Symposium on Motivation* (Vol. 38). Lincoln: University of Nebraska Press.

Bandura, Albert (1991). Social cognitive theory of moral thought and action. In W. M. Kurtines & J. L. Gewirtz (eds.), *Handbook of moral behavior and development* (Vol. 1): *Theory.* Hillsdale, NJ: Erlbaum.

Bandura, Albert (1994). Self-efficacy. In *Encyclopedia of human behavior* (Vol. 4). Orlando, FL: Academic Press.

Bandura, Albert (1999). Moral disengagement in the perpetration of inhumanities. *Personality and Social Psychology Review, 3,* 193–209.

Bandura, Albert; Ross, Dorothea; & Ross, Sheila A. (1963). Vicarious reinforcement and imitative learning. *Journal of Abnormal and Social Psychology, 67,* 601–607.

Banks, Martin S. [with Philip Salapatek] (1984). Infant visual perception. In P. Mussen (series ed.), M. M. Haith & J. J. Campos (vol. eds.), *Handbook of child psychology* (Vol. 2): *Infancy and developmental psychobiology* (4th ed.). New York: Wiley.

Bardach, Ann Louise (1993, August). Tearing the veil. *Vanity Fair,* 123–127, 154–158.

Barinaga, Marcia (1992). Challenging the "no new neurons" dogma. *Science, 255,* 1646.

Barlow, David H. (1996). Health care policy, psychotherapy research, and the future of psychotherapy. *American Psychologist, 51,* 1050–1058.

Barlow, David H.; Chorpita, Bruce F.; & Turovsky, Julia (1996). Fear, panic, anxiety, and disorders of emotion. In D. A. Hope et al. (eds.), *Nebraska Symposium on Motivation* (Vol. 40): *Perspectives on anxiety, panic, and fear.* Lincoln: University of Nebraska Press.

Barnett, Rosalind C., & Rivers, Caryl (1996). *She works, he works: How two-income families are healthier, happier, and better off.* San Francisco: HarperCollins.

Barondes, Samuel H. (1998). *Mood genes: Hunting for origins of mania and depression.* New York: W. H. Freeman.

Barrish, Barbara M. (1996). The relationship of remembered parental physical punishment to adolescent self-concept. *Dissertation Abstracts International, Section B, 57,* 2171.

Bartlett, Frederic C. (1932). *Remembering.* Cambridge, England: Cambridge University Press.

Bashore, Theodore R.; Ridderinkhof, K. Richard; & van der Molen, Maurits W. (1997). The decline of cognitive processing speed in old age. *Current Directions in Psychological Science, 6,* 163–169.

Bauer, Patricia J., & Dow, Gina A. (1994). Episodic memory in 16- and 20-month-old children: Specifics are generalized but not forgotten. *Developmental Psychology, 30,* 403–417.

Baum, William M. (1994). *Understanding behaviorism: Science, behavior, and culture.* New York: Addison-Wesley.

Baumeister, Roy F. (2000). Gender differences in erotic plasticity: The female sex drive as socially flexible and responsive. *Psychological Bulletin, 126,* 347–374.

Baumrind, Diana (1991). Parenting styles and adolescent development. In R. Lerner, A. C. Petersen, & J. Brooks-Gunn (eds.), *The encyclopedia of adolescence.* New York: Garland.

Baxter, Lewis R.; Schwartz, Jeffrey M.; Bergman, Kenneth S.; et al. (1992). Caudate glucose metabolic rate changes with both drug and behavior therapy for obsessive–compulsive disorder. *Archives of General Psychiatry, 49,* 681–689.

Bechara, Antoine; Dermas, Hanna; Tranel, Daniel; & Damasio, Antonio R. (1997). Deciding advantageously before knowing the advantageous strategy. *Science, 275,* 1293–1294.

Beck, Aaron T. (1976). *Cognitive therapy and the emotional disorders.* New York: International Universities Press.

Beck, Aaron T. (1988). Cognitive approaches to panic disorder: Theory and therapy. In S. Rachman & J. D. Maser (eds.), *Panic: Psychological perspectives.* Hillsdale, NJ: Erlbaum.

Beck, Aaron T. (1991). Cognitive therapy: A 30-year retrospective. *American Psychologist, 46,* 368–375.

Becker, Ernest (1973). *The denial of death.* New York: Free Press.

Becker, Judith V.; Skinner, Linda J.; Abel, Gene G.; & Cichon, Joan (1984). Time-limited therapy with sexually dysfunctional sexually assaulted women. *Journal of Social Work and Human Sexuality, 3,* 97–115.

Becker, Marshall H. (1993). A medical sociologist looks at health promotion. *Journal of Health and Social Behavior, 34,* 1–6.

Beebe, B.; Gerstman, L.; Carson, B.; et al. (1982). Rhythmic communication in the mother–infant dyad. In M. Davis (ed.), *Interaction rhythms: Periodicity in communicative behavior.* New York: Human Sciences Press.

Beer, Jeremy M.; Arnold, Richard D.; & Loehlin, John C. (1998). Genetic and environmental influences on MMPI factor scales: Joint model fitting to twin and adoption data. *Journal of Personality and Social Psychology, 74,* 818–827.

Bekenstein, Jonathan W., & Lothman, Eric W. (1993). Dormancy of inhibitory interneurons in a model of temporal lobe epilepsy. *Science, 259,* 97–100.

Bell, Derrick (1992). *Faces at the bottom of the well: The permanence of racism.* New York: Basic Books.

Bellugi, Ursula; Bihrle, Amy; Neville, Helen; et al. (1992). Language, cognition, and brain organization in a neuro-developmental disorder. In M. R. Gunnar et al. (eds.), *Developmental behavioral neuroscience: The Minnesota Symposia on Child Psychology.* Hillsdale, NJ: Erlbaum.

Belsky, Jay; Campbell, Susan B.; Cohn, Jeffrey F.; & Moore, Ginger (1996). Instability of infant parent attachment security. *Developmental Psychology, 32,* 921–924.

Belsky, Jay; Hsieh, Kuang-Hua; & Crnic, Keith (1996). Infant positive and negative emotionality: One dimension or two? *Developmental Psychology, 32,* 289–298.

Bem, Sandra L. (1993). *The lenses of gender.* New Haven, CT: Yale University Press.

Benet-Martínez, Verónica, & John, Oliver P. (1998). *Los Cinco Grandes* across cultures and ethnic groups: Multitrait multimethod analyses of the Big Five in Spanish and English. *Journal of Personality and Social Psychology, 75,* 729–750.

Benjamin, Jessica (1988). *The bonds of love: Psychoanalysis, feminism, and the problem of domination.* New York: Pantheon.

Benjamin, Ludy T., Jr. (1998). Why Gorgeous George, and not Wilhelm Wundt, was the founder of psychology: A history of popular psychology in America. Invited address presented at the National Institute on the Teaching of Psychology, St. Petersburg Beach.

Berenbaum, Sheri A., & Snyder, Elizabeth (1995). Early hormonal influences on childhood sex-typed activity and playmate preferences: Implications for the development of sexual orientation. *Developmental Psychology, 31,* 31–42.

Berger, F.; Gage, F. H.; & Vijayaraghavan, S. (1998). Nicotinic receptor-induced apoptotic cell death of hippocampal progenitor cells. *Journal of Neuroscience, 18,* 6871–6881.

Berkowitz, Leonard (1999). Evil is more than banal: Situationism and the concept of evil. *Personality and Social Psychology Review, 3,* 246–253.

Bernieri, Frank J.; Gillis, John S.; Davis, Janet M.; & Grahe, Jon E. (1996). Dyad rapport and the accuracy of its judgment across situations: A lens model analysis. *Journal of Personality and Social Psychology, 71,* 110–129.

Bernstein, Anne E., & Warner, Gloria M. (1993). *An introduction to contemporary psychoanalysis.* New York: Jason Aronson.

Berry, John W. (1994). Acculturation stress. In W. J. Lonner & R. S. Malpass (eds.), *Psychology and culture.* Needham Heights, MA: Allyn & Bacon.

Berry, John W. (1998). Acculturation strategies: Theory, measurement and application. Paper presented at the annual meeting of the International Association for Cross-Cultural Psychology, Bellingham, WA.

Besalel-Azrin, V.; Azrin, N. H.; & Armstrong, P. M. (1977). The student-oriented classroom: A method of improving student conduct and satisfaction. *Behavior Therapy, 8,* 193–204.

Best, Deborah L., & Williams, John E. (1993). Cross-cultural viewpoint. In A. E. Beall & R. J. Sternberg (eds.), *The psychology of gender.* New York: Guilford Press.

Betancourt, Hector, & López, Steven R. (1993). The study of culture, ethnicity, and race in American psychology. *American Psychologist, 48,* 629–637.

Bettelheim, Bruno (1967). *The empty fortress.* New York: Free Press.

Beyerstein, Barry L. (1996). Graphology. In G. Stein (ed.), *The encyclopedia of the paranormal.* Amherst, NY: Prometheus Books.

Beyerstein, Barry L. (1999). Fringe psychotherapies: The public at risk. In W. Sampson (ed.), *A guide to alternative medicine.* London: Gordon and Breech.

Bianchi, Suzanne, & Robinson, John (2000). Paper presented at the annual meeting of the Population Association of America, Los Angeles.

Birdwhistell, Ray L. (1970). *Kinesics and context: Essays on body motion communication.* Philadelphia: University of Pennsylvania Press.

Bishop, Katherine M., & Wahlsten, Douglas (1997). Sex differences in the human corpus callosum: Myth or reality? *Neuroscience and Biobehavioral Reviews, 21,* 581–601.

Bjork, Daniel W. (1993). *B. F. Skinner: A life.* New York: Basic Books.

Blakemore, Colin, & Cooper, Grahame F. (1970). Development of the brain depends on the visual environment. *Nature, 228,* 477–478.

Blass, Thomas (1993). What we know about obedience: Distillations from 30 years of research on the Milgram paradigm. Paper presented at the annual meeting of the American Psychological Association, Toronto.

Blass, Thomas (ed.) (2000). *Obedience to authority: Current perspectives on the Milgram paradigm.* Mahwah, NJ: Erlbaum.

Blatt, Sidney J.; Auerbach, John S.; & Levy, Kenneth N. (1997). Mental representations in personality development, psychopathology, and the therapeutic process. *Review of General Psychology, 1,* 351–374.

Bleuler, Eugen (1911/1950). *Dementia praecox or the group of schizophrenias.* New York: International Universities Press.

Bliss, T. V., & Collingridge, G. L. (1993). A synaptic model of memory: Long-term potentiation in the hippocampus. *Nature, 361*(6407), 31–39.

Blos, Peter (1962). *On adolescence.* New York: Free Press.

Blouin, J. L.; Dombroski, B. A.; Nath, S. K.; et al. (1998). Schizophrenia susceptibility loci on chromosomes 13q32 and 8p21. *Nature Genetics, 20,* 70–73.

Blum, Deborah (1997). *Sex on the brain: The biological differences between men and women.* New York: Viking.

Bodenheimer, Thomas (2000, May 18). Uneasy alliance—clinical investigators and the pharmaceutical industry [Health policy report]. *New England Journal of Medicine, 342,* 1539–1544.

Boesch, Cristophe (1991). Teaching among wild chimpanzees. *Animal Behavior, 41,* 530–532.

Bohannon, John N., & Stanowicz, Laura (1988). The issue of negative evidence: Adult responses to children's language errors. *Developmental Psychology, 24,* 684–689.

Bohannon, John N., & Symons, Victoria (1988). Conversational conditions of children's imitation. Paper presented at the biennial Conference on Human Development, Charleston, South Carolina.

Bolshakov, Vadim Y., & Siegelbaum, Steven A. (1994). Postsynaptic induction and presynaptic expression of hippocampal long-term depression. *Science, 264,* 1148–1152.

Bond, Rod, & Smith, Peter B. (1996). Culture and conformity: A meta-analysis of studies using Asch's (1952b, 1956) line judgment task. *Psychological Bulletin, 119,* 111–137.

Bosworth, H. B., & Schaie, K. Warner (1999). Survival effects in cognitive function, cognitive style, and sociodemographic variables in the Seattle Longitudinal Study. *Experimental Aging Research, 25,* 121–139.

Bothwell, R. K., Deffenbacher, K. A., & Brigham, J. C. (1987). Correlation of eyewitness accuracy and confidence: Optimality hypothesis revised. *Journal of Applied Psychology, 72,* 691–698.

Bouchard, Claude; Tremblay, A.; Despres, J. P.; et al. (1990, May 24). The response to long-term overfeeding in identical twins. *New England Journal of Medicine, 322,* 1477–1482.

Bouchard, Thomas J., Jr. (1995). Nature's twice-told tale: Identical twins reared apart—what they tell us about human individuality. Paper presented at the annual meeting of the Western Psychological Association, Los Angeles.

Bouchard, Thomas J., Jr. (1997a). The genetics of personality. In K. Blum & E. P. Noble (eds.), *Handbook of psychiatric genetics.* Boca Raton, FL: CRC Press.

Bouchard, Thomas J., Jr. (1997b). IQ similarity in twins reared apart: Findings and responses to critics. In R. J. Sternberg & E. Grigorenko (eds.), *Intelligence: Heredity and environment.* New York: Cambridge University Press.

Bouchard, Thomas J., Jr., & McGue, Matthew (1981). Familial studies of intelligence: A review. *Science, 212,* 1055–1058.

Bousfield, W. A. (1953). The occurrence of clustering in the recall of randomly arranged associates. *Journal of General Psychology, 49,* 229–240.

Bowen, Murray (1978). *Family therapy in clinical practice.* New York: Jason Aronson.

Bower, Gordon H., & Clark, M. C. (1969). Narrative stories as mediators of serial learning. *Psychonomic Science, 14,* 181–182.

Bowers, Kenneth S.; Regehr, Glenn; Balthazard, Claude; & Parker, Kevin (1990). Intuition in the context of discovery. *Cognitive Psychology, 22,* 72–110.

Bowlby, John (1958). The nature of the child's tie to his mother. *International Journal of Psycho–Analysis, 39,* 350–373.

Bowlby, John (1969). *Attachment and loss* (Vol. 1): *Attachment.* New York: Basic Books.

Bowlby, John (1973). *Attachment and loss* (Vol. 2): *Separation.* New York: Basic Books.

Boysen, Sarah T., & Berntson, Gary G. (1989). Numerical competence in a chimpanzee (*Pan troglodytes*). *Journal of Comparative Psychology, 103,* 23–31.

Brainerd, C. J.; Reyna, V. F.; & Brandse, E. (1995). Are children's false memories more persistent than their true memories? *Psychological Science, 6,* 359–364.

Brannon, Elizabeth M., & Terrace, Herbert S. (1998). Ordering of the numerosities 1 to 9 by monkeys. *Science, 282,* 746–749.

Brauer, Markus; Wasel, Wolfgang; & Niedenthal, Paula (2000). Implicit and explicit components of prejudice. *Review of General Psychology, 4,* 79–101.

Breggin, Peter R. (1991). *Toxic psychiatry.* New York: St. Martin's Press.

Breland, Keller, & Breland, Marian (1961). The misbehavior of organisms. *American Psychologist, 16,* 681–684.

Brennan, Patricia A., & Mednick, Sarnoff A. (1994). Learning theory approach to the deterrence of criminal recidivism. *Journal of Abnormal Psychology, 103,* 430–440.

Brewer, Marilynn B. (1993). Social identity, distinctiveness, and in-group homogeneity. *Social Cognition, 11,* 150–164.

Brewer, Marilynn B. (1999). The psychology of prejudice: Ingroup love or outgroup hate? *Journal of Social Issues, 55,* 429–444.

Brewer, Marilynn B., & Gardner, Wendi (1996). Who is this "we"? Levels of collective identity and self representations. *Journal of Personality and Social Psychology, 71,* 83–93.

Brigham, John C., & Malpass, Roy S. (1985). The role of experience and contact in the recognition of faces of own- and other-race persons. *Journal of Social Issues, 41,* 139–155.

Brockner, Joel, & Rubin, Jeffrey Z. (1985). *Entrapment in escalating conflicts: A social psychological analysis.* New York: Springer-Verlag.

Brodsky, Annette M. (1982). Sex, race, and class issues in psychotherapy research. In J. H. Harvey & M. M. Parks (eds.), *Psychotherapy research and behavior change* (Vol. 1): *The APA Master Lecture Series.* Washington, DC: American Psychological Association.

Brody, Nathan (1990). Behavior therapy versus placebo: Comment on Bowers and Clum's meta-analysis. *Psychological Bulletin, 107,* 106–109.

Bromberger, Joyce T., & Matthews, Karen A. (1996). A "feminine" model of vulnerability to depressive symptoms: A longitudinal investigation of middle-aged women. *Journal of Personality and Social Psychology, 70,* 591–598.

Brooks-Gunn, J. (1986). Differentiating premenstrual symptoms and syndromes. *Psychosomatic Medicine, 48,* 385–387.

Brown, George W. (1993). Life events and affective disorder: Replications and limitations. *Psychosomatic Medicine, 55,* 248–259.

Brown, Jonathon D. (1991). Staying fit and staying well. *Journal of Personality and Social Psychology, 60,* 555–561.

Brown, Robert, & Middlefell, Robert (1989). Fifty-five years of cocaine dependence [Letter]. *British Journal of Addiction, 84,* 946.

Brown, Roger (1986). *Social psychology* (2nd ed.). New York: Free Press.

Brown, Roger; Cazden, Courtney; & Bellugi, Ursula (1969). The child's grammar from I to III. In J. P. Hill (ed.), *Minnesota Symposium on Child Psychology* (Vol. 2). Minneapolis: University of Minnesota Press.

Brown, Roger, & Kulik, James (1977). Flashbulb memories. *Cognition, 5,* 73–99.

Brown, Roger, & McNeill, David (1966). The "tip of the tongue" phenomenon. *Journal of Verbal Learning and Verbal Behavior, 5,* 325–337.

Brown, Ryan P., & Josephs, Robert A. (1999). A burden of proof: Stereotype relevance and gender differences in math performance. *Journal of Personality and Social Psychology, 76,* 246–257.

Brown, Steven P. (1996). A meta-analysis and review of organizational research on job involvement. *Psychological Bulletin, 120,* 235–255.

Brownell, Kelly D., & Rodin, Judith (1994). The dieting maelstrom: Is it possible and advisable to lose weight? *American Psychologist, 49,* 781–791.

Buck, Ross (1984). *The communication of emotion.* New York: Guilford Press.

Buck, Ross, & Teng, Wan-Cheng (1987). Spontaneous emotional communication and social biofeedback: A crosscultural study of emotional expression and communication in Chinese and Taiwanese students. Paper presented at the annual meeting of the American Psychological Association, New York.

Budiansky, Stephen (1998). *If a lion could talk: Animal intelligence and the evolution of consciousness.* New York: Free Press.

Burgess, Cheryl A.; Kirsch, Irving; Shane, Howard; et al. (1998). Facilitated communication as an ideomotor response. *Psychological Science, 9,* 71–74.

Burke, Deborah M.; MacKay, Donald G.; Worthley, Joanna S.; & Wade, Elizabeth (1991). On the tip of the tongue: What causes word finding failures in young and older adults? *Journal of Memory and Language, 30,* 237–246.

Burstyn, Linda (1995, October). Female circumcision comes to America. *Atlantic Monthly,* 28–35.

Bushman, Brad J. (1995). Moderating role of trait aggressiveness in the effects of violent media on aggression. *Journal of Personality and Social Psychology, 69,* 950–960.

Bushman, Brad J.; Baumeister, Roy; & Stack, Angela D. (1999). Catharsis, aggression, and persuasive influence: Self-fulfilling or self-defeating prophecies? *Journal of Personality and Social Psychology, 76,* 367–376.

Buss, David M. (1994). *The evolution of desire: Strategies of human mating.* New York: Basic Books.

Buss, David M. (1995). Evolutionary psychology: A new paradigm for psychological science. *Psychological Inquiry, 6,* 1–30.

Buss, David M. (1996). Sexual conflict: Can evolutionary and feminist perspectives converge? In D. M. Buss & N. Malamuth (eds.), *Sex, power, conflict: Evolutionary and feminist perspectives.* New York: Oxford University Press.

Bussey, Kay, & Bandura, Albert (1992). Self-regulatory mechanisms governing gender development. *Child Development, 63,* 1236–1250.

Butcher, James N.; Lim, Jeeyoung; & Nezami, Elahe (1998). Objective study of abnormal personality in cross-cultural settings: The MMPI-2. *Journal of Cross-Cultural Psychology, 29,* 189–211.

Butler, S.; Chalder, T.; Ron, M.; et al. (1991). Cognitive behaviour therapy in chronic fatigue syndrome. *Journal of Neurology, Neurosurgery & Psychiatry, 54,* 153–158.

Buunk, Bram; Angleitner, Alois; Oubaid, Viktor; & Buss, David M. (1996). Sex differences in jealousy in evolutionary and cultural perspective: Tests from the Netherlands, Germany, and the United States. *Psychological Science, 7,* 359–363.

Byne, William (1993). Sexual orientation and brain structure: Adding up the evidence. Paper presented at the annual meeting of the International Academy of Sex Research, Pacific Grove, CA.

Byne, William (1995). Science and belief: Psychobiological research on sexual orientation. *Journal of Homosexuality, 28,* 303–344.

Cabezas, A.; Tam, T. M.; Lowe, B. M.; et al. (1989). Empirical study of barriers to upward mobility of Asian Americans in the San Francisco Bay area. In G. Nomura (ed.), *Frontiers of Asian American studies.* Pullman: Washington State University Press.

Cahill, Larry; Prins, Bruce; Weber, Michael; & McGaugh, James L. (1994). ß-Adrenergic activation and memory for emotional events. *Nature, 371,* 702–704.

Cain, Kathleen M., & Dweck, Carol S. (1995, January). The relation between motivational patterns and achievement cognitions through the elementary school years. *Merrill-Palmer Quarterly, 41,* 25–52.

Camera, Wayne J., & Schneider, Dianne L. (1994). Integrity tests: Facts and unresolved issues. *American Psychologist, 49,* 112–119.

Campbell, Anne (1993). *Men, women, and aggression.* New York: Basic Books.

Campbell, Frances A., & Ramey, Craig T. (1995). Cognitive and school outcomes for high risk students at middle adolescence: Positive effects of early intervention. *American Educational Research Journal, 32,* 743–772.

Campbell, Jennifer; Trapnell, Paul D.; Heine, Steven J.; et al. (1996). Self-concept clarity: Measurement, personality correlates, and cultural boundaries. *Journal of Personality and Social Psychology, 70,* 141–156.

Campbell, Joseph (1949/1968). *The hero with 1,000 faces* (2nd ed.). Princeton, NJ: Princeton University Press.

Campbell, W. Keith, & Sedikides, Constantine (1999). Self-threat magnifies the self-serving bias: A meta-analytic integration. *Review of General Psychology, 3,* 23–43.

Campos, Joseph J.; Barrett, Karen C.; Lamb, Michael E.; et al. (1984). Socioemotional development. In P. H. Mussen (series ed.), M. M. Haith & J. J. Campos (vol. eds.), *Handbook of child psychology* (Vol. 2): *Infancy and developmental psychobiology* (4th ed.). New York: Wiley.

Canetto, Silvia S. (1992). Suicide attempts and substance abuse: Similarities and differences. *Journal of Psychology, 125,* 605–620.

Caramazza, Alfonso, & Hillis, Argye E. (1991, February 28). Lexical organization of nouns and verbs in the brain. *Nature, 349,* 788–790.

Carver, Charles S., & Baird, Eryn (1998). The American dream revisited: Is it *what* you want or *why* you want it that matters? *Psychological Science, 9,* 289–292.

Carver, Charles S.; Pozo, Christina; Harris, Suzanne D.; et al. (1993). How coping mediates the effect of optimism on distress: A study of women with early stage breast cancer. *Journal of Personality and Social Psychology, 65,* 375–390.

Carver, Charles S., & Scheier, Michael F. (1999). Optimism. In C. R. Snyder (ed.), *Coping: The psychology of what works.* New York: Oxford University Press.

Cassingham, Randy (1998). The Skeptics Society 1997 Dumbth award for the dumbest thing anyone did in 1997. *Skeptic, 6*(2), 14–15.

Cattell, Raymond B. (1965). *The scientific analysis of personality.* Baltimore: Penguin.

Cattell, Raymond B. (1973). *Personality and mood by questionnaire.* San Francisco: Jossey-Bass.

Ceci, Stephen J., & Bruck, Maggie (1995). *Jeopardy in the courtroom: A scientific analysis of children's testimony.* Washington, DC: American Psychological Association.

Cejka, Mary Ann, & Eagly, Alice H. (1999). Gender-stereotypic images of occupations correspond to the sex segregation of employment. *Personality and Social Psychology Bulletin, 25,* 413–423.

Celis, William, III (1993, August 1). Down from the self-esteem high. *New York Times,* Education Section.

Cermak, Laird S., & Craik, Fergus I. M. (eds.) (1979). *Levels of processing in human memory.* Hillsdale, NJ: Erlbaum.

Chambless, Dianne L., & the Division 12 Task Force (1996). An update on empirically validated therapies. *The Clinical Psychologist, 49,* 5–18.

Chambless, Dianne L.; & the Task Force on Psychological Interventions (1998). Update on empirically validated therapies: II. *The Clinical Psychologist, 51,* 3–16.

Chance, June E., & Goldstein, Alvin G. (1995). The other-race effect in eyewitness identification. In S. L. Sporer, G. Koehnken, & R. S. Malpass (eds.), *Psychological issues in eyewitness identification.* Hillsdale, NJ: Erlbaum.

Chance, Paul (1988, October). Knock wood. *Psychology Today,* 68–69.

Chance, Paul (1989, November). The other 90%. *Psychology Today,* 20–21.

Chance, Paul (1999). *Learning and behavior* (4th ed.). Pacific Grove, CA: Brooks/Cole.

Chang, Edward C. (1998). Dispositional optimism and primary and secondary appraisal of a stressor. *Journal of Personality and Social Psychology, 74,* 1109–1120.

Cheney, Dorothy L., & Seyfarth, Robert M. (1985). Vervet monkey alarm calls: Manipulation through shared information? *Behavior, 94,* 150–166.

Chipuer, Heather M.; Rovine, Michael J.; & Plomin, Robert (1990). LISREL modeling: Genetic and environmental influences on IQ revisited. *Intelligence, 14,* 11–29.

Chodorow, Nancy (1978). *The reproduction of mothering.* Berkeley: University of California Press.

Chodorow, Nancy (1992). *Feminism and psychoanalytic theory.* New Haven, CT: Yale University Press.

Choi, Incheol; Nisbett, Richard E.; & Norenzayan, Ara (1999). Causal attribution across cultures: Variation and universality. *Psychological Bulletin, 125,* 47–63.

Chomsky, Noam (1957). *Syntactic structures.* The Hague, Netherlands: Mouton.

Chomsky, Noam (1980). Initial states and steady states. In M. Piatelli-Palmerini (ed.), *Language and learning: The debate between Jean Piaget and Noam Chomsky.* Cambridge, MA: Harvard University Press.

Chorney, M. J.; Chorney, K.; Seese, N.; et al. (1998). A quantitative trait locus associated with cognitive ability in children. *Psychological Science, 9,* 159–166.

Chorpita, Bruce F., & Barlow, David H. (1998). The development of anxiety: The role of control in the early environment. *Psychological Bulletin, 124,* 3–21.

Chrisler, Joan C. (2000). PMS as a culture-bound syndrome. In J. C. Chrisler, C. Golden, & P. D. Rozee (eds.), *Lectures on the psychology of women* (2nd ed.). New York: McGraw-Hill.

Christensen, Andrew, & Jacobson, Neil S. (2000). *Reconcilable differences.* New York: Guilford.

Chua, Streamson C., Jr.; Chung, Wendy K.; Wu-Peng, S. Sharon; et al. (1996). Phenotypes of mouse *diabetes* and rat *fatty* due to mutations in the OB (leptin) receptor. *Science, 271,* 994–996.

Cialdini, Robert B. (1993). *Influence: The psychology of persuasion.* New York: Quill/Morrow.

Cialdini, Robert B.; Trost, Melanie R.; & Newsom, Jason T. (1995). Preference for consistency: The development of a valid measure and the discovery of surprising behavioral implications. *Journal of Personality and Social Psychology, 69,* 318–328.

Cinque, Guglielmo (1999). *Adverbs and functional heads: A cross-linguistic approach.* New York: Oxford University Press.

Cioffi, Frank (1998). *Freud and the question of pseudoscience.* Chicago, IL: Open Court.

Clark, David M., & Ehlers, A. (1993). An overview of the cognitive theory and treatment of panic disorder. *Applied and Preventive Psychology, 2,* 131–139.

Clark, Margaret S.; Milberg, Sandra; & Erber, Ralph (1987). Arousal state dependent memory: Evidence and some implications for understanding social judgments and social behavior. In K. Fiedler & J. P. Forgas (eds.), *Affect, cognition and social behavior.* Toronto, Canada: Hogrefe.

Clopton, Nancy A., & Sorell, Gwendolyn T. (1993). Gender differences in moral reasoning: Stable or situational? *Psychology of Women Quarterly, 17,* 85–101.

Coats, Erik J.; Janoff-Bulman, Ronnie; & Alpert, Nancy (1996). Approach versus avoidance goals: Differences in self-evaluation and well-being. *Personality and Social Psychology Bulletin, 22,* 1057–1067.

Coffey, C. E. (1993). Structural brain imaging and ECT. In C. E. Coffey (ed.), *The clinical science of electroconvulsive therapy.* Washington, DC: American Psychiatric Association.

Cohen, David B. (1999). *Stranger in the nest: Do parents really shape their child's personality, intelligence, or character?* New York: Wiley.

Cohen, Dov (1998). Culture, social organization, and patterns of violence. *Journal of Personality and Social Psychology, 75,* 408–419.

Cohen, Dov; Nisbett, Richard E.; Bowdle, Brian F.; & Schwarz, Norbert (1996). Insult, aggression, and the Southern culture of honor: An "experimental ethnography." *Journal of Personality and Social Psychology, 70,* 945–960.

Cohn, Lawrence D. (1991). Sex differences in the course of personality development: A meta-analysis. *Psychological Bulletin, 109,* 252–266.

Cole, David (1999). *No equal justice: Race and class in the American criminal justice system.* New York: New Press.

Collins, Allan M., & Loftus, Elizabeth F. (1975). A spreading-activation theory of semantic processing. *Psychological Review, 82,* 407–428.

Collins, Barry E., & Brief, Diana E. (1995). Using person-perception vignette methodologies to uncover the symbolic meanings of teacher behaviors in the Milgram paradigm. *Journal of Social Issues, 51,* 89–106.

Collins, Bud (1981, August 30). Rivals at Flushing Meadows. *The New York Times Magazine,* 71.

Colman, Andrew (1991). Crowd psychology in South African murder trials. *American Psychologist, 46,* 1071–1079.

Comas-Díaz, Lillian, & Greene, Beverly (1994). *Women of color: Integrating ethnic and gender identities in psychotherapy.* New York: Guilford Press.

Condon, William (1982). Cultural microrhythms. In M. Davis (ed.), *Interaction rhythms: Periodicity in communicative behavior.* New York: Human Sciences Press.

Connors, Gerard J.; Carroll, Kathleen M.; DiClemente, Carlo C.; et al. (1997). The therapeutic alliance and its relationship to alcoholism treatment participation and outcome. *Journal of Consulting and Clinical Psychology, 65,* 588–598.

Cooper, M. Lynne; Shapiro, Cheryl M.; & Powers, Anne M. (1998). Motivations for sex and risky sexual behavior among adolescents and young adults: A functional perspective. *Journal of Personality and Social Psychology, 75,* 1528–1558.

Copi, Irving M., & Burgess-Jackson, Keith (1992). *Informal logic* (2nd ed.). New York: Macmillan.

Corder, E. H.; Saunders, A. M.; Strittmatter, W. J.; et al. (1993). Gene dose of apolipoprotein E type 4 allele and the risk of Alzheimer's disease in late onset families. *Science, 261,* 921–923.

Coren, Stanley (1996). Daylight saving time and traffic accidents. *New England Journal of Medicine, 334,* 924.

Corkin, Suzanne (1984). Lasting consequences of bilateral medial temporal lobectomy: Clinical course and experimental findings in H. M. *Seminars in Neurology, 4,* 249–259.

Corkin, Suzanne; Amaral, David G.; Gonzalez, R. Gilberto; et al. (1997). H. M.'s medial temporal lobe lesion: Findings from magnetic resonance imaging. *Journal of Neuroscience, 17,* 3964–3979.

Cose, Ellis (1994). *The rage of a privileged class.* New York: HarperCollins.

Cosmides, Leda; Tooby, John; & Barkow, Jerome H. (1992). Introduction: Evolutionary psychology and conceptual integration. In J. H. Barkow, L. Cosmides, & J. Tooby (eds.), *The adapted mind: Evolutionary psychology and the generation of culture.* New York: Oxford University Press.

Costa, Paul T., Jr.; McCrae, Robert R.; Martin, Thomas A.; et al. (1999). Personality development from adolescence through adulthood: Further cross-cultural comparisons of age differences. In V. J. Molfese & D. Molfese (eds.), *Temperament and personality development across the life span.* Hillsdale, NJ: Erlbaum.

Cowen, Emory L.; Wyman, Peter A.; Work, William C.; & Parker, Gayle R. (1990). The Rochester Child Resilience Project (RCRP): Overview and summary of first year findings. *Development and Psychopathology, 2,* 193–212.

Crain, Stephen (1991). Language acquisition in the absence of experience. *Behavioral & Brain Sciences, 14,* 597–650.

Cramer, Phebe (2000). Defense mechanisms in psychology today. *American Psychologist, 55,* 637–646.

Crawford, Mary, & Marecek, Jeanne (1989). Psychology constructs the female: 1968–1988. *Psychology of Women Quarterly, 13,* 147–165.

Crews, Frederick (1995). *The memory wars: Freud's legacy in dispute.* New York: New York Review of Books.

Crews, Frederick (ed.) (1998). *Unauthorized Freud: Doubters confront a legend.* New York: Viking.

Crick, Francis, & Mitchison, Graeme (1995). REM sleep and neural nets. *Behavioural Brain Research, 69,* 147–155.

Crick, Nicki R.; Werner, Nicole E.; Casas, Juan F.; et al. (1999). Childhood aggression and gender: A new look at an old problem. In D. Bernstein (ed.), *Nebraska Symposium on Motivation* (Vol. 45): *Gender and motivation.* Lincoln: University of Nebraska Press.

Critser, Greg (1996, June). Oh, how happy we will be: Pills, paradise, and the profits of the drug companies. *Harper's,* 39–48.

Crocker, Jennifer, & Major, Brenda (1989). Social stigma and self-esteem: The self-protective properties of stigma. *Psychological Review, 96,* 608–630.

Croizen, Jean-Claude, & Claire, Theresa (1998). Extending the concept of stereotype threat to social class: The intellectual underperformance of students from low socioeconomic backgrounds. *Personality and Social Psychology Bulletin, 24,* 588–594.

Cross, William E. (1971). The Negro-to-Black conversion experience: Toward a psychology of Black liberation. *Black World, 20,* 13–27.

Cross, William E. (1991). *Shades of Black: Diversity in African-American identity.* Philadelphia, PA: Temple University Press.

Cross, William E., Jr., & Fhagen-Smith, Peony (1996). Nigrescence and ego identity development: Accounting for differential black identity patterns. In P. B. Pedersen, J. G. Draguns, W. J. Lonner, & J. E. Trimble (eds.), *Counseling across cultures* (4th ed.). Thousand Oaks, CA: Sage.

Cubelli, Roberto (1991, September 19). A selective deficit for writing vowels in acquired dysgraphia. *Nature, 353,* 209–210.

Culbertson, Frances M. (1997). Depression and gender: An international review. *American Psychologist, 52,* 25–31.

Currie, Elliot (1998). *Crime and punishment in America.* New York: Henry Holt.

Curtiss, Susan (1977). *Genie: A psycholinguistic study of a modern-day "wild child."* New York: Academic Press.

Curtiss, Susan (1982). Developmental dissociations of language and cognition. In L. Obler & D. Fein (eds.), *Exceptional language and linguistics.* New York: Academic Press.

Cutler, Brian L., & Penrod, Steven D. (1995). *Mistaken identification: The eyewitness, psychology, and the law.* New York: Cambridge University Press.

Czeisler, C. A.; Shanahan, T. L.; Klerman, E. B.; et al. (1995). Suppression of melatonin secretion in some blind patients by exposure to bright light. *New England Journal of Medicine, 332,* 6–11.

Dadds, Mark R.; Bovbjerg, Dana H.; Redd, William H.; & Cutmore, Tim R. H. (1997). Imagery in human classical conditioning. *Psychological Bulletin, 122,* 89–103.

Daly, Martin, & Wilson, Margo (1983). *Sex, evolution, and behavior* (2nd ed.). Belmont, CA: Wadsworth.

Damasio, Antonio R. (1990). Category-related recognition defects as a clue to the neural substrates of knowledge. *Trends in Neurosciences, 13,* 95–98.

Damasio, Antonio R. (1994). *Descartes' error: Emotion, reason, and the human brain.* New York: Grosset/Putnam.

Damasio, Antonio R. (1999). *The feeling of what happens: Body and emotion in the making of consciousness.* New York: Harcourt Brace.

Damasio, Hanna; Grabowski, Thomas J.; Frank, Randall; et al. (1994). The return of Phineas Gage: Clues about the brain from the skull of a famous patient. *Science, 264,* 1102–1105.

Damasio, Hanna; Grabowski, Thomas J.; Tranel, Daniel; et al. (1996). A neural basis for lexical retrieval. *Nature, 380,* 499–505.

Darley, John M. (1993). Research on morality: Possible approaches, actual approaches [Review of *Handbook of moral behavior and development*]. *Psychological Science, 4,* 353–357.

Darley, John M. (1995). Constructive and destructive obedience: A taxonomy of principal agent relationships. *Journal of Social Issues, 51*(3), 125–154.

Darwin, Charles (1859/1964). *On the origin of species* [a facsimile of the first edition, edited by Ernst Mayer, 1964]. Cambridge, MA: Harvard University Press.

Darwin, Charles (1872/1965). *The expression of the emotions in man and animals.* Chicago: University of Chicago Press.

Darwin, Charles (1874). *The descent of man and selection in relation to sex* (2nd ed.). New York: Hurst.

Dasen, Pierre R. (1994). Culture and cognitive development from a Piagetian perspective. In W. J. Lonner & R. S. Malpass (eds.), *Psychology and culture.* Needham Heights, MA: Allyn & Bacon.

Dasgupta, Nilanjana (1999). Exposure to admired group members reduces implicit prejudice. Paper presented at the annual meeting of the American Psychological Society, Denver.

Daum, Irene, & Schugens, Markus M. (1996). On the cerebellum and classical conditioning. *Psychological Science, 5,* 58–61.

Davey, Graham C. (1992). Classical conditioning and the acquisition of human fears and phobias: A review and synthesis of the literature. *Advances in Behaviour Research and Therapy, 14,* 29–66.

Davidson, Richard J. (1995). Cerebral asymmetry, emotion, and affective style. In R. J. Davidson & K. Hugdahl (eds.), *Brain asymmetry.* Cambridge, MA: MIT Press.

Davis, David B. (1984). *Slavery and human progress.* New York: Oxford University Press.

Dawes, Robyn M. (1994). *House of cards: Psychology and psychotherapy built on myth.* New York: Free Press.

Dawes, Robyn M.; Faust, David; & Meehl, Paul E. (1989). Clinical versus actuarial judgment. *Science, 243,* 1668–1674.

Dawson, Neal V.; Arkes, Hal R.; Siciliano, C.; et al. (1988). Hindsight bias: An impediment to accurate probability estimation in clinicopathologic conferences. *Medical Decision Making, 8*(4), 259–264.

Dean, Geoffrey (1987, Spring). Does astrology need to be true? Part II. The answer is no. *Skeptical Inquirer, 11,* 257–273.

Deaux, Kay (1985). Sex and gender. *Annual Review of Psychology, 36,* 49–81.

Deaux, Kay, & Major, Brenda (1990). A social-psychological model of gender. In D. L. Rhode (ed.), *Theoretical perspectives on sexual difference.* New Haven, CT: Yale University Press.

de Bono, Edward (1971). *The dog exercising machine.* New York: Touchstone.

de Bono, Edward (1985). *de Bono's thinking course.* New York: Facts on File.

Deci, Edward L.; Koestner, Richard; & Ryan, Richard M. (1999). A meta-analytic review of experiments examining the effects of extrinsic rewards on intrinsic motivation. *Psychological Bulletin, 125,* 627–668.

Deci, Edward L., & Ryan, Richard M. (1987). The support of autonomy and the control of behavior. *Journal of Personality and Social Psychology, 53,* 1024–1037.

Deffenbacher, Jerry L.; Dahlen, Eric R.; Lynch, Rebekah S.; et al. (1998). Application of Beck's cognitive therapy to general anger reduction. Paper presented at the annual meeting of the American Psychological Association, San Francisco.

de Lacoste-Utamsing, Christine, & Holloway, Ralph L. (1982). Sexual dimorphism in the human corpus callosum. *Science, 216,* 1431–1432.

DeLoache, Judy S. (1995). Early understanding and use of symbols: The model model. *Current Directions in Psychological Science, 4,* 109–113.

Dement, William (1978). *Some must watch while some must sleep.* New York: W. W. Norton.

Dement, William C., & Vaughan, Christopher (1999). *The promise of sleep.* New York: Delacorte.

Dennett, Daniel C. (1991). *Consciousness explained.* Boston: Little, Brown.

de Rivera, Joseph (1989). Comparing experiences across cultures: Shame and guilt in America and Japan. *Hiroshima Forum for Psychology, 14,* 13–20.

Deutsch, Morton (1949). An experimental study of the effects of cooperation and competition among group processes. *Human Relations, 2,* 199–231.

Deutsch, Morton (1980). Fifty years of conflict. In L. Festinger (ed.), *Retrospections on social psychology.* New York: Oxford University Press.

Devanand, Devangere P.; Dwork, Andrew J.; Hutchinson, Edward R.; et al. (1994). Does ECT alter brain structure? *American Journal of Psychiatry, 151,* 957–970.

Devine, Patricia G. (1995). Breaking the prejudice habit: Progress and prospects. Award address presented at the annual meeting of the American Psychological Association, New York.

Devine, Patricia G.; Evett, Sophia R.; & Vasquez-Suson, Kristin A. (1996). Exploring the interpersonal

dynamics of intergroup contact. In R. M. Sorrentino & E. T. Higgins (eds.), *Handbook of motivation and cognition* (Vol. 3): *The interpersonal context.* New York: Guilford Press.

Devlin, B.; Daniels, Michael; & Roeder, Kathryn (1997). The heritability of IQ. *Nature, 388,* 468–471.

de Waal, Frans (1997, July). Are we in anthropodenial? *Discover,* 50-53.

De Wolff, Marianne, & van Ijzendoorn, Marinus H. (1997). Sensitivity and attachment: A meta-analysis on parental antecedents of infant attachment. *Child Development, 68,* 571–591.

Dewsbury, Donald A. (1996). Animal research: Getting in and getting out. *The General Psychologist, 32,* 19–25.

Diamond, Jared (1997). *Guns, germs, and steel: The fates of human societies.* New York: W. W. Norton.

Diamond, Marian C. (1993, Winter–Spring). An optimistic view of the aging brain. *Generations, 17,* 31–33.

Dickinson, Alyce M. (1989). The detrimental effects of extrinsic reinforcement on "intrinsic motivation." *The Behavior Analyst, 12,* 1–15.

Dien, Dora S. (1982). A Chinese perspective on Kohlberg's theory of moral development. *Developmental Review, 2,* 331–341.

Dien, Dora S. (1999). Chinese authority-directed orientation and Japanese peer-group orientation: Questioning the notion of collectivism. *Review of General Psychology, 3,* 372–385.

Digman, John M. (1996). The curious history of the five-factor model. In J. S. Wiggins (ed.), *The five-factor model of personality: Theoretical perspectives.* New York: Guilford Press.

Digman, John M., & Shmelyov, Alexander G. (1996). The structure of temperament and personality in Russian children. *Journal of Personality and Social Psychology, 71,* 341–351.

DiLalla, David.; Carey, Gregory; Gottesman, Irving I.; & Bouchard, Thomas J., Jr. (1996). Heritability of MMPI personality indicators of psychopathology in twins reared apart. *Journal of Abnormal Psychology, 105,* 491–499.

di Leonardo, Micaela (1987). The female world of cards and holidays: Women, families, and the work of kinship. *Signs, 12,* 1–20.

Dinges, David F.; Whitehouse, Wayne G.; Orne, Emily C.; et al. (1992). Evaluating hypnotic memory enhancement (hypermnesia and reminiscence) using multitrial forced recall. *Journal of Experimental Psychology: Learning, Memory, and Cognition, 18,* 1139–1147.

Dinnerstein, Dorothy (1976). *The mermaid and the Minotaur: Sexual arrangements and human malaise.* New York: Harper & Row.

Dinsmoor, James A. (1992). Setting the record straight: The social views of B. F. Skinner. *American Psychologist, 47,* 1454–1463.

Dollard, John, & Miller, Neal E. (1950). *Personality and psychotherapy: An analysis in terms of learning, thinking, and culture.* New York: McGraw-Hill.

Domhoff, G. William (1996). *Finding meaning in dreams: A quantitative approach.* New York: Plenum.

Doty, Richard M.; Peterson, Bill E.; & Winter, David G. (1991). Threat and authoritarianism in the United States, 1978–1987. *Journal of Personality and Social Psychology, 61,* 629–640.

Dovidio, John F.; Gaertner, Samuel L.; & Validzic, Ana (1998). Intergroup bias: Status, differentiation, and a common in-group identity. *Journal of Personality and Social Psychology, 75,* 109–120.

Downey, Geraldine; Freitas, Antonio L.; Michaelis, Benjamin; & Khouri, Hala (1998). The self-fulfilling prophecy in close relationships: Rejection sensitivity and rejection by romantic partners. *Journal of Personality and Social Psychology, 75,* 545–560.

Druckman, Daniel, & Swets, John A. (eds.) (1988). *Enhancing human performance: Issues, theories, and techniques.* Washington, DC: National Academy Press.

Dweck, Carol S. (1992). The study of goals in psychology. *Psychological Science, 3,* 165–167.

Dweck, Carol S., & Sorich, Lisa A. (1999). Mastery-oriented thinking. In C. R. Snyder (ed.), *Coping: The psychology of what works.* New York: Oxford University Press.

Dym, Barry, & Glenn, Michael L. (1993). *Couples: Exploring and understanding the cycles of intimate relationships.* New York: HarperCollins.

Eaton, William W.; Bilker, Warren; Haro, Josep M.; et al. (1992a). Long-term course of hospitalization for schizophrenia: II. Change with passage of time. *Schizophrenia Bulletin, 18,* 229–241.

Eaton, William W.; Mortensen, Preben B.; Herrman, Helen; et al. (1992b). Long-term course of hospitalization for schizophrenia: I. Risk for rehospitalization. *Schizophrenia Bulletin, 18,* 217–228.

Ebbinghaus, Hermann M. (1885/1913). *Memory: A contribution to experimental psychology* (H. A. Ruger & C. E. Bussenius, trans.). New York: Teachers College Press, Columbia University.

Eberlin, Michael; McConnachie, Gene; Ibel, Stuart; & Volpe, Lisa (1993). Facilitated communication: A failure to replicate the phenomenon. *Journal of Autism and Developmental Disorders, 23,* 507–530.

Eccles, Jacquelynne S. (1993). Parents and gender-role socialization during the middle childhood and adolescent years. In S. Oskamp & M. Costanzo (eds.), *The Claremont Symposium on Applied Social Psychology: Gender issues in contemporary society.* Newbury Park, CA: Sage.

Eccles, Jacquelynne S.; Jacobs, Janis E.; & Harold, Rena D. (1990). Gender role stereotypes, expectancy effects, and parents' socialization of gender differences. *Journal of Social Issues, 46,* 183–201.

Eckensberger, Lutz H. (1994). Moral development and its measurement across cultures. In W. J. Lonner & R. Malpass (eds.), *Psychology and culture.* Needham Heights, MA: Allyn & Bacon.

Edelson, Marshall (1994). Can psychotherapy research answer this psychotherapist's questions? In P. F. Talley, H. H. Strupp, & S. F. Butler (eds.), *Psychotherapy research and practice: Bridging the gap.* New York: Basic Books.

Edwards, Carolyn P. (1987). Culture and the construction of moral values. In J. Kagan & S. Lamb (eds.), *The emergence of morality in young children.* Chicago: University of Chicago Press.

Edwards, Kari, & Smith, Edward E. (1996). A disconfirmation bias in the evaluation of arguments. *Journal of Personality and Social Psychology, 71,* 5–24.

Ehrenreich, Barbara (1978). *For her own good: 150 years of the experts' advice to women.* New York: Doubleday.

Eichenbaum, Luise, & Orbach, Susie (1983). *Understanding women: A feminist psychoanalytic approach.* New York: Basic Books.

Eisenberg, Nancy (1995). Prosocial development: A multifaceted model. In W. M. Kurtines & J. L. Gewirtz (eds.), *Moral development: An introduction.* Boston: Allyn & Bacon.

Eisenberg, Nancy; Fabes, Richard A.; Murphy, Bridget; et al. (1996). The relations of children's dispositional empathy-related responding to their emotionality, regulation, and social functioning. *Developmental Psychology, 32,* 195–209.

Eisenberger, Robert, & Cameron, Judy (1996). Detrimental effects of reward: Reality or myth? *American Psychologist, 51,* 1153–1166.

Eisenberger, Robert; Rhoades, Linda; & Cameron, Judy (1999). Does pay for performance increase or decrease perceived self-determination and intrinsic motivation? *Journal of Personality and Social Psychology, 77,* 1026–1040.

Ekman, Paul (1994). Strong evidence for universals in facial expressions: A reply to Russell's mistaken critique. *Psychological Bulletin, 115,* 268–287.

Ekman, Paul; Friesen, Wallace V.; O'Sullivan, Maureen; et al. (1987). Universals and cultural differences in the judgments of facial expression of emotion. *Journal of Personality and Social Psychology, 53,* 712–717.

Ekman, Paul, & Heider, Karl G. (1988). The universality of a contempt expression: A replication. *Motivation and Emotion, 12,* 303–308.

Elbert, T.; Pantev, C.; Wienbruch, C.; et al. (1995, October 13). Increased cortical representation of the fingers of the left hand in string players. *Science, 270,* 305–307.

Elliot, Andrew J., & Sheldon, Kennon M. (1998). Avoidance personal goals and the personality-illness relationship. *Journal of Personality and Social Psychology, 75,* 1282–1299.

Elliott, Robert, & Morrow-Bradley, Cheryl (1994). Developing a working marriage between psychotherapists and psychotherapy researchers: Identifying shared purposes. In P. F. Talley, H. H. Strupp, & S. F. Butler (eds.), *Psychotherapy research and practice: Bridging the gap.* New York: Basic Books.

Ellis, Albert (1993). Changing rational-emotive therapy (RET) to rational emotive behavior therapy (REBT). *Behavior Therapist, 16,* 257–258.

Ellis, Albert, & Blau, Shawn (1998). Rational emotive behavior therapy. *Directions in Clinical and Counseling Psychology, 8,* 41–56.

Elshtain, Jean B. (1987). *Women and war.* New York: Basic Books.

Endler, Norman S. (1990). *Holiday of darkness.* New York: Wiley-Interscience.

Ennis, Robert H. (1985). Critical thinking and the curriculum. *National Forum, 65*(1), 28–30.

Epstein, Robert; Kirshnit, C. E.; Lanza, R. P.; & Rubin, L. C. (1984, March 1). "Insight" in the pigeon: Antecedents and determinants of an intelligent performance. *Nature, 308,* 61–62.

Epstein, Seymour (1994). Integration of the cognitive and the psychodynamic unconscious. *American Psychologist, 49,* 709–724.

Erikson, Erik H. (1950/1963). *Childhood and society* (2nd ed.). New York: W. W. Norton.

Erikson, Erik H. (1982). *The life cycle completed.* New York: W. W. Norton.

Eriksson, P. S.; Perfilieva, E; Bjork-Eriksson, T.; et al. (1998). Neurogenesis in the adult human hippocampus. *Nature Medicine, 4,* 1313–1317.

Eron, Leonard D. (1982). Parent-child interaction, television violence, and aggression of children. *American Psychologist, 37,* 197–211.

Eron, Leonard D. (1995). Media violence: How it affects kids and what can be done about it. Invited address presented at the annual meeting of the American Psychological Association, New York.

Ervin-Tripp, Susan (1964). Imitation and structural change in children's language. In E. H. Lenneberg (ed.), *New directions in the study of language.* Cambridge, MA: MIT Press.

Esterson, Allen (1993). *Seductive mirage: An exploration of the work of Sigmund Freud.* New York: Open Court.

Evans, Christopher (1984). *Landscapes of the night* (Edited and completed by Peter Evans). New York: Viking.

Ewart, Craig K. (1995). Self-efficacy and recovery from heart attack. In J. E. Maddux (ed.), *Self-efficacy, adaptation, and adjustment: Theory, research, and application.* New York: Plenum.

Exner, John E. (1993). *The Rorschach: A comprehensive system* (Vol. 1): *Basic foundations* (3rd ed.). New York: Wiley.

Eyferth, Klaus (1961). [The performance of different groups of the children of occupation forces on the Hamburg-Wechsler Intelligence Test for Children.] *Archiv für die Gesamte Psychologie, 113,* 222–241.

Eysenck, Hans J. (1993, August). Psychoanalysis: Pseudo-science [Letter to the editor]. *Monitor, 4,* 68.

Fackelmann, Kathleen (1998, August 22). Stroke rescue: Can cells injected into the brain reverse paralysis? *Science News, 154,* 120–122.

Fagan, Joseph F., III (1992). Intelligence: A theoretical viewpoint. *Current Directions in Psychological Science, 1,* 82–86.

Fagot, Beverly I. (1985). Beyond the reinforcement principle: Another step toward understanding sex role development. *Developmental Psychology, 2,* 1097–1104.

Fagot, Beverly I. (1993, June). Gender role development in early childhood: Environmental input, internal construction. Invited address presented at the annual meeting of the International Academy of Sex Research, Monterey, CA.

Fagot, Beverly I.; Hagan, R.; Leinbach, Mary D.; & Kronsberg, S. (1985). Differential reactions to assertive and communicative acts of toddler boys and girls. *Child Development, 56,* 1499–1505.

Fagot, Beverly I., & Leinbach, Mary D. (1993). Gender-role development in young children: From discrimination to labeling. *Developmental Review, 13,* 205–224.

Fairchild, Halford H. (1985). Black, Negro, or Afro-American? The differences are crucial! *Journal of Black Studies, 16,* 47–55.

Falk, Ruma, & Greenbaum, Charles W. (1995). Significance tests die hard: The amazing persistence of a probabilistic misconception. *Theory & Psychology, 5*(1), 75–98.

Fancher, Robert T. (1995). *Cultures of healing.* New York: W. H. Freeman.

Fausto-Sterling, Anne (1985). *Myths of gender: Biological theories about women and men.* New York: Basic Books.

Fausto-Sterling, Anne (2000). *Sexing the body: Gender politics and the construction of sexuality.* New York: Basic Books.

Fazio, Russell H.; Jackson, Joni R.; Dunton, Bridget C.; & Williams, Carol J. (1995). Variability in automatic activation as an unobtrusive measure of racial attitudes: A bona fide pipeline? *Journal of Personality and Social Psychology, 69,* 1013–1027.

FDA Drug Bulletin (1990, April). Two new psychiatric drugs. *20*(1), 9.

Feather, N. T. (1966). Effects of prior success and failure on expectations of success and subsequent performance. *Journal of Personality and Social Psychology, 3,* 287–298.

Feeney, Dennis M. (1987). Human rights and animal welfare. *American Psychologist, 42,* 593–599.

Fein, Steven, & Spencer, Steven J. (1997). Prejudice as self-image maintenance: Affirming the self through derogating others. *Journal of Personality and Social Psychology, 73,* 31–44.

Feingold, Alan (1988). Cognitive gender differences are disappearing. *American Psychologist, 43,* 95–103.

Feltus, M. S., & Gardner, D. M. (1999). Second generation antipsychotics for schizophrenia. *Canadian Journal of Clinical Pharmacology, 6,* 187–195.

Festinger, Leon (1957). *A theory of cognitive dissonance.* Evanston, IL: Row, Peterson.

Festinger, Leon (1980). Looking backward. In L. Festinger (ed.), *Retrospections on social psychology.* New York: Oxford University Press.

Festinger, Leon, & Carlsmith, J. Merrill (1959). Cognitive consequences of forced compliance. *Journal of Abnormal and Social Psychology, 58,* 203–210.

Festinger, Leon; Pepitone, Albert; & Newcomb, Theodore (1952). Some consequences of deindividuation in a group. *Journal of Abnormal and Social Psychology, 47,* 382–389.

Festinger, Leon; Riecken, Henry W.; & Schachter, Stanley (1956). *When prophecy fails.* Minneapolis: University of Minnesota Press.

Fiez, J. A. (1996). Cerebellar contributions to cognition. *Neuron, 16,* 13–15.

Fincham, Frank D.; Beach, Steven R. H.; Harold, Gordon T.; & Osborne, Lori N. (1997). Marital satisfaction and depression: Different causal relationships for men and women? *Psychological Science, 8,* 351–357.

Fischer, Ann R., & Good, Glenn E. (1998). New directions for the study of gender role attitudes: A cluster analytic investigation of masculinity ideologies. *Psychology of Women Quarterly, 22,* 371–384.

Fischer, Ann R.; Tokar, David M.; Good, Glenn E.; & Snell, Andrea F. (1998). More on the structure of male role norms. *Psychology of Women Quarterly, 22,* 135–155.

Fischhoff, Baruch (1975). Hindsight is not equal to foresight: The effect of outcome knowledge on judgment under uncertainty. *Journal of Experimental Psychology: Human Perception and Performance, 1,* 288–299.

Fishbein, Harold D. (1996). *Peer prejudice and discrimination.* Boulder, CO: Westview Press.

Fisher, Kathleen (1985, March). ECT: New studies on how, why, who. *APA Monitor, 16,* 18–19.

Fisher, Ronald J. (1994). Generic principles for resolving intergroup conflict. *Journal of Social Issues, 50,* 47–66.

Fisher, S. E.; Vargha-Khadem, F.; Watkins, K. E.; et al. (1998). Localisation of a gene implicated in a severe speech and language disorder. *Nature Genetics, 18,* 168–170.

Fisher, Sarah; Guenin, Krista; Alter, R. J.; & Flannagan, Jeff (1999). Sweet and enduring: Quantity and consistency of long-term autobiographical memories. Paper presented at the annual meeting of the American Psychological Society, Denver.

Fiske, Alan P., & Haslam, Nick (1996). Social cognition is thinking about relationships. *Current Directions in Psychological Science, 5,* 143–148.

Fivush, Robyn, & Hamond, Nina R. (1991). Autobiographical memory across the school years: Toward reconceptualizing childhood amnesia. In R. Fivush & J. A. Hudson (eds.), *Knowing and remembering in young children.* New York: Cambridge University Press.

Flavell, John H. (1993). Young children's understanding of thinking and consciousness. *Current Directions in Psychological Science, 2,* 40–43.

Flavell, John H. (1996). Piaget's legacy. *Psychological Science, 7,* 200–203.

Flavell, John H.; Green, F. L.; & Flavell, E. R. (1990). Developmental changes in young children's knowledge about the mind. *Cognitive Development, 5,* 1–27.

Flynn, James R. (1987). Massive IQ gains in 14 nations: What IQ tests really measure. *Psychological Bulletin, 95,* 29–51.

Flynn, James R. (1999). Searching for justice: The discovery of IQ gains over time. *American Psychologist, 54,* 5–20.

Foa, Edna, & Emmelkamp, Paul (eds.) (1983). *Failures in behavior therapy.* New York: Wiley.

Fogelman, Eva (1994). *Conscience and courage: Rescuers of Jews during the Holocaust.* New York: Anchor Books.

Fordham, Signithia (1991, Spring). Racelessness in private schools: Should we deconstruct the racial and cultural identity of African-American adolescents? *Teachers College Record, 92,* 470–484.

Forgas, Joseph P. (1998). On being happy and mistaken: Mood effects on the fundamental attribution error. *Journal of Personality and Social Psychology, 75,* 318–331.

Forgas, Joseph P., & Bond, Michael H. (1985). Cultural influences on the perception of interaction episodes. *Personality and Social Psychology Bulletin, 11,* 75–88.

Fouts, Roger [with Stephen T. Mills] (1997). *Next of kin: What chimpanzees have taught me about who we are.* New York: Morrow.

Fouts, Roger S., & Rigby, Randall L. (1977). Man-chimpanzee communication. In T. A. Seboek (ed.), *How animals communicate.* Bloomington: University of Indiana Press.

Fox, Ronald E. (1994). Training professional psychologists for the twenty-first century. *American Psychologist, 49,* 200–206.

Frankl, Victor E. (1955). *The doctor and the soul: An introduction to logotherapy.* New York: Knopf.

Franklin, Anderson J. (1993, July/August). The invisibility syndrome. *Family Therapy Networker,* 33–39.

Franklin, Karen (1998). Psychosocial motivations of hate crimes perpetrators: Implications for educational interventions. Paper presented at the annual meeting of the American Psychological Association, San Francisco, CA.

Franz, Carol E. (1997). Stability and change in the transition to midlife: A longitudinal study of midlife adults. In M. E. Lachman & J. B. James (eds.), *Multiple paths of midlife development.* Chicago: University of Chicago Press.

Freed, C. R.; Breeze, R. E.; Rosenberg, N. L.; & Schneck, S. A. (1993). Embryonic dopamine cell implants as a treatment for the second phase of Parkinson's disease: Replacing failed nerve terminals. *Advances in Neurology, 60,* 721–728.

Freedman, Jonathan L. (1988). Television violence and aggression: What the evidence shows. In S. Oskamp (ed.), *Applied social psychology annual* (Vol. 8): *Television as a social issue.* Newbury Park, CA: Sage.

Freud, Anna (1967). *Ego and the mechanisms of defense (The writings of Anna Freud, Vol. 2)* (rev. ed.). New York: International Universities Press.

Freud, Sigmund (1900/1953). The interpretation of dreams. In J. Strachey (trans. and ed.), *The standard edition of the complete psychological works of Sigmund Freud* (Vols. 4 and 5). London: Hogarth Press.

Freud, Sigmund (1905a). Fragment of an analysis of a case of hysteria. In J. Strachey (ed.), *Standard edition* (Vol. 7). London: Hogarth.

Freud, Sigmund (1905b). Three essays on the theory of sexuality. In J. Strachey (ed.), *Standard edition* (Vol. 7). London: Hogarth.

Freud, Sigmund (1908). Civilized sexual morality and modern nervousness. In J. Strachey (ed.), *Standard edition* (Vol. 9). London: Hogarth.

Freud, Sigmund (1920/1960). *A general introduction to psychoanalysis* (Joan Riviere, trans.). New York: Washington Square Press.

Freud, Sigmund (1920/1963). The psychogenesis of a case of homosexuality in a woman. In S. Freud, *Sexuality and the psychology of love.* New York: Collier Books.

Freud, Sigmund (1923/1962). *The ego and the id* (Joan Riviere, trans.). New York: W. W. Norton.

Freud, Sigmund (1924a). The dissolution of the Oedipus complex. In J. Strachey (ed.), *Standard edition* (Vol. 19). London: Hogarth.

Freud, Sigmund (1924b). Some psychical consequences of the anatomical distinction between the sexes. In J. Strachey (ed.), *Standard edition* (Vol. 19). London: Hogarth.

Freud, Sigmund (1930/1962). *Civilization and its discontents* (J. Strachey, ed. and trans.). New York: W. W. Norton.

Freud, Sigmund (1933). Femininity. In J. Strachey (ed.), *Standard edition* (Vol. 22). London: Hogarth.

Freud, Sigmund (1961). *Letters of Sigmund Freud, 1873–1939* (Ernst L. Freud, ed.). London: Hogarth.

Freyd, Jennifer J. (1996). *Betrayal trauma: The logic of forgetting childhood abuse.* Cambridge, MA: Harvard University Press.

Friedman, William; Robinson, Amy; & Friedman, Britt (1987). Sex differences in moral judgments? A test of Gilligan's theory. *Psychology of Women Quarterly, 11,* 37–46.

Friedrich, W. (1998). Normative sexual behavior in children: A contemporary sample. *Pediatrics, 101,* 4.

Frieze, Irene Hanson, & McHugh, Maureen C. (1998). Measuring feminism and gender role attitudes. *Psychology of Women Quarterly, 22,* 349–352.

Frome, Pamela M., & Eccles, Jacquelynne S. (1998). Parents' influence on children's achievement-related perceptions. *Journal of Personality and Social Psychology, 74,* 435–452.

Gage, Fred H.; Kempermann, G.; Palmer, T. D.; et al. (1998). Multipotent progenitor cells in the adult dentate gyrus. *Journal of Neurobiology, 36,* 249–266.

Gagnon, John, & Simon, William (1973). *Sexual conduct: The social sources of human sexuality.* Chicago: Aldine.

Galanter, Marc (1989). *Cults: Faith, healing, and coercion.* New York: Oxford University Press.

Gallo, Fred (1998). *Energy therapies.* Washington, DC: American Psychological Association.

Galotti, Kathleen (1989). Approaches to studying formal and everyday reasoning. *Psychological Bulletin, 105,* 331–351.

Gao, Jia-Hong; Parsons, Lawrence M.; Bower, James M.; et al. (1996). Cerebellum implicated in sensory acquisition and discrimination rather than motor control. *Science, 272,* 545–547.

Garb, Howard N. (1999). Call for a moratorium on the use of the Rorschach Inkblot Test in clinical and forensic settings. *Assessment, 6,* 313–315.

Garb, Howard N.; Florio, Colleen M.; & Grove, William M. (1998). The validity of the Rorschach and the Minnesota Multiphasic Personality Inventory: Results from meta-analyses. *Psychological Science, 9,* 402–404.

Garb, Howard N.; Wood, James M.; & Nezworski, M. Teresa (2000). Projective techniques and the detection of child sexual abuse. *Child Maltreatment, 5,* 161–168.

Garcia, John, & Koelling, Robert A. (1966). Relation of cue to consequence in avoidance learning. *Psychonomic Science, 4,* 23–124.

Garcia, Julio; Helms, Wes; & Garcia, Lisette (undated). White men can't jump. Manuscript in preparation, Tufts University, Department of Psychology.

Garcia-Marques, Leonel, & Mackie, Diane M. (1999). The impact of stereotype-incongruent information on perceived group variability and stereotype change. *Journal of Personality and Social Psychology, 77,* 979–990.

Gardner, Howard (1983). *Frames of mind: The theory of multiple intelligences.* New York: Basic Books.

Gardner, Howard (1992). Scientific psychology: Should we bury it or praise it? *New Ideas in Psychology, 10,* 179–190.

Gardner, Howard (1995). Perennial antinomies and perpetual redrawings: Is there progress in the study of mind? In R. L. Solso & D. W. Massar (eds.), *The science of the mind: 2001 and beyond.* New York: Oxford University Press.

Gardner, R. Allen, & Gardner, Beatrice T. (1969). Teaching sign language to a chimpanzee. *Science, 165,* 664–672.

Garmezy, Norman (1991). Resilience and vulnerability to adverse developmental outcomes associated with poverty. *American Behavioral Scientist, 34,* 416–430.

Garry, Maryanne; Manning, Charles G.; & Loftus, Elizabeth F. (1996). Imagination inflation: Imagining a childhood event inflates confidence that it occurred. *Psychonomic Bulletin & Review, 3,* 208–214.

Garven, Sena; Wood, James M.; & Malpass, Roy S. (2000). Allegations of wrongdoing: The effects of reinforcement on children's mundane and fantastic claims. *Journal of Applied Psychology, 85,* 38–49.

Garven, Sena; Wood, James M.; Malpass, Roy S.; & Shaw, John S., III (1998). More than suggestion: The effect of interviewing techniques from the McMartin Preschool case. *Journal of Applied Psychology, 83,* 347–359.

Gay, Peter (1988). *Freud: A life for our time.* New York: W. W. Norton.

Gazzaniga, Michael S. (1967). The split brain in man. *Scientific American, 217*(2), 24–29.

Gazzaniga, Michael S. (1983). Right hemisphere language following brain bisection: A 20-year perspective. *American Psychologist, 38,* 525–537.

Gazzaniga, Michael S. (1985). *The social brain: Discovering the networks of the mind.* New York: Basic Books.

Gazzaniga, Michael S. (1988). *Mind matters.* Boston: Houghton Mifflin.

Gazzaniga, Michael S. (1998). *The mind's past.* Berkeley: University of California Press.

Geary, David C. (1995). Reflections of evolution and culture in children's cognition: Implications for mathematical development and instruction. *American Psychologist, 50,* 24–37.

Geis, Florence L. (1993). Self-fulfilling prophecies: A social psychological view of gender. In A. E. Beall & R. J. Sternberg (eds.), *The psychology of gender.* New York: Guilford Press.

Gerbner, George (1988). Telling stories in the information age. In B. D. Ruben (ed.), *Information and behavior* (Vol. 2). New Brunswick, NJ: Transaction Books.

Gergen, Kenneth J. (1973). Social psychology as history. *Journal of Personality and Social Psychology, 26,* 309–320.

Gergen, Kenneth J. (1994). Exploring the postmodern: Perils or potentials? *American Psychologist, 49,* 412–416.

Gerson, Kathleen (1993). *No man's land: Men's changing commitments to family and work.* New York: Basic Books.

Gibson, Eleanor, & Walk, Richard (1960). The "visual cliff." *Scientific American, 202,* 80–92.

Gillham, Jane E.; Reivich, Karen J.; Jaycox, Lisa H.; & Seligman, Martin E. P. (1995). Prevention of depressive symptoms in schoolchildren: A two-year follow-up. *Psychological Science, 6,* 343–351.

Gilligan, Carol (1982). *In a different voice.* Cambridge, MA: Harvard University Press.

Gilmore, David D. (1990). *Manhood in the making: Cultural concepts of masculinity.* New Haven, CT: Yale University Press.

Gladue, Brian A. (1994). The biopsychology of sexual orientation. *Current Directions in Psychological Science, 3,* 150–154.

Glanzer, Murray, & Cunitz, Anita R. (1966). Two storage mechanisms in free recall. *Journal of Verbal Learning and Verbal Behavior, 5,* 351–360.

Gleaves, David H. (1996). The sociocognitive model of dissociative identity disorder: A reexamination of the evidence. *Psychological Bulletin, 120,* 42–59.

Glenmullen, Joseph (1993). *The pornographer's grief and other tales of human sexuality.* New York: HarperCollins.

Gobodo-Madikizela, Pumla (1994). The notion of the "collective" in South African "political" murder cases: The "deindividuation" argument revisited. Paper presented to the biennial conference of the American Psychology and Law Society, Santa Fe, NM.

Goddard, Henry H. (1917). Mental tests and the immigrant. *Journal of Delinquency, 2,* 243–277.

Gold, Paul E. (1987). Sweet memories. *American Scientist, 75,* 151–155.

Goldin-Meadow, S., & Mylander, C. (1998). Spontaneous sign systems created by deaf children in two cultures. *Nature, 391,* 279–281.

Goldman, Alan (1994, Winter). The centrality of "Ningensei" to Japanese negotiating and interpersonal relationships: Implications for U.S.-Japanese communication. *International Journal of Intercultural Relations, 18,* 29–54.

Goldman-Rakic, Patricia S. (1996). Opening the mind through neurobiology. Invited address at the annual meeting of the American Psychological Association, Toronto, Canada.

Goldstein, Michael J. (1987). Psychosocial issues. *Schizophrenia Bulletin, 13*(1), 157–171.

Goldstein, Michael, & Miklowitz, David (1995). The effectiveness of psychoeducational family therapy in the treatment of schizophrenic disorders. *Journal of Marital and Family Therapy, 21,* 361–376.

Goodman, Gail S.; Qin, Jianjian; Bottoms, Bette L.; & Shaver, Phillip R. (1995). Characteristics and sources of allegations of ritualistic child abuse. Final report to the National Center on Child Abuse and Neglect, Washington, DC. Executive summary and complete report available from NCCAN, 1-800-394-3366.

Gore, P. M., & Rotter, Julian B. (1963). A personality correlate of social action. *Journal of Personality, 31,* 58–64.

Goren, C. C.; Sarty, J.; & Wu, P. Y. (1975). Visual following and pattern discrimination of face-like stimuli by newborn infants. *Pediatrics, 56,* 544–549.

Gorn, Gerald J. (1982). The effects of music in advertising on choice behavior: A classical conditioning approach. *Journal of Marketing, 46,* 94–101.

Gottesman, Irving I. (1991). *Schizophrenia genesis: The origins of madness.* New York: W. H. Freeman.

Gottesman, Irving I. (1994). Perils and pleasures of genetic psychopathology. Distinguished Scientist Award address presented at the annual meeting of the American Psychological Association, Los Angeles.

Gottfried, Adele Eskeles; Fleming, James S.; & Gottfried, Allen W. (1994). Role of parental motivational practices in children's academic intrinsic motivation and achievement. *Journal of Educational Psychology, 86,* 104–113.

Gould, Elizabeth; Beylin, A.; Tanapat, Patima; et al. (1999). Learning enhances adult neurogenesis in the hippocampal formation. *Nature Neuroscience, 2,* 260–265.

Gould, Elizabeth; Tanapat, Patima; McEwen, Bruce S.; et al. (1998). Proliferation of granule cell precursors in the dentate gyrus of adult monkeys is diminished by stress. *Proceedings of the National Academy of Science, 95,* 3168–3171.

Gould, James L., & Gould, Carol G. (1995). *The animal mind.* San Francisco: W. H. Freeman.

Gould, Stephen Jay (1987). *An urchin in the storm.* New York: W. W. Norton.

Gould, Stephen Jay (1994, November 28). Curveball [review of *The Bell Curve*, by Richard J. Herrnstein and Charles Murray]. *The New Yorker,* 139–149.

Gould, Stephen Jay (1996). *The mismeasure of man* (rev. ed.). New York: W. W. Norton.

Gourevich, Philip (1998). *We wish to inform you that tomorrow we will be killed with our families: Stories from Rwanda.* New York: Farrar, Straus & Giroux.

Graf, Peter, & Schacter, Daniel A. (1985). Implicit and explicit memory for new associations in normal and amnesic subjects. *Journal of Experimental Psychology: Learning, Memory, and Cognition, 11,* 501–518.

Graham, Jill W. (1986). Principled organizational dissent: A theoretical essay. *Research in Organizational Behavior, 8,* 1–52.

Graham, Sandra (1994). Motivation in African Americans. *Review of Educational Research, 64,* 55–117.

Green, Donald P.; Glaser, Jack; & Rich, Andrew (1998). From lynching to gay bashing: The elusive connection between economic conditions and hate crime. *Journal of Personality and Social Psychology, 75,* 82–92.

Green, Gina (1996a). Behavioral treatment of autistic persons: A review of research from 1980 to the present. *Research in Developmental Disabilities, 17,* 433–465.

Green, Gina (1996b). Early behavioral intervention for autism: What does research tell us? In C. Maurice, G. Green, & S. C. Luce (eds.), *Behavioral intervention for young children with autism: A manual for parents and professionals.* Austin, TX: Pro-Ed.

Greenberg, Roger P.; Bornstein, Robert F.; Greenberg, Michael D.; & Fisher, Seymour (1992). A meta-analysis of antidepressant outcome under "blinder" conditions. *Journal of Consulting and Clinical Psychology, 60,* 664–669.

Greenberg, Roger P.; Bornstein, Robert F.; Zborowski, Michael J.; et al. (1994). A meta-analysis of fluoxetine outcome in the treatment of depression. *Journal of Nervous and Mental Disease, 182,* 547–551.

Greenberger, Dennis, & Padesky, Christine A. (1995). *Mind over mood: A cognitive therapy treatment manual for clients.* New York: Guilford Press.

Greene, Robert L. (1986). Sources of recency effects in free recall. *Psychological Bulletin, 99,* 221–228.

Greenough, William T. (1984). Structural correlates of information storage in the mammalian brain: A review and hypothesis. *Trends in Neurosciences, 7,* 229–233.

Greenough, William T. (1991). The animal rights assertions: A researcher's perspective. *Psychological Science Agenda* (American Psychological Association), *4*(3), 10–12.

Greenough, William T., & Anderson, Brenda J. (1991). Cerebellar synaptic plasticity: Relation to learning vs. neural activity. *Annals of the New York Academy of Sciences, 627,* 231–247.

Greenough, William T., & Black, James E. (1992). Induction of brain structure by experience: Substrates for cognitive development. In M. Gunnar & C. A. Nelson (eds.), *Behavioral developmental neuroscience* (Vol. 24): *Minnesota Symposia on Child Psychology.* Hillsdale, NJ: Erlbaum.

Greenwald, Anthony G.; McGhee, Debbie E.; & Schwartz, Jordan L. K. (1998). Measuring individual differences in implicit cognition: The Implicit Association Test. *Journal of Personality and Social Psychology, 74,* 1464–1480.

Griffin, Donald R. (1992). *Animal minds.* Chicago: University of Chicago Press.

Groebel, Jo, & Hinde, Robert (eds.) (1989). The Seville statement on violence. In *Aggression and war: Their biological and social bases.* Cambridge, England: Cambridge University Press.

Groneman, Carol (2000). *Nymphomania: A history.* New York: W. W. Norton.

Gross, Paul R., & Levitt, Norman (1994). *Higher superstition: The academic left and its quarrels with science.* Baltimore: Johns Hopkins University Press.

Grove, William M., & Meehl, Paul E. (1996). Comparative efficiency of formal (mechanical, algorithmic) and informal (subjective, impressionistic) prediction procedures: The clinical/statistical controversy. *Psychology, Public Policy, and Law, 2,* 293–323.

Gudykunst, William B., & Ting-Toomey, Stella (1988). *Culture and interpersonal communication.* Newbury Park, CA: Sage.

Guglielmi, R. Sergio (1999). Psychophysiological assessment of prejudice: Past research, current status, and future directions. *Personality and Social Psychology Review, 3,* 123–157.

Guilford, J. P. (1950). Creativity. *American Psychologist, 5,* 444–454.

Gupta, S.; Mosnik, D.; Black, D. W.; et al. (1999). Tardive dyskinesia: Review of treatments past, present, and future. *Annals of Clinical Psychiatry, 11,* 257–266.

Gur, R. E.; Maany, V.; Mozley, P. D.; et al. (1998). Subcortical MRI volumes in neuroleptic-naive and treated patients with schizophrenia. *American Journal of Psychiatry, 155,* 1711–1717.

Guralnick, M. J. (ed.) (1997). *The effectiveness of early intervention.* Baltimore: Brookes.

Haber, Ralph N. (1970, May). How we remember what we see. *Scientific American, 222,* 104–112.

Haier, Richard J.; Siegel, Benjamin V., Jr.; MacLachlan, Andrew; et al. (1992). Regional glucose metabolic changes after learning a complex visuospatial/motor task: A positron emission tomographic study. *Brain Research, 570,* 134–143.

Haier, Richard J.; Siegel, Benjamin V., Jr.; Nuechterlein, Keith; et al. (1988). Cortical glucose metabolic rate correlates of abstract reasoning and attention studied with positron emission tomography. *Intelligence, 12,* 199–217.

Haimov, I., & Lavie, P. (1996). Melatonin—A soporific hormone. *Current Directions in Psychological Science, 5,* 106–111.

Hall, Edward T. (1959). *The silent language.* Garden City, NY: Doubleday.

Hall, Edward T. (1976). *Beyond culture.* New York: Anchor.

Hall, Edward T. (1983). *The dance of life: The other dimension of time.* Garden City, NY: Anchor Press/Doubleday.

Hall, Edward T., & Hall, Mildred R. (1990). *Understanding cultural differences.* Yarmouth, ME: Intercultural Press.

Halpern, Diane (1995). *Thought and knowledge: An introduction to critical thinking* (3rd ed.). Hillsdale, NJ: Erlbaum.

Halpern, Diane (1998). Teaching critical thinking for transfer across domains. *American Psychologist, 53,* 449–455.

Halpern, Diane F. (2000). *Sex differences in cognitive abilities* (3rd ed.). Hillsdale, NJ: Erlbaum.

Haney, Craig; Banks, Curtis; & Zimbardo, Philip (1973). Interpersonal dynamics in a simulated prison. *International Journal of Criminology and Penology, 1,* 69–97.

Haney, Craig, & Zimbardo, Philip (1998). The past and future of U.S. prison policy: Twenty-five years after the Stanford Prison Experiment. *American Psychologist, 53,* 709–727.

Hanna, Elizabeth, & Meltzoff, Andrew N. (1993). Peer imitation by toddlers in laboratory, home, and day-care contexts: Implications for social learning and memory. *Developmental Psychology, 29,* 701–710.

Hardie, Elizabeth A. (1997). PMS in the workplace: Dispelling the myth of cyclic function. *Journal of Occupational and Organizational Psychology, 70,* 97–102.

Harding, Courtenay M.; Zubin, Joseph; & Strauss, John S. (1992). Chronicity in schizophrenia: Revisited. *British Journal of Psychiatry, 161*(Suppl. 18), 27–37.

Hare, Robert D. (1965). Temporal gradient of fear arousal in psychopaths. *Journal of Abnormal Psychology, 70,* 442–445.

Hare, Robert D. (1993). *Without conscience: The disturbing world of the psychopaths among us.* New York: Pocket Books.

Hare-Mustin, Rachel T. (1991). Sex, lies, and headaches: The problem is power. In T. J. Goodrich (ed.), *Women and power: Perspectives for therapy.* New York: W. W. Norton.

Hare-Mustin, Rachel T., & Marecek, Jeanne (1990). Gender and the meaning of difference: Postmodernism and psychology. In R. Hare-Mustin & J. Marecek (eds.), *Psychology and the construction of gender.* New Haven, CT: Yale University Press.

Haritos-Fatouros, Mika (1988). The official torturer: A learning model for obedience to the authority of violence. *Journal of Applied Social Psychology, 18,* 1107–1120.

Harkins, Stephen G., & Szymanski, Kate (1989). Social loafing and group evaluation. *Journal of Personality and Social Psychology, 56,* 934–941.

Harlow, Harry F. (1958). The nature of love. *American Psychologist, 13,* 673–685.

Harlow, Harry F., & Harlow, Margaret K. (1966). Learning to love. *American Scientist, 54,* 244–272.

Harlow, Harry F.; Harlow, Margaret K.; & Meyer, D. R. (1950). Learning motivated by a manipulation drive. *Journal of Experimental Psychology, 40,* 228–234.

Harmon-Jones, Eddie, & Allen, J. B. (1998). Anger and frontal brain activity: EEG asymmetry consistent with approach motivation despite negative affective valence. *Journal of Personality and Social Psychology, 74,* 1310–1316.

Harmon-Jones, Eddie; Brehm, Jack W.; Greenberg, Jeff; et al. (1996). Evidence that the production of aversive consequences is not necessary to create cognitive dissonance. *Journal of Personality and Social Psychology, 70,* 5–16.

Harris, Judith R. (1998). *The nurture assumption.* New York: Free Press.

Harris, Marvin (1985). *Good to eat: Riddles of food and culture.* New York: Simon & Schuster.

Harris, Marvin (1997). *Culture, people, nature* (7th ed.). New York: Longman.

Harris, Naomi G. Singer; Bellugi, Ursula; Bates, Elizabeth; et al. (1997). Contrasting profiles of language development in children with Williams and Down syndromes. *Developmental Neuropsychology, 13,* 345–370.

Hart, John, Jr.; Berndt, Rita S.; & Caramazza, Alfonso (1985, August 1). Category-specific naming deficit following cerebral infarction. *Nature, 316,* 339–340.

Hasher, Lynn, & Zacks, Rose T. (1984). Automatic processing of fundamental information: The case of frequency of occurrence. *American Psychologist, 39,* 1372–1388.

Hatfield, Elaine, & Rapson, Richard L. (1996). *Love and sex: Cross-cultural perspectives.* Boston: Allyn & Bacon.

Hattori, M.; Fujiyama, A.; Taylor, T. D.; et al. (2000). The DNA sequence of human chromosome 21. *Nature, 405,* 311–319.

Hauser, Marc (2000). *Wild minds: What animals really think.* New York: Holt.

Hawkins, Scott A., & Hastie, Reid (1990). Hindsight: Biased judgments of past events after the outcomes are known. *Psychological Bulletin, 107,* 311–327.

Heinrichs, R. Walter (1993). Schizophrenia and the brain: Conditions for a neuropsychology of madness. *American Psychologist, 48,* 221–233.

Helson, Ravenna, & McCabe, Laurel (1993). The social clock project in middle age. In B. F. Turner & L. E. Troll (eds.), *Women growing older.* Newbury Park, CA: Sage.

Helson, Ravenna; Roberts, Brent; & Agronick, Gail (1995). Enduringness and change in creative personality and the prediction of occupational creativity. *Journal of Personality and Social Psychology, 6,* 1173–1183.

Henry, Bill; Caspi, Avshalom; Moffitt, Terrie E.; & Silva, Phil A. (1996). Temperamental and familial predictors of violent and nonviolent criminal convictions: Age 3 to age 18. *Developmental Psychology, 32,* 614–623.

Herdt, Gilbert (1984). *Ritualized homosexuality in Melanesia.* Berkeley: University of California Press.

Herek, Gregory M. (1998). The social psychology of homophobias and heterosexisms. Invited address presented at the annual meeting of the American Psychological Association, San Francisco.

Herek, Gregory M. (1999). Interpersonal contact and sexual prejudice. Paper presented at the annual meeting of the American Psychological Society, Denver.

Herek, Gregory M., & Capitanio, J. P. (1996). "Some of my best friends": Intergroup contact, concealable stigma, and heterosexuals' attitudes toward gay men and lesbians. *Personality and Social Psychology Bulletin, 22,* 412–424.

Herman, Louis M.; Kuczaj, Stan A.; & Holder, Mark D. (1993). Responses to anomalous gestural sequences by a language-trained dolphin: Evidence for processing of semantic relations and syntactic information. *Journal of Experimental Psychology: General, 122,* 184–194.

Herman, Louis M., & Morrel-Samuels, Palmer (1996). Knowledge acquisition and asymmetry between language comprehension and production: Dolphins and apes as general models for animals. In M. Bekoff & D. Jamieson et al. (eds.), *Readings in animal cognition.* Cambridge, MA: MIT Press.

Herrnstein, Richard J., & Murray, Charles (1994). *The bell curve: Intelligence and class structure in American life.* New York: Free Press.

Higgins, E. Tory (1998). Promotion and prevention: Regulatory focus as a motivational principle. *Advances in Experimental Social Psychology, 30,* 1–46.

Higley, J. D.; Hasert, M. L.; Suomi, S. J.; & Linnoila, M. (1991). A nonhuman primate model of alcohol abuse: Effects of early experience, personality, and stress on alcohol consumption. *Proceedings of the National Academy of Science, 88,* 7261–7265.

Hill, James O., & Peters, John C. (1998). Environmental contributions to the obesity epidemic. *Science, 280,* 1371–1374.

Hilts, Philip J. (1995). *Memory's ghost: The strange tale of Mr. M. and the nature of memory.* New York: Simon & Schuster.

Hirsch, Helmut V. B., & Spinelli, D. N. (1970). Visual experience modifies distribution of horizontally and vertically oriented receptive fields in cats. *Science, 168,* 869–871.

Hirst, William; Neisser, Ulric; & Spelke, Elizabeth (1978, January). Divided attention. *Human Nature, 1,* 54–61.

Hobson, J. Allan (1988). *The dreaming brain.* New York: Basic Books.

Hobson, J. Allan (1990). Activation, input source, and modulation: A neurocognitive model of the state of the brain mind. In R. R. Bootzin, J. F. Kihlstrom, & D. L. Schacter (eds.), *Sleep and cognition.* Washington, DC: American Psychological Association.

Hobson, Robert F. (1985). *Forms of feeling: The heart of psychotherapy.* London: Tavistock.

Hockett, Charles F. (1960). The origins of speech. *Scientific American, 203,* 89–96.

Hodges, Ernest V. E., & Perry, David G. (1999). Personal and interpersonal antecedents and consequences of victimization by peers. *Journal of Personality and Social Psychology, 76,* 677–685.

Hoffman, Martin L. (1989). Empathy, social cognition, and moral action. In W. Kurtines & J. Gewirtz (eds.), *Moral behavior and development* (Vol. 1): *Advances in theory, research, and application.* Hillsdale, NJ: Erlbaum.

Hoffman, Martin L. (1994). Discipline and internalization. *Developmental Psychology, 30,* 26–28.

Hofstede, Geert, & Bond, Michael H. (1988). The Confucius connection: From cultural roots to economic growth. *Organizational Dynamics,* 5–21.

Holmes, David S. (1990). The evidence for repression: An examination of sixty years of research. In J. L. Singer (ed.), *Repression and dissociation.* Chicago: University of Chicago Press.

Hooker, Evelyn (1957). The adjustment of the male overt homosexual. *Journal of Projective Techniques, 21,* 18–31.

Hooper, Judith (1999, February). A new germ theory. *Atlantic,* 41–53.

Hoptman, Matthew J., & Davidson, Richard J. (1994). How and why do the two cerebral hemispheres interact? *Psychological Bulletin, 116,* 195–219.

Horner, Althea J. (1991). *Psychoanalytic object relations therapy.* New York: Jason Aronson.

Horney, Karen (1926/1973). The flight from womanhood. Reprinted in J. B. Miller (ed.), *Psychoanalysis and women.* New York: Brunner/Mazel.

Horney, Karen (1945). *Our inner conflicts.* New York: W. W. Norton.

Horney, Karen (1967). *Feminine psychology.* New York: W. W. Norton.

Hornstein, Gail (1992). The return of the repressed: Psychology's problematic relations with psychoanalysis, 1909–1960. *American Psychologist, 47,* 254–263.

Horowitz, Mardi J. (1988). *Introduction to psychodynamics: A new synthesis.* New York: Basic Books.

Howard, George S. (1991). Culture tales: A narrative approach to thinking, cross-cultural psychology, and psychotherapy. *American Psychologist, 46,* 187–197.

Howe, Mark L., & Courage, Mary L. (1993). On resolving the enigma of infantile amnesia. *Psychological Bulletin, 113,* 305–326.

Howe, Mark L.; Courage, Mary L.; & Peterson, Carole (1994). How can I remember when "I" wasn't there? Long-term retention of traumatic experiences and emergence of the cognitive self. *Consciousness and Cognition, 3,* 327–355.

Hrdy, Sarah B. (1988). Empathy, polyandry, and the myth of the coy female. In R. Bleier (ed.), *Feminist approaches to science.* New York: Pergamon.

Hrdy, Sarah B. (1994). What do women want? In T. A. Bass (ed.), *Reinventing the future: Conversations with the world's leading scientists.* Reading, MA: Addison-Wesley.

Hubbard, Ruth (1990). *The politics of women's biology.* New Brunswick, NJ: Rutgers University Press.

Hubbard, Ruth, & Wald, Elijah (1993). *Exploding the gene myth.* Boston: Beacon Press.

Hubel, David H., & Wiesel, Torsten N. (1962). Receptive fields, binocular interaction and functional architecture in the cat's visual cortex. *Journal of Physiology* (London), *160,* 106–154.

Hubel, David H., & Wiesel, Torsten N. (1968). Receptive fields and functional architecture of monkey striate cortex. *Journal of Physiology* (London), *195,* 215–243.

Hughes, Judith M. (1989). *Reshaping the psychoanalytic domain: The work of Melanie Klein, W. R. D. Fairbairn, & D. W. Winnicott.* Berkeley: University of California Press.

Hughes, Robert (1993). *The culture of complaint: The fraying of America.* New York: Oxford University Press.

Hultsch, David F.; Hertzog, Christopher; Small, Brent J.; & Dixon, Roger A. (1999). Use it or lose it: Engaged lifestyle as a buffer of cognitive decline in aging? *Psychology and Aging, 14,* 245–263.

Hunt, Morton M. (1993). *The story of psychology.* New York: Doubleday.

Hunter, John E. (1997). Needed: A ban on the significance test. *Psychological Science, 8,* 3–7.

Huntington's Disease Collaborative Research Group (1993). A novel gene containing a trinucleotide repeat that is expanded and unstable on Huntington's disease chromosomes. *Cell, 72,* 971–983.

Hupka, Ralph B. (1981). Cultural determinants of jealousy. *Alternative Lifestyles, 4,* 310–356.

Hupka, Ralph B. (1991). The motive for the arousal of romantic jealousy. In P. Salovey (ed.), *The psychology of jealousy and envy.* New York: Guilford Press.

Hur, Yoon-Mi; McGue, Matt; & Iacono, William G. (1998). The structure of self-concept in female preadolescent twins: A behavioral genetic approach. *Journal of Personality and Social Psychology, 74,* 1069–1077.

Hyde, Janet S.; Fennema, Elizabeth; & Lamon, Susan J. (1990). Gender differences in mathematics performance: A meta-analysis. *Psychological Bulletin, 107,* 139–155.

Hyde, Janet S., & Linn, Marcia C. (1988). Gender differences in verbal ability: A meta-analysis. *Psychological Bulletin, 104,* 53–69.

Hyman, Ira E., Jr., & Pentland, Joel (1996). The role of mental imagery in the creation of false childhood memories. *Journal of Memory and Language, 35,* 101–117.

Iaccino, James F. (1994). *Psychological reflections on cinematic terror: Jungian archetypes in horror films.* Westport, CT: Praeger/Greenwood.

Inglehart, Ronald (1990). *Culture shift in advanced industrial society.* Princeton, NJ: Princeton University Press.

Irons, Edward D., & Moore, Gilbert W. (1985). *Black managers: The case of the banking industry.* New York: Praeger/Greenwood.

Islam, Mir Rabiul, & Hewstone, Miles (1993). Intergroup attributions and affective consequences in majority and minority groups. *Journal of Personality and Social Psychology, 64,* 936–950.

Izard, Carroll E. (1994). Innate and universal facial expressions: Evidence from developmental and cross-cultural research. *Psychological Bulletin, 115,* 288–299.

Jacklin, Carol N., & Reynolds, Chandra (1993). Gender and childhood socialization. In A. E. Beall & R. J. Sternberg (eds.), *The psychology of gender.* New York: Guilford Press.

Jacobs, Janis E., & Eccles, Jacquelynne S. (1985). Gender differences in math ability: The impact of media reports on parents. *Educational Researcher, 14,* 20–25.

Jacobsen, Paul B; Bovbjerg, Dana H.; Schwartz, Marc D.; et al. (1995). Conditioned emotional distress in women receiving chemotherapy for breast cancer. *Journal of Consulting & Clinical Psychology, 63,* 108–114.

Jacobson, John W.; Mulick, James A.; & Schwartz, Allan A. (1995). The history of facilitated communication: Science, pseudoscience, and anti-science. *American Psychologist, 50,* 750–765.

James, Jacquelyn B., & Lewkowicz, Corinne J. (1997). Themes of power and affiliation across time. In M. E. Lachman & J. B. James (eds.), *Multiple paths of midlife development.* Chicago: University of Chicago Press.

James, William (1890/1950). *Principles of psychology* (Vol. 1). New York: Dover.

Jancke, Lutz; Schlaug, Gottfried; & Steinmetz, Helmuth (1997). Hand skill asymmetry in professional musicians. *Brain and Cognition, 34,* 424–432.

Jang, Kerry L.; McCrae, Robert R.; Angleitner, Alois; et al. (1998). Heritability of facet-level traits in a cross-cultural twin sample: Support for a hierarchical model of personality. *Journal of Personality and Social Psychology, 74,* 1556–1565.

Janis, Irving L. (1982). *Groupthink: Psychological studies of policy decisions and fiascoes* (2nd ed.). Boston: Houghton Mifflin.

Janis, Irving L. (1989). *Crucial decisions: Leadership in policymaking and crisis management.* New York: Free Press.

Janis, Irving L.; Kaye, Donald; & Kirschner, Paul (1965). Facilitating effects of "eating-while-reading" on responsiveness to persuasive communications. *Journal of Personality and Social Psychology, 1,* 181–186.

Jenkins, Jennifer M., & Astington, Janet W. (1996). Cognitive factors and family structure associated with theory of mind development in young children. *Developmental Psychology, 32,* 70–78.

Jenkins, Sharon Rae (1994). Need for power and women's careers over 14 years: Structural power, job satisfaction, and motive change. *Journal of Personality and Social Psychology, 66,* 155–165.

Jensen, Arthur R. (1969). How much can we boost IQ and scholastic achievement? *Harvard Educational Review, 39,* 1–123.

Jensen, Arthur R. (1981). *Straight talk about mental tests.* New York: Free Press.

Johnson, Marcia K. (1995). The relation between memory and reality. Paper presented at the annual meeting of the American Psychological Association, New York.

Johnson, Mark H.; Dziurawiec, Suzanne; Ellis, Hadyn; & Morton, John (1991). Newborns' preferential tracking of face-like stimuli and its subsequent decline. *Cognition, 40,* 1–19.

Johnson, Robert, & Downing, Leslie (1979). Deindividuation and valence of cues: Effects of prosocial and antisocial behavior. *Journal of Personality and Social Psychology, 37,* 1532–1538.

Jones, Edward E. (1990). *Interpersonal perception.* New York: Macmillan.

Jones, James M. (1991). Psychological models of race: What have they been and what should they be? In J. D. Goodchilds (ed.), *Psychological perspectives on human diversity in America.* Washington, DC: American Psychological Association.

Jones, James M. (1997). *Prejudice and racism* (2nd ed.). New York: McGraw-Hill.

Jones, Mary Cover (1924). A laboratory study of fear: The case of Peter. *Pedagogical Seminary, 31,* 308–315.

Jones, Russell A. (1977). *Self-fulfilling prophecies.* Hillsdale, NJ: Erlbaum.

Jones, Steve (1994). *The language of genes.* New York: Anchor/Doubleday.

Jones, Steve (2000). *Darwin's ghost: "The Origin of Species" updated.* New York: Random House.

Judd, Charles M.; Park, Bernadette; Ryan, Carey S.; et al. (1995). Stereotypes and ethnocentrism: Diverging interethnic perceptions of African American and white American youth. *Journal of Personality and Social Psychology, 69,* 460–481.

Jung, Carl (1967). *Collected works.* Princeton, NJ: Princeton University Press.

Kaczynski, Richard (1997). The satanic ritual abuse controversy: A case of groupthink? Paper presented at the annual meeting of the American Psychological Association, Chicago.

Kagan, Jerome (1984). *The nature of the child.* New York: Basic Books.

Kagan, Jerome (1989). *Unstable ideas: Temperament, cognition, and self.* Cambridge, MA: Harvard University Press.

Kagan, Jerome (1993). The meanings of morality. *Psychological Science, 4,* 353, 357–360.

Kagan, Jerome (1994). *Galen's prophecy: Temperament in human nature.* New York: Basic Books.

Kagan, Jerome (1998a). How we become what we are. Paper presented at the annual meeting of the Family Therapy Network Symposium, Washington, DC.

Kagan, Jerome (1998b). *Three seductive ideas.* Cambridge, MA: Harvard University Press.

Kagan, Jerome, & Lamb, Sharon (eds.) (1987). *The emergence of morality in young children.* Chicago: University of Chicago Press.

Kagan, Jerome, & Moss, Howard (1962). *Birth to maturity.* New York: Wiley.

Kahneman, Daniel, & Treisman, Anne (1984). Changing views of attention and automaticity. In R. Parasuraman, D. R. Davies, & J. Beatty (eds.), *Varieties of attention.* New York: Academic Press.

Kameda, Tatsuya, & Sugimori, Shinkichi (1993). Psychological entrapment in group decision making: An assigned decision rule and a groupthink phenomenon. *Journal of Personality and Social Psychology, 65,* 282–292.

Kandel, Eric R., & Schwartz, James H. (1982). Molecular biology of learning: Modulation of transmitter release. *Science, 218,* 433–443.

Kanter, Rosabeth Moss (1977/1993). *Men and women of the corporation.* New York: Basic Books.

Kaplan, Meg S.; Morales, Miguel; & Becker, Judith V. (1993). The impact of verbal satiation of adolescent sex offenders: A preliminary report. *Journal of Child Sexual Abuse, 2,* 81–88.

Karasek, Robert, & Theorell, Tores (1990). *Healthy work: Stress, productivity, and the reconstruction of working life.* New York: Basic Books.

Karau, Steven J., & Williams, Kipling D. (1993). Social loafing: A meta-analytic review and theoretical integration. *Journal of Personality and Social Psychology, 65,* 681–706.

Karney, Benjamin, & Bradbury, Thomas N. (2000). Attributions in marriage: State or trait? A growth curve analysis. *Journal of Personality and Social Psychology, 78,* 295–309.

Karni, Avi; Tanne, David; Rubenstein, Barton S.; et al. (1994). Dependence on REM sleep of overnight improvement of a perceptual skill. *Science, 265,* 679–682.

Kashima, Yoshihisa; Yamaguchi, Susumu; Kim, Uichol; et al. (1995). Culture, gender, and self: A perspective from individualism-collectivism research. *Journal of Personality and Social Psychology, 69,* 925–937.

Kasser, Tim, & Ryan, Richard M. (1996). Further examining the American dream: Correlates of financial success as a central life aspiration. *Personality and Social Psychology Bulletin, 22,* 280–287.

Katigbak, Marcia S.; Church, A. Timothy; & Akamine, Toshio X. (1996). Cross-cultural generalizability of personality dimensions: Relating indigenous and imported dimensions in two cultures. *Journal of Personality and Social Psychology, 70,* 99–114.

Katz, Phyllis A., & Ksansnak, Keith R. (1994). Developmental aspects of gender role flexibility and traditionality in middle childhood and adolescence. *Developmental Psychology, 30,* 272–282.

Katz, Stuart, & Lautenschlager, Gary J. (1994). Answering reading comprehension items without passages on the SAT-I, the ACT, and the GRE. *Educational Assessment, 2,* 295–308.

Kaufman, Joan, & Zigler, Edward (1987). Do abused children become abusive parents? *American Journal of Orthopsychiatry, 57,* 186–192.

Kaye, Kenneth (1977). Toward the origin of dialogue. In H. R. Schaffer (ed.), *Studies in mother-infant interaction.* New York: Academic Press.

Keating, Caroline F. (1994). World without words: Messages from face and body. In W. J. Lonner & R. Malpass (eds.), *Psychology and culture.* Needham Heights, MA: Allyn & Bacon.

Keller, Martin B.; McCullough, James P.; Klein, Daniel N.; et al. (2000, May 18). A comparison of nefazodone, the cognitive behavioral-analysis system of psychotherapy, and their combination for the treatment of chronic depression. *New England Journal of Medicine, 342,* 1462–1470.

Kelman, Herbert C., & Hamilton, V. Lee (1989). *Crimes of obedience: Toward a social psychology of authority and responsibility.* New Haven, CT: Yale University Press.

Kempermann, G.; Brandon, E. P.; & Gage, F. H. (1998). Environmental stimulation of 120/SvJ mice causes increased cell proliferation and neurogenesis in the adult dentate gyrus. *Current Biology, 8,* 939–942.

Kendall-Tackett, Kathleen A.; Williams, Linda Meyer; & Finkelhor, David (1993). Impact of sexual abuse on children: A review and synthesis of recent empirical studies. *Psychological Bulletin, 113,* 164–180.

Kenny, Michael G. (1986). *The passion of Ansel Bourne: Multiple personality in American culture.* Washington, DC: Smithsonian Press.

Kenrick, Douglas T., & Trost, Melanie R. (1993). The evolutionary perspective. In A. E. Beall & R. J. Sternberg (eds.), *The psychology of gender.* New York: Guilford Press.

Kernberg, Otto F. (1976). *Object relations theory and clinical practice.* New York: Jason Aronson.

Kerr, Norbert L. (1995). Norms in social dilemmas. In D. Schroeder (ed.), *Social dilemmas: Perspectives on individuals and groups.* Westport, CT: Praeger.

Kessler, Ronald C.; McGonagle, Katherine A.; Zhao, Shanyang; et al. (1994). Lifetime and 12-month prevalence of DSM-III-R psychiatric disorders in the United States: Results from the National Comorbidity Study. *Archives of General Psychiatry, 51,* 8–19.

Kessler, Ronald C.; Sonnega, A.; Bromet, E.; et al. (1995). Posttraumatic stress disorder in the National Comorbidity Survey. *Archives of General Psychiatry, 52,* 1048–1060.

Kihlstrom, John F. (1994). Hypnosis, delayed recall, and the principles of memory. *International Journal of Clinical and Experimental Hypnosis, 40,* 337–345.

Kihlstrom, John F. (1995). From a subject's point of view: The experiment as conversation and collaboration between investigator and subject. Invited address presented at the annual meeting of the American Psychological Society, New York.

Kihlstrom, John F., & Harackiewicz, Judith M. (1982). The earliest recollection: A new survey. *Journal of Personality, 50,* 134–148.

Kim, Karl H. S.; Relkin, Norman R.; Lee, Kyoung-Min; & Hirsch, Joy (1997). Distinct cortical areas associated with native and second languages. *Nature, 388,* 171–174.

King, Patricia M., & Kitchener, Karen S. (1994). *Developing reflective judgment: Understanding and promoting intellectual growth and critical thinking in adolescents and adults.* San Francisco: Jossey-Bass.

Kinsbourne, Marcel (1982). Hemispheric specialization and the growth of human understanding. *American Psychologist, 37,* 411–420.

Kirsch, Irving, & Lynn, Steven Jay (1995). The altered state of hypnosis: Changes in the theoretical landscape. *American Psychologist, 50,* 846–858.

Kirsch, Irving; Montgomery, G.; & Sapirstein, Guy (1995). Hypnosis as an adjunct to cognitive behavioral psychotherapy: A meta-analysis. *Journal of Consulting and Clinical Psychology, 63,* 214–220.

Kirsch, Irving, & Sapirstein, Guy (1998). Listening to Prozac but hearing placebo: A meta-analysis of antidepressant medication. *Prevention & Treatment, 1, Article 0002a,* posted electronically June 26, 1998 on the website of the American Psychological Association.

Kirschenbaum, B.; Nedergaard, M.; Preuss, A.; et al. (1994). In vitro neuronal production and differentiation by precursor cells derived from the adult human forebrain. *Cerebral Cortex, 4,* 576–589.

Kitchener, Karen S., & King, Patricia M. (1990). The Reflective Judgment Model: Ten years of research. In M. L. Commons (ed.), *Models and methods in the study of adolescent and adult thought* (Vol. 2): *Adult development.* Westport, CT: Greenwood Press.

Kitchener, Karen S.; Lynch, Cindy L.; Fischer, Kurt W.; & Wood, Phillip K. (1993). Developmental range of reflective judgment: The effect of contextual support and practice on developmental stage. *Developmental Psychology, 29,* 893–906.

Klein, Donald F. (1980). Psychosocial treatment of schizophrenia, or psychosocial help for people with schizophrenia? *Schizophrenia Bulletin, 6,* 122–130.

Klein, Stanley B., & Kihlstrom, John F. (1998). On bridging the gap between social-personality psychology and neuropsychology. *Personality and Social Psychology Review, 2,* 228–242.

Kleinman, Arthur (1988). *Rethinking psychiatry: From cultural category to personal experience.* New York: Free Press.

Klerman, Gerald L.; Weissman, Myrna M.; Rounsaville, Bruce J.; & Chevron, Eve S. (1984). *Interpersonal psychotherapy of depression.* New York: Basic Books.

Klima, Edward S., & Bellugi, Ursula (1966). Syntactic regularities in the speech of children. In J. Lyons & R. J. Wales (eds.), *Psycholinguistics papers.* Edinburgh, Scotland: Edinburgh University Press.

Kluft, Richard P. (1987). The simulation and dissimulation of multiple personality disorder. *American Journal of Clinical Hypnosis, 30,* 104–118.

Kluft, Richard P. (1993). Multiple personality disorders. In D. Spiegel (ed.), *Dissociative disorders: A clinical review.* Lutherville, MD: Sidran.

Kluger, Richard (1996). *Ashes to ashes: America's hundred-year cigarette war, the public health, and the unabashed triumph of Philip Morris.* New York: Knopf.

Kohlberg, Lawrence (1964). Development of moral character and moral ideology. In M. Hoffman & L. W. Hoffman (eds.), *Review of child development research.* New York: Russell Sage Foundation.

Kohlberg, Lawrence (1976). Moral stages and moralization: The cognitive-developmental approach. In T. Lickona (ed.), *Moral development and behavior.* New York: Holt, Rinehart and Winston.

Kohlberg, Lawrence (1984). *Essays on moral development* (Vol. 2): *The psychology of moral development: The nature and validity of moral stages.* San Francisco: Harper & Row.

Köhler, Wolfgang (1925). *The mentality of apes.* New York: Harcourt, Brace.

Köhler, Wolfgang (1959). Gestalt psychology today. Presidential address to the American Psychological Association, Cincinnati. [Reprinted in E. R. Hilgard (ed.), *American psychology in historical perspective: Addresses of the presidents of the American Psychological Association, 1892–1977.* Washington, DC: American Psychological Association, 1978.]

Kohn, Alfie (1992). *No contest: The case against competition* (rev. ed.). Boston: Houghton Mifflin.

Kohn, Alfie (1993). *Punished by rewards.* Boston: Houghton Mifflin.

Kohn, Melvin, & Schooler, Carmi (1983). *Work and personality: An inquiry into the impact of social stratification.* Norwood, NJ: Ablex.

Kolb, B., & Whishaw, I. Q. (1998). Brain plasticity and behavior. *Annual Review of Psychology, 49,* 43–64.

Kolbert, Elizabeth (1995, June 5). Public opinion polls swerve with the turns of a phrase. *The New York Times, 144,* A1.

Koocher, Gerald P.; Goodman, Gail S.; White, C. Sue; et al. (1995). Psychological science and the use of anatomically detailed dolls in child sexual-abuse assessments. *Psychological Bulletin, 118,* 199–222.

Korn, James H. (1998). *Illusions of reality: A history of deception in social psychology.* New York: State University of New York Press.

Kosslyn, Stephen M. (1980). *Image and mind.* Cambridge, MA: Harvard University Press.

Kozak, Michael J.; Liebowitz, Michael R.; & Foa, Edna B. (2000). Cognitive-behavior therapy and pharmacotherapy for OCD: The NIMH-sponsored collaborative study. In W. K. Goodman, M. Rudorfer, & J. Maser (eds.), *Treatment challenges in obsessive compulsive disorder.* Mahwah, NJ: Erlbaum.

Kring, Ann M., & Gordon, Albert H. (1998). Sex differences in emotion: Expression, experience, and physiology. *Journal of Personality and Social Psychology, 74,* 686–703.

Kroll, Barry M. (1992). *Teaching hearts and minds: College students reflect on the Vietnam War in literature.* Carbondale: Southern Illinois University Press.

Krumhansl, Carol L. (2000). Rhythm and pitch in music cognition. *Psychological Bulletin, 126,* 159–179.

Krupa, David J.; Thompson, Judith K.; & Thompson, Richard F. (1993). Localization of a memory trace in the mammalian brain. *Science, 260,* 989–991.

Kuhn, Deanna; Weinstock, Michael; & Flaton, Robin (1994). How well do jurors reason? Competence dimensions of individual variation in a juror reasoning task. *Psychological Science, 5,* 289–296.

Kunda, Ziva (1990). The case for motivated reasoning. *Psychological Bulletin, 108,* 480–498.

Kurdek, L. A. (1987). Sex role self schema and psychological adjustment in coupled homosexual and heterosexual men and women. *Sex Roles, 17,* 549–562.

Kurtines, William M., & Gewirtz, Jacob L. (eds.) (1991). *Handbook of moral behavior and development* (Vols. 1–3). Hillsdale, NJ: Erlbaum.

Kutchins, Herb, & Kirk, Stuart A. (1997). *Making us crazy: DSM. The psychiatric bible and the creation of mental disorders.* New York: Free Press.

LaFromboise, Teresa; Coleman, Hardin L. K.; & Gerton, Jennifer (1993). Psychological impact of biculturalism: Evidence and theory. *Psychological Bulletin, 114,* 395–412.

Lakoff, Robin T., & Coyne, James C. (1993). *Father knows best: The use and abuse of power in Freud's case of "Dora."* New York: Teachers College Press.

Landrine, Hope (1988). Revising the framework of abnormal psychology. In P. Bronstein & K. Quina (eds.), *Teaching a psychology of people.* Washington, DC: American Psychological Association.

Lane, Charles (1994, December 1). The tainted sources of "The Bell Curve." *New York Review of Books,* 14–18.

Langer, Ellen J. (1989). *Mindfulness.* Reading, MA: Addison-Wesley.

Langer, Ellen J.; Blank, Arthur; & Chanowitz, Benzion (1978). The mindlessness of ostensibly thoughtful action: The role of placebic information in interpersonal interaction. *Journal of Personality and Social Psychology, 36,* 635–642.

Langer, Ellen J., & Moldoveanu, Mihnea (2000). The construct of mindfulness. *Journal of Social Issues, 56,* 1–9.

Latané, Bibb; Williams, Kipling; & Harkins, Stephen (1979). Many hands make light the work: The causes and consequences of social loafing. *Journal of Personality and Social Psychology, 37,* 822–832.

Laumann, Edward O., & Gagnon John H. (1995). A sociological perspective on sexual action. In R. G. Parker & J. H. Gagnon (eds.), *Conceiving sexuality: Approaches to sex research in a postmodern world.* New York: Routledge.

Laumann, Edward O.; Gagnon, John H.; Michael, Robert T.; & Michaels, Stuart (1994). *The social organization of sexuality.* Chicago: University of Chicago Press.

Laursen, Brett, & Collins, W. Andrew (1994). Interpersonal conflict during adolescence. *Psychological Bulletin, 115,* 197–209.

Lazarus, Richard S. (1991). Cognition and motivation in emotion. *American Psychologist, 46,* 352–367.

LeDoux, Joseph E. (1994, June). Emotion, memory, and the brain. *Scientific American, 220,* 50–57.

LeDoux, Joseph E. (1996). *The emotional brain.* New York: Simon & Schuster.

Leibel, Rudolph L.; Rosenbaum, Michael; & Hirsch, Jules (1995). Changes in energy expenditure resulting from altered body weight. *New England Journal of Medicine, 332,* 621–628.

Lent, James R. (1968, June). Mimosa cottage: Experiment in hope. *Psychology Today,* 51–58.

Leonard, S.; Gault, J.; Moore, T.; et al. (1998, July 10). Further investigation of a chromosome 15 locus in schizophrenia: Analysis of affected sibpairs from the NIMH Genetics Initiative. *American Journal of Medical Genetics, 81,* 308–312.

Lepowsky, Maria (1994). *Fruit of the motherland: Gender in an egalitarian society.* New York: Columbia University Press.

Lepper, Mark R.; Greene, David; & Nisbett, Richard E. (1973). Undermining children's intrinsic interest with extrinsic rewards. *Journal of Personality and Social Psychology, 28,* 129–137.

Lepper, Mark R.; Henderlong, Jennifer; & Gingras, Isabelle (1999). Understanding the effects of extrinsic rewards on intrinsic motivation—Uses and abuse of meta-analysis: Comment on Deci, Koestner, and Ryan (1999). *Psychological Bulletin, 125,* 669–676.

Leproult, Rachel; Copinschi, Georges; Buxton, Orfeu; & Van Cauter, Eve (1997). Sleep loss results in an elevation of cortisol levels the next evening. *Sleep, 20,* 865–870.

Leproult, Rachel; Van Reeth, Olivier; Byrne, Maria M.; et al. (1997). Sleepiness, performance, and neuroendocrine function during sleep deprivation: Effects of exposure to bright light or exercise. *Journal of Biological Rhythms, 12,* 245–258.

Lerner, Harriet G. (1989). *The dance of intimacy.* New York: Harper & Row.

Lerner, Melvin J. (1980). *The belief in a just world: A fundamental delusion.* New York: Plenum.

Levenson, Leah (1983). *With wooden sword: A portrait of Francis Sheehy-Skeffington, militant pacifist.* Boston: Northeastern University Press.

Levenson, Robert W. (1992). Autonomic nervous system differences among emotions. *Psychological Science, 3,* 23–27.

Levine, Joseph, & Suzuki, David (1993). *The secret of life: Redesigning the living world.* Boston: WGBH Educational Foundation.

Levine, Robert V.; Martinez, Todd S.; Brase, Gary; & Sorenson, Kerry (1994). Helping in 36 U.S. cities. *Journal of Personality and Social Psychology, 67,* 69–82.

Levinson, D. F.; Mahtani, M. M.; Nancarrow, D. J.; et al. (1998). Genome scan of schizophrenia. *American Journal of Psychiatry, 155,* 741–750.

Levitan, Alexander A., & Ronan, William J. (1988). Problems in the treatment of obesity and eating disorders. *Medical Hypnoanalysis Journal, 3,* 131–136.

Levy, Becca (1996). Improving memory in old age through implicit self-stereotyping. *Journal of Personality and Social Psychology, 71,* 1092–1107.

Levy, David A. (1997). *Tools of critical thinking: Metathoughts for psychology.* Boston: Allyn & Bacon.

Levy, Jerre (1985, May). Right brain, left brain: Fact and fiction. *Psychology Today,* 38–39, 42–44.

Levy, Jerre; Trevarthen, Colwyn; & Sperry, Roger W. (1972). Perception of bilateral chimeric figures following hemispheric deconnection. *Brain, 95,* 61–78.

Levy, Robert I. (1984). The emotions in comparative perspective. In K. R. Scherer & P. Ekman (eds.), *Approaches to emotion.* Hillsdale, NJ: Erlbaum.

Levy-Lehad, Ephrat; Wasco, Wilma; Poorkaj, Parvoneh; et al. (1995). Candidate gene for the chromosome 1 familial Alzheimer's disease locus. *Science, 269,* 973–977.

Lewis, Dorothy O. (ed.) (1981). *Vulnerabilities to delinquency.* New York: Spectrum Medical and Scientific Books.

Lewis, Dorothy O. (1992). From abuse to violence: Psychophysiological consequences of maltreatment. *Journal of the American Academy of Child and Adolescent Psychiatry, 31,* 383–391.

Lewis, Michael (1992). *Shame: The exposed self.* New York: Free Press.

Lewis, Michael (1997). *Altering fate: Why the past does not predict the future.* New York: Guilford Press.

Lewontin, Richard C. (1970). Race and intelligence. *Bulletin of the Atomic Scientists, 26*(3), 2–8.

Lewontin, Richard C.; Rose, Steven; & Kamin, Leon J. (1984). *Not in our genes: Biology, ideology, and human nature.* New York: Pantheon.

Lewy, Alfred J.; Ahmed, Saeeduddin; Jackson, Jeanne L.; & Sack, Robert L. (1992). Melatonin shifts human circadian rhythms according to a phase response curve. *Chronobiology International, 9,* 380–392.

Lichtenstein, Sarah; Slovic, Paul; Fischhoff, Baruch; et al. (1978). Judged frequency of lethal events. *Journal of Experimental Psychology: Human Learning and Memory, 4,* 551–578.

Lickona, Thomas (1983). *Raising good children.* New York: Bantam.

Liepert, J.; Bauder, H.; Miltner, W. H.; et al. (2000). Treatment-included cortical reorganization after stroke in humans. *Stroke, 31,* 1210–1216.

Lifton, Robert J. (1986). *The Nazi doctors: Medical killing and the psychology of genocide.* New York: Basic Books.

Lightdale, Jenifer R., & Prentice, Deborah A. (1994). Rethinking sex differences in aggression: Aggressive behavior in the absence of social roles. *Personality and Social Psychology Bulletin, 20,* 34–44.

Lilienfeld, Scott O. (1993, Fall). Do "honesty" tests really measure honesty? *Skeptical Inquirer, 18,* 32–41.

Lilienfeld, Scott O. (1999, September/October). Projective measures of personality and psychopathology: How well do they work? *Skeptical Inquirer,* 32–39.

Lillard, Angeline (1998). Ethnopsychologies: Cultural variations in theories of mind. *Psychological Bulletin, 123,* 3–32.

Lin, Keh-Ming; Poland, Russell E.; & Chien, C. P. (1990). Ethnicity and psychopharmacology: Recent findings and future research directions. In E. Sorel (ed.), *Family, culture, and psychobiology.* New York: Legas.

Linday, Linda A. (1994). Maternal reports of pregnancy, genital, and related fantasies in preschool and kindergarten children. *Journal of the American Academy of Child and Adolescent Psychiatry, 33,* 416–423.

Lindsay, D. Stephen, & Read, J. Don (1994). Psychotherapy and memories of childhood sexual abuse: A cognitive perspective. *Applied Cognitive Psychology, 8,* 281–338.

Lindvall, O.; Sawle, G.; Widner, H.; et al. (1994). Evidence for long-term survival and function of dopaminergic grafts in progressive Parkinson's disease. *Annals of Neurology, 35,* 172–180.

Linton, Marigold (1978). Real-world memory after six years: An in vivo study of very long-term memory. In M. M. Gruneberg, P. E. Morris, & R. N. Sykes (eds.), *Practical aspects of memory.* London: Academic Press.

Linville, P. W.; Fischer, G. W.; & Fischhoff, B. (1992). AIDS risk perceptions and decision biases. In J. B. Pryor & G. D. Reeder (eds.), *The social psychology of HIV infection.* Hillsdale, NJ: Erlbaum.

Lipstadt, Deborah E. (1994, Spring). Denying the Holocaust: The fragility of memory. *Brandeis Review,* 30–33.

Lissner, L.; Odell, P. M.; D'Agostino, R. B.; et al. (1991, June 27). Variability of body weight and health outcomes in the Framingham population. *New England Journal of Medicine, 324*(26), 1839–1844.

Locke, Edwin A., & Latham, Gary P. (1990). Work motivation and satisfaction: Light at the end of the tunnel. *Psychological Science, 1,* 240–246.

Locke, Edwin A.; Shaw, Karyll; Saari, Lise; & Latham, Gary (1981). Goal-setting and task performance: 1969–1980. *Psychological Bulletin, 90,* 125–152.

Loehlin, John C. (1992). *Genes and environment in personality development.* Newbury Park, CA: Sage.

Loehlin, John C.,: Horn, J. M.; & Willerman, L. (1996). Heredity, environment, and IQ in the Texas adoption study. In R. J. Sternberg & E. Grigorenko (eds.), *Intelligence: Heredity and environment.* New York: Cambridge University Press.

Loewen, E. Ruth; Shaw, Raymond J.; & Craik, Fergus I. (1990). Age differences in components of metamemory. *Experimental Aging Research, 16*(1–2), 43–48.

Loftus, Elizabeth F. (1996). Memory distortion and false memory creation. *Bulletin of the American Academy of Psychiatry and the Law, 24*(3), 281–295.

Loftus, Elizabeth F., & Greene, Edith (1980). Warning: Even memory for faces may be contagious. *Law and Human Behavior, 4,* 323–334.

Loftus, Elizabeth F., & Ketcham, Katherine (1994). *The myth of repressed memory.* New York: St. Martin's Press.

Loftus, Elizabeth F.; Miller, David G.; & Burns, Helen J. (1978). Semantic integration of verbal information into a visual memory. *Journal of Experimental Psychology: Human Learning and Memory, 4,* 19–31.

Loftus, Elizabeth F., & Palmer, John C. (1974). Reconstruction of automobile destruction: An example of the interaction between language and memory. *Journal of Verbal Learning and Verbal Behavior, 13,* 585–589.

Loftus, Elizabeth F., & Pickrell, Jacqueline E. (1995). The formation of false memories. *Psychiatric Annals, 25,* 720–725.

Loftus, Elizabeth F., & Zanni, Guido (1975). Eyewitness testimony: The influence of the wording of a question. *Bulletin of the Psychonomic Society, 5,* 86–88.

Lonner, Walter J. (1995). Culture and human diversity. In E. Trickett, R. Watts, & D. Birman (eds.), *Human diversity: Perspectives on people in context.* San Francisco: Jossey-Bass.

Lonner, Walter J., & Malpass, Roy S. (1994). When psychology and culture meet: An introduction to cross-cultural psychology. In W. J. Lonner & R. S. Malpass (eds.), *Psychology and culture.* Needham Heights, MA: Allyn & Bacon.

López, Steven R. (1989). Patient variable biases in clinical judgment: Conceptual overview and methodological considerations. *Psychological Bulletin, 106,* 184–203.

López, Steven R. (1995). Testing ethnic minority children. In B. B. Wolman (ed.), *The encyclopedia of psychology, psychiatry, and psychoanalysis.* New York: Henry Holt.

Lott, Bernice, & Maluso, Diane (1993). The social learning of gender. In A. E. Beall & R. J. Sternberg (eds.), *The psychology of gender.* New York: Guilford Press.

Louie, Therese A. (1999). Decision makers' hindsight bias after making favorable and unfavorable feedback. *Journal of Applied Psychology, 84,* 29–41.

Lovaas, O. Ivar (1977). *The autistic child: Language development through behavior modification.* New York: Halsted Press.

Lovaas, O. Ivar; Schreibman, Laura; & Koegel, Robert L. (1974). A behavior modification approach to the treatment of autistic children. *Journal of Autism and Childhood Schizophrenia, 4,* 111–129.

Luengo, M. A.; Carrillo-de-la-Peña, M. T.; Otero, J. M.; & Romero, E. (1994). A short-term longitudinal study of impulsivity and antisocial behavior. *Journal of Personality and Social Psychology, 66,* 542–548.

Luepnitz, Deborah A. (1988). *The family interpreted: Feminist theory in clinical practice.* New York: Basic Books.

Lugaresi, Elio; Medori, R.; Montagna, P.; et al. (1986, October 16). Fatal familial insomnia and dysautonomia with selective degeneration of thalamic nuclei. *New England Journal of Medicine, 315,* 997–1003.

Luhrmann, T. M. (2000). *Of two minds: The growing disorder in American psychiatry.* New York: Knopf.

Luria, Alexander (1968). *The mind of a mnemonist* (L. Soltaroff, trans.). New York: Basic Books.

Luria, Alexander R. (1980). *Higher cortical functions in man* (2nd rev. ed.). New York: Basic Books.

Lutz, Catherine (1988). *Unnatural emotions.* Chicago: University of Chicago Press.

Lykken, David, & Tellegen, Auke (1996). Happiness is a stochastic phenomenon. *Psychological Science, 7,* 186–189.

Lytton, Hugh, & Romney, David M. (1991). Parents' differential socialization of boys and girls: A meta-analysis. *Psychological Bulletin, 109,* 267–296.

Lyubomirsky, Sonja; Caldwell, Nicole D.; & Nolen-Hoeksema, Susan (1998). Effects of ruminative and distracting responses to depressed mood on retrieval of autobiographical memories. *Journal of Personality and Social Psychology, 75,* 166–177.

Maas, James B. (1998). *Power sleep.* New York: Villard.

Maccoby, Eleanor E. (1998). *The two sexes: Growing up apart, coming together.* Cambridge, MA: Belknap Press/Harvard University Press.

MacKavey, William R.; Malley, Janet E.; & Stewart, Abigail J. (1991). Remembering autobiographically consequential experiences: Content analysis of psychologists' accounts of their lives. *Psychology and Aging, 6,* 50–59.

MacKinnon, Donald W. (1968). Selecting students with creative potential. In P. Heist (ed.), *The creative college student: An unmet challenge.* San Francisco: Jossey-Bass.

MacLean, Paul (1993). Cerebral evolution of emotion. In M. Lewis & J. M. Haviland (eds.), *Handbook of emotions.* New York: Guilford Press.

Macrae, C. Neil; Milne, Alan B.; & Bodenhausen, Galen V. (1994). Stereotypes as energy-saving devices: A peek inside the cognitive toolbox. *Journal of Personality and Social Psychology, 66,* 37–47.

Maddux, James E. (ed.) (1995). *Self-efficacy, adaptation, and adjustment: Theory, research, and application.* New York: Plenum.

Maddux, James E. (1996). The social-cognitive construction of difference and disorder. In D. F. Barone, J. E. Maddux, & C. R. Snyder (eds.), *Social cognitive psychology: History and current domains.* New York: Plenum.

Maddux, James E., & Mundell, Clare E. (1997). Disorders of personality. In V. Derlega, B. Winstead, & W. Jones (eds.), *Personality: Contemporary theory and research* (2nd ed.). Chicago: Nelson-Hall.

Madigan, Carol O., & Elwood, Ann (1984). *Brainstorms and thunderbolts.* New York: Macmillan.

Maguire, Eleanor A.; Gadian, David G.; Johnsrude, Ingrid S.; et al. (2000). Navigation-related structural change in the hippocampi of taxi drivers. *Proceedings of the National Academy of Sciences, 97,* 4398–4403.

Major, Brenda; Spencer, Steven; Schmader, Toni; et al. (1998). Coping with negative stereotypes about intellectual performance: The role of psychological disengagement. *Personality and Social Psychology Bulletin, 24,* 34–50.

Malamuth, Neil, & Dean, Karol (1990). Attraction to sexual aggression. In A. Parrot & L. Bechhofer (eds.), *Acquaintance rape: The hidden crime.* Newark, NJ: Wiley.

Malinosky-Rummell, Robin, & Hansen, David J. (1993). Long-term consequences of childhood physical abuse. *Psychological Bulletin, 114,* 68–79.

Manning, Carol A.; Hall, J. L.; & Gold, Paul E. (1990). Glucose effects on memory and other neuropsychological tests in elderly humans. *Psychological Science, 1,* 307–311.

Mansfield, Elizabeth D., & McAdams, Dan P. (1996). Generativity and themes of agency and community in adult autobiography. *Personality and Social Psychology Bulletin, 22,* 721–731.

Marcus, Gary F.; Pinker, Steven; Ullman, Michael; et al. (1992). Overregularization in language acquisi-

tion. *Monographs of the Society for Research in Child Development, 57*(Serial No. 228), 1–182.

Marcus, Gary F.; Vijayan, S.; Rao, S. Bandi; & Vishton, P. M. (1999, January 1). Rule learning by seven-month-old infants. *Science, 283,* 77–79.

Marcus-Newhall, Amy; Pedersen, William C.; Carlson, Mike; & Miller, Norman (2000). Displaced aggression is alive and well: A meta-analytic review. *Journal of Personality and Social Psychology, 78,* 670–689.

Marino, Raul, Jr., & Cosgrove, G. Rees (1997). Neurosurgical treatment of neuropsychiatric illness. *Psychiatric Clinics of North America, 20,* 933–943.

Markus, Hazel R., & Kitayama, Shinobu (1991). Culture and the self: Implications for cognition, emotion, and motivation. *Psychological Review, 98,* 224–253.

Marshall, Grant N.; Wortman, Camille B.; Vickers, Ross R., Jr.; et al. (1994). The five-factor model of personality as a framework for personality-health research. *Journal of Personality and Social Psychology, 67,* 278–286.

Masand, P. S. (2000). Side effects of antipsychotics in the elderly. *Journal of Clinical Psychiatry, 61*(Suppl. 8), 43–49.

Maslow, Abraham H. (1971). *The farther reaches of human nature.* New York: Viking.

Masten, Ann S., & Coatsworth, J. Douglas (1998). The development of competence in favorable and unfavorable environments. *American Psychologist, 53,* 205–220.

Masters, William H., & Johnson, Virginia E. (1966). *Human sexual response.* Boston: Little, Brown.

Mather, Mara; Shafir, Eldar; & Johnson, Marcia K. (2000). Misremembrance of options past: Source monitoring and choice. *Psychological Science, 11,* 132–138.

Matsumoto, David (1996). *Culture and psychology.* Pacific Grove, CA: Brooks-Cole.

Mawhinney, T. C. (1990). Decreasing intrinsic "motivation" with extrinsic rewards: Easier said than done. *Journal of Organizational Behavior Management, 11,* 175–191.

Maxfield, Michael, & Widom, Cathy S. (1996). The cycle of violence: Revisited 6 years later. *Archives of Pediatric and Adolescent Medicine, 150,* 390–395.

May, Rollo (1994). *The discovery of being: Writings in existential psychology.* New York: W. W. Norton.

Mayer, John D.; McCormick, Laura J.; & Strong, Sara E. (1995). Mood-congruent memory and natural mood: New evidence. *Personality and Social Psychology Bulletin, 21,* 736–746.

Mazza, James J.; Reynolds, William M.; & Grover, Jennifer H. (1995). Exposure to violence, suicidal ideation and depression in school-based adolescents. Paper presented at the annual meeting of the American Psychological Association, New York.

Mazzoni, Guiliana A. L.; Loftus, Elizabeth F.; Seitz, Aaron; & Lynn, Steven J. (1999). Changing beliefs and memories through dream interpretation. *Applied Cognitive Psychology, 13,* 125–144.

McAdams, Dan P. (1988). *Power, intimacy, and the life story: Personological inquiries into identity.* New York: Guilford Press.

McClearn, Gerald E.; Johanson, Boo; Berg, Stig; et al. (1997). Substantial genetic influence on cognitive abilities in twins 80 or more years old. *Science, 176,* 1560–1563.

McClelland, David C. (1961). *The achieving society.* New York: Free Press.

McClelland, David C. (1987). Characteristics of successful entrepreneurs. *Journal of Creative Behavior, 3,* 219–233.

McClelland, David C.; Atkinson, John W.; Clark, Russell A.; & Lowell, Edgar L. (1953). *The achievement motive.* New York: Appleton-Century-Crofts.

McClelland, James L. (1994). The organization of memory: A parallel distributed processing perspective. *Revue Neurologique, 150,* 570–579.

McConnell, James V. (1962). Memory transfer through cannibalism in planarians. *Journal of Neuropsychiatry, 3*(Monograph Suppl. 1).

McCord, Joan (1992). The Cambridge-Somerville study: A pioneering longitudinal-experimental study of delinquency prevention. In J. McCord & R. E. Tremblay (eds.), *Preventing antisocial behavior: Interventions from birth through adolescence.* New York: Guilford Press.

McCrae, Robert R. (1987). Creativity, divergent thinking, and openness to experience. *Journal of Personality and Social Psychology, 52,* 1258–1265.

McCrae, Robert R., & Costa, Paul T., Jr. (1988). Do parental influences matter? A reply to Halverson. *Journal of Personality, 56,* 445–449.

McCrae, Robert R., & Costa, Paul T., Jr. (1996). Toward a new generation of personality theories: Theoretical contexts for the five-factor model. In J. S. Wiggins (ed.), *The five-factor model of personality: Theoretical perspectives.* New York: Guilford Press.

McCrae, Robert R., & Costa, Paul T., Jr. (1997). Personality trait structure as a human universal. *American Psychologist, 52,* 509–516.

McDonald, Kim A. (1998, August 14). Scientists consider new explanations for the impact of exercise on mood. *Chronicle of Higher Education,* A15–A16.

McDonough, Laraine, & Mandler, Jean M. (1994). Very long-term recall in infancy. *Memory, 2,* 339–352.

McFarlane, Jessica; Martin, Carol L.; & Williams, Tannis M. (1988). Mood fluctuations: Women versus men and menstrual versus other cycles. *Psychology of Women Quarterly, 12,* 201–223.

McFarlane, Jessica, & Williams, Tannis M. (1994). Placing premenstrual syndrome in perspective. *Psychology of Women Quarterly, 18,* 339–373.

McGaugh, James L. (1990). Significance and remembrance: The role of neuromodulatory systems. *Psychological Science, 1,* 15–25.

McGaugh, James L. (1999). Making memories that linger: Emotional arousal, stress hormones and brain systems. Invited address at the annual meeting of the Western Psychological Association, Irvine.

McGlynn, Susan M. (1990). Behavioral approaches to neuropsychological rehabilitation. *Psychological Bulletin, 108,* 420–441.

McGrath, Ellen; Keita, Gwendolyn P.; Strickland, Bonnie; & Russo, Nancy F. (eds.) (1990). *Women and depression: Risk factors and treatment issues.* Washington, DC: American Psychological Association.

McGregor, Ian, & Holmes, John G. (1999). How storytelling shapes memory and impressions of relationship events over time. *Journal of Personality and Social Psychology, 76,* 403–419.

McGue, Matt; Bouchard, Thomas J., Jr.; Iacono, William G.; & Lykken, David T. (1993). Behavioral genetics of cognitive ability: A life-span perspective. In R. Plomin & G. E. McClearn (eds.), *Nature, nurture, and psychology.* Washington, DC: American Psychological Association.

McGue, Matt, & Lykken, David T. (1992). Genetic influence on risk of divorce. *Psychological Science, 3,* 368–373.

McGuinness, Diane (1993). Sex differences in cognitive style: Implications for math performance and achievement. In L. A. Penner, G. M. Batsche, & H. Knoff (eds.), *The challenge in mathematics and science education: Psychology's response.* Washington, DC: American Psychological Association.

McHugh, Paul R. (1993a). History and the pitfalls of practice. Unpublished paper, Johns Hopkins University, Department of Psychiatry.

McHugh, Paul R. (1993b, December). Psychotherapy awry. *American Scholar,* 17–30.

McKee, Richard D., & Squire, Larry R. (1992). Equivalent forgetting rates in long-term memory for diencephalic and medial temporal lobe amnesia. *Journal of Neuroscience, 12,* 3765–3772.

McKee, Richard D., & Squire, Larry R. (1993). On the development of declarative memory. *Journal of Experimental Psychology: Learning, Memory, and Cognition, 19,* 397–404.

McKim, Margaret K.; Cramer, Kenneth M.; Stuart, Barbara; & O'Connor, Deborah L. (1999). Infant care decisions and attachment security: The Canadian Transition to Child Care Study. *Canadian Journal of Behavioural Science, 31,* 92–106.

McLeod, Beverly (1985, March). Real work for real pay. *Psychology Today,* 42–44, 46, 48–50.

McNally, Richard J. (1996). Cognitive bias in the anxiety disorders. In D. A. Hope et al. (eds.), *Nebraska Symposium on Motivation* (Vol. 40): *Perspectives on anxiety, panic, and fear.* Lincoln: University of Nebraska Press.

McNally, Richard J. (1998). Panic attacks. In *Encyclopedia of mental health* (Vol. 3). New York: Academic Press.

McNaughton, B. L., & Morris, R. G. M. (1987). Hippocampal synaptic enhancement and information storage within a distributed memory system. *Trends in Neuroscience, 10,* 408–415.

McNeill, David (1966). Developmental psycholinguistics. In F. L. Smith & G. A. Miller (eds.), *The genesis of language: A psycholinguistic approach.* Cambridge, MA: MIT Press.

Mealey, Linda (1996). Evolutionary psychology: The search for evolved mental mechanisms underlying complex human behavior. In J. P. Hurd (ed.), *Investigating the biological foundations of human morality* (Vol. 37). Lewiston, NY: Edwin Mellen Press.

Medawar, Peter B. (1979). *Advice to a young scientist.* New York: Harper & Row.

Medawar, Peter B. (1982). *Pluto's republic.* Oxford, England: Oxford University Press.

Mednick, Martha T. (1989). On the politics of psychological constructs: Stop the bandwagon, I want to get off. *American Psychologist, 44,* 1118–1123.

Mednick, Sarnoff A. (1962). The associative basis of the creative process. *Psychological Review, 69,* 220–232.

Mednick, Sarnoff A.; Huttunen, Matti O.; & Machón, Ricardo (1994). Prenatal influenza infections and adult schizophrenia. *Schizophrenia Bulletin, 20,* 263–267.

Medvec, Victoria H.; Madey, Scott F.; & Gilovich, Thomas (1995). When less is more: Counterfactual thinking and satisfaction among Olympic medalists. *Journal of Personality and Social Psychology, 69,* 603–610.

Meeus, Wim H. J., & Raaijmakers, Quinten A. W. (1995). Obedience in modern society: The Utrecht studies. *Journal of Social Issues, 51,* 155–175.

Meindl, J. R., & Lerner, M. J. (1985). Exacerbation of extreme responses to an out-group. *Journal of Personality and Social Psychology, 47,* 71–84.

Menon, Tanya; Morris, Michael W.; Chiu, Chi-yue; & Hone, Ying-yi (1999). Culture and the construal of agency: Attribution to individual versus group dispositions. *Journal of Personality and Social Psychology, 76,* 701–717.

Mercer, Jane (1988, May 18). Racial differences in intelligence: Fact or artifact? Talk given at San Bernardino Valley College, San Bernardino, CA.

Merskey, Harold (1992). The manufacture of personalities: The production of MPD. *British Journal of Psychiatry, 160,* 327–340.

Merskey, Harold (1995). The manufacture of personalities: The production of multiple personality disorder. In L. M. Cohen, J. N. Berzoff, & M. R. Elin (eds.), *Dissociative identity disorder: Theoretical and treatment controversies.* Northvale, NJ: Jason Aronson.

Merton, Robert K. (1948). The self-fulfilling prophecy. *Antioch Review, 8,* 193–210.

Meyer-Bahlburg, Heino F. L.; Ehrhardt, Anke A.; Rosen, Laura R.; et al. (1995). Prenatal estrogens and the development of homosexual orientation. *Developmental Psychology, 31,* 12–21.

Meyerowitz, Beth E., & Chaiken, Shelley (1987). The effect of message framing on breast self-examination attitudes, intentions, and behavior. *Journal of Personality and Social Psychology, 52,* 500–510.

Mickelson, Kristin D.; Kessler, Ronald C.; & Shaver, Phillip R. (1997). Adult attachment in a nationally representative sample. *Journal of Personality and Social Psychology, 73,* 1092–1106.

Milgram, Stanley (1963). Behavioral study of obedience. *Journal of Abnormal and Social Psychology, 67,* 371–378.

Milgram, Stanley (1974). *Obedience to authority: An experimental view.* New York: Harper & Row.

Miller, George A. (1956). The magical number seven, plus or minus two: Some limits on our capacity for processing information. *Psychological Review, 63,* 81–97.

Miller, Joan G. (1999). Cultural psychology: Implications for basic psychological theory. *Psychological Science, 10,* 85–91.

Miller, Neal E. (1978). Biofeedback and visceral learning. *Annual Review of Psychology, 29,* 421–452.

Miller, Neal E. (1985). The value of behavioral research on animals. *American Psychologist, 40,* 423–440.

Miller-Jones, Dalton (1989). Culture and testing. *American Psychologist, 44,* 360–366.

Milner, Brenda (1970). Memory and the temporal regions of the brain. In K. H. Pribram & D. E. Broadbent (eds.), *Biology of memory.* New York: Academic Press.

Milner, J. S., & McCanne, T. R. (1991). Neuropsychological correlates of physical child abuse. In J. S. Milner (ed.), *Neuropsychology of aggression.* Norwell, MA: Kluwer Academic.

Minuchin, Salvador (1984). *Family kaleidoscope.* Cambridge, MA: Harvard University Press.

Mischel, Walter (1966). A social-learning view of sex differences in behavior. In E. E. Maccoby (ed.), *The development of sex differences.* Stanford, CA: Stanford University Press.

Mischel, Walter (1973). Toward a cognitive social learning reconceptualization of personality. *Psychological Review, 80,* 252–253.

Mischel, Walter (1984). Convergences and challenges in the search for consistency. *American Psychologist, 39,* 351–364.

Mischel, Walter (1990). Personality dispositions revisited and revised: A view after three decades. In L. A. Pervin (ed.), *Handbook of personality: Theory and research.* New York: Guilford Press.

Mischel, Walter, & Shoda, Yuichi (1995). A cognitive affective system theory of personality: Reconceptualizing situations, dispositions, dynamics, and invariance in personality structures. *Psychological Review, 102,* 246–268.

Mishkin, Mortimer, & Appenzeller, Tim (1987). The anatomy of memory. *Scientific American, 256,* 80–89.

Mishkin, M.; Suzuki, W. A.; Gadian, D. G.; & Vargha-Khadem, F. (1997). Hierarchical organization of cognitive memory. *Philosophical Transactions of the Royal Society of London, B: Biological Science, 352,* 1461–1467.

Mistry, Jayanthi, & Rogoff, Barbara (1994). Remembering in cultural context. In W. J. Lonner & R. Malpass (eds.), *Psychology and culture.* Needham Heights, MA: Allyn & Bacon.

Mitchell, D. E. (1980). The influence of early visual experience on visual perception. In C. S. Harris (ed.), *Visual coding and adaptability.* Hillsdale, NJ: Erlbaum.

Mitchell, Stephen A. (1993). *Hope and dread in psychoanalysis.* New York: Basic Books.

Mithers, Carol L. (1994). *Reasonable insanity: A true story of the seventies.* Reading, MA: Addison-Wesley.

Modestin, J.; Stephan, P. L.; Erni, T.; & Umari, T. (2000, May 5). Prevalence of extrapyramidal syndromes in psychiatric inpatients and the relationship of clozapine treatment to tardive dyskinesia. *Schizophrenia Research, 42,* 223–230.

Modigliani, Andre, & Rochat, François (1995). The role of interaction sequences and the timing of resistance in shaping obedience and defiance to authority. *Journal of Social Issues, 51,* 107–125.

Moffitt, Terrie E. (1993). Adolescence-limited and life-course-persistent antisocial behavior: A developmental taxonomy. *Psychological Review, 100,* 674–701.

Moore, Timothy E. (1995). Subliminal self-help auditory tapes: An empirical test of perceptual consequences. *Canadian Journal of Behavioural Science, 27,* 9–20.

Moore, Timothy E., & Pepler, Debra J. (1998). Correlates of adjustment in children at risk. In G. W. Holden, R. Geffner, et al. (eds.), *Children exposed to marital violence: Theory, research, and applied issues.* Washington, DC: American Psychological Association.

Moorhead, Gregory; Ference, Richard; & Neck, Chris P. (1991). Group decision fiascoes continue: Space shuttle *Challenger* and a revised groupthink framework. *Human Relations, 44,* 539–550.

Morelli, Gilda A.; Rogoff, Barbara; Oppenheim, David; & Goldsmith, Denise (1992). Cultural variation in infants' sleeping arrangements: Questions of independence. *Developmental Psychology, 28,* 604–613.

Morris, Michael W., & Peng, Kaiping (1994). Culture and cause: American and Chinese attributions for social and physical events. *Journal of Personality and Social Psychology, 67,* 949–971.

Morrison, Ann M., & Von Glinow, Mary Ann (1990). Women and minorities in management. *American Psychologist, 45,* 200–208.

Moscovici, Serge (1985). Social influence and conformity. In G. Lindzey & E. Aronson (eds.), *Handbook of social psychology* (Vol. 2, 3rd ed.). New York: Random House.

Moscovitch, Morris; Winocur, Gordon; & Behrmann, Marlene (1997). What is special about face recognition? Nineteen experiments on a person with visual object agnosia and dyslexia but normal face recognition. *Journal of Cognitive Neuroscience, 9,* 555–604.

Muehlenhard, Charlene L. (1988). "Nice women" don't say yes and "real men" don't say no: How miscommunication and the double standard can cause sexual problems. *Women & Therapy, 7,* 95–108.

Muehlenhard, Charlene L., & Cook, Stephen (1988). Men's self-reports of unwanted sexual activity. *Journal of Sex Research, 24,* 58–72.

Mueller, Claudia M., & Dweck, Carol S. (1998). Praise for intelligence can undermine children's motivation and performance. *Journal of Personality and Social Psychology, 75,* 33–52.

Mulick, James (1994, November/December). The non-science of facilitated communication. *Science Agenda* (APA newsletter), 8–9.

Müller, Ralph-Axel; Courchesne, Eric; & Allen, Greg (1998). The cerebellum: So much more [Letter]. *Science, 282,* 879–880.

Myers, Ronald E., & Sperry, R. W. (1953). Interocular transfer of a visual form discrimination habit in cats after section of the optic chiasm and corpus callosum. *Anatomical Record, 115,* 351–352.

Nash, Michael R. (1987). What, if anything, is regressed about hypnotic age regression? A review of the empirical literature. *Psychological Bulletin, 102,* 42–52.

Nash, Michael R. (1994). Memory distortion and sexual trauma: The problem of false negatives and false positives. *International Journal of Clinical and Experimental Hypnosis, 42,* 346–362.

Nash, Michael R., & Nadon, Robert (1997). Hypnosis. In D. L. Faigman, D. Kaye, M. J. Saks, & J. Sanders (eds.), *Modern scientific evidence: The law and science of expert testimony.* St. Paul, MN: West.

Nathan, Debbie (1994, Fall). Dividing to conquer? Women, men, and the making of multiple personality disorder. *Social Text, 40,* 77–114.

Nathan, Debbie, & Snedeker, Michael (1995). *Satan's silence: Ritual abuse and the making of a modern American witch hunt.* New York: Basic Books.

Needleman, Herbert L.; Riess, Julie A.; Tobin, Michael J.; et al. (1996). Bone lead levels and delinquent behavior. *Journal of the American Medical Association, 275,* 363–369.

Needleman, Herbert L.; Schell, Alan; Bellinger, David; et al. (1990). The long-term effects of exposure to low doses of lead in childhood: An 11-year follow-up report. *New England Journal of Medicine, 322,* 83–88.

Neher, Andrew (1996). Jung's theory of archetypes: A critique. *Journal of Humanistic Psychology, 36,* 61–91.

Neisser, Ulric (ed.) (1998). *The rising curve: Long-term gains in IQ and related measures.* Washington, DC: American Psychological Association.

Neisser, Ulric, & Harsch, Nicole (1992). Phantom flashbulbs: False recollections of hearing the news about *Challenger.* In E. Winograd & U. Neisser (eds.), *Affect and accuracy in recall: Studies of "flashbulb memories."* New York: Cambridge University Press.

Nelson, Thomas O., & Dunlosky, John (1991). When people's judgments of learning (JOLs) are extremely accurate at predicting subsequent recall: The "delayed JOL effect." *Psychological Science, 2,* 267–270.

Newcombe, Nora S.; Drummey, Anna Bullock; Fox, Nathan A.; et al. (2000). Remembering early childhood: How much, how, and why (or why not). *Current Directions in Psychological Science, 9,* 55–58.

Newman, Leonard S., & Baumeister, Roy F. (1994). "Who would wish for the trauma?" Explaining UFO abductions. Paper presented at the annual meeting of the American Psychological Association, Los Angeles.

NICHD Early Child Care Research Network (1997). The effects of infant-child care on infant-mother attachment security (Results of the NICHD study of early child care). *Child Development, 68,* 860–879.

Nickerson, Raymond S. (1998). Confirmation bias: A ubiquitous phenomenon in many guises. *Review of General Psychology, 2,* 175–220.

Nigg, Joel T., & Goldsmith, H. Hill (1994). Genetics of personality disorders: Perspectives from personality and psychopathology research. *Psychological Bulletin, 115,* 346–380.

Nisbett, Richard E. (1993). Violence and U.S. regional culture. *American Psychologist, 48,* 441–449.

Nisbett, Richard E., & Ross, Lee (1980). *Human inference: Strategies and shortcomings of social judgment.* Englewood Cliffs, NJ: Prentice-Hall.

Nolen-Hoeksema, Susan, & Girgus, Joan S. (1994). The emergence of gender differences in depression during adolescence. *Psychological Bulletin, 115,* 424–443.

Nonaka, S.; Hough, C. J.; & Chuang, De-Maw (1998, March 3). Chronic lithium treatment robustly protects neurons in the central nervous system against excitotoxicity by inhibiting N-methyl-D-aspartate receptor-mediated calcium influx. *Proceedings of the National Academy of Sciences, 95,* 2642–2647.

Oatley, Keith, & Jenkins, Jennifer M. (1996). *Understanding emotions.* Cambridge, MA: Blackwell.

Ofshe, Richard J., & Watters, Ethan (1994). *Making monsters: False memory, psychotherapy, and sexual hysteria.* New York: Scribners.

Ogden, Jenni A., & Corkin, Suzanne (1991). Memories of H. M. In W. C. Abraham, M. C. Corballis, & K. G. White (eds.), *Memory mechanisms: A tribute to G. V. Goddard.* Hillsdale, NJ: Erlbaum.

Ogden, Thomas H. (1989). *The primitive edge of experience.* New York: Jason Aronson.

Olds, James (1975). Mapping the mind onto the brain. In F. G. Worden, J. P. Swazy, & G. Adelman (eds.), *The neurosciences: Paths of discovery.* Cambridge, MA: Colonial Press.

Olds, James, & Milner, Peter (1954). Positive reinforcement produced by electrical stimulation of septal area and other regions of the rat brain. *Journal of Comparative and Physiological Psychology, 47,* 419–429.

Olin, Su-Chin S., & Mednick, Sarnoff A. (1996). Risk factors of psychosis: Identifying vulnerable populations premorbidly. *Schizophrenia Bulletin, 22,* 223–240.

Oliner, Samuel P., & Oliner, Pearl M. (1988). *The altruistic personality: Rescuers of Jews in Nazi Europe.* New York: Free Press.

Oliver, Roland (1992). *The African experience.* New York: HarperCollins.

O'Reilly, Jane (1980). *The girl I left behind.* New York: Macmillan.

Ó Scalaidhe, Séamas P.; Wilson, Fraser A. W.; & Goldman-Rakic, Patricia S. (1997). Areal segregation of face-processing neurons in prefrontal cortex. *Science, 278,* 1135–1138.

Paige, Karen E., & Paige, Jeffery M. (1981). *The politics of reproductive ritual.* Berkeley: University of California Press.

Panksepp, Jack; Herman, B. H.; Vilberg, T.; et al. (1980). Endogenous opioids and social behavior. *Neuroscience and Biobehavioral Reviews, 4,* 473–487.

Parker, Gwendolyn M. (1997). *Trespassing: My sojourn in the halls of privilege.* Boston: Houghton Mifflin.

Parks, Randolph W.; Loewenstein, David A.; Dodrill, Kathryn L.; et al. (1988). Cerebral metabolic effects of a verbal fluency test: A PET scan study. *Journal of Clinical & Experimental Neuropsychology, 10,* 565–575.

Parsons, Michael W., & Gold, Paul E. (1992). Glucose enhancement of memory in elderly humans: An inverted-U dose response curve. *Neurobiology of Aging, 13,* 401–404.

Patterson, Francine, & Linden, Eugene (1981). *The education of Koko.* New York: Holt, Rinehart and Winston.

Patterson, Gerald R.; Forgatch, Marion S.; Yoerger, Karen L.; & Stoolmiller, Mike (1998). Variables that initiate and maintain an early-onset trajectory for juvenile offending. *Development and Psychopathology, 10,* 531–547.

Patterson, Gerald R.; Reid, John; & Dishion, Thomas (1992). *Antisocial boys.* Eugene, OR: Castalia.

Paul, Richard W. (1984, September). Critical thinking: Fundamental to education for a free society. *Educational Leadership,* 4–14.

Pellegrini, Anthony D., & Galda, Lee (1993). Ten years after: A reexamination of symbolic play and literacy research. *Reading Research Quarterly, 28,* 163–175.

Pendergrast, Mark (1995). *Victims of memory* (2nd ed.). Hinesburg, VT: Upper Access Press.

Peplau, Letitia A., & Conrad, Eva (1989). Beyond non-sexist research: The perils of feminist methods in psychology. *Psychology of Women Quarterly, 13,* 379–400.

Peplau, Letitia A., & Gordon, Steven L. (1985). Women and men in love: Gender differences in close heterosexual relationships. In V. O'Leary, R. Unger, & B. Wallston (eds.), *Women, gender, and social psychology.* Hillsdale, NJ: Erlbaum.

Peplau, Letitia A., & Spalding, Leah (2000). The close relationships of lesbians, gay men and bisexuals. In C. Hendrick & S. Hendrick (eds.), *Close relationships: A sourcebook.* Thousand Oaks, CA: Sage.

Peplau, Letitia A.; Spalding, Leah R.; Conley, Terri D.; & Veniegas, Rosemary C. (1999). The development of sexual orientation in women. *Annual Review of Sex Research, 10,* 70–99.

Pepperberg, Irene (2000). *The Alex papers: The cognitive and communicative abilities of grey parrots.* Cambridge, MA: Harvard University Press.

Perdue, Charles W.; Dovidio, John F.; Gurtman, Michael B.; & Tyler, Richard B. (1990). Us and them: Social categorization and the process of intergroup bias. *Journal of Personality and Social Psychology, 59,* 475–486.

Perloff, Robert (1992, Summer). "Where ignorance is bliss, 'tis folly to be wise." *The General Psychologist Newsletter, 28,* 34.

Pert, Candace B., & Snyder, Solomon H. (1973). Opiate receptor: Demonstration in nervous tissue. *Science, 179,* 1011–1014.

Pesetsky, David (1999). Introduction to symposium: "Grammar: What's Innate?" Paper presented at the annual meeting of the American Association for the Advancement of Science, Anaheim.

Peterson, Christopher (2000). The future of optimism. *American Psychologist, 55,* 44–55.

Peterson, Lloyd R., & Peterson, Margaret J. (1959). Short-term retention of individual verbal items. *Journal of Experimental Psychology, 58,* 193–198.

Peterson, Marilyn R. (1992). *At personal risk: Boundary violations in professional–client relationships.* New York: W. W. Norton.

Pettigrew, Thomas F. (1997). Generalized intergroup contact effects on prejudice. *Personality and Social Psychology Bulletin, 23,* 173–185.

Pettigrew, Thomas F. (1998). Intergroup contact theory. *Annual Review of Psychology, 49,* 65–85. Palo Alto, CA: Annual Reviews.

Pfungst, Oskar (1911/1965). *Clever Hans (The horse of Mr. von Osten): A contribution to experimental animal and human psychology.* New York: Holt, Rinehart and Winston.

Phillips, D. P.; Ruth, T. E.; & Wagner, L. M. (1993, November 6). Psychology and survival. *Lancet, 342*(8880), 1142–1145.

Phinney, Jean S. (1990). Ethnic identity in adolescents and adults: Review of research. *Psychological Bulletin, 108,* 499–514.

Phinney, Jean S. (1996). When we talk about American ethnic groups, what do we mean? *American Psychologist, 51,* 918–927.

Piaget, Jean (1929/1960). *The child's conception of the world.* Paterson, NJ: Littlefield, Adams.

Piaget, Jean (1952a). *The origins of intelligence in children.* New York: International Universities Press.

Piaget, Jean (1952b). *Play, dreams, and imitation in childhood.* New York: W. W. Norton.

Piaget, Jean (1984). Piaget's theory. In P. Mussen (series ed.) & W. Kessen (vol. ed.), *Handbook of child psychology* (Vol. 1): *History, theory, and methods* (4th ed.). New York: Wiley.

Pinker, Steven (1994). *The language instinct: How the mind creates language.* New York: Morrow.

Piper, August, Jr. (1997). *Hoax and reality: The bizarre world of multiple personality disorder.* Northvale, NJ: Jason Aronson.

Plant, E. Ashby, & Devine, Patricia G. (1998). Internal and external motivation to respond without prejudice. *Journal of Personality and Social Psychology, 75,* 811–832.

Plomin, Robert (1989). Environment and genes: Determinants of behavior. *American Psychologist, 44,* 105–111.

Plomin, Robert; Corley, Robin; Caspi, Avshalom; et al. (1998). Adoption results for self-reported personality: Evidence for nonadditive genetic effects? *Journal of Personality and Social Psychology, 75,* 211–218.

Plomin, Robert; Corley, Robin; DeFries, J. C.; & Fulker, D. W. (1990). Individual differences in television viewing in early childhood: Nature as well as nurture. *Psychological Science, 1,* 371–377.

Plomin, Robert, & DeFries, John C. (1985). *Origins of individual differences in infancy: The Colorado Adoption Project.* New York: Academic Press.

Plous, Scott L. (1991). An attitude survey of animal rights activists. *Psychological Science, 2,* 194–196.

Plous, Scott L. (1996). Attitudes toward the use of animals in psychological research and education: Results from a national survey of psychologists. *American Psychologist, 51,* 1167–1180.

Plutchik, Robert; Conte, Hope R.; Karasu, Toksoz; & Buckley, Peter (1988, Fall/Winter). The measurement of psychodynamic variables. *Hillside Journal of Clinical Psychology, 10,* 132–147.

Poole, Debra A. (1995). Strolling fuzzy-trace theory through eyewitness testimony (or vice versa). *Learning and Individual Differences, 7,* 87–93.

Poole, Debra A., & Lamb, Michael E. (1998). *Investigative interviews of children.* Washington, DC: American Psychological Association.

Poole, Debra A.; Lindsay, D. Stephen; Memon, Amina; & Bull, Ray (1995). Psychotherapy and the recovery of memories of childhood sexual abuse: U.S. and British practitioners' opinions, practices, and experiences. *Journal of Consulting and Clinical Psychology, 63,* 426–437.

Pope, Kenneth S. (1996). Memory, abuse, and science: Questioning claims about the false memory syndrome epidemic. *American Psychologist, 51,* 957–974.

Postmes, Tom, & Spears, Russell (1998). Deindividuation and antinormative behavior: A meta-analysis. *Psychological Bulletin, 123,* 238–259.

Potter, W. James (1987). Does television viewing hinder academic achievement among adolescents? *Human Communication Research, 14,* 27–46.

Poulin-Dubois, Diane; Serbin, Lisa A.; Kenyon, Brenda; & Derbyshire, Alison (1994). Infants' intermodal knowledge about gender. *Developmental Psychology, 30,* 436–442.

Powell, Russell A., & Boer, Douglas P. (1994). Did Freud mislead patients to confabulate memories of abuse? *Psychological Reports, 74,* 1283–1298.

Powell, Russell A., & Boer, Douglas P. (1995). Did Freud misinterpret reported memories of sexual abuse as fantasies? *Psychological Reports, 77,* 563–570.

Pratkanis, Anthony, & Aronson, Elliot (1992). *Age of propaganda: The everyday use and abuse of persuasion.* New York: W. H. Freeman.

Premack, David, & Premack, Ann James (1983). *The mind of an ape.* New York: W. W. Norton.

Punamaeki, Raija-Leena, & Joustie, Marja (1998). The role of culture, violence, and personal factors affecting dream content. *Journal of Cross-Cultural Psychology, 29,* 320–342.

Pynoos, R. S., & Nader, K. (1989). Children's memory and proximity to violence. *Journal of the American Academy of Child and Adolescent Psychiatry, 28,* 236–241.

Radetsky, Peter (1991, April). The brainiest cells alive. *Discover, 12,* 82–85, 88, 90.

Radke-Yarrow, Marian; Zahn-Waxler, Carolyn; & Chapman, M. (1983). Prosocial dispositions and behavior. In P. Mussen (series ed.), *Handbook of child psychology* (Vol. 4): *Socialization, personality, and social development* (3rd ed.). New York: Wiley.

Raine, Adrian (1996). Autonomic nervous system factors underlying disinhibited, antisocial, and violent behavior: Biosocial perspectives and treatment implications. *Annals of the New York Academy of Sciences, 794,* 46–59.

Raine, Adrian; Brennan, Patricia; & Mednick, Sarnoff A. (1994). Birth complications combined with early maternal rejection at age one year predispose to violent crime at age 18 years. *Archives of General Psychiatry, 51,* 984–988.

Raine, Adrian; Meloy, J. R.; Bihrle, S.; et al. (1998). Reduced prefrontal and increased subcortical brain functioning assessed using positron emission tomography in predatory and affective murderers. *Behavioral Science and Law, 16,* 319–332.

Ramey, Craig T., & Ramey, Sharon L. (1998). Early intervention and early experience. *American Psychologist, 53,* 109–120.

Rathbun, Constance; DiVirgilio, Letitia; & Waldfogel, Samuel (1958). A restitutive process in children following radical separation from family and culture. *American Journal of Orthopsychiatry, 28,* 408–415.

Rechtschaffen, Allan; Gilliland, Marcia A.; Bergmann, Bernard M.; & Winter, Jacqueline B. (1983). Physiological correlates of prolonged sleep deprivation in rats. *Science, 221,* 182–184.

Redd, W. H.; Dadds, M. R.; Futterman, A. D.; et al. (1993). Nausea induced by mental images of chemotherapy. *Cancer, 72,* 629–636.

Redelmeier, Donald A., & Tversky, Amos (1996). On the belief that arthritis pain is related to the weather. *Proceedings of the National Academy of Sciences, 93,* 2895–2896.

Reid, R. L. (1991). Premenstrual syndrome. *New England Journal of Medicine, 324,* 1208–1210.

Rescorla, Robert A. (1988). Pavlovian conditioning: It's not what you think it is. *American Psychologist, 43,* 151–160.

Restak, Richard (1983, October). Is free will a fraud? *Science Digest, 91*(10), 52–55.

Restak, Richard M. (1994). *The modular brain.* New York: Macmillan.

Reynolds, Brent A., & Weiss, Samuel (1992). Generation of neurons and astrocytes from isolated cells of the adult mammalian central nervous system. *Science, 255,* 1707–1710.

Reynolds, Meredith A. (1998). Childhood sexual play games. Paper presented at the annual meeting of the American Psychological Association, San Francisco.

Rice, George; Anderson, Carol; Risch, Neil; & Ebers, George (1999, April 23). Male homosexuality: Absence of linkage to microsatellite markers at Xq28. *Science, 284,* 665–667.

Rice, Mabel L. (1989). Children's language acquisition. *American Psychologist, 44,* 149–156.

Ridley-Johnson, Robyn; Cooper, Harris; & Chance, June (1983). The relation of children's television viewing to school achievement and I.Q. *Journal of Educational Research, 76,* 294–297.

Rind, Bruce, & Tromovitch, Philip (1997). A meta-analytic review of findings from national samples on psychological correlates of child sexual abuse. *Journal of Sex Research, 34,* 237–255.

Rind, Bruce; Tromovitch, Philip; & Bauserman, Robert (1998). A meta-analytic examination of assumed properties of child sexual abuse using college samples. *Psychological Bulletin, 124,* 22–53.

Ristau, Carolyn A. (ed.) (1991). *Cognitive ethology: The minds of other animals.* Hillsdale, NJ: Erlbaum.

Roberts, John E.; Gotlib, Ian H.; & Kassel, Jon D. (1996). Adult attachment security and symptoms of depression: The mediating roles of dysfunctional attitudes and low self-esteem. *Journal of Personality and Social Psychology, 70,* 310–320.

Roe, R. A.; Zinovieva, I. L.; Dienes, E.; & Ten Horn, L. A. (1998). Test of a model of work motivation in the Netherlands, Hungary and Bulgaria. Paper presented at the annual meeting of the International Association for Cross-Cultural Psychology, Bellingham, WA.

Roediger, Henry L., & McDermott, Kathleen B. (1995). Creating false memories: Remembering words not presented in lists. *Journal of Experimental Psychology: Learning, Memory, & Cognition, 21,* 803–814.

Rogers, Carl (1951). *Client-centered therapy: Its current practice, implications, and theory.* Boston: Houghton Mifflin.

Rogers, Carl (1961). *On becoming a person.* Boston: Houghton Mifflin.

Rogers, Ronald W., & Prentice-Dunn, Steven (1981). Deindividuation and anger-mediated interracial aggression: Unmasking regressive racism. *Journal of Personality and Social Psychology, 41,* 63–73.

Rogoff, Barbara, & Chavajay, Pablo (1995). What's become of research on the cultural basis of cognitive development? *American Psychologist, 50,* 859–877.

Rosch, Eleanor H. (1973). Natural categories. *Cognitive Psychology, 4,* 328–350.

Rosen, R. D. (1977). *Psychobabble.* New York: Atheneum.

Rosenthal, Robert (1966). *Experimenter effects in behavioral research.* New York: Appleton-Century-Crofts.

Rosenthal, Robert (1994). Interpersonal expectancy effects: A 30-year perspective. *Current Directions in Psychological Science, 3,* 176–179.

Rosenzweig, Mark R. (1984). Experience, memory, and the brain. *American Psychologist, 39,* 365–376.

Ross, Colin (1995). The validity and reliability of dissociative identity disorder. In L. M. Cohen, J. N. Berzoff,

& M. R. Elin (eds.), *Dissociative identity disorder: Theoretical and treatment controversies.* Northvale, NJ: Jason Aronson.

Ross, Michael (1989). Relation of implicit theories to the construction of personal histories. *Psychological Review, 96,* 341–357.

Rotter, Julian B. (1966). Generalized expectancies for internal versus external control of reinforcement. *Psychological Monographs, 80*(Whole No. 609), 1–28.

Rotter, Julian B. (1982). *The development and applications of social learning theory: Selected papers.* New York: Praeger.

Rotter, Julian B. (1990). Internal versus external control of reinforcement: A case history of a variable. *American Psychologist, 45,* 489–493.

Roueché, Berton (1984, June 4). Annals of medicine: The hoof-beats of a zebra. *The New Yorker,* 71–86.

Rowe, John W., & Kahn, Robert L. (1998). *Successful aging.* New York: Pantheon.

Rowe, Walter F. (1993, Winter). Psychic detectives: A critical examination. *Skeptical Inquirer, 17,* 159–165.

Rubin, Jeffrey Z. (1994). Models of conflict management. *Journal of Social Issues, 50,* 33–45.

Ruggiero, Vincent R. (1988). *Teaching thinking across the curriculum.* New York: Harper & Row.

Ruggiero, Vincent R. (1997). *The art of thinking: A guide to critical and creative thought* (5th ed.). New York: HarperCollins.

Rumbaugh, Duane M. (1977). *Language learning by a chimpanzee: The Lana project.* New York: Academic Press.

Rumbaugh, Duane M.; Savage-Rumbaugh, E. Sue; & Pate, James L. (1988). Addendum to "Summation in the chimpanzee (*Pan troglodytes*)." *Journal of Experimental Psychology: Animal Behavior Processes, 14,* 118–120.

Rumelhart, David E., & McClelland, James L. (1987). Learning the past tenses of English verbs: Implicit rules or parallel distributed processing. In B. MacWhinney (ed.), *Mechanisms of language acquisition.* Hillsdale, NJ: Erlbaum.

Rumelhart, David E.; McClelland, James L.; & the PDP Research Group (1986). *Parallel distributed processing: Explorations in the microstructure of cognition* (Vols. 1 and 2). Cambridge, MA: MIT Press.

Rushton, J. Philippe (1988). Race differences in behavior: A review and evolutionary analysis. *Personality and Individual Differences, 9,* 1009–1024.

Rusting, Cheryl L., & DeHart, Tracy (2000). Retrieving positive memories to regulate negative mood: Consequences for mood-congruent memory. *Journal of Personality and Social Psychology, 78,* 737–752.

Ryan, Richard M.; Chirkov, Valery I.; Little, Todd D.; et al. (1999). The American dream in Russia: Extrinsic aspirations and well-being in two cultures. *Personality and Social Psychology Bulletin, 25,* 1509–1524.

Ryle, Gilbert (1949). *The concept of mind.* London: Hutchinson.

Rymer, Russ (1993). *Genie: An abused child's flight from silence.* New York: HarperCollins.

Sack, Robert L., & Lewy, Alfred J. (1997). Melatonin as a chronobiotic: Treatment of circadian desynchrony in night workers and the blind. *Journal of Biological Rhythms, 12,* 595–603.

Sackett, Paul R. (1994). Integrity testing for personnel selection. *Current Directions in Psychological Science, 3,* 73–76.

Sacks, Oliver (1985). *The man who mistook his wife for a hat and other clinical tales.* New York: Simon & Schuster.

Sacks, Oliver (1995). Musical ability. *Science, 268,* 621.

Saffran, J. R.; Aslin, R. N.; & Newport, E. L. (1996). Statistical learning by 8-month-old infants. *Science, 274,* 1926–1928.

Sagan, Eli (1988). *Freud, women, and morality: The psychology of good and evil.* New York: Basic Books.

Sagarin, Brad; Cialdini, Robert B.; & Rice, William E. (1998). Creating critical consumers: Instilling resistance to unethical persuasion. Paper presented at the annual meeting of the American Psychological Association, San Francisco.

Sahley, Christie L.; Rudy, Jerry W.; & Gelperin, Alan (1981). An analysis of associative learning in a terrestrial mollusk: I. Higher-order conditioning, blocking, and a transient US preexposure effect. *Journal of Comparative Physiology, 144,* 1–8.

Salthouse, Timothy A. (1998). The what and where of cognitive aging. Address presented at the annual meeting of the American Psychological Association, San Francisco.

Samelson, Franz (1979). Putting psychology on the map: Ideology and intelligence testing. In A. R. Buss (ed.), *Psychology in social context.* New York: Irvington.

Sandler, A. D.; Sutton, K. A.; DeWeese, J.; et al. (1999). Lack of benefit of a single dose of synthetic human secretin in the treatment of autism and pervasive developmental disorder. *New England Journal of Medicine, 341,* 1801–1806.

Sapolsky, Robert M. (1997). *The trouble with testosterone: And other essays on the biology of the human predicament.* New York: Touchstone.

Sarason, Irwin G., & Sarason, Barbara R. (1999). *Abnormal psychology* (9th ed.). Upper Saddle River, NJ: Prentice-Hall.

Savage-Rumbaugh, E. Sue, & Lewin, Roger (1994). *Kanzi: The ape at the brink of the human mind.* New York: Wiley.

Savage-Rumbaugh, E. Sue; Shanker, Stuart; & Taylor, Talbot (1998). *Apes, language and the human mind.* New York: Oxford University Press.

Scarborough, Elizabeth, & Furumoto, Laurel (1987). *Untold lives: The first generation of American women psychologists.* New York: Columbia University Press.

Scarr, Sandra (1993). Biological and cultural diversity: The legacy of Darwin for development. *Child Development, 64,* 1333–1353.

Scarr, Sandra; Pakstis, Andrew J.; Katz, Soloman H.; & Barker, William B. (1977). Absence of a relationship between degree of white ancestry and intellectual skill in a black population. *Human Genetics, 39,* 69–86.

Scarr, Sandra, & Weinberg, Robert A. (1994). Educational and occupational achievement of brothers and sisters in adoptive and biologically related families. *Behavioral Genetics, 24,* 301–325.

Schachter, Stanley, & Singer, Jerome E. (1962). Cognitive, social, and physiological determinants of emotional state. *Psychological Review, 69,* 379–399.

Schacter, Daniel L. (1996). *Searching for memory: The brain, the mind, and the past.* New York: Basic Books.

Schacter, Daniel L. (1999). The seven sins of memory: Insights from psychology and cognitive neuroscience. *American Psychologist, 54,* 182–203.

Schacter, Daniel L.; Chiu, C.-Y. Peter; & Ochsner, Kevin N. (1993). Implicit memory: A selective review. *Annual Review of Neuroscience, 16,* 159–182.

Schacter, Daniel L.; Reiman, E.; Curran, T.; et al. (1996). Neuroanatomical correlates of veridical and illusory recognition memory: Evidence from positron emission tomography. *Neuron, 17,* 267–274.

Schaie, K. Warner (1994). The course of adult intellectual development. *American Psychologist, 49,* 304–313.

Schank, Roger C. [with Peter Childers] (1988). *The creative attitude.* New York: Macmillan.

Schank, Roger C., & Abelson, Robert P. (1995). Knowledge and memory: The real story. In R. S. Wyer, Jr., et al. (eds.), *Advances in social cognition* (Vol. 8): Hillsdale, NJ: Erlbaum.

Schein, Edgar; Schneier, Inge; & Barker, Curtis H. (1961). *Coercive persuasion.* New York: W. W. Norton.

Schmolck, H.; Buffalo, E. A.; & Squire, L. R. (2000). Memory distortions develop over time: Recollections of the O. J. Simpson trial verdict after 15 and 32 months. *Psychological Science, 11,* 39–45.

Schnell, Lisa, & Schwab, Martin E. (1990, January 18). Axonal regeneration in the rat spinal cord produced by an antibody against myelin-associated neurite growth inhibitors. *Nature, 343,* 269–272.

Schuessler, Jennifer (2000, April). Monkeys who think, and the cognitive neuroscientist who loves them. *Lingua Franca,* 56–64.

Schulkin, Jay (1994). Melancholic depression and the hormones of adversity: A role for the amygdala. *Current Directions in Psychological Science, 3,* 41–44.

Schulman, Michael, & Mekler, Eva (1994). *Bringing up a caring child* (rev. ed.). New York: Doubleday.

Schulz, S. C. (2000). New antipsychotic medications: More than old wine in new bottles. *Bulletin of the Menninger Clinic, 64,* 60–75.

Schuman, Howard, & Scott, Jacqueline (1989). Generations and collective memories. *American Journal of Sociology, 54,* 359–381.

Schwartz, Barry, & Reilly, Martha (1985). Long-term retention of a complex operant in pigeons. *Journal of Experimental Psychology: Animal Behavior Processes, 11,* 337–355.

Schwartz, Jeffrey; Stoessel, Paula W.; Baxter, Lewis R.; et al. (1996). Systematic changes in cerebral glucose metabolic rate after successful behavior modification treatment of obsessive-compulsive disorder. *Archives of General Psychiatry, 53,* 109–113.

Scofield, Michael (1993, June 6). About men: Off the ladder. *New York Times Magazine,* 22.

Scribner, Sylvia (1977). Modes of thinking and ways of speaking: Culture and logic reconsidered. In P. N. Johnson-Laird & P. C. Wason (eds.), *Thinking: Readings in cognitive science.* Cambridge, England: Cambridge University Press.

Seeman, Philip.; Guan, Hong-chang; & Van Tol, Hubert H. (1993). Dopamine D4 receptors elevated in schizophrenia. *Nature, 365,* 441–445.

Segall, Marshall H.; Dasen, Pierre R.; Berry, John W.; & Poortinga, Ype H. (1999). *Human behavior in global perspective: An introduction to cross-cultural psychology* (2nd ed.). Boston, MA: Allyn & Bacon.

Seidenberg, Mark S. (1997). Language acquisition and use: Learning and applying probabilistic constraints. *Science, 275,* 1599–1603.

Seidenberg, Mark S., & Petitto, Laura A. (1979). Signing behavior in apes: A critical review. *Cognition, 7,* 177–215.

Seif, Ellie (1979, June). A young mother's story. *Redbook, 49,* 165–167.

Seifer, Ronald; Schiller, Masha; Sameroff, Arnold; et al. (1996). Attachment, maternal sensitivity, and infant temperament during the first year of life. *Developmental Psychology, 32,* 12–25.

Seligman, Martin E. P. (1975). *Helplessness: On depression, development, and death.* San Francisco: W. H. Freeman.

Seligman, Martin E. P. (1991). *Learned optimism.* New York: Knopf.

Seligman, Martin E. P., & Hager, Joanne L. (1972, August). Biological boundaries of learning: The sauce-béarnaise syndrome. *Psychology Today,* 59–61, 84–87.

Seligman, Martin E. P.; Schulman, Peter; DeRubeis, Robert J.; & Hollon, Steven D. (1998). The prevention of depression and anxiety. Paper presented at the annual meeting of the American Psychological Association, San Francisco.

Sellers, Robert M.; Smith, Mia A.; Shelton, J. Nicole; et al. (1998). Multidimensional model of racial identity: A reconceptualization of African American racial identity. *Personality and Social Psychology Review, 2,* 18–39.

Serbin, Lisa A.; Powlishta, Kimberly K.; & Gulko, Judith (1993). The development of sex typing in middle childhood. *Monographs of the Society for Research in Child Development, 58*(2, Serial No. 232), v–74.

Serpell, Robert (1994). The cultural construction of intelligence. In W. J. Lonner & R. S. Malpass (eds.), *Psychology and culture.* Needham Heights, MA: Allyn & Bacon.

Shapiro, A. Eugene, & Wiggins, Jack G. (1994). A PsyD degree for every practitioner. *American Psychologist, 49,* 207–210.

Shapiro, Deane H.; Schwartz, Carolyn E.; & Astin, John A. (1996). Controlling ourselves, controlling our world. *American Psychologist, 51,* 1213–1230.

Shatz, Marilyn, & Gelman, Rochel (1973). The development of communication skills: Modifications in the speech of young children as a function of listener. *Monographs of the Society for Research in Child Development, 38*(5, Serial No. 152), 1–37.

Shaywitz, Bennett A.; Shaywitz, Sally E.; Pugh, Kenneth R.; et al. (1995). Sex differences in the functional organization of the brain for language. *Nature, 373,* 607–609.

Shedler, Jonathan; Mayman, Martin; & Manis, Melvin (1993). The illusion of mental health. *American Psychologist, 48,* 1117–1131.

Shepard, Roger N., & Metzler, Jacqueline (1971). Mental rotation of three-dimensional objects. *Science, 171,* 701–703.

Shepperd, James A. (1995). Remedying motivation and productivity loss in collective settings. *Current Directions in Psychological Science, 4,* 131–140.

Sherif, Muzafer (1958). Superordinate goals in the reduction of intergroup conflicts. *American Journal of Sociology, 63,* 349–356.

Sherif, Muzafer; Harvey, O. J.; White, B. J.; Hood, William; & Sherif, Carolyn (1961). *Intergroup conflict and cooperation: The Robbers Cave experiment.* Norman, OK: University of Oklahoma Institute of Intergroup Relations.

Sherman, Bonnie R., & Kunda, Ziva (1989). Motivated evaluation of scientific evidence. Paper presented at the annual meeting of the American Psychological Society, Arlington, VA.

Sherman, Jeffrey W., & Bessenoff, Gayle R. (1999). Stereotypes as source-monitoring cues: On the interaction between episodic and semantic memory. *Psychological Science, 10,* 106–110.

Shermer, Michael (1997). *Why people believe weird things: Pseudoscience, superstition, and other confusions of our time.* New York: W. H. Freeman.

Shermer, Michael (2000). *How we believe: The search for God in an age of science.* New York: W. H. Freeman.

Shermer, Michael, & Grobman, Alex (2000). *Denying history.* Berkeley, CA: University of California Press.

Sherrington, R.; Rogaev, E. I.; Liang, Y.; et al. (1995). Cloning of a gene bearing missense mutation in early-onset familial Alzheimer's disease. *Nature, 375,* 754–760.

Sherwin, Barbara B. (1988). A comparative analysis of the role of androgen in human male and female sexual behavior: Behavioral specificity, critical thresholds, and sensitivity. *Psychobiology, 16,* 416–425.

Sherwin, Barbara B. (1998a). Estrogen and cognitive functioning in women. *Proceedings of the Society for Experimental Biological Medicine, 217,* 17–22.

Sherwin, Barbara B. (1998b). Use of combined estrogen-androgen preparations in the postmenopause: Evidence from clinical studies. *International Journal of Fertility & Women's Medicine, 43,* 98–103.

Shih, Margaret; Pittinsky, Todd L.; & Ambady, Nalini (1999). Stereotype susceptibility: Identity salience and shifts in quantitative performance. *Psychological Science, 10,* 80–83.

Shin, Lisa M.; Kosslyn, Stephen M.; McNally, Richard K.; et al. (1997). Visual imagery and perception in post-traumatic stress disorder. *Archives of General Psychiatry, 54,* 233–241.

Showalter, Elaine (1997). *Hystories: Hysterical epidemics and modern culture.* New York: Columbia University Press.

Shweder, Richard A.; Mahapatra, Manamohan; & Miller, Joan G. (1990). Culture and moral development. In J. W. Stigler, R. A. Shweder, & G. Herdt (eds.), *Cultural psychology: Essays on comparative human development.* Cambridge, England: Cambridge University Press.

Sidanius, Jim; Pratto, Felicia; & Bobo, Lawrence (1996). Racism, conservatism, affirmative action, and intellectual sophistication: A matter of principled conservatism or group dominance? *Journal of Personality and Social Psychology, 70,* 476–490.

Siegler, Robert (1996). *Emerging minds: The process of change in children's thinking.* New York: Oxford University Press.

Silverstein, Brett, & Perlick, Deborah (1995). *The cost of competence: Why inequality causes depression, eating disorders, and illness in women.* New York: Oxford University Press.

Sinclair, Lisa, & Kunda, Ziva (1999). Reactions to a Black professional: Motivated inhibition and activation of conflicting stereotypes. *Journal of Personality and Social Psychology, 77,* 885–904.

Singer, Margaret T.; Temerlin, Maurice K.; & Langone, Michael D. (1990). Psychotherapy cults. *Cultic Studies Journal, 7,* 101–125.

Skal, David J. (1993). *The monster show: A cultural history of horror.* New York: W. W. Norton.

Skinner, B. F. (1938). *The behavior of organisms: An experimental analysis.* New York: Appleton-Century-Crofts.

Skinner, B. F. (1948). Superstition in the pigeon. *Journal of Experimental Psychology, 38,* 168–172.

Skinner, B. F. (1948/1976). *Walden Two.* New York: Macmillan.

Skinner, B. F. (1956). A case history in the scientific method. *American Psychologist, 11,* 221–233.

Skinner, B. F. (1961, November). Teaching machines. *Scientific American,* 91–102.

Skinner, B. F. (1972). The operational analysis of psychological terms. In B. F. Skinner (ed.), *Cumulative record* (3rd ed.). New York: Appleton-Century-Crofts.

Skinner, B. F. (1978). *Reflections on behaviorism and society.* Englewood Cliffs, NJ: Prentice-Hall.

Skinner, B. F. (1983). *A matter of consequences.* New York: Knopf.

Skinner, B. F. (1987). What is wrong with daily life in the Western world? In B. F. Skinner (ed.), *Upon further reflection.* Englewood Cliffs, NJ: Prentice-Hall.

Skinner, B. F. (1990). Can psychology be a science of mind? *American Psychologist, 45,* 1206–1210.

Skinner, B. F., & Vaughan, Margaret (1984). *Enjoy old age.* New York: W. W. Norton.

Skinner, J. B.; Erskine, A.; Pearce, S. A.; et al. (1990). The evaluation of a cognitive behavioural treatment programme in outpatients with chronic pain. *Journal of Psychosomatic Research, 34,* 13–19.

Skreslet, Paula (1987, November 30). The prizes of first grade. *Newsweek,* 8.

Slavin, Robert E., & Cooper, Robert (1999). Improving intergroup relations: Lessons learned from cooperative learning programs. *Journal of Social Issues, 55,* 647–663.

Smith, Carolyn A.; Lizotte, Alan J.; Thornberry, Terence P.; et al. (1997). Resilient youth: Identifying factors that prevent high-risk youth from engaging in delinquency and drug use. In J. Hagan (ed.), *Delinquency and disrepute in the life course.* Greenwich, CT: JAI Press.

Smith, James F., & Kida, Thomas (1991). Heuristics and biases: Expertise and task realism in auditing. *Psychological Bulletin, 109,* 472–489.

Smith, M. Brewster (1994). Selfhood at risk: Postmodern perils and the perils of postmodernism. *American Psychologist, 49,* 405–411.

Smith, N.; Tsimpli, I.-M., & Ouhalla, J. (1993). Learning the impossible: The acquisition of possible and impossible languages by a polyglot savant. *Lingua, 91,* 279–347.

Smith, Peter B., & Bond, Michael H. (1994). *Social psychology across cultures: Analysis and perspectives.* Boston: Allyn & Bacon.

Smither, Robert D. (1998). *The psychology of work and human performance* (3rd ed.). New York: Longman.

Snow, Margaret E.; Jacklin, Carol N.; & Maccoby, Eleanor (1983). Sex-of-child differences in father-child interaction at one year of age. *Child Development, 54,* 227–232.

Snowdon, Charles T. (1997). The "nature" of sex differences: Myths of male and female. In P. A. Gowaty (ed.), *Feminism and evolutionary biology.* New York: Chapman and Hall.

Snyder, James J., & Patterson, Gerald R. (1995). Individual differences in social aggression: A test of a reinforcer model of socialization in the natural environment. *Behavior Therapy, 26,* 371–391.

Snyder, Robert A. (1993, Spring). The glass ceiling for women: Things that don't cause it and things that won't break it. *Human Resource Development Quarterly,* 97–106.

Sommer, Robert (1969). *Personal space: The behavioral basis of design.* Englewood Cliffs, NJ: Prentice-Hall.

Sommer, Robert (1977, January). Toward a psychology of natural behavior. *APA Monitor.* (Reprinted in *Readings in psychology 78/79.* Guilford, CT: Dushkin, 1978.)

Sorce, James F.; Emde, Robert N.; Campos, Joseph; & Klinnert, Mary D. (1985). Maternal emotional signaling: Its effect on the visual cliff behavior of 1-year-olds. *Developmental Psychology, 21,* 195–200.

Spanos, Nicholas P. (1996). *Multiple identities and false memories: A sociocognitive perspective.* Washington, DC: American Psychological Association.

Spanos, Nicholas P.; Burgess, Cheryl A.; & Burgess, Melissa F. (1994). Past-life identities, UFO abductions, and satanic ritual abuse: The social construction of memories. *International Journal of Clinical and Experimental Hypnosis, 42,* 433–446.

Spanos, Nicholas P.; Menary, Evelyn; Gabora, Natalie J.; et al. (1991). Secondary identity enactments during hypnotic past-life regression: A sociocognitive perspective. *Journal of Personality and Social Psychology, 61,* 308–320.

Spelke, Elizabeth S.; Breinlinger, Karen; Macomber, Janet; & Jacobson, Kristen (1992). Origins of knowledge. *Psychological Review, 99,* 605–632.

Speltz, Matthew L.; Greenberg, Mark T.; & Deklyen, Michelle (1990). Attachment in preschoolers with disruptive behavior: A comparison of clinic-referred and nonproblem children. *Development and Psychopathology, 2,* 31–46.

Spence, Janet T. (1985). Gender identity and its implications for concepts of masculinity and femininity. In T. Sonderegger (ed.), *Nebraska Symposium on Motivation.* Lincoln: University of Nebraska Press.

Spence, Janet T., & Hahn, Eugene D. (1997). The Attitudes Toward Women Scale and attitude change in college students. *Psychology of Women Quarterly, 22,* 17–36.

Sperry, Roger W. (1964). The great cerebral commissure. *Scientific American, 210*(1), 42–52.

Sperry, Roger W. (1982). Some effects of disconnecting the cerebral hemispheres. *Science, 217,* 1223–1226.

Spiegel, David (2000, May/June). Suffer the children: Long-term effects of sexual abuse. *Society, 37,* 18–20.

Spilich, George J.; June, Lorraine; & Renner, Judith (1992). Cigarette smoking and cognitive performance. *British Journal of Addiction, 87,* 113–126.

Spitz, Herman H. (1997). *Nonconscious movements: From mystical messages to facilitated communication.* Mahwah, NJ: Erlbaum.

Sporer, Siegfried L.; Penrod, Steven; Read, Don; & Cutler, Brian (1995). Choosing, confidence, and accuracy: A meta-analysis of the confidence-accuracy relation in eyewitness identification studies. *Psychological Bulletin, 118,* 315–327.

Springer, Sally P., & Deutsch, Georg (1998). *Left brain, right brain: Perspective from cognitive neuroscience.* New York: W. H. Freeman.

Squier, Leslie H., & Domhoff, G. William (1998). The presentation of dreaming and dreams in introductory psychology textbooks: A critical examination with suggestions for textbook authors and course instructors. *Dreaming, 8,* 149–168.

Squire, Larry R. (1987). *Memory and the brain.* New York: Oxford University Press.

Squire, Larry R., & Zola-Morgan, Stuart (1991). The medial temporal lobe memory system. *Science, 253,* 1380–1386.

Staats, Carolyn K., & Staats, Arthur W. (1957). Meaning established by classical conditioning. *Journal of Experimental Psychology, 54,* 74–80.

Stajkovic, Alexander D., & Luthans, Fred (1998). Self-efficacy and work-related performance: A meta-analysis. *Psychological Bulletin, 124,* 240–261.

Stanne, Mary Beth; Johnson, David W.; & Johnson, Roger T. (1999). Does competition enhance or inhibit motor performance: A meta-analysis. *Psychological Bulletin, 125,* 133–154.

Stanovich, Keith (1996). *How to think straight about psychology* (4th ed.). New York: HarperCollins.

Staples, Brent (1994). *Parallel time.* New York: Pantheon.

Staub, Ervin (1996). Cultural–social roots of violence. *American Psychologist, 51,* 117–132.

Staub, Ervin (1999). The roots of evil: Social conditions, culture, personality, and basic human needs. *Personality and Social Psychology Review, 3,* 179–192.

Staudinger, Ursula M.; Fleeson, William; & Baltes, Paul B. (1999). Predictors of subjective physical health and global well-being: Similarities and differences between the United States and Germany. *Journal of Personality and Social Psychology, 76,* 305–319.

Steele, Claude M. (1992, April). Race and the schooling of Black Americans. *Atlantic Monthly,* 68–78.

Steele, Claude M. (1997). A threat in the air: How stereotypes shape intellectual identity and performance. *American Psychologist, 52,* 613–629.

Steele, Claude M., & Aronson, Joshua (1995). Stereotype threat and the intellectual test performance of African-Americans. *Journal of Personality and Social Psychology, 69,* 797–811.

Steinberg, Laurence D. (1990). Interdependence in the family: Autonomy, conflict and harmony in the parent-adolescent relationship. In S. S. Feldman & G. R. Elliott (eds.), *At the threshold: The developing adolescent.* Cambridge, MA: Harvard University Press.

Steinberg, Laurence D.; Dornbusch, Sanford M.; & Brown, B. Bradford (1992). Ethnic differences in adolescent achievement: An ecological perspective. *American Psychologist, 47,* 723–729.

Steiner, Robert A. (1989). *Don't get taken!* El Cerrito, CA: Wide-Awake Books.

Stenberg, Craig R., & Campos, Joseph (1990). The development of anger expressions in infancy. In N. Stein, B. Leventhal, & T. Trabasso (eds.), *Psychological and biological approaches to emotion.* Hillsdale, NJ: Erlbaum.

Stephan, K. M.; Fink, G. R.; Passingham, R. E.; et al. (1995). Functional anatomy of the mental representation of upper movements in healthy subjects. *Journal of Neurophysiology, 73,* 373–386.

Stephan, Walter G. (1999). *Reducing prejudice and stereotyping in schools.* New York: Teachers College Press.

Stephan, Walter G.; Ageyev, Vladimir; Coates-Shrider, Lisa; et al. (1994). On the relationship between stereotypes and prejudice: An international study. *Personality and Social Psychology Bulletin, 20,* 277–284.

Stephens, Mitchell (1991, September 20). The death of reading. *The Los Angeles Times Magazine,* 10, 12, 16, 42, 44.

Stern, Daniel (1985). *The interpersonal world of the infant.* New York: Basic Books.

Stern, Marilyn, & Karraker, Katherine H. (1989). Sex stereotyping of infants: A review of gender labeling studies. *Sex Roles, 20,* 501–522.

Sternberg, Robert J. (1988). *The triarchic mind: A new theory of human intelligence.* New York: Viking.

Sternberg, Robert J.; Wagner, Richard K.; Williams, Wendy M.; & Horvath, Joseph A. (1995). Testing common sense. *American Psychologist, 50,* 912–927.

Sternberg, Robert J., & Williams, Wendy M. (1997). Does the GRE predict meaningful success in the graduate training of psychologists? A case study. *American Psychologist, 52,* 630–641.

Stevenson, Harold W.; Chen, Chuansheng; & Lee, Shin-ying (1993, January 1). Mathematics achievement of Chinese, Japanese, and American children: Ten years later. *Science, 259,* 53–58.

Stevenson, Harold W., & Stigler, James W. (1992). *The learning gap.* New York: Summit.

Stewart, Abigail J., & Ostrove, Joan M. (1998). Women's personality in middle age: Gender, history, and midcourse corrections. *American Psychologist, 53,* 1185–1194.

Stimpson, Catherine (1996, Winter). Women's studies and its discontents. *Dissent, 43,* 67–75.

Stokes, L.; Leetz, R.; Gerr, F.; et al. (1998). Neurotoxicity in young adults 20 years after childhood exposure to lead: The Bunker Hill experience. *Occupational and Environmental Medicine, 55,* 507–516.

Stoller, Robert J. (1985). *Observing the erotic imagination.* New Haven, CT: Yale University Press.

Straus, Murray A., & Kantor, Glenda Kaufman (1994). Corporal punishment of adolescents by parents: A risk factor in the epidemiology of depression, suicide, alcohol abuse, child abuse, and wife beating. *Adolescence, 29,* 543–561.

Strickland, Bonnie R. (1965). The prediction of social action from a dimension of internal-external control. *Journal of Social Psychology, 66,* 353–358.

Strickland, Bonnie R. (1989). Internal-external control expectancies: From contingency to creativity. *American Psychologist, 44,* 1–12.

Strickland, Bonnie R. (1995). Research on sexual orientation and human development: A commentary. *Developmental Psychology, 31,* 137–140.

Strickland, Tony L.; Lin, Keh-Ming; Fu, Paul; et al. (1995). Comparison of lithium ratio between African-American and Caucasian bipolar patients. *Biological Psychiatry, 37*, 325–330.

Strickland, Tony L.; Ranganath, Vijay; Lin, Keh-Ming; et al. (1991). Psychopharmacological considerations in the treatment of black American populations. *Psychopharmacology Bulletin, 27*, 441–448.

Stunkard, Albert J. (ed.) (1980). *Obesity*. Philadelphia: Saunders.

Sue, Stanley (1998). In search of cultural competence in psychotherapy and counseling. *American Psychologist, 53*, 440–448.

Sulloway, Frank J. (1992). *Freud, biologist of the mind: Beyond the psychoanalytic legend* (rev. ed.). Cambridge, MA: Harvard University Press.

Sundstrom, Eric; De Meuse, Kenneth P.; & Futrell, David (1990). Work teams: Applications and effectiveness. *American Psychologist, 45*, 120–133.

Suomi, Stephen J. (1987). Genetic and maternal contributions to individual differences in rhesus monkey biobehavioral development. In N. Krasnegor, E. Blass, M. Hofer, & W. Smotherman (eds.), *Perinatal development: A psychobiological perspective*. New York: Academic Press.

Suomi, Stephen J. (1991). Uptight and laid-back monkeys: Individual differences in the response to social challenges. In S. Branch, W. Hall, & J. E. Dooling (eds.), *Plasticity of development*. Cambridge, MA: MIT Press.

Super, Charles A., & Harkness, Sara (1994). The developmental niche. In W. J. Lonner & R. Malpass (eds.), *Psychology and culture*. Needham Heights, MA: Allyn & Bacon.

Susser, Ezra; Neugebauer, Richard; Hoek, Hans W.; et al. (1996). Schizophrenia after prenatal famine: Further evidence. *Archives of General Psychiatry, 53*, 25–31.

Symons, Donald (1979). *The evolution of human sexuality*. New York: Oxford University Press.

Tabandeh, H.; Lockley, S. W.; Buttery, R.; et al. (1998). Disturbance of sleep in blindness. *American Journal of Ophthalmology, 126*, 707–712.

Taffel, Ronald (1990, September/October). The politics of mood. *Family Therapy Networker*, 49–53, 72.

Tajfel, Henri; Billig, M. G.; Bundy, R. P.; & Flament, C. (1971). Social categorization and intergroup behavior. *European Journal of Social Psychology, 1*, 149–178.

Tajfel, Henri, & Turner, John C. (1986). The social identity theory of intergroup behavior. In S. Worchel & W. G. Austin (eds.), *Psychology of intergroup relations*. Chicago: Nelson-Hall.

Tangney, June P.; Wagner, Patricia E.; Hill-Barlow, Deborah; et al. (1996). Relation of shame and guilt to constructive versus destructive responses to anger across the lifespan. *Journal of Personality and Social Psychology, 70*, 797–809.

Taubes, Gary (1998). As obesity rates rise, experts struggle to explain why. *Science, 280*, 1367–1368.

Tavris, Carol (1987, January). How to succeed in business abroad. *Signature*, 86–87, 110–113.

Tavris, Carol (1989). *Anger: The misunderstood emotion* (2nd ed.). New York: Simon & Schuster/Touchstone.

Taylor, Donald M., & Porter, Lana E. (1994). A multicultural view of stereotyping. In W. J. Lonner & R. Malpass (eds.), *Psychology and culture*. Needham Heights, MA: Allyn & Bacon.

Taylor, Shelley E. (1998). *Health psychology* (4th ed.). New York: McGraw-Hill.

Terrace, H. S. (1985). In the beginning was the "name." *American Psychologist, 40*, 1011–1028.

Thase, Michael E.; Greenhouse, J. B.; Frank, E.; et al. (1997). Treatment of major depression with psychotherapy or psychotherapy-pharmacotherapy combinations. *Archives of General Psychiatry, 54*, 1009–1015.

Thoma, Stephen J. (1986). Estimating gender differences in the comprehension and preference of moral issues. *Developmental Review, 6*, 165–180.

Thomas, Alexander, & Chess, Stella (1984). Genesis and evolution of behavioral disorders: From infancy to early adult life. *American Journal of Psychiatry, 141*, 1–9.

Thomassen, R.; van Schaick, H. W.; & Blansjaar, B. A. (1998). Prevalence of dementia over age 100. *Neurology, 50*, 283–286.

Thompson, Richard F. (1986). The neurobiology of learning and memory. *Science, 233*, 941–947.

Thorndike, Edward L. (1898). Animal intelligence: An experimental study of the associative processes in animals. *Psychological Review Monograph Supplement, 2*(Whole No. 8).

Thorndike, Edward L. (1903). *Educational psychology*. New York: Columbia University Teachers College.

Thornhill, Randy, & Palmer, Craig T. (2000). *A natural history of rape: Biological bases of sexual coercion*. Cambridge, MA: MIT Press.

Thornton, E. M. (1984). *The Freudian fallacy: An alternative view of Freudian theory*. Garden City, NY: Dial.

Tiefer, Leonore (1995). *Sex is not a natural act and other essays*. Boulder, CO: Westview Press.

Todes, Daniel P. (1997). From the machine to the ghost within: Pavlov's transition from digestive physiology to conditional reflexes. *American Psychologist, 52*, 947–955.

Tolman, Edward C. (1938). The determiners of behavior at a choice point. *Psychological Review, 45*, 1–35.

Tolman, Edward C. (1948). Cognitive maps in rats and men. *Psychological Review, 55*, 189–208.

Tolman, Edward C., & Honzik, Chase H. (1930). Introduction and removal of reward and maze performance in rats. *University of California Publications in Psychology, 4*, 257–275.

Tomasello, Michael (1999). *The cultural origins of human cognition*. Cambridge, MA: Harvard University Press.

Torrey, E. Fuller (1988). *Surviving schizophrenia* (rev. ed.). New York: Harper & Row.

Torrey, E. Fuller; Bowler, Ann E.; Taylor, Edward H.; & Gottesman, Irving I. (1994). *Schizophrenia and manic-depressive disorder*. New York: Basic Books.

Tougas, Francine; Brown, Rupert; Beaton, Ann M.; & Joly, Stéphane (1995). Neosexism: Plus ça change, plus c'est pareil. *Personality and Social Psychology Bulletin, 21,* 842–849.

Traub, James (1993, June 7). The hearts and minds of City College. *The New Yorker,* 42–53.

Triandis, Harry C. (1994). *Culture and social behavior.* New York: McGraw-Hill.

Triandis, Harry C. (1995). *Individualism and collectivism.* Boulder, CO: Westview Press.

Triandis, Harry C. (1996). The psychological measurement of cultural syndromes. *American Psychologist, 51,* 407–415.

Trimble, Joseph E., & Medicine, Beatrice (1993). Diversification of American Indians: Forming an indigenous perspective. In U. Kim & J. W. Berry (eds.), *Indigenous psychologies: Research and experience in cultural context.* Newbury Park, CA: Sage.

Trivers, Robert (1972). Parental investment and sexual selection. In B. Campbell (ed.), *Sexual selection and the descent of man.* New York: Aldine de Gruyter.

Tulving, Endel (1985). How many memory systems are there? *American Psychologist, 40,* 385–398.

Tversky, Amos, & Kahneman, Daniel (1973). Availability: A heuristic for judging frequency and probability. *Cognitive Psychology, 5,* 207–232.

Tversky, Amos, & Kahneman, Daniel (1981). The framing of decisions and the psychology of choice. *Science, 211,* 453–458.

Twenge, Jean M. (1997). Attitudes toward women, 1970–1995: A meta-analysis. *Psychology of Women Quarterly, 21,* 35–51.

Tyler, Tom R. (1997). The psychology of legitimacy: A relational perspective on voluntary deference to authorities. *Personality and Social Psychology Review, 1,* 323–345.

Uchida, K., & Toya, S. (1996). Grafting of genetically manipulated cells into adult brain: Toward graft-gene therapy. *Keio Journal of Medicine* (Japan), *45,* 81–89.

Unger, Rhoda (1990). Imperfect reflections of reality: Psychology constructs gender. In R. T. Hare-Mustin & J. Marecek (eds.), *Making a difference: Psychology and the construction of gender.* New Haven, CT: Yale University Press.

Usher, JoNell A., & Neisser, Ulric (1993). Childhood amnesia and the beginnings of memory for four early life events. *Journal of Experimental Psychology: General, 122,* 155–165.

Vaillant, George E. (ed.) (1992). *Ego mechanisms of defense.* Washington, DC: American Psychiatric Press.

Valenstein, Elliot (1986). *Great and desperate cures: The rise and decline of psychosurgery and other radical treatments for mental illness.* New York: Basic Books.

Valenstein, Elliot (1998). *Blaming the brain: The truth about drugs and mental health.* New York: Free Press.

Valian, Virginia (1998). *Why so slow? The advancement of women.* Cambridge, MA: MIT Press.

Van Boven, Leaf; Kamada, Akiko; & Gilovich, Thomas (1999). The perceiver as perceived: Everyday intuitions about the correspondence bias. *Journal of Personality and Social Psychology, 77,* 1188–1199.

Van Cantfort, Thomas E., & Rimpau, James B. (1982). Sign language studies with children and chimpanzees. *Sign Language Studies, 34,* 15–72.

Vandenberg, Brian (1985). Beyond the ethology of play. In A. Gottfried & C. C. Brown (eds.), *Play interactions.* Lexington, MA: Lexington Books.

van Praag, H.; Kempermann, G.; & Gage, F. H. (1999). Running increases cell proliferation and neurogenesis in the adult mouse dentate gyrus. *Nature Neuroscience, 2,* 266–270.

Vandello, Joseph A., & Cohen, Dov (1999). Patterns of individualism and collectivism across the United States. *Journal of Personality and Social Psychology, 77,* 279–292.

Verhaeghen, Paul, & Salthouse, Timothy A. (1997). Meta-analyses of age-cognition relations in adulthood: Estimates of linear and nonlinear age effects and structural models. *Psychological Bulletin, 122,* 231–249.

Vertosick, Frank T. (1997, October). Lobotomy's back. *Discover,* 66–72.

Von Lang, Jochen, & Sibyll, Claus (eds.) (1984). *Eichmann interrogated: Transcripts from the archives of the Israeli police.* New York: Random House.

Voyer, Daniel; Voyer, Susan; & Bryden, M. P. (1995). Magnitude of sex differences in spatial abilities: A meta-analysis and consideration of critical variables. *Psychological Bulletin, 117,* 250–270.

Wagenaar, Willem A. (1986). My memory: A study of autobiographical memory over six years. *Cognitive Psychology, 18,* 225–252.

Walker, Anne (1994). Mood and well-being in consecutive menstrual cycles: Methodological and theoretical implications. *Psychology of Women Quarterly, 18,* 271–290.

Walker, Lawrence J.; de Vries, Brian; & Trevethan, Shelley D. (1987). Moral stages and moral orientations in real-life and hypothetical dilemmas. *Child Development, 58,* 842–858.

Walker-Andrews, Arlene S. (1997). Infants' perception of expressive behaviors: Differentiation of multimodal information. *Psychological Bulletin, 121,* 437–456.

Waller, Niels G.; Kojetin, Brian A.; Bouchard, Thomas J., Jr.; et al. (1990). Genetic and environmental influences on religious interests, attitudes, and values: A study of twins reared apart and together. *Psychological Science, 1,* 138–142.

Wang, Alvin Y.; Thomas, Margaret H.; & Ouellette, Judith A. (1992). The keyword mnemonic and retention of second-language vocabulary words. *Journal of Educational Psychology, 84,* 520–528.

Wark, Gillian R., & Krebs, Dennis (1996). Gender and dilemma differences in real-life moral judgment. *Developmental Psychology, 32,* 220–230.

Washburn, David A., & Rumbaugh, Duane M. (1991). Ordinal judgments of numerical symbols by macaques (*Macaca mulatta*). *Psychological Science, 2,* 190–193.

Watson, John B. (1913). Psychology as the behaviorist views it. *Psychological Review, 20,* 158–177.

Watson, John B. (1925). *Behaviorism.* New York: W. W. Norton.

Watson, John B., & Rayner, Rosalie (1920). Conditioned emotional reactions. *Journal of Experimental Psychology, 3,* 1–14.

Watters, Ethan, & Ofshe, Richard (1999). *Therapy's delusions.* New York: Scribner.

Webb, Wilse B., & Cartwright, Rosalind D. (1978). Sleep and dreams. In M. Rosenzweig & L. Porter (eds.), *Annual Review of Psychology, 29,* 223–252.

Webster, Richard (1995). *Why Freud was wrong.* New York: Basic Books.

Weiner, Bernard (1986). *An attributional theory of motivation and emotion.* New York: Springer-Verlag.

Weiss, Bahr; Dodge, Kenneth A.; Bates, John E.; & Petitt, Gregory S. (1992). Some consequences of early harsh discipline: Child aggression and a maladaptive social information processing style. *Child Development, 63,* 1321–1335.

Weisz, John R.; Rothbaum, Fred M.; & Blackburn, Thomas C. (1984). Standing out and standing in: The psychology of control in America and Japan. *American Psychologist, 39,* 955–969.

Weisz, John R.; Weiss, Bahr; Alicke, Mark D.; & Klotz, M. L. (1987). Effectiveness of psychotherapy with children and adolescents: A meta-analysis for clinicians. *Journal of Consulting and Clinical Psychology, 55,* 542–549.

Weisz, John R.; Weiss, Bahr; Han, Susan S.; et al. (1995). Effects of psychotherapy with children and adolescents revisited: A meta-analysis of treatment outcome studies. *Psychological Bulletin, 117,* 450–468.

Wells, Gary L. (1993). What do we know about eyewitness identification? *American Psychologist, 48,* 553–571.

Wells, Gary L.; Small, Mark; Penrod, Steven; et al. (1998). Eyewitness identification procedures: Recommendations for lineups and photospreads. *Law and Human Behavior, 22,* 602–647.

Werner, Emmy E., & Smith, R. S. (1992). *Overcoming the odds: High risk children from birth to adulthood.* Ithaca, NY: Cornell University Press.

West, Candace, & Zimmerman, Don H. (1991). Doing gender. In J. Lorber & S. A. Farrell (eds.), *The social construction of gender.* Newbury Park, CA: Sage.

West, Maxine M. (1998). Meta-analysis of studies assessing the efficacy of projective techniques in discriminating child sexual abuse. *Child Abuse & Neglect, 22,* 1151–1166.

West, Melissa O., & Prinz, Ronald J. (1987). Parental alcoholism and childhood psychopathology. *Psychological Bulletin, 102,* 204–218.

Westen, Drew (1998). The scientific legacy of Sigmund Freud: Toward a psychodynamically informed psychological science. *Psychological Bulletin, 124,* 333–371.

Wheeler, David L. (1998, September 11). Neuroscientists take stock of brain-imaging studies. *Chronicle of Higher Education,* A20–A21.

Whisman, Mark A. (1993). Mediators and moderators of change in cognitive therapy of depression. *Psychological Bulletin, 114,* 248–265.

White, Judith B., & Langer, Ellen J. (1999). Horizontal hostility: Relations between similar minority groups. *Journal of Social Issues, 55,* 537–560.

Whitehurst, Grover J.; Arnold, David S.; Epstein, Jeffrey N.; et al. (1994). A picture book reading intervention in day care and home for children from low-income families. *Developmental Psychology, 30,* 679–689.

Whitehurst, Grover J.; Falco, F. L.; Lonigan, C. J.; et al. (1988). Accelerating language development through picture book reading. *Developmental Psychology, 24,* 552–559.

Whiting, Beatrice B., & Edwards, Carolyn P. (1988). *Children of different worlds: The formation of social behavior.* Cambridge, MA: Harvard University Press.

Whiting, Beatrice B., & Whiting, John (1975). *Children of six cultures.* Cambridge, MA: Harvard University Press.

Wickelgren, Ingrid (1997). Estrogen stakes claim to cognition [Research news]. *Science, 276,* 675–678.

Widner, H.; Tetrud, J.; Rehncrona, S.; et al. (1993). Fifteen months' follow-up on bilateral embryonic mesencephalic grafts in two cases of severe MPTP-induced Parkinsonism. *Advances in Neurology, 60,* 729–733.

Wiggins, Jerry S. (ed.) (1996). *The five-factor model of personality: Theoretical perspectives.* New York: Guilford Press.

Williams, Kipling D., & Karau, Steven J. (1991). Social loafing and social compensation: The effects of expectations of co-worker performance. *Journal of Personality and Social Psychology, 61,* 570–581.

Williams, Walter (1986). *The spirit and the flesh: Sexual diversity in American Indian culture.* Boston: Beacon Press.

Willie, Charles V.; Rieker, Patricia P.; Kramer, Bernard M.; & Brown, Bertram S. (eds.) (1995). *Mental health, racism, and sexism* (rev. ed.). Pittsburgh: University of Pittsburgh Press.

Willis, Sherry L. (1987). Cognitive training and everyday competence. In K. W. Schaie (ed.), *Annual review of gerontology and geriatrics* (Vol. 7). New York: Springer.

Wilner, Daniel; Walkley, Rosabelle; & Cook, Stuart (1955). *Human relations in interracial housing.* Minneapolis: University of Minnesota Press.

Wilson, Edward O. (1975). *Sociobiology: The new synthesis.* Cambridge, MA: Belknap/Harvard University Press.

Wilson, Edward O. (1978). *On human nature.* Cambridge, MA: Harvard University Press.

Wilson, G. Terence, & Fairburn, Christopher G. (1993). Cognitive treatments for eating disorders. *Journal of Consulting and Clinical Psychology, 61,* 261–269.

Windholz, George, & Lamal, P. A. (1985). Köhler's insight revisited. *Teaching of Psychology, 12,* 165–167.

Winnicott, D. W. (1957/1990). *Home is where we start from.* New York: W. W. Norton.

Wittchen, Hans-Ulrich; Kessler, Ronald C.; Zhao, Shanyang; & Abelson, Jamie (1995). Reliability and clinical validity of UM-CIDI DSM-III-R generalized anxiety disorder. *Journal of Psychiatric Research, 29,* 95–110.

Wittig, Michele A., & Grant-Thompson, Sheila (1998). The utility of Allport's conditions of intergroup contact for predicting perceptios of improved racial attitudes and beliefs. *Journal of Social Issues, 54,* 795–812.

Wood, James M.; Lilienfeld, Scott O.; Garb, Howard N.; & Nezworski, M. Teresa (2000). The Rorschach Test in clinical diagnosis: A critical review, with a backward look at Garfield (1947). *Journal of Clinical Psychology, 56,* 395–430.

Wood, James M.; Nezworski, M. Teresa; & Stejskal, William J. (1996). The comprehensive system for the Rorschach: A critical examination. *Psychological Science, 7,* 3–10.

Wood, Robert, & Bandura, Albert (1989). Impact of conceptions of ability on self-regulatory mechanisms and complex decision making. *Journal of Personality and Social Psychology, 56,* 407–415.

Wood, Wendy; Lundgren, Sharon; Ouellette, Judith A.; et al. (1994). Minority influence: A meta-analytic review of social influence processes. *Psychological Bulletin, 115,* 323–345.

Wooley, Susan; Wooley, O. Wayne; & Dyrenforth, Susan (1979). Theoretical, practical, and social issues in behavioral treatments of obesity. *Journal of Applied Behavior Analysis, 12,* 3–25.

Wright, Daniel B. (1993). Recall of the Hillsborough disaster over time: Systematic biases of "flashbulb" memories. *Applied Cognitive Psychology, 7,* 129–138.

Wright, R. L. D. (1976). *Understanding statistics: An informal introduction for the behavioral sciences.* New York: Harcourt Brace Jovanovich.

Wurtman, Richard J. (1982). Nutrients that modify brain function. *Scientific American, 264*(4), 50–59.

Wygant, Steven A. (1997). Moral reasoning about real-life dilemmas: Paradox in research using the Defining Issues Test. *Personality and Social Psychology Bulletin, 23,* 1022–1033.

Yalom, Irvin D. (1980). *Existential psychotherapy.* New York: Basic Books.

Yalom, Irvin D. (1989). *Love's executioner and other tales of psychotherapy.* New York: Basic Books.

Yalom, Irvin D. (1995). *The theory and practice of group psychotherapy* (4th ed.). New York: Basic Books.

Yang, Kuo-shu, & Bond, Michael H. (1990). Exploring implicit personality theories with indigenous or imported constructs: The Chinese case. *Journal of Personality and Social Psychology, 58,* 1087–1095.

Yapko, Michael (1994). *Suggestions of abuse: True and false memories of childhood sexual trauma.* New York: Simon & Schuster.

Yoder, Janice D. (1999). *Women and gender: Transforming psychology.* Upper Saddle River, NJ: Prentice-Hall.

Yoder, Janice D., & Kahn, Arnold S. (1993). Working toward an inclusive psychology of women. *American Psychologist, 48,* 846–850.

Young, Malcolm P., & Yamane, Shigeru (1992). Sparse population coding of faces in the inferotemporal cortex. *Science, 256,* 1327–1331.

Young-Eisendrath, Polly (1993). *You're not what I expected: Learning to love the opposite sex.* New York: Morrow.

Zajonc, Robert B. (1968). Attitudinal effects of mere exposure. *Journal of Personality and Social Psychology, 9*(Monograph Suppl. 2), 1–27.

Zhang, Yiying; Proenca, Ricardo; Maffei, Margherita; et al. (1994). Positional cloning of the mouse obese gene and its human homologue. *Nature, 372*(6505), 425–432.

Zilbergeld, Bernie (1983). *The shrinking of America: Myths of psychological change.* Boston: Little, Brown.

Zimbardo, Philip G. (1970). The human choice: Individuation, reason, and order versus deindividuation, impulse, and chaos. In W. J. Arnold & D. Levine (eds.), *Nebraska Symposium on Motivation, 1969.* Lincoln: University of Nebraska Press.

Zimbardo, Philip G., & Leippe, Michael R. (1991). *The psychology of attitude change and social influence.* New York: McGraw-Hill.

Zorrilla, L. T.; Cannon, T. D.; Kronenberg, S.; et al. (1997, December 15). Structural brain abnormalities in schizophrenia: A family study. *Biological Psychiatry, 42,* 1080–1086.

CREDITS

TEXT, TABLES AND FIGURES

Chapter 2: Page 50 (Fig. 2.1) From *Understanding statistics: An informational introduction for the behavior sciences* by R.L.D. Wright. Copyright © 1976 Harcourt Brace & Company. Reprinted by permission. *Chapter 3:* Page 85 (Fig. 3.3) Monkmeyer Press / p. 89 (Fig. 3.4) Harlow Primate Laboratory / p. 97 Adapted from Evolutionary Psychology: A new paradigm for psychological science by David M. Buss, in *Psychological Inquiry, 6,* 1–30 (1995). *Chapter 5:* (Fig. 5.2) Adapted from Reinforcement schedules and behavior from Teaching Machines by B. F. Skinner, *Scientific American,* November 1961. Copyright © 1961 by Scientific American, Inc. Reprinted with permission of Margaret C. Gladbach / p. 209 (Fig. 5.3) from Intrinsic Motivation: How to turn play into work by D. Greene and M.R. Lepper, *Psychology Today,* September 1974. Reprinted with permission from *Psychology Today.* Copyright © 1974 Sussex Publishers, Inc. *Chapter 6:* Page 222 (Fig. 6.1) From Introduction and removal of reward and maze performance in rats by E.C. Tolman and C.H. Honzik from *Psychology, 4* (1930). Copyright © 1930 The Regents of the University of California. Reprinted by permission of University of California Press. / p. 234 (Fig. 6.2) From Mueller, Claudia M. & Dweck, Carol S. (1998). Praise for intelligence can undermine children's motivation and performance. *Journal of Personality and Social Psychology, 75,* 33–52. Copyright © 1998 by the American Psychological Association. Reprinted with permission. *Chapter 7:* Page 276 Edward de Bono (1971). *The dog exercising machine.* New York: Touchstone. Copyright © 1970 The Cognitive Research Trust. Reprinted by permission of Gillian Aitken Associates, London. / p. 303 Puzzle Solutions from *Conceptual blockbusters* by James L. Adams. Copyright © 1986 by James L. Adams. Reprinted by permission of Basic Books. *Chapter 8:* Page 325 (Fig. 8.3), From A piece of the semantic memory network–a later view. In *Cognitive psychology and information processing: An introduction* by Lachman et al., 1979. Reprinted by permission of Lawrence Earlbaum Associates, Inc. / p. 334 (Fig. 8.6) From I remember it well: A forgetting curve for personal events by Marigold Linton. *Psychology Today,* July 1979. Reprinted with permission of *Psychology Today.* Copyright © 1979 by Sussex Publishers, Inc. *Chapter 10:* Page 428 (Fig. 10.3) From R. Rogers and S. Prenttice-Dunn, 1981. *Journal of Personality and Social Psychology, 41,* p. 68. Copyright © 1981 by the American Psychological Association. Reprinted with permission. *Chapter 11:* Pages 450–451 from Psychotherapy in action: How one therapist reached a withdrawn boy. In *Forms off Feeling* by Robert Hobson. Reprinted by permission of Tavistock Publications. *Chapter 12:* Page 505 (Fig. 12.1) Antisocial personality disorder by Robert Hare from *Journal of Psychology,* 1965. Reprinted with permissions of the Helen Dwight Reid Educational Foundation. Published by Helref Publications, 1319 Eighteenth St. NW, Washington, DC 20036-1802. Copyright © 1965.

PHOTOGRAPHS AND CARTOONS

Chapter 1: Page 7 Punch/Rothco / p. 14 Archives of the History of American Psychology The University of Akron / p. 31 Burnt Offerings by Don Addis. By permission of Don Addis and Creators Syndicate. *Chapter 2:* Page 36 Alan Carey/Image Works / p. 42 Art Resource, NY/Giuseppe Arcimboldo [1527-930, "Vertumnus (Emperor Rudolf II)]." 1590. Oil on wood, 70.5 x 57.5 cm. Stocklosters Slott, Sweden. *Chapter 3:* Page 91 Stock Boston / p. 110 Sidney Harris. *Chapter 4:* Page 133 Copyright © 2000 The New Yorker Collection from cartoonbank.com. All rights reserved. / p. 136 (L) Hank Morgan/Science Source/Photo Researchers, Inc. , (R) Dr. Michael E. Phelps/ Massiotta UCLA School of Medicine / p. 137 Howard Sochurek, Inc. / p. 162 Sidney Harris. *Essay 1:* Page 178 Reprinted with special permission King Features Syndicate. *Chapter 5:* Page 194 King Features Syndicate / p. 204 Liason Agency, Inc. / p. 210 Copyright © The New Yorker Collection 1986 Lee Lorenz from catoonbank.com. All rights reserved. *Chapter 6:* Page 231 Liaison Agency, Inc./ p. 248 (L) Stock Boston, (R) Betsy Lee. *Essay 2:* Page 258 Sidney Harris / p. 261 Cartoonists & Writers Syndicate/cartoonweb.com. *Chapter 7:* Page 281 (L) Monkmeyer Press, (R) Marcia Weinstein / p. 298 Georgia State University/LRC. *Chapter 8:* Page 307 The Far Side Copyright © 1993 Farworks, Inc. / p. 311 Dr. Elizabeth Loftus / p. 315 Sidney Harris / p. 332 Sidney Harris. *Essay 3:* Page 350 Mary Hancock / p. 355 United Media/United Feature Syndicate, Inc. *Chapter 9:* Page 371 Sidney Harris / p. 376 P.G. Zimbardo, Inc. / p. 377 AP/Wide World Photos / p. 383 AP/Wide World Photos. *Chapter 10:* Page 399 (L) M. Dalmasso/Gamma Liaison, (R) Shahn Kermani/Gamma Liaison / p. 410 Sidney Harris / p. 417 (L) National Anthropological Archives/Smithsonian Institution, (R) Library of Congress / p. 419 King Features Syndicate.

NAME INDEX

SUBJECT INDEX